WAPPING WHARF.COM

The Darlings of Wapping Wharf Launderette E.1.

A Small Faces and related magazine

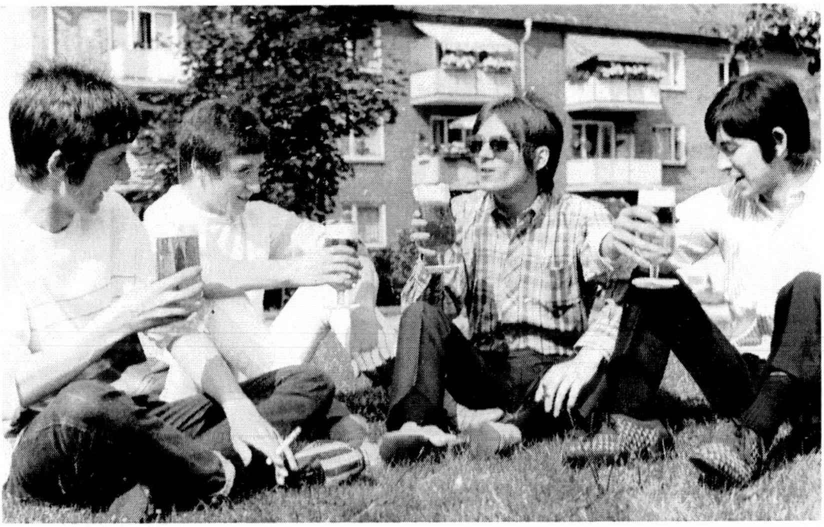

The Small Faces are probably remembered more for their sharp clothes than anything else; but they were one of the few mod bands to become more than a cult and they kept completely in touch with the changing times through their music. By the time they split in early 1969 they had encompassed R&B, psychedelia, soul, pop, comedy and music hall yet without ever falling into the trap of pretentiousness that afflicted so many of their contemporaries. Their records still provide a breath of fresh air and sum up the musical adventurousness and confidence that made the sixties such an exciting era in pop history.

Someone, somewhere said the bloke who wrote the song 'Gloria in Excelsis' would be turning in his grave if he heard 'My Mind's Eye': Well, I'll certainly be chuffed to bits if somebody revives one of our songs in a couple of years time   -Steve Marriott 1966.

John Hellier, I really love that little ol' magazine of yours   -Ronnie Lane 1997.

FIRST PUBLISHED 2018

ISBN: 978-0-9956533-3-7

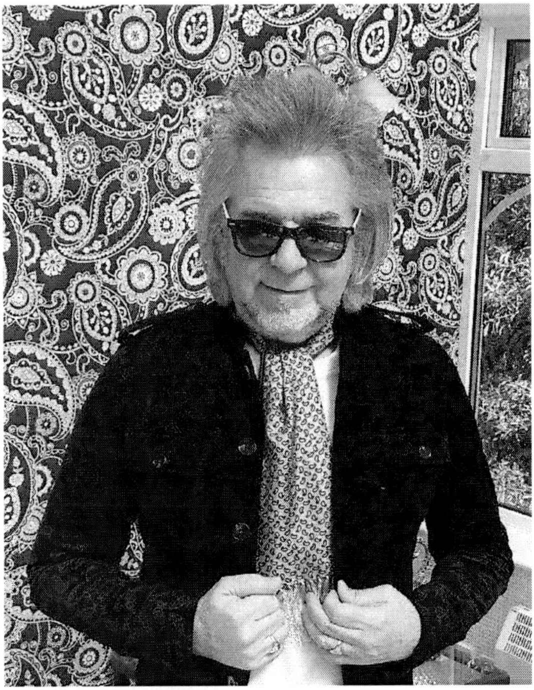

Wapping Wharf head honcho
JOHN HELLIER

The boss at Wapping Wharf Records & Promotions who counts amongst his biggest triumphs the staging of sold-out memorial shows for Ronnie Lane and Steve Marriott at the Royal Albert Hall and London Astoria respectively. He has also staged successful Small Faces Conventions in London since 1997 as well as annual Christmas Mod Balls at the 100 Club. His record company, in conjunction with Carlton Sandercock and the Steve Marriott estate, have been paramount in keeping Steve's memory alive with a string of tasteful rarities albums including the best selling 'Rainy Changes' collection. John has also co-written several books including the highly acclaimed Ronnie Lane and Steve Marriott biographies, Can You Show Me A Dream? and All Too Beautiful, both with Paolo Hewitt and has made numerous television and radio appearances for the BBC, ITV and Sky including Soul Britannia, South Bank Show, Vinyl Frontier, Inside Out, Oh You Pretty Things, Rock Routes and many, many more....... Original mod: Still flying the flag.

A LETTER FROM THE EDITOR

The Small Faces are everywhere, still. Although three quarters of the band have sadly passed: Steve in April 1991, Ronnie in June 1997 and Mac in December 2014, the cliché is authentic and the legend really does live on. It endures because we live in the age of rewind. Digital re-mastering, Blu-ray technology, MP3s, CDr, CD Rom etc. etc. etc. Nobody dies anymore, bands no longer split up, and the song goes on forever but with the Small Faces that wasn't always the case. The Mod Revival of 1979, kicked off by the movie 'Quadrophenia', revolved around The Who and throughout the whole of the eighties and early nineties The Small Faces were largely forgotten.

There was the occasional compilation album or two but virtually nothing in print; so as a fan since 1965 just imagine my joy when I stumbled across a fanzine called 'Darlings of Wapping Wharf Launderette' around 1993. It was produced by two guys, Steve Chamberlain from Merseyside and Stuart Wright from Dagenham, on a shoe string budget and was an incredibly basic cut and paste job, but it excited me. I wrote to them and told them of my delight and offered to write a story for issue 2. They took me up on my offer and further contributions from myself appeared in issues 3 and 4, after which the fanzine was on the verge of folding due mainly to the fact that very few people were buying it. I just couldn't stand by and see it die so I stepped in and took over the editorship from issue 5. I took it upmarket with a new glossy 40 page format and have never looked back, from that moment onwards the popularity and readership soared. By issue 20 it was the biggest selling self published fanzine in the country, overtaking the established Eric Clapton magazine 'Where's Eric' and was attracting readers worldwide. Fans were purchasing from literally every continent on the planet and with the advent of the internet it has grown in stature and sales ever since. 40 issues on, it was time for a 'Best Bits' compilation in the form of an A5 book and here we are!

Fans have often said to me over the years 'Surely you'll soon run out of things to write about' but that's never been the case. As the readership increased the feedback from those same readers also increased and interesting stories suitable for print were stock piled. Also of course, this Small Faces fanzine is really a Small Faces and related fanzine and all of the off-shoot bands before and after also feature.

This book has no index, it doesn't need an index; after the introduction it's simply a collection of some of the best articles to grace the pages of 40 issues of Wapping Wharf. It doesn't need to be read from start to finish, simply flick through the pages and read at random. Likened to a record it becomes a literary version of a 'Greatest Hits' album!

I'd like to thank every single fan that has ever contributed a story and every single fan that has ever purchased a copy of the magazine but VERY special thanks go out to my graphic designer for the last quarter of a century, Brian Guy. Most of the original artwork, at least 95% of it, on these scanned pages is his. The man is a professional of the highest order and I cannot speak highly enough of him; both as a person and for his wonderful work............ Thank you sir.

JOHN HELLIER (MAY 2018) **jjhellier@aol.com**

AN INTRODUCTION

CALL IT SOMETHING NICE..........a fan's pilgrimage

By David Mullaney

East London was slowly becoming aglow. The long lines of terraced houses off the High Street were dark, but the bricks on the higher buildings were tinged in orange and some appeared to dance with fire. Dawn was slowly sapping the deep indigo from the sky and the moony -most that had hung over the Pimlico church steeple, by the hotel I had left an hour or so before, was lower in the horizon and fading. Despite the early hour there was a buzz of activity around East Ham underground station and the street was filled with traffic. I was headed up the road with map, camera and notes; walking against the flow. I had no time for error and stopped to check with one of the underground staff outside the station just to make sure I was headed for Manor Park. "Far from home, aren't we?" he responded with a friendly, quizzical smile noting my accent. "It's a pilgrimage of sorts" I told him; and so it was. I was back in London for the first time in decades and going to the places I was determined to see if I ever came back.

I grew up in London in the late 1960s. My family had moved there from the suburbs of New York when my father was offered a promotion to the firm's London office. I found London a fascinating place and quickly fell in love with it. A favourite past time was to get on a bus, any bus, go to the upper deck and see the many neighbourhoods of London unfold as the tree branches scraped the side of the vehicle. I developed affection for the underground, as well, and delighted in travelling to such exotic sounding places as Shepherds Bush, St. John's Wood and Elephant and Castle. Charles Dickens portrayal of the East End in Oliver Twist captured my imagination and my interest in East London was further fuelled by accounts of Sherlock Holmes' adventures in the docklands, especially his forays to the foggy streets and alleys of Limehouse. The opening chapter of a book about Jack the Ripper, read one day surreptitiously behind the stiles in Harrods's bookstore, painted a frightening picture of Whitechapel in 1888. The image of the East End that I had construed in my mind seemed worlds removed but the underground map showed it to be only a short tube trip away. I had to go see for myself.

After overcoming some initial hesitation due to images in my young imagination of being attacked by street ruffians and other unsavoury characters, my exploration of London quickly expanded east. I knew I was very privileged to be living in South Kensington and I suppose this guilty knowledge coupled with mild teenage rebellion against my parents made me eschew West London and turn east, an area I wanted to identify with but, of course, had no hope of ever being part of. My early forays to the East End only whetted my appetite to see and learn more. I traipsed from Spitalfields to Bow, wandered from Hackney Wick to Wapping and explored from Shoreditch to the Isle of Dogs. In retrospect, it is all rather embarrassing and I was a true poser, but my experiences in East London enriched my life in many ways and, not least of which, led me to the Small Faces and their music.

It was the cover of the initial Decca album and the accompanying liner notes that first made me take notice. They, the band, looked the way I wanted to look at 15. Four rather cherubic faces with just a hint of menace against that enigmatic background of a dark wall and kids' graffiti made me want know more, only later did I learn the true meaning of the 'cigarettes" poking out of the chalked faces. So, too, with the liner notes which were brief and succinct. There was just enough information to make it maddeningly incomplete. Who was who on the cover? And which one had that incredible voice?! If the cover hinted at a tinge of toughness the music inside confirmed it. This was not the melodic polish of the Beatles, the blues of the Stones or the pop of a dozen other bands, it was more akin to the Who, it verged on being anarchic at times but never surrendered melody and still had plenty of hooks. Even the overtly commercial "Sha La La La Lee" had real bite. Energy and exuberance constantly jumped out, song after song, and if the band was physically small in stature they collectively made for a very big presence. The drumming sometimes went without rules and the organ really moved the band. I loved the ominous bass on "It's Too Late" and "You Need Lovin'" which kept on simmering on high until it just boiled over completely. In retrospect some of the album pre-dated punk by a good decade or so and over arcing the entire performance was that electrifying, riveting, powerful, soulful voice. Steve Marriott may have come from Stepney, as Tony Bainbridge wrote, but somewhere there had to be roots in Memphis or the depths of Alabama or maybe in Detroit. Amazing, too, that such a voice could emanate from someone so young. No one on the cover looked out of his teens yet! I loved the music, they were from the East End of London and they looked sharp. I was hooked.

My interest in and devotion to all things Small Faces grew throughout my teenage years. I came to love the band like no other and earned the moniker "small face" in school. Subsequent albums and singles made me more of fan and I couldn't wait for their next release. Their musical mix of R&B, blue-eyed soul, pure pop and hard rock, psychedelia, East End music hall, vaudeville, and whimsy was irresistible. I liked their cheeky humour and the way they wore their cockney heritage on their sleeves. If my musical tastes predictably expanded as an adult and became far more eclectic, my loyalty to the Small Faces never waned. The Small Faces had been an integral part of my youth. I also strongly associated them with London, a city that I loved. It might be months now if not years between actually listening to one of their records, but when I do, I am reminded how good they are and how proud I am to be a fan.

When the idea of a London trip with a dear friend promised to become more of a reality than a dream, I dug out the scraps of information I had collected over the years. One rainy Friday night over a few beers and with "From the Beginning" playing in the background, I put together an itinerary. The J60 Music Bar seemed a logical place to start and the worn copy of my old London A-Z showed it right in Marriott's East London stomping ground and close to the mythical Itchycoo Park (assuming it was Little Ilford Park after all). John and Paolo's book proved an invaluable guide to Steve's early life in Manor Park and although Ronnie Lane might have been born down the road in Plaistow, a quick look on the internet showed he had once lived at 385 Romford Road, a definite must see, and close by in Forest Gate. Kenney Jones' Stepney and the Small Faces group home in Westmoreland Terrace would require their own separate trips another day but the Ruskin Arms, once owned by Jimmy Winston's parents and the rehearsal space for the early Small Faces, was conveniently located just up the road from East Ham underground station. Minutes after having spoken to the station attendant, I found myself standing in front of its mock Tudor facing faster than expected.

My breath clouded its window with condensation as I peered in. In honour of the photograph session that graced the covers of the two Decca LPs I drew cartoon faces which quickly sagged and dripped away on the glass. The Ruskin Arms was closed at this early hour, a shame as I would have loved a cup of tea and bacon sandwich. The pub included a hotel and I envisioned staying the night in such hallowed surroundings upon any subsequent London visit. The J60 Music Bar, comparable to the Woolton church where McCartney first met Lennon, was just up the street and closed, too. It now masqueraded as a dry goods store. My imagination went into overdrive as I stood outside its shuttered entrance. I pictured Ronnie Lane and his dad on that Saturday morning many years ago encountering a chirpy shop assistant with boundless energy and enthusiasm named Steve Marriott. Ronnie and Steve seemed to have hit it off right away and my eyes followed the way up the High Street that they would take later that same afternoon (as the story goes) to listen to Marriott's collection of American R&B records in his parents council flat in Daines Close.

Strone Road, its entrance marked by a red brick church with a steeple as shunted as the tree that stood by its side, was the location of Marriott's first Manor Park address and just around the corner. I was impressed by how close everything was to each other in this part of Small Faces' London and how neighbourhood based their origin had been. Kenney Jones, who lived in Stepney, a few miles south and close to the Thames, was even a frequent visitor to the J60 Music Bar which must have been a very happening place. Still in shadows, Strone Road's parallel lines of nearly identical terraced houses stretched well into the distance, probably unchanged since the area was first developed. I reminded myself this was the very same view that greeted Steve Marriott every time he romped down the street. I stood outside Marriott's childhood home at number 308 taking pictures and hoping the curious residents would invite me in for a peek inside. Sadly, there were neither fluttering curtains nor peering faces within beckoning with a warm welcome. The door remained unopened. I paused again at number 241 the home of Rene Tungate "the Dockers' Delight" and the inspiration for that classic Small Faces song. "Rene" with its witty cockney lyrics and extended jam helped make 'Ogdens Nut Gone Flake' the perfect album that it remains. Strone Road was still mostly quiet at this hour but I imagined a loud and rambunctious Steve Marriott carrying on here as if he were lord of the manor.

I walked to Monega, young Marriott's local primary school, and then on to Sandringham Secondary with its Victorian aura of iron gates, spires and gables, and cupola now beginning to shine in the rising sun. I half expected to hear a chorus of "Food, Glorious Food" emanating from behinds its latticed windows. As I walked past, I was relieved to find no smoke rising above the venerable old building and the fire brigade nowhere in sight. While checking the internet for its exact spelling and later reminding myself of the route I took that morning, I came across the Sandringham website which includes a nice video of the school narrated by its students decked out in smart maroon jumpers. Despite Marriott's negative experiences of it and it of him, Sandringham seems like a very welcoming and progressive place where a diverse population gets an excellent education. If these articulate and thoughtful youngsters are anything to go by, Britain's future is in good hands. Not surprisingly, the website makes no reference to the rumour of a young, bored Steve Marriott almost setting the school ablaze while putting out his cigarette in the back of class one day.

Romford Road in Forest Gate appeared not much different to my eyes than the non-descript sprawl in outer districts of US cities. Only the iconic red double-decker bus's reminded me I was still in London, even the local McDonalds did not seem out of place. Chagrined as I was to see the golden arches defacing Ronnie's old neighbourhood I was glad of its restroom. The tea I had bought in the cafe by the East Ham underground station this cold morning had gone right through me. I considered knocking on the door of 365 Romford Road, Plonk's former home and the place he must have lived when he first met a precocious Steve Marriott and came away with that Harmony bass, but as it was barely 7am I thought better of it. Hoping to see a horse drawn caravan or maybe a lorry belonging to Ronnie's dad, I expectantly peeked up the dirt drive to the back. Instead, a large satellite dish dominated the view and brought me back to earth. Undeterred, I gazed up to the second floor and in my mind's eyes saw the wooden hills of Bedfordshire leading up to it.

By all reports Ronnie was a lovely man, well-liked by all lucky enough to know him. In interviews he seems warm and charming with a great sense of humour. The endearing looks he gives Marriott in the 'Colour Me Pop' video and his swinging feet shuffles while playing bass indicate a man with his heart and perspective in the right place. Marriott and Rod Stewart may have been the dominant front men in his bands but I found it inspiring and reassuring that Ronnie, too easily overlooked by the casual fan, was essential to their spirit and, as Rod Stewart admitted, the heart and soul of the Faces. The Faces minus Marriott were never the same as when they were 'Small' but there were still occasional hints to the Small Faces grand tradition mostly courtesy of Ronnie Lane. When he left the Faces in 1973 I lost all interest in them even though Jones and McLagan remained.

Ronnie quit the Faces at the height of their popularity to follow an unconventional path eschewing rock stardom and extravagance. If that decision left him with peace of mind as a man true to his values, it also began a slow descent into financial difficulties that would plague Lane for the rest of his life. It also led him to the best music of his career. The Passing Show, short-lived and financially doomed as it may have been, and his band Slim Chance, tight knit despite its revolving door membership, seemed the perfect vehicles for Ronnie to deliver his hybrid brand of unpretentious folk/rock/roots music tinged with beautiful touches of Appalachia and the Celtic fringe. Stricken with disabling multiple sclerosis, Lane demonstrated a heroic lack of self-pity even when restricted to a wheelchair. He comes across as an inspirational figure able to laugh in the face of adversity. His four albums recorded with Slim Chance and on his own are standouts and show that Ronnie saw life in a different, more intimate way than most.

A fifth album, *Rough Mix,* recorded with old pal Pete Townshend, reveals Ronnie at the top of his game while sadly approaching the end of his recording career. His voice, too often under appreciated, is at its soulful best on his three master strokes – "Annie", "Nowhere to Run" and "April Fool" – giving them added poignancy. Lyrical images of north stars shrouded in dust and cobwebs, rusted wheels going nowhere, dreams that once roamed freely now being put to bed, and colours long faded when Jack Frost comes to call haunt these songs and, given the onset of MS, seem frighteningly autobiographical.

Steve Marriott was also not averse to quit a band while on top. After the number one success of 'Ogden's Nut Gone Flake', Marriott left the Small Faces to follow his hard rock and R&B muse. In the process he achieved his goals of losing his hated teen idol image and playing black music. By the end, the man who had starred at the Palladium, played before thousands at Hyde Park and filled arenas throughout America was playing one night stands in pubs. Yet, he seemed happy doing it. In retrospect I grudgingly admired his decision to leave the Small Faces when he did. Marriott was probably right. Had they continued Small Faces might very well have overstayed their welcome and not become the venerated legends they are now. Marriott seemed to instinctively know that the band's time had come and he, at least, bored and stale, needed to follow a new direction. "Itchycoo Park", "Lazy Sunday", "HappyDaysToyTown", "I Feel Much Better" and "All Our Yesterdays", could only have come from a band in the heights of its youthful exuberance. "Midgets on manoeuvres", to borrow Marriott's description of the bands' antics, surely was a very young man's game. The playfulness and joy that exudes from so much of their music may have faded away had they continued to grow up together. That aside, the beautiful and acoustic "Autumn Stone" and "Red Balloon" plus Lane's subsequent compositions give some tantalizing hints at the musical directions the Small Faces might have been headed to next. I would have loved to have heard a complete 1862, the album they tentatively began but never finished.

I only saw Steve Marriott perform live once. It was during a Humble Pie "farewell tour" in 1974 at the Pittsburgh Civic Arena, a soulless indoor sports arena and an awful place for a concert. In the aftermath of the Small Faces break-up I had tried to become a Humble Pie fan simply out of allegiance to Marriott, but never really liked the band very much. All the magic and humour of the Small Faces was missing from Humble Pie and not even Marriott's presence could make up for it. I had never seen the Small Faces in concert – a huge regret – but I had seen the Faces several times and was now determined to see Steve Marriott at least once. The music was loud and raw and the audience very much the same. The smell on the floor was a mix between marijuana and vomit, and the stage was too often obscured by fat assed girls on their boy friends' shoulders. The surroundings were not my cup of tea but Marriott on stage fascinated me. His performance was nothing less than mesmerizing. High frantic energy throughout as if he was plugged into a socket with energy on full amps. Marriott's cockney humour was evident as he bantered with the crowd between songs and he came across the exact way I imagined him to be – cocky and tough, quick minded and funny, charming yet edgy, and very blunt. He could be quite talkative but suddenly the chatter would cease and the strut began. A few boogie blues chords on his guitar would beckon the band to join in and Marriott would again ascend to a different world as he started to sing. How his voice could keep up night after night at that intensity I don't know. There were several mandatory but well-deserved encores and the crowd became louder and more boisterous between each as they demanded more. During the last encore Marriott seemed irritated. Maybe he felt the band had given all they could for the evening and enough was enough. Or perhaps he was embarrassed by the chanting of the crowd imploring the band to keep going and not pack it in. As the last crashing chords faded my strongest memory of the night is Marriott reassuring the audience with a scowl "Don't worry somebody will come quick enough to take our place."

Now, after a quick bus ride up Romford Road, I was standing in front of Steve Marriott's house at 9 Daines Close. The TV cable guys stopped rummaging in the van and looked on perplexed as I took some pictures. "Hi", I said, "Steve Marriott used to live here. I'm a big fan." What I hoped would be both an explanation and ice breaker was met with a hard stare from the older of the two. "Who?" He asked. It almost seemed a challenge. Then, to my relief, he began to hum and sing his own version of the chorus to "All or Nothing". "Is that him?" He asked. "My brother followed some band he was in." Rob, probably in his late 40s, was from Romford and, it turned out, a big Beach Boys fan. His older brother, we determined, had liked Steve Marriott when he was in Humble Pie. Rob seemed less impressed that Steve Marriott had lived here than with the fact, negatively or positively I wasn't sure, that I had come all the way to Manor Park to see his house. Admittedly, there wasn't a lot to see. Daines Close was a cluster of 4-story council flats at the end of the road, electric pylons rose above it and the morning trains ran at the back: Well maintained and landscaped, it was short on atmosphere and straddled the border between urban and suburban. "Now if I was you I'd be off to California, sun, fun, girls and good vibrations," he laughed. We chatted for a while and then that hard look that I had earlier misread returned to his face. "Is this what you expected? You sure came a long way to see it." I wasn't sure how to answer. Instead, I countered with a question for him. "Ever heard of an Itchycoo Park around here?" Rob responded with a smile which again was hard to fathom. His expression told me no but in farewell he wished me well in finding it. The younger man, bored by it all, had long since gone back to the screen on his phone.

The girls I met on the Dersingham Avenue on the way to Little Ilford Park hadn't heard of Itchycoo Park, either. The looks on their faces told me they had me pegged as a likely paedophile. In their delightful mix of Caribbean cockney patter, they stated in no uncertain terms that they weren't about to talk to strangers. Nevertheless, they were only too eager to ask me about Australia. "Sorry to disappoint you girls; I'm from America." I could almost hear Marriott laughing in the distance.

Of all the places on my itinerary it was Itchycoo Park that I most wanted to see. As a fifteen-year-old the song had risen to mythical proportions in my teenage mind and even to this day that beautiful melody and Ronnie Lane's pastoral lyrics sung in Steve's "soft" voice bring me back to my teenage years in London like no other. Sorry, Mac, I have to disagree with you on this one. Marriott's softer side definitely has its appeal. The tea refused to quit and I relieved myself deep in the rhododendrons with Marriott's full approval, I'm sure. I think it was he who once said "Itchycoo Park" was just a "piss take" of a song, an assessment he used for some of his and the band's best work.

By now the sun had peeked well beyond the trees and was rising above Little Ilford Park. There were many shades of green to rest my eyes but no dreaming spires in sight unless the electric pylons stretching to the south counted. It was all nice enough but, if I was honest with myself, pretty unremarkable, too. Underwhelmed and fighting a feeling of anti-climax, I wandered behind the older turbaned gentlemen walking along the path of the park's perimeter, when a minor revelation came. The reality of Itchycoo Park might not match up to the romantic images I had of it, but to all the neighbourhood kids surely it was a special place. I imagined the goals scored here by young aspiring footballers, "ducks fed with a bun" by toddlers under a warm sun, family get-togethers and first kisses in the shadows and just as the lyrics hinted, no doubt Little Ilford Park had been the place where virginity had been lost, drugs discovered and school skipped – "Why go learn the words of fools", surely part of Marriott's lyrical contribution.

Marriott would object to any over analysis but "Itchycoo Park" has invited more than a few interpretations. Ronnie Lane's idyllic West Country imagery transposed to gritty East London, a commentary on social class and privilege, an East End send up of the "summer of love", a nostalgic look at childhood memories, an exclamation of cockney pride, a proclamation of teenage rebellion, or just a pretty pop song with a catchy chorus. All true, I'm sure, but in a mere 2 minutes and 47 seconds 'Itchycoo Park' succinctly evokes the right of adolescent passage from innocence to discovery. Marriott's impassioned vocals highlight all the nuances of the lyrics. Beginning in a soft, almost pre-adolescent voice he revs up to maximum power singing as if he has grown up and experienced things unimagined a short time before. As good as Marriott is vocally on "Itchycoo Park" I still associate the song with Ronnie Lane. Maybe somewhere there is a demo of Ronnie on acoustic guitar singing lead in his vulnerable, soulful way.

I passed the mosque on Church Road and then crossed over the humped bridge spanning the tracks below. Walking back to East Ham station I was already making plans to visit Kenney Jones' Stepney neighbourhood the following morning.

No fog swirled around hazy gas lit lamps in murky early morning Whitechapel but still I found myself lost in its deep shadows. It had looked easy enough on the map yet somehow coming out of Aldgate East station I had missed the turn for Commercial Street. I wandered up Whitechapel High Street towards the London Hospital, once the home of the Elephant Man, and realizing I had gone much too far cut across New Road to Commercial Street. Losing time, I took the bus to Limehouse and walked back to and up Bromley Road to the British Prince.

The British Prince Pub had come up under a site called "Lost Pubs in Stepney" accompanied by the sad announcement that it had closed for business in 2006 or 2007. This was disappointing news, indeed. Another dream dashed as I had envisioned nursing a pint one night in The British Prince while listening to an East End sing-along in the very place where Kenney Jones, an aspiring drummer from the neighbourhood, had first met Ronnie Lane. Sad, too, that yet another neighbourhood institution was gone for good. But, maybe not! With its freshly painted sides and a sign that still read The British Prince it looked as if the pub might be up and running again. Bromley Road with its squat row houses and church steeple in the distance was my very image of the East End. I half expected to see Alf Garnett of "Till Death Do Us Part" fame come out the door in cloth cap carrying a pigeon cage. Instead, my eyes met a well-coifed woman in a snappy business suit with leather satchel coming down the street. Before I could ask about The British Prince, the woman had gotten into a late model navy blue BMW and drove past, the engine purring nicely. It looked as if this part of the East End was gentrifying. It made sense with London's astronomical housing prices and Stepney's proximity to the centre of London. I wondered if her destination was an office in one of the City's modern tower blocks rising not far to the west. With no one else in sight to ask, I departed the British Prince hoping it would be alive and kicking later in the day. My next stop on the itinerary was Havering Street and the home of Kenney Jones, the man whose broken drum stick I had once possessed.

Much to my surprise the drumstick came into my possession with considerable ease. I might have missed seeing the Small Faces live but I was determined not to make the same mistake with the Faces. My first attempt was a "no-go". My good friend Mike Clarke, who bore more than a passing resemblance to Ronnie Lane, and I bought tickets to see them through the mail at a polytechnic college towards the end of the Piccadilly Line on London's western fringe. I forget who we did see that night but it certainly was not the Faces who never showed up or maybe were never booked in the first place. Nevertheless, they got a great review in one of the music papers which gave Mike and me a good laugh.

The advertisement shortly thereafter in the *Melody Maker* announcing the Faces first London appearance at the Lyceum looked more promising. It was a Sunday night in February of 1970, I think. Not only did the Faces show up but they were fantastic. As soon as they came on it was obvious that they had presence. They just took over the stage. In direct contrast to many of the name groups I'd seen, the Faces actually seemed to be enjoying themselves and were determined not to take the evening's proceedings too seriously. No backs turned to the audience or long, boring jams on this occasion. Rod Stewart couldn't wait to make friends with the crowd and Ronnie Lane, after a few numbers, assured those assembled that it was our lucky night; so far they were sounding much better than in recent rehearsals. They cavorted like a bunch of mischievous brothers and were only too happy to include the audience in the jokes. Rod fawned over everyone in the band and there were more than a few warm embraces. I was fortunate to see the Faces live many times again. Never did they fail to create a bond with the audience and even a sense of community among it.

I only remember three songs from that night. As Woody played the closing riff to "Flying", the band gathered by his side with arms outstretched to create their own personal spotlight. Ronnie Lane sang the opening verse of "Devotion" with Rod's arm firmly draped around his shoulder, and later Ronnie took lead vocal and played guitar on "Stone" while Rod sat playing the banjo. They probably played their entire first album, 'First Step',_but no other song stayed with me. It's the atmosphere of the night I remember more than the music. When the lights came up and the small crowd dispersed, I struck up my nerve to go to the stage. Kenney Jones had broken more than a few drumsticks that night and I asked a roadie if I could have one. Without a word and to my delight he tossed me one. Sadly, if the records survived many moves, Kenney Jones' drumstick did not. It probably found its way to the bottom of a box in storage unceremoniously thrown away without me there to rescue it.

I recognized Havering Street right away from the'Lazy Sunday' video but forgot which house was Kenney Jones'. I had figured it out once from the video but had since forgotten how many doors it was from the end of the block. The man I asked in the stylish leather jacket smiled, held up his hands and politely muttered that he did not speak English. His accent sounded Polish or Russian. No one else appeared and I watched a train rumble across the bridge at the end of the street. I had the impression that Jones had been very connected to his old neighbourhood and wondered if he ever came back. He seemed the most down to earth member of the band a perception only reinforced by the few interviews of him I'd seen. Even at the height of their fame, Jones had elected to stay at home in Stepney commuting each day in his cherished mini to the house in Pimlico shared by his band mates. Too often he arrived only to wait for Marriott, Lane and McLagan to wake up. In the music videos Kenney Jones seems oddly detached as the band grooves and cavorts around him. Younger than the others and only too willing to relinquish the spotlight, Jones at first glimpse appears the least invested. Yet, he was highly regarded by the others not only as a musician but as a person. The ever mischievous and cynical Marriott even recognized Jones' inherent goodness and honesty. "If Kenney said it, it must be true," Marriott once remarked about him. Kenney Jones, now the only Small Face still alive, always proclaimed his pride in the band and remorse in its demise. "I wish we'd never broken up", he once proclaimed. Marriott effectively ended the Small Faces; storming off the Alexandra Palace stage in a temper tantrum one New Year's Eve. His discontent had been evident for months. Lane and McLagan, to my knowledge, never voiced any nostalgia for the band, although Mac along with Kenney worked

hard to regain its lost royalties and took great care in supervising subsequent compilation releases. It's a shame really, as they all said on more than one occasion, that they were fated to come together and play music. Kenney Jones continues to be the keeper of the Small Faces flame and its biggest champion. Good for you, Kenney!

No mini pulled up with Kenney Jones in it and I decided against knocking on doors to inquire about him. I'd seen what I had come for and it was time to leave the past behind and return to the present. I took a final picture of Havering Street, waiting for another train to cross the bridge to complete the picture. The dog crossing the street was in the frame, too, but left before I pressed the shutter.

The wind was up and it was raining. The cool breeze was a welcome relief to what had been an unseasonably warm and sunny week. By now it was very late and I was standing across from 22 Westmoreland Terrace, the spot I had first visited nearly a week before. On that first evening in London I had made a bee-line to see the iconic Pimlico house where the Small Faces had lived together for a year playing music, smoking dope and racing cars on their Scalextric track. Now, on our last night in London, I was back.

Unable to sleep I had gotten up to walk away the restlessness. I found my way for a last look at the old house off Brompton Road to again to be in the company of my parents, now long gone, and visualize that 15-year-old kid I once had been coming out the door. After coming back to the present, I decided to make 22 Westmoreland Terrace my final night cap of the evening. My Small Faces pilgrimage had begun here so it only seemed fitting for a last look and it was on the way back. Westmoreland Terrace was dark and deserted and only a few lights shone behind curtained windows. I sat on the curb and imagined Kenney Jones' chequered mini parked nearby. A kaleidoscope of thoughts and emotions raced through my mind. It had been a good visit. It was fun to play tourist and not only relive London as a cherished memory of my youth but now more to celebrate it as the wonderful extraordinary city that it is. Hilarie, a true Anglophile, had also had a good time and that was important. It was good, too, to be going home to America. As much as I had loved living in London and wanted so desperately to be a true Londoner I had always known deep down that I was really only a passionate visitor. London was a temporary love affair, one that ultimately proved tiring. Living abroad is exciting and enriching and I have had the good fortune to do it several times, but there is a nagging sense of unreality to it. Inevitably the expatriate is a foreigner despite his best efforts to pass as a native. Tomorrow we would fly out of Heathrow and I imagined somewhere over the Atlantic crossing an imaginary line where I would cease to be a tourist just as many years before I had shed the label of expat. There was something real and exciting about that. I bid the Small Faces good night and headed back to the hotel.

Occasionally I hear London calling and think about going back. A visit to the Ruskin Arms is certainly high on the agenda; I fantasize finding myself sitting next to Jimmy Winston. "Fancy a drink, mate?" No doubt my knock on the door of 22 Westmoreland Terrace will be answered by a warm invitation to come in, take a look, and have a chat over tea. Definitely, another pint at the British Prince (if it actually has re-opened) is called for; maybe Kenney comes over from Surrey every once in a while to sit in on drums, just for old time's sake. I'd like to find a kid on Church Road whose face lights up in recognition when I ask about Itchycoo Park or a Pakistani shopkeeper on Manor Park High Street humming "It's Too Beautiful". A trip out to Barnes and the Olympic

Studios is in order just to check the dust bins one more time. The tapes of "Be My Baby" and "If You Think You're Groovy" with Marriot on lead vocal must be there somewhere. I'll make a special point to visit Mac's neighbourhood in Hounslow and, as the planes make their final approaches to Heathrow, pay respects to the man Bainbridge's liner notes referred to as "one of the leading organists in the country" and whereabouts is Wapping Wharf launderette anyway, the place as immortalized in "All Our Yesterday's"? It must exist, if only in my imagination. As the Thames flows by I can hear the band now: Kenney lays down the beat, Ronnie's bass and Mac's B-3 pump away, Steve busks the opening lines in his cockney best and Ronnie takes over on lead vocal completing the magic.

"Ah, fish cakes, cabbage and mash....... Ah, the world is mine!"

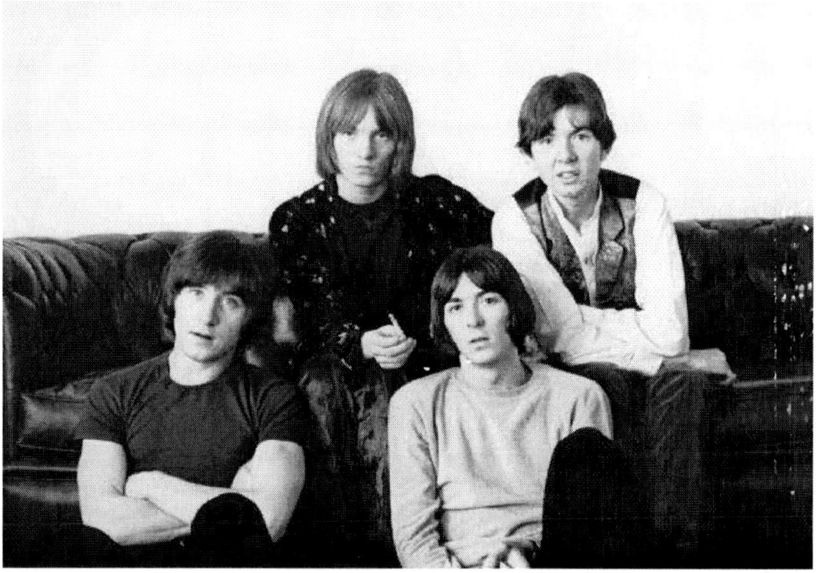

THE GLORY YEARS

John Hellier and Kent Benjamin talk to Steve, Mac, Kenney and Ronnie about what was best described as Beatlemania all over again. By 1966 they were Pop Stars of the highest order!

BY 1966 THE BEATLES AND ROLLING STONES WERE PRETTY MUCH OFF THE ROAD WHILST THE SMALL FACES WERE KEPT CONSTANTLY BUSY TOURING AND DOING TV AND RADIO WORK. STEVE AND RONNIE BOTH COLLAPSED AT ONE POINT DUE TO STRAIN. WHAT WERE THE GIGS LIKE BACK THEN? WHAT WAS THE AUDIENCE BREAKDOWN.....MORE GIRLS THAN GUYS?

Mac: More girls definitely. Sometime you'd have guys there kinda getting the needle too, because their girlfriend was looking at and drooling over us. There were some guys there just for the music but the girls were just there for our look. More girls than guys though.

Ronnie: We were Teenyboppers. We were in our late teens. It was weird, really weird, not like anything I've experienced before or since. We'd have thousands of chicks screaming and if they got hold of you they'd tear you to pieces, man.

DID THAT MEAN YOU HAD TO BE CAREFUL WHO YOU APPROACHED?

Ronnie: Well..........not that careful.

HOW LONG WOULD YOU GUYS PLAY FOR?

Mac: It got shorter and shorter the bigger you became. It's like the more famous you are, the less you have to pay for equipment. We didn't have to buy equipment by 1966. We'd start off playing about an hour, then it became forty minutes, then twenty minute slots. We'd play a few minutes then someone would break through the barrier and it would get out of control and we'd have to quit.

COULD YOU HEAR YOURSELVES?

Mac: We couldn't hear much, it was screaming. We would go on and play all the hits and more but they wouldn't listen. It was just screaming, you know. It was a funny old scene; it was like they were watching television. Girls would literally pee in their knickers and we saw girls in the front row fiddling themselves! They didn't seem to grasp that we could see them, I mean they're in the front row! And it was overwhelming; it wasn't the smell of the pee. It's like strippers, now I know how they feel when there are guys out front touching themselves as if they can't be seen. It was ugly, it was horrible......we were sex objects! It's like a kid with television, they're watching something but have no connection with it at all. I saw that all over again in later years with Rod.

Kenney: We couldn't hear ourselves. Girls would sit in front and diddle themselves. It never went away until we buried ourselves in the studio a lot but it haunted us. Although we had to like it I suppose as it was their way of showing appreciation. You couldn't knock it on the one hand but it became irritating on the other. All we wanted to do was play to them and say "listen to the music and then scream at the end but it never happened that way.

Steve: It was mad. It was a bunch of noise, a bunch of screaming little girls. It wasn't like today where people actually listen. It was just a screaming row. The PAs were sort of archaic; you could never hear a thing. Monitors to me were people that brought the milk around at school! I had to stick my finger in my ear to hear myself properly. It wasn't welcomed, it wasn't pleasant, and they were watching something that wasn't happening. We were just a screen.

Ronnie: There's nothing more a young kid could want, get a hit record and that kind of thing. Whew! The Teenybopper thing became quite enormous really, because after getting the first hit record we never heard ourselves again on stage. It was screaming all the time, you know. I thought it was great to begin with but it wasn't good for the music.

DID YOU WANT TO BE TREATED MORE LIKE MUSICIANS?

Mac: These were pubescent girls. They were only 11-12-13-14 years old, very unpleasant. You'd go on and it would be...oh! Fuck this...they're screaming and fiddling so we'll play whatever we want to play. We'd play just anything, we'd just jam. Jam on one chord, organ solo for ten days and Kenney and Ronnie doing this Cuban/Latin thing.

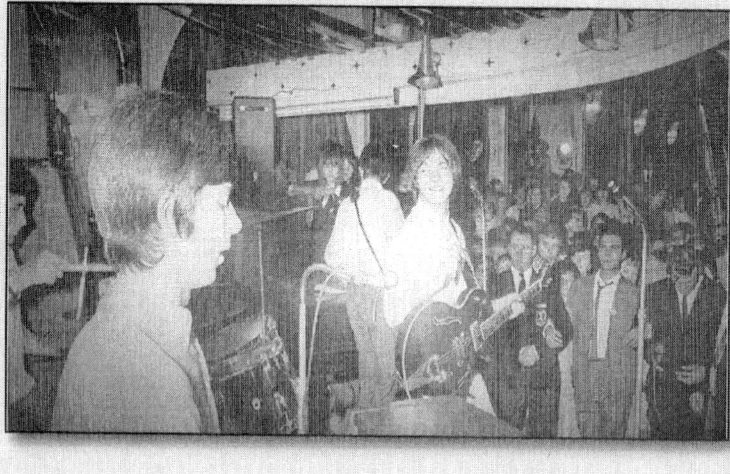

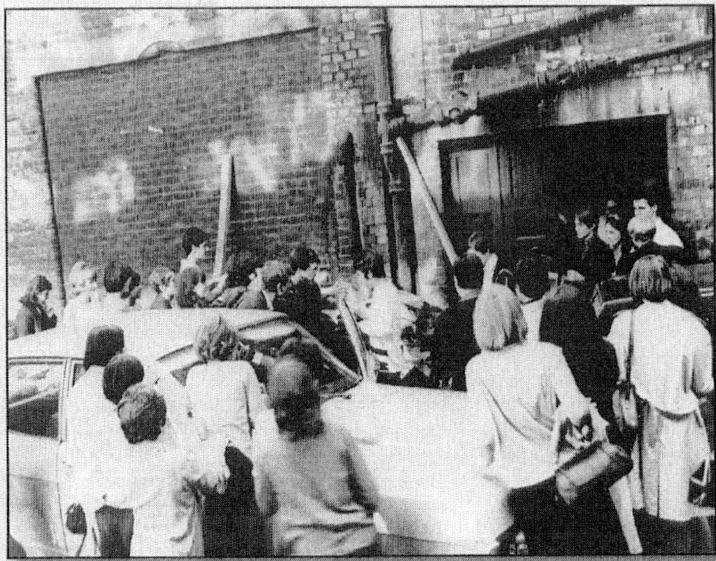

WHAT BRITISH BANDS REALLY FORGED A RELATIONSHIP WITH THE SMALL FACES?

Mac: The Who were mates but the Beatles were already Rock Gods and we didn't bump into them. I used to hang around with the Stones but I didn't really know them back then. Well I knew Brian and Mick a little bit; they were the friendliest of the bunch, never spoke to the others.

Kenney: Ronnie and Steve used to bump into McCartney quite a lot in the hippy, trippy days. They used to go the same clubs places like the Ad Lib and Scotch Of St James, I never used to go. I saw John Lennon walk through Olympic studios once. I sort of said hello and walked out. I think they were all big fans of the Small Faces.

Mac: Ha Ha, they'd probably never even heard of us! I almost met John Lennon in the studio when the Stones were recording We Love You and he and Paul were doing backing vocals. I was in the studio next door laying down piano tracks and John stuck his head around the door. I looked down at the piano and when I looked back up again he was gone. The kids in the 90s were either Blur or Oasis fans but not both. In those days it was the Beatles or Stones. I was a Stones fan. The Beatles got the big push though, also the Beatles were not from London and the Stones were so I could go see them a lot. One time at the Station Hotel in Richmond, I think, the Beatles came down to check them out. I was there that night. At the time the Stones hadn't even made a record but they had a big reputation. This would have been around spring or summer 1963. I went on to work with some of them later on, well all of them except John. I wrote a song for George called Far East Man and Paul used to come and watch the Faces after we covered Maybe I'm Amazed. I first heard that record of his when I and Ronnie were in a car going from Connecticut to New York City. It came on the radio but they didn't say who it was by. I thought that's the type of stuff that McCartney should be recording without knowing it was him.

Kenney: I'm good friends now with Ringo and Paul and I see George now and then as well. I got to play with Paul in the Rockestra Charity gig, so did Ronnie.

HOW DID YOU FEEL WHEN ALL OR NOTHING REACHED NUMBER ONE IN 1966?

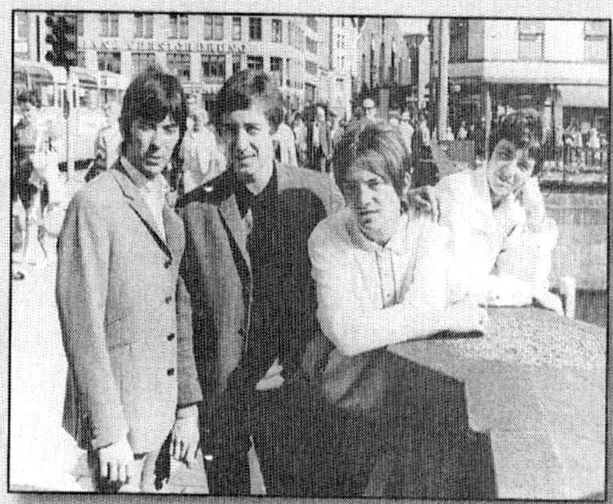

Mac: I don't remember but I'm sure I must have felt pretty damn good.

Kenney: It was an amazing feeling, it was history. We had a joint number one with the Beatles Yellow Submarine at one point. I'll never forget on Top Of The Pops they had our pictures joined together, like cut in half. Half my face and half Ringo's. I've still got a picture of it somewhere, yeah fantastic.

DON ARDEN GOT THIS REPUTATION AS BEING A CROOK. DO YOU THINK THAT REPUTATION WAS DESERVED?

Mac: Well, like I say in my book you've got to give Don Arden credit where credit is due. He was a great manager and did a lot for the band. He was a great manager in the old school way, a bit like Colonel Tom Parker, in the same way you never knew where the money was and you never got the money. Bills got paid, you got fed and you worked hard. Our parents realised something amiss was going on. We got wages every week but where was the money for the hit records? Behind our backs all the parents had a meeting with Don. He was too clever for them and fobbed them off. He threw a red herring in front of them and said (gangsters voice) "Well people in Show Business spend money and they've spent theirs" "Oh! And by the way they're all on heroin!" That shut them up, didn't it? When they were all done crying, they left. Then they were attacking us. It was bollocks we weren't on heroin. We left Don shortly afterwards.

HOW DID YOU COME TO SIGN FOR ANDREW LOOG OLDHAMS PRESTIGIOUS NEW RECORD LABEL IMMEDIATE RECORDS?

Ronnie: Steve was mates with Andrew and he knew the Stones as well and I suppose he went to him and anyway, we signed up with Andrew. After Decca Records it was like heaven, you know, and everything was laid on for us. We could have as much studio time as we wanted. It was a dream to start with but we never made any money from Immediate Records, I don't think anybody did.

Steve: Me and Ronnie did a bit of teamwork on the shopping around for a new manager and agent. We flitted around and tried a few different contacts including Chris Blackwell at Island Records. He said that whoever took us on would have to give us 100% of their time and he didn't have time. He liked us but he had Stevie Winwood and his new band Traffic and that was so time consuming that there would not be any time left for us.

WITH THE CHANGE OF RECORD LABEL CAME A CHANGE OF MUSICAL DIRECTION. HOW DID THAT COME ABOUT?

Ronnie: Well by 1967 we were more thoughtful with our lyrics, it was called Psychedelia, and I was spiked at this party with Beatles manager, Brian Epstein. This weird guy came out with a plate of cut up oranges on it and he passed them out to his guests. I thought this is funny! A funny party ain't it? But I had a bit of orange as everybody else was indulging. About an hour later strange things started to happen. I didn't know what I'd been given, if I'd been given anything at all. At first it was quite frightening but then it turned into something quite beautiful.

Steve: When we were with Decca we were in the studio for just three days to make a complete album. With Immediate they were both our manager and our record company so it suited their purposes as managers to have us in the studio as long as possible. They gave us time to experiment and progress because in those days you didn't have all the electronic gadgetry you've got now. We used to have tape loops running around the back of fucking chairs and back onto the machine to get the desired effect. It was great for that reason you had to experiment because no fucking machine was going to do it for you. I suppose it could look like we set out to become an album band but no, not at all. We practically lived in the studio all the time we were with Andrew.

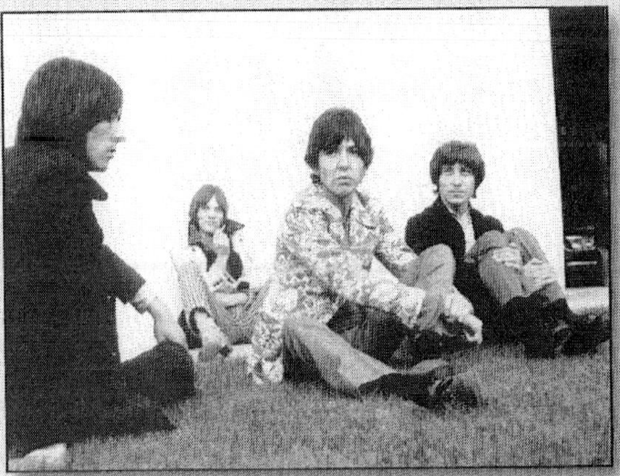

Kenney: What happened was we were given more studio time to do whatever we wanted. Andrew Oldham would just encourage us to stay and play and do whatever needed doing.

WHAT ABOUT THE TV SHOW WHERE STEVE APPARENTLY STOLE THE TAPES AND RAN OFF DOWN THE ROAD WITH THEM?

Mac: I think that happened in Italy. We'd been messed around and hung up, I vaguely remember that. We were cheeky lads. I do remember once we were in Paris and the cameramen were drunk and they bumping into each other and rolling about laughing. They dented my organ and we all walked out. I think we did a promotion tour in Italy and they were fucking us around. We did a take for a TV show and we wanted to hear it so we just took the tape and walked right out. Actually Steve didn't take it, it was Andrew Oldham.

ANY RECOLLECTIONS OF THE COOL PROMO VIDEOS THAT YOU MADE, PARTICULARLY THE ITCHYCOO PARK FOOTAGE ON THE BEACH?

Kenney: That was great fun that one. We shot that down at Camber Sands in Sussex. Don't forget that in those days it was unheard of to do a video. The word video hadn't been invented! They could be sent out across the world for showing, great promotion. I remember driving Andrew's little mini around the beach all day, I fell in love with it. We just fucked around on the beach all day; I seem to remember Pat (PP) Arnold being there with us. We did another Itchycoo Park film in Chiswick Park in London. We all lived near there so it was convenient. I have vague memories of others, there was one where three of us were dressed in policeman's uniforms and chasing Steve. That was in Regents Park. There was one that was shot for Lazy Sunday in my Mum and Dad's house in the East End, well in the back garden anyway. An irate old lady

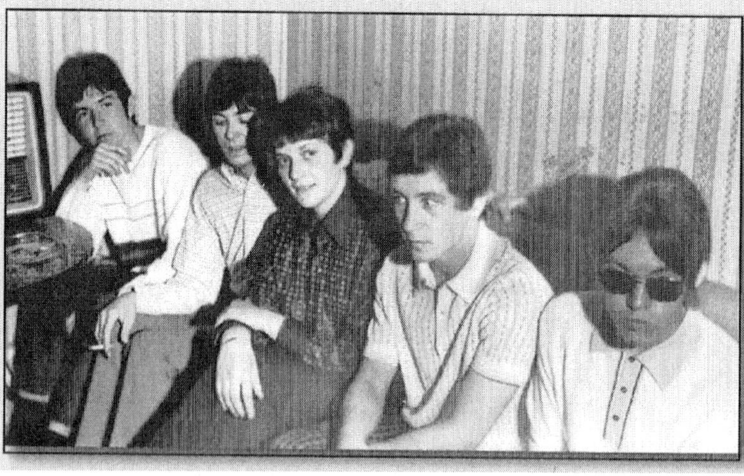

knocks on the front door and then they go through to the back where we had an outside lavvy. I think some of that film was also shot at Steve's gaff in Chiswick down by the river.

ANY RECOLLECTIONS OF THE INFAMOUS TOUR DOWN UNDER WHERE YOU BROUGHT THE WRATH OF THE AUSTRALIAN GOVERNMENT DOWN ON YOU?

Steve: Well it was a bad rap. We did a press conference and I put out my cigarette on the most obvious place, the floor. It was the only place you could, there were no ashtrays. They picked on that calling us Dirty Old Englishmen! I was seen to scratch behind my ears so they said I'd caught mange off of my dogs. The Australian trip was a total disaster. It was fun though, midgets on manoeuvres. We had a lot of laughs but we came away owing money. Smashed up rooms and stuff like that had to be paid for. Then it was New Zealand, in Wellington it was my 21st birthday and they gave me the only suite in the hotel, which was really nice of them. Me and Keith Moon and a Who road manager called Wiggy destroyed the place. I'll tell you how it happened. EMI had given me a little portable record player as a birthday present so I'd gone out and bought a bunch of great records. They're so far behind over there you could still get stuff that you couldn't get any longer at home. I started playing it and it fed back into itself and made a terrible humming noise that you couldn't get rid of so I just threw it over the balcony. Wiggy went down and got it and I threw it over again and before you knew it there were chairs, TVs, settees,, mirrors......everything was going over the balcony, the whole fucking deal. There was quite an audience watching as it all came down. It was ridiculous, I was hurting with laughter, it was so funny at the time.......pissed as newts! We'd be lying on the floor gasping for breath and someone would see something that wasn't broken, then break it and sling it over the balcony and it would all start again. Anyway, we were lying there wondering what to do and then we just passed out. When we came to we could see what we'd done, there was nothing left in the room it was all on the pavement. I think Ronnie and Pete (Townshend) were there at the beginning and Pete said to Ronnie "This'll end in the nick" and they split and left the three of us to do it. We were the culprits I'm afraid, so I had a great idea "Let's say somebody broke into our room and complain about it". So that's what we did and the police were there interviewing us and all that. We got one policeman drunk in our room and actually wore his helmet while we continued the rampage. Keith Moon rings up the reception and says "Look, what kind of security do you have? Our room has been broken into and vandalised and we paid good money for these......" The police came again but Wiggy, who was totally bald, had been seen throwing an armchair over the balcony. There was this wig hanging by the bed and they're talking to him "Do you know a bald man?" and he'd say "No". It was as simple as that and we got away with it. I thought "great"; the next night would be cool. They spent all day re-furnishing the place, putting in new French windows and everything. Come the evening, Keith comes up and says "They done a good job" and immediately put an ashtray through the French windows and off it all goes again. Furniture over the balcony, the lot. We didn't get away with this time, no chance. The second time it was like "Oh God we can't possibly get away with it" so instead Keith put on his bravado, which was always funny to watch. We were drinking champagne, still celebrating twenty-one, and the manager came up in his dressing gown. It was late, about three in the morning, and he said "I know it was you this time, who has done this?" And Keith put the manager's dressing gown cord in his drink and said "I did it". Like, whatcha gonna do about it? "Moons the name". So I think he took most of the rap for that, which he should have done really.

Ronnie: We got on the aeroplane early one morning for the flight to New Zealand, we'd been up raving the night before and I fell asleep on the plane. There was an Australian support band also aboard and they'd brought some cans of beer on with them. They started drinking and in those days it was illegal to consume alcohol on the flight and a couple of the stewardesses took a very dim view of it. We'd had a load of bad press anyway and they were obviously influenced by this and they refused to serve us any coffee. I'd woken up and I was sitting with ex Manfred Mann singer Paul Jones, who was also part of the tour. He certainly was not one of us geezers from the East End; he spoke properly with a bit of a plum in his mouth. He started to demand coffee in a very loud voice which made the stewardesses burst into tears. They complained to the Pilot and the incident was reported. The Pilot had obviously been reading the newspapers as well and knew what a load of scallywags we were. He made an unscheduled landing at an airport on route and when we landed there were all these Police and television cameras there waiting for us. I said to everybody " Go out with your hands on your head and it'll look like the plane was hijacked, it'll look really good on the telly". That's what we did. Apart from the trouble that trip is where I got to know Pete very well and it turned into a religious thing as well. I was reading a couple of Sufi books and he was reading about this guy called Meher Baba that had this thing called Sufism Reorientated. That's where I started to learn about Baba and he seemed like an alright guy. Pete and I had fun, the beginning of a long and close friendship. My song "Stone" (aka Evolution) came directly from Meher Baba's teachings.

Steve: I think Paul Jones was our spokesman 'cos he spoke proper English. "It didn't really have anything to do with us" he was saying and we were making raspberries behind him. Terrible slags we were, terrible liars. I think they let us do one more show then we were deported. The Police saw us out of the country! New Zealand was enjoyable. We got to the airport and Pete Townshend immediately smashed one press guy's camera, he threw it. Oh, here we go again! They kind of understood because I don't think they're keen on Australians either.

STEVE MARRIOTT** interviewed by **JOHN HELLIER, MARCH 1985

IAN McLAGAN & KENNEY JONES** interviewed by **JOHN HELLIER, FEBRUARY 2001

RONNIE LANE** interviewed by **KENT BENJAMIN, JUNE 1989

Real Fun:

An Exclusive Interview With Ian McLagan

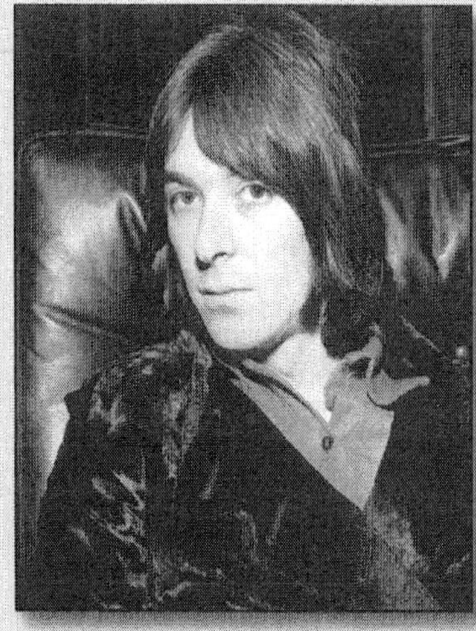

"It all comes down to having fun. Real fun. Over the years, I've been asked to play on different people's records, but I have turned them down. I just told them I was busy. They were people I didn't particularly like. Even if I was broke, I just couldn't do it. I was invited to audition for The Grateful Dead, and having never really listened to them much, I bought one of their records to hear their music. My wife came home that night to find me sitting there in the dark, with a very sad face. She asked me, "What's the matter?" and I replied, "Oh, nothing. I've just been listening to this band and I cannot bear them! I just couldn't do it." The potential was there for huge amounts of money, but she said, "Mac, you can't do it. If it puts you in that sort of mood, forget it!"
– Ian 'Mac' McLagan

Born Ian Patrick McLagan, May 12, 1945 in West Middlesex Hospital, Isleworth, Middlesex, Ian 'Mac' McLagan is today best known as a founding member of two iconic bands: The Small Faces and The Faces. In the 1960s McLagan played keyboards and sang backing vocals as a member of The Small Faces, following earlier stints with The Muleskinners and The Boz People. He joined the group in November 1965, replacing Jimmy Winston, and played his debut with The Small Faces at London's Lyceum Theatre on November 2 of that year. After Steve Marriott left the group in 1969, singer Rod Stewart and virtuoso guitarist Ronnie Wood joined the band, which emerged as The Faces. After The Faces split up in 1975, McLagan worked as a keyboard player for The Rolling Stones, where his signature B3 organ sound was a highlight on both the band's studio work and their tours. McLagan also worked on various Ronnie Wood projects, including The New Barbarians. In addition, he has built an impressive resume of session work, backing such notable artists as Bob Dylan, Bruce Springsteen, Joe Cocker, Bonnie Raitt, Chuck Berry, Jackson Browne, Paul Westerberg, Melissa Etheridge, Frank Black, John Mayer, Izzy Stradlin and Nikki Sudden. McLagan has also released several solo albums. An in-demand player, since 1977 he has served as bandleader with his own Bump Band, which played at the 2006 Austin City Limits Music Festival and opened for The Rolling Stones in Austin, Texas in 2006. Currently, Mac and his band play a regular weekly gig at the Lucky Lounge in Austin, Texas, where the band enjoy a devout following among the patrons of Austin's city nightlife club scene. In addition, since 1997 McLagan has been a member of Billy Bragg's band. In 1973, McLagan developed a relationship with Kim Kerrigan, the young, estranged wife of Keith Moon. After she divorced Moon in 1975, the two lived together and later married on October 9, 1978, one month after Moon died at the age of 32. On August 2, 2006 Kerrigan died in a traffic accident in Travis County, Texas, aged 57. Her car was hit by a truck, and she was pronounced dead at the scene.

First, I want to congratulate you on the induction of The Small Faces/The Faces into the Rock & Roll Hall of Fame. Were you excited about that induction? Well, first I want to say that those are two separate bands; they are not the same band! The Hall may think they are, but they are not. You know, as long as Madonna's in there for dancing and miming, then it just makes a joke of the whole thing!

I've read that Booker T. Jones was the driving force behind your picking up the B3 organ. Is that true? Yeah, absolutely. I heard Green Onions and it changed my life, really. I just wanted to play that sound, you know! He's brilliant, and he's just got a new album out, The Road From Memphis. The roots are back in him, it's brilliant!

What was it about growing up in post-war England that resulted in such a plethora of outstanding, legendary British musicians and singers? What was it about that post-war atmosphere that resulted in this? The music in England at that time was crap, that's why! Well, the music in America at that time was crap too. You had stuff like "How Much Is That Doggie In The Window?" and it was all very middle-of-the-road rubbish. Then we heard the Blues, Soul and R& B, and it touched our hearts! We didn't know where that came from, but we just wanted to hear it and wanted to hear it now.

You've been quoted as saying that right up until you reached your teens; the British adolescents didn't have their own unique style in clothing, music, or much else. We take it for granted these days that you can wear any colour…well, I mean, back when I was a kid, you actually wore small versions of your dad's clothes. It was dark blues and browns, miserable clothes. There just weren't any clothes for kids, not like now. Even babies then wore these zero size, adult clothes; either that or they were naked.

What do you think about The Small Faces Ultimate Collection? There are so many collections you know; I'm not sure which one that is. There's been so many that I get confused. I'm sure I've seen it, but it's hard to keep up. Right now, they are working on a really good Small Faces collection that covers the Decca and Immediate periods. It has alternate tracks. This guy in England has researched it and has found all kinds of stuff they never knew existed. Kenney (Jones) and I are very keen to get that out.

How does that music sound to you now, Mac? It sounds a little old to me, frankly. I'm not that influenced by it. The music I was influenced by still sounds as fresh as the day I first heard it. Stuff that I'm on, I see the faults and I hear the stuff that I may have played better. I just don't think that the (Small Faces) records are as interesting as the records that turned me on. But I'm proud of them, just not quite so excited by them.

Do you have a favourite Small Faces or Faces song, and if you do, then why is it your favourite? Well, my favourite Small Faces song is Tin Soldier. I think that track is really well-played, well-written, well-sung, well-recorded and well-produced. I'm real pleased with that; I think it's as good as we got. In fact, the funny thing is that Booker T. & the MGs obviously like it because they included licks from it into a song called Carnaby Street. For years I thought that we must have stolen that from them, and then the author of the book about Stax Records (Soulsville USA: The Story of Stax Records) interviewed me for another project, the Small Faces DVD All or Nothing 1965-1968. I asked him about that, and he said, "No, no, no! You were first!" So they borrowed Tin Soldier, and knowing that really knocked me out!

That's a real compliment. That's more than just a compliment. That's something that needs to be on one's tombstone!

You've been quoted as saying that you're having some trouble remembering some of those older songs. It depends on what the song is, but sometimes they disappear from the memory. Maybe we only played them a few times.

Do you have a favourite memory or story from your days with either The Small Faces or The Faces? When I think of The Small Faces, I think of us on the road. We were the closest pals, same as The Faces. But since there were only the four of us, we were very tight. We lived together and we did everything together for three or four years. But you know a favourite memory keeps coming back: it's just us in the car, going to gigs. Kenney used to sit in the front, and Ronnie, Steve and I would sit in the back. We used to smoke, listen to music, laugh and giggle, and had the best time! We'd get to the gig and we'd play music, then we'd leave the gig and we'd listen to music. Then we'd go back to the hotel and we'd play music, then we'd listen to music. It's all we did, and it was fabulous! You can't have a better life, and also we were playing shows that were jam-packed with people. It was very rewarding in that way. We didn't get the money that we thought we were getting, but it's sort of irrelevant when we were having the best time and the people who came to our shows were having the best time too; the best time we could give them, anyway. So it was just…it's just a ton of memories. But it was just the feeling of us being in the car, listening to music and having a damn good time!

What bands were you in before The Small Faces? I was in a band called The Mule Skinners. That was my first band. We were formed at art school; the four or five of us were at art school together. I was with that band for a couple of years, and then I got an offer to join another band and be paid for it, which was pretty good. I was sort of managing the band. I booked the gigs and I booked the van. I'd book the guy that would drive the van, and I'd rent gear. I was kind of in charge of everything. I wasn't the best, the most talented. After a while it got kind of tiring, and I got called to join a band that was going to pay me and provide me a place to live and the music was okay. It turned out that was The Boz People. The lead singer was Boz Burrell, who went on to become a bass player with Bad Company. So I was with them for about six months, then I quit because they weren't keen to work and it was frustrating; I wanted to get on with it. Then I got an offer to join The Small Faces the following day. I joined immediately on November 1, 1965.

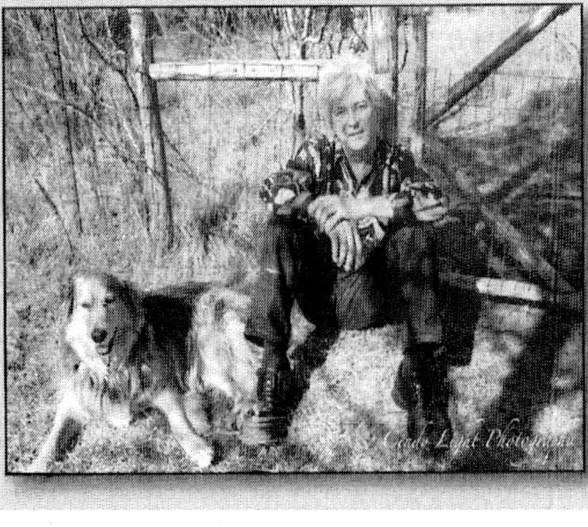

Do you still enjoy playing those classics from that period? Well, I don't play many of them, frankly. I very rarely do All or Nothing and I don't do Tin Soldier as it's too complex: two guitars, keyboards and Steve Marriott's voice. It's all too much bother! I play Glad and Sorry, but I don't do it too often. It's really hard to replicate Steve's voice.

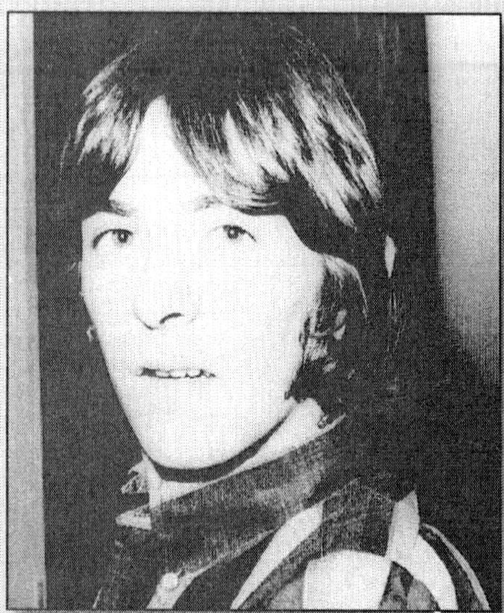

Do you feel like your music has only just begun to reach its potential that your best work is still ahead? I do! I mean, I hope that's true. The point of it is I enjoy what I do. I'm still writing, recording…you know, I have a keyboard right here (Mac plays a few mean licks on his organ) and I have a piano right here (plays his piano) and I also have the grand piano right here! (Plays some hot New Orleans style boogie) I love what I do, you know! I'm blessed, I'm a lucky guy! So many people in this world don't do what they like, but I love what I do.

Mac, you'll live to be 100 doing what you love to do, and doing it well! Well, as long as I'm healthy. I'd like to be old! I'd like to be healthy when I die!

It's a lot better than the alternative, as my granny used to say, LOL. Now, I know from reading your autobiography (All the Rage) that your relationship with The Rolling Stones goes way, way back. You've done two tours with them. Do you still keep in touch with them? Not really. I mean, I speak to Charlie (Watts) every now and then, and of course I speak to Ronnie (Wood) all the time. Keith (Richards) has been known to call me, and I've been known to call him. I don't really…I see Bill (Wyman) every now and again. But you know those are busy, busy boys!

You've been living in Austin, Texas since 1994. I've read that the reason you moved there from Los Angeles wasn't because of Ronnie Lane, as many fans believe. Rather, you moved there because of earthquakes in California. Yeah, well that last one really knocked me out! That was it!

Was that the 1994 quake, Mac? Yeah, the Northridge one. The news media said that it was the "big one" on January 17: the day of the earthquake. Then the next day they said it wasn't. I looked at Kim and said "Okay, we're out!" She'd wanted to leave anyway, and I guess that was all I needed. I was done! We were gone! We arrived here on May 21 '94, so that's 18 years ago.

Tell me about your band's past and current members. My bass player now is Jon Notarthomas, and on solo tours he comes with me. For me, 'Solo' actually means me solo part of the time and duo the rest of the time. Mark Andes left about three years ago. Don Harvey and 'Scrappy' Jud Newcomb have been with me since I moved here 18 years ago.

Are you maintaining your Thursday night residency at The Lucky Lounge in Austin, Texas? Yes, since last October. Prior to that, The Faces were on the road touring. Scrappy too.

You've been turning out amazing projects with your band (The Bump Band). I know that your album Never Say Never received glowing reviews. After all these years in the music biz, that must

be gratifying for you. It is, yes. It was nice to get some recognition as a writer, and the next one hopefully will keep that moving, you know. I haven't stopped. I actually had hoped to get an album out before the Faces tour, but there wasn't enough time. It's especially gratifying at this late stage when a lot of my contemporaries aren't writing and are relaxing on their laurels. I have no laurels to relax on, I'm building my laurels.

Over the years, your sound has been known for the B3 organ. Yet on your album Never Say Never, it got relegated to the backburner. I think it's only heard on two tracks. Why is that? It wasn't intentional. I wrote most of my songs on piano. There just wasn't a place for organ. I wanted to keep it simple. It was actually on three things, but I took it off one of them. It just wasn't necessary. On my next album, of the six songs we've already got, three of them already have B3 on 'em. I don't write on the organ, never have. It's a strange instrument. If you hit a piano the note dies out, whereas if you hit an organ the note's there until you stop. It kind of makes it difficult to write. I don't know, maybe I'll never write on the organ.

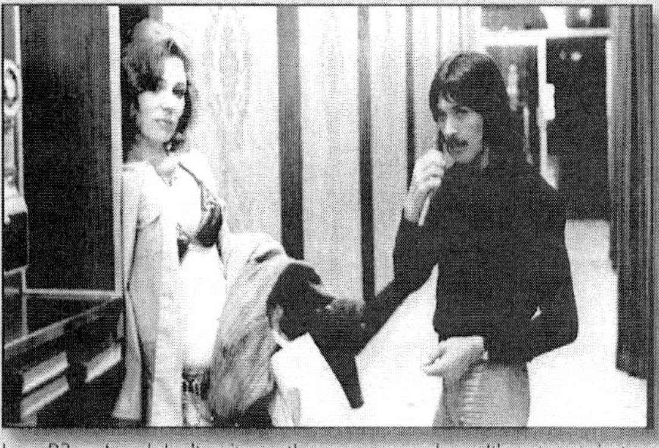

The story behind the album's title track, that's very emotional: the story of your beloved wife's untimely death. I read an amazing account of yours, where you said that you actually saw her spirit appear to you as clear as day. I saw her. Absolutely! It's the second line in the song: "I can see you standing in the shade. The sun is glistening, blinding my view." The sun wasn't glistening, I was crying, and I couldn't see. Everything, everything was glistening! You see what I mean? It actually happened. In fact, it's happened a couple of times. I saw her in The Lucky Lounge one night, near the stage! That's the last verse: "I can see you standing in the crowd. I can see your face in the crowd, and I've been listening to an angel's cry."

When did you see her appear at The Lucky Lounge? A couple of weeks after she died. You know, it's not rare. I went to grief counselling, and I sat with a lot of people who had lost their wives and husbands and whatever. I mentioned this, and they just gathered around and hugged me, and so many of them said, "We've all experienced it" so it's quite common. We're not used to the 'other world' and we don't know anything about it. Who knows what happens after death. I know there is something. She hadn't disappeared, I didn't invent it. I saw her twice. I only wish I could see her again!

You've been quoted as saying that the song Killing Me With Love was written for Kim when she was still alive. Yeah, I used to play that for her.

How did that album come about? Well, actually I had already recorded…Killing Me With Love it was quite old. That was the earliest. In fact, George Reiff was my bass player when that was cut. On several tracks I had already started recording. I woke up one day and thought about doing an album, writing songs. I'd always planned to do it, and I looked at the date and realized that Ronnie Lane's 60th birthday was only a couple of months away. I thought it would be nice to have an album of his out on his birthday, to play those songs to him on his birthday. So I shelved what became Never Say Never temporarily, and we started recording Ronnie's songs, and put Spiritual Boy out on April 1. We played it at a gig at a cinema here in Austin, and then they played the documentary of his life, and we then played a few more songs. It was a magic night! That was in April, and Kim died in August 2006. After that, I didn't do anything for a while. Then, when I did start writing, I went back to see what I had, and we already had quite a few tracks. We cut some of them, and I just got down to work. It kept me sane at that point just to keep working. Actually, I haven't stopped ever since, so I must be very sane, LOL.

Speaking of Ronnie Lane, fans and critics alike have noted the special care that you've taken over the years to keep his life and his music alive and vital. Can you tell readers what this means to you? Ronnie was the heart of Small Faces and Faces. He was the glue. He was the reason The Faces started. Ronnie Wood called him up and asked him what he was doing after Steve (Marriott) had left. So they got together and I got together with them, then Kenney got together with us. Then Rod came in and we had a band. But Ronnie Lane was the beginning of Faces and his songs meant a lot to me. The reason he left was because of Rod basically, Ronnie wasn't gonna be singing any of those songs live. He never did. He only sang a couple over a period of three or four years. He knew Ooh La La was his swan song. Most of the songs were his, but he knew he wasn't gonna get to sing any of them, so he quit. He never got the recognition he should have. He went solo, made records and had some success. But not big success, not success in America. He deserves more. He deserves better! When I put the box set together, I tried to address that fact with notes about him. Even today I still play his songs in my show, because they mean so much to me and so much to a lot of people. But there are people who don't know about him, so I've got to tell people.

I've heard that the Ronnie Lane/Steve Marriott song writing partnership was much like that of Lennon/McCartney in that each wrote their songs separate from the other, then they came together for the final product. The thing is there were all kinds of variations. Steve would have a song that Ronnie would add to, and vice versa. Sometimes they wrote together, and sometimes I was there with them writing, but I didn't get credit. Eventually I did, though.

You've played in bands with arguably two of the greatest singers that the UK has ever produced: Steve Marriott and Rod Stewart. Can you compare those two experiences? Actually, I've played in three, because The Rolling Stones have one hell of a fucking singer too! The difference between Steve and Rod...well, they're both so cool to play with! I'm pretty much spoiled. I wouldn't pick one over the other. I think they were both so great and unique. There are lots of great English singers who don't get the recognition they deserve. People like Terry Reid, Joe Cocker, etc.

Was it difficult for the band when Rod began to have success as a solo artist? No. It helped us! Are you kidding me? We had more people coming to the shows. We did more TV, more gigs. It was all positive.

You've been quoted as saying that Itchycoo Park has dated very quickly. Can you elaborate on why you feel that's so? Our recording of it has dated very quickly. I realized that Ronnie Lane would have sung it much slower and with more feeling than "It's all too BEA-UUU-TI-FUL!" which makes it sound like a comic song! When I recorded it on Spiritual Boy I played it at a slower tempo so that you could hear the lyrics and I could express myself a little bit more in the lyrics. It's a very special song. It's not just about getting high. It's about education and privilege in England. What he's really saying is "I haven't got money. I haven't been to Oxford or Cambridge. I don't believe that education really matters. I haven't got England's wonderful scenery. I have a nettle patch in the East End of London and it's beautiful, and I do get it!" and that's really what the song is all about! He's saying that he has a nettle patch but it's enough for him, and he loves every leaf! It's a much deeper song than most people realize! That's Ronnie Lane for you!

Over the years, the fans have speculated on the possibility of a Faces reunion that would include Rod Stewart. You've been quoted as saying it's not going to happen. Oh no! I've never said it's not going to happen! Rod's decided he's not going to do it right now, but the door is open. We extend our open arm to him! We want him to do it, for fuck's sake! At the moment, he's got other plans. I respect that. We would like it if he would change his mind, but if he doesn't, he doesn't. Life moves on.

Over the years, many Faces fans have wondered why there's been no re-release of those classic albums. Do you know why they haven't been re-released? I do, yeah. Lawyers! They've been sitting there with extra tracks, covers already designed, for about three years…four years now! Sitting there, while meanwhile Warner Brothers disappeared! There's no such thing as Warner Brothers anymore to spearhead the releases. So I'm afraid that the lawyers, as always, got in the way and are holding it up. They're still there, waiting. And you'd think that with Faces there on tour, they would at least try to get them re-released! Don't ya think?!

Who owns the rights to all that material, Mac? It depends on what you mean by 'rights.' Warner Brothers have the rights to the recordings. Warner Chappelle, who had the publishing, have just folded. So I don't know where we stand, but I'm sure we'll find out soon. We'll get a letter from a lawyer, LOL.

You have a wonderful quote: "The next autobiography that I write won't be written until I'm on my deathbed!" It will be written long before, but it will probably be called Burning Bridges. When I go, the truth comes out! It may not be for a long time, because I don't want to be around when that shit hits the fan! But I will tell the truth about every fucker! I do try to tell the truth, I really do! A lot of stories develop over the years, but the truth is the best thing. Before that book comes out, there'll be another book, which I've started to write: a book about Kim. It will be all about her life. People need to know about Kim. In another way, she is like Ronnie Lane. People need to know about Ronnie Lane and they need to know about Kim McLagan. She was beautiful. Absolutely beautiful.

Do you have a tentative title for her book? No, not yet.

Well, I want to read that one I'm looking forward to it. I've written some, but I need to get to it when I don't have other things to do.

In the last few years, you've become increasingly well-known for your paintings. You've gotten great reviews; you've done some gallery shows. Indeed! A couple of gallery shows. I've printed twelve of the paintings on 5"x7" postcards, and I'm gonna take them around to gigs and hope to sell them as small versions of what I do.

You've been quoted as saying there's a direct connection between your debilitating bouts of migraine headaches and your painting. How has one influenced the other? When I get a migraine, the first sign is this visual effect they call the 'aura'. It's a flashing…it's just a horrible thing where you can't see properly. You only see the aura. I decided I was going to try to capture it because it's just so debilitating. The idea is that you take medication, close the blinds, lie down and wait for it to go. I don't do that anymore. Instead, I take my medication and try to draw what I can see. Sometimes I paint at the same time. The result of that was seventy-five to eighty paintings of auras. It wasn't like I was becoming an artist – I've always painted – but this was me trying to capture something that no one else could see. People have tried to capture the auras, but they haven't been successful. I've seen about a dozen paintings of people's auras, and they're not successful. I've done much better, I think. Anyway, it's been some relief just to say to the migraine, "You're fucking with me, I'm gonna fuck with you!" It's called "paint from pain" and Van Gogh knew all about it!

You're best known for your prowess on the Hammond B3 organ. Are there any particular makes/models of organ you recommend, and if so, then why? Well, the B3 itself is a model, and I have several of them. The thing is that the B3, C3 and A3 are exactly the same: they're just a pump box. It's just that one is made for church; one is made for home, and so on. The B3 is slightly lighter than the C3 or the A3, and looks better onstage. It's just a magic piece of instrument; a combination of mechanics and music.

During your days with The Small Faces and Faces, what makes/models of keyboards did you play? In the early days of Small Faces, I already had an L102. In fact, I'm looking at my L102 right now, the one I bought last year. It's made in 1963, and that's a nice little organ. Then I got an M102 which is slightly bigger, better sounding, and that too was in the Small Faces days. Then when Faces formed, I bought the organ I'm standing in front of, which is the one I use onstage ever since. Every Bump Band gig, (the recording of) Maggie May, Faces gigs except for the current Faces because I rent. This one I've had since 1969 and she's my baby, yeah, she's my BABY! When you hear a Hammond organ on one of my records or a Faces record or one of Rod's records, it's this one you hear.

When you look back at your long and highly influential career, what are you the most proud of? Most proud of my own albums, actually. Especially Never Say Never and Spiritual Boy. I'm just proud of them; I think I do good work! And the next one is going to be even better!

As you look back over your career, is there anything that you would have done differently? No. No regrets! I've been lucky to have a career in music, and it continues. I play the music I love, I turn down work I don't want, and I've got a nice place to live. I had the love of a wonderful woman for 33 years. Everything's ok!

Arguably, you're one of Rock's best-known, most respected keyboard players. Do you have any advice for up and coming musicians who want to achieve the best possible sound from their instrument? It all comes from the love of the music. The music guides you. I love music. I just love to play. I mean, the thing is if you're in the position to do something that you love, and then you don't look at it much harder because you won't even feel it, LOL. The only advice I've got is this: people, if you love music, then don't look at it as a business. Don't think, "Oh! I'll make money!" because there's no money to be made in music unless you get very lucky! I do sessions, that's where I get my money. It's not as rewarding as playing what I like to play live onstage, but I don't make much money out of that. Follow your heart in everything and be lucky, and accept luck when you get it!

SHIRLEY PENA (May 2012)

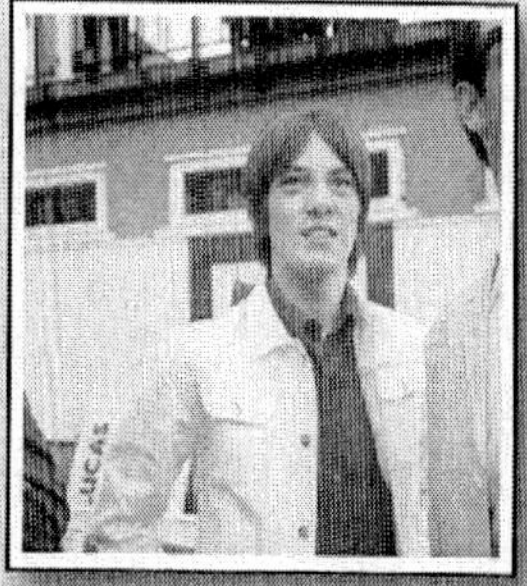

POP THINK IN..... STEVE MARRIOTT (1966)

"We'll be able to get plastic sitars in our Cornflakes soon"
Steve airs his opinions on.........

STAR STATUS: I don't really know much about it. It's all in other people's minds and you don't know how big or small you are in their minds. You can never really tell what people think. It doesn't worry us and we can only do our best.

SOUL SINGING: Everyone's got soul but as far as negro soul singing goes only negroes can do it. But white artists can interpret coloured soul into their own. You don't have to be born on the wrong side of the tracks.

LOONERS: Should form a private club where everyone can go and have a loon.

THE WHO: A gas. I can't really understand their personal basis, the friendship basis, but I don't want to understand. Their music is great and always will be.

VIOLENCE: Don't like it. I've had many a kick before I was in the group. Where I come from, London's East End, violence was the "in" thing. Since I've been in the group I've realised how stupid it all is. There's just no need for it. Violence equals vegetable. Never go out in the East End after midnight. It's a terrible place. The thing is I used to be one of them and when I think back the whole thing was stupid.

NOISE: Love it. I love noise! At the right time, of course, not when you've got an headache. I like to hear records played full blast because it's the only way to listen to the music and I always play as loud as I can and I like to talk as loud as I can. I can't stand people who talk softly and whisper. Noise in general is a gas! There will never be too much noise.

ATOMIC WAR: Hope it never happens. It doesn't scare me because you'd never know what happened but it's horrible to think about.

SIR WINSTON CHURCHILL: I think he was fantastic. The whole group were cut up when he died. Plonk digs him the most. I'm not too keen on his son, Randolph Churchill, from what I've heard of him.

SUCCESS: Is a very nice thing. It must be everybody's aim to be successful. People say we are but once again it's all in people's minds. I suppose we are successful but we'd be happy no matter what we are. A lot of things come with success like Kenny, our drummer, going down with nervous exhaustion.

FAILURE: I was a failure at school completely but I was happy. Failure is a horrible word. I don't think anybody is really a failure. It's what other people make of them.

FRIENDS: I haven't got very many mainly because I don't want very many. True friends that is. I've got hundreds that call themselves friends but they are not always people I want to be friends with. The group are friends and I'm very friendly with my Mum! I'm not friendly with the Noise Abatement Society! Once you've had a hit record you've got hundreds of friends that you didn't even know before.

FRUSTRATION: This can cover a lot of things. Musically I'm happy. I feel sorry for frustrated people who don't have peace of mind. Women are my frustration, nothing else!

INVOLVEMENT: Cor, you've picked some things for me! Don't get involved with things that don't concern you because it leads to frustration.

LSD: Something I don't know much about, except for what I read in the Sunday papers. It's a mind drug and a short cut.

CARS: I think I'd kill myself if I had one because I love speed. If I go up north to Manchester I have a car to shoot about in but I put it in a ditch last week. You've got to be a genius to drive in London.

YAKKING BIRDS: Pills give a lot of these birds the rabbits. If I meet a yakking bird I say "Oh, I'm sorry I've got an appointment". I try to keep out of their way but when a bird starts rabbiting look at her eyes that way you'll always suss them out.

BABIES: I don't really want any.

BRIAN JONES: I've only met him a few times and he's been completely on his own scene. I think he's a gas, a really nice fella but unless you're also on his scene you can't get through to him. I think he's very talented and has a lot to do with the sound of the Stones.

SCREAMING LORD SUTCH: A big influence. I used to go to watch him at the Wykeham Hall in Romford. He always had a good band and people should admire him as an entertainer because that's exactly what he is, an entertainer.

RELIGION: I don't believe in religion and I don't think you have to go to church to be religious. You can believe in God while sitting on the khazi. English religion is very sad. We talk about it in the group all the time. We can never understand why religion here is full of repentance while in America, in the negro States, religion is happy and smiling with happy songs. Here it is very hypocritical because everybody repents then carries on with more adultery. I don't dig religion at all.

TV ADS: There's always a lovely looking bird eh? Some are great. I like ones where they take time to knock you out. I don't like bird seed ads though mainly because I don't like bird seed.

SPOONS: My Dad plays them. Really, he's great! Fred Scuttle for President!

FRENCH FAGS: Do my lungs in. When you wake up in the morning with that parrot cage mouth feeling you know you've had a French fag. It's all they smoke in France, funnily enough.

PURPLE HEARTS: Things of the past. There are so many pills now that people refer to as Purple Hearts. I think they're a drag. Pills do you in eventually.

RAGA ROCK: Most ridiculous term I've ever heard used. It's all over blown and inflated. I like Ravi Shankar, he plays a good sitar but there's plenty of good music as well as Indian, Japanese or African music. The point is we'll be able to get plastic sitars in our Cornflakes soon. If it doesn't let up the same will happen to Indian music that happened to Folk.

FAT FACES: Fat people have more character in their faces and they all seem happy. Maybe it all comes back to Father Christmas!

(First published in Melody Maker 1966)

WE ARE THE MODS!!

John Hellier talks to Steve Marriott, Kenney Jones and Ian McLagan about THE ACE FACE years.

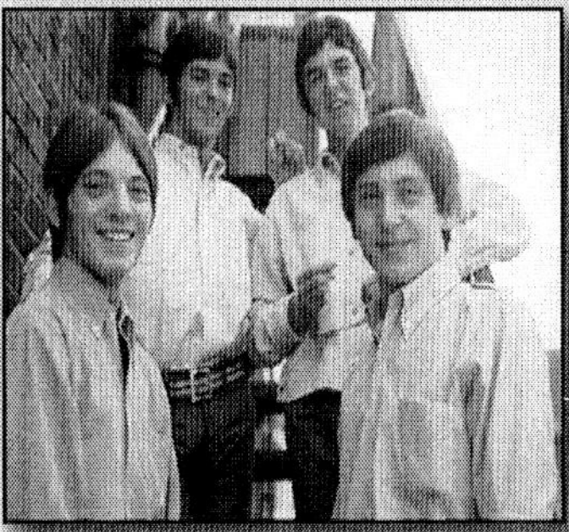

THE WHO ALWAYS TRIED TO PRESENT THEMSELVES AROUND 1964/1965 AS MODS BUT THE SMALL FACES WERE REAL MODS?

MAC: By then Roger was a real Mod. Pete had only just got out of art school so couldn't afford the clothes and John, of course, wasn't. Yeah, Daltrey was a Mod, he was quite a heavy little tough bastard! I wasn't a Mod until I joined the Small Faces. I was at art school, like Pete, and didn't have any money for clothes. It was like a brown corduroy jacket and jeans for me. I wasn't interested in Mods. There was a couple of guys at art school who had the parkas and scooters. I liked the clothes, well apart from the parkas. I thought they were stupid.

STEVE: I was a Mod, I had my anorak (a parka). I think to establish yourself, in the very early stages, clothes can really set an image for you, really work for you or it can make you a laughing stock. It was a cool thing while it lasted but it's over now. Kids are always searching for something new and I think music has taken over from the image nowadays.

WERE ALL THE GUYS IN THE BAND MODS PRE-SMALL FACES (WELL, OTHER THAN MAC)?

KENNEY: We were all Mods before we formed the band, when we met up we were already Mods. We had all identified individually with what we wanted to be before we had actually met. It was absolutely amazing that when we all bumped into each other we all looked the same. Same taste in clothes, same taste in music and the same outlook generally. We were the first young generation to be born after the war and I remember growing up as a kid in black and white. Everyone wore black, white or sometimes grey. Our generation were the first to wear bright colours. We always wore bright things and it was acceptable to dye your hair as well. A lot of Mods actually dyed their hair blonde. It wasn't called dyed, it was called bleaching your hair back then. We actually used bleach, no hair dye from the chemist.

STEVE: I was one from around 1963. There weren't a lot of Mods to begin with, only a few around where I was living. I used to save up all my dough and go down to Carnaby Street. The funny thing about the street was that it was only a handful of dingy little shops early on and they used to import all their stuff from France. An actor mate of mine, who I used to hang around with at the Square Ring coffee bar in Manor Park, first turned me on to the place. He'd always turn up wearing all the latest gear but it was expensive. I had to save up for it. But really, we used to get laughed at. Me and Ronnie and Jimmy, Kenney wasn't really a Mod, used to get wolf whistles from geezers on building sites and my ol' man didn't like that. I mean it did take a lot of courage in those days. I think there are more Mods now (1985) than there was then, well to begin with anyway. Now every gig I play I see Mods. In the 60s it was a very select crowd. If you went up North there were no Mods up there at all to begin with but eventually they took it up and Manchester and Sheffield did become very Mod indeed. It was nice to be different, well that's the way I felt about it anyway. It's all to do with mates as well. I mean you look around and there's always one geezer that looks different. You clock him, ask him where he got the gear, he tells you, and you become a Mod without really thinking about it. That's the way it went.

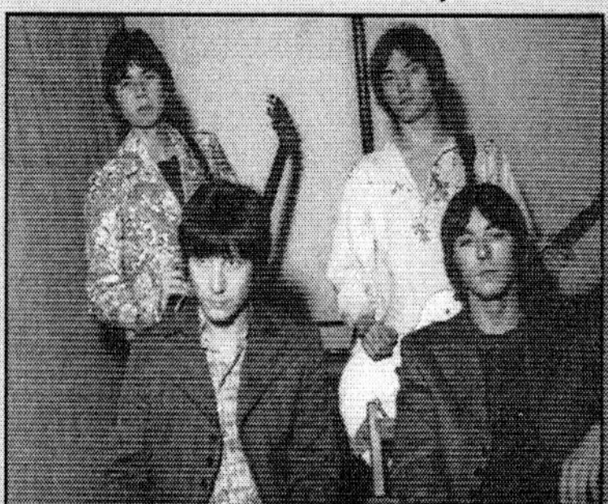

KENNEY: I had my Mini then. I'd get home, park outside and all I did was clean it, polish it and put clocks and stuff on it. It was my extension of a scooter really.

<u>DID YOU ENJOY THE MOD IMAGE THAT THE BAND PROMOTED?</u>

MAC: Yeah, we could go down Carnaby Street and fill a taxi with shirts and jackets and hats and stuff. I just wish I had kept some of the gear. I remember a beautiful suede jacket with a leather collar. Actually Kenney wore it on an album sleeve picture and then he gave it to me and I wore it for years. And some of the shoes and suits.......Yeah!

KENNEY: I do that all the time. My mother had a load of stuff. It was all either given away or auctioned off for charity. There's nothing left now.

STEVE: We never tried to impress an image, it was just the way we were. I think the difference between us and groups like The Who was that they actually had managers that saw Mod and deliberately dressed them like that. We were just of the street. The Small Faces were what they were before anyone discovered them. We were just a little Moddy band whereas The Who actually got things bought for them. I thought The Who were great, it's only in retrospect that you can look back and see that Pete Meaden, a great mate of mine, and Kit Lambert kitted them out. But then you had the legitimate Mod bands like The Action they were of the same age as us and they were just off the streets as well, they were not groomed. There were a lot of bands that were groomed though, bands like Grapefruit and Johns Children, they were sent to go and get all these clothes from a particular shop. There was a lot of rotten, horrible bands that had a lot of money spent on them and they amounted to fuck all really. Out of that quagmire of bands the Small Faces came to the top because they were legitimate and I think it showed.

THE SMALL FACES WERE ABOUT SO MUCH MORE THAN JUST THE MUSIC TO MOST FANS. THE OVERALL IMAGE WAS ONE OF PERFECTION. DO YOU AGREE?

MAC: Well the clothes were a lot of fun. It was great to be able to have a lot of great clothes and shoes and always have a choice of what to wear. I don't have that choice these days. I wish I did, if I see clothes I won't buy them. I mean Rod just goes out and spends $7000 on clothes just like it was nothing but the music was the focus of the Small Faces. The core of it was Muddy Waters, Marvin Gaye, Booker T, Otis influenced. That's what the band was all about it wasn't the clothes.

STEVE: Mod meant money. A way of life gone wrong. It went up its own arse. As soon as too much money gets involved the people who are in it can't get into anymore, as soon as it starts to cost money if you see what I mean. Mod never really did cost money at first. You'd buy the cheapest things but in the style you wanted and then they'd start producing it because they realised there's a demand for it and then up the price. The whole original idea was to be individual and as soon as they started mass marketing the stuff and up pricing the hell out of it then the thing of being an individualist is lost. Mod was individual at the time, it's like saying that you want to be an individual but within a group. That's a contradiction but it's a good one. You want to be an individual but just a little bit, not too much just a little niche. It is down to the individual what they want to wear

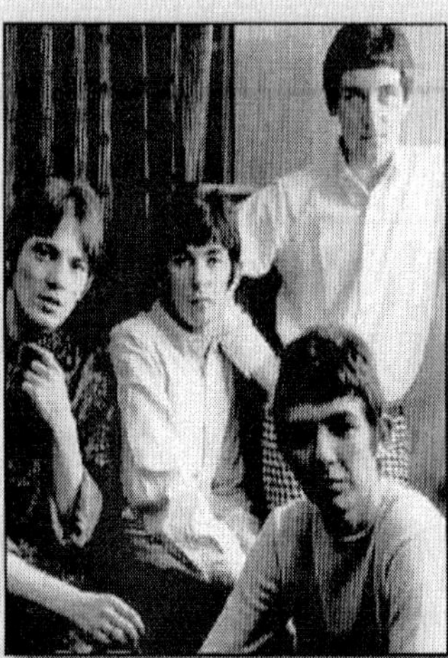

within some set rules. There were some set rules, no doubt about it, like the length of trousers, colour of socks, length and style of hair, that kind of thing. That was the code that said you were a Mod. The rest of what you covered your body with was up to you. But then it all got out of hand and, like anything, as soon as it got out of hand all was lost.

DO YOU STILL FOLLOW THE MOD MOVEMENT A LITTLE BIT?

KENNEY: Oh yeah, the great thing about the Mod movement is that it'll never die. Even if it goes out of fashion there will always be that spark movement and that'll always keep it alight. Every time it comes back it gets stronger because it's the sentiment behind the movement of the Mods, not just fashions but a movement that says "We are here, take notice of us we're just people in a group and we're having fun and it's alright to have fun! Nothing wrong with it and if we get a bit outrageous we don't mean to upset anybody. Stay cool!

ARE YOU GUYS THE GODFATHERS OF MOD?

KENNEY: I think it's great that we're finally seen as that. Over the years everybody has been hyping the Beatles and the Stones and there we were all the time. Everybody realises, all these years later, that if not musically the Small Faces made the biggest fashion statement of the 60s. We were ahead of our time, of that I'm sure.

STEVE: The media gave us the name and called us Mods. We didn't know what the fuck it was, y'know, we just liked button downs and when I look back on it now it was fucking great! But I couldn't do it myself now. I'd be like a cartoon of myself, a parody. No, I'll leave it up to others to carry that flag. If I did it now I'd look stupid. I'd be like an old man dressed up in young clothes. It would be stupid.

STEVE MARRIOTT interviewed by JOHN HELLIER in March 1985
IAN McLAGAN & KENNEY JONES interviewed by JOHN HELLIER in February 2001

ALEXANDRA PALACE AND OUT!!

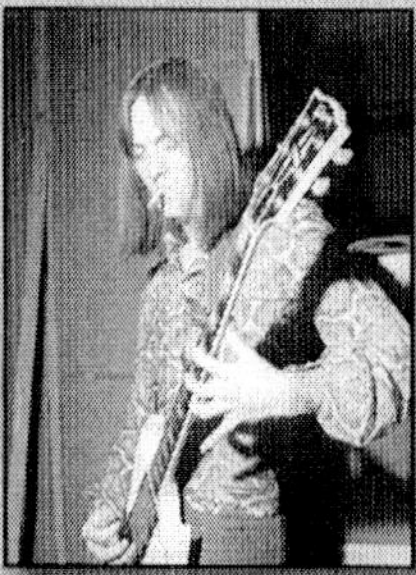

Steve Marriott's own account of that now legendary New Years Eve gig that signalled the end of the road for The Small Faces....as told to John Hellier in 1985.

Steve recalls...The band had just returned to England from a recording session in Paris with "the French Elvis" Johnny Hallyday. We were booked for a New Years Eve bash at Alexandra Palace along with John Mayall, Joe Cocker and Amen Corner. I asked the others if Peter Frampton could stay as he'd been recording with us in Paris and I thought he'd add something very special to the band. He'd be another influence, another player that I could do dual things with. I wanted him in the Small Faces and I wanted him to do that Ally Pally gig with us. Peter was up for it after all we were his favourite band in the whole wide world. When I put the suggestion to the others they all gave the idea a unanimous thumbs down! That was a big downer for me and then that New Years Eve gig went badly, so very badly! It was horrendously bad!! Nobody was looking at each other, it was a total shambles. Alexis Korner got up and played, that was my idea I must admit but at the time I thought it would work. I just thought " This is terrible", I slung my guitar to the floor and did a very unprofessional thing, I just walked off. The set wasn't even finished but it was near to the end. The sound was the worst we'd ever had. I left the Small Faces that night really although we still had a few gigs to do contractually, but that was it. It was embarrassing and it showed that we weren't at all together live on stage still. We had become too involved with recording and we couldn't transfer it over. We were very mediocre and nobody seemed bothered about it. Peter could and would have changed that.

At the time Ronnie and his Mrs. were living in a barn at the back of my place which was embarrassing. I had this little country cottage (Beehive) and there was a barn at the back of it on the same ground and that's where they lived. He was in the process of moving out but it took about three months which was awful because there was a definite bad feeling which there needn't have been to be honest. I talked to him afterwards about it all and he just couldn't understand why I had to go. I wasn't getting good vibes and the band were too loose. Years later after Ron left The Faces he finally knew and he said to me I now know how you felt but I didn't at the time. You can't you see because dissatisfaction is for the individual.

RONNIE LANES BRIEF ACCOUNT OF THE ALEXANDRA PALACE FARCE.

"Steve went on stage that night in a foul mood and we knew something was up. He had been throwing real wobblers all week and then halfway through the set he just threw his guitar down and walked off leaving us there like three lemons! We looked at each other and it was like...well see ya! There was this almighty row afterwards, Mac went particularly wild and was screaming. Steve just simply said that he couldn't do it anymore, he felt we couldn't cross over from being a Pop band to something heavier. He felt it was too difficult which was wrong because we had it all and were going that way naturally and I'll always remember when it was announced in the music papers, it said " Steve quits to play with better musicians" which broke my heart because I always thought we were alright!

THE CONCEPT ALBUM....
as a new art form.

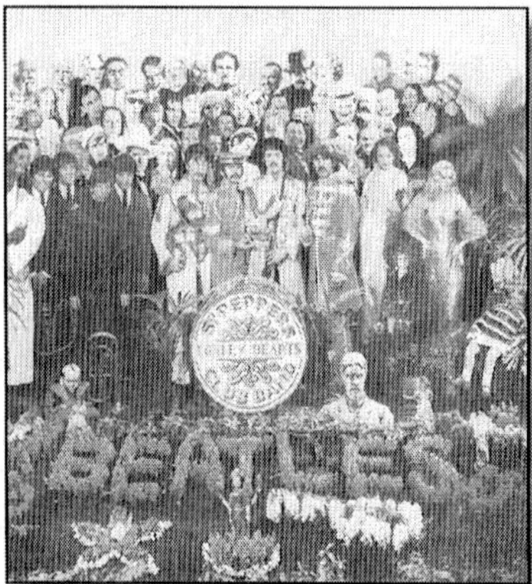

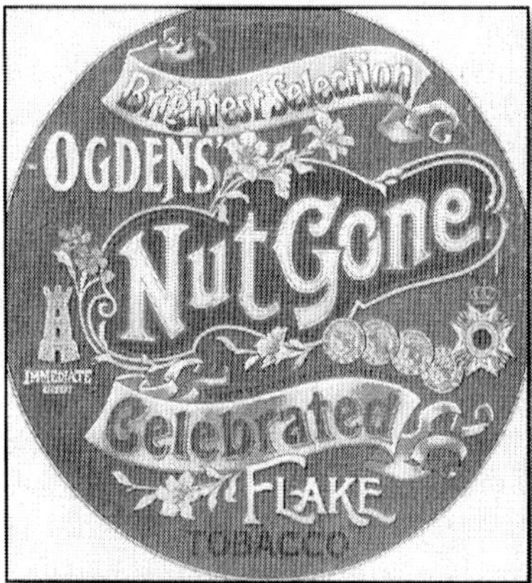

A comparison between Ogden's Nut Gone Flake and Sgt. Pepper

On the 1st June 1967 the Beatles released the album Sgt. Pepper's Lonely Hearts Club Band and the whole production and recording techniques of popular music were blown apart A new term also came about from the release of this album, the term "concept album". An album that told a story or had a theme. This to some extent was denied by the Beatles camp but it certainly registered as doing so with several other bands and musicians of the time.

Some of the content of Sgt. Peppers songs are influenced by elements of traditional British culture and of "high culture". For example, the title itself: the military connection, the marching band, the music hall overtones, the fairground organ, the use of brass instruments and it's incorporating of classical music arrangement techniques in the shaping of the songs plus the experimental use of new instruments such as the Mellotron, a fore runner of the Synthesizer. The band also indulged in experimental recording techniques such as double-tracking, over-dubbing and tape splicing. Add to that George Harrison's Indian musical cultural influence on the album with use of the Sitar and Delrouba (a kind of violin). By 1967 they had the time, the money and most importantly, unlimited musical and technological resources to be as idiosyncratic as they liked.

Everything about the album reeked of the "Swinging London" scene in the late 60s, they were no longer a Mersey Beat group. Dressed in Edwardian costume the reproduction posters could be found adorning the walls of Carnaby Street and Kings Road clothing boutiques. There was indeed a shop in Carnaby Street called "I Was Lord Kitcheners Valet" that sold military style tunics of the ilk of that on the album cover and inside sleeve. The LP, with Peter Blake artwork, slotted them in alongside London's elite and the emerging upper classes such as David Bailey and Lord Snowdon. Rich young socialites were now becoming part of the new scene..Rock and Roll had started to become intellectualized.

While all of this was going on around the streets of Chelsea and Knightsbridge another band from a very different area of London were set on proving their own worth musically. The Small Faces came from a very strong working class background (East End 'erberts!) and were very much part of the London Mod scene. Up until now much of the music press (wrongly I might add) dismissed them as a twee Pop band but by late1967 they were signed to the newly formed and very adventurous Immediate record label and were planning a concept album of their own (albeit only one side of the record). Their 1968 masterpiece Ogden's Nut Gone Flake was (and still is) a treasure.

The album is as distinctive in its appearance as the Beatles Sgt. Pepper. It has a circular gatefold sleeve and the printed front cover depicts a tobacco tin. In a recent edition of Mojo magazine Lois Wilson described it as "...one of the most elaborate sleeve designs in Rock history". There are lots of similarities and coincidences in the making of the two albums. Some are minor but some situations are reflective. It bugs me that in 2012 the album is remembered more for the round sleeve than the music itself. Compared to the adulation afforded to the song writing and production on Sgt. Pepper this album, although lauded at the time, has not held the lofty position as the definitive period piece. There are circumstances that influenced this. The Beatles had conquered the American market so were much more "international" than our East End fab four but as far as being the "definitive period piece" from a totally British angle, this I feel is arguable.

Let's highlight a few of those

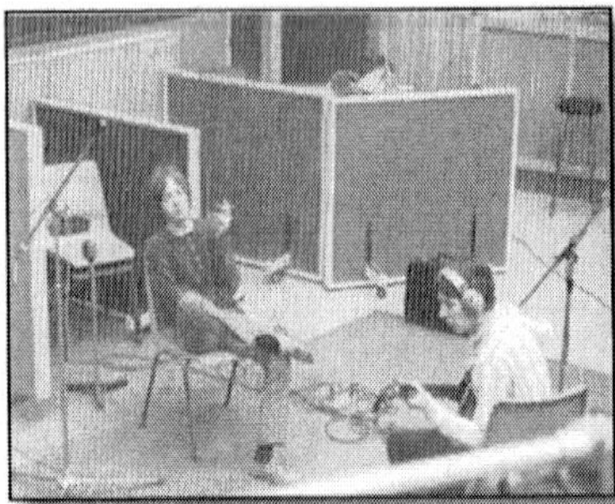

coincidences. The Small Faces had recently signed to Andrew Loog Oldham's Immediate Records after having previously been with Decca. Similarly to the Beatles they had grown tired of the endless pop merry-go-round of single releases and soul destroying tours. In the halcyon days of 1967 the Small Faces had progressed and ventured naturally from Mod to Psychedelia and as with the Beatles there were two main songwriters in the band. Marriott and Lane were both multi instrumentalists. Marriott possessing arguably the best white Soul voice this country has ever produced. As a guitar player his skill was shamefully overlooked, he was also a fine keyboard player and played a mean Blues harmonica. Ronnie Lane also sang lead vocals and was an incredibly solid bass player very much with a style of his own and also handled guitar as well on a lot of the studio sessions. In Ian McLagan they had a keyboard player that suited the style brilliantly moving from Booker T influenced Soul to some straight forward boogie woogie playing. Lastly, there was the solid and dependable Kenney Jones filling the drum stool They were sharp, sussed and wore their working class roots on their sleeves. Steve and Ronnie especially seemed to treat the "ass licking" side of the music business with the contempt that it deserved and treated a lot of the glitzy Chelsea set with mocking tongue in cheek humour but when it came to capturing a period with great songs through the simple fact of being "real" they were second to none.

Eventually they met a sound engineer who was willing to experiment with sound, instruments and technology in the studio...one Glyn Johns. They began recording sounds and then playing them back alongside other tracks out of synch, creating "phasing". This experimentation coming together brilliantly in the classic Itchycoo Park which was released on 4th August 1967. As with the Beatles releasing the double A side Strawberry Fields Forever and Penny Lane as a taster for Sgt. Pepper this was a taster for Ogden's. Similarity again in the fact that the Beatles had taken cherished childhood areas of Liverpool and wrote classic songs around them, so Steve and Ronnie took what many people say is a piece of wasteland in Manor Park in London's East End and with a certain amount of satire transferred the "trippy, hippy" California happenings and re-located them to "Swinging London" but the working class East End of it. They followed that with yet another classic single Tin Soldier before the tag "hippy" could be attached to them. The recordings continued into 1968. The band having the idea of mixing tracks they had been working on during the latter part of '67 with the idea of a concept to one side of the next album.

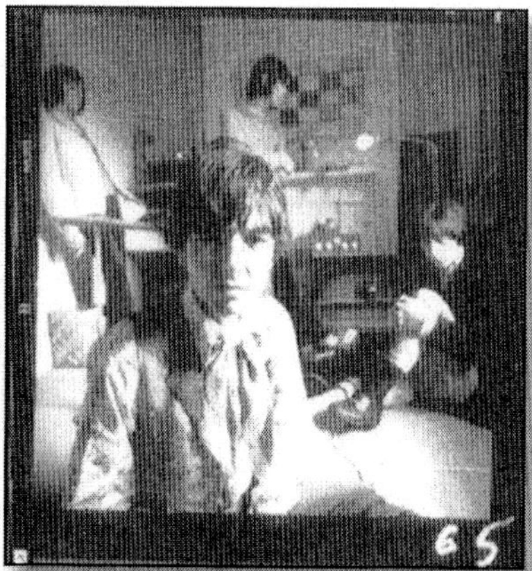

The Beatles with Sgt. Pepper not only released an LP of inspirational songs but also turned the whole presentation of their finished product into a piece of Art, by the fact that the album cover is as famous as the songs that feature on it. The sleeve was a talking point and artist Peter Blake gained worldwide recognition for his work.

The creative juices of the Small Faces were bubbling over with ideas on what the title and cover of their album should be, again with streetwise sensibilities playing it's part. An ex employee of Decca Records, who was now working for Immediate, mentioned the idea of releasing an album in a round sleeve. Ronnie had the idea of a tobacco tin. This, of course, having interwoven meanings given the era, culture and social class values of the band. The brand Ogden's being their favoured loose tobacco for rolling their joints with, also the tobacco tin being a particular working class artefact and a very British one at that. A small link to the Beatles again is the fact that the Ogden's Tobacco Company was Liverpool based. Andrew Oldham rang the company and asked them to send a catalogue of their tobacco tin designs. The guys in the band chose Ogden's Nut Brown Flake but changed the name to Ogden's Nut Gone Flake... a little in joke as when it was mixed with marijuana it blew your mind when you smoked the stuff! The cover opens up to reveal humour and serious representation again running side by side. There's Psychedelic illustrations along with a packet of cigarette papers, brand name SUS, no explanation needed. The rear cover depicting the weight of the tobacco tin- a 1lb box. The cover also folded out into four gatefold inner pictures of the band members. Another little link with the Sgt. Pepper album is, on the front cover there are four small coins featuring the faces of the individual band members as coins of the realm and also a medal. This is similar to the subtle Britishness and Empire Pop Art noted on Pepper.

The round cover has probably, over the years, overlapped the albums content in acclaim. For me they go hand in hand. The B side was the concept side. The songs based around the story of Happiness Stan and his quest to find the missing half of the moon. He travels on a giant fly and meets such characters as Mad John and finally discovers "Happydaystoytown". Mad, yes, and with the narrative supplied by the king of gobbledegook Stanley Unwin. It's a charming piece of work that combines Psychedelia, Hard Rock and Music Hall. There is a natural injection of humour into the songs and performances. The non concept side of the album also contained a wide variety of genres ranging from Music Hall (Rene, The Dockers Delight and Lazy Sunday) to Psychedelia (Long Ago's And Worlds apart) to arguably Steve's finest ever love song (Afterglow). Ogden's hit the top of the album charts and stayed there for six weeks and spent a total of 19 weeks in the top ten.

The song content, in my opinion, is as ambiguous as anything on Sgt. Pepper. It doesn't bring us the mystical east flavouring of George Harrisons Indian music influence but instead it gives us a mystical East End flavouring of Swinging London in 1968. It's an excellent example of a period piece of work that incorporates all the elements of the "new art school" of the time. Art design, photography, presentation and the musical composition of the songs mixes classical instrument arrangements with new studio technology, inspired natural musical talent, excellent Pop sensibility and song crafting for the first time. A sense of humour that enabled them to combat the self indulgent musical masturbation by musicians that riddled the oncoming "Progressive Rock Music" era.

To conclude my discussion...Both albums are premier examples of how Popular music fusing with past musical origins, new technology and other forms of artistic expression i.e.; photography and design, came together to extend the boundaries of what people perceived as Art. More importantly, especially in the case of the Small Faces, it proved that creativity should not be allowed to be hindered by social class.

GARY O'DEA..........

MICK TAYLOR PRESENTS........ THE UNIVERSAL: *THE STORY*

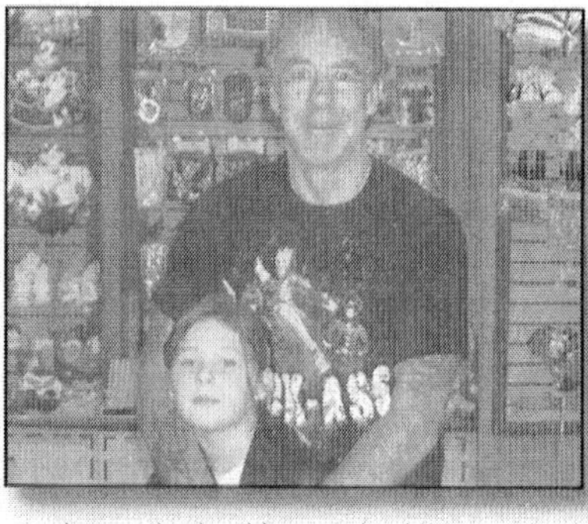

"The Universal" started life as a demo in Steve Marriott's garden in Marlow, Buckinghamshire, whilst he was having a boiled egg for breakfast. (The cottage was once owned by the famous author Jerome K Jerome who wrote 'Three Men In A Boat'). The finished track wasn't intended to be given a 'live' feeling but Steve Marriott said "I tried to better The Universal in the studio but couldn't do it so I had to use the cassette I used in the garden. Makes sense doesn't it?"

Originally released in 'mono' format on Immediate single IM 069 on June 28th 1968 it reached number 16 in the UK charts and stayed on the charts for 11 weeks. The 'stereo' mix was first issued on the two LP set "The Autumn Stone". At this present time the single is worth £9 (white label) and £12 for the pink label.

What's both amusing and amazing is that the live version (in the garden) feels as though all the sound effects like the twittering birds, dogs, traffic are waiting there for their cue to come in. Everything fitted in perfectly. Firstly you hear Steve setting up the tape recorder with the birds twittering followed by the sound of a car horn, followed by Steve on guitar. The dogs on the track are Steve's dogs Seamus and Rufus and if you listen to them they come in on perfect timing with barks - talented musical dogs!

In the 'Olympic' studio the Small Faces added drums, trombone, clarinet, guitar and bass. McLagan's Hammond didn't appear at all. In fact McLagan said later in an interview that "The Universal was all Steve and I didn't appear on it" (obviously Ronnie and Kenney played bass and drums). Until Mac's statement there was a rumour that Mac played the lead guitar solo but it's since been established it could have been Big Jim Sullivan although this is unconfirmed. When the Small Faces did the song on Top Of The Pops Steve sung live vocal over the backing track whilst the other members mimed. Mac always mimed the electric guitar solo bit. Big Jim Sullivan did actually play on a lot of the Immediate sessions and its been officially recorded he played a 12 string guitar on 'Itchycoo Park' plus guitars on the Billy Nicholls album 'Would You Believe'.

The song itself is a thoughtful country flavoured track based mainly around the A, D & E guitar chords on acoustic guitar. When the electric guitar bursts in for a solo I think it's exceptional and intense. Knowing what the song is about and its clever word play I just find the song pretty awe-inspiring.

The Universal came about because Andrew Loog Oldham at Immediate wanted to release another single to keep sales going after the 'Ogden's Nut Gone flake album. Although Steve wanted to release 'Afterglow (Of Your Love)' as the next single, Andrew wanted something new and fresh. Marriott offered him 'Hello The Universal', a song that Steve had recently recorded.

As a kid I absolutely loved this song and still do. I'd say it was amongst my top 5 Small Faces tracks. I distinctly remember Steve Marriott saying in a music paper about the Universal - "The people out there like comedy records such as Lazy Sunday so I'm giving them another one". Steve said in an interview later "The Universal was a right piss-take. I think that's one of the funniest and best songs I've ever written. At the time it went like a fuckin' bucket - down. People didn't understand it at all. Maybe it has a certain laughter value. I recorded it in the back garden and you can even hear the roadies arriving to take us to a gig and my wife Jenny coming in from shopping and shouting "Hello Steve". Steve did actually say in another interview though that his dog barking was at the arrival of a roadie - Dave.....and when Jenny came home from shopping, she is saying "Hello Dave". When I transcribed the lyrics for this story I listened to the stereo version to try and hear what Jenny is saying and she does indeed say "Hello Dave".

Talking of live version's, The Universal is the only track yet to be released as a live version from the concert gig "Live at Newcastle". All other tracks from that gig have been released, firstly on the 'Autumn Stone' and 'In Memoriam' vinyl albums and then later on CD format.

At the time of the Small Faces recording 'The Universal' Steve Marriott took time off to appear on The Easybeats track, "Good Times" (from their "Vigil" album released June 1968) plus Steve and Ronnie helped Skip Bifferty on the "Man In Black" 45. Ronnie arranging and Steve producing but neither played on the session.

The lyrics to the Universal dwelled on his feelings about stardom and Steve Marriott said "People were saying that 'Universal' was a send up of Bob Dylan but didn't realise that it's a serious record which proves that they don't listen to it because if they did they would understand what it was about. It's about getting up in the morning and going outside and saying hello to the universal"

Released in June of 1968, as simply 'The Universal', the press greeted this idiosyncratic song with some scepticism and initial sales were hardly encouraging....To promote it, Keith Altham was called to the band's country hideaway where he met a defensive-sounding Marriott. 'The song was supposed to be called 'Hello The Universal' Marriott told him, a fact he would repeat again and again in every interview. 'But it escaped before we could put it right. The whole idea of the song was a kind of 'Good Morning' to life. The secret of nearly all of our records is that we are really just being ourselves, that's what it's all about....

In the Melody Maker, Marriott also went on the defensive. In the piece, writer Chris Welch refers to the bad reviews given the single, one calling it 'an ill-timed catastrophe.' 'You were right,' Marriott agreed. 'It is a catastrophe - musically, it's a weird follow up which we recorded because we liked it and because it's different from anything else. We wanted it to be the most terrible production. We wanted a really evil sound and as far as we are concerned we've got it perfectly - and it's good. Listen to it a few times and it will grow on you. Anyway Ringo Starr liked it and Keith Moon said some nice things about it so it can't be all bad.'

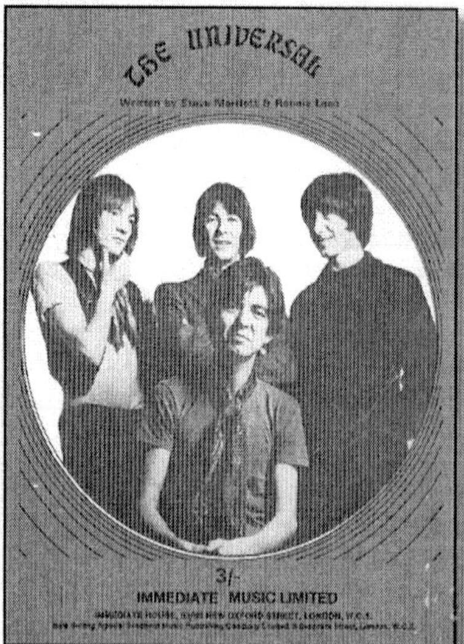

I've heard 3 versions of the Universal. Stereo, mono, and another version that turned up years later with different drumming. I've compared both stereo and mono versions from the Small Faces box set "The Immediate Years":

MONO: The mono version has an extended intro (4 seconds) before Steve comes in with guitar. This version lasts 2 minutes and 42 seconds. It also finishes with a guitar and trombone ending.
STEREO: What's interesting about this version is that Steve's voice echoes as if double tracked but it sounds like his voice is bouncing off his cottage walls. This version ends differently and finishes with a clarinet and trombone instead of guitar. 2 minutes & 38 seconds long.

VERSION 3 (Alternate take?): Entirely different drumming pattern. I'm very wary though whether the 'different drumming' version is really Kenney Jones or just some re-mixed studio trickery. It basically sounds like the stereo mix with vocals slowed down and another bass drum added over the top of the original. Good version though. Oddly enough this version can be found on the 1982 "Rod Stewart - Riding High" album on Italy's Joker label under the title of "Red Balloon".

Last but not least, for the first time in 'Mick Taylor Presents' I'm going to have a competition for some lucky reader. Over the last few months I've managed to collect most of the original 60s Small Faces sheet music (except 'I've Got Mine & Afterglow) thanks to my good friend Brent Cunliffe. To win the original 60s sheet music for 'The Universal' (pictured here and great for framing), PLUS a CD copy of all 3 versions of The Universal. All you have to do is tell me what the B-side of The Universal was..... Send answer to: Nutgone@aol.com - all winners will be put in a hat (or Stanley Unwin's crown; 0) and a final winner announced. Good luck.
And now, for your delight...

THE UNIVERSAL

There's such a lot of good ways to be bad,
And so many bad ways to be good,
Haven't paid my rent yet,
I hate to tell them sorry,
But I haven't got the money any more.

Just for today I thought I'd leave love alone -
Hold hands with day,
And if I'm so bad,
Why don't they take me away.

Just like what you hear,
With a shell pressed to your ear,
That's the sea in the trees in the morning,
Hello the universal,

Good morning Steve,
Well you won't believe me today...
Working doesn't seem to be,
The perfect thing for me,
So I continue to play,

And If I'm so bad,
Why don't they take me away.

Well a hippy trippy name dropper came through my door -
He said "I just bumped in to Mick",
He told me "do you know where to score"
No, not me friend...
I mind my own,
And my own minds me,

Well, My love is at the foot of your hand,
Come what may,
But if June comes first,
Please won't you take me away....

SPECIAL THANKS: John Hellier * Brent Cunliffe (for all the Small Faces original 60s sheet music).
Iain McGonigal.
STAY COOL WON'T YOU!

THE FRANTIKS

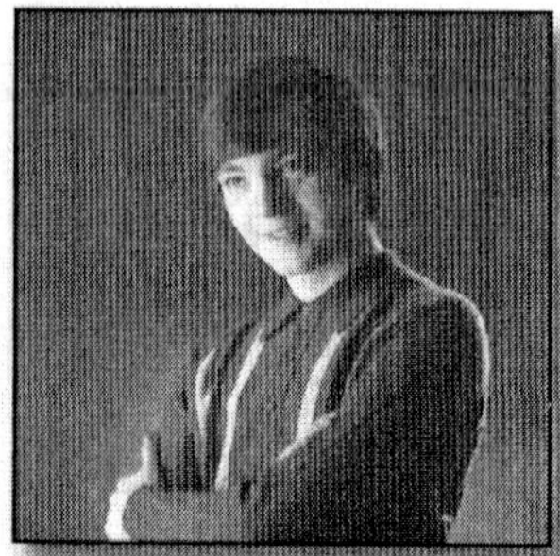

Denis Thompson tells the story of Steve Marriott's musical beginnings.....

I'm from Barking, East London, originally and got interested in playing the guitar when a cousin of mine came to stay with us. He was a good guitar player and had three guitars. He was substantially older than I and he taught me how to play. I was in a local music shop one day when I met a guy called Dave Findlayson, he was a drummer but not in a band. He invited me to his house along with another guy called Johnny Herve. We were all pretty young and musically didn't really know what we were doing. Because none of us could sing we learnt a few instrumentals like Walk Don't Run and some Shadows and Duane Eddy tracks. We even got as far as a few pub gigs in this form, just two guitars and drums, no bass, no vocals. At a coffee bar in East Ham that we used to frequent we paled up with a fella called Colin Fuller. Incidentally the coffee bar owner, who was a pro.wrestler, was the guy that used to get us the gigs, a regular one being the dance hall above the row of shops where his coffee bar was located. Colin joined the band and we started to learn vocals. Dave Findlayson sang lead with me on backing vocals. This band was called The Moonlights

One day whilst playing at the local dance hall we were first introduced to Steve Marriott by the wrestler. Steve jumped up and done a couple of Buddy Holly numbers with us. He had a great voice, even back then, and we invited him to join the group. He agreed, he was our vocalist only, he didn't play any instruments with The Moonlights. We became very popular locally and worked every weekend. My Dad had bought us some equipment and a van so we were able to compete with all the other local bands....and of course, we had Steve. Dave the drummer left and was replaced by Tony McIntyre who was so much better. We were now, arguably, the best band in the Eastern suburbs of London. We met and signed with Tony Calder and he took us to the next level. We started playing nationally and were very much in demand.

Steve was having problems at home with his Mum and Dad, although I always got on very well with them. He moved out and moved in with my Mum and Dad for a few months until all blew over with his parents. Steve was great to get along with. There were no drugs and no drinking and despite not having much money he was always dressed to the nines. At first we'd wear suits on stage but gradually as we matured we went for more individual looks. I don't ever remember Steve wearing jeans. Tony Calder had been a big influence on the way we looked. Our set list changed as we went from Cliff Richard and the Shadows to more a Beatles type thing. We did a few of their numbers such as Twist And Shout and I Saw Her Standing There also some Eddie Cochran tunes Cut Across Shorty, Summertime Blues and of course, lots of Chuck Berry and Bo Diddley, even some very early Stevie Wonder material plus of course, Ray Charles What'd I Say but we always ended with Got My Mojo Working. We were moving more and more towards bluesy stuff and we were regulars playing at the Elephant and Castle. The Moonlights were a happy band, there was never any arguing. Off stage Steve was learning the guitar and harmonica; he had a one in a million talent of being able to teach himself to a very high standard within, literally, weeks. He was still getting acting gigs, as well, and I used to go with him to film sets.

One day we were rehearsing at Tony McIntyre's house when our manager Tony Calder arrived with Tony Meehan of the Shadows. We had learned to play a very raucous version of Cliff Richards Move It. Meehan loved it and wanted to record it. He also suggested we change our name to THE FRANTIKS in keeping with the style of music we were playing. We did go on to record Move It but it was never released... Shame, I'd love to hear it now. Around this time (1963) Tony Calder got us signed as singer Jess Conrad's backing group. It was a good gig and we would back Jess whenever he went on tour. He realised Steve's ability and brought Steve right into his own vocal style. Together they were really good. We opened for the Rolling Stones, Searchers and other big bands of the day. Master Marriott was very high energy, always wanting to play longer. His age (16) was not a factor in the group. His guitar playing had come on in leaps and bounds and ill feeling began to grow between Steve and Johnny as Steve felt he was now good enough to play his instrument with the band. Eventually both Johnny and I left the group to join ranks with Bobby Christo and the Rebels, a local band that had a recording contract and recorded with Joe Meek, a very nasty man that made the hairs stand up on the back of my neck. We recorded several songs, the most notable being Other Side Of The Tracks.

Steve remained a very good friend and had re-formed the group into The Moments. They were pretty good but mostly ego driven, they used to rehearse at the keyboard players house and I would go round and watch. I remember seeing Ritchie Blackmore round there one time. The story that Steve was kicked out of that band is ridiculous. He could now play every instrument in the group including a mean harmonica and they could not come to terms with his popularity. Make no bones about it that band was Steve Marriott AND the Moments. Myself and Steve had seen a band in a pub in Rainham that we both rated very highly. That band was Ronnie Lane's band. Steve left the Moments and was between gigs when he met Ronnie. You know the rest of that story......

I remember one day I left my van at Bobby Christos' house. Steve and I went round to get it. A neighbour thought we were stealing the van and called the Police. They stopped us in Barking and slapped us in a cell at the Police Station. Steve thought this was hilarious; he had his harmonica with him and started playing the Jailhouse Blues. The cops thought this was funny and he just kept playing until my Dad came and got us out.

I continued playing with Bobby and switched to bass when the bass player left. Tony Jackson had left the Searchers and formed his own band, The Vibrations. The drummer with the Rebels went for the audition and became Tony's drummer. After a few months I had joined them on bass and stayed until 1966. I remember one night the Small Faces were on Ready Steady Go and Steve collapsed, he went home to his parent's house and called me the next morning. I went to his parent's home and we walked into town, I was disgusted to find out how much money he was making. I was making much more with Tony. I would speak to him every month or so but it was clear he was sinking into the business, getting very cynical and taking far too many drugs. I eventually lost contact with Steve. Years later I was living in Baltimore, USA and playing with a good little band there. One of the guys in the band said that Steve was playing Washington, about an hours drive from us. I called the Stadium and left a message for Steve, he was opening for AC/DC. Steve called me and said to meet him but I was playing myself that night so never did.........

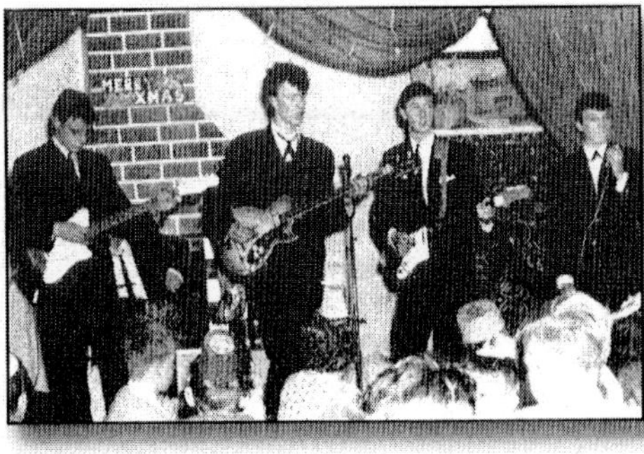

STEVE MARRIOTT....
Disc Jockey EXTRAORDINAIRE!

Steve hosts his own "Radio 2 Sounds Of The Sixties Show" (23/05/87). He selects and plays 20 classics from the best era of 'em all. Steve did manage to break the rules though (we wouldn't have expected anything else!) and threw in a couple from the 1950s. Take it away, Stevie........

Hello, I'm welcoming you to "Sounds Of The Sixties" (Steve with his beautiful broad Cockney accent).

Whatcha Gonna Do About It -Small Faces 1965
It was our first hit back in 1965 and if you hear a little bit of this going on (makes noises of opening a paper bag), it's only me. I'm trying to nosh some cheese and biscuits down me that were kindly supplied by the BBC. Now here is something from my childhood hero ....

Heartbeat –Buddy Holly 1959
He has got to be the biggest influence of my youth. I used to run about the room wearing a pair of thick glasses. No glass in them, just the rims and a tennis racket that I used to mime with. I made a record once called "Give Her My Regards", copying him and it was diabolical. It was a really rotten record. Anyway, we're not going to play that. Now how about some Motown magic........

Ain't Too Proud To Beg –Temptations 1966
Well what a smashing song that is and we all tried our hand at getting that sound you know....all the bands in the mid 60s. The best ones at it were The Action. I think they became Ace later on. They were an amazing band. Anyway, enough rabbiting from me........

On The Rebound –Floyd Cramer 1961
I must admit I had forgotten how good that was and it had slipped my mind that it went to number 1. Here is another huge influence. We were talking about influences before and this guy was up there with the best for me. It is the sadly missed and much loved Muddy Waters........

I Just Wanna Make Love To You –Muddy Waters 1954
Well that is Muddy singing a Willie Dixon song. It's been my pleasure to play with Muddy a couple of times and he was always a gentleman, a true gentleman. Anyway let's change the mood a little with a big hit from Dusty Springfield. This was her first big solo hit.......

I Only Want To Be With You –Dusty Springfield 1963
Funny story about Dusty, when we used to do "Top Of The Pops" with her, she would stand about three feet from us and just stare at us....put us off a bit and I asked her afterwards why she did it? She was short sighted, you know. That was all it was, just wanted to get a better view. Must have been all the eye make up eh? This next song is of special significance if you are or were a Mod. When I was a nipper this was our Mod National Anthem. It was called......

You Can't Sit Down –Phil Upchurch Combo 1961
Great record! It is funny how the organ figured so much in those days. A lot of instrumentals, a lot of Hammond organ work. There is more coming up later but I won't give the game away. I won't also give the game away about this! See if you can guess who it is?.......

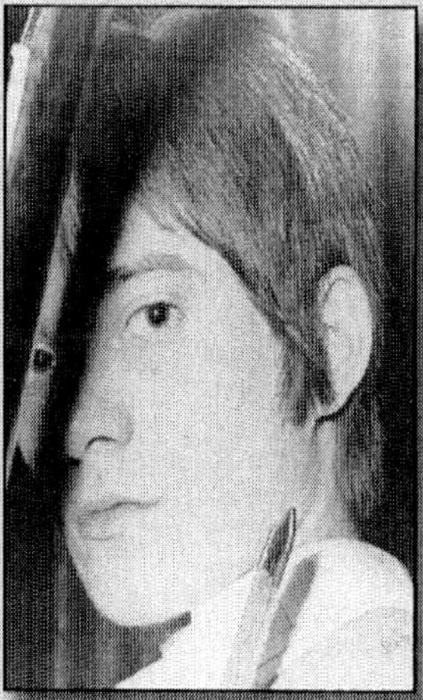

A Hard Days Night –Peter Sellers 1965
Well did you win a bread knife or did you lose your beer money? Own up! That was actually Peter Sellers doing the Beatles song. Great! A bit of Larry Olivier in there and it was produced by George Martin, who also did the string parts. It proves Ol' George has a sense of humour, doesn't it? Fabulous stuff! And now some old mates of mine.......

Somebody Help Me –Spencer Davis Group 1966
That was written by Jackie Edwards as we pointed out earlier to each other in the studio here and he also wrote Keep On Running. So they had a couple of hits from Jackie Edwards, I would have liked to have heard him sing them. And now onto some even older mates of the dooming variety…and Peter of the Townshend variety.....

Happy Jack –The Who 1966
Great record innit? When that was out we were touring Australia together and we got bunged out at gun-point after my 21st birthday, but that is another story. Time to be self indulgent.......

Lazy Sunday –Small Faces 1968
Oh there is another halfpence for me. Marvellous stuff! That was me and Ronnie Lane doing our Arthur Mullard impressions. It's amazing what you can do with a few sound effects and a tuning fork, innit? And here is Chuck Berry.....

Come On –Chuck Derry 1960
Great track, it was the Stones first single wasn't it? And we have had three Stones covers on this programme. We've also had Ain't Too Proud To Beg that they did on an album and I Just Wanna Make Love To You. Jolly good taste! Anyway cap an ear hole of some big band Jazz featuring Jimmy Smith esquire.....

Walk On The Wild Side –Jimmy Smith 1962
Well how about that then? I used to drive my Mother mad with that blaring down the hall! Thank you Leonard Bernstein, he wrote it anyway. This next one, whenever I read or think about it I think of Hale and Pace. I do Ron Ron..I do Ron Ron.......

Da Doo Ron Ron –The Crystals 1963
Nice isn't it? A Phil Spector masterpiece. Now is the all time master of Soul music, Mr Sam Cooke.......

Shake –Sam Cooke 1964
Absolutely marvellous record. We used to open up with that every night with the Small Faces in the 60s. We used to try and do it justice. I don't think we ever really did, not like that anyway. At least we had a go at it..aah! This next geezer, the only time I used to meet him was around my girlfriends flat. He had a room in the same house and we never said a dicky bird to each other. We used to look each other up and down, we both had hit records in the charts, but we didn't like to say anything to each other…it was very odd! Later on, of course we did and I grew to love and admire him.

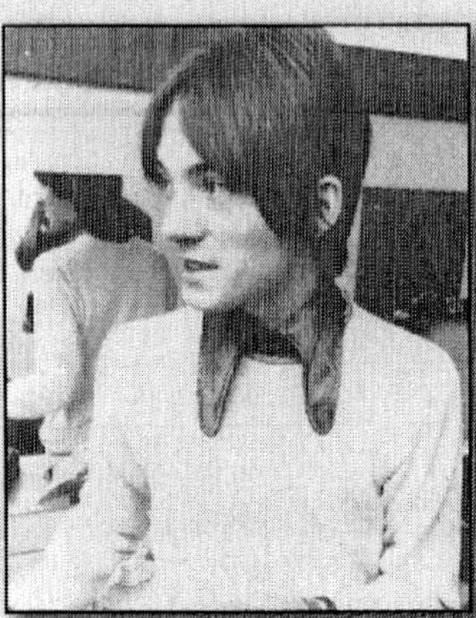

The Wind Cries Mary –Jimi Hendrix Experience 1967
Wow! And now for another record that used to drive my Mother mad…….

Green Onions –Booker T and the MGs 1962
My favourite all-time record! The MGs by the way stands for Memphis Group and that is what they were. They made all their records in this old cinema in Memphis. They were also responsible for backing all the artists that came out of Stax Records people like Wilson Pickett, Otis Redding and Rufus Thomas. Steve Cropper, the bands guitar player wrote classics like In The Midnight Hour and Mr Pitiful and they were the Small Faces biggest influence. Anyway, here is dear ol' Marianne…..

Come And Stay With Me –Marianne Faithful 1965
Marvellous stuff, me darlin'….They're going to do this to me in a minute, they're coming to take me away!......

They're Coming To Take Me Away (Ha Ha) –Napoleon XIV 1966
Cor, dear, dear, dear, that was Napoleon XIV. I wonder what his Mother thought of him? Eh still, back to reality here is Wilson Pickett with the Memphis Group……

Land Of A Thousand Dances –Wilson Pickett 1966
Well that's your lot, because the clock has beaten us. I hope you have enjoyed listening to my choice of records as much as I've had playing them and remember I'm always available for bookings!
Ta Ta.

1862

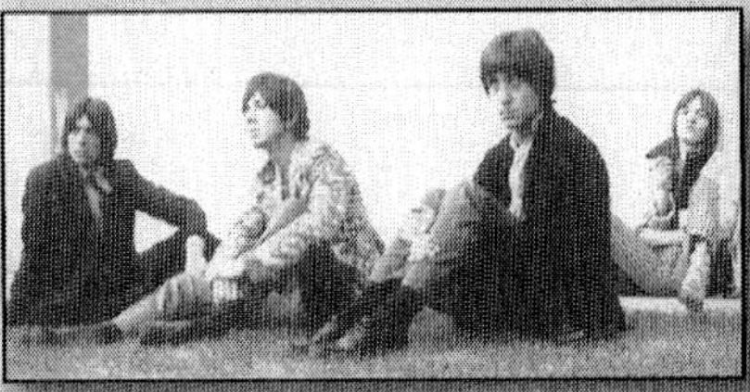

1862 is the Small Faces album that never was. Steve Marriott, in a 1985 interview, told me the story behind the album that was intended to be the follow up to the best selling Ogden's Nut Gone Flake. The project was aborted when Steve left the band high and dry after storming offstage midway through a New Years Eve gig at Alexandra Palace in North London (31/12/68). The band never entered a recording studio again and officially split, after a European tour, in the spring of 1969.

I suppose comparisons can be made with the story of Brian Wilson's proposed Pet Sounds follow up Smile, which took 35 years to eventually emerge. Difference being 1862 was left very much unfinished. The track listing shows several "working titles" consisting of backing tracks only. Although these tracks are unfinished they are of excellent quality and are a fine testimony to the growing musicianship of the band. One track, in particular, deserves special mention and that is Steve's haunting ballad Wrist Job. That's Wrist Job as in suicidal, knowing Steve's lavatorial humour as I do, for years I thought the title referred to something very different!

In late 1968 Steve and Ronnie, with the help of an advance from Immediate Records, bought Beehive Cottage, a 16th century listed thatched cottage in the heart of Steve's beloved Essex countryside. Next door was a small derelict church hall. Steve had a vision of purchasing it with a view to converting it into a recording studio. The idea was to record the next album there and shoot the album sleeve outside with the band standing in the doorway underneath the building date 1862. However planning permission was denied and the dream, like the band itself, died a death. Incidentally that same church hall still stands derelict to this very day, some 40 years after the event.

A couple of bits of nice trivia; One particular track was completed but untitled at the time of recording. When an engineer enquired as to what to label it as, Ronnie shrugged his shoulders and said I dunno...call it something nice! Job done! Before Steve's move to Beehive Cottage he recorded what was to be the bands last 45 in the garden of his home in Marlow, Buckinghamshire on a portable cassette recorder (incidentally that house was once owned by distinguished literary figure Jerome J Jerome, he of Three Men In A Boat fame). The recording which comes complete with dogs a barking and overhead aircraft noise was called "Hello The Universal". Immediate Records mistakenly left the "Hello" off of the original single version, Steve was none too pleased. If this lovely little album is ever commercially released I would like to think that this track would eventually get its original and correct title.

Proposed track listing: Wham Bam Thank you Mam, Buttermilk Boy, Bang, Hello The Universal, Donkey Rides A Penny A Glass, Wrist Job, Stone, Wide Eyed Girl On The Wall, Collibosher, Red Balloon, The Autumn Stone, What You Will, Every Little Bit Hurts.

JOHN HELLIER (2009)

DON ARDEN - THE AL CAPONE OF POP

A LOOK AT THE LIFE AND TIMES OF THE SMALL FACES FIRST MANAGER. ALTHOUGH THE BANDS RELATIONSHIP WITH HIM WAS FRAUGHT WITH NEGATIVITY, STEVE MARRIOTT ALWAYS REFERRED TO HIM AS "MR. BIG" AND ALWAYS SAID "NO DON ARDEN, NO SMALL FACES!"

Don Arden, the most notorious of all British pop-rock music managers, died in Los Angeles in 2007 after a long illness aged 81. In a career that spanned 60 years, he promoted and managed some of the biggest names in pop music. His ruthless business dealings and willingness to intimidate both his charges and his competitors earned him the nickname "the Al Capone of pop". Arden was born Harry Levy in Cheetham Hill, Manchester. He would describe the neighbourhood as "a Jewish ghetto" and recall "my family were good Yiddisher folk - poor but very hard-working". He left school aged 13, determined to work in show business and adopted the name Don Arden to avoid encountering anti-Semitism from bookers. During the second world war, the teenage Arden found work as a stand-up comic and singer on the vaudeville circuit, entertaining the troops before he was drafted.

With the war over, Arden returned to vaudeville, and contemporaries remember him as a gifted comic whose imitations of Enrico Caruso and Al Jolson were excellent. But his bad temper and aggressive approach alienated bookers to such an extent that he began working as a promoter, initially booking Hebrew folk-song contests. In the early 1950s he settled in Brixton, south London, marrying Irish ballet teacher Hope Shaw, and returned to performing briefly as a member of the Black and White Minstrels.

In 1959, Arden promoted the first UK tour of American rockabilly singer Gene Vincent, who was so impressed by his British following that he shifted to the UK, employing Arden as his manager. Arden kept Vincent busy touring western Europe, but the two men parted in 1965 amid much acrimony, so setting a pattern for Arden's working relationships. By then he had begun to earn considerable sums by promoting package tours of American 1950s rock'n'roll artists, yet the onset of Beatlemania caused him to lose £100,000 on one 10-week tour as British teenagers declared US artists passé. Arden set off in search of young British talent and met the Newcastle-based band the Animals, whose manager, Mike Jeffrey, was looking for an influential agent. Arden brought the band to London and helped secure them a recording deal. Their huge immediate success benefited Arden - now their worldwide agent - but he soon fell foul of Jeffrey, so sold his rights to book the band and began managing the Nashville Teens. Arden offered little artistic direction to the Teens,

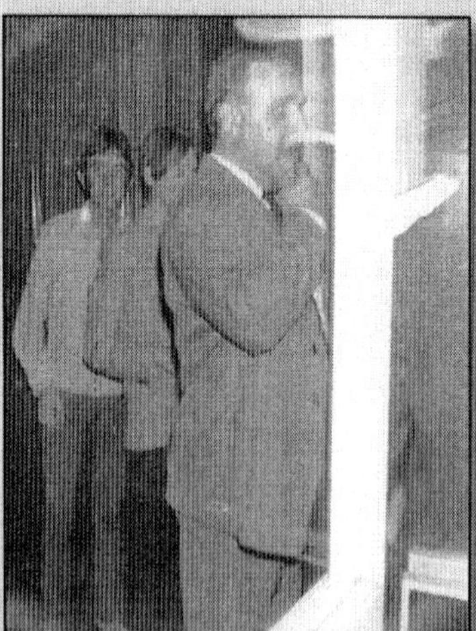

instead keeping them on a gruelling tour schedule. When band pianist John Hawken chastised him in his Carnaby Street office for the meagre sums he advanced the group, Arden began to strangle the musician before attempting to throw him from the second storey window, shouting: "You're going over, John, you're going over." The distraught Hawken freed himself and fled, but this story is not untypical of those concerning Arden's handling of anyone who challenged him. In 1965 he signed Cockney teenagers the Small Faces and ensured their debut single was a hit by outlaying several hundred pounds to chart fixers. Arden kept the highly successful band on a £20-a-week salary while cocooning them in pop star luxury. When the band demanded to see their royalty statements in 1966, he countered by informing their parents that the band were drug addicts. Hearing that Australian entrepreneur Robert Stigwood was interested in the band, he and his heavies paid Stigwood a visit with Arden hanging Stigwood off his fourth-floor balcony as a warning. The Small Faces eventually won their freedom, but all attempts at retrieving royalties due from Arden found them locked in court battles, finally receiving payment only in 1977. Arden briefly attempted to revive his singing career in 1967 before returning to management with Amen Corner. A similar pattern of hits and disputes followed leading to a threat of assassination - which Arden took seriously and resolved by threatening certain of those involved with his gun-carrying heavies. All this helped give rise to rumours that Arden was connected to the mafia, rumours that he encouraged. Arden then took over managing the Move, and out of this band came the Electric Light Orchestra, which went on to sell millions of albums internationally, generating huge wealth for Arden. He settled in Los Angeles, purchasing Howard Hughes' mansion in 1972. Again, the relationship ended acrimoniously.

In 1979 Arden found himself under scrutiny from the BBC Radio 4 Checkpoint programme, and so he threatened the investigative journalist Roger Cook. By 1980 Arden was managing Ozzy Osbourne after the singer's split from Black Sabbath. Osbourne left his wife to marry Arden's daughter Sharon - she, having worked for Don since her teens, had inherited his tough management skills - and when the couple left Arden to go it alone in 1982, Don ensured that much litigation followed. In 1986 Arden and son David were charged (as Harry and David Levy) with blackmailing and imprisoning an accountant who they had fallen out with. The sensational court case found a jury declaring David guilty, while Don was acquitted. Arden soldiered on, managing the declining Black Sabbath while Sharon Osbourne turned her husband (and, subsequently, children and herself) into a hugely profitable enterprise.

Osbourne had told her children that their grandfather was dead, and they first saw him when she began screaming abuse at the elderly Arden upon encountering him on a Los Angeles street.

In 2004 Arden published his autobiography, Mr Big: Ozzy, Sharon and My Life As the Godfather of Rock, to modest interest.

Sharon Osbourne's 2005 autobiography Extreme sold two million copies and, although she was reconciled with her now ailing father, portrayed him as a villainous, if occasionally generous, man. His wife Hope predeceased him. He is survived by Sharon and David.

Don Arden (Harry Levy), artists' manager and promoter, born January 4 1926; died July 21 2007

John Hellier 2009

A FEW YEARS IN THE SMALL FACES WILL BE ENOUGH FOR ME!

Steve Marriott talks with Bill Harry (April 1967).

Remarkably sunny summer day in London. Cool breezes, girls in their summer dresses, the usual crammed streets, traffic jams, never ending array of traffic lights on red. The taxi literally crawled to Steve Marriott's new flat near Baker Street. Lift to the 5th floor, inside, past a black and white cat that winked at me, along a small passageway crammed with boxes labelled Decca, guitar cases and amplifiers.

The living room was fairly large and decorated with extremely good taste. Fine furniture that must add a few extra bob to the rent. Antique gold carpets. Two speaker cabinets. A Hohner electric pianette. A Vortexion stereo tape. On the wall two prints - an abstract and a print of an Indian dancer. A few other people in the room sipping coffee.

I looked at Steve's bookcase above his TV set. Someone once said you can understand a person to some extent by the books he reads. There were four red leather bound volumes of Hans Anderson's Fairy Tales; Anya Secto's "Avalon"; Colin Wilson's "Beyond The Outsider"; "The Rubaiyat Of Omar Khayyam"; four James Bond adventures; The New English Bible; Two volumes of Pelican's "Illustrated English Social History"; "Learning To Ride"; "Batman Versus The Joker"; Spike Milligan's "The Little Pot Boiler" and "Silly Verse For Kids; Julie Feiffer's "Sick Sick Sick" and a large handsome volume entitled "Classical Dances And Costumes Of India".

Steve came in smiling, even though his accountant was perched up in the corner, hard at work. He lit a cigarette, on the window ledge there were half a dozen tins of Benson and Hedges. He's one of the few lead singers I know who smokes. He'd been entertaining press people throughout the day. "My voice is a bit hoarse. I've been talking non stop since eleven this morning ... and I've got a recording session tonight."

Having studied his library, I asked him what sort of discs were in his record collection. "Records. I like everything really, there's no limit. I've got every sort of record "The Plastic Suite" to Mingus. It's just a matter of opening your mind to it. Music is music; you can't hate a particular kind. Those people who say they dislike a style of music probably haven't listened to it."

One reason why Steve looked so chirpy, he'd found out the value of having a genuine holiday. "This is the first time I've had a holiday in a year, last time I went to Manchester! This time I spent a week in Portugal and I'm going back. It was so good that I've made up my mind to have more than one holiday a year. I forgot completely about the whole business. I suddenly realised I was on a deserted beach and there was absolutely nothing to do, nothing to think about except "this is it". I must admit that on the last day I got a bit frustrated because I wanted something to do."

Steve talked of the future. "I'm becoming a lot more interested in other sides of the business and that's my main aim. I don't want to remain in a group for more than a few years. When you begin you want to taste success in a group, then you want to try and experiment and become successful in other fields. Record producing, arranging and song writing are much more interesting anyway. Song writing is more of a steady career, so is record producing.

"We all feel like this and we'll remain together for a long time. Ronnie and I are great walls for each other; we bounce ideas off each other all the time. We used to have great fun together and we get on well mentally together. We have rows, but we don't boil up. He's as temperamental as I am.

We've been song writing for 18 months now and some of our songs are very nice. We've written for people like Chris Farlowe and Marianne Faithfull. As far as record producing goes it's orchestras I want to get hold of and get away from the usual line-up of three guitars and drums.

"Plonk and I write individually under the company name Marriott/Lane. But we also get together to work on particular songs. If you did it by yourself you'd mess your mind up. Get too hung up, too involved with your own ideas, which sometimes are not too good. Some of the songs I write are true experiences that I feel strongly about. I also like to put myself in someone else's position. This approach to song writing is interesting. It's like character acting. I imagine I'm someone else, create situations and wonder how I would react to them. NICE yeah!

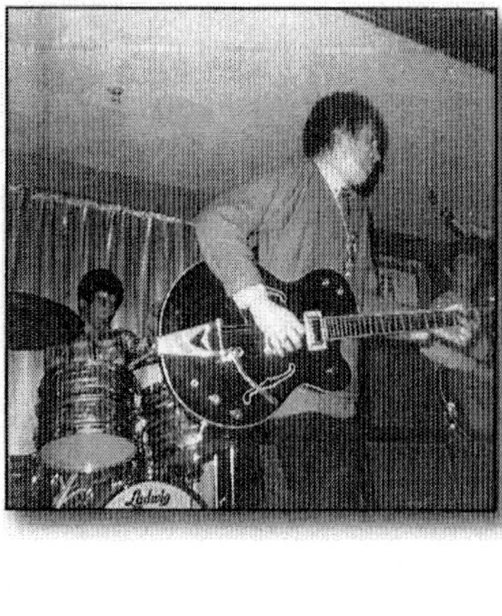

FIRST PUBLISHED
IN RECORD MIRROR
29/04/67.

ITCHYCOO PARK

Ronnie Lanes own take on his "Summer of love" anthem.

The first Small Faces single written by Marriott and Lane, "I Got Mine", flopped on release as the follow up to "Whatcha Gonna Do About It" in late 1965. The group were pushed away from their R&B roots into Pop for their next release, "Sha La La La Lee", written by Mort Schuman and Kenny Lynch. But Marriott and Lane (who speaks below) caught on quickly, and over the next two years their songs ensured the group were in the charts more weeks than they were out of it. "Itchycoo Park", a paen to a patch of grass in the East End, was an antidote to the anthems of the Summer of love.

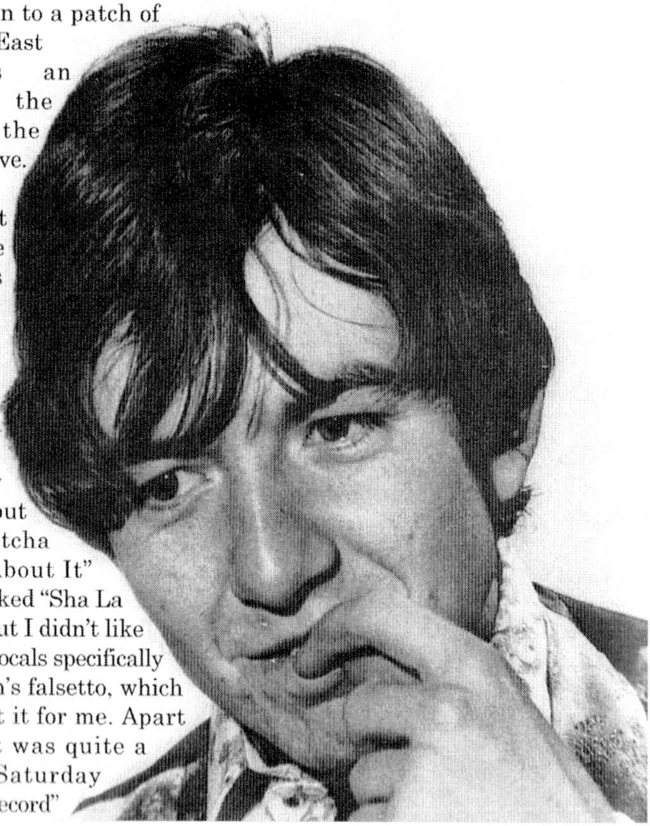

"The first Immediate album was the first one that we were proud of, well some of it anyway. I had previously liked the debut single "Whatcha Gonna Do About It" and I quite liked "Sha La La La Lee" but I didn't like the backing vocals specifically Kenny Lynch's falsetto, which totally spoilt it for me. Apart from that it was quite a good little Saturday night dance record"

"At the time we didn't really mind. We were pleased to have some money in our pockets, because we'd driven around for about a year, living in the back of an old black maria, playing for nothing and living on brown sauce rolls. We used to wake up in the morning, look around and think "my God!" All the windows would be steamed up and there'd be heaps of old socks. But then we started to get all fucked up with things like "Hey Girl". It didn't take long for the rot to set in. We were young and impressionable and we got manipulated. But we were happy. We had twenty quid a week in our pockets, we had accounts down Carnaby Street at all the clothes shops, we didn't want anymore. We were like a bunch of old women at a jumble sale when we walked into a shop. Some of the stuff we never even wore. We lived on the road and all the expenses were paid for. In actual fact we often had money left over from that twenty quid! And we were out of our boxes most of the time."

"We were working a lot on the road then, there was a lot of screaming going on and musically the band just stopped developing. The funny thing was we were quite a good little live band when we started out, but we didn't hear ourselves for about two years. Literally, we never heard a note we played. It was like curtains open, wiggle your arse for half an hour and screaming. We hadn't been playing that long together anyway. We were always in a car. We seemed to live in this Jaguar. We were always on the road. It was alright at the time because it was all new and I suppose we thought this is what it was all about. That was what happened if you got successful, that was it."

"It was with Immediate Records that we started getting more involved with studio techniques. Things started really moving then and it was utter joy to work with producer Glyn Johns. Our new manager Andrew Loog Oldham had a lot of influence over us, but then again we were very impressionable. Andrew was a pretty moody fucker. He'd swan around in shades and his limousine and he was quite amusing really. He was very camp and had this camp humour and we used to knock these little things out. That's when we started getting into those little cameos like "Itchycoo Park", which a piss-take in actual fact, but it ended up sounding so good that it went past the fact that it was meant to be a joke."

“In the early days Steve was far more the driving force than I was because I hadn’t even considered writing songs until Steve sat down and said “I’ve got an idea”, and we started working on it. I thought it was pretty amazing that this guy could actually think of his own material. He educated me a lot, Steve. We’d get the ideas individually and present them to each other. We didn’t write a lot of stuff together, we more or less finished off more stuff together than we actually wrote together. It was a chemical thing. You couldn’t really say that he did this and I did that, it was like alchemy. A good chemical mix. When we got together something used to happen, whether it fell out of my head or his head. We’d come up with something to knock each other out, I suppose, and once the ball got rolling it used to sort of finish itself, once we’d sat down together. Looking back on it, the things that I remember most are the things that Steve would turn up and sit down and play and knock me out with.”

“Itchycoo Park” basically came from me. I lifted it from a hymn ”God Be In My Head” and I got the theme for the words in a hotel somewhere. There was a magazine in the room with a rambling account of some place in the country and it was about “dreaming spires” and a “bridge of sighs” and I just thought they were nice lines. It wasn’t me that came up with “I feel inclined to blow my mind, get hung up feed the ducks with a bun, they all come out to groove about, be nice and have fun in the sun!” That was Steve, but the more poetic stuff was mine. By then we’d turned totally into a recording band. We couldn’t go out and do those things on stage. We’d do it in the studio for a laugh, but Steve wasn’t prepared to get up on stage and make an arse of himself like that.”

“When we were on stage, it had to be the Mod Soul thing. We did play “Itchycoo Park” a couple of times, but if you bought a record we were playing it wasn’t necessarily so that you’d go and see us play what was on that record, if you get my drift. We more or less treated the two things as totally separate entities”

JOHN PIDGEON SPEAKING WITH RONNIE LANE, 1990.

"MAD" ANN MOODY INTERVIEW

by John Hellier (31st October 2002)

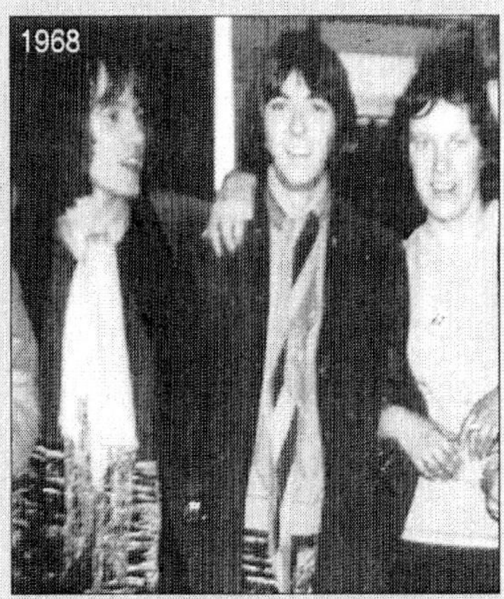

Forty years after the event "Mad" Ann Moody is revered by mods everywhere as the Small Faces most fanatic fan. Her revelations about following them on the road have been well documented in both the Steve Marriott and Ian McLagan biographies. Kenney once quoted " She's the only person I know that could move faster than an E-Type Jag, she was totally crazy, she would jump on the car and hold on by the windscreen wipers!"

Ann reminisces about those Swinging Sixties.

JH WHEN DID YOU FIRST MEET THE GUYS?

ANN It was September 1966 in Birmingham. I was already a fan and had all the early records but it wasn't until Mac joined the band that they really caught my eye. Back in the 1960's all teenage girls had their favourite pop star and Mac was mine. It had nothing to do with musical ability it was just the way he looked. It was at that first gig in Birmingham that I saw them leave by the stage door and I just instinctively run after the car. They stopped at traffic lights and wound the window down. I just said, "You won't forget me will you?" and for some reason they never did. From there on afterwards I followed them absolutely everywhere they played.

JH HOW DID YOU TRAVEL AROUND THE COUNTRY?

ANN Well I was only sixteen but I used to hitchhike with my friend and fellow fan, Rita.

You could do that in those days, certainly couldn't do it now. After a few gigs they got to know us well and they obviously took a shine because they would always leave backstage passes for us. Bur even with the backstage pass it was sometimes difficult to get past their road manager, Terry, he was really horrible. He wouldn't let anybody near them, looking back on it now I suppose he was only doing his job, but he was horrible! He was eventually sacked after the group caught him stealing from them. His replacement was a guy with a famous name, Dave Clarke, he was lovely.

JH WHAT WAS THE MOST OUTRAGEOUS THING YOU EVER DONE IN ORDER TO SEE THE BOYS?

ANN I remember one particular evening in Newcastle. For some reason I hadn't been able to get backstage and I was waiting outside the venue for them. Because of heavy traffic I actually lost sight of their car so I just laid down in the middle of a very busy dual carriageway, mad or what! When I think about it now it makes me whinge but that's what you had to do in those heady days

JH WITH YOUR BACKSTAGE PASS YOU MUST HAVE BEEN THE ENVY OF HUNDREDS OF OTHER FANS?

ANN They couldn't believe it. A member of the road crew would come outside, find us and take us in. Ronnie even put an ad. in a local paper in the area that they were playing, Northampton I think it was. It read, "looking forward to seeing Ann and Rita again". A lot of the female fans were all dressed beautifully and looked just like models from a fashion magazine and they'd look on amazed that ordinary fans like Rita and myself were shown favour by the band. A lot of those girls tried just about every trick in the book to reach the dressing room but very few were successful.

JH HOW DID THE GROUP REACT TO HYSTERICAL SCREAMING FANS?

ANN Well it was just like Beatles being in town, it really was. You couldn't hear them on stage at all, well not from the front, anyway. They could have been playing just about anything and nobody would have been any the wiser. From where I was standing in the wings the sound was just decipherable. At first they loved all the female attention, especially Steve, but it soon became a nuisance.

JH CAN YOU REMEMBER ANY OF THE SONGS THAT THEY PLAYED LIVE?

ANN Well when I first met them "All Or Nothing" was number one in the charts and they always played that one. I can't really remember the songs; "Whatcha Gonna Do About It" was always in there and a bit later on I remember "Tin Soldier".

JH DID YOU EVER SEE THEM IN THE STUDIO OR WRITING SONGS?

ANN Oh no, never. It was just the shows really.

JH WHAT WERE THEIR INDIVIDUAL PERSONALITIES LIKE?

ANN Steve was a bit of a Jack The Lad but he was lovely with the fans and always looked after them with autographs and the like. He was difficult to get close to though. We were both the same birth sign, Aquarius, and we would fight and argue a lot albeit in a friendly manner. It was nothing too serious, just differences of opinion on things such as music. Steve could be moody at times and I recall, even back then, arguments with Ronnie. The two that I was closest to were Ronnie and Mac. Ronnie was just like a brother to me. I just cannot find words special enough for him, we got on so well. Mac was just lovely in EVERY respect. Kenney was very deep and extremely hard to get to know, he still is. I saw him last year at Dingwalls in Camden and he's still exactly the same. There's always a quiet one in every band and with the Small Faces it was Kenney. He was still a lovely guy, he looked after me, they all did.

JH DID YOU EVER VISIT ANY OF THEM IN THEIR HOMES?

ANN Amazingly I never went to Westmoreland Terrace or any of their houses. I didn't want to invade their private lives. I did visit Mac's mum and dad at their home in Hounslow in 1967. I asked Mac first and he arranged it for me. His dad was in the garage most of the day fixing his car. He was lovely I just stood there and chatted to him while he worked. His mum showed me the family photograph album and cooked me dinner. All in all a lovely day to remember. Mac's still got a photo of me and his mum sitting in their front room. I only ever went the once but it was really nice.

JH ARE THEIR ANY PARTICULAR INCIDENTS THAT YOU REMEMBER?

ANN There was a time at a gig in Kelso in Scotland when I had an accident. I was knocking on a door rather heavily and I put my hand through a glass window. I was taken to hospital in Edinburgh. Much to my surprise the four of them came to visit me there with their chauffeur Dave Clarke. The following day I was discharged and Dave drove me to see the lads at a hotel near Newcastle.

JH WHAT WAS THE MOOD LIKE IN THE DRESSING ROOM, PARTY TIME OR WHAT?

ANN No, not really. They were always high-spirited but not destructful, as you would read. Always smoking hash but I never, ever, saw anything stronger than that.

JH DID YOUR PARENTS KNOW THAT YOU WERE HITCHHIKING AROUND THE COUNTRY?

ANN Oh no, I'd just say I was staying with friends. I got caught out a few times but not very often. As I said before it was a different age and certainly wasn't considered as dangerous as it would nowadays. These 60's stories have made me quite famous, you know. Fans often stop me when I'm around Carnaby Street.

JH DID YOU SEE THE SMALL FACES BREAK-UP COMING?

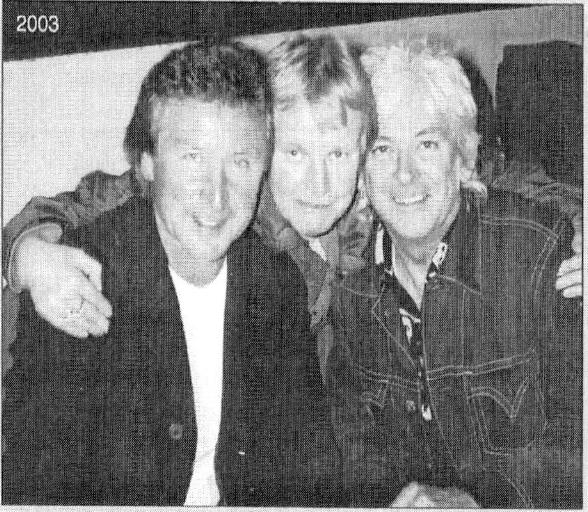

ANN Well yeah, I suppose I did. By 1968 Steve had developed itchy feet and was ready to try something new. The rest of them were pretty gutted when he left to form Humble Pie.

JH WHAT ARE YOUR OWN FAVOURITE SMALL FACES RECORDS?

ANN My favourite singles are "All Or Nothing" and "Tin Soldier" and I also love Ronnie's "Just Passing". My favourite album is definitely the first Decca LP. I had it autographed by all four of them but it was destroyed along with all my other Small Faces memorabilia in a flood at my home in 1984. I bought another copy for £75 recently but it's not the same is it?

JH DID YOU FOLLOW THE FACES AND HUMBLE PIE ON TOUR?

ANN I only saw Humble Pie once and that was at the Roundhouse in Chalk Farm. I remember taking a nice photo of Steve and Jenny there. I used to follow the Faces more because of Ronnie and Mac. I saw their first gig in Sheffield. I turned up and found my name on the guest list. They were absolutely great and Ronnie Wood was totally mad! Backstage at Faces gigs were much wilder than previously at Small Faces gigs. It was quite frightening at times, Rod and Woody were really loud and I saw Ronnie Lane completely legless on many an occasion. I moved to London in the mid seventies and met up with Steve again around the time of the Small Faces re-union, even got to baby sit for Toby. Even though all the later bands were great, the magic of those teenage days in the 1960's was missing. Great times, great memories.

THANKYOU ANN, A SPECIAL FAN INDEED!

Trivia! Trivia!

DID YOU KNOW THAT..............According to the new Don Arden book "Mr. Big", the ol' crook himself was fuming when he heard that the Small Faces had got into the habit of throwing jackets into the crowd at the end of their shows. He told them "Do you know how much they fucking cost? If you had told me that you wanted to throw stuff to the audience I could have got a good deal on some monogrammed handkerchiefs!

DID YOU KNOW THAT.............Jimi Hendrix Experience bass player, Noel Redding, used to take a portable record player on tour with him along with a few favourite albums. One of them was the first Small Faces Decca album which, according to roadie Georgie Butler, was played non stop.

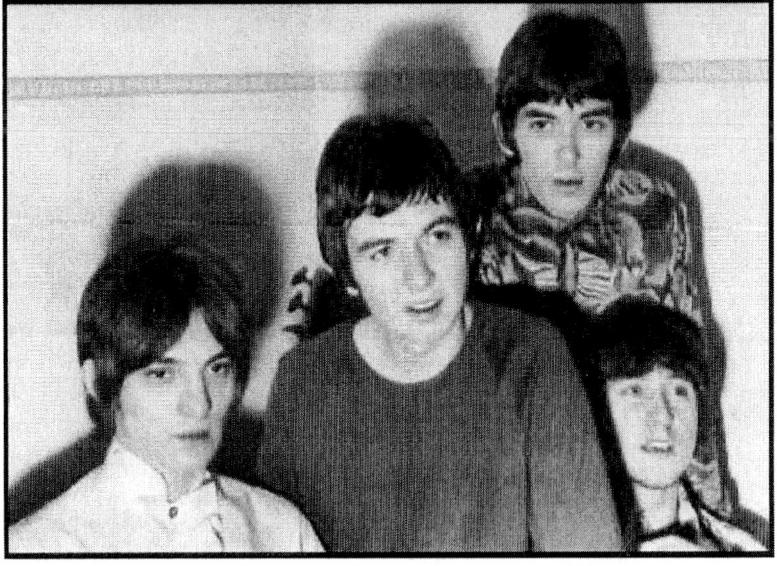

LET'S DANCE

Andrew "Loog" Oldham tells the story of the hit record that never was.

I was asked to produce a new Humble Pie album. A&M Records had agreed to my fee - with all expenses, travel and even my colleague Eddie allowed as par for the slate – what everybody had forgotten to tell me was that the group was no longer. Humble Pie had broken up!

The first two nights only two Piemen showed, drummer Jerry Shirley and bassist Greg Ridley. The third night guitarist Dave "Clem" Clempson, who had replaced Peter Frampton, arrived, but we were still no-go without Mr Marriott. "Steve's having problems" explained Greg. Mr Greg Ridley looked like a wild plainsman. Tight, frayed jeans and well worn suede cowboy boots, tall, well built, healthily gaunt, blond-along curly hair. When he pulled his Jim Bowie knife out of his boots or britches, offered you a line off its blade and told you he'd kill for you, you were inclined to believe him.

"I think he'll come to the sessions if first you'd go out to his house in Essex for a talk".
Greg was a man of few words, so Jerry Shirley had finished the thought for him. So to Essex Eddie and I went. Steve was ranting and raving. He'd had it up to here with A&M records, up to there with Dee Anthony. He'd worked four straight......well four years on the trot and was tired and broke. He had just learned that the real estate, a compound named Rock's Rest that he thought he owned with the rest of the group somewhere in the Bahamas, wasn't his at all.

I cannot recall why and how logic prevailed but Steve agreed to come and work on the album, which would be titled Street Rats. He'd come to town and grind out an album if I'd come out to his home studio and make a solo Steve and Greg effort on the side, then take it to New York, mix it and guard it till it was deemed releasable. I said yes. Steve said yes and the last Humble Pie album got underway.

The studio was booked around the clock and we were supposed to clock in at 7pm each evening. By nine o'clock Humble Pie started to drift in from their Essex marginal rock n roll manors but nothing would really get started until they had ordered and received some terrible coke. This was madness. Their attention span was non-existent. Steve would get bored on the run throughs, a wired cocker cockney spaniel in retreat, so the woodsman - Greg Ridley - would take over the singing chores, which would end up as his end run duty on 40% of the final record, while Steve wished himself out of the deal he'd made with his devil via me. We cut basic tracks that were note-for-note rave-ups of well known Beatles songs: Paperback Writer, Rain and a couple of others. I let him change Paperback Writer into his own Street Rats, but drew the line at letting him plagiarise Drive My Car, We Can Work It Out and Rain.

Steve didn't care. The insidious madness grew. Then he did a couple of breathtaking vocals, incredible I'll-show-you-don't-count-me-out performances, each of them delivered in one tasty take. This just served to frustrate yours truly, mind in pride and a lump in the throat, and the on looking Piemen, ears boggling, at two takes of reminder as to how great he could be.

I then went out to Essex and stayed there a good week. The sounds Steve had come up with for Steve and Greg's now titled "Joint

Effort" were fresher, had a great vital groove and were much better than anything we'd produced at Olympic for Humble Pie. It was like Steve's little big mod jazz funk James Brown East End review! Actually, that labelling doesn't do it justice - it was an up instant groove, clever, new money from an old mint.

I went back to the studio, Olympic Sound Studios, to finish Street Rats. Steve Marriott turned up on Friday and sang his three songs for me, then went home, slugging out of the side of his mouth that wasn't smiling "That's all you're f****** getting Andrew, so don't come back asking for no more".

I did ask for more and I got it. It was the second week of recording at Olympic, thought the clock was already down three and I still had an album to fill. I had the band playing grooves, anything they felt like. Out of nowhere they hit a figure that was pure Steve Marriott, evoking his life's musical structure from All Or Nothing, through Stax and back to Lazy Sunday. It strutted, walked and talked good. He knew it and he felt it, it was right there in the pocket. The little cockneymeister shook his head and pranced up to the mike in his brown flared-bottomed trousers. He began to sing and I felt my earth move as Steve started in on Chris Montez's hit from 1962 Let's Dance.

In the control room I couldn't believe it. This was the hit moment I'd been waiting for, and it gained ground as Stevie wailed on, I could already smell hit, hear it on the radio. A hit single! I liked it. Steve needed a hit, I needed a hit. The tape was rolling. They got through the first time round, they didn't f*** it up, it stayed on the money, hit the second verse; just as simple.....it worked! Oh, for God's sake, I don't ask for much, just let 'em finish is all I ask. You'll have your own weapon; you'll have your own dance. I was here there and everywhere in that moment. I was past, present and future - that's how it feels when you hear the whole nine yards. Steve turned to me in the control room, saw me getting off, smiling, praying he'd continue and finish the whole deal, chapter and verse.

Suddenly he shouted "Hold it" like a sergeant major, and Greg, Jerry and Clem did, and with that went this magic sound. "Got you that time, didn't I, Oldham? ....you think I'd do that f****** song?" "You got me Steve - you really got me" "Hey Andrew, what would you like us to do next for ya, Sha La La La Lee?"

With that Steve threw down his guitar. The feedback felt like an award of applause and before you could say "they're coming to take me away ha ha" he jumped off the mike stand and walked out of the studio. "Well" said Jerry "that's one boy that's not coming back tonight "He's just scared about what he's good at" said Greg "You wait, he'll hear on the radio. Grand Funk Railroad will do "Locomotion" and it'll be number one" "Don't think Steve didn't know what was going on, Andrew" said Jerry

Maybe Steve was right - for himself. He sure played Let's Dance like a f******* hit, but he could not stand the idea of standing up, getting f***** over and hurt again.

ANDREW OLDHAM

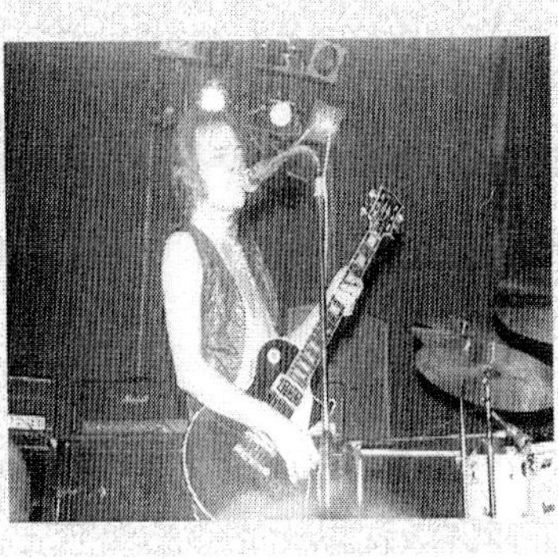

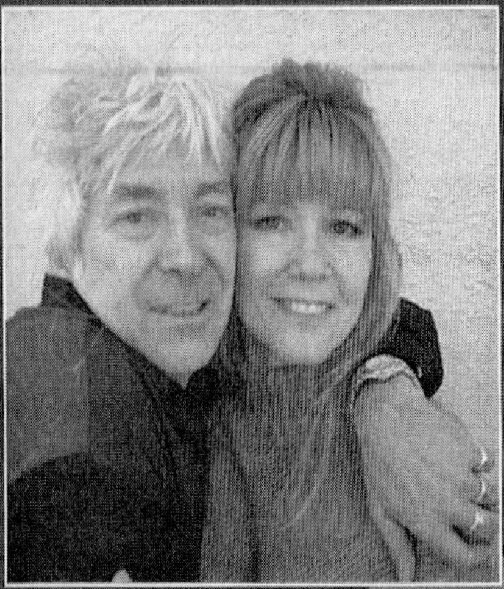

KIM McLAGAN

Kim, beloved wife of Ian McLagan, was tragically killed in a road accident on Wednesday 2nd August 2006 in Austin, Texas. Kim was very well known in her own right in the Swingin' London of the 1960's. She was a model who was married to Who hell-raiser Keith Moon (and bore him his only child, Mandy). Kim was best pals with Patti Boyd Harrison and even appeared in the pre-video clip of "All You Need Is Love". Unlike the entourage-laden bands of today, who pretty much keep in their own circle, the British bands of the 60's all hung out together.

TO MAC: Where angels hide there are words I don't know, I can't find them. There's nothing I can say to help you or get you through the day. The words that might heal you escape me. There's nothing I can write to help you or get you through the night. You're not alone, she'll always be there, right by your side singing lullaby's and when you dream she'll always be where the Angels hide in paradise.

FROM MAC: She is my shining light and always will be. Her life was a testament to love and healing and everyone who met her felt the glow from this warm, loving and giving being. She means everything to me but I know we'll be together again in a better place. She is a flower and a dream and finally the Angel she always was. She leaves behind Mandy, our loving daughter and two grand-daughters, Sam and Jess, her devoted brother Dermot, my son Lee, who loved her as his own mother. Her family and friends are spread all over the world but the outpouring of love for her is just a reflection of the love she gave. She said "You get what you give" and as always she's absolutely right. Kim is an Angel, finally.

DAVID ESSEX AND KENNEY OFF THE WALL........

"The record company were already looking for another album and single and I suspect that it was going back to music, after the break of filming, although pretty whacked, that helped me cope. The backing vocals had been finished for my single "America" originally by The Persuasions. It was released in May 1974, and although it charted, it never made the top 10 in the UK, probably because the lyric was too personal.

This wasn't the case in France, where the song became the biggest foreign hit ever, staying at number 1 for months. Curious to know why, I asked a French record executive what could be the reason. He told me his theory - the chorus of America goes 'America, America - ca ca', and 'ca ca' is apparently the French equivalent of poo poo [shit]. This obviously appealed to the xenophobic French. And I thought it was just a catchy song...

I've spent a fair deal of time in the South of France, which is one of my favourite places. One time when I was there I met up with my good friend Kenney Jones, the ex-drummer of the Small Faces. One night Kenney and I went out for a drink in a club in St Tropez. At the end of the night Kenney and I decided to head back to the villa I'd rented next to Jean-Michael Jarre, but not before relieving ourselves against a wall. There I was quietly answering the call of nature, when from out of nowhere an arm went round my neck and I was dragged away - still with my flies wide open and it swaying in the breeze :-)...

My mistake seems to have been that the wall selected belonged to a Police station. Once inside, with my flies safely done up, I was quizzed and rebuked until one burly policeman recognised me: 'Daveed Esseex - America - ca ca.' He then brokered a deal - I would be let off from a night in a police cell if I gave them a rendition of 'America'. Faced with little choice, I climbed up on to the table and sang it. It felt like some strange initiation ceremony for the Foreign Legion. Kenney could hardly keep a straight face as the local constabulary joined in".

David Essex (2006)

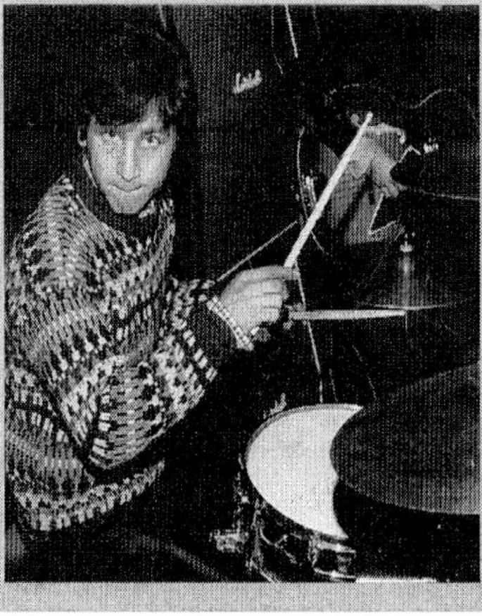

GREEN CIRCLES

Nick Jones at a Small Faces recording session.

"Everybody do the paranoia" hissed Steve Marriott as he sloped across the room of the Small Faces Pimlico pad. Resembling an unlikely gang of underwater karate experts, mimicking the great Wilson, Keppel and Betty, the remaining Faces followed about the room in slow motion. The squeamish may find the Small Faces latest war cry a little cruel, Napoleon XIV didn't stay unbanned, but then the Faces live in a compact, happy, air-tight little world of life, thought, ideas and music.

Steve, Mac, Plonk and mate Mick, a kind of hidden Small Face that you never hear about, lounged about in front of the TV. Kenney was out underneath his Mini. Someone stealthily moved to the record player and put on a sound. After about one third of a bar of Bobby Parker's Barefootin' they were all grooving along with the record, listening hard and digging. Downstairs, faint shuffling, step-treading and the occasional "eeeeeek" came floating under the front door. "They must be soaking wet by now, they've been out there for hours" thought Stevie of the handful of fans clustered under the front porch. "They'll have all the neighbours out soon" said Mac, visualising angry next-doors chasing the bedraggled girls down the street.

The Small Faces recording session wasn't booked until 11pm. "The girls have usually gone by about 9 o'clock" continued Mac, "that means it's a free passage to the awaiting mini-cab", he laughed. Talk of the session prompted the boys to tumble slowly downstairs, via the kitchen for bread and jam first.

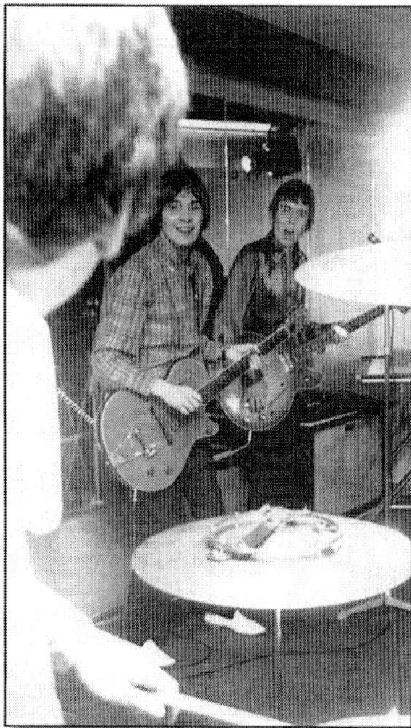

The dining table stood majestically in the middle of chaos. Tape recorders, miles of tape all over the place, guitars, speakers and an old piano. On to a tape recorder whirled a rough backing track- just drums, bass, piano and guitar- of the bands newest composition. "We based it on a dream that Mick had. He saw this geezer, a nice bloke actually, walking about with this green aura round him" explained Steve, "by the time we've added all the sounds it'll be a gas. We're not sure yet whether Ronnie or me is going to do the lead vocal." "It's a gas" breathed dreamer Mick (O'Sullivan). The boys concentrated on Green Circles, remembering their parts and adding little bits. Ideas were flowing freely and Steve was dancing excitedly by the time he'd thought of all the sounds that could be incorporated.

At 11pm, clutching brandy- Napoleon, of course- guitar cases and other oddments of mystery and imagination, four small, happy, Small Faces bounded into the recording studio. "I love this place," sighed Steve, rushing up to the control room and saying hello to John the engineer, before switching the lights on and generally grooving about. "We've forgotten the tape for John," cried Plonk. Disaster! How could they describe to John what kind of sound they wanted on Green Circles? Marriott went into action, "A nice big jangle on Mac's piano, Rock n Roll bass and a deep crisp drum sound," When the bass drum boom was satisfactory and Plonk's bass speaker crackle was eliminated the first backing track was laid down.

Recording was under way. Strictly no entry when the red light is on. "Circles of greeeeeeen," hummed Mr. Marriott over engineer John's shoulder. Kenney's drums exploded from the battery of huge speakers in the control room. Plonk sang out the melodically eerie bass line. No more "everybody do the paranoia," no more "neighbours," no more "Sha La La La Lee," no more "My Minds Eye". The past is blocked out completely for the moment. There's only one way- forwards. Each record is that bit better.

"Our outlook is one of happiness

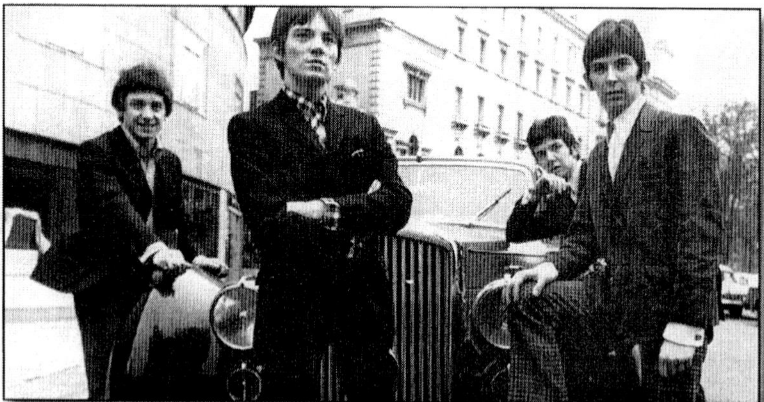

and well-being," said Steve "and this must come through with your music. We are living and we want our music to too. Superficially a number like Green Circles sounds sinister but we want people to listen. If they listen, and they can think, they'll get a kick out of it." Lunacy broke through again. "Orlright was it?" beamed Plonk. "Can't I take the bottom off this piano." laughed Mac. Kenney sat quietly in the corner and watched. The boys listened to the playback. Discussed it. More ideas; adding, subtracting, louder, softer, harder, longer. Brandy!

Back into the studio. Shouting, joking, falling about. Red light, another layer of bass from Ronnie, 12 string guitar from Steve and more jangle from Mac, now with a stripped down piano. The sound began to grow as the different sounds went on. Another track, another idea. Green Circles was getting better. Stevie was back in the studio falling about with a load of enormous chimes. In with the bells, in with the conga drums. More depth and a bit further forward. By 3am the backing track is mixed. A mess of machines and a mass of electricity. They tried the vocals. First Plonk then Steve doing the lead. "The old voice box begins to crack by this time," said Mac. "No, it's not right." "I'm tired," volunteered the engineer. "Right," answered Steve. Too tired!

"Home!" came the cry. Snoring road manager is awoken. Red light off. And the green circles grew and they all lived happily ever after.

Originally published in
Melody Maker 17/12/66

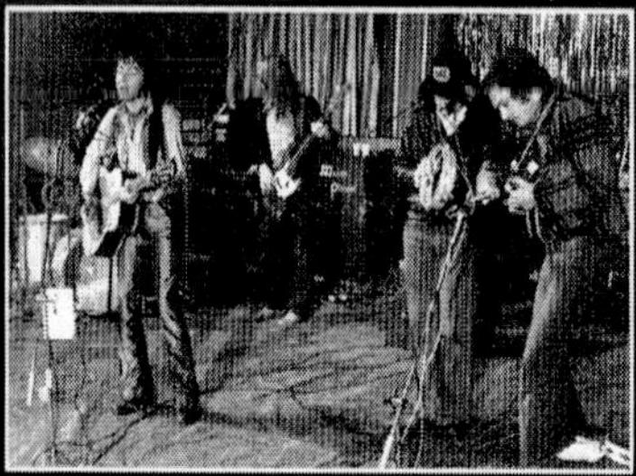

A TRIP DOWN RONNIE LANE

As a fan of the Small Faces for many a moon it is only recently I've begun to delve into and fully appreciate the rich tapestry of Ronnie Lane's post Small Faces song-writing. The moving documentary "The Passing Show – The life & music of Ronnie Lane' wonderfully portrays a musician and a beautiful person who never really received his dues.

Ronnie Lane was the heart and soul of the Small Faces and later, The Faces. It was whilst in the Faces his song-writing flair began to fully bloom with beautiful heartfelt numbers like 'Debris' and 'Glad And Sorry'. Miles away from the boozy and lad-dish reputation the Faces had nurtured these tracks portrayed a more earthy and reflective side that was pure Ronnie Lane.

Lane turned his back on the fame and fortune at his feet with the Faces and went onto live a gypsy style life on a farm. It was here, I wrongly assumed, the Ronnie Lane story ended. But he would continue recording, creating some remarkable solo material that oozed simplicity and charm with a lovely hint of melancholy. The country tinged lilt of his finest compositions should have made him one of the our most treasured country rock singers but a run of continuous bad luck and a lack of interest in the bullshit surrounding the music biz meant his work remains sadly under-appreciated.

My favourite footage of the Small Faces shows the band wandering round the streets and shops of London (which is shown in the first part of the film) in the sixties. The band looked the dogs' bollocks and would make heads turn today. They were dressed smartly in timeless, classic mod suits with mighty fine haircuts. Ronnie Lane, in particular, looks equally dapper and cheekily cocksure. Youth and style captured on film for generations to copy. Priceless!

It's an image that any mod would hold dear to his/her heart but with the passing of time I've begun to dig some of the more reflective and poignant recordings Ronnie would go onto make which were a million miles away from this bold and inspirational image.

Inspired by the movie I began to delve into the Ronnie Lane back catalogue and with deep joy indeed I discovered many nuggets and musical gems, the best of which I've compiled onto my own favourite eighty minute compilation.

So, are you sitting 2 square and comflee bold on your botty? Then I'll begin...

Although the Lane/Marriott song-writing partnership yielded loads of classic songs and some wonderful vocals, the real Ronnie Lane character evolved during his time with the Faces so my compilation kicks off here with a select bunch of tracks featuring our Ron.

Plonk & The Faces

Ronnie wrote two tracks on the debut Faces album, First Step (1970), alongside a couple of joint Lane/Ronnie Wood efforts. I've plumped for 'Stone' which has a loose Stonesy vibe but Ronnie adds a touch of wry humour to this story telling, toe tapping ditty.

His first real classic was on the Faces second album, Long Player (1971). 'Tell Everyone' was actually sung by Rod Stewart for this album but the version that stands out for me is Lane's own version that was included on the 1974 album 'Anymore For Anymore'. Surprisingly Lane's voice is far better suited to this romantic lament than Rod's. Ronnie Lane's best work had wonderful simple but evocative couplets and this song is no exception. Add to that a wistful, laidback voice and lines like "To wake up with you, it makes my morning so bright/Wipes the sleep from my eyes, have you tell me your dream" simply ooze soul when handled by Ronnie. It just sounds more believable when you hear him sing his version.

Meanwhile, back in 1971, the country homage to life on the road is captured in 'Richmond' in which Lane in his finest adopted western drawl wishes he was back home in Richmond with some great picking by Ronnie Wood on slide guitar. If Rod Stewart added the boozy euphoria to the Faces most uplifting songs, Lane provided the morning after the night before soundtrack.

The two contrasting voices of Lane and Stewart are both captured best on the live version of Maybe I'm Amazed (written by Paul McCartney). Both voices, though contrasting, sound equally soulful and the Faces make this song their own.

The second stone cold classic track Ronnie Lane wrote and this time sung himself whilst in the Faces was 'Debris', a song about Ronnie's childhood memories. 'Debris' is a classic ballad with lyrics that skilfully portray touching images of family life and a time long forgotten.

As with all these selected tracks the musicianship is first class. This track and the more jovial 'You're So Rude', co-written with Ian McLagan, make it onto the compilation. Both are taken from the album, 'A Nod's As Good As A Wink'.

The final Faces album to feature Ronnie Lane song-writing was Ooh La La (1973) and the stand out album track was 'Glad and Sorry', Once again Ronnie's vocals lead on this self-penned track and includes the classic, immortal line, "Can you show me a dream, can you show me one that's better than mine?"

Lane co-wrote the title track 'Ooh La La' with Ronnie Wood and Wood takes the lead vocals on the album. Lane cut a great version for a BBC session with his next band Slim Chance.

Slim Chance

After quitting the Faces, Ronnie formed Slim Chance. Shunning the increasingly bloated and emotional vacuum of the heavier sounds most bands in the 70s were succumbing to, Plonk searched for a more rustic and simple acoustic sound to channel his deeply soulful laments such as the yearning, elegance of 'Done This One Before' and 'Don't You Cry For Me'.

'Anymore for Anymore', released in 1974, is a classic album and it's hard to pick just a few songs for this compilation but I've plumped for the single 'How Come' (the BBC session version edges it for me) alongside, The Poacher, the aforementioned version of, 'Tell Everyone' and the country tinged cover 'Roll On Babe'. Special mention too for the rich melodies of 'Don't You Cry For Me' and 'Anymore For Anymore' two faultless examples of the most enchanting and affectionate of songs.

You have to dig a bit deeper into the rest of the back catalogue, Ronnie Lane went onto record albums and tracks with members of Slim Chance as well as Ronnie Wood, Pete Townsend, Steve Marriott and Eric Clapton.

One of the best stories from the Passing Show is how Eric Clapton was captured by the charm of Ronnie Lane and he speaks lovingly about his dear friend revealing that his own record 'Wonderful Tonight' was both inspired and written down on Ronnie's farm. It would have been great to have heard Ronnie doing his version of this song.

'Anniversary' is my favourite track from 1975's Ronnie Lane's Slim Chance album. The title track from 'One For The Road' (1076) is the pick from this album. Eric Clapton featured heavily on the 1979 album 'See Me' and the duo penned the lovely track 'Barcelona'. The stand out track from the album Lane cut with Ronnie Wood, 'Mahoney's Last Stand' was the country influenced 'Just For A Moment'. Better still was a couple of tracks Ronnie cut with Pete Townsend for the 'Rough Mix' album. April Fool (Ronnie's birthday) and the tearjerker 'Annie' – written about a much loved neighbour.

We're down to the final two tracks that don't feature on any of the above albums but can be found on the compilation, 'Kuschty Rye: The Singles 1973-1980' on Pilot records. This compilation is probably the best starting point for anyone starting out collecting Ronnie Lane's solo work. The single 'Kuschty Rye' and 'Done This One Before' wrap up my compilation. 'Done This One Before' is another classic Lane composition. It was previously only available as a B-side to the single 'How Come'. Laidback, achingly dreamlike soul, seemingly effortless but, packed with an understated emotion that Lane had a knack of producing.

Finally, special mention for the compilation of BBC sessions, 'You Can Never Tell'. Amongst the many great versions of classic Lane tracks is his bubbly version of 'Ooh La La' and it's so full of jaunty, optimism you can't help but fall in love with it. What a great way to finish any album and to best remember Ronnie Lane.

I'm sure I've overlooked some other classic Ronnie Lane moments. Perhaps enough for a volume two if you also consider the Small Faces tracks Ronnie contributed most to.

Much of Ronnie Lane's music has an added poignant feel largely down to his impoverished lifestyle and his subsequent battle with MS (an illness I can personally relate to as my grandmother also had the same). Listening to Ronnie Lane speak and sing you can't help but succumb to his near mystical charm and down to earth innocence. Watch 'The Passing Show' and you will have tears rolling down your face by the end I promise. God bless Ronnie Lane. Thanks for showing me the dream.

Track listing for my "A Trip Down Ronnie Lane" compilation:

1. Tell Everyone
2. Done This One Before
3. The Poacher
4. Roll On Babe
5. Anymore For Anymore
6. Kuschty Rye
7. Annie
8. April Fool
9. Just For A Moment
10. Anniversary
11. Barcelona
12. Don't You Cry For Me
13. One For The Road
14. How Come (BBC session)
15. Ooh La La (BBC session)
16. Debris
17. Glad & Sorry
18. Maybe I'm Amazed (Live)
19. Richmond
20. Stone
21. You're So Rude

BY PAUL RITCHIE www.ready-steady-go.org.uk

OGDEN'S NUT GONE FLAKE
– The making of *BY JOHN HELLIER (OCTOBER 2008)*

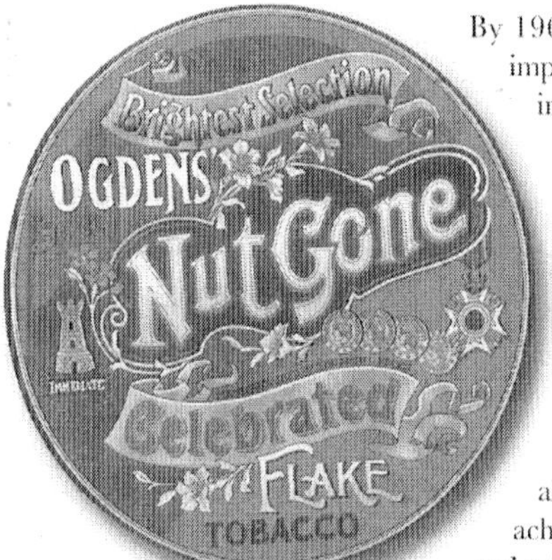

By 1968, the album had assumed a far greater importance within Rock culture. Singles were still important but albums, post Sgt. Pepper, were now the medium to conquer. To reflect its lofty position the music press began running lengthy stories about such events as the band Traffic moving to the country to write and record their debut album. Steve Marriott thoroughly approved of this shift in music. Bands would now be judged by artistic standards not by the size of their pop stardom. By creating an outstanding new album he firmly hoped that the band could now achieve two goals in one; lose the screaming girls and gain musical respect. They got what they wanted.

The Small Faces had recently arrived back from the infamous tour of Australia and New Zealand and were looking for ideas for the next Immediate album, as yet still untitled. For inspiration they decided to rent three cabin cruisers on the Thames and casually drift along the famous river whilst working on ideas for new songs. Over the course of a week they drifted from Henley to Maidenhead and back many times. During the day they'd play, they'd jump from boat to boat and although quite unintentially they'd cause havoc amongst other boating clientele. After crashing into another vessel they were declared "scum of the river" by some guy posing as Horatio Hornblower who was sporting a blue blazer with gold buttons, white trousers and a Captains hat! Aside from the sky larking, they did, in fact, get to do some work and gems such as "Happy Days Toytown" "Happiness Stan" "The Journey" and "Hungry Intruder" were written or developed on that trip.

Earlier in the year the band had a big hit single with a track that Steve had written about problems with his neighbours entitled Lazy Sunday. The problems were probably of his own making though as he himself must have been the original "neighbour from hell" with a sound system from Olympic studios in the front room of his two bedroom flat! Steve's extreme cockney accent on that disc was the result of a music paper story stating that Allan Clarke, lead singer of the Hollies, had said that Steve Marriott only ever sung with a false American accent. Steve thought I'll show him and delivered the most sparkling cockney accent ever! It was a classic track (still is) and found it's way onto Side One of the new (still untitled) album alongside new tracks such as an instrumental version of the bands second single I've Got

Mine (eventually the title track of the album), Afterglow.....always one of Steve's favourite Small Faces songs although he dismissed it at the time as just another soppy love song for some soppy tart!, An Ian McLagan song Long Ago's And Worlds Apart, Song Of A Baker, possibly their hardest hitting rocker to date and the hilarious Rene (The Dockers Delight) straight from the music hall and a true story! Rene Tungate was a neighbour of Steve's in his youth and according to Steve himself she was one sandwich short of a picnic! She did, in fact, have several children of every shape and colour and had a reputation locally for being easy meat. Steve would regularly bunk off school to go to her house for sexual encounters. "She taught me everything my mother used to clout me for" he once said.

Side Two of the new album would be groundbreaking, it would be conceptual (some 12 months or so before The Who's Tommy) and would tell the tale of Happiness Stan and his quest to find the missing half of the moon. Happiness Stan is accompanied by a gossiping giant fly. He meets the old and allegedly crazy hermit Mad John and in the end he discovers Happy Days Toytown. This story would need narration and according to Steve who better to do it than his boyhood hero Spike Milligan. Spike was approached but passed on the idea. Ronnie then came up with the idea of asking Stanley Unwin, who was at that time appearing in a TV advert for Gales Honey. Stanley had never heard of the Small Faces but was up for the task. It was an inspired move Stanley was ideal for the job and, in hindsight, should have been first choice anyway. His speciality lay in the re-making of the English language with linguistic twists and turns unique to himself only. He called it Unwinese and it provided a lot of clever humour. When Stanley first met the band at Olympic studios he asked them to provide him with some phrases and they gave him things like "Where at man" and "Stay cool" and he popped those into the dialogue. He warmed to the band quickly and made them laugh and remembers that the band also had their own sort of language. There was plenty of laughter, chuckling and replacing of words in the studio which resulted in a very relaxed atmosphere. Stanley's narration linked the following songs, Happiness Stan (named after Ronnie's father), Rollin' Over, The Hungry Intruder, Mad John and Happy Days Toytown.

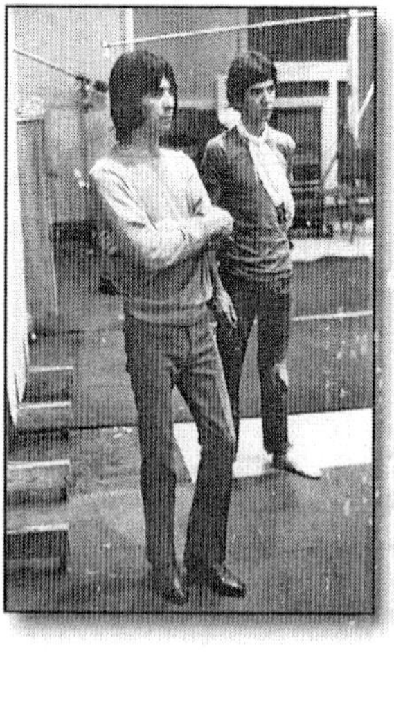

Back in London and back in Immediate Records office in New Oxford Street it was Steve that suggested the whole tobacco tin theme for the sleeve. "Can we do it like Ogden's?" he said. Ogden's was a popular tobacco firm that produced their goods in a tin. Andrew Loog Oldham, the bands manager, arranged for the tobacco company to send illustrations of every tobacco tin they had ever produced. One of them was called Ogden's Nut Brown Flake which was quickly changed by Steve to Ogden's Nut Gone Flake. The band's preferred tobacco brand for mixing their marijuana joints used to be Ogden's Flake and according to them whenever they smoked the stuff their nuts would go! Hence Ogden's Nut Gone Flake. The unusual packaging also included a round sleeve which would annoy shop keepers as it kept rolling off the shelves! As the cover is unfolded it features four jazzed-up black and white pictures of the band members. One of them shows Mac with a cat, behind him is Ronnie sitting with his banjo, Kenney is holding an ice cream wafer and Steve is grinning in his "George the cleaner" guise. Photographer Gerard Mankowitz had asked them to bring various things from home that they liked and were visually interesting. Steve totally forgot to bring anything but decided to dress up in things that he found in the studio. He ended up as a manic lavatory cleaner!

To promote the album in the music press Andrew Loog Oldham and, his business partner, Tony Calder concocted a controversial advert parodying the Lords Prayer. It was great publicity but had certain vicars and politicians up in arms about the Bibles words being abused for "pop" promotion. Steve was to say "We simply borrowed it from God and changed the words a little".

SMALL FACES
WHICH WERE IN THE STUDIOS
HALLOWED BE THY NAME
THY MUSIC COME
THY SONGS BE SUNG
ON THIS ALBUM AS THEY COME FROM YOUR HEADS
WE GIVE YOU THIS DAY OUR DAILY BREAD
GIVE US THY ALBUM IN A ROUND COVER
AS WE GIVE THEE 37/9d
LEAD US INTO THE RECORD STORES
FOR NICE IS THE MUSIC, THE SLEEVE AND THE STORY
FOR EVER AND EVER.....AMEN.

The glowing reviews, advertising and excitement over the package in addition to this being the bands first album for over a year meant that it sold over 20,000 copies on the first day of release (24th May 1968) and crashed into the album charts at number 9. One week later it was number 1 and stayed there for six weeks. The album stayed in the UK charts for 19 weeks in total, proving to be Immediate Records best selling album ever giving the band the musical respect that they had craved and putting them in the same album league as the Beatles, Beach Boys and Rolling Stones. Add to all this, the band recorded a Colour Me Pop TV special featuring the second side of the album complete with Professor Stanley Unwin et al. That piece of footage remains the finest ever testimony to the East End of London's own fab four.

Of course, fans and critics now expected a live rendition of this masterpiece but that never happened. This was a substantial mistake as Steve would admit later. "We had spent best part of a year in the studio and our recording experience had developed in leaps and bounds. We were all keenly interested in the technical possibilities, in the art of recording. We let down the people that wanted to hear Ogden's played live. We were still sort of rough and ready and in the end the audience became uninterested as far as our stage show was concerned.

It was our own fault because we could have sussed it all out if we had only used our brains. We could have taken Stanley Unwin on tour with us, maybe a string section as well, and it would have been fab. But we didn't do it; we stuck to the concept that had been successful for a long time, which was our kiss of death". Shortly afterwards The Small Faces were no more.

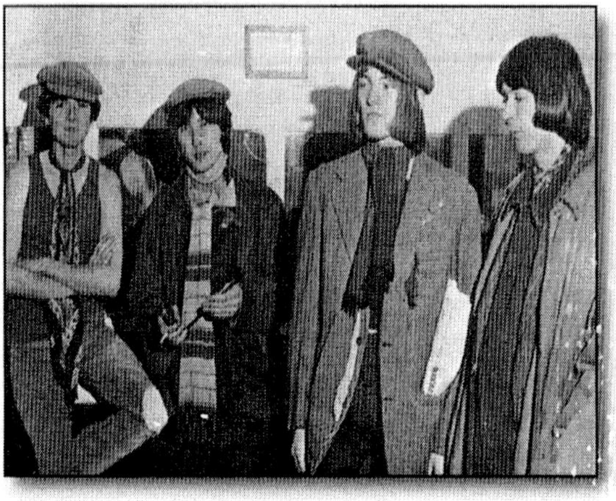

OGDEN'S QUOTES:

STEVE MARRIOTT (1969): We cleaned up every award in the book for it and Andrew collected them. We caught him on the stairs at Immediate's offices, his arms full of bits of plastic- Best Artwork, Best Design, Best Album.....

Anything that made us laugh we liked. God knows how it worked but it did and I'm very proud of it and the other guys are too. We didn't know a thing about the Lords Prayer advert until we saw it in the music papers and frankly we got the horrors at first. We realised that it could be taken as a serious knock against religion but on thinking it over, we didn't feel it was particularly good or bad it was just another form of advertising.

PETE TOWNSHEND (1969): Ogden's Nut Gone Flake was a world shaking record. When they first played it to me the only material I had heard to which it could be compared to were concept pieces like Pet Sounds or Sgt. Pepper. I was jealous of the Small Faces sound; they were becoming a real extraordinary sonic force to be reckoned with.

KENNEY JONES (1968): Really this album is just the beginning of things. Before we used to be with Immediate we'd turn out albums like sausages. They'd stick us up against a brick wall somewhere and take a picture for the sleeve. We could never work up much pride into what we were putting in with that kind of system. Now we've got better lyrics and better ideas. On stage we use six brass players including trumpets, saxophone and trombones. When we go to the studio these days we don't have to worry about wasting half an hour. We recorded some of the tracks on Ogden's as many as ten times.

BARRY HEWITT INTERVIEW

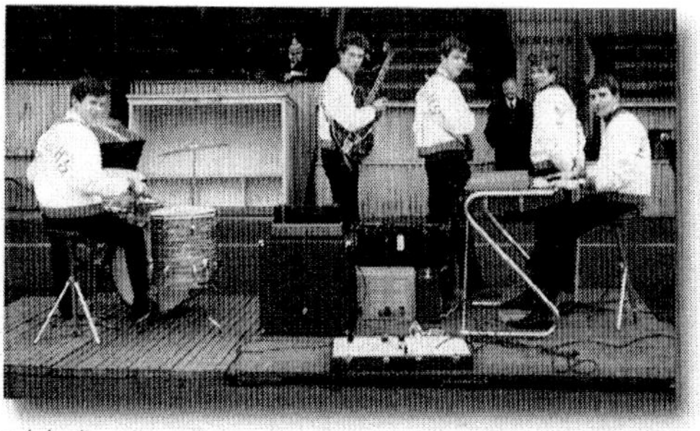

BY JOHN HELLIER.

Steve Marriott's Moments- The EP was issued on 22nd September by Acid Jazz Records (licensed from Wapping Wharf Records). It features two previously unreleased tracks "Good Morning Blues" and "You'll Never Get Away From Me" along with mega rare "You Really Got Me" and "Money Money" which were originally released as a single in 1964 by World Records in the USA. The two unreleased tracks were recently discovered by the Moments bass player, Barry Hewitt. I caught up with him recently and asked about those heady pre-Small Faces days.

JH: WHEN AND HOW DID YOU FIRST MEET STEVE MARRIOTT?

BH: First met Steve around 1963 in an East End coffee bar called the Square Ring. All the local groups of the day would go there and spend hours over one cup of coffee. A definate meeting place for local musicians. Steve was in a group, can't remember the name (Frantiks) when he asked Allen (Ellett) if he could join ours. We were always the Moments but such was Steve's reputation locally that promoters would bill us as Steve Marriott's Moments. That was never the official name of the band. The Faces had a similar situation in the 70s with Rod Stewart. The Moments were a going concern before I joined but I joined before Steve.

JH: DO YOU RECALL GIGGING?

BH: We were on the road all the time and worked a lot of gigs for promoter, Arthur Howes. We often supported chart names of the day such as the Animals and Billy J Kramer. We even supported Freddie And The Dreamers! We built up a big following, well Steve did, he was very charismatic even back then. A typical Moments set would consist of R&B covers. Things like My Babe, Leaving Here, Ooh Poo Pa Doo, You Can't Sit Down, Send Me Some Lovin', lots of James Brown songs but not the obvious ones. We'd do Just Me And You and I Don't Mind; also remember several Rufus Thomas, Chuck Berry and Bo Diddley songs and would you believe it a number called Whatcha Gonna Do About It, this was a Doris Troy song not the same number that was recorded by the Small Faces later. One of Steve's girlfriends of the day, actress Adrienne Posta, would often join us as guest vocalist. She was great and everybody fancied the pants off her!

JH: YOU RECORDED "YOU REALLY GOT ME" FOR A US LABEL, WHY? AND WERE THE KINKS AN INFLUENCE?

BH: Can't remember how You Really Got Me came about but it was never considered for UK release, after all the Kinks had had a number one hit here with it so nobody would have bought ours! The Kinks were not really an influence. Back then their stage act consisted of US covers as ours did. This was pre-Waterloo Sunset you know! There was absolutely no game plan; we were just kids, not long out of school, having fun.

JH: WERE THE BAND MODS?

BH: It seemed like every working class kid in the East End was a Mod. It was no big deal and you didn't consciously set out to be one, you just fell into it. It was the fashion of the day. We bought our gear (clothes) in Woolworths!

JH: WHY DID STEVE GET KICKED OUT OF THE BAND?

BH: Steve was voted out because he was hard work you know. He'd adopted a lot of attitude and although he was a great front man he was an inferior musician compared to the rest of us. Johnny Weider, our guitarist, had previously played with Johnny Kidd and the Pirates and was as good as it got. Allen had toured Europe with Jackie Lynton and really Steve was a novice in comparison. He was always a great singer though and looking back now he was the one member that was destined for bigger things. The Moments actually split up very soon after Steve went so we didn't go on to achieve anything without him.

JH: HOW DID THESE TWO UNRELEASED TRACKS TURN UP AFTER SOME 40 ODD YEARS?

BH: The acetate has been in my possession for years and years. Just sitting in a drawer, doing nothing. The tracks are time pieces, I think they sound 44 years old, which they are, but that's not to take anything away from them. Steve's voice though very distinctive was still to reach the soulful peak that it did a few years later. All I can remember about them is that they were recorded in a very basic studio somewhere near the Holloway Road in North London. Can't even remember the name. We didn't have a record deal and certainly never considered an album. In those days you had to have at least a couple of hit 45s before you done that. They were cut very quickly; we were only in the studio for half a day. I think it was funded by Tony Calder but can't be sure. Joe Meek turned up and showed interest in recording us but nothing ever came of it.

JH: ARE THERE ANY MORE RECORDINGS LIKELY TO BE UNEARTHED?

BH: Nothing else that I can remember featuring Steve. We recorded a few things before Steve joined but goodness knows where they are now. There is another track in existence called Touch Of The Blues but that was one of our keyboard player Allen Ellett's songs. Allen used to do all the lead vocals before Steve. Even after Steve joined he would still do a lot of lead vocals. He was upset about the group being billed as Steve Marriott's Moments. Touch Of The Blues was Jerry Lee Lewis meets the Dave Clark 5! Don't think Steve was even on it but can't be sure of that.

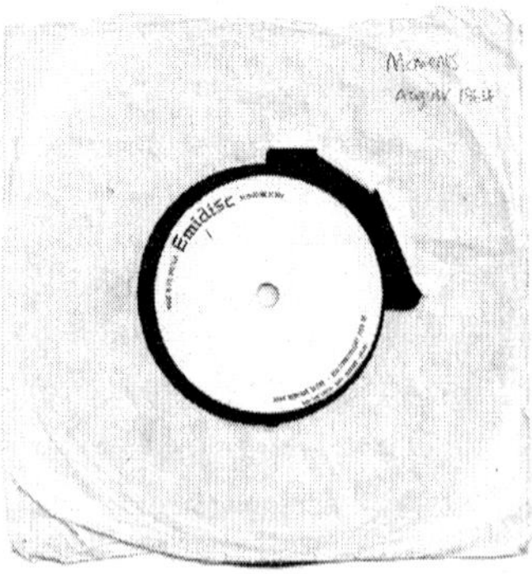

STEVE MARRIOTT TOOLED UP!

You'd expect a man with such fabulous taste in the sharpest togs to show equal discernment when it came to guitars and Steve Marriott didn't disappoint. Neither did he shy away from customising his guitars to make them exactly right. His main Small Faces guitars were a sunburst Fender Telecaster with a Gibson humbucker in the neck position for a meatier sound, a Gretsch Tennessean semi-acoustic and a 1959 Gretsch Jet Fire Bird with Filtertrons and a disarmed Bigsby (this guitar seems to switch between red and white finishes, or were their two?) . These guitars were generally played through Marshall, Selmer, Vox AC30 or Fender Showman amps, though with the re-formed Small Faces he used a Fender Twin Reverb. Steve used few effects, one notable exception being a primitive wah-wah that he shackled to Ian McLagan's piano for the instrumental title track of Ogden's Nut Gone Flake.

In Humble Pie, Steve enlarged his tool collection to include a late 50's sunburst Les Paul Standard (he removed the pickup covers to reveal all-black coils) and a black '57 Custom. Like many Custom fanciers, he found the added middle pickup interfered with his picking so he took it out and added Grover machines for better tuning. Steve also had a nose for other Gibsons and Epiphones. An Epiphone Coronet with a single white P90 and an added new extra curvey scratchplate, a Dwight, essentially a Coronet carrying the name of an American music store. He loved this one for its extra powerful pick-up and a late 50's double cut Les Paul Junior (later with the white Dwight scratchplate added).

Other Gibsons included a 335 favoured for solo tours from 1983 onwards including Packet Of Three duties, an archtop (believed to be an all-gold ES295) that he eventually presented to Alexis Korner and a Gibson Melody Maker. New Fenders in the rack included a stripped but otherwise all original 1955 Esquire with a black scratchplate (used on the Small Faces reunion) and a super early '54 Stratocaster, serial number 0062, which he liked but never used on stage (in fact he cannibalised the Strat's neck and slapped it onto his old Telecaster, now stripped back to a natural finish). Later he bought another Strat, a sunburst model with an early 60s rosewood fingerboard, as ever with the tremolo disabled and with a gold Gibson speed knob on the upper volume pot.

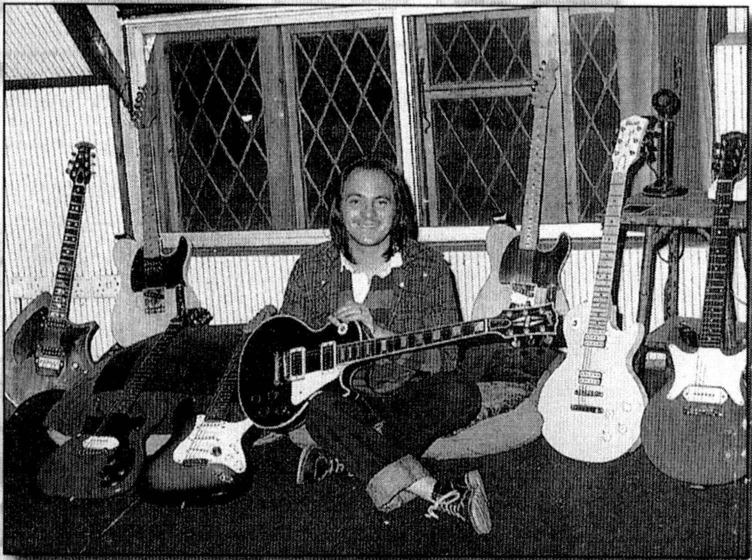

Steve Marriott's collection also included an original orange G-brand Gretsch 6120. He had three Ibanez electrics; a white Les Paul copy called a Deluxe '59 with a maple fingerboard; a Gibson/Epiphone Howard Roberts archtop copy with a single pickup, three knobs and an oval soundhole, strung with super light strings and used on Itchycoo Park: and an Artist semi acoustic, like a plush sunburst 335. He was so impressed with Ibanez that he posed for endorsement shots in 1983. He also had a weirdly shaped, mahogany finished Ovation Breadwinner much used in the studio during the mid to late '70s.

The Midgets many acoustics included his beloved 1937 Martin 000-18, a 1970's all-maple Gibson Gospel and a lovely '60s Epiphone Frontier dreadnought with a huge, ornate scratchplate. He also had matching '70s Ovations in six and twelve string form and a custom item by Crispian Mellor with a heart shaped soundhole, which can be heard on Humble Pie's 1973 album Eat It.

Steve's guitar collection was his pride and joy but sadly by the time he returned from his excile in America, in the early 1980's, they had all been disposed of courtesy of the taxman (and various drug dealers) but hey, that's another story.

COURTESY OF ULI TWELKER

SMALL FACES **NEWS**

The 2007 Small Faces Convention will be held at the Carling Academy, Islington, London on Sunday 9th September. For further details jjhellier@aol.com

The Jones Gangs successful US single "Angel" has been released as a single in the UK and is receiving lots of favourable reviews and airplay.

BBC Radio Two recently featured an hour long Small Faces documentary entitled "Whatcha Gonna Do About It". Narrated by Billy Bragg the programme was broadcast on February 17th.

Macs devoted wife Kim was tragically killed in a road accident in Austin on 2nd August last year. See page 11.

"Rough Mix" the Ronnie Lane/Pete Townshend album from 1977 has been released on cd for the first time by Eel Pie Records.

BBC London recently featured a Ronnie Lane Special hosted by mega Small Faces fan Robert Elms.

The excellent Ronnie Lane documentary "The Life And Music Of" has been shown twice on BBC4 and is now available to purchase through Eagle Rock Records.

Kenney Jones is to open an international chain of Polo clubs in both the USA and the Middle East. Cor Blimey, what would Stevie Marriott have made of that!

April 6th 2006 was declared Ian McLagan day, in his home town of Austin in Texas, by Mayor Will Wynn.

Wapping Wharfs John Hellier was interviewed for a Steve Marriott feature on BBC 1 televisions "Inside Out" late last year. Mainly focused on Steve's controversial death in 1991 it was broadcast on September 8th.

June 4th sees the tenth anniversary of Ronnie Lane's sad passing. Coming soon a definitive book on Ronnie's Austin years by Paul Snyder.

Marks and Spencer's current television advertising campaign features the Small Faces classic "Itchycoo Park" along with some retro footage featuring Twiggy amongst others.

Out now on Wapping Wharf Records "Wham Bam" by Steve Marriott's All-Stars from 1976. The last ever recordings from Steve's Clear Sound studios.

Fillmore East/West owner Bill Graham has recently stated that he is to make over 700 hours of audio and visual tapes from the 70's available for commercial release. Both the Faces and Humble Pie played these two venues on a regular basis so hopefully some of those will emerge.

AN INTERVIEW

WITH SMALL FACES FAN CLUB SECRETARY PAULINE CORCORAN

BY JOHN HELLIER (24th August 2011)

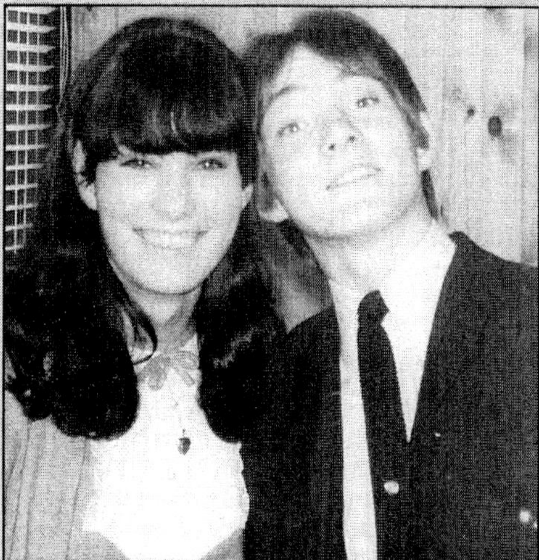

Pauline ran the fan club from late 1965 until just before the bands demise. Here she reminisces about working with the coolest band on the planet. An enviable job indeed.

JH: HOW DID YOU GET THE JOB IN THE FIRST PLACE?

PC: I wanted to change my job as I hated the previous one so much. I went to loads of employment agencies and told them that I wanted to work in either the theatre or the music business. They both appealed to me and sounded exciting. Anyway, one of them sent me for an interview with Don Arden in Carnaby Street. I had never heard of him before but one of my friends told me that the job vacancy was for running the Who's fan club. I loved Roger Daltrey so I was very excited about the prospect, however when I got to the interview I was told it wasn't for them at all. It was for a new group called The Small Faces. Their first single Whatcha Gonna Do About It had just been released and Don, during the half hour interview, told me that they were going places. Don was very convincing and told me that he purposely wanted a non-fan for the job so as not to be in awe of the boys, just be there to do a good job. He said "Can you start on Monday?" and I did.

JH: WHEN DID YOU FIRST MEET THE BOYS?

PC: I met them immediately I started my new job in the office. They were a bunch of fun loving guys and always messing around. Don told me to go and see them play so I went to the Marquee in Wardour Street and was very impressed. I hadn't realised just how good they were. The place was rammed and there were screaming hysterical girls and I just felt so proud to be working with them and being part of the team. Steve and I clicked straight away and it was Steve that always led the way in the band.

JH: WHAT DID AN AVERAGE WORKING DAY CONSIST OF?

PC: Well as soon as I got in the postman would arrive. Stacks of letters, sack loads of them. That took hours to sort out. There would be fan club application forms and I'd need to sort all the postal orders and stuff. There would also be the phone calls to be answered ten to the minute. Fans would ring constantly. Don also managed other bands such as The Animals and Nashville Teens. Steve and Ronnie used to really dig the Nashville Teens; they were very impressed with them. Don soon had me writing quarterly newsletters which I loved doing but fitting it all in was sometimes nigh on impossible. I'd write out a draft then Don would go through it. When you read them now they are so corny but that's what it was like back then. The readership went from 800 to 10,000 very quickly. Fans would often come in off the street and I'd get them helping out with enveloping. One would staple pages together and then pass to another who would fold, then another would put into an envelope and lastly somebody would put the stamp on. It was just like a conveyor belt in a factory; it was the most stressful part of the job and had to be done whilst still answering the phone and whatever. The Small Faces did use to help out though and the fans just loved that. They'd be sitting on the floor sorting out the letters and the boys would walk in……

Don was a marvellous boss and would always take me to lunch on a Friday along with other members of the staff. We'd all go to the Shakespeare's Head in Carnaby Street and would always have three hours. That was our treat. Great days! To work in Carnaby Street alone was a dream for any 16 year old girl. All the boutiques…..

JH: WHY WAS JIMMY WINSTON SACKED?

PC: I was never told the reason. I was told to tell the fans that Jimmy was leaving the band of his own accord. The atmosphere was terrible in the office but thinking back on it he was always on the outside. Steve and Jimmy both wanted to be front man, something or somebody had to give. Jimmy was a bit more grounded than the others, he was the serious one. Ian did fit in better with the band. Steve was always far and away the most popular member with the fans. The others were all equal second. Don continued to manage Jimmy for awhile afterwards.

JH: ON BOXING DAY 1965 DON MOVED THE BAND INTO 22 WESTMORELAND TERRACE. WHAT ARE YOUR MEMORIES OF THE HOUSE?

PC: Well I used to go round there regularly. I'm actually quite surprised at the "Party Central" label that it has these days. I don't remember any parties; they'd normally just be sitting around playing guitars or listening to music. I remember being asked to play Scalectrix with them and I remember Steve cooking bacon sandwiches even though they had a live in house keeper. I would pop over there for many different reasons and at different times of the day. Don sent

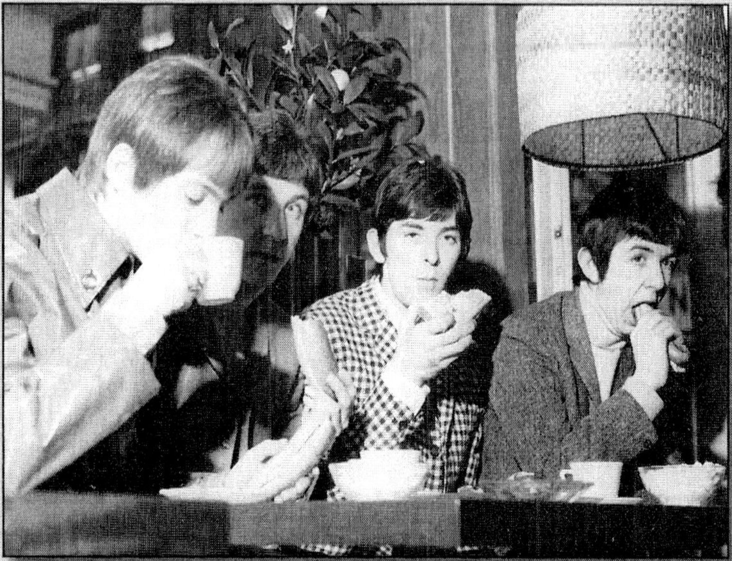

me there once to take Steve some money. He told me "Don't post it, make sure he answers the door". I was banging on the door and shouting "Steve, open this door" when the next door neighbour came out and told me to "clear off and leave those poor boys alone". Obviously thought I was a crazy fan. There are also stories about the boys inviting female fans into the house for whatever. I was not aware of that, they all had beautiful girlfriends.

JH: DID YOU EVER GO TO GIGS WITH THEM OR CLOTHES SHOPPING?

PC: Clothes shopping, oh yes. When it was my lunchtime they'd drag me out. They'd go mad, they wouldn't take one shirt off the rail they'd take handfuls in all different colours. They must have spent an absolute fortune. Shoes, leather jackets…they'd just help themselves. A lot of the clothes never even got worn; there were always loads of shirts still in wrappers around the house. Sometimes they'd say "What size is your brother? Here take these for him". He was only about 15 and I'd bring him home all these Small Faces clothes. He was over the moon, still talks about it today. . Fans would just stare at them whilst shopping but they never got any hassle in the street unlike gigs… I used to travel with them quite a lot in the beginning but after awhile I started travelling on my own, the hysteria was frightening. I remember one particular time in Lewisham when I was travelling home with them. There were literally hundreds and hundreds of girls outside the venue. There were bouncers but not enough of them to cope with those numbers. I got in the car first but the boys literally got clawed to bits, they really did. Inside the car it was so claustrophobic with fans pressing their faces and bodies up to the window. It's amazing how the windows weren't smashed. After that I told Don that I couldn't travel with them anymore. They loved all the adulation but then it got too aggressive. You couldn't hear a note they played above the screaming girls. That did frustrate them, I know it did. One minute I'm working with a group I'd never heard of and now all this….

JH: DID THEY ALWAYS DRESS WELL OR WAS IT JUST FOR THE BENEFIT OF A PHOTO SHOOT?

PC: Oh no, they were always dressed very smartly in a Mod casual type of way. I'd quite often go round the house unexpected at all times of the day and they'd always look immaculate. Most managers would say to their band "You've gotta look smart 24/7" Don Arden never had to do that.

JH: DID YOU ATTEND ANY OF THE TV SHOWS THAT THEY DID?

PC: Yes lots. I remember Steve collapsing while they were doing Hey Girl on Ready Steady Go. He was carried, like you'd carry a child, back to his dressing room. He just sat there with towels wrapped all around him and he was shaking, he was so pale. I said to him "Are you OK?" and he said "I'm sorry". I didn't know what to make of that. On another occasion when we were all in the canteen at Ready Steady Go with my Mum, who was a make up artist at the studio, Steve said "I'll have to pop round and see the family" Mum said " Well come on over after you've finished here" as we lived close by. I never expected him to but a bit later on he said to me "Come on Pauline, let's go see the family". We walked into the house and my two brothers and their girlfriends were there. My Mum was expecting him so she'd cooked him dinner. The others all gasped "Oh God!" "We've got a Pop star in our house". Steve had dinner, had a couple of beers and stayed for a few hours. We all had a great laugh, he was so sociable. Next day Steve was telling the others that he'd met my family so Ronnie said "Well can I come, can I come today?" and I said NO! I told him "Ronnie I love you but I can't take you back to meet my family". He took it all in his stride but I think he was a bit put out.

JH: I UNDERSTAND THAT RONNIE HAD A CRUSH ON YOU?

PC: Well yes, but he was always so stoned. More so than the other three, he was always away with the fairies. I loved him as a friend. At one time he wanted to come and visit my parents and I had to say no. He said "Why?" I couldn't take him home to meet my friends and family, they would have clicked the moment he walked through the door that he was stoned. Too many joints that's all. My Mum knew them all anyway through her job at Ready Steady Go. Once on a trip to Birmingham with Don Arden and the Small Faces he invited me to his hotel room. Don told them very firmly "If anyone of you goes near her room tonight I'll break your legs!" Don was very protective of me. I was a 16 year old virgin and he looked after me. Ronnie would ring my room, about half past 12, when I was in bed and say "Do you wanna come over?" I'd say "Do you know what time it is?" He'd say "You don't have to get changed, come as you are" He was a lovable character but definitely not boyfriend material.

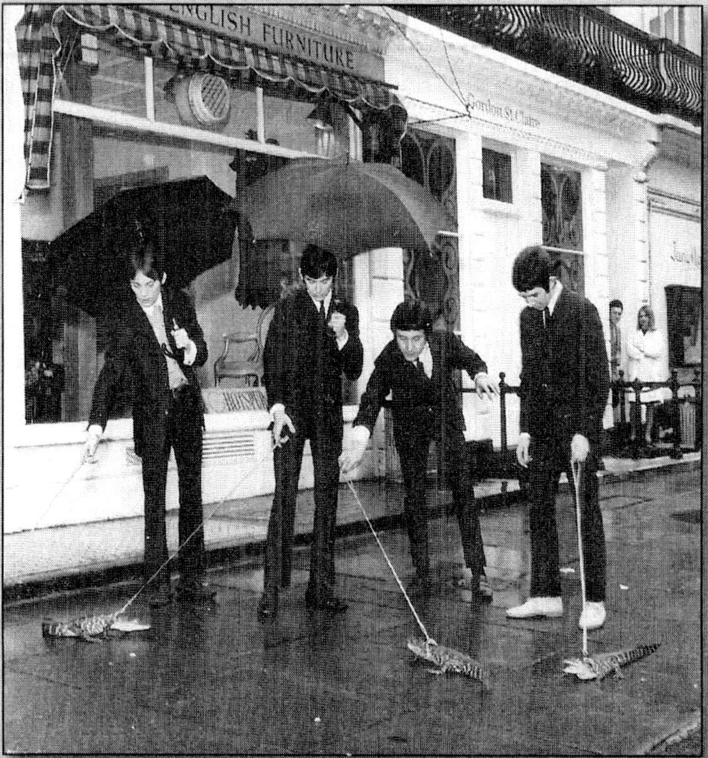

JH: THE BAND WAS FAMOUSLY PHOTOGRAPHED WITH SOME BABY ALLIGATORS, HOW DID THAT COME ABOUT?

PC: Well apparently Ronnie had said in a magazine that he would like an alligator as a pet. Then one day a special delivery guy came into the office with a big box addressed to the fan club. When we first opened the box we thought that they were stuffed alligators or toy ones. I went to pick one up and they all moved. Everybody screamed! We didn't expect them to be real. Kenney run out first and Don came in to see what all the fuss was about. He took one look but he didn't look surprised. He was laughing, next thing I know Don's on the phone to a photographer and he took the boys up the road for some pics. It's funny how all the alligators had leads! Once the photos were taken they were all put back into the box and he got somebody from the RSPCA to come and take them away. It was almost certainly one big publicity stunt although we were never told that. The official story was that they were from a group of fans but what fans would think to do that. It was around this time that the boys were filmed driving around Belgravia in a jeep. I was following behind with the fella that was videoing them. Kenney wasn't there, according to the others he was still in bed. That was fun and after awhile they got out of the jeep and went walk around. They were skylarking and doing Harry Worth impersonations in shop windows. They then looked into one boutique and startled two girls working there who were so obviously in awe of the group. There were little old ladies shopping and thinking...what's going on!

JH: DO YOU RECALL THE TIME THAT STEVE FIRST BECAME A FATHER IN 1966.

PC: Yeah, one day he threw his arms around my neck and was hysterically sobbing. I thought that perhaps one of his parents had died. I asked him what was the matter but he was crying so hard he couldn't talk. "I've made a fan pregnant and she's under age" I took him into Don's office. He was in Don's office for a couple of hours and when they came out Steve was still sobbing. Don had his arm around him and was saying things along the line of "Don't worry, I'll sort everything. You won't have to worry about this anymore, just forget about it". My thoughts were that they were going to arrange an abortion and pay her off. After that Steve never mentioned it again until about six months later. He came in with a bottle of champagne and a load of paper cups and handed them all around and declared "I've just become a Dad, I've got a daughter". I thought Oh God, what a turn around because he was ecstatic, absolutely ecstatic. A couple of weeks afterwards I asked him if he had seen his daughter and he said no. I asked again about a week later and again he said no, so I thought that was the time to shut up as he was quite obviously upset about it. Neither of us ever mentioned it again.

JH: DON ARDEN HAD BEEN NICKNAMED THE AL CAPONE OF POP; DID YOU SEE A DARKER SIDE OF THE MAN?

PC: We were all working one day when Don came storming into the office. "Right listen; I'm gonna say this once and only once. You've all got to get under your desks. I'm gonna lock you in, unplug the phones and turn the lights off and not one of you is to even breathe until I give a sign. He locked us all in and went downstairs and locked the outside doors and then locked himself in his office. One of Dons enemies was on his way, obviously Don had his gun ready, which he normally kept locked away in a drawer in his desk. After about half an hour he unlocked the door and said "Right back to work" it was as if it were just a normal day at work. I remember Stella, our switchboard girl, saying to me while we were under the desk "Are you going to tell your Mum about this?" I said "You must be joking; she wouldn't let me back here again". I said to Stella "Are you going to tell your Mum?" She said "No way, this is fun!"

JH: HOW DID YOU PERCEIVE DON AS YOUR BOSS?

PC: He was great to work for and very kind and generous towards the girls in the office. I remember being off sick for about two weeks, but I wasn't really sick. I'd been filming, as an extra, in Georgie Girl. Quite a few months later Don said to me "That time you were sick a while back, what was the matter?" I said I had flu. He replied "Well I was sitting in a cinema last night watching the worst film I'd ever seen in my life when my wife nudged me and said

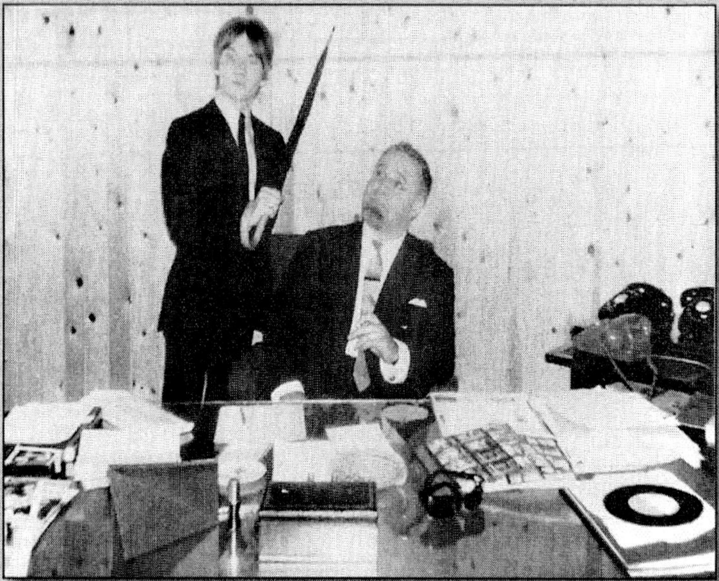

"Look who's up there" and who did I see? I saw Pauline, looking very well in the film". He said explain yourself. I told him my Mum wouldn't let me give up the film work as it paid quite well. "We'll make a pact right now; you'll keep your job but let me know in the future when you get a film job as I obviously won't pay you for that time. Just be honest with me from now on BUT any offers you get have got to come through me first". I used to do modelling as well but was only allowed to do so if I mentioned the Small Faces fan club. He was very good natured about it…yeah, a brilliant boss.

JH: ARE THERE ANY PARTICULAR SMALL FACES STORIES THAT STICK IN YOUR MIND FROM THE DON ARDEN ERA?

PC: I had a really bad road crash on the motorway and was very seriously ill. I'd crushed nearly every bone in my body and the Small Faces came to see me in hospital in Edgware. First time, Steve and my boyfriend Neil come to visit but I was so high on morphine I didn't even know they were there. Apparently they both sat by my bed holding one hand each and trying to talk to me. Both gave me a kiss or so the nurses told me the next day. They said you had the two most gorgeous guys sitting on your bed yesterday and we were taking bets amongst ourselves as to which one was your boyfriend as they both kissed you goodbye. A couple of days later all the boys came in and ended up signing autographs for all the nurses and patients.

JH: WHAT HAPPENED TO MAKE THEM LEAVE DON AND SIGN FOR IMMEDIATE RECORDS?

PC: I don't know I just noticed all of a sudden the Small Faces weren't coming to the office anymore and Don was ignoring their calls. I knew then something was obviously wrong and that went on for quite a few weeks. Don called me into the office one day and told me that they were going to Immediate Records and told me that I had the choice of going with them or staying put. He didn't tell me why, he only ever told me what he wanted to tell me. I was never, ever involved in the business side of things. I went to Immediate with the boys and the fan club continued at the offices in New Oxford Street but it was very much the end of a golden era for me. Life had been fun in Don's Carnaby Street office but life now in New Oxford Street was miserable. Andrew Loog Oldham's right hand man Tony Calder made it quite clear that he didn't want me there. My new office was no bigger than a broom cupboard. I said that I couldn't work in there. Calder just shrugged his shoulders and told me that if I didn't like it I knew what I could do. They made me feel very uncomfortable. I never really got to know Andrew Loog Oldham but when I did meet him occasionally he seemed lovely, much nicer than Tony Calder. Unlike Carnaby Street the boys very rarely came to the office as they were in the studio most of the time. It was the beginning of the end really. Fans still used to turn up and I'd smuggle them in at lunchtime and they'd still ask all sorts of questions about the boys but after an hour I'd be ushering them out before Calder and Co. got back.

JH: DID YOU CONTINUE WITH THE NEWSLETTERS AT IMMEDIATE AND HOW DID IT ALL END FOR YOU?

PC: Tony Calder told me that he didn't want all the crap that I'd been writing previously. It was Don Arden that told me to write all that crap! He always said write as though your writing to your best friend, make it cheerful. The fans used to love it. When I used to give a draft to Tony Calder he'd just say "You can cut this out and cut that out" so I used to alter it around best I could. You can see in the letters that I was depressed about the situation. The readership numbers soon plummeted. At Don's we'd get 4 or 5 sackfuls every day but very soon it was down to half a sack, then down to a couple of carrier bags. The fans were growing up and the band themselves wanted to be taken more seriously as musicians therefore shedding any teeny bop image they may have had. At Carnaby Street the mail was predominantly all female but now it was more of an even mix. Eventually I ended up working from home but I always stayed in touch with the fans by chatting on the telephone but by now the demand for newsletters had dwindled so much that a decision was taken to discontinue it and therefore my job with them ended. Steve was OK about it and said that we must stay in touch and that we did for awhile. I'd visit him and Jenny, his new wife, at his idyllic Essex countryside home, Beehive Cottage. I remember fondly sitting in the garden with the two of them (and all of their dogs) just sipping tea. So very English and so very normal. Don Arden got me a new job running the Amen Corner fan club. They were very big at that time but nowhere near as big as the Small Faces had been during their Don Arden days. Still it was a job and a very enjoyable one at that.

THE ULTIMATE PIECES OF SMALL FACES MEMORABILIA

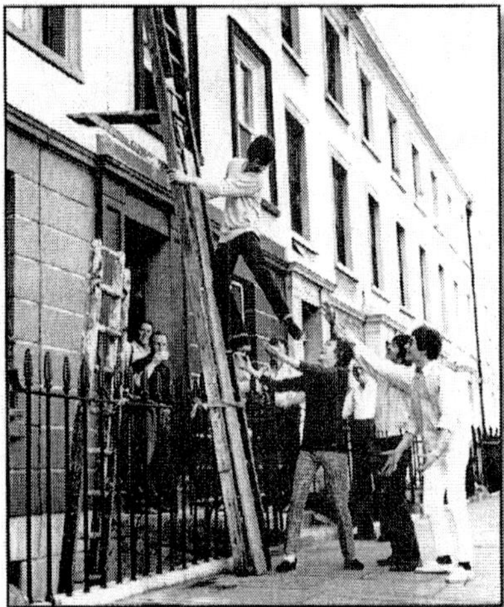

For sale: 22 Westmoreland Terrace, Pimlico, London SW1. The Small Faces lived here from Boxing day 1965 to Boxing day 1966 and it was nicknamed by the music press and fans alike "Party Central". It was here that Brian Epstein famously first introduced the band to LSD and it was here that many of Steve and Ronnies songs were constructed in the midst of the night. It is a 5 bedroom Victorian town house spread over four floors and is probably THE address that every Mod in the whole wide world would love to live. The dream is now possible...one little snag £2,500.000 required. All that's needed (in most cases) is a lottery win! jjhellier@aol.com Genuine enquiries only please.

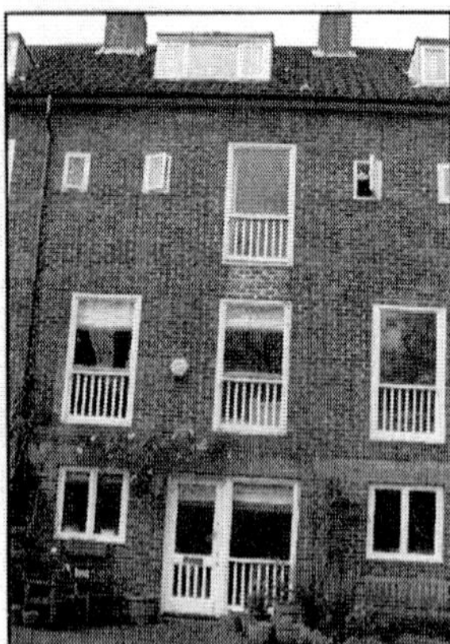

For sale: 10 Eyot Green, Chiswick, London W4. Steve Marriott lived here in 1967 and famously wrote Lazy Sunday in the house after endless arguments with neighbours who didn't appreciate the fact that they had a noisy Pop Idol living next door to them. Steve had a sound system in the small lounge from Olympic studios, he must have been the original neighbour from hell eh? It's a 4 bedroom townhouse that backs on to the River Thames and available at a mere £1.1 million pounds. Compared with Westmoreland Terrace , a snip!
jjhellier@aol.com Genuine enquiries only please.

RONNIE LANE: MOHAIR SUIT TO A GYPSY EAR-RING!

Did you ever hear of The Passing Show winding its way through the English countryside in the Summer of 1974, clowns, jugglers, dancers and Rock musicians, like some ancient caravan winding its way through the Sahara desert bringing amusement and entertainment to wandering nomads that they came across. Well, so it was for Ronnie Lanes travelling revue "The Passing Show".

The notion of a successful Rock musician starting his solo career with a travelling circus is a little strange, what makes it even more bizarre is that Ronnie Lane had just left one of the worlds most successful live bands The Faces. It is a mark of the mans determination and romanticism that such a plan would be conceived and then constructed. Unlike his time in The Small Faces, Ronnie's time in The Faces had been financially lucrative. Together with Kenney Jones, Ronnie Wood, Ian McLagan and superstar vocalist Rod Stewart, Ronnie was part of one of the worlds most sort after Rock bands filling football stadiums all over the world.

As well as being an accomplished musician Ronnie was also a very gifted songwriter, co-writing many of The Small Faces classic 60s songs with Steve Marriott such as Itchycoo Park, Green Circles and Tin Soldier. He was also responsible for most of The Faces introspective outings such as Ooh La La, Debris and Glad And Sorry. It was his desire to record and perform his own songs that led him ultimately to leave The Faces in the spring of 1973. Ronnie was always denied the opportunity to take lead vocals on stage with The Faces (with the exception of one line at the beginning of the McCartney cover Maybe I'm Amazed).

Ronnie was quoted in the book Happy Boys Happy as saying "We've been working together for eight years and the whole thing seemed like a never ending story. then one morning I woke up and asked myself why I went along with all these hectic schedules. Then I thought of singing my own songs in pubs, I did and had a lot of fun with that. Those experiences also made me realise that my songs weren't suitable for The Faces anymore and that was when I split".

Ronnie had his heart set on softer, more thoughtful music which was at odds with The Faces good time Rock n Roll stomps. With earnings from The Faces he set about building the pastoral life of his dreams. He purchased a farm called "Fishpool" on the Welsh border near Shrewsbury and purchased a mobile studio in which most of his solo work would be recorded. The studio was converted from a mobile home with the help of engineer Ron Nevison. Lane formed his band Slim Chance with eight talented musicians, the aim was to play Acoustic and Folk influenced music. They set to work on Ronnie's first studio album Anymore For Anymore, which was released in August 1974.

Anymore For Anymore is a real gem of an album, full of lovely melodic songs that express Lane's quest for a simpler life. Songs such as Roll On Babe and the title track amble along like a summer stroll down a country lane. Then there's the interesting American Folk song Amelia Earhart, music hall inspired songs such as Bird In A Gilded Cage not to mention the sophisticated pop of The Poacher which is still played frequently on radio today. Unfortunately for all its charm the album failed to sell well and wasn't even released in the U.S.

To promote the album Ronnie was set on getting The Passing Show on the road, having parted company with Faces manager Billy Gaff. Management duties now fell to his new brother in law, Paul Lambert. The launch party for the first single How Come took place on Clapham Common in a tent hired from circus owner Gerry Cottle. This was a great success and the carnival atmosphere suited Ronnie's new fans to a tee. Unfortunately, The Passing Show would not live up to this fine start. As anyone who has organised even a touring holiday will know the potential for things to go wrong is high and there's no replacement for experience. Hence the omens weren't good when Paul Lambert was dispatched to London to check out the vans and tent that were being hired from retired Circus owner Wally Luckings. The equipment and vehicles were rather old and poorly maintained, they continually broke down and then before the first show on 27th May 1974 in Marlow the established duo Gallagher and Lyle left, leaving Ronnie and the rest of his band, Slim Chance, in the lurch. Luckily support act Robin Lucas and Drew McCullough stepped in.

Despite some wonderful performances that were well received, the show was not to last long. After only two months on the road Ronnie had to close the show and revert to touring the more conventional college circuit. He said "I couldn't hold it up...because I didn't have any more money. It was as simple as that. We were flogging everything in the end just to buy enough diesel to move the show and I had to worry about the toilets and the firemen coming round and saying "This ain't right......."

Ronnie lived the dream but lost all of his hard earned Faces money. Quote his lyrics from The Poacher "I've no use for riches and I've no use for power"......Even without money Ronnie did become a much richer man!

John Hellier (Oct.2011)

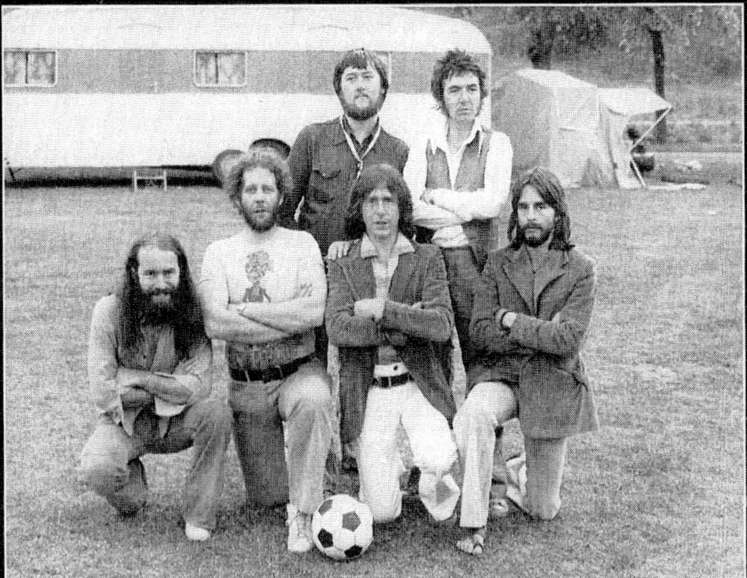

OVERWHELMED BY VOLUME

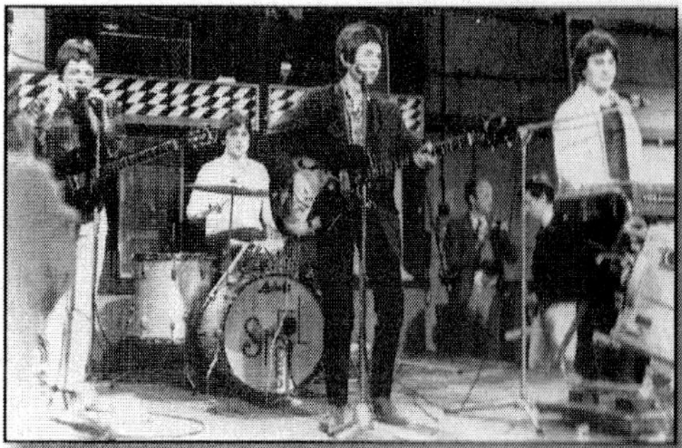

Lou Cleaves reminisces about his Steve Marriott introduction.

Just a small contribution and maybe a flavour of the times, 1964/1965. My brother and I started a group (we were called groups, not bands in those days) in 1964. I was 14 years old and it was very much against the advice of my Father who thought we should stop wasting our time and get a career.

We were booked at the White Swan along the East India Dock Road, later to gain notoriety as the Gay club which Michael Barrymore famously came out. We were to play until 9pm and then dash around the corner to the Dockers Club and play there until 11 o'clock. I took to the stage with my Lucky Seven Egmond guitar, my brother had his Watkins Rapier and we had one Reslo microphone between four of us. In the audience that night was a sharply dressed Mod who was seated to the left of the stage and as the night wore on and drink took its toll, he began to heckle us. Undaunted we continued our show and were later reassured by most people that this guy was pissed and knew absolutely nothing.

We used to rehearse in the basement of a shop in Bow, East London, but we became too loud with our Vox AC 30s and Foundation bass amps so we looked around for alternative rehearsal space. We had been going to a youth club in East Ham called the Kensington Club, just a wooden hut really. We asked if we could rehearse there and were pointed towards a brand new building opposite, which was to be the new premises. It was a purpose built brick building with sound proofed rehearsal rooms. This was ideal for us and the only payment required was for us to play a once monthly gig there for nothing. It's on Wordsworth Avenue in East Ham and it's still there to this day. Rehearsing in the brand new youth club was brilliant, however one night the club started to vibrate in a way we had never experienced. A girl friend of mine came in the room and quite excitedly said "You have just got to see this". We abandoned our rehearsal to see what was happening. The Kensington Club itself was a medium sized room with a very low stage at one end with a gallery at the top which is where the rehearsal rooms were.

I watched the first number by this group and was overwhelmed by the volume and I was totally spellbound by the singer. This was a totally new experience for me. Nothing in my life had ever come close to the excitement (and energy) that they were creating. By the time they launched into a number that they announced as being their forthcoming debut single (Whatcha Gonna Do About It) I realised that this was the way to go and that we needed a radical rethink.

In a word they were awesome and Steve Marriott was a total star and I was his biggest fan since that day in the summer of 1965 in the Kensington Youth Club. I talked to them about amps and guitars after the show and Steve told me that his biggest influence was Steve Cropper, who of course I started listening to after that. Oh, and the drummer that night was Kenny Jones, who had heckled us in the White Swan. My girlfriend knew Jimmy Winston through her sister and told me that he was really an actor. In later years I'd see him in several TV shows including 70s favourite Budgie. She also lived in the turning opposite the J60 guitar shop in Manor Park. I met Steve in there many times (he used to work there) and he was always ready to chat about music and give advice when asked for......Thanks for the memories, mate.

L.C. (LOU AND THE DIAMONDS)

STEVE MARRIOTT INTERVIEW

BY JOE GENUA (1983)

PART ONE

The first of a two part interview with Steve conducted in 1983 in Australia. Here he talks frankly about the many faces of Steve Marriott.... be it Mod, Psychedelia, Hard Rock, Boogie or even Acoustic. The recurring theme being that he was always trying to change and never remain static, that is change to what he wanted; not to whatever was dictated to him and for that he always deserved utmost respect.

JG: *You started performing as an actor in things like "Oliver" and "Peter Pan". Was that your original ambition?*

SM: No, not at all, it was my mother's ambition for me. What happened was that I burnt my school down and the only school that would accept me was drama school. My mother knew Lionel Bart, who wrote "Oliver", and I auditioned for the part and got it. I didn't know what I was getting into really except that I enjoyed performing in front of an audience. At that stage I had no choice in the matter.

JG: *Was your 1963 record "Give Her My Regards" your first?*

SM: No, I was recording before that. I made demos for Andrew Oldham and playing in a band called The Frantiks. In those days they used to introduce you on stage and you had to run from the back of the hall. Now if you happened to knock some bloke's beer you'd get flattened. So sometimes only half the band would arrive in tact or indeed on stage. Hilarious times. The first single I ever did was with The Frantiks and it was a cover of Cliff Richards "Move It". It made number one in Malaysia! (One of Steve's famous fibs, I suspect))

JG: *Was Buddy Holly a big influence?*

SM: Buddy Holly was an influence on just about all of my generation. When I approached Carlin Music Publishers with some songs that I'd written they suggested the Buddy Holly route as they liked my voice better than the songs. That's how I ended up with "Give Her My Regards" hiccups and all.

JG: *Your next single "You Really Got Me" with The Moments was more R&B influenced?*

SM: By then I was very into American R&B.

JG: *Who have been your greatest influences?*

SM: Ray Charles, James Brown, Muddy Waters, BB King, Chuck Berry, Little Richard, Jimmy Reed. In those days I was one of the privileged few to realise what Black music was all about. My favourite white singer was Eddie Cochran. Loved everything he ever done.

JG: *You still continued to act in films like "Be My Guest", "Live It Up" and "Dateline Diamonds". They're not highly regarded are they?*

SM: Sure, they're a load of bloody rubbish. They were David Hemmings showcase pieces and I

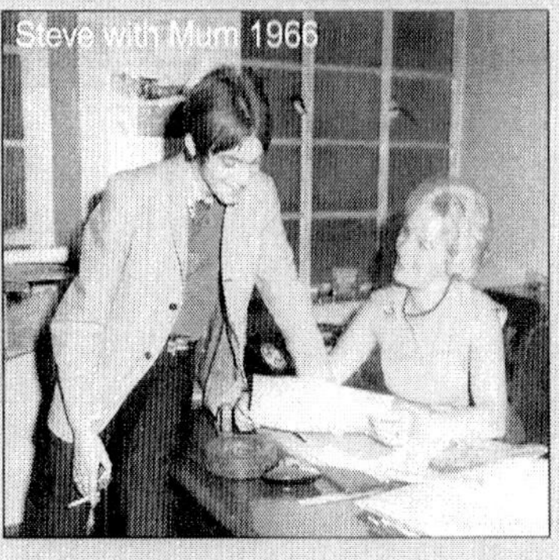
Steve with Mum 1966

played the part of a joker. Me all over!

JG: *Well we come to 1965 and the Small Faces. After formation of only a couple of months you find yourselves in the charts with "Whatcha Gonna Do About It". It was also around this time that Mod took off in London.*

SM: Well we were street kids really as compared to The Who's image which was manufactured. That's not to put them down they've always been a fabulous group but the truth of the matter is that they were made to look like Mods but we were the real deal. At the time Kim Lambert (who went on to become The Who's manager) was interested in us and that gave The Who the horrors as we were playing the same sort of material and attracting the same sort of audience. In the end Kim got The Who and we got Don Arden and an account at a clothes shop. What a deal!

JG: *That's interesting because at the time you were being compared with The Who and were described as a cheap copy?*

SM: They were being taught and shown what to do to create an image. We were straight off the street and broke. We had no money to smash guitars up and stuff like that. All we had was ourselves and I don't think you can compare what was of the streets to what was manufactured.

JG: *How did the group get together?*

SM: I sold Ronnie a bass guitar and I took over the payments of a guitar he had previously bought. I couldn't play for toffee so I used a lot of feedback which again brought comparisons with The Who. That wasn't fair because Pete could play the guitar and I couldn't. Anyway I went to a gig with Ronnie and Kenny when they were in a band called The Outcasts. I smashed the pub piano and they got the sack from their residency. We just sat on the kerb outside and decided to start a new band there and then. We just needed a keyboard player and I roped in Jimmy.

JG: *After your first hit record was there a lot of pressure to come up with another quickly?*

SM: Yeah, it was ridiculous. We were just kids taking Speed and Hash and we didn't know what was going on. We were on £20 a week and even after our third hit we were still on £20 a week.......and an account at a clothes shop.

JG: *Did you think of yourselves as a Mod band in the early days?*

SM: Absolutely. It was my lifestyle. It was what I lived for, dunno why but I did. Mod music though wasn't us it was James Brown, it was Rufus Thomas, it was Otis and all those cats.

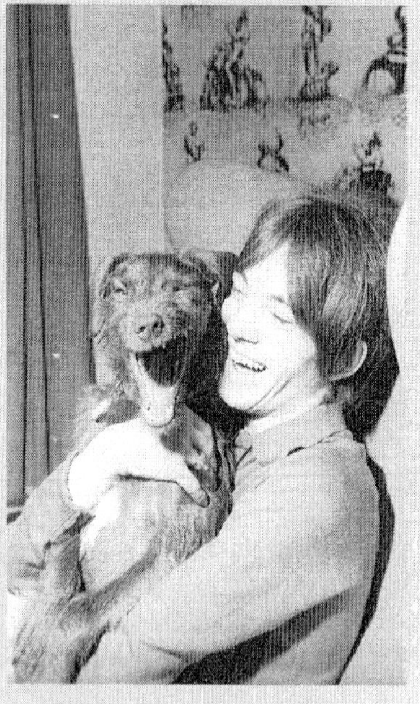

JG: *There were so many good bands and so much good music being made back then what was it like being part of it all?*

SM: It was great, fucking great. Unfortunately I feel the 70's and 80's have missed out. The music was our lifestyle not just background stuff.

JG: *Once Jimmy Winston left and Mac joined the hits began to come but there was no big album success until "Ogden's".*

SM: Jimmy didn't leave he was kicked out. The only reason he was there in the first place was because he had a van and a Vox organ, he had lots more money than the rest of us. Our second single "I've Got Mine", which we produced ourselves, flopped. The record company didn't believe in it and didn't promote it properly which was a shame as it was one of the best things we ever done. The next single "Sha La La La Lee" was a big hit but it was the only one of our records that I really hated and was ashamed of doing.

JG: *How did the song writing team of yourself and Ronnie work and what do you think of your Small Faces songs now?*

SM: Fucking great. Ronnie would be the wall to my music and would sort of add his talent to what I had already done. I would do the denture work and Ronnie would cement it in.

JG: *Diversity seemed to be the catchphrase of the Small Faces with songs like "Hey Girl", "Understanding", "I Can't Dance With You" and "My Minds Eye".*

SM: Well yeah, I've always tried to do different things all the time as I've never wanted to get pigeon-holed. It's always changed and will continue to change for as long as I make music.

JG: *You left Decca and joined Immediate. What was the difference between an established traditional label and a new independent?*

SM: With Immediate we could produce our own stuff. We knew what we wanted and how to get it on the mixing board. Also we owned part of Immediate as we had shares in it. It was great until they got the accountants in then it got too much like a record company. All the artists there got on well and it was a gas working with the likes of Chris Farlowe and PP Arnold.

JG: *Again the diversity of the material continued?*

SM: Yeah, like I said I never want to be pigeon-holed. I suppose I am a bit by now but I don't want it that way and I want to defeat them all and for that I'm my own worst enemy. If I went with the crowd I'd be a fuckin' millionaire by now but there ain't no fun in that. The fun is fucking them up.

JG: *Would you agree that "Ogden's Nut Gone Flake" was the pinnacle of both yours and the Small Faces careers?*

SM: The pinnacle of the Small Faces career yes but not mine. Believe it or not I think I still have to reach it. I probably won't but I feel I still have much to offer. It was because I couldn't top "Ogden's" that I left the band and we've all since talked about it many times and now agree it was the best thing to do at the time.

JG: *With all the success that you had with the Small Faces did you come to expect it with every new release?*

SM: I never ever expected success. I was happy for as long as I could do what I wanted to do.

JG: *Did you ever find the Mod tag limited you or the band and were you confined by it.*

SM: No, because it was a label that we wanted. If it was the record company or the managers idea we would have kicked against it, but no we wanted it. We weren't confined by it because it was our lifestyle; it was us as we really were. It wasn't just an image. How on earth can you be confined by your own lifestyle?

JG: *What was it like to be a Mod in the 60's? What did you do and what were you involved with>*

SM: Basically we were weekend ravers who'd dance, dress, take pills, smoke hash and occasionally get into a fight. We tried to avoid the violence but had to contend with Rockers and Skinheads and they were dangerous boys. We had the scooters, Vespas preferably as Lambrettas were shite, but they had vans which held about six of the bastards. They were older than us as well. Ronnie and me got a right pasting the day before we auditioned for Don Arden. Every time I hit a high note my lip split open, claret everywhere!

TO BE CONTINUED.

STEVE MARRIOTT INTERVIEW

BY JOE GENUA (1983)

PART TWO

The second and final part of an interview with Steve conducted in Australia in 1983. Part one (featured in issue 29) spoke of the early years and the Small Faces, here Steve talks candidly about life after 1968.

JG: Almost immediately after leaving the Small Faces you team up with Peter Frampton, Greg Ridley and Jerry Shirley to form Humble Pie in 1969. It started with a hit single "Natural Born Bugie" and the since regarded "progressive" album "As Safe As Yesterday Is".

SM: Actually I originally formed Humble Pie for Peter Frampton as he always used to come round to me and Ronnie and whine about the fact that he wanted to be in a real group. By the time I got the musicians together for him I thought it was a time for change myself so I joined them as well. As for the first album, well they may say its "progressive" now but at the time everybody said it was a load of old shit! The first couple of Humble Pie albums, the Immediate ones, were like the Small Faces really. Most of the new material on them was written while I was still in the Small Faces.

JG: At this stage did you realise there would be friction between yourself and Peter?

SM: Nah, but I wish he hadn't sung so much. I never liked his voice and he always wrote wimpish songs and I'd say to him "Do you really want to sing this, Pete?" When he left it was a relief.

JG: It was after the second album that Immediate Records folded and the group fell into low spirits.

SM: We broke them with all the publicity, equipment and more. They didn't have the turnover to cope. At least Andrew Oldham had the decency to warn us two months in advance so we had the time to negotiate a contract with A&M. We were at a quandary in which way to go musically though.

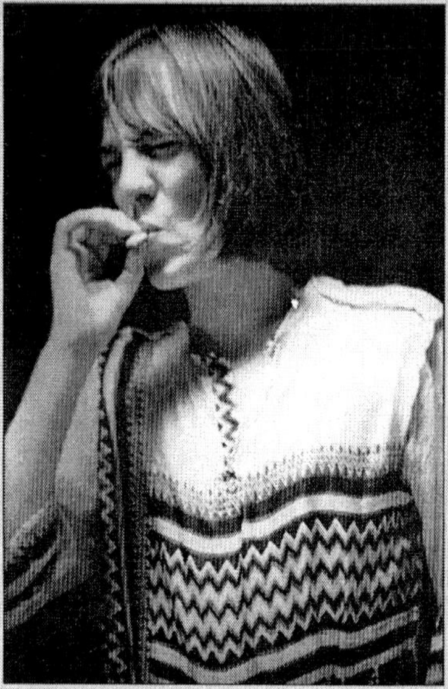

JG: After Frampton left you really broke big in the States with the "Humble Pie", "Rock On" and "Rockin' The Fillmore" albums but the direction was towards harder rock. Why?

SM: Well, because in America you had to do that to get across and you had to record material that you could play on stage as opposed to recording for the sake of it as we did originally. So it was a matter of writing music that we could play live.

JG: But that way aren't you catering to the audience?

SM: No, just catering to ourselves. If they'd buy it that's fine, but we weren't catering to anybody but ourselves. We couldn't play fuckin' great stadiums with acoustic guitars. We tried it with the first few tours but it didn't work.

JG: Why is it that every band has an inbuilt mechanism to make it big in the USA?

SM: To us it was just another country. We didn't think we were going to make it in America. It was just good living at the time but looking back I wish we hadn't have made it.

JG: Was "Rockin' The Fillmore" and "Smokin'" the high point of Humble Pie?

SM: Without a doubt, yes, that is commercially. I thought "Eat It" was a more interesting album although it wasn't as well produced as the others. It was the first stuff that I did myself in my own studio; I did all the technics myself. "Smokin'" was decent but "Eat It" better.

JG: You had album success but not with singles. Why?

SM: America wasn't a singles market for an R&B based band. We'd have singles in the R&B based charts but not the national charts. We always scored with the albums. Radio in the States is shithouse as it's so segregated. FM used to be good but now it's exactly the same as the AM stations.

JG: Around this time critics claimed your voice was in decline and had deteriorated.

SM: Not really, but when you're touring for nine months of the year something's gotta give. They blame everything but the work. If they had wanted my voice not to deteriorate then they should have got me off the road for awhile.

JG: It was claimed that your music was taking a heavier and heavier stance.

SM: Bollocks! "Eat It" was half acoustic and half electric and that was the direction I wanted to go by then. I got panned because they said I didn't give the people what they wanted. "Eat It" was a change of direction but people don't like breaking formulas.

JG: After the hiatus the quality of the recorded work was declining sharply with the release of both "Thunderbox" and "Street Rats" and in 1975 the band broke up.

SM: I absolutely hated "Street Rats" and I didn't even want to go to the sessions. I'd already left the band in spirit. A&M wanted harder Rock albums but I was recording much more interesting stuff at home so I just said "Fuck it, I'm out". By then I didn't have any artistic control. "Street Rats" was by far and away our worst ever record and I just thought what was I bothering for.

JG: Does the Rock business become a tiring game? A sort of circus after all the time that you've been in the business.

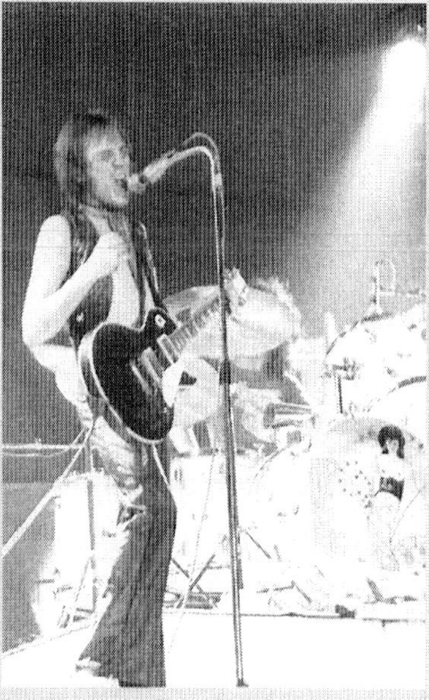

SM: If it gets like that then you should quit. I still enjoy myself. The problem is the older you get the harder it gets as the mind is forever 18 but the body is 36.

JG: In 1976 you released your first solo album "Marriott" but as one critic put it, it nearly severed Anglo-American music relations as the album had an American side and an English side.

SM: Yeah, it was an awful album. The concept was the producers, not mine. I had already recorded and produced those songs myself but A&M said it was just like a demo so they spent 300,000 dollars to re-record it and it came out like a pile of shit!

JG: In 1977 you re-formed the Small Faces without Ronnie Lane. What's the story there?

SM: Ronnie wouldn't do it. What happened was we done a video for "Itchycoo Park" as it had been re-released and we sort of fell in love with each other again and said lets do a record. So we made "Playmates" and it was a totally new sound for us. It was slagged off because it was released during the height of Punk and I suppose it sounded like fish out of water at that particular time. We followed it with "78 In The Shade" but that wasn't as good. We had a complete lack of promotion and broke up again.

JG: By 1978 there was a Mod resurgence with bands such as the Jam and the Chords claiming the Small Faces as a major influence. Did it make you proud that you were not forgotten and that your work was an inspiration to younger bands?

SM: That's all you want and yeah, it made me feel great. It's what makes this crazy business worthwhile.

JG: Did you think the Mod resurgence was healthy?

SM: Yeah, I think anything that shakes up the system for a while is good. That's why I liked Punk. Mind you I hated the music but the ideas were great.

JG: But Punk formed to rebel against what your generation of musicians stood for and the impersonality and lack of values it had.

SM: Yes but it's the circuit that exists and you found that the Pistols played the same circuit so it was really so contradictory. It is the American circuit; I used to feel fuckin' sick when we played stadiums. I used to come on stage and literally be in tears and I couldn't work out why. Then I realised it was unfulfilling, like singing to a void.

JG: The Jam and specifically Paul Weller mould themselves to you visually as you were in the Small Faces. What do you think of them and have they progressed the Mod idea at all?

SM: I think they've contributed to a whole heap of younger kids who weren't old enough to be in it originally. They've taken large chunks of the Who and ourselves but have managed to form their own identity. Paul Weller's lyrics are very good, you've got to have guts to say the things the way he does and I admire that.

JG: Well what about the new line up of Humble Pie?

SM: It's NOT Humble Pie. Promoters have taken it upon themselves to call us that. It's got nothing to do with Humble Pie.

JG: What are the musicians like in the new band?

SM: I've known them for years and they're friends of mine. They're excellent musicians to play with.

JG: Just to sidetrack I've heard that Ronnie has MS.

SM: Yes he has but it's only his body that is sick and not his mind and I'll carry him anywhere he wants to go. He's determined to beat it and he always thinks positively. He's very determined and his spirit has sharpened.

JG: You recently did an album with him (Majik Mijits). What's it like?

SM: It's very Small Faces like, which is exactly what I tried to avoid when I reformed the group but writing with Ronnie you get the sort of material that is bound to sound like the Small Faces. Ronnie and I are of the same mind and it was easy to record with him after so much time.

JG: Rock'n'Roll has always been projected as a young mans sport. How does Steve Marriott fit in today?

SM: I don't. I'm a type of flag bearer, I think if you can live it out as long as I have or as long as other people have then you just become a standard bearer. You become unique, I guess, and the ultimate thing is to try to be unique or to last long enough to make people realise that maybe you are a little unique.

ANYBODY THAT HAS FOLLOWED STEVE MARRIOTT'S CAREER COULD ONLY AGREE THAT STEVE MARRIOTT IS INDEED UNIQUE AND THAT'S SOMETHING WE SHOULD ALL BE BLOODY THANKFUL FOR.

IAN McLAGAN TRIBUTE..........by Jeff Slate

(December 2014)

I first saw Ian McLagan, fittingly seated behind a keyboard, with the Rolling Stones in 1981. There was obviously a lot going on around him, Mick preening, Keith chopping at his guitar and Ronnie Wood playing to the crowd, but I couldn't take my eyes off of him. I'd discovered the Small Faces about a year before after being given the U.S. compilation "There Are But Four Small Faces" by the guitarist in my first band. It had changed my life, now; here was the bands inimitable keyboardist in the flesh.

I don't remember much more than flashes of that first sighting but I have a clear recollection of seeing Mac again in the nineties, when he joined Billy Bragg on tour to promote an album of Woody Guthrie lyrics that Bragg and Wilco had set to music as Mermaid Avenue. It was a great show and Mac's organ was the glue that held it all together while seemingly floating above it at the same time.

But when I got word that Mac had died in a hospital in his adopted hometown of Austin, Texas, after suffering a stroke the day before, neither of those memories leapt to mind. Instead, heartbroken, I thought back to a few more personal encounters. I first met Mac about 15 years ago on one of his frequent trips to New York City in support of his solo career. My band at the time had built up a bit of a name for itself, mining the same vein as the Small Faces and Faces, and I thought I was kind of a big deal. I wasn't, of course, and besides Mac had seen it all before but when one of his minders

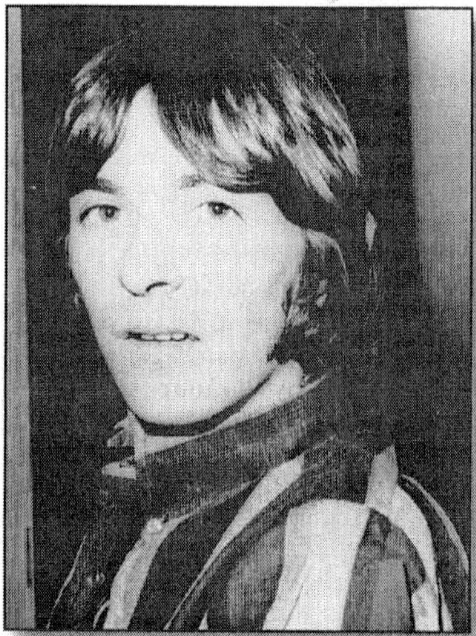

introduced us, he was kind and supportive and, much to my enjoyment, he put me in my place with wit and charm and (literally) a wink.

Not long after that Mac sent me a copy of the Faces Box Set, signed to me and the band. Later he sent his book and a copy of a Small Faces compilation, also both signed. Each time I thanked him sincerely and we kept up a correspondence by email.

Over the years I interviewed Mac about one project or another and I came to believe that he knew my love for his work and playing was sincere. I'm sure I made it clear that I wanted to work with him but what I remember most vividly is that he always made me laugh, and laugh, and laugh. Even when he would go on about one of the many times in the music business in which he'd been screwed, we still ended up laughing together in the end.

Then, not long ago, I reconnected with Mac's former band mate in the Small Faces and Faces, Kenney Jones. I'd met Kenney in 1993 through Pete Townshend but hadn't seen him since. We spotted each other across a crowded party and picked up right where we'd left off. There were a few special Small Faces projects in the works, Kenney told me, and asked if I'd lend a hand. I said yes before he'd finished the question. Over the next year or so I got to talk to both Kenney and Mac quite a bit and it was my honour to collect recollections of the Small Faces from Paul Weller amongst others for the Here Come The Nice Immediate Years Box Set as well as a fabulous introduction to the liner notes from Pete. I remember when I circulated Pete's email address to everybody, it was wonderful and we were all elated. Of course, Mac also didn't miss the chance to point out that Pete had spelled his name wrong. We had another good laugh.

Along the way I mentioned to both Kenney and Mac that I was recording new material and that I really wanted both of them to play on it. They were very supportive and almost matter of fact about it "Of course, I'll play on your record" Mac said to me when I sheepishly pressed him on the phone one day. "It's what I do".

Both Kenney and Mac were set to record their parts last Spring (2014) but I had so many things on my plate and I, of course, didn't want to seem in any way entitled to having them help me out and things just dragged on. June passed and Mac promised he'd record his parts in August when he came back from a UK tour.

He called me from the car one night after his return on the way to a barbeque in Austin with a friend. We talked about everything but the recordings and laughed, and laughed. In fact I remember laughing so hard that I had tears in the corners of my eyes.

We put of those sessions yet again and now there are tears of a different sort. I wouldn't be as bold as to say Mac was my friend, because he had so many and because it always thrilled me when we talked that he knew who I was and what I was up to and cared that things were going well.

I put the Small Faces on my turntable last night after I got the news of Mac's sudden untimely death. He touched my life in a meaningful way with his music and I'll always have that and cherish it and those songs we were going to work on together will always feel a little empty to me without his special touch on them, but right now all I can remember is how he made me laugh. I'm sure that's how he'd want it to be.

RIP Mac

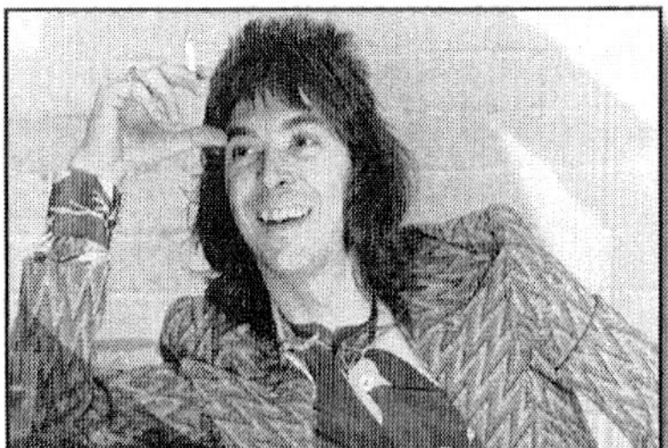

ROCK 'N' ROYAL

BY REBECCA HARDY

Kenney Jones played in three of the biggest bands of the 1960s and 1970s and trashed hotels with Keith Moon but while others fell by the wayside, he now lives the good life on a 250 acre Polo club.

Kenney Jones is sitting on the terrace at Hurtwood Park, the Polo club he owns in Ewhurst, Surrey, sipping a Coke. A few months ago Prince Charles was here. The two men, it seems, are unlikely friends. Kenney, drummer and original member of the Small Faces, the Faces and later on the Who, is the son of a lorry driver from the East End of London. "I have a good chuckle about it sometimes" says Kenney "it's like the Prince and the pauper. Although I'm not a pauper, I am from Stepney and he's the next King of England and here we are playing Polo together. Prince Charles is a really great guy, a really nice man. His sense of humour is fantastic. We're both Goons fans and we're also the same age, which we do have a chuckle about sometimes. About three years ago, we were playing Polo and he said "I don't know how long I can keep doing this, I'm 56 this year" I said yeah, I know what you mean I am too. He scratched his head a bit there because I suppose I do look a bit younger than him". Kenney, now 59, appears remarkably unravaged by show-biz excess. In jeans and t-shirt, he is still instantly recognisable from pictures taken decades ago. His hair is still cut in a hedgehoggy mullet, but shorter.

Kenney used to trash hotel rooms with the Who's drummer Keith Moon, who died in 1978, and drank himself senseless with the Rolling Stones Ronnie Wood. Today, Ronnie remains a friend and they are both part of Rock aristocracy. Princes William and Harry are regular players at Kenney's 250 acre Polo club. Jodie Kidd is a friend as are Mike Rutherford and David Essex. Eric Clapton and Ringo Starr are neighbours. Eric, he says, invested well in property. "He's been living here since the day dot. He lives up on the hill and bought his place for £12,000, now it's worth billions. Ringo is a good friend. He doesn't drink so isn't one to go out socialising but he comes over at Christmas".

Kenney lives in a 14th century farmhouse, a mass of polished floors, beams, huge sofas and family photographs. He is married for a second time and says he is monogamous. He votes Tory and complains about stealth taxes. "If everyone paid a lower level across the

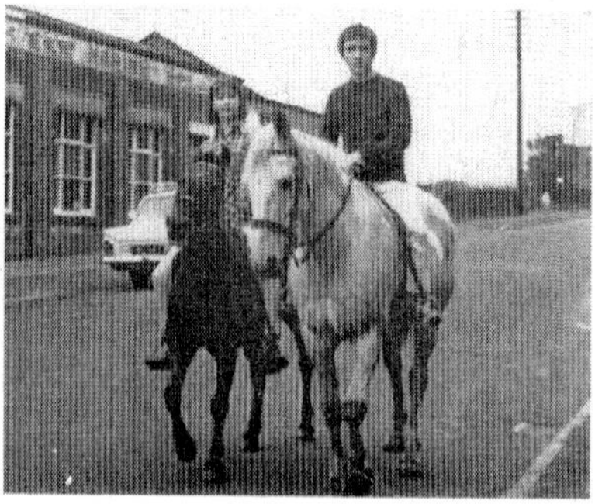

board it would be fine" he says "to penalise someone for making a success of their life is not right". He has six children: Dylan, 35 and Jesse, 30 from his first marriage and Casey 19, Jay 18, Cody 12 and Erin 9 from his second marriage to former model Jayne.

"When I was with the Small Faces, you couldn't not be into girls" he says "we had our first hit when I was only 17 and they were throwing themselves at us. On the road there would be flings. It would be "she looks nice, why not?" I didn't do any more than anyone else was doing, or any less. With my own kids I watch their every move. I want to know where they're going and what they're up to. I know what goes on at parties, so I worry. They want to do no more than we did. It's part of growing up. They will discover sex and discover different things".

Kenney's second child, Jesse, was expelled from Hurtwood House School at 15 for smoking marijuana. "The whole bloody school was doing it. He was at a party and they did random blood testing. Basically, because he was my son, that's the way it went. Of course, I was furious. He got over it and went on to college. I don't like drugs; I've always been a drinking man. Every band I've ever been in did all kinds of stuff including Acid. I had my drink spiked once with LSD and that wasn't a very nice experience. The only thing I took was the odd "blues"; it's Mod stuff to keep you awake. Everyone was doing that in the sixties".

Kenney, of course, was not just a child of the sixties. He and his Rock'n'Roll friends WERE the sixties. Kenney was 17 when he had his first major hit with the Small Faces. He taught himself to play the drums with a kit bought on HP that stood in the front room of his parent's simple terraced house. He says playing the drums made him feel ecstatic. It was pretty much the first thing he'd been good at. He is dyslexic and suffered terribly at school where the condition was not recognised. "My parents were called into the school and told that I had a lazy brain. When I was about ten, we all had to write an essay. The teacher came in and said to the class "I must read you this from Kenney Jones", I thought "Oh God, she's chosen me" I was beaming. She read it like I'd written it, which was terrible because I couldn't spell properly. She demoralised me in front of the whole class. I felt so bad. I didn't know what I had until someone gave it a name. Even in the Small Faces I didn't know. When we used to go on tour in Europe we had to fill in all these forms. I began to find my way around dyslexia. I'd say to the guys in the band "that's a stupid question isn't it? what would you put?" and they'd say yes or no, so I'd write yes or no. They'd finish their forms ages before me and I'd be embarrassed by that. It went on for years and years. Slowly I learned to deal with the problem. You start to think laterally. It's why I call dyslexia a gift. You have to think in another way and what you find along the way can be more interesting.

Kenney was driving to the stables in Epping Forest, where he used to ride (a passion since the age of 14) when he heard his first record on the radio, Whatcha Gonna Do About It. Within months the band were household names. "When I first heard it on the radio I felt like a million dollars, absolutely amazing" he says "soon we were on television and word started spreading. It was mad, like the Beatles. We couldn't walk down the street without being mobbed. I was still hanging out with my mates in the East End and after about six months I felt a bit of hostility from them. They said it had gone to my head. I suppose it did. I'd be a bit "look at me, I've done it". From that moment on I decided I wasn't going to be like that. For years and years I've got back to the East End every Sunday to have a lunchtime drink because that's sacred in the East End, especially with my dad liking his drink. There came a time when I couldn't do that because we were off touring so I drifted away, but the thought has stayed with me. I've never been one to brag about anything.

Indeed, Kenney's mother still lives in the house in Stepney that was his childhood home. Kenney adores his parents, who were quiet, no frills, people, but hugely proud of their son. His father, Sam, died of leukaemia ten years ago. "It was the worst kind and he was dead within ten days of being diagnosed. In hospital they did some tests. I'd taken mum home to get some stuff and when we got back the look on his face was horrific. They'd actually told him he had leukaemia without us being there. He couldn't deal with it. I stayed with him one night. I sat in the chair and let him sleep. He was moaning and groaning as if he was talking to someone. Then he called me and said" Ken, I need to go to loo" I lifted him up, he put his arms around me and went. He was so heavy I landed on the floor. I was calling him not to go, to stay with us, but he wanted to go. He was a typical East End drinking man and loved by everybody. My mum's still waiting for him to walk through the door. She's coping because she has too, but every time I go there it's "I miss Daddy, he did so much for me" It's a really sad affair. When I open the door I know he's there somewhere. Sometimes I forget he's dead.

"There have been so many deaths. Life becomes more precious. You think "this is no time for people to go" Steve Marriott and Ronnie Lane both went before their time and Keith Moon. I was with him the night before he died. We were at the premiere of the film The Buddy Holly Story. That evening I was at a table with David Frost, Paul and Linda McCartney, Paul's brother and Moonie. Moonie and I were talking drums. He also told me that he hadn't had a drink, or anything else, for two months. He said he was on special drugs to stop him drinking. For once, he wasn't loony. I went home and the next day, when I turned on the TV, the first thing on the news was that Keith had died of a drug overdose. He'd gone home from the premiere, taken his nightly dose of medicine, woken up and thinking it was morning taken another. The drugs slowed his heart down".

During those hell raising Rock'n'Roll years, Kenney was always known as the quiet one and shy. Perhaps that's why he has survived. "On tour I'd get homesick" he says " sometimes I wanted to phone home because all I wanted was a friendly voice and sometimes I couldn't get through, so I'd get angry and take it out on things around me. Once in Melbourne, when the Small Faces were touring with the Who we all went to Keith Moons room. He had all these snare drums. I said "What do you need all those for?"

He said "I'll show you". He picked one up and threw it through the window. It crashed into the centre of the High Street and rolled down the road. We legged it to the bar!

Kenney stopped touring in the late 1980s. He had fallen in love with his second wife, Jayne. He says of his volatile first marriage to Jan, "Nobody wants a divorce, but we just couldn't get along. We argued too much and drifted apart. I'm very old fashioned and believed that you only get married once. I never in a million years dreamed of splitting up a family, but it was unbearable. When you've got kids any divorce is painful and does leave scars". The marriage ended in 1982. The kids had some emotional problems after the divorce. Dylan and Jesse came to live with me when they were about nine or ten. With my first marriage, my mind was focused on being a musician and I was always away. I like to think that I'm more understanding now and have more time for my family. In fact, I'm with them as much as I can be. Jayne makes me feel wanted. I feel I can trust her and she can trust me. I've been as honest as the day is long. I've not had affairs because I don't need to. Between us we've created something nice, another family. We rely on each other and it works. "She's had plenty of times when she could have got up and walked out, but she hasn't. I'm not the easiest person to live with. I can get moody. I worry about silly little things like if the field is going to cut in time for a Polo match".

"I don't think of myself as a Rock star. I'm just someone who learnt to play the drums and learnt to ride a horse at 14. They are just two hobbies that have gone side by side. I never dreamed I'd end up with all of this" he says, sweeping his eyes across the Polo fields and club house. "or that I'd end up knowing the likes of the future King. He's a music lover too. At the end of the day we're all human. That's one of the nice things about Polo. You can be out there with a King or Queen or anybody famous, but you're all equal when you play the game".

A NICE INSIGHT INTO THE PRIVATE LIFE OF KENNEY JONES. CAN'T HELP WONDERING WHAT STEVIE MARRIOTT WOULD HAVE MADE OF IT THOUGH.

CHALK AND CHEESE EH!

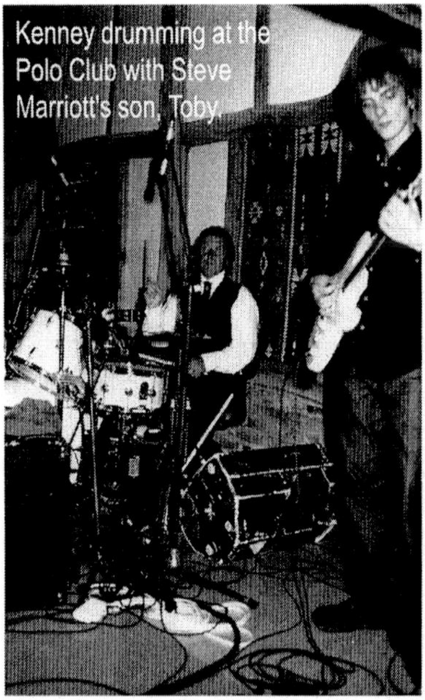
Kenney drumming at the Polo Club with Steve Marriott's son, Toby.

SMALL FACES AT THE BEEB

The Small Faces guested on 41 television and 21 radio programmes for the BBC between August 23rd 1965 and August 22nd 1968. Here is the complete check list of their appearances.

TV

Date	Studio	Programme	Transmitted
6th Sept.1965	TV theatre	Gadzooks	Live
16th Sept.1965	Studio 2	Top Of The Pops	Live
30th Sept.1965	Studio 2	Top Of The Pops	Live
7th Oct.1965	Studio 2	Top Of The Pops	Live
10th Nov.1965	Studio 2	Crackerjack	Nov.12th
17th Feb.1966	Studio 2	Top Of The Pops	Live
24th Feb.1966	Studio 2	Top Of The Pops	Live
10th Mar.1966	Studio 2	Top Of The Pops	Live
6th Apr.1966	Studio 2	A Whole Scene Going	Live
26th May 1966	Studio 2	Top Of The Pops	Live
11th Aug.1966	Lime Grove	Top Of The Pops	Live
18th Aug.1966	Lime Grove	Top Of The Pops	Later same night on V.T.
1st Sept.1966	Lime Grove	Top Of The Pops	Live
8th Sept.1966	Lime Grove	Top Of The Pops	Live
10th Oct.1966	IBC	The Managers	Oct.23rd
10th Nov.1966	Lime Grove	Top Of The Pops	Live
16th Nov.1966	Lime Grove	Top Of The Pops (2 performances)	Nov.17th and Nov.24th
1st Dec.1966	Lime Grove	Top Of The Pops	Live
13th Dec.1966	Lime Grove	Top Of The Pops	Dec.26th
15th Feb.1967	Lime Grove	Top Of The Pops	Never screened
31st May 1967	Lime Grove	Top Of The Pops	June 1st
13th June 1967	Dickenson Road	Dee Time	Live
22nd June 1967	Lime Grove	Top Of The Pops	Live
23rd Aug.1967	Lime Grove	Top Of The Pops	Aug.24th
5th Sept.1967	Dickenson Road	Dee Time	Live
7th Sept.1967	Lime Grove	Top Of The Pops	Sept.24th
10th Dec.1967	Studio G	Twice A Fortnight	Dec.16th
3rd Jan.1968	Studio A	All Systems Freeman	Never screened
4th Jan.1968	TV Centre	Crackerjack	Jan.5th
4th Jan.1968	Lime Grove	Top Of The Pops	Live
11th Jan.1968	Lime Grove	Top Of The Pops	Live
6th Apr.1968	Studio G	Dee Time	Live
11th Apr.1968	Studio G	Top Of The Pops	Later same night on V.T.
11th Apr.1968	Studio 4	My Generation	Never screened
18th Apr.1968	Studio G	Top Of The Pops	Live

25th Apr.1968	Studio G	Top Of The Pops	Live
21st June 1968	Studio B	Colour Me Pop	Later same night on V.T.
26th June 1968	Studio G	Top Of The Pops	June 27th
11th July 1968	Studio G	Top Of The Pops	Live
22nd Aug. 1968	Studio G	Top Of The Pops	Live

This listing refers to the original transmissions and not any subsequent repeats.
Note: Studios 2, 4 and B are at Television centre, Wood Lane, London.
Studio G is at Lime Grove, Shepherds Bush, London.
Dickenson Road is in Manchester.
Studio A was at the re-furbished Dickenson studio, Manchester.
IBC Studio at Portland Place, London W1

RADIO

Date	Studio	Programme	Transmitted
23rd Aug.1965	Aeolian Hall	Saturday Club	Sept.4th
11th Sep.1965	Studio 1	Top Of The Pops	Later same day(Marriott only)
22nd Oct.1965	Camden	Joe Loss Show	Live
14th Jan.1966	Playhouse	Joe Loss Show	Live
1st Mar.1966	Paris	Pop In	Live
11th Mar.1966	Playhouse	Joe Loss Show	Live
14th Mar.1966	Aeolian Hall	Saturday Club	March 19th
28th Mar.1966	Bush House	Hit 66	Live
28th Mar.1966	Bush House	Good Morning	April 7th
3rd May 1966	Playhouse	Saturday Club	May 7th
10th June 1966	Playhouse	Joe Loss Show	Live
22nd June 1966	Playhouse	Parade Of The Pops	Live
11th July 1966	Bush House	Pop Profile	Later same day
30th Aug.1966	Paris	Saturday Club	Sept 3rd
18th Nov.1966	Playhouse	Joe Loss Show	Live
19th Apr.1967	BBC Reception	Pop Interview	July 25th
4th Aug.1967	Broadcasting House	Where It's At	Aug.5th (Marriott/Lane only)
12th Jan.1968	Broadcasting House	Scene And Heard	Jan.13th (Marriott/Lane only)
4th Apr.1968	Broadcasting House	Scene And Heard	Live (Marriott only)
9th Apr.1968	Piccadilly 1	Top Gear	Apr.14th
26th Apr.1968	Studio 2	Top Of The Pops	Live (Jones only)

Note: Aeolian Hall was at New Bond Street, London.
Studio 1 and 2 were at Kensington House, Shepherds Bush, London.
Playhouse Theatre was at Northumberland Avenue, London.
Paris Studios were at Lower Regent Street, London.
Bush House was at Aldwych, London.
Piccadilly 1 was at 201 Piccadilly, London.

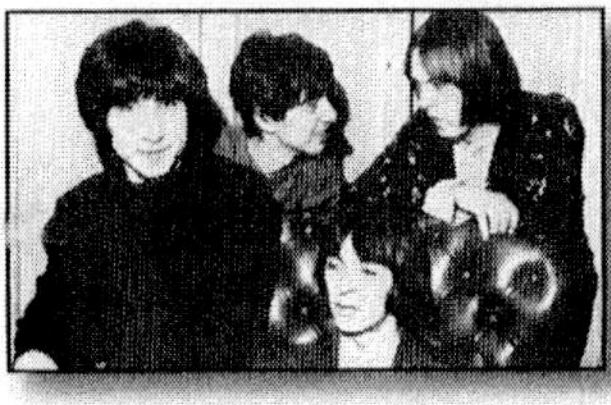

IAN MCLAGAN

Ronnie Lane just pulled up
In an old circus wagon
Loaded up the Hammond
And his friend Ian McLagan
'Where we goin' Ron?
And why's this wagon flying?'
'Just trust me you should leave
You were never one for crying.'
Through the veil and past the stars
Where giant gardens grow
Everything made clear at last
And nothing left to know
Above the ancient pyramids
And just past Tower Bridge
Everywhere and somewhere else
The circus wagon skids
To a halt to a halt
Get out good sir and walk
Your flag is flown
Our love is shown
All hearts your way do shine
Rise all rise all
This ain't no curtain call
Rise and greet your brother
Who in this house resides
As spirits gather round
Filling up with love and sound
The river brings the spirits
Of those who dared to live and drown
To the place of all creation
Inside the heart of time
Ancient jubilation
Common spirits intertwine
Far above the clouds
And far above the rain
Eternity does beckon
To a loud and brash refrain
The circus wagon swaggers
Taking friends down to the lane

Bucks Burnett
December 3, 2014

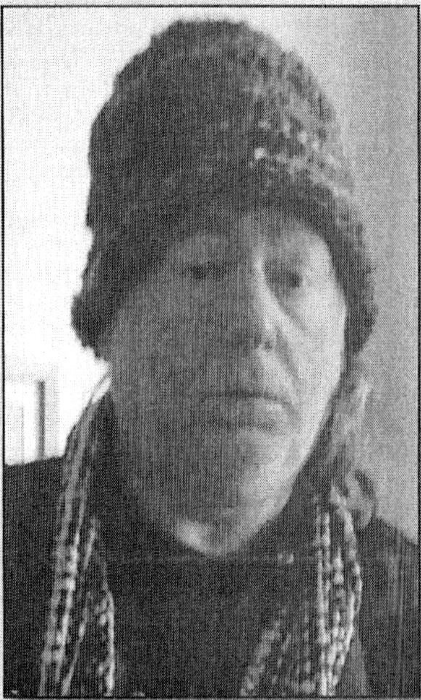

Ronnie Lanes butler, chauffeur and very best friend during his Texas days, Bucks Burnett.

I'D NEVER HAVE BOUGHT OUR RECORDS!

STEVE MARRIOTT reminisces with Dave Thompson (1982)

"I dunno, I'd never have bought our records" Steve Marriott laughed. "The Small Faces were a great band and they were exactly the sort of group I'd have gone to see if I'd not been with them. But those records, the early ones especially, they weren't exactly great, were they?

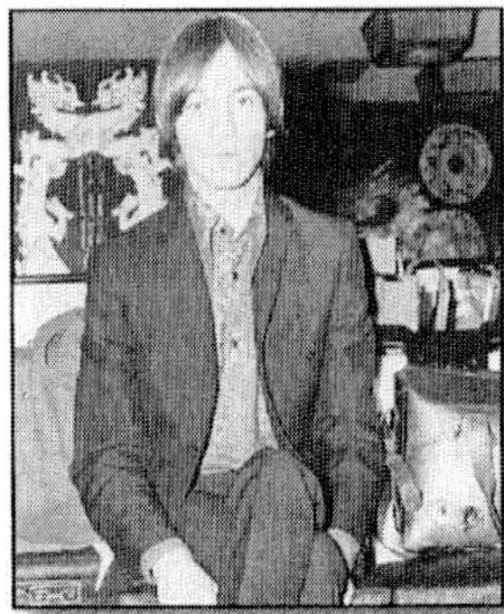

In 1982 Steve Marriott was just on the verge of re-launching his career. Of course, he was always just on the brink of launching his career, but this time there was something really believable about his plans, the sense that this time things might start going right for him. It was about time, an attempt to re-form Humble Pie had collapsed a year earlier, the victim of both record company inactivity and the bands inability to tour while Marriott underwent hospital treatment first for the fingers he crushed in a Chicago doorway and then for the ulcer he discovered in Dallas. Before that, it was a Small Faces revival which collapsed in disarray. But a raunchy guest appearance on Johnny Thunders So Alone album had won him over with the Punk crowd and Paul Weller's regards from the confines of the Jam hadn't hurt him either. Marriott appreciated their support.

"I've got to stop going backwards all the time" he laughed "or it'll be the fucking Artful Dodger next and I won't I look a sight?"

As a child actor, Marriott had appeared in the London production of Lionel Bart's Oliver, but to see him 20 years on it was difficult to believe so much time had passed. Wreathed in cigarette smoke, a scruffy hat balanced jauntily on a scruffy head over a scruffy jacket and cackling loudly at the slightest provocation, he remained the consummate Victorian waif, a gypsy, a joker and one of the greatest performers Britain has ever produced. What more could an Artful Dodger be?

Peter Frampton once told me "The first time I met Steve, I just recognized pure Soul, the natural stuff that he had" That natural stuff literally bleeds from Marriott's greatest records; even today, after all the bards and bleeding hearts that have been thrown up by Rock's self-conscious embracing of its own place in legend, nobody has ever successfully eclipsed Marriott's passion. He always had time to talk to the fans, even ones that broached him unexpectedly in any one of London's watering holes he favoured, asked for a few words for a book they were writing and then spent 20 minutes wrestling with a plainly broken cassette tape recorder. Who said the art of note taking was dead?

His speech shot out at tangents. In conventional interview situations he always sounded considered and sharp. Off duty though, he let his thoughts go where they would and if you couldn't keep up it was just bad luck on you. He moved so fast and jumped so far, that a speed typist could not get a word in edgeways. But the gist of it was simple.

"The problem was we signed for Don Arden. Fuck the money and everything else. The problem was Arden knew what he wanted from us before he'd ever heard of us, which is why he gave us Ian Samwell (ex Cliff Richard songwriter who wrote Move It amongst others). He was a great bloke and did his best, but he just didn't get the black thing. Arden wanted a Pop band which played Mod and he didn't understand that we were the opposite of that and he didn't get it when we started fighting back and doing stuff like the Booker T things we did on stage. If he'd had it all his way we'd have been doing Sha La La La Lee forever.

It is, of course, no secret that the Small Faces loathed their third single and second hit record. Steve and Ronnie, the bands principle songwriters, had been kicked out of singles market after their second single and first self composed 45 flopped. Sha La La La Lee, a Kenny Lynch/Mort Shuman composed nonsense turned their fortunes around completely but it also lacked the bands spirit. Little of what they played on record had anything to do with what they played on stage. And as the bands hit making stock rose, little of what they played on stage had anything to do with what they'd started out dreaming of.

"We couldn't hear a fucking thing because of all the screaming" Marriott recalled. "We'd go out and it was a shambles every night. I'd be playing one key, or one song, Mac would be playing another, Ronnie would be playing another and every night it was like that. Every hit record we had just made it worse, because we'd have to drop something else we liked to fit it in. We were miserable and Don Arden knew it."

It would take £12,000 to extract the Small Faces from Don Arden's management, which is what promoter Harold Davison paid for them in late '66. A matter of months later, they were on the move again to Andrew Loog Oldham and his thriving Immediate record label. Steve and Ronnie had first approached Chris Blackwell's Island records but he passed on them. "There were two ways of looking at Immediate" Marriott reflected "One was that they ripped us off, just as Arden did, to the point where I've not seen one penny from the Faces, while there are record companies all over the globe who are probably making a fortune from our old records. But the other is that Andrew gave us everything we wanted; unlimited studio time, unlimited creative powers, he let us write whatever we wanted, he let us produce and he let us make two albums without even questioning what we were doing once we got in there. Yeah, the money we should have earned would have set us up for life but that's what the musical freedom did, it set us up for life."....and with remarkable serendipity, a punter in the bar, where we're seated, plays Itchycoo Park on the jukebox. Marriott responds with a loud "Awright mate!" "....otherwise we wouldn't be sitting here listening to this, would we?".

For the Small Faces, their Immediate years were a period of unrivalled creativity, not only within their own frame of reference, but many other bands as well. Packed off to a cottage in the country to work on what Andrew Oldham, at least, was already convinced would be their masterpiece. A well as writing and producing for a string of other Immediate talents, the Small Faces defined the summer of Psychedelic bloom like no other band in the country.

The Beatles, Stones and Kinks were all, more or less, at the peak of their powers, but across the string of singles which began with Here Come The Nice, an 18 month blink of the historical eye, the Small Faces not only zapped the spirit of the time, they spiked it's morning tea as well.

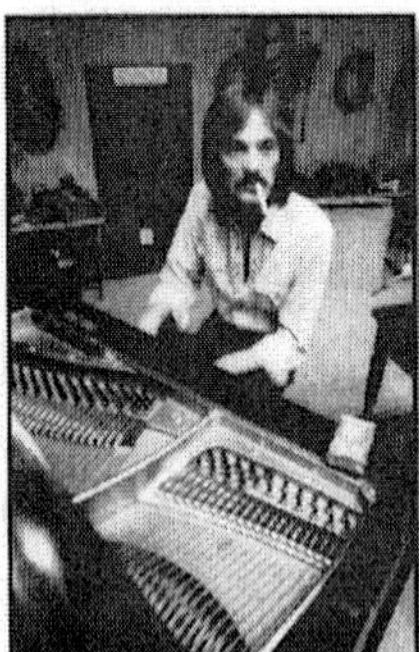

Steve roared " Did we ever! We were out of our boxes but the fucking funniest thing was nobody got it.".... "He's always there when I need some speed" " How fucking obvious can you get and there we were on Top Of The Pops, while those other poor sods, the sugar lumps lot were banned (The Smoke, whose song "My friend Jack eats sugar lumps" lyric won an outright ban on the BBC). That was probably the best thing to come out of the Don Arden era, he gave us this image...Sha La La, butter wouldn't melt in our mouths. We could have got away with murder. Itchycoo Park was an acid trip. The first Immediate album was an acid trip.

And then there was Ogden's. Marriott's grin faded. "I had an awful fight with Andrew when he said Lazy Sunday was the single. It was an album track, it was me taking the piss because I'd had this fight

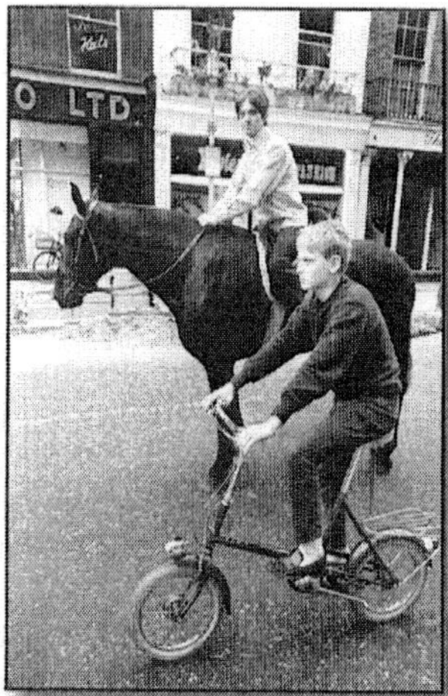

with the Hollies about never singing in my own voice, and they were right because my own voice is Cockney and I'd never sung in Cockney. So I did it for a laugh, for an album track, and because it cracked everybody up. If we'd done the song straight, like it was written, it would never have been a hit but because it was this funny, jokey novelty thing, we were stuck with it."

Ogden's other downfall, of course, was that it was impossible to duplicate live. The band did tackle a couple of cuts, Song Of A Baker and Lazy Sunday for BBC radio but only Baker and Rolling Over made it into the live set. Even the famous and often boot-legged footage of the band performing side two's epic tale of Happiness Stan on the BBC TV Colour Me Pop offered nothing more than a mime job. Marriott reflected " If we'd had any gumption at all we'd have booked narrator Stanley Unwin, hired a string section and gone out on the road with it. Instead we carried on fucking around, just crashing about on stage and putting up with the screaming. It was horrible. Andrew was losing interest in Immediate, so he didn't give us any pointers; all we had was this awful formula which had been successful for years and was now becoming an albatross which wouldn't fly away.

Worse was still to come, however. The Small Faces first (and as it transpired, last) post-Ogden's single The Universal was universally condemned as a failed in-joke. The sound of Steve playing live in his garden, his dog barking and his wife calling in the background was just too pastoral, too rural, and too weird, even for the heads freed by Sgt. Pepper and Ogden's. The Universal barely scraped the top 20; its b-side the eternal flame of Donkey Rides A Penny A Glass barely got heard and Steve utterly discouraged by his first taste of personal failure says "I did take it personally because that song was the best I'd ever written; I just thought "Fuck it!" He not only announced intentions of quitting the band but intentions of quitting as front man, as well. Everything came to a head at the Alexandra Palace gig on New Year's Eve and apart from a few contractual dates in early '69; the Small Faces were no more.

It would be another two years, well into the life of Humble Pie, before Steve returned to the front of stage, and even longer it seems before the Small Faces legacy was finally seen for what it was. Their 1976 re union was generally regarded as a desperate attempt to retrieve some dignity from four careers that had recently nose dived. It was not until pub rocker Little Bob Story and the Sex Pistols Great Rock n Roll Swindle soundtrack resuscitated their own ragged covers of Whatcha Gonna Do About It that anybody even thought twice about the Small Faces again; not until the Jam covered Get Yourself Together did respectability re-attach itself to their memory and not until Marriott turned up on a Johnny Thunders album to breathe fresh air into Daddy Rolling Stone, did anybody remember he still possessed one of the greatest voices in British Rock. There are the people who still crack up when they hear Lazy Sunday, still jump around when they hear Tin Soldier and still fall into dreamland when Itchycoo Park drifts by. It was only later, once a tragic fate had taken its awful toll on the group with the sad passing of Steve and Ronnie, that the lyrics took on deeper resonance, despite the fact that Steve had been living them out for two decades.

"What becomes of me" he sang "is meant to be, so I'll just groove along quite naturally". And that's exactly what he did.

HAD ME A REAL GOOD TIME

Party time with The Faces.........

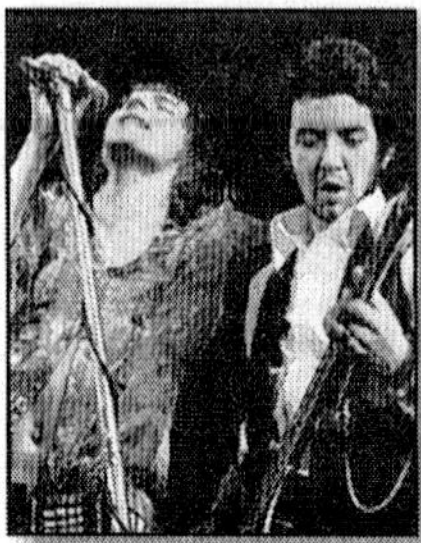

Growing up in the sixties I got to listen to a lot of fab music from the likes of the Beatles, Stones, Kinks, The Who and many more. One of my favourite bands was the Small Faces. I love singles such as All Or Nothing, Tin Soldier, Itchycoo Park and Lazy Sunday. I also loved the way these East End Mods looked and acted on stage. Stevie was a true star and had been a child actor previously. He had the most dynamic voice and it was a total surprise to me when he left the band to form Humble Pie with guitarist Peter Frampton from the Herd.

I had been too young to get to see the Small Faces live and by the time of my teens I was a regular gig goer at places like the London Lyceum and Marquee Club where I got to see Rory Gallagher's Taste, Led Zeppelin and others. I heard that what was left of the Small Faces had joined up with Rod Stewart and Ronnie Wood from Jeff Becks band to form a new outfit. I loved Rod anyway and eagerly went along to the Marquee to see the Faces.

The band still had Small Faces written on the amps, they liked to drink on stage, they liked to have fun on stage. They were merry and I absolutely loved every minute of it. I fell in love with this band and promised myself to get to see them at every opportunity. I remember Rod telling the audience that this band loved Motown, in an age where it was fashionable to be heavy this band were for real.

I remember being excited when I saw the Faces play Flying on TV in a show that later became The Old Grey Whistle Test. The song is still my favourite Faces track and would feature on their debut album First Step. That album was a mix of great songs like Around The Plynth and filler instrumentals. I loved it but it never made a deep impression in the charts. Rod also had a solo deal at the time and was well known in the States through his work with Jeff Beck. His first solo album had been recorded before the Faces really took off and his second one, Gasoline Alley, featured Woody and Mac from the band as well as his old Beck stalwart Micky Waller on drums. Rod's choice of songs on those albums was a perfect mix of Folk, Blues and Soul with a sprinkling of Bob Dylan and Eddie Cochran. Rod never wrote many songs himself although his Gasoline Alley was a classic indeed. He seemed to have two quite separate careers but always insisted the Faces was his main priority.

The Faces second album called Long Player had a great version of Paul McCartney's Maybe I'm Amazed on it. Once again the album seemed to miss the mark despite having great moments. Ronnie Lane had continued his Rock n Roll gypsy style that he had when he formed a brilliant song writing partnership with Steve Marriott. Marriott had new found fame when his Rockin' The Fillmore album hit the charts and Rod's next solo album Every Picture Tells A Story was an absolute classic. The guys in the Faces wanted it known they were more than just his backing band. Their next album A Nods As Good As A Wink proved their worth, their finest album by a long chalk from which came their hit single and anthem Stay With Me which made them regulars on the Top Of The Pops TV show

I had tickets to see the Faces supporting the Kinks at the Lyceum and the Kinks pulled out due to Dave Davies being ill so the Faces ended up headlining. I also saw them with the Who at the Oval cricket ground and again later on at the Weeley festival along with T Rex and Status Quo. There was another time with Badfinger at the London Coliseum. All great gigs.

I loved the band, still do, but when Ronnie left, after the fourth album Ooh La La, to be replaced by Japanese bass player Tetsu it was never quite the same. Even Rod has been quoted as saying "Ronnie Lane was the heart and soul of the Faces". Rod and Woody had both previously said that " All the Faces ever wanted to be was the Rolling Stones" so following a poor live album, Woody went on to join his dream band. As a unit this was the end of the road for my dream band.

ALAN BUTCHER (2011)

MICK TAYLOR
(with a little help from PP Arnold) presents......
TIN SOLDIER, the story.

Without a doubt, "Tin Soldier" was one of the greatest song's ever released from the Small Faces. It's certainly in my top 3 and always seems to be voted their top song in many survey's and poll votes. The making of Tin Soldier began around Oct/November 1967 and from Monday Nov 27th through to Saturday Dec 9th the band were booked into Olympic Studios to finalise their latest recording and release this brilliant track on the unsuspecting world...

Tin Soldier/I'm Only Dreaming: Single released 1st December 1967 [Immediate IM052]. Enters the chart at N025 and stays in the charts for three months peaking at number 25. The first 50,000 copies came in a colour picture sleeve.

NME 9th Dec 1967: "A complete break away from "Itchycoo Park". Tin Soldier reverts to the earthy, raucous sound and energetic beat that typified most of the Small Faces early hits. Don't be mislead by the title - it isn't a protest song. It refers to a boy/girl relationship and is an analogy rather like 'putty in your hands'. The song starts slowly and builds remorselessly to a frenzied climax with Steve Marriott shouting the Blues until you think his lungs are going to burst. The song has a tremendous sense of urgency and excitement."

I remember seeing the Small Faces with PP Arnold on Top Of The Pops performing 'Tin Soldier' and the sheer energy of it all was a complete blast. The combination of PP with the Small Faces was just

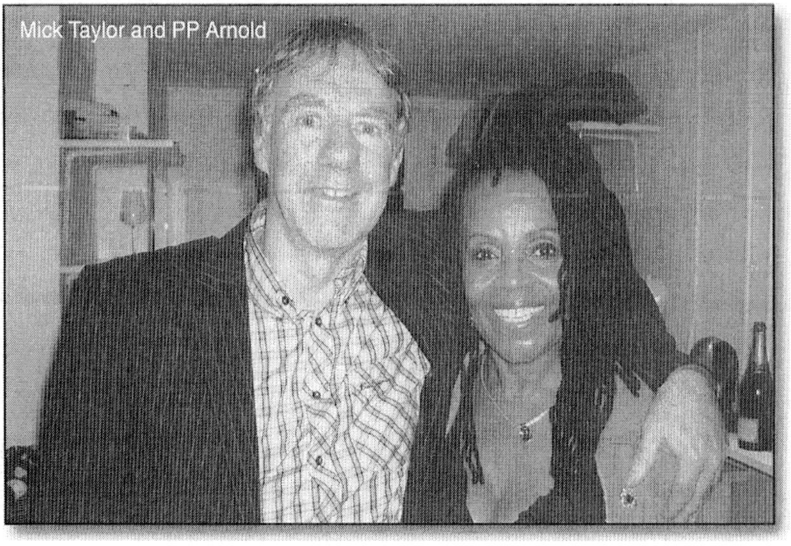

Mick Taylor and PP Arnold

awesome. I was about 15 at the time. The Small Faces were and still are my all-time favourite band. PP Arnold was one of my favourite 60s female singers after that, and little did I know at that time I would, years later, become a personal friend of Pats and now run the Fan site for her. (http://www.facebook.com/home.php?#!/pages/PP-Arnold/478119865157.)

Of all the collaborations PP Arnold has done with Steve Marriott, it is probably true to say the most famous is her collaboration with the Small Faces on 'Tin Soldier'. Steve's idea of adding PP to backing vocals was a touch of class and it would be a crime not to involve Pat with this article, so exclusively for you Pat tells her story about the recording of this classic.

"Steve Marriott a.k.a. the little Tin Soldier and I hit it off straight away. It wasn't just a physical connection with us, although we were attracted to one another, it was much more than that. We're connected on a deep Soul level. Ronnie, Mac and Kenny were all lovely and friendly but the connection was with Steve and I. The Small Faces and myself were all about the same age, a few years younger than a lot of our peers and we were also a little bit shorter in stature, but not in Spirit. I was instantly comfortable with them as they were all very dapper in the Ivy League Mod fashion that was the same style that my brothers were into back home in Los Angeles. Steve, Ronnie, Mac and Kenny were all super trendy, super cool and fine, fine, fine, but Steve was the cutest and was without a doubt the engine that powered and drove their creativity. I felt really at home in their company.

I was the new female hot property at Immediate records and The Small Faces were Andrew Oldham's hot new replacement for the Rolling Stones. Steve wasted no time getting to know me and we would spend hours jamming and singing R&B and Soul classics together. He told me how his grandmother had introduced him to the music of Ray Charles at a very early age. He had inherited her love of the music of black America from her. His raw, powerful, soulful, emotional vocal style, matched my natural, raw soulful gospel style perfectly and we instantly became true Soul Brother and Sister.

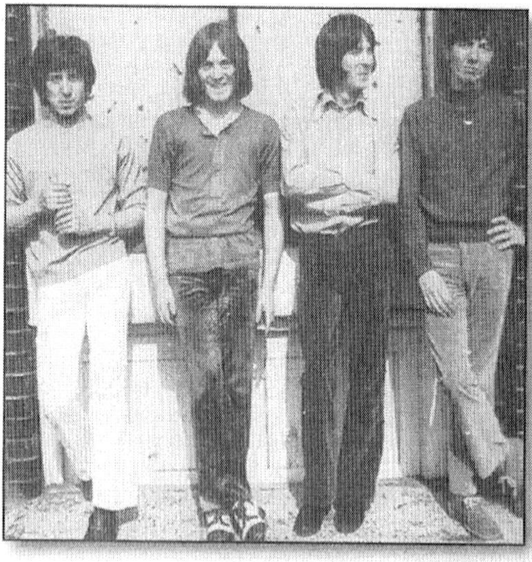

Steve was great fun, a real mischievous, cheeky joker with an abundance of hyper energy. He had a great sense of humour and we all spent many great evenings together just hanging out jamming, laughing, smoking great hashish and listening to all the latest Soul, R&B, Blues and Rock and Roll releases of the day. There was such an abundance of great artists and influences of the time, all individual and unique in style. There was so much going on around us, you couldn't help but be inspired daily by the music revolution that was taking place. The boys were energetic, happy liggers and loved to get high, hangout and make music. We all were happy to be a part Andrew Oldham's Immediate

Record label. We adopted the Motown policy of everybody working together for the good of the label and it was only natural that the Small Faces and I would collaborate with one another.

Steve invited me down to Olympic Studios one evening, where we would always record, and the serious fun of making music was on. By the end of an incredible electrically charged cosmic evening, the band had worked their magic on the new track, Tin Soldier, Steve, Mac, Ronnie and I laid down those historic backing vocals and "Tin Soldier" was in the can, and a good time was had by all. It was all too beautiful! As far as I know, Steve wrote the song for his girlfriend Jenny." ... PP x

Many thanks to Pat for those 'Groovy' words. You'll also be interested to know that PP Arnold is currently writing her autobiography under the working title's of "The First Cut" or "Now I Can Tell You How I Feel" and many more exclusive stories of Steve Marriott and the Small Faces will be unbound - NICE!

Not surprisingly, "Tin Soldier" has been covered by a whole host of top artists, including Paul Weller, Todd Rundgren, Uriah Heep, Lou Gramm of Foreigner, Black Crowes, Ozzie Osbourne and not least, Steve Marriott's 80s re-incarnation of Humble Pie.

In my opinion the song owes a lot to the superb Hammond playing of one Ian McLagan. His keyboard work sounding more like riffs than chords - superb!

Ian McLagan recalls: "My personal favourite Marriott/Lane song is 'Tin Soldier' partly because it's a great song but mainly because everything came together in the recording. From Steve's count in at the top, the rich sound Glyn got on each of the instruments, the beautiful lyrics and everyone's performance."

The lyrics were written with Steve's girlfriend of the time, Jenny Rylance, in mind. Steve says: "The meaning of the song 'Tin Soldier' is about getting into someone's mind - not their body. It refers to a girl I used to talk to all the time and she gave me a buzz. The song was to give her a buzz in return. I'd tried every trick in the book to pull her and couldn't, so I wrote her that song and she married me! (laughs)"

I understand Steve's meaning. The song was full of poetic images with words like "I am a little tin soldier that wants to jump into your fire", "All I need is your whispered hello's", "Your eyes, they are deeper than time", "A dream passing by in the sky", "Smiles melting the snow", "All I want to do is sit with you, 'cause I love you." - What girl wouldn't fall in love after that? Although the song was meant as a romantic mind blowing gesture - the BBC begged to differ. They wanted Steve to remove the last line of the song from all radio and TV performances because they thought the words said "All I want to do is sleep with you, 'Cause I love you." Steve Marriott exploded "I actually said "sit" with you, not "sleep" with you. God almighty - if it wasn't the press misunderstanding them it was the fucking authorities!" The misunderstanding was cleared up and Tin Soldier played in its original entirety.

Ian McLagan continues: "Tin Soldier had all the raw excitement of the Small Faces 'live' on stage, even up to Kenney's signature drum fill at the end. I played three keyboards on the track including Olympics beautiful Steinway grand, my old flat top Wurlitzer electric piano and a recently bought Hammond M100 that replaced my first L100. Ronnie played such a subtle bass, full of melody and right on the money. The chorus was myself, Pat Arnold, Steve and Ronnie. Steve borrowed my Fender Telecaster for that track because he wanted to bend the third string above the nut on the intro, and he couldn't do that on his Gretsch. Tin Soldier was always great to play live but listening to the record is three minutes and twenty seconds of goose bumps for me. Steve's vocal is chilling, and the final build gets me going every time. I can hardly listen to the record without a tear".

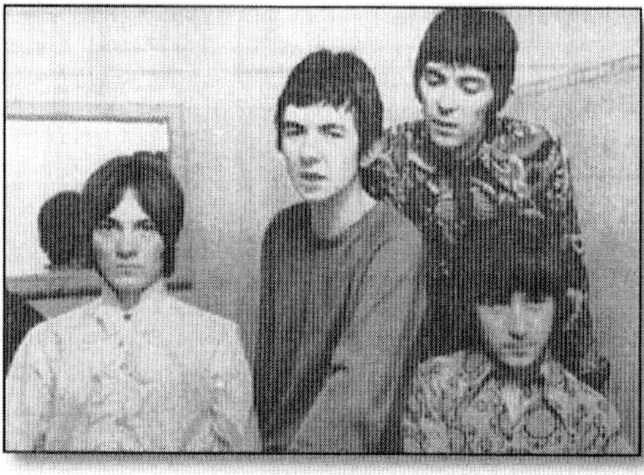

Kenney Jones recalls: "If You Think You're Groovy" (PP Arnold) and "Would You Believe" (Billy Nicholls) were done at the same time as the "Tin Soldier" sessions, Jones says: "You can tell by the very distinctive drum sound, which stayed very similar right up to 'Ogden's'."

According to Charly Records: "The Small Faces had in fact recorded their own version of "If You Think You're Groovy" which was originally intended for inclusion on their forthcoming album however this was shelved along with two other tracks, a cover version of the Ronettes "Be My Baby", and "Love Is Here And Now Your Gone", neither of which have ever surfaced."

Paul Weller also recalls: "I became aware of the Small Faces around the time of Tin Soldier. I think it was late 1967 and I remember seeing them on Top Of The Pops with PP Arnold. They were the most complete band with this great look. The whole image thing came together quite naturally and, of course, the music was just fantastic. Steve's voice had a lot of maturity and that was in their playing too and the look and the sound just blew me away, it was totally unique."

Mollie Marriott also has her say on her father's 'Tin Soldier' ...

MOLLIE: "Well everyone knows I'm more of a Humble Pie fan than Small Faces as they have that rock edge which I love but Tin Soldier is my all time favourite SF song!! The intro is one of the best and the simple piano chords send a shiver down my back every time! It's one of those songs that you could play at Glastonbury and the intro alone would get the crowd going mad! I was very fortunate to sing Tin Soldier with PP at one of the Small Faces Conventions and I actually mimed the first half as I thought 'Jesus I can't sing with this chick' . I was only 15 at the time and she shoved the microphone in my face and said ' I know what you're doing now SING!!' Her vocals on that song are legendary as are my Fathers."

Regular readers will know by now that I'm one for dissecting Small Faces tracks, finding alternates and writing about them.... so here goes .

The tracks/alternates are as follows

1. Original mono single with 1,2,3,4 count in timed at [3:18] with a natural end.

2. Stereo version, first available on the 1967 USA Immediate album "There Are But Four" and timed at [3:20]. There isn't much difference lyric wise between the two versions but Steve is yelling different backing vocals/words in parts.

3. An instrumental version, recorded for miming on TV appearances with a live vocal over the top, appears on the J60 bootleg CD "All Or Nothing". It has the same form and natural end but runs 5 seconds slower than the mono version at [3:23]

4. Another instrumental version which first appeared on the Springboard album "Rod Stewart" under the title of "Anything" has only organ, bass and drums (SP-4030). It also appeared on the 1991 CD "Quite Naturally Rare". Apparently Steve was playing keyboards to boost Mac's organ, a masterful RnB track. It was also re-issued on the German Line Label LP "Small Faces Rarities" (LMLP 5283 AS). The first ever CD release of this instrumental version was aired on the Immediate 4-CD Box Set from Charly Records.

5. The Charly "Immediate Years" 1995 box set boasts a half vocal, half instrumental version. It's unknown why it exists although it could be another TV performance backing track but in any case it was first released on the USA 2-LP set "Small Faces - Big Music" album in 1984 on the Complete label. Charly Records dubbed this version with noise reduction from a very clean copy of that 2 LP set for the Immediate Years collection.

6. The Charly Records "Immediate Years" 1995 box set also boasts a 'live' version from Newcastle City Hall, 1968 which was first aired in December 1969 on the German vinyl album 'In Memoriam' . The "In Memoriam" album also included 4 other live tracks from this gig whilst the UK album 'The Autumn Stone', released at the same time, only included 3 of those tracks. The Charly box set includes all of the 5 live tracks and for the first time on CD release as a continuous piece instead of being separated by fade-ups and fade-outs as on the vinyl albums.

7. TV version - from the BBC 1967 programme "Twice in a Fortnight" - available on a 1995 bootleg CD entitled "There Are But Three" . This version was recorded on Sunday December 10th, 1967 and because of the BBC TV miming (vocal) ban the Small Faces recorded a live vocal over a specially recorded instrumental backing track which was then aired on December 16th.

8. Last but never least. On 14th May 2012, Universal and Charly released their "Small Faces Official Re-masters Series -Deluxe Editions". Rob Caiger, who master-minded the project unearthed lots of alternate takes and mixes including a 15 minute plus work in progress version which will be available soon on a new box-set. In the meantime, lets finish with what is generally regarded to be the Small Faces finest.

TIN SOLDIER [Stereo version]

1,2,3,4,
Come on,
Ha...

I am a little tin soldier that wants to jump into your fire,
You, are a look in your eye,
A dream passing by in the sky,

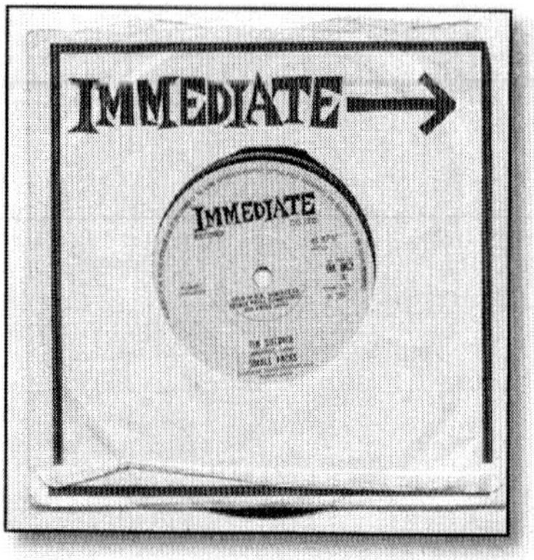

Oh I don't understand,
And all I need is treat me like a man,
Cause I ain't no child,
Take me like I am...
I gotta know that I belong to you,
I'd do anything that you want me to,
I'll sing any song that you want me to sing to you,

Ooph,
Woh...

I don't need no - aggravation,
I just got to make you,
Ahh, gotta listen,
I just got to make you -
Yeah - my occupation...

I gotta know that I belong to you [Woh, yeah, yeah,]
I'll do anything that you want to do [Yeah yeh]
I'll sing any song that you want me to sing to you.

All I need is your whispered hello,
Smiles melting the snow, nothing heard,
Your eyes, they're deeper than time,
Say of love that won't rhyme without words,

So now I've lost my way,
I need help to show me things to say,
So give me your love before mine fades away...

Ha, yeah yeah,
I gotta know that I belong to you [Woh, yeah yeah],
I'll do anything that you want to do [Well I'll sing any song]
I'll sing any song that you want me to sing to you...

Oh yeah, Oh yeah,
Listen -
I just want some reaction,
Someone to give me satisfaction,
All I want to do is sit with you,
'Cause I love you.

(Marriott/Lane)

Many thanks to: PP Arnold, Ian McLagan, Kenney Jones, Paul Weller, Mollie Marriott, Iain McGonigal, John Hellier.

STAY COOL..................................Mick T.

STEVE MARRIOTT SPEAKS OUT.....

Keith Altham interviews Steve at Beehive Cottage (May 1969)

CAN YOU TELL US EXACTLY WHY YOU DECIDED TO LEAVE THE SMALL FACES?

When you start with a group like the Small Faces you are playing for yourselves. Everyone is very together. Then someone decides you are the spokesman for the group. Suddenly you are pulled out in front as someone special – you are. "The ten by eight glossy teen scream of the year". Every time you go on stage you play a selection of past hits, most of which you would like to forget. I got tired of being an ego-freak or whatever people thought I was. We weren't playing for ourselves anymore. It was just time for a change. "I'm not a super-musician or anything like that, but I know I can do some better things with our new group. I do a little bit of everything- singing, composing, entertaining, and playing. That enables me to get together a final produce sometime, which with the help of better musicians I can improve upon.

YOU MUST HAVE AT LEAST TWENTY CATS IN THIS HOUSE AND HALF A DOZEN DOGS, NOT TO MENTION THE GEESE AND THE DUCKS OUTSIDE. HOW DID YOU EVER GET SO FOND OF ANIMALS?

I don't know, man. Even as a kid I used to dig ducks. I had a chicken called Hamilton that used to sit on my shoulder. There are no "aggros" with animals. You give them love and affection and they give it back without any ulterior motives. It all began as a bit of an accident. I got lumbered with a cat that belonged to an ex-girlfriend. That was Smelly Arfur. Then I went down to the Shepherds Bush market one morning and bought my dog, Shamus. Then I met Jenny who had a dog called Love, and Shamus and Love got on well together. Then there was this skinny Alsatian that looked all ill and poorly, that I couldn't resist. Animals are creatures; I don't treat them as human beings. I mean what animal in it's right mind wants to be wrapped up in a pink jacket when it has a perfectly good coat of it's own? Freedom is the only thing I try to give them and food, of course. Zoos just sicken me, there's nothing more sad than to see a huge great hairy Gorilla rolling around in two yards of space. Vivisection is another thing I feel very strongly about. I know there are probably arguments about having to experiment on animals but I just can't stand the idea. It's horrible. I'd probably cudgel a vivisectionist if I met one.

HAVING BEEN SO SUCCESSFUL OVER THE YEARS, WHY AREN'T YOU RICH?

'Cos we spent it all. No, we spent a lot. Never really knew the value of money, never really cared. We probably never saw a lot of the money we should have. There were some very bad scenes but it's a groove being poor anyway.

NOW THAT YOU ARE MORE DOMESTICATED AND SPENDING MORE TIME AT HOME HOW MUCH BRAIN DAMAGE DO YOU GET FROM THINGS LIKE THE TV?

Quite a lot from things like the Ken Dodd show and those Palladium type shows. They are all so Workers Playtime mentality. I don't believe it. The only shows I really dig are The Untouchables and those science fiction plays. Oh, and the Survival series. I'm not very sport conscious.

DO YOU THINK MANAGERS ARE BECOMING OBSOLETE IN POP?

What you have to get is someone who will look after you before he will look after himself and that's very difficult. In my opinion in their job the artist must come before their personal interest.

HOW MUCH RESPECT DO YOU HAVE FOR FANS?

I've been a fan; I was a Buddy Holly fan. Used to save all his pictures and get the album covers. Fan is such a silly word. I want people to respect me for something more than just my face. If they like what I do or enjoy my songs I would prefer it to stop there. I don't really want a fan club in the accepted sense. If you've been a teen scream you know what it's like to have fans. I suppose there has to be a compromise. Give, but not too much take.

NUF NIS AND REEB (SPELL IT BACKWARDS FOR THE MESSAGE) WAS ALWAYS THE WAR CRY FOR THE SMALL FACES, IS IT STILL YOUR ATTITUDE?

It never really was. It was in defiance of what you really believe. Just something to shout about. A joke to keep you going. More a war cry for abroad than anywhere else.

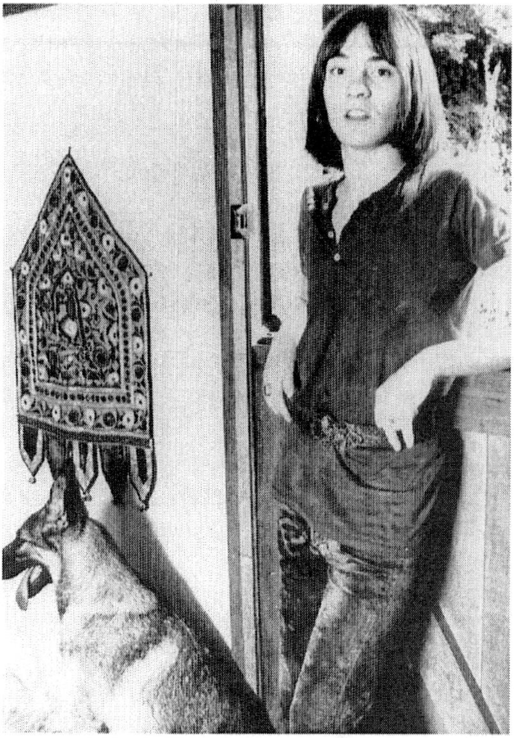

WHY DO YOU THINK SO MANY MARRIAGES GO WRONG IN POP?

Possibly because it is so difficult for the wife to accept that music to a musician is a way of life. It has to come first so often that your wife must occasionally feel neglected. It hurts a woman's pride. It's just something you have to learn to live with, you can't fight it.

THIS HAS ALL GOT TOO SERIOUS, WHAT MAKES YOU LAUGH ABOUT LIFE?

Frankie Howard, Tommy Cooper, Marty Feldman, Peter Sellars, Stanley Unwin and Keith Moon. Moony is the world's greatest practical joker, he's evil. Stink bombs in the crack of your door, hotel hose pipe under your door and books above it. You're guaranteed to end up in trouble if you're a friend of Keith's.

WHAT MAKES YOU AFRAID?

When I was a kid, it used to be Policemen. Adults used to frighten you by threatening you with fetching one. Now I feel kind of sorry for them. Some of them I have met have been a gas, I mean they really don't like what they do but they don't know how to do anything else. Our Police are a great deal better than other places in the world, but giving a Policeman a gun is rather like giving a nutter an axe! Planes are about the only thing that really scare me today. It's no use people saying that it's no more dangerous than a car or a taxi. If you are driving one of those you have a chance, and "you're" driving. I've had bad experiences in planes flying over the North Pole in storms and engines catching fire. It just gives me the horrors. After a flight on a plane I'm shattered. Everywhere by boat for me.

HOW DO YOU FEEL ABOUT CHILDREN?

I don't know if I would make a good father yet. I don't know that I would be able to bring up a child that was able to adjust in our present society. I would want my child to grow up free. Free from all the bias and conditioning that most of us go through. Not force-feed it with my ideas and my prejudices and opinions. I couldn't cope yet.

COLOUR PREJUDICE, DOES IT MEAN ANYTHING TO YOU?

It's so stupid, what can you say? It's almost as thick from one end or the other. That is the Black Power Movement are just as stupid in thinking all white men are devils as the reverse. It makes no difference to me whether a man is purple, pink, red, green or beige. Man is a man, except some of them have got more rhythm!

AND NOW A WILFRED PICKLES QUESTION. IF YOU WERE NOT YOU WHO WOULD YOU LIKE TO BE?

Ray Charles, which is a Wilfred Pickles answer!

DO YOU THINK THERE IS ANY DANGER IN POP MUSIC OUT-GROWING ITSELF? CAN IT BECOME TOO CLEVER?

Of course it can. Feel is the most important thing in any group. When people get really freaked out on technique and electronics they should go and listen to an early Muddy Waters album. That man plays the world's most useless guitar but with such feeling that it doesn't matter. Feel is what it's all about.

THIS INTERVIEW WAS ORIGINALLY PUBLISHED IN RAVE MAGAZINE 1969.

A FANS EYE VIEW

Original 60s fan, Margaret Bennett, reminisces about crafty meetings with her favourite band, The Small Faces in 1966.

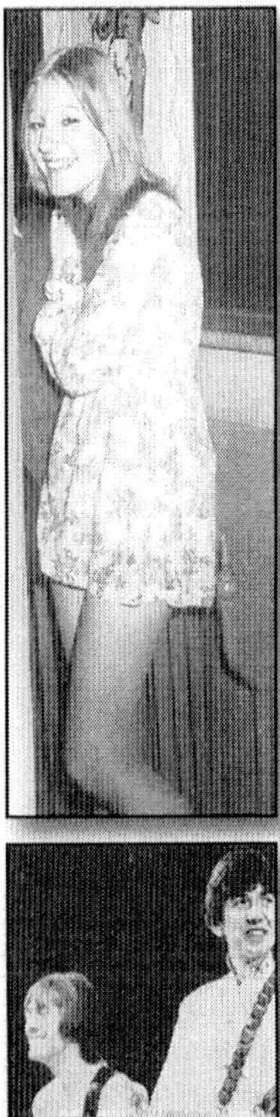

John, as you know the Small Faces were my local band, so I tried to get to see them as much as possible and often went to Steve's Mum and Dad's flat in Daines Close to see if he was in. He never was, but his sister Kay always spoke to us, which was really nice.

The first time I met the boys was at the Marquee Club in Wardour Street in London's West End. I was with some friends and we had queued up for hours so that we could be at the front, which we were, the height of the stage was just below knee level, and the more the people poured in, the more we were pushed against the stage and this was still way before the time they were due to appear. It got to the point where I couldn't move my legs and the stage was really digging into me. Unknown to me a bouncer must have been watching and the next thing I knew was being lifted up by my arms and away from the stage area and taken to a small room. I don't know why but I didn't think at the time to walk out and try to get back to the stage. I just sat there in disbelief that I had lost my place and therefore had lost any chance of seeing the Small Faces. Anyway, after what seemed to be a lifetime to me, the door opened and in they came!! Imagine the scenario; think of somebody in the world you would do anything to meet, but in reality knew you never had a chance, then there they were standing alongside you. I just stood there frozen, mesmerized, not believing what my eyes were seeing, it was just like a dream. They all smiled at me and I just about managed a smile back. I had a colour picture of them and another which I had copied on a new fangled machine in work called a photo copier. They were a new invention and were as big as an arm chair in those days and they only printed in black and white. I eventually got my legs working and went over to Kenney, Ian and Ronnie to ask them to sign the pics for me, which they did. When I got to Steve I handed the pictures over, staring at him like I was in a daze. He signed the colour one then looked at the other one for a bit and said, 'ere did you draw these yerself, I said no and explained about the photocopier to which he said, that's good innit. They then went on stage and I could see them from the room I was in, they did a few songs but I can't for the life of me remember what they were. Anyway, they came off the stage and back into the room for a few minutes. Then the door opened, they all waved and Steve said see ya luv, then they were gone.

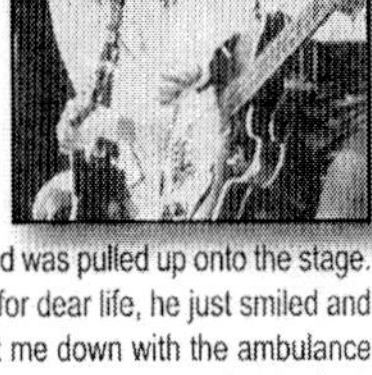

I walked out in a daze, met up with my friends who didn't know where I had been. I told them I had just met the Small Faces and talked to Steve. Oh, how I wish we had had mobile phones in those days, they didn't believe me until I showed them the signed pictures, how jealous were they?

So that was the first, and probably the last, time I met them, ah, but onto the Uppercut Club, close to Ronnie Lane's childhood home in East London. Again we got there very early to be at the front, this time though the stage was very high, up to your shoulders, so we were looking up at them while they were playing. I noticed that as the girls were fainting, probably to do with the heat, the crowd being tightly packed and of course, the Small Faces presence, they were being lifted up and carried across the stage to the ambulance people. The idea came to me to do the same, knowing I would have to pass Steve. I performed the most wonderful fainting act ever! You couldn't fall to the ground because it was jammed tight with people, anyway I was noticed and was pulled up onto the stage. As I was carried past Steve I suddenly came to life, I grabbed him round the neck and held on for dear life, he just smiled and the bouncers eventually got me off of him (it took two of them though!) Luckily they didn't put me down with the ambulance crew because they realised I'd faked it. There was no room at the front, from where I came, so they put me sort of at the back of the stage area but to the side, I could still see them so that was OK by me. They finished playing and again they were waiting right by me ready to go. I was feeling much braver this time and managed to blurt out a few words. Steve remembered I was the one who'd grabbed him previously and said, bleedin' clever that girl and winked........ then, gone again.

I didn't get a photograph but have two beautiful memories to keep with me forever.

JH: Thank you for sharing the experience, Margaret It's always a joy to hear a fans eye account of meeting the guys back in the day

A to B. E to D. *By GARY KENT:*

the last man to see and speak with Steve Marriott EVER!!

LATE SUMMER IN 2009. My wife and I are in the back of a cab to Stansted Airport. It's the early evening rush hour and thankfully our cabbie knows a twisty, picturesque route through the leafy lanes to cut out any M11 snags. He knows Turkey too by the sounds of it, and tales are a-plenty from the front seat, shrinking any pre-flight jitters as well as journey time. Chat makes time fly. As planes get bigger, lower and louder above, something hits me, out of the blue. A red, a stop light. A set of traffic lights – innocuous enough – but surely odds-on winner of the least necessary set of lights at a country junction. Nonetheless, these lights are tagged in my head as that good old déjà vu descends, consuming me, puzzling me. It's green. We go. Luggage, baggage, the departure lounge. The Turkey trip comes and goes. Years pass. One day that junction will reveal more...

"It's some sort of a party, but it's wound down now." Wally mumbles, half asleep. "Give the address out on the radio and someone'll pinch the fare off you."

It's 1991. In a life before I start taking writing and music seriously, I drive a taxi for a while. Wally, the cab office owner, is a fighter, and he struggles to prop up his dog-eared cab service with aid in the shape of a nightly bottle of Bell's, 40 Superkings Black and me. Scars on his arms, legs and possibly his back - from yesteryear's skin grafts - tell of a fiery business dispute going out of hand in his own former life. He also survives a heart attack just four months back, which is when I step in, manning phones, driving. Meanwhile Wally recuperates in between the Black Lion and underneath the cab office counter. But Wally's self-destructive bent will end within the next twenty-four hours when luck will finally call time on him.

It's been a steady night so far and I grab the last of the bookings – or what I think will be the last – which takes me into Central London around midnight, one o'clock-ish. I'm thinking I might get some kip soon. But now there's another pick-up. I hear Wally calling out my name on the radio over and over, but he can't hear my response. Not until I reach the Waterworks roundabout can he get me, and he intriguingly instructs me to return to the office. I'm worried and do as I'm told. "It's a pick-up out in Ongar." He says, raising himself. There's me thinking he's having one of his funny turns. Ongar? That's a bit out in the sticks isn't it? "Yeah, but I've had a chat with him. He's alright. He's just a bit pissed..." Translated, this means the punter is probably as pickled as Wally. But is he a puker, I wonder? "Naah. He's gonna be alright. Just a bit pissed." adds Wally. "Listen. He knows it's out of our area and it's going further out an' all that. But he's gonna wait for you. He's got money. It's roughly thirty quid. Don't worry."

Thirty quid and a valet? Vomiting drunks, or coming within an inch of your life? Which is best? Three weeks back, I pull up at one of Wally's late night pick-ups and knock to be greeted with a nutter, barefoot, top-off: he's had a phone call - someone's on his way over to 'do' him – but they send him a cab to shit him up. I knock, and here's Rambo, knife in hand, threatening. What a laugh. A false alarm for both Rambo and myself.

I explore the Ongar to Chelmsford road seeking a posh name of a posh house no doubt, easing up at every tree break, gap and gateway. It's here. I turn into the 'in and out' driveway, tick over and wait. There's a glow at the door, shapes appear. In he gets, into the back seat. This fellah. "You know Saffron Walden...? S'alright. I'll show yer." I love trying to suss out these creatures of the night. I mean, how has this chap ended up here tonight? Whose party? How come he hasn't arranged a taxi beforehand? And if he came by taxi, why not book a return with the driver? But why sit in the back? Most people on their own, sit in the front with me, glad of the company. Perhaps he knows he's going to honk? And most people chat, eh? Not this chap. No small talk whatsoever. Not even the ubiquitous ice-breaker, 'are you busy tonight, driver?' Yes I am, thank you. Thank you for asking. Driving, yawning, driving, yawn... country roads, half an hour in, a red light - yes, that one – not a soul in sight. We wait. A pub set back on the corner, a few houses beyond. It's still red. And still nothing from the back seat. I can't see him either. He's right in the corner on the nearside, out of the range of my mirror. I can't turn around, can I? I could angle the mirror a bit so I can see him? No, that looks bad, like I'm spying on him. Or shall I? Shall I say something? While I move the mirror?

"Is it straight over these lights?"
"Straight on. I'll tell you where to go."
"Is it much further?"
"Naah, not far."

Past houses of people asleep, wishing I was one of those tucked up in slumber. Trees, more trees. Villages, verges, and then another directive from the back seat. I catch a glimpse of his eyes in my mirror: he looks thoroughly fucked off, gazing out into space. Eyes hardened by anger, softened by despair, consumed in thought. Weary, worn-out. What's his worry? Is he skint? But he must have a few bob living out here? Well-heeled, like that posh old Ongar gaff. Well-Brewstered. Surely money can buy happiness, can't it? And he's still not doing the small-talk. This bloke can't be not sociable – he's just come from a party. Then again, Wally did say he's a bit pissed. Not that I can smell it in the front. Eons pass and roads become lanes and lanes become narrower. My headlights snake round a tiny hamlet dotted with cottages and there's a junction. Is it left or right? Which is it to be? None of the above.

"This'll do. Just 'ere mate. Just 'ere."

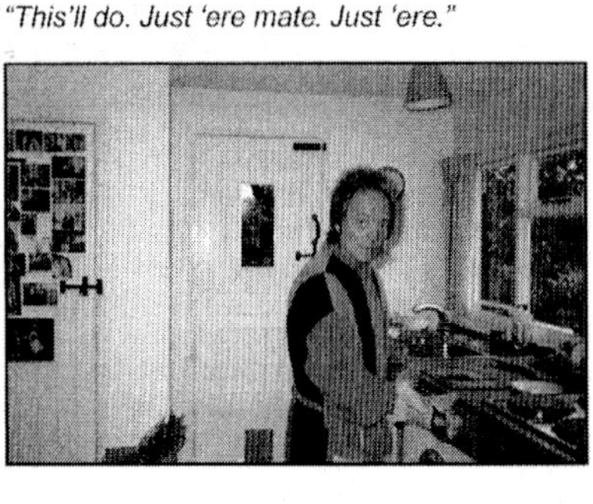

Mick's here. He's mad into his music. But tonight he's suited and booted: he's trying to get me into some network marketing free enterprise thing. It's gone midnight when he leaves. He plonks his whiteboard back in the boot of his car. "It's nice out here, innit?" he says, taking a sniff of late night air.

It's 1996. Me and my missus live out in amongst those sticks now. In Ongar. "'Ere, didn't Stevie Marriott live out this way? Once upon a long ago? In Moreton, that's it. Stevie, phew. He was b-rrrrilliant wasn't he? Stevie? You've heard of Stevie Marriott ain'tcha?" I've not, but Mick has, by the sounds of it... "Small Faces,? Humble Pie? Stevie Marriott was amazin'. He used to drink in The White Hart. He was a Mod icon, saw him, amazin'. Y'know his wife, Toni? She knocked some kid down in Norff Weald? Drunk. Phh... But Stevie Marriott – yeah - he was b-rrrrilliant..." Mick's hyperbole fails to excite me because I have no clue just who Mick is banging on about. It's all Stevie or nothing. Why don't I know? "Yeah, Mod icon... Marriott... Stevie... Humble... Stevie... Small... Pie... Stevie... b-rrrrilliant."

Mick plays in bands, like me. And like me, he will never escape music. As a kid, I'm ruled by pop royalty Queen, plus some old 45's in my older sister's collection. She's got The Beatles, the Stones and the Kinks. Punk comes along in my Year IV - It's 1977 - and bang! It blows my mind! Not the spitting, mind. 1979, it's the Mod revival. But with the year below us commandeering it, (turning up in parkas with fur bits looking like Davey Crocket,) we blank it so as we don't mix with the riff-raff. Bailing out of school before it bins me, I find myself helping out my band from the punk zone, The Stranglers at their Thames HQ. Later, I hang with Steve, an Essex Mod, and attempt to hang on to his Parka on the back of his Lambretta. Once, he hands me a bike chain: "Ere, use this!' He then proceeds to launch into a pack of scooter boys he's invented a vendetta with, screaming 'Chaaaarrge!!' No wonder we get chased everywhere from then on. On his sister's old Dansette record player, he only spins the old and the new, The Jam and The Who; never the Small Faces. By '82 I'm almost grown-up, and with a different 'in-crowd' of the electronic era at the Cariba in Conduit Street, Lord's in

Ilford and Jaffa in Romford Market, suitably attired in Bowie pegs and wedge haircut - before suddenly it's 'Aciiieeeed!' spewing out from poxy pill-popping Ecstasy-ridden raves disguised as venues next to some stinky Essex sewage plant: a distasteful scene in a tasteless era. Music is dead.

The naughty '90's; Brit Pop is the new cultural movement, but nothing much to shout about. Then marriage, then mortgage and then a beer belly. Where does time go? Musically, I start looking for that buzz, the bolt, the charge. It only leaves the retro route: The Beatles' Sgt. Peppers and the White Album, loads of Hendrix, all of the Kinks and.... Tad-dah! Cue drum roll! Ladies and gentlemen, I finally discover the Small Faces! My new favourite band mean so much to me. So much more than John, Paul, George, Ringo, Jimi, Ray, Dave Dee, Dozy, Beaky, Mick and Titch! My new quest leads me to 'The Ultimate Collection' and the 'Essential Collection.' Then 'Ogden's' Nut Gone Flake,' 'Classic Small Faces': 'Dateline Diamonds' off EBay, Steve with his Packet of Three live at Camden Palace, but best of all, the 'Steve Marriott Memorial Concert' at the Astoria with Peter Frampton and his Humble Pie replacement Clem Clempson doing an amazing (not hyperbole) 'I Don't Need No Doctor.' Oh, and a Humble Pie comp, plus 'Live at the Fillmore'. Ultimately, it's Steve's creative force within the Small Faces that binds me the most. That original, early mercurial flash of inspiration and chemistry; like Paul Weller's golden five year lifespan of The Jam, (and to a lesser extent, Style Council or solo stuff). Similarly, The Stranglers first four LPs during 1977-9 (over anything since); and a pre-1977 Dr. Feelgood with Wilko Johnson, who quite simply, 'does it right.'

I don't know why, but I often cry after playing 'Tin Soldier'. I can't picture many artists out there who match that emotion. Then there's the 'rinky-dinky-doo-ness' of 'Lazy Sunday'; amazing how the band mix heartfelt and humour, as well as pop and groove. Oasis become The Beatles, but Blur blossom - as a Small Faces hybrid - tipping their tit-fer-tats with some aplomb. The Small Faces will always be the guv'nors of the Cockney knees-up: 'What'cha Gonna Do About It?,' 'Sha-La-La-La-Lee,' 'Itchycoo Park,' and 'Lazy Sunday'; sheer unadulterated pop in 'Get Yourself Together,' 'I'm Only Dreaming,' 'Here Come The Nice'; quirky corkers such as 'Up The Wooden Hills To Bedfordshire,' 'I Feel Much Better,' 'Long Agos And Worlds Apart'; rich groove-infused numbers like 'It's Too Late,' 'I've Got Mine,' 'Understanding,' 'I Can't Dance With You,' 'E To D,' 'Afterglow (Of Your Love),' 'Wham Bam Thank You Mam' and magnificent pec-pumped anthems of 'All Or Nothing,' 'Song Of A Baker,' and my tear-filled 'Tin Soldier'. All works of a genius. Or genii, Plonk, Kenny and Mac included. Back in the day. the Small Faces album gets applause a-plenty whereas Sgt. Pepper gets critical and cultural acclaim in the lysergic haze of the Summer of Love. So what outfit can anyone name from the Summer of Ecstasy? The Prodigy? SL2? Forget it. But then again, if you know you were there, then you weren't really there...

For a spot of bath-time inspiration, there's nothing more satisfying than dipping into any of two tantalising publications: 'Small Faces & Other Stories' by Uli Twelker & Roland Schmitt; and 'Steve Marriott: All Too Beautiful' by Paolo Hewitt & John Hellier; I implore you get hold of these books – if you haven't already. Particularly Hewitt & Hellier's tome, even if it's just to find out what Steve tapes in a voice message for the Marriott fan in a coma! Steve Marriott's early days make captivating reading: growing up in London's East End like me, I can't help align alongside the man. The parental dismay when a son chooses an alternative path to the status quo – in Steve's case, he ditches the acting. In my case, I ditch everything. At school, Steve (allegedly) torches the class room – a crime I find myself accused of in my final days of school (allegedly) – with a head filled with not much more than music and hope and ether from the chemistry lab (allegedly, natch).

But it is Steve's last day on this planet that provides the saddest, most poignant thrust: he's forty-four years of age, no longer that Mod icon of old, plenty of pop hits from the past, with his money siphoned off in all other directions but his. Suddenly a last chance saloon of a deal worth a staggering £3 million alongside former Humble Pie colleague Peter Frampton means financial security that Steve can only dream of before. 1991 certainly looks like Steve's great comeback. So how come he and wife Toni bail out and head home before completing the recordings? Maybe clues lie in booze, pills and powder? Perhaps the pressure of having too much money, mixed with an intrinsic fear of fame? For the flight home, Steve's flying anxiety means more booze, pills and powder to numb his senses. But the couple squabble on the plane, enough for a stewardess to implore they keep it down.

At Heathrow, a pal picks them up and Steve seems pleased to be back in Blighty, although he appears agitated with his missus. After checking on Steve's dream narrow boat at The Maltings at Sawbridgeworth, the couple return to their rented house in Arkesden, near Saffron Walden late afternoon. It's been burgled recently. Instead of succumbing to excess and jet-lag, Steve's malevolent alter-ego makes an ugly appearance: this he names - and blames – Melvin, the bald-headed wrestler; he goes into one, smashing everything in sight. Rescue comes when another friend collects them for a meal at the Straw Hat restaurant in Sawbridgeworth. Here, Steve tucks into possibly his last meal – his favourite, roast lamb and mint sauce – and more booze and more bickering between the couple leads to a request from staff to calm it. It's very late when the couple head south to Ongar, to the house of their friend, entertainment promoter Brian Shaw. With Steve's final day soaked in drink and drugs, you might be yet again forgiven for assuming that once up the wooden hills, he's likely to be in the land on nod almost immediately. But some time later, Steve's up and about. He's downstairs, and in need of a taxi to take him back home to Arkesden.

Once inside, who knows what happens. Apart from around six-thirty in the morning, smoke is seen billowing from the house. They say Steve accidentally lets go of a cigarette in bed. If only the fag is the self-extinguishing roll-up variety as opposed to a flight duty-free one Steve has. If only Steve turns to the out door and not the closet door he is found at. If only Steve gets out of the right side of the bed instead of the wrong side.

All this seems at odds with the man on stage, the hyperactive performer with gallons of talent. But it's clear that Steve wrestles with his demons. Warm, witty and generous, charming company for the most part. Obnoxious, rude and volatile at other times, and then there's that alter-ego, Melvin. Maybe mind-bending binges in the past unbalance the chemistry of the brain and confusion leads to coping mechanisms that for most people are hard to accept. Meanwhile, Steve's contemporaries play to stadiums, live a champagne lifestyle, and hop from young model to young model – blondes have more fun – while Steve covers the small club and pub circuit. It's

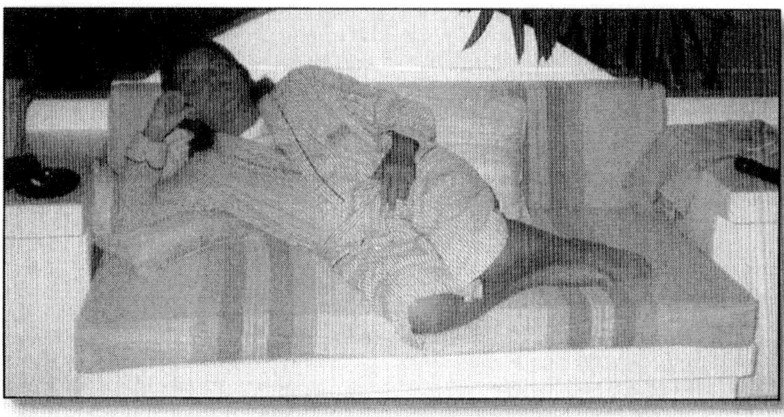

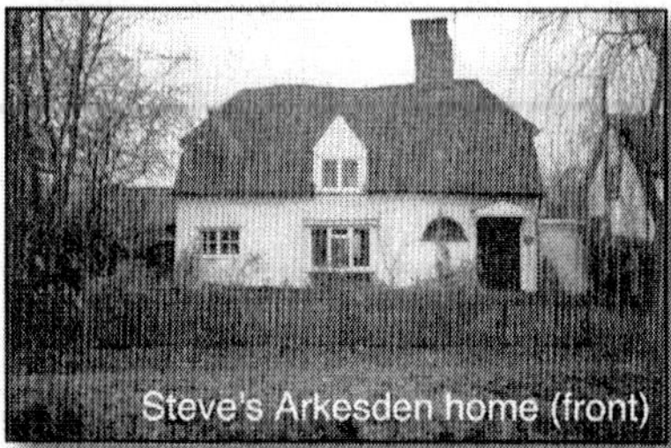

Steve's Arkesden home (front)

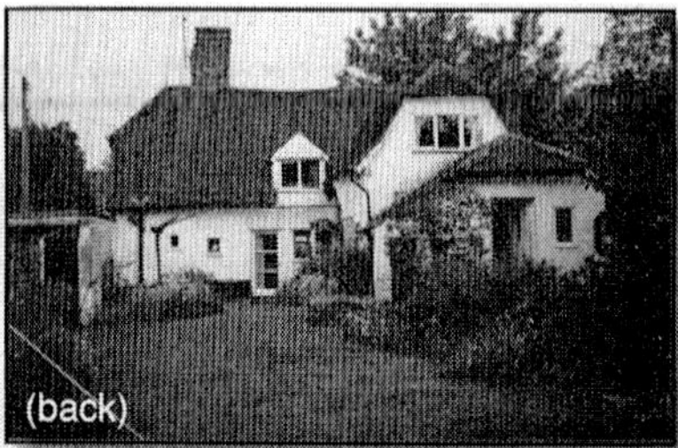

(back)

pitiful. He must feel hard done by? I just wish I could have met the man. But now it will have to be in the afterlife. And not when Melvin's around, naturally.

"You live in Ongar don't you? I used to run a pub near you. The White Hart, in Moreton - "

I'm in the present. I'm having a coffee. A work colleague – Tracey - sits down opposite. I can't resist asking her if anyone well-known ever came into The White Hart, Steve Marriott's one-time local. "Dunno. There was a chap called Brian Shaw, an entertainments promoter." She says, "He used to bring friends in all the time. He lived near you. He had a nice house in Ongar. We had some great parties there..."

Brian Shaw? Entertainment promoter? The friend of Steve's? And he lives in Ongar...? Suddenly I feel my heart racing, bordering atriofibrilation almost. Books spin round in my mind, and I see Steve getting into the taxi... but was it me at the wheel that April night in 1991? Surely not. But Tracey fails to recall the name of the Ongar house. "It was a long time ago." She's right - and so are her directions - when I locate the gaff on the way home from work. There it is, King's Ridden. That must be it. It's there. The Ongar pick-up. The 'in and out' driveway. My head is in overdrive. My reflection is red. I fathom a sea of possibilities and probabilities. I need to think. The following morning, I catch Tracey in the corridor at work. "That's it, King's Ridden. I've been racking my brain all last night..."

Neither book in my bookcase mentions the house name. There's no place to stop, and no point in knocking. But the 'in and out' driveway does look right. The front door too. The cab journey to north Essex somewhere with the man of misery in the back, not speaking. And those sad, subdued eyes gazing out into space. The junction! Those traffic lights! The pause before green is unforgettably tense as I fail to weigh him up. The mirror. The lanes. It's Arkesden where he gets out. My synaesthesia says it's Steve Marriott. I don't know whether to laugh or cry. Celebrate or commiserate. If only the cunt invited in his cabbie that night for a little tipple? Then again, I was so tired I could have fallen asleep on a phone line. And he was jet-lagged, pilled-up. Then there would have been two of us snuffed it in the flames. So I met Steve Marriott hours before he died, and I didn't even know. Why didn't I know? Why didn't he say something? Why wasn't I into the Small Faces? What if he'd said 'Don't you know who I am?' Could he have said that? I can't help imagining a trigger, say, to lose his rag on the night, to bring Melvin out in the back of the cab? 'Ere, can I smoke in your cab, mate?' No, sorry. 'What? Don't you know who I am?'

I would have let him smoke, for the record: I only start smoking myself six months prior. That's because it's in my dusty diaries, down from my loft. On top of the pile, 1990: Thursday March 29th – Gig with Candyflip at the Astoria – The day I am lured to the weed. Ah, here it is. 1991. April. Friday, 19th April 1991 - Nothing of any note. Saturday 20th – Car broke down, called RAC. Sunday 21st, - Got car towed to garage. Alf died today. As you can see, I am no Anne Frank. Memo to self: 'track down Brian Shaw.'

A hurried search online. An email is sent off asking a Brian Shaw - an entertainments promoter - if he ever lived at King's Ridden and was also a friend of Steve Marriott. Let's see. I leave my numbers. It's a long shot. Suddenly, it's the landline ringing. A voice goes: "Yes. And yes. But why do you want to know?" I relay my total recall of my night in question, careful not to crow-bar any mitigating energy, however vague it comes across. But Brian seems certain I was there: "It's funny," he says, "we never thought of tracking down the cab driver at the time." When I pry a little more, I am reminded of it being twenty-two years on from the event, and that not everyone's memory is in such great detail. Interestingly, he did recall they did wait a considerable length of time for the taxi to turn up. I wonder if I did call at his house, but collect another guest? To which Brian says that no one else got a cab from there that night. There are just three of them, with their two guests, Steve and Toni, with Toni asleep in bed. He then recalls how all hell breaks loose the following morning after the phone call to say Steve is dead. Toni has yet to find out. I wonder why Steve gets a taxi home on his jacks. "Quite simply, Steve Marriott was his own man. Nobody told him what to do. Whatever he wanted to do, he did it." Brian then wraps up the phone call: "I must say though. I've always believed that I was the last person to see Steve alive, but now I'm almost certainly convinced it's you." It is me. The past becomes my present. My mind flicks back and forth to that consequential night in April 1991. I see my doodling pen quivering, and feel my throat close up. It's me. It's my epiphany. I hear those words:"This'll do. Just 'ere mate. Just 'ere." See? I do become his mate, now he's home. Fare on the seat. Figure fading in the darkness. I feel like I should retrace the journey. Or not?

The Odyssey: I've never been to Saffron Walden until a work meeting pops up. It's sunny late afternoon when it finishes, and the chore simply has to be made worthy by swerving to nearby Arkesden. With the sun resting peacefully on this rather posh little village, I can see the attraction for Steve: the desire to retreat to an idyll after all the mania and mayhem of playing in sweaty dives. That, plus the Axe & Compasses pub directly opposite.

Steve's one-time abode out near Ongar – Beehive Cottage in Moreton - is just as tranquil. But hard times force him and first wife Jenny to pilfer spuds from a neighbouring farmer's field. It is here Steve builds his Clear Sound Studio in the adjacent out building and records Humble Pie. Up the road and round a bend is his second home - The White Hart - after the studio, that is. According to legend, Steve is known to steer his horse to the pub and make the return journey the same way, only this time navigation is entirely equestrian-led.

Quite possibly, just like Moreton, the residents of Arkesden rapidly outgrow any novelty there may once have been of having a rock star in their midst. In the books - Gell, the erstwhile Axe & Compasses' landlord - is a particular focus of Steve and one Christmas, Steve scales a ladder to Gell's bedroom window to shout out Christmas carols. Which is sweet, but not so much at two o'clock in the morning!

I pull up on the pub forecourt as the last afternoon customers leave. Outside, I focus my camera at Sexton's, the penultimate resting place for Steve. It's funny. I can almost hear him crunching his way cross the tarmac to the pub in his Converse trainers and dressing gown for a bottle of brandy from Gell, while barred. "Hello? Can I help you?" Today's crunching belongs to Gell's successor who appears from around the side. Although not a publican at the time, by sheer coincidence, today's landlord is actually on his way to work. Early that fateful morning, he spots smoke from Arkesden and calls 999. "It was thick black smoke. So I phone the Fire Brigade. Then, I'm listening to Radio One, and just after the news, there's an announcement saying Steve Marriott has died in a fire at his home in Arkesden. I couldn't believe it. It was terrible. I was so shocked. Oddly enough, a year on, I become the landlord of Steve's pub." Over ensuing evenings, our landlord is filled in with tales of Steve. Like, how his body was burned through the floor after setting himself alight in the en-suite. If Sexton's had an en-suite, that is. Another has a more cheery tale: during one of the times Steve is barred from the boozer, he enters with peace in mind. He apologises to Gell for his swearing and bad behaviour in the past, and insists on buying a round of drinks for all of those present. The publican still is wary, but Steve promises to curb his profanities. After everyone is served, Steve raises his glass to Gell and he says: "CHEERS - AND HERE'S TO YOU - YOU OLD CUNT!!!"

Opposite, and bang next door to Sexton's, is the former village Post Office. An old red telephone box outside is now shelved out full of books to borrow. A pleasant, elderly lady pulls up and gets out of her car. This former Post Mistress was indeed Steve Marriott's neighbour: "Someone in the village told me Steve Marriott had moved in and he's my new neighbour." She says. "But I'd never heard of him! It was my son who knew him when I phoned him up. He said: 'What? Steve Marriott has moved in next door to you?!!! Wow!!!' He just couldn't believe it!" She also recalls phoning the Fire Brigade on that April morning in 1991 after first smelling smoke and then witnessing the fire just feet away. The operator tells her that they can't send anyone yet despite relaying the severity of the fire, as well as the proximity of the blaze to her own place. But they do come. "For quite some time after the fire," she says, "Steve Marriott's fans used to turn up with flowers and pictures and all sorts. Although many weren't quite sure which house to leave them at, as the house across the road also suffered a fire six months previously."

Accident? Arson, even? One of the two. Who knows? I still can't believe Steve was in the back of my car, and it's only now I know. The past is the past, but more so than ever, it is very much my present. And in quiet moments, I can't help reflecting on Steve's final few hours on this planet in the leafy corner of North Essex, between taxi and Sexton's. Sometimes I lie awake, gazing up at the ceiling, thinking. I find myself in a similar silence to that dark Arkesden night, like a film reel, softly flickering in slow motion: the shutting of the car door, the doleful figure disappearing away from me along the willow-lashed lane. Inside, and closure. Shutting the world outside out forever. Upstairs, into peace and solitude and a final respite. Again those saddened eyes appear in my moonlit mirror as I steer out of the twilight zone, heading back to civilisation and daybreak, breakfast and a bed. I switch on the early morning radio and I hear a familiar tune. A rave from the grave. But this time, the song is sung directly at me:

'I picked him up on a Friday night, Sha-La-La-La-Lee, yeah.
I knew everything's gonna be alright, Sha-La-La-La-Lee, yeah, Sha-La-La-La-Lee.
I asked him where he wanted to go, Sha-La-La-La-Lee, yeah.
Well we went some place I don't know, Sha-La-La-La-Lee, yeah, Sha-La-La-La-Lee.'

Yeah! Good night, Steve. May you rest in peace with the rest of the ravers.

Gary Kent is vocalist-guitarist-songwriter of The Feb 21s at:
http://www.reverbnation.com/ thefeb21s

https://myspace.com/feb21s

He also edits 'The Burning Up Times' Stranglers' fanzine at: www.strangled.co.uk

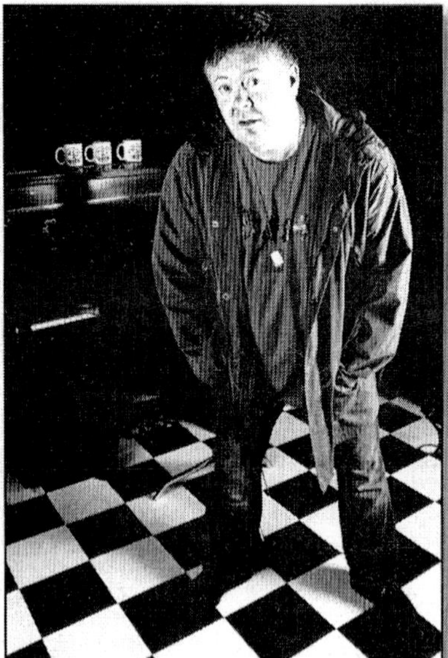

RONNIE LANE remembered..........

by John Pidgeon

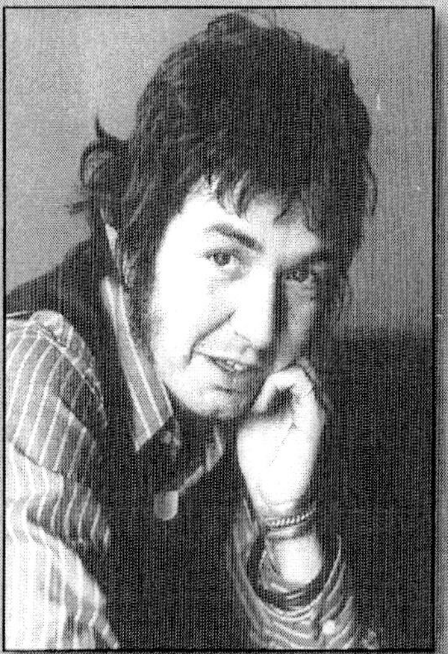

It may well have been his Song Of A Baker on the Small Faces Ogden's Nut Gone Flake album that first had me believing that Ronnie Lane was wise beyond his years. The opening line caught my attention. "There's wheat in the field and water in the stream" he sang, which had me wondering, "A song that opens with the basic ingredients of bread? That's not something you hear every day." Then, as the theme unfolded, I realised that it was about more than baking. What the singer was saying was that as long as there's wheat in the field and water in the stream, there's no reason why you should ever go hungry or thirsty, provided you're prepared to make the effort to turn that wheat into flour and to fetch drinking water from the stream. In essence, and without finger-wagging, Song Of A Baker was preaching the benefits of self-sufficiency and in 1968 that struck me as deep for a pop song. Ronnie even made the "loafs texture and... flavour" a rhyme for the bakers "labour". I found out later that he had borrowed his theme from a Sufi parable. To have considered the writing of a Muslim mystic suitable source material was impressive erudition from a 21-year-old from East London.

I guessed the song was Ronnie's because he sang it rather than Steve Marriott, as clear an assertion of ownership as John Lennon singing Strawberry Fields Forever or Paul McCartney Eleanor Rigby, and it was because of that conclusion, no doubt, that I listened more closely than usual to the lyrics. Like Lennon-McCartney, the joint Marriott-Lane credit was essentially a convenience, since few of their songs were either written in the same room or derived from equal input. Across a handful of singles or the two sides of an album those individually unequal contributions would balance up but more importantly, as writers, each needed the others spur. The songs that emerged from their association could not have been written in isolation, only with the direct or indirect input of the partner. We would come up with something to knock each other out, he explained, so, with Itchycoo Park, the Small Faces most famous song, Ronnie had knocked Steve out with a melody he had lifted from a hymn, God Be In My Head and words he had concocted after reading a magazine article about the attractions of Oxford, which had spotlighted the city's Dreaming Spires and its Bridge of Sighs. It wasn't me that came up with "I feel inclined to blow my mind, get hung up, feed the ducks with a bun" that wasn't me, he protested, though arguably Marriott's tongue-in-cheek, East Enders take on the spirit of '67 contributed as much to the songs success as Ronnie's verses.

The real worth of the melody and poetry that Ronnie brought to their partnership was only revealed once Steve Marriott had abandoned the Small Faces to form Humble Pie. Whereas Ronnie continued to develop as a songwriter, his one-time mentor atrophied. In fact, it's hard to come up with a single notable song with Marriott's name on after the Small Faces' melancholy cheerio, The Universal.

Humble Pie's American fans were at least partly to blame for his slump. After all, it was they who cheered his black-white-boy shtick and whooped and hollered at his vocal histrionics and hyperactive posturing and if all it took to send an audience into an orgasmic frenzy and propel an album as unimaginative as 1972's Smokin' into the US top ten was a handful of overloud blues chords, a repertoire of - for a pint-sized Cockney - improbably throaty growls and trills, and a stage persona prone to throw extravagant shapes, why bother with the hard slog of actually writing words and a tune?

Ronnie's songs, meanwhile, fitted the born-again Faces perfectly, nowhere more obviously than on the group's third and most cohesive album, A Nods As Good As A Wink To A Blind Horse. Despite sharing their blokey, anti-intellectual, working-class-and-proud-of-it philosophy, his songs are not only musically less flamboyant than the Rod Stewart-Ron Wood rockers, but lack their rampant hedonism. Even in a song about sex, where the road-wise roué of Stay With Me trades a groupies promise to be gone by the morning for a post-coital cab fare home, Ronnie, in You're So Rude, was reliving an in flagrante teenage fumble in the front room of his parents house; while in Debris, as if consciously counterbalancing the rowdy bravado of Too Bad, Ronnie explores childhood memories of his father, underpinning the evident reality of both these songs by setting them with chronological precision on a Sunday morning and evening and, in lines like "Oh, you was my hero", by deliberately expressing himself in vernacular that would have earned him a detention from his English teacher.

If you're going to be on the road, you might as well be on the road, he once told me, because if you don't totally accept that you're on the road and that's it, that's your lot, private jets back to London for a few hours a day ain't going to make it home. What's wrong with life on the road? I can't understand this rushing there and rushing back business.

True to his word, he would do his best not to rush on the Faces' US tour in the spring of 1973, renting a Winnebago camper whenever time and distance allowed. Even so, somewhere between Minneapolis and New York an unarguable truth hit him: this wasn't why he had learned to play guitar, not this uninspiring, sapping routine of travel, gig, hotel, no. The equally inescapable consequence was that he would have to leave the group.

Once he had started thinking that way, it wasn't hard to come up with other reasons for not staying in the Faces. He was in no doubt that Rod held back his best songs, as he had most recently with True Blue, for his own solo records. He would not turn a blind eye to the looming shadow of Rod's solo success, which he recognized as a threat, not just to the longevity, but to the very entity of the Faces. He couldn't ignore the slow, but unstoppable spread of separate billing on posters "Rod Stewart and the Faces" by promoters bothered

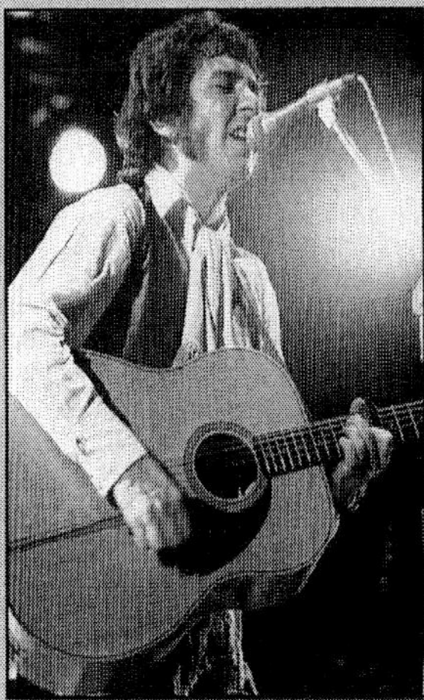

more by the prospect of missing a single potential ticket sale than bruising musicians egos. And he felt gagged as a singer, especially on stage, where his vocal role was reduced to backing harmonies and the opening verse of Maybe I'm Amazed and not in my key either, you can guess whose key it was in. He was also frustrated by the slow progress of the Faces follow-up to A Nods As Good As A Wink, especially Rod's infrequent attendance at sessions and unhelpful appraisal of tracks necessarily recorded in his absence and when Ooh La La was eventually released, he was disappointed by its critical reception, and appalled by Rod's faithless distancing of himself from the record.

On 12 May 1973, as the Faces were waiting to go on stage at the Civic Centre in Roanoke, West Virginia, Ronnie said the words that had been used countless times by different members of the band, but until now only in fun, parodying a pop star's foot-stamping tantrum at a trivial setback, like a lukewarm cup of tea or a brandy-and-coke with no ice; I'm leaving the group! He left no one in doubt that he meant it. During the set he spat an obscenity at Ian McLagan, the keyboard player retaliating with a vicious kick which left 10,000 West Virginians wondering whether it was part of the act. One more US date, four nights to fulfil in London, then Ronnie was gone.

Fortuitously, the timing of his exit from the Faces and his decision to pursue a more eclectic, rootsier music closely followed the surge of a forceful undercurrent in London's music community. Either bruised by the business or uninterested in what it had to offer, bands like Brinsley Schwarz, Kilburn and the High Roads, Bees Make Honey and Eggs Over Easy had deliberately taken a detour from the well-mapped highway to Hitsville onto a musical B-road, where they could perform, freed from the pressures of commerce or fashion, on an array of interchangeable instruments, a seemingly off-the-cuff mix of R&B, Rockabilly, Country, Jazz, even post-war, pre-Rock'n'Roll Jump Jive - styles altogether too diverse to lump together under any more meaningful banner than the name of the modest venues where the bands chose to play. Pub rock, as it was known, was to provide three key members of Ronnie's next band, Slim Chance: Bees Make Honey's Ruan O'Lochlainn (saxophone, keyboards, guitar); Charlie Hart (keyboards, fiddle, accordion) from Ian Dury's ramshackle first band, Kilburn and the High Roads; while the group Steve Simpson (guitar, mandolin, fiddle) left behind became pub-rock regulars as Meal Ticket. Slim Chance brought a broad musicality to the melodic charm, conversational lyrics, and subtle themes of Ronnie's songs and bolstered by this band, his voice, by his own 1975 description an instrument I only picked up eighteen months ago, grew strong, emotive and sure, able to skip nimbly and sure-footedly along the melody lines. Whenever he sang, it was hard not to smile, harder still not to join in.

The multi-instrumental abilities of O'Lochlainn, Hart and Simpson weren't employed to impress, but to allow Ronnie to follow diverse musical directions and to provide his material with an apparently infinite variety of sympathetic settings. On record the unseen interchange of instruments was efficient but owing in part to that invisibility, unremarkably low-key. On stage, however, once his musicians had freed themselves from the recorded arrangements and made the songs their own, a Slim Chance gig was an intoxicating event, a cross between a pub sing-song and a country hoedown. The set was not only neatly balanced, but, in the manner of pub rockers, wilfully challenged the convention that confines set lists to past hits and excerpts from the current album. Naturally, Ronnie didn't ignore How Come, his first (and only substantial) solo hit, or its bafflingly underachieving follow-up, The Poacher, but both were enormously enhanced in live performance.

The chorus of How Come became impossible not to sing along with, such an audible show of public affection endowing it with a far heftier status than that of a single that hadn't quite made the top ten, while the somewhat prissy oboe and string arrangement that had made The Poacher a lightweight 45 was replaced by the duelling fiddles of O'Lochlainn and Simpson to create a show-stopping knees-up. Oldies Ronnie had revived, like Fats Domino's Blue Monday and Chuck Berry's You Never Can Tell (both on 1975's Ronnie Lane's Slim Chance album), were there too, but several live Slim Chance highlights, notably covers of the Rolling Stones Sweet Virginia and Leroy Van Dyke's Walk On By, never made it onto record.

His new-found freedom meant he could even find room for the forty-year-old Depression ballad, Brother, Can You Spare Me A Dime, a song weighed with poignant meaning in the wake of 1974's Passing Show, an ill-judged attempt to take his music to the people, when a caravan of decrepit circus vehicles limped from town to town with insufficient advance publicity to attract enough paying customers to the big top, pushing him to the very edge of financial ruin. What bailed him out was the American Airstream caravan, sleek as a cigar tube, that he had had kitted out as a mobile recording studio during his last days with the Faces. Hired out to Led Zeppelin, The Who and Bad Company, it generated enough income to disguise, albeit temporarily, his fragile finances.

In the autumn of 1975 Ronnie used that mobile studio to record a third album at his farm on the Welsh borders. With One For The Road he created something unique in British music: a genuine form of native country music, no capitals, no inverted commas, not anglicized Nashville, just music that came out of the country and could not conceivably have been created anywhere else. When that record didn't sell, he had to let the band go, unable to fund the full-time wages of five musicians and a road crew from his own, diminishing income.

Broke, he approached Pete Townshend for a loan. An old pal and, like Ronnie, a follower of Meher Baba, Townshend turned him down, but proposed instead that they should make a record together, which, if for no other reason than that it represented half a solo album by the leader of The Who, was bound to generate record company interest and, with it, an advance: a financial boost for Ronnie without the burden of debt. Although Rough Mix was less than a true collaboration, with only the title track co-written by Townshend and Lane, the album contained the most enchanting, sublime song Ronnie ever wrote.

It's a cliché to call a song timeless, but Annie sounded as old as the century. It could also have been the work of Leadbelly, Woody Guthrie or George Gershwin. Or a century older and by John Newton or Charles Wesley, since, sung in church by a choir, it would certainly have sounded like a hymn. Expressed most directly in its God bless us all plea, the song was infused throughout with a hymnal tone, its melody uplifting, its message that in spite of mortality, life was ongoing, that even in death was optimism. A hymn by Ronnie Lane would almost be worth going to church for.

An unforeseen outcome of the Rough Mix sessions was an immediate opportunity for Ronnie to resuscitate Slim Chance, opening for Eric Clapton on his spring 1977 tour. Clapton, whose acoustic work on the Rough Mix sessions highlighted the selfless restraint and sensitivity he could bring to a supporting role in the recording studio and earned him a co-writers credit on Annie, had fallen under Ronnie's spell, envying the freewheeling eclecticism and determinedly low-key approach that offered an antidote to the pyrotechnics commanded by Clapton's own audiences. The guitarist even adopted Ronnie's Romany look of bucolic shirt, scarf and waistcoat.

In his early thirties the symptoms of multiple sclerosis became harder to ignore, and the next time I saw him he walked as if he was permanently tipsy. Being forced by the remorseless creep of immobility to accept the role of observer rather than participant intensified the aura of wisdom that had surrounded Ronnie as long as I had known him. More than ever, he came across like an ancient sage, one with a long life time's knowledge and experience to impart, the appearance of a younger man adopted to disguise his age. But if increased wisdom was a side effect of MS, it was a cruel trade-off.

In 1984, Julia (my wife) and I had a son who was born too soon and lived for a day and a half. Ronnie telephoned with a question. You know when you see a baby bird dead on the ground? Well, if you look up, there'll be a nest, and in that nest there'll be more, healthy babies. It's like a little Pidgeon has fallen out of the nest. There'll be more, you'll see. There was more solace, humanity and hope in that succinct analogy than in a hundred Bible stories or Sunday sermons. Julia and I weren't short of love or support, but nothing made the future look less bleak than the simple, life-affirming image suggested by Ronnie.

He was living in Kentish Town, but within weeks had moved to Texas, where he had been promised regular access to hyperbaric oxygen treatment in Houston. Because the claims made in some quarters for HBO treatment encouraged unreasonable expectations for what it could achieve, the therapy was controversial, but Ronnie knew, having tried it in London, that spending an hour a week in a sealed chamber where the normal amount of oxygen in the air was multiplied many times worked for him. It wasn't a cure for MS, but it alleviated some of the symptoms. Undeniably, it made him feel better.

I was keen to visit him, but hard up. Someone told me you could fly for free as a DHL courier in exchange for escorting their mail sacks through customs, so I signed up for the Houston run. There was a 48-hour stop-over, and I spent two nights at the house Ronnie shared

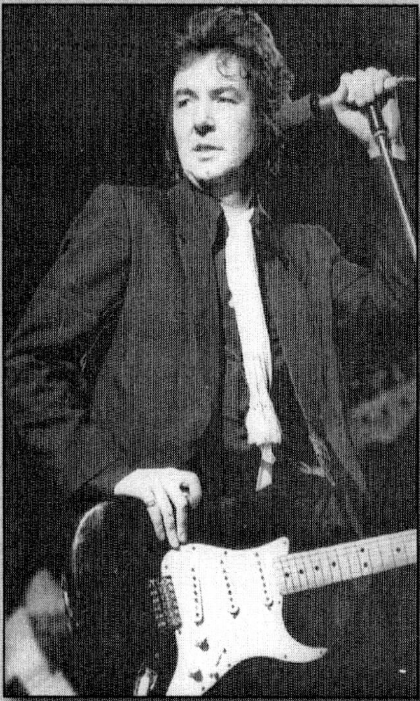

with his carer, James "Big Bucks" Burnett, an amiably goofy young Texan who drove Ronnie to and from his weekly sessions at the HBO Medical Centre and for a daily swim at the YMCA. I was happy to be able to tell Ronnie that Julia was pregnant again, and repeated our thanks for the help and hope he had given us.

There's another Pidgeon in the nest. He tilted his head as he looked at me, one eye slightly off to one side, his bony fingers cupped over the top of his walking stick. You sure it was me that said that?

Part of Ronnie's exercise regime was a daily walk, but even though spring had not yet turned to summer, Houston's climate was debilitating, and I watched him wilt, oppressed by the cloying humidity, so I was relieved to learn that he had moved to Austin, 130 miles west, in Texas' more temperate hill country. I visited him there in March 1990. He had signed up for a short tour of Japan, a bold undertaking for someone whose central nervous system was under daily attack. Having recruited a band of Austin musicians, he twisted Ian McLagan's arm to play keyboards. I'd wanted to record them both for my Radio 1 series, Classic Albums, for which the Small Faces Ogden's Nut Gone Flake was an overdue candidate, and figured that, with Mac at his side, Ronnie would be a livelier interviewee than on his own. I was right. The interview, recorded at Ronnie's house between rehearsals, was punctuated with laughter and impromptu repartee, hilarity I hadn't heard from them since 1973.

But, back in Austin two years later, when I phoned him to say I was in town and would love to drop by, he replied, "No, that won't be possible". "I only want to pop in to say hello". "Sorry, mate". "See you then, Ronnie". Click. Silence.

Like George Harrison, Ronnie Lane played in the shade of louder talents. Like him too, he left an undeniably impressive body of work. His influence is quiet, but enduring. Ronnie Lane mattered, and still does. And I haven't even mentioned his bass-playing.........................JP

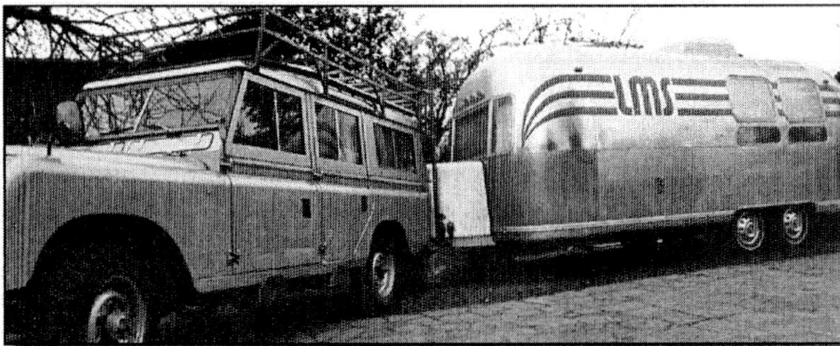

RONNIE LANE'S LONG LOST MOBILE STUDIO.

On the afternoon of 14th September 2009 I got a telephone call from good friend and colleague Mark Cunningham (Total Production) with a message along the lines of "You'll never guess in a million years where I am?" "standing inside the LMS (Lanes Mobile Studio)".

Ronnie Lanes mobile recording studio, lost for the past 30 years, had turned up at a trade show at Earls Court in West London. It was last heard of in the early 1980s when Ronnie, being stone broke, sold it to get funds to re-locate to the States in search of better medical expertise for treatment of Multiple Sclerosis, a disease which he had recently inherited from his mother.

At that time the LMS was in a pretty poor condition having been vandalised by yobs whilst parked outside the council house that Plonk was living in at the time in Kentish Town, North London, along with partner, Boo Oldfield.

Many people including Brother Stan and documentary maker Rupert Williams had spent years seeking it out with no joy and all the time it had been less than 40 miles from London stored on a farm in West Sussex.

Now lovingly restored by owner Mark St. John (Pretty Things manager) it is in full working "analogue" order. A bit of a looker too, it's the classic US Airstream model. Mark St John invited me to the trade show to give it the once over and has even offered its services to record a very special Ogden's show that Mark Cunningham and myself are planning for London later this year.   WOW!

John Hellier

PETE TOWNSHEND

.... MEMORIES OF THE LMS.

The Who's main man speaks exclusively with Wapping Wharf about his memories of Ronnie Lane's mobile studio.

Ronnie's Mobile was one of the projects that fell loosely into the scope of TrackPlan, a company run by John Allcock, Ted Fletcher and myself to provide studio facilities to musicians. Ron Nevison had done some work for Trackplan I think, working on a recommended acoustic treatment for Ronnie Wood's home studio (now my home studio), and left to work exclusively in LMS as engineer. It was natural for me to turn to LMS when recording Quadrophenia because I had helped design it and specify the equipment. The Who were waiting on Ramport Studios control room to be completed, but needed to begin tracks so we used LMS for the tracks of quite a few songs on Quadrophenia. At that time it was an 8 track rig, but that suited us because I was using 8 track for my home studio, so we could get straight to work on reels I brought from home.

The first job for LMS was the best. We took the Airstream down to Cornwall to Porthallow, and recorded the rough sea around a rock, in quadrophonic. The tapes still exist and they are magnificent. We didn't want the generator to spoil the sound so we plugged the studio into a light socket in a public toilet on the beach. I'm amazed it didn't blow it up. Four brand new Neuman U87 mikes were set up as the tide came in and crashed all over them. They continued to work OK, amazingly.

Ron Nevison and Ronnie's manager for the Airstream who's name was also Ron something (fabulous hippy kind of bloke but I've forgotten his name) did the final equipping of the Airstream outside Ronnie's house in Richmond where I now live. I haven't strayed very far from my roots and I think about Ronnie, Susie, Katie, Ron Wood, his son Jessie, Krissy Wood, Ron Nevison, Meher Baba (who visited a nearby hotel in 1932) and of course the Airstream whenever I look out of my window.

I have a big Airstream myself that I use as a studio, but mine is used partly as a sound booth, partly as a video studio, and partly as a technical workshop. I'm really glad LMS has a retro analogue desk. It was first equipped with a Helios desk, and that was partly what gave it such an amazing sound. Cadac made the desks at Wessex studios where I made my first two solo albums Empty Glass and Chinese Eyes, and they are also really beautiful desks.

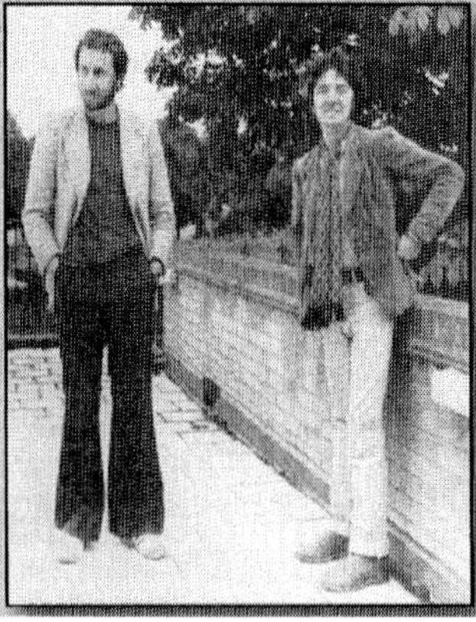

A word about Ronnie Lane. He and I went through a short period from 1967 to 1976 when we were incredibly close friends. He was really supportive of my home recording efforts, and was far more enthusiastic about my solo work than anything I ever did within the Who. We both knew that in some ways I wasn't strong enough emotionally to be in a band like the Who, and that it would eventually take its toll. We also knew that he didn't belong in a band like the Faces, and of course that also took its toll. We both were lucky to do such good work in our bands, separately as solo artists and together on Rough Mix. The band that we should have created together was beyond my conception at the time, and exists only in an alternate reality, but he was a true inspiration and encouraging musical friend to me.
PT (Feb 2010)

FROM THE BEGINNING

STEVE MARRIOTT IN HIS OWN WORDS

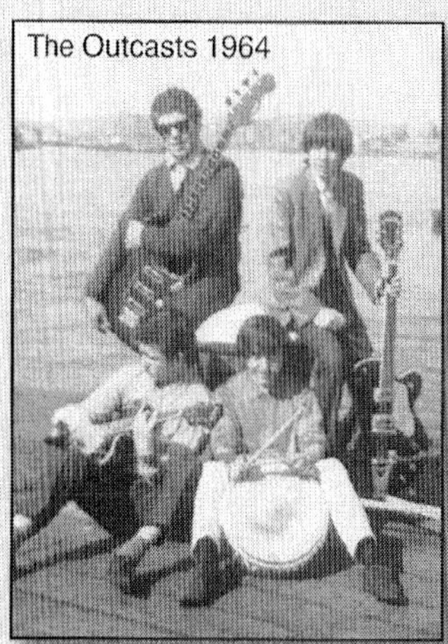

Steve talks with John Hellier about the formation of the Small Faces (Feb.1984)

When Kenney met me he said he'd had a dream or something and he got in the van and I was sitting there as a friend of Ronnie's and he sort of backed off and I said "Whatsa matter?" to him and he said "You ain't gonna believe this. I've never seen you before but I had this dream and your face was in it". It's weird innitt? He said he dreamed that they were playing somewhere huge and he said" You were there!" and it was Ronnie and him and me, he couldn't see anybody else. Strange...that's something we've never been able to explain. It sounds ridiculous but Kenney's too straight to make up anything like that and he told me about it straight away on route to their gig in Bermondsey. Small Faces were a fated group!

The Outcasts were Ronnie's group when I first met him in the music shop that I had taken a Saturday job in. We got paralytic when Ronnie had me first play with them. I don't know if was nerves or what or friendship or both. We got paralytic and then went on stage. I can't remember much about it but I'm told that I smashed the piano up or something...Jerry Lee Marriott impressions! I was banging the shit out of it, jumping on top of it and because of that they ended up losing their residency that they had in the pub. George was their singer (George Cambridge) but I can't remember much about him. He was there, sang a little bit and that was about all. He looked more like a plumber, or something, than a singer. Ronnie and Kenney left the Outcasts, I think, so we said "Let's form a band of our own". Either that or they semi left and semi got booted out because of our rowdy showing that night. Around the same time Ronnie lost his day job at Selmer's because he was trying to get me a free PA for my group The Moments. I'd go down there and he'd be testing PA's and shouting like "Free PA for Marriott" and they sacked him for it.

I remember the next job he had was running errands for the War Office or summink like that, might have been the Home Office. We were sitting in the Giaconda, in Denmark Street, looking at maps of Polaris submarine bases. We opened the tube and it had brown sauce all over it before we'd rolled it back up again. I think Ronnie had to deliver it somewhere, it was on its way from A to B and just sort of got diverted..we couldn't believe it. I don't think we had planned to meet there that day. He knew I used to hang out there and I think he may have just popped in. I'd hang out there because it was Tin Pan Alley and there were studios there. If people wanted demo's made they'd just pop their head in and say " Can anybody play drums?" and someone would say "Yeah, I can". We'd put our hand up immediately for anything. It was a few quid in your pocket. I'd do anything; drums, vocals, harmonicas, backing vocals, bass..anything. I don't really remember any of the things I worked on, most of it was foul! There were some good writers around and they favoured me for singing their demo's. They were, I think, publishers demo's not recordings as such.

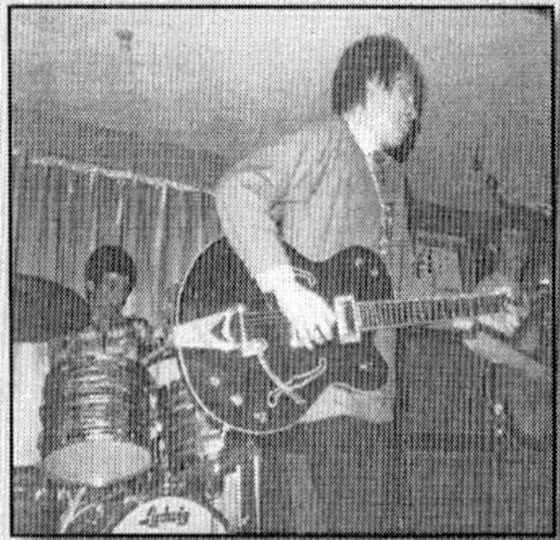

Did Ronnie tell you of the job we had washing up at Lyons Corner House? I was only there a couple of days, four I think, and I didn't drop anything I just got pissed off with it and the staff there were mad. My hands went all brown and the skin started falling off because of the bleach they used to wash their shit up with. I used to wash them and Ronnie would rack them and push them through a shower. It was a nightmare, just a conveyor belt of eggs and bacon and shit. It was 'orrible, I think we got 8 quid a week and Ronnie stayed on another couple of days to get his full weeks wages. I pissed off, I couldn't handle it. There used to be this mad Scotsman who used to go around with a knife all the time when he was working in there and this other mad woman used to turn on all the gas taps and giggle. It was crazy! and the Scotsman would pick up a carving knife. and yell "I'll fucking kill the bitch" and go after the one that turned the taps on. Fucking bedlam!

I found Jimmy Winston. He used to come to the J60 music shop, the same way as Ronnie, but he was more of a regular. His parents were the tenants of the Ruskin Arms, my local. It was a great pub, I remember being invited round there and he was mucking about on a guitar. He was proficient on guitar, more so than me at the time. His family were much more well off than mine, so he had some decent equipment. I didn't even have a guitar until I took over Ronnie's payments. I was playing mostly piano at the time. He had an organ too you see and a van...the van was the big thing! He was quite a bit older than me and he used to fight a lot. He was always getting into fights, over chicks probably. Always in a scuffle.

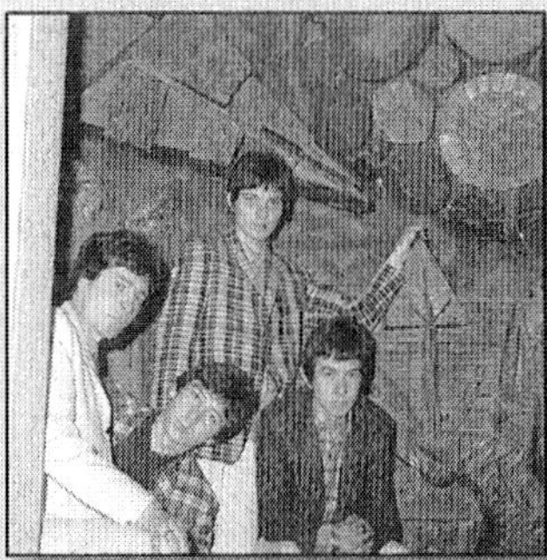

Basically the Small Faces formed for bar mitzvahs and weddings as a generalism. Any chance to play, we'd play. We weren't trying to make it big, it was a hobby, just something we done for fun. I think we only done one wedding, it was in Loughton. We played at this chicks wedding and I remember her jumping over the balcony! This was before we went North but it wasn't a proper gig. This was where I was living with me mate Mick O'Sullivan and his friends from acting school. Ronnie would sleep there sometimes and when Kenney came over we'd have a little play. Mick got a writing credit on one of our songs later on when he lived with us in Pimlico. I got a Marshall, either a 50 watt or 100 watt, the old ones with the big cooker knobs on, it was black and white. It was massive for those days. We were loud, notoriously loud! If you can't play...play loud!

We had an agent, a guy called Terry the Egg, I don't know where he came from and he ended up doing some roadie work for us, driving us around. We'd done about four gigs in London before we went North, including the wedding and some East End working men's clubs. In Manchester we did the Twisted Wheel, an R&B club. That was the first gig on the trip. I don't think they'd ever seen Mods before. There were a few on the border but not quite as into it as we were at the time. We were all dressing Mod at the time, it didn't have anything to do with money, it had everything to do with how you wore what you had, you know. We were totally into it, we weren't into scooters at all, it was all about the look and the music. During that Manchester gig some bastard lent our black van out for an hour and came back with a fuckin' load of leather coats in the back, they done a job while we were playing. Me and Ronnie both got a leather coat out of it!

In Sheffield they kicked us out after a couple of numbers. It was a working man's club and all these old geezers were shouting out while we were playing. I do remember one old lady in there though, she must have been at least forty, started screaming when I announced we were going to do a song by James Brown. She loved it! She was hip! so we kind of played to her only. She was the only one in the audience who knew what we were doing. Anyway, the guvnor slung us off, paid us off and told us to piss off! We also played at the Esquire Club, a trendy Blues club and the Mojo Club, the biggest club we'd played up until then. They put us up for the night. It was a GREAT club, really was, and was owned by Peter Stringfellow. It was a Mod club with a very appreciative crowd. I think we only played there once before the hit record but they adopted us, we were their band it was as if they'd discovered us. They'd always go totally berserk when we went back there later and it was such a special place for us because they gave us a break when nobody else was willing to do so.

We played the Cavern Club in Leicester Square that same weekend after we got back to London. I think we went down there ourselves and blagged the guy for the gig. I remember the manager, some Irish guy, kept saying " Can you do two more?" so we'd have to repeat a couple. We only knew about five or six songs but they'd last ages as we just went into a jam, we had energy, a lot of energy and flair and that was sorely missing from the scene. The numbers were never played the same twice. We went down well and he saw the crowd reaction and put us on again. It turned into a little residency for about six weeks. We were little Mods and by that time devout. We became arm-flingers and feedback players and I think it had a lot of charisma just to look at. Little people with a BIG noise!

We had that place packed every time we played there. Kit Lambert came down to see one gig and got a lot of flak from the Who because he wanted to take us on at one point and then Maurice King and then finally Don Arden. He was the one that actually got a hold on us. A chick from Arden's office spotted us, his secretary. She just happened to be around. I'd seen her before at the Starlight Club that Maurice King used to own near Oxford Street and that chick had seen me down there, too. We'd done some rehearsals down there when we first got together and before any gigs at all. Maurice King was very interested in signing me as a solo singer at the time and I chatted him up to let us rehearse there. Kenney's playing at the time wasn't too clever at all. Up until then I was used to playing with older people. Small Faces were all sort of the same age and obviously less experienced than my previous band members in the Moments. He was OK but I didn't realise it was the material that he had been playing. He set his drums up and we were just farting around and he just went berserk! For about half an hour he made me and Ronnie just kill ourselves laughing! and we were giving him encouragement "Go on, my son!" He really opened up. He was like a different drummer and just got better and better. Today he's one of the best drummers around. It was a real eye-opener and there was no looking back. Every song we did he swung like Hanratty (convicted murderer who was hung in the 1960s), it was like a revelation, we couldn't believe it especially Ronnie who had played with him longer than me.

So Don Arden's secretary asked for my number at the house I was staying at in Loughton. I don't think we were on the phone though, 'cos I remember going to telephone boxes to

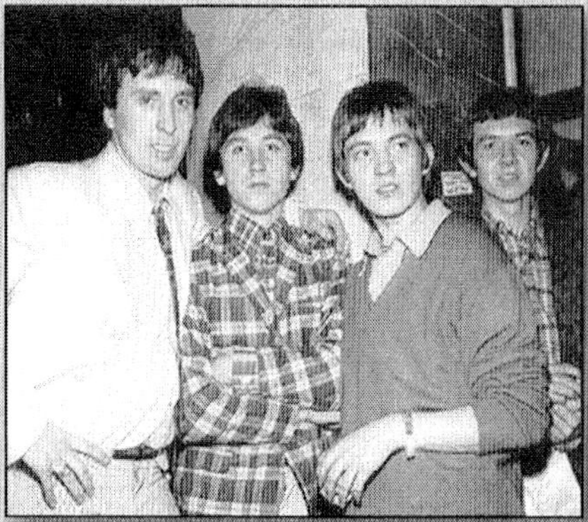

make calls. They got hold of my Mother instead. I'd make a call to my Mum once a week to be sure she didn't worry too much, me living away from the family home was still frightening for her, I think. So she said this office had been trying to get hold of me, Don Arden, whoever he is. I knew about him and had seen his name on Blues posters because he used to bring over guys like Jimmy Reed and John Lee Hooker to play in London. I was very impressed and told Ronnie about it. We called them and he sent his main man, Pat Meehan to see us play at the Cavern.

As it happened Ronnie and I had just taken a terrible beating. We were a bit exhausted and it was freezing. We got off a bus and there was this van following us with about six or seven geezers in it. They were older than us and looked like Greasers, whatever. We were Mods and they obviously took objection to that. They jumped out of the van and beat the shit out of us. They hit me with a bottle, I found that out later, had no idea at the time. Still got scar on my forehead (shows me).They did Ronnie with a bit of wood that had a nail in it, so he actually had a hole in his forehead. We were covered in claret and kicked to bits. We found out later that a couple of boys from Loughton had gone down to Tottenham and smashed up a few cafes and stuff so this was the return visit. We were just unlucky bystanders. In a state of shock we couldn't stop laughing about it to each other. We were blowing bubbles with blood and still we were laughing. We went to Woodford Hospital and we were still laughing! This nurse came over to us and shouted " Be quiet, this is a hospital!!" which hurt us that much more because we couldn't stop laughing again. They threw us out saying it was a maternity hospital anyway. and we didn't have any right to be in there! Anyway, next day we had the audition, playing at the Cavern Club for Don Arden. It was fucking hilarious! Every time Ronnie hit a high note his fucking stitches would open up and the blood would pour down his face. My face looked like a gargoyle, two black eyes, very fat lips and a stitched up head. They like us apparently! I think this was the last time we played the Cavern. Don Arden immediately gave us a gig a few nights later at the Wykeham Hall in Romford....he refused to pay us, said we were too loud!!

The start of things to come.

TRACK BY TRACK

"SMALL FACES" by the Small Faces.

Original UK release
Decca LK 4790
CD UK release
Deram 844 634-2 with bonus tracks.

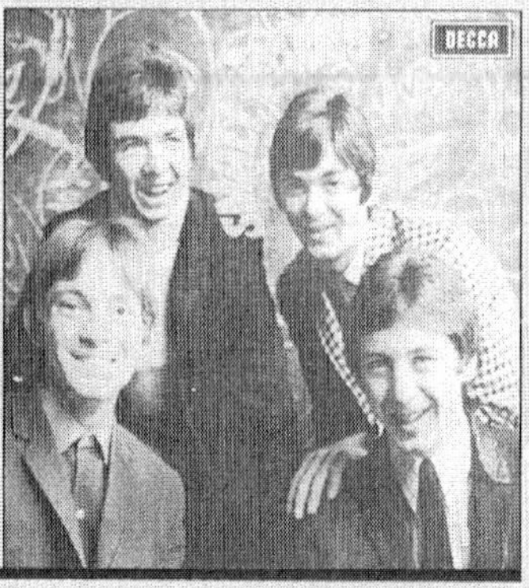

The Small Faces debut album in 1966 was recorded in just three days under modest circumstances. The songs were a mixed bag of group compositions as well as outside material, but still mainly indebted to Rhythm and Blues.

SHAKE: With this Sam Cooke tribute the Small Faces used to open their gigs in the early days. One of the few fast numbers sung by Ronnie.

COME ON CHILDREN: One of the first Marriott/Lane compositions, extremely wild and rough, a showcase for Steve the shouter. The song's structure was arranged suitably simple and rhythmic, with hand clapping typical of the era.

YOU BETTER BELIEVE IT: A memorable, soulful Marriott/Lane number. B-side of the "I've Got Mine" single. An attractive group composition with an unusual acoustic guitar. Features fine organ work from Jimmy Winston.

ONE NIGHT STAND: A melancholic beat number with a beautiful melody.

WHATCHA GONNA DO ABOUT IT: The polished single version as opposed to the rougher alternative version that appeared on a French e.p. This number stayed in Steve's set right up until the end.

SORRY SHE'S MINE: An unspectacular Kenny Lynch composition, nicely naïve with typical beat references.

E TO D: A very dynamic, unrefined bastard consisting of just two chords i.e. "from E to D" Written by Steve and Ronnie, it has snappy guitar riffs and Steve's almost shrieking voice. The song presents untypical but contemporary words which point in the direction of "All Or Nothing". " Sometimes I feel like a frustrated child/ I've got everything I want/ There's nothing that I need/ I can't stop my brain from running wild". It's hardly surprising that this number tends to appear under the title "Running Wild" from time to time, especially on US compilations.

YOU NEED LOVING: A blues orientated Marriott/Lane song, which supposedly was shaped upon Willie Dixon's "You Need Love". Muddy Waters had recorded this number by his former bass player in 1962 for Chess Records. Anyway, the Small Faces revamped the thing from scratch and with Steve's treatment it developed into something of it's own. It was Led Zeppelin who really stole parts of "You Need Loving" for their "Whole Lotta Love" and Robert Plant quite impressively copies Steve's phrasing. He actually met Steve backstage in Atlanta in the 70s and said sorry! In 1987 Willie Dixon sued Led Zeppelin for plagiarism and they settled out of court. Interestingly enough Marriott/Lane's " You Need Loving! wasn't even mentioned!

DON'T STOP WHAT YOU'RE DOING: In a way this is the "lightweight" counterpart to the Tamla Motown standard "Baby Don't Do It" which the Small Faces also had in their live set (and which Steve's Humble Pie mark two re-recorded in 1980). This isn't terribly exciting.

OWN UP: An instrumental band effort with a classic blues chord sequence. Hard-hitting, crashing guitar riffs combined with Mac's warm organ improvisations.

SHA-LA-LA-LA-LEE: The rather frowned upon hit single as the final number. Nothing but a beat period piece. With Steve very much in command they manage to induce quite a lot of fire into a mediocre song. There was a rumour that Steve had managed to find out which shops were going to get interviewed for the charts for the crucial weekend and he sent his friends to buy the single copies accordingly. After "Payola" here was "Buyola" !

This debut album appeared in the shops at the end of May 1966, just in time for their UK tour in June. It climbed as far as a respectable number 3 and stayed in the British album charts for six months.

Album review by Uli Twelker and Roland Schmitt.
Authors of the wonderful "Happy Boys Happy" Small Faces and beyond book.

NO KISSING, CUDDLING OR CLOSE EMBRACING.

AN INSIGHT INTO THE SMALL FACES AND WHO TOUR OF AUSTRALIA AND NEW ZEALAND IN 1968 BY A FAN THAT WAS THERE.

In late January 1968 The Who, The Small Faces and Paul Jones, ex lead singer of Manfred Mann, came to New Zealand as part of their first tour down-under. It was controversial as you will see.

For the New Zealand leg of the trip, concerts were scheduled for Auckland (29th January) and Wellington (31st January). Tickets went on sale for two shows per day in each city, a matinee show and an evening show. I managed to get a ticket for the matinee show in Wellington which was to be held in the Wellington town hall.

Getting to Wellington was a long trip and took around 24 hours. First there was the train ride from Invercargill to Lyttelton which in those days of steam would have taken about 12 hours, stops included. The next leg from Lyttelton to Wellington was by overnight ferry, the Wahine. As fate would have it the Wahine foundered a couple of months later in April 1968 at the entrance to Wellington harbour with the loss of 56 lives. In Wellington I stayed at the Peoples Palace which is a budget hotel located on Upper Cuba Street. The original hotel is still there and is now part of a large hotel complex.

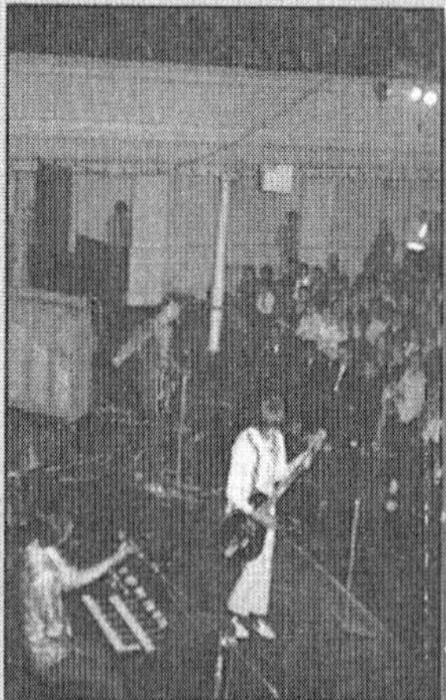

Although the controversy of the tour is now well documented the concert goers at the time knew nothing of what was happening or about to happen. The following piece sums it up nicely........

The "Big Show" tour by The Who, Small Faces and Paul Jones should have been a dream ticket but the only Australia/New Zealand visit by both of these legendary bands was unfortunately a disaster in many respects. Almost from the moment they stepped off the plane both groups ran into conflicts with the establishment and the media, who saw them as a dangerous and corrupting influence. The rebellious image of the "Orrible Oo" naturally attracted the attention of the Australian press who had long since acquired a well-earned reputation for being difficult, insensitive and often downright provocative. Even the media friendly Monkees ran into problems with belligerent Aussie journalists during their tour later the same year when they were aggressively grilled about their attitude to the Vietnam war.

The hostility of the Aussie press corporation is recounted by both Ian McLagan, who devotes a whole chapter to the tour in his biography "All The Rage", and by Keith Moons biographer Tony Fletcher. Both describe the hostility which erupted after a jet-lagged McLagan told Aussie journalists to "Fuck Off!" when questioned about his recent UK drug bust. This resulted in the touring party being harassed on a daily basis by the press.

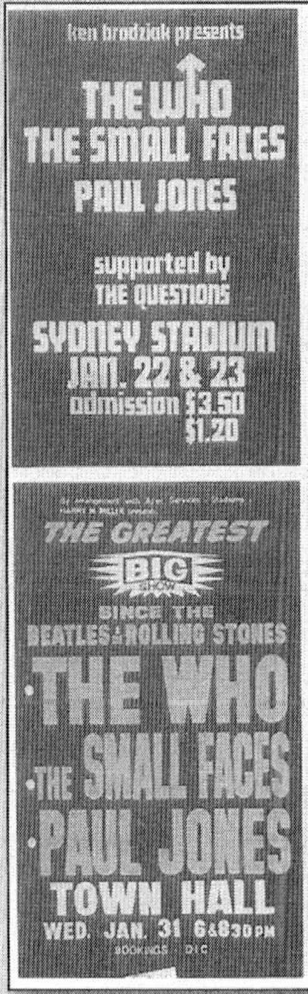

According to Rock historian Paul Conn there were constant conflicts with the promoters over the "appalling" sound system. Fletcher and McLagan both mention problems at the Sydney concert. The stadiums revolving stage was actually pushed around manually and when Steve Marriott got "pissed off" with the men pushing it they simply left it in one place, to the considerable annoyance of group and audience alike. By the next day the press had the bands pegged as "bad tempered louts". Several other incidents upset the establishment including Pete Townshend allegedly punching out at an Australian journalist (who could blame him?), altercations between band members and aggressive "fans" and the groups public expressions of frustration with the concert arrangements.

Not all of the tour was a bad experience though. Ian McLagan fondly recalls their reception in Adelaide, where the groups were met by a troop of expatriate English

Mods who gave them a "scootercade" escort into the city, took them to a pub and then down to the beach.

The problems and frustration finally come to a head during the flight back to Sydney from Adelaide on the 28th January. Ansett Airlines in those days did not permit in-flight drinking but, according to McLagan, members of Paul Jones Australian backing band had smuggled bottles of beer onto the plane and were passing it around. A stewardess complained to Who roadie, Bob Pridden, who was evidently in no mood for a lecture and told her, in no uncertain terms, where to get off. The stewardess immediately complained to the pilot who radioed ahead and arranged for the touring party to be intercepted by airport security and police at Sydney's Essendon airport. The party was escorted off the plane and into a first class lounge...where to their great amusement they were served with drinks! After which they were escorted on to their flight to New Zealand.

Prime Minister John Gorton sent Pete Townshend a telegram telling The Who never to come back to Australia. Townshend reportedly sent back a fruity reply and left Australia swearing never to return. Once in New Zealand things calmed down briefly although they again ruffled establishment feathers in Auckland when Keith Moon and Steve Marriott indulged in their famous penchant for wrecking hotel rooms.

There was a comical postscript to the story in the year 2000 when Roger Daltrey and John Entwhistle returned to Australia as part of another "Big Show", the Ultimate Rock Symphony Tour which included guitarist Simon Townshend, younger brother of Pete. It was reported in the Sydney press that at one of the shows Daltrey made a pointed reference to the events of the '68 tour and the telegram from the Prime Minister. He vented his anger by smashing a guitar on stage. Unfortunately instead of using his own guitar Daltrey inadvertently grabbed Simon Townshend's prized 2000 dollar Maton acoustic guitar and reduced it to matchwood!

To be honest I can't remember a great deal about the actual concert itself, other than Paul Jones opening the show followed by Small Faces and lastly The Who, but they've all been very well documented in the Keith Moon biography "Dear Boy", Ian McLagan's biography "All The Rage" and the excellent Andy Neill publication "A Fortnight Of Furore" from 1998. All of which are worth searching out.

TOM BLAINEY

GIVE HER MY REGARDS

THE FIRST EVER STEVE MARRIOTT REVIEW FROM THE 1963 MUSIC MAGAZINE "POP WEEKLY"........REPRODUCED WORD FOR WORD WITH KIND PERMISSION FROM AUTHOR OF THE PIECE, ANGELA SLAYDON.

NEW TO YOU.....STEVE MARRIOTT

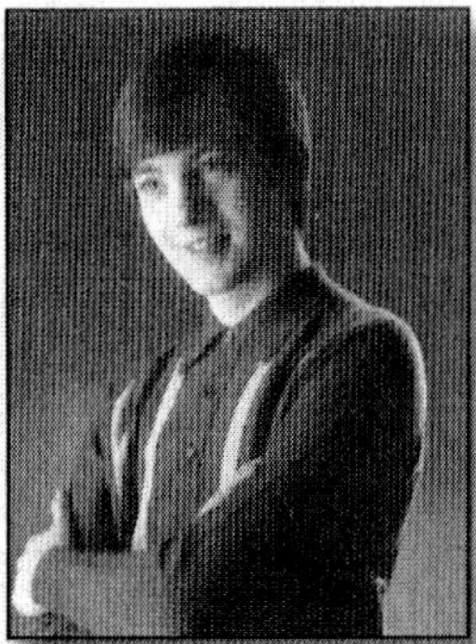

Nuthin' but nuthin comes easily in the pop music business. You've gotta have a heart, talent....and persistency, which the likeable Steve Marriott, now out on Decca with Give Her My Regards, has in abundance.

Come back a few months. Steve wrote a song called Imaginary Love and felt sure it might have possibilities if only he knew how to go about getting it published. He talked to his aunt, who was once secretary to impresario Jack Hylton. She suggested he took it down Tin Pan Alley, alias Denmark Street, off of London's Charing Cross Road.

Steve was then only 15 but he went to every publisher he could find. Nobody was even remotely interested.....except to wonder at a young chap like that having so much nerve.

Back he went to his Auntie Sheila. She rang Mr. Hylton, who gave her the address of a publishing company in Savile Row. Steve went along clutching his demo disc. Said the publisher; "The song, well that's OK but the voice, that's terrific. How'd you like to record?"

The outcome is a new disc on Decca recorded by former song star Franklyn Boyd for Belinda Recordings. Looks like it's going to be a good seller.......

So now, at 16, Steve had achieved a great deal in show business. East Ham born, at the age of 11 he was given a plastic ukulele by his Dad. At 12 he was given a proper guitar for a Christmas present. The same year he auditioned for Oliver and stayed in the West End production for a year. Steve said " That smell of grease paint was all I needed. I signed on for the Italia Conti acting school and I'm still there".

He's been in Peter Pan, he's been on the telly with Sid James and Mr.Pastry and on the radio in Mrs. Dales Diary and also made a film with Peter Sellers and Eric Sykes called Heavens Above which will soon be on general release. Whenever Steve can get away from his acting activities he's seen playing with his own group, the Moonlights at London clubs such as the Flamingo.

Give a listen to his debut disc. A snappy, fast-beater, good lyrics, happy tune with just a touch of the Buddy Holly's about it. Enough anyway to make comparisons justifiable. Steve said "I must admit, I think Buddy Holly was the greatest and I suppose my voice is very similar to his. I certainly don't try to copy his style, in a way though it's flattering for me to be even mentioned in the same breath as that late great American star."

Over the past year, Steve has picked up a handy salary what with his acting, singing and song writing activities but his mother won't stand for any wild spending. "It's all banked, my mother gives me a pound a week pocket money. That just about keeps me going".

Steve also finds time to collect animals. He remembers, not so long ago, hatching a ducks egg in front of the fire at home. His only difficulty is keeping and looking after all the variety of animals he takes a fancy to. Steve said "Apart from that, I guess my favourite occupation is going down to the café at home and just talking with my friends. And girls, of course, I was checking up just the other day and I reckon I must have had over 50 girlfriends since I was 11. Funny the effect some of them have on me. When the last one left me I felt so sad I just sat down and wrote sad songs. Before I knew where I was I'd put about thirty of them on paper".

But there's nothing sad now about Steve's all-round show business career. The Decca folk are rootin' for his disc and he has the experience to build on any success he gets.

PS: He's a good looker, as well.

Sadly the single Give Her My Regards/Imaginary Love (Decca F11619) didn't sell very well and Steve had to wait a further two years before tasting commercial success with the Small Faces. In recent times a number of pre-Small Faces Steve Marriott tracks have surfaced none better than the most recent. An Austrian fan currently living in Guatemala contacted Wapping Wharf (the wonders of the internet) with a late 1964 demo disc featuring our Stevie on vocals. Steve was cutting demos for songwriter Barry Mason at the famous Regent Sound studio in Tin Pan Alley and this particular track called "Give All She's Got" features a prominent Hammond organ and a vocal performance by Steve that's as good as anything he ever done! Quite a statement eh? But, on this track, the 17 year old cockney sounds like a middle aged black man. Take my word for it this performance is pure class and it'll see the light of day next year on a Wapping Wharf Steve Marriott Anthology. NICE!!

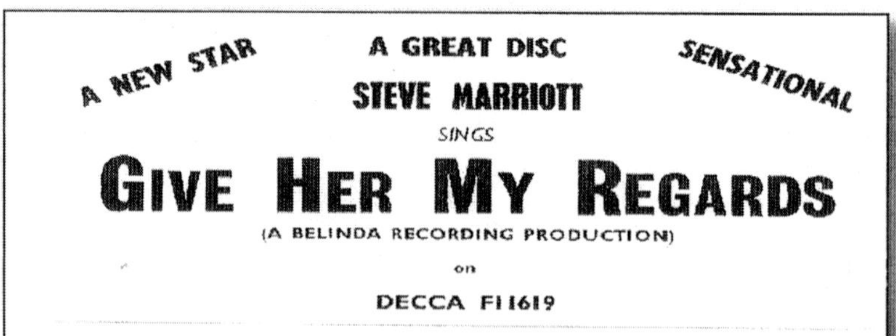

TALE OF AN AGEING MOD

SMALL FACES FAN, EILEEN WILLIAMS FROM ROMFORD, ESSEX LOOKS BACK WITH FOND MEMORIES OF TEENAGE LIFE IN THE MOST EXCITING ERA OF THEM ALL, THE MID 60S.

I was very fortunate to be born when I was. The second world war was over and Great Britain was indeed great. In the1960s England must have been the most exciting place on earth. My friend Joan and I grew up together and attended the same school in Romford. Most Saturdays we'd jump on the train and head for Carnaby Street. In those days it was very different to what it is now, the shops and boutiques were small and costly. If we saw something we wanted to purchase we normally had to put a deposit on it and pay off the remainder by weekly instalments until the balance was cleared, no such thing as credit cards in those days. Musically we started off loving Buddy Holly and Elvis but then moved on to The Who, Yardbirds, Booker T and many others. In 1964 we became Mods, we were never bored, we lived for music, dancing and clothes. We'd spend many hours in the booth at Wells record store in Romford listening to our favourite discs and most weekends it was on the back of a boyfriend's scooter and down to Brighton.

Our taste in music was heightened one night at one of our local haunts, the Willow Rooms. Main group on the bill was local favourites Scrooge and the Misers but it was the support band that made most impact on us. The vocalist was Steve Marriott (with the Moments) and out of this diminutive Gent came a voice that tore into your soul. He was electric and completely blew us away. After that we followed him and his group everywhere we could. Another band we followed was the Outcasts. We first saw them at a church hall in Forest Gate. This was our first sighting of Ronnie Lane and Kenny Jones. We were kept very busy following both of these bands and occasionally the two bands would play together. It was shear heaven and so were the parties we used to go to, only wish I could go back to some of them. I was grounded several times but as soon as I was shut in, I would just climb out the bedroom window, good job we lived in a bungalow. Joan wasn't so lucky; our drainpipe antics had us in hysterics.

When the Small Faces formed in 1965 we went to loads and loads of their gigs and when Mac joined Joan fell in love with him. We hitch hiked to many venues; you could do that in those days. This was the swinging sixties and you could do just about anything. My favourite singles of theirs are Tin Soldier, Itchycoo Park and Afterglow. They were just so stylish but when the teen hysteria kicked in it caused problems. They couldn't hear what they playing; shame, and Steve and Ronnie together must have been the greatest song writing team ever!

I was at the Alexandra Palace gig on New Years Eve 1968 when Steve decided to leave the band. Initially we were both upset as Steve is THE greatest vocalist of them all but I also loved the Jeff Beck Group and when I heard that Rod and Ronnie Wood were to join the remaining band I was in seventh heaven.

I saw Steve with Humble Pie at the Marquee club and again in 1973 at the Kursaal Ballroom in Southend. In 1977 I went to Newcastle where he'd kicked off the Small Faces second time around tour. It was a great show but there was a bit of heckling. Steve dealt with that very efficiently and soon had the audience eating out of his hand. The next show was in Leeds but after that my own work as an entertainer clashed with the tour and I didn't see anymore until Hammersmith Odeon.

As for the Faces, well that really was something else. Joan said I was on a mission; she was probably right as I hardly ever missed a show. One day in 1973 I was working at a holiday camp in Norfolk and only had one day off a week but if the Faces were playing that day was spent on a train travelling to wherever they were. My favourite Faces album is "Nods", that band were so hot at the time that if you got too close you would burst into flames!

In 1973 when Ronnie Lane left the soul of the band seemed to go with him. Tetsu replaced Ronnie but it was never the same. Now I was following Ronnie and his group Slim Chance. Shortly after this I suffered a nervous breakdown and hit rock bottom. Music was my only aid, so I wrote to Ronnie, who was then living at Fishpool, through his fan club and received a beautiful letter back. Ronnie's letter inspired me to get better and slowly I recovered. Thanks Ronnie. I'd hoped to see his Passing Show but I was working abroad and by the time I'd returned it had folded. Still I was still able to follow Slim Chance and had many a great night listening to them at different venues around the country. I love The Poacher, Barcelona, Richmond, How Come, Roll On Babe….the list is endless and my favourite Ronnie album is See Me from 1980.

In 1982 I started to do dance marathons for charity and in August 1984 began a five day, four night Belly Dance marathon for the charity Bliss. It was hard going especially in the hours of early morning. However a member of the Red Cross had the answer. Between the hours of 3am and 7am we played the Small Faces to which I would dance to. At 07.00 we resumed the Belly Dance music and I danced for 106 hours. We raised £1300 for Bliss and I got my name in the Guinness Book Of Records. Couldn't have done it without the boys. Thanks guys or as Steve would have said NICE!

My son, Ian was an avid Small Faces fan. He was in the Royal Navy and when on leave would always treat us to a rendition of Lazy Sunday and Happy Days Toytown. Sadly, he died in 1993 in a tragic accident. Steve and Ronnie also went before their time but they will never be forgotten and incidentally Joan is still in love with Mac. I think the plaque in Carnaby Street in the bands honour is wonderful. Thanks boys for all the pleasure you've given me and all of your other fans. I extend the same to Rod and Ronnie, of course. I love you all.

EILEEN (an ageing Mod)
Ps: Still can't get to sleep at night until I've had a burst of Small Faces on my headset first.

SMALL FACES: TRAVEL IS A NIGHTMARE (and other things!)

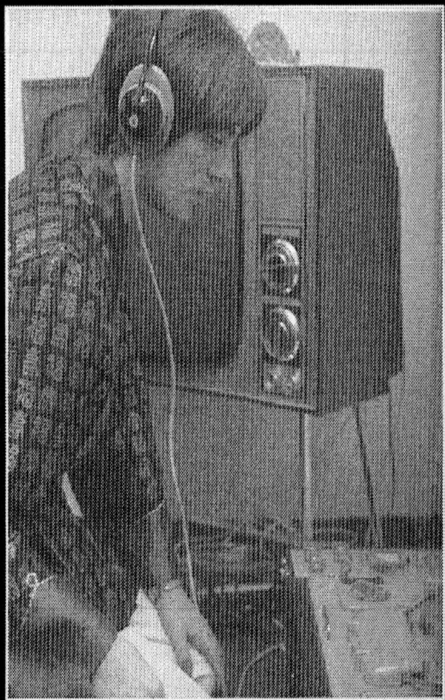

Keith Altham speaks with Ronnie Lane and Dad.

The Small Faces most often through no fault of their own find great difficulty in getting from place to place ie; interviews, photographic sessions and gigs and so it was last week that I went to them or rather to Ronnie "Plonk" Lanes pad just off Earls Court. What with a lively discussion between him and his father on the Beatles new philosophy of life (Ronnie is one of "yeractual" meditators), a sneak preview of the new Beach Boys Smiley Smile LP and his lovely girlfriend Sue to look at…it proved a very pleasant rainy afternoon.

Having relieved me of my raincoat, Ronnie settled into his armchair and talked of the Small Faces travelling problems. "Last week we arrived in Norwich to find the promoter had us down to play the day before" said Ronnie "all the publicity was for the day previous so only a few kids turned up. Then we missed at gig at Streatham completely. That was because we were returning from a Paris TV show and Stevie's French taxi driver missed the airport! At least the driver missed the turn off on the motorway and because it was a motorway they had to go right to the end to turn round, by which time the plane had gone. Anyway, by that time we'd realised we were at the wrong airport and had to drive to the right one. Poor Steve arrived in London around midnight with no money in his pocket, he was stranded. We'll have to make it up to them and play the gig another time.".

Seeing the Small Faces on stage is becoming something of a rarity these days and I asked Ronnie if this was a deliberate policy to play less ballrooms and clubs. This week they are off promoting in Europe and next month there are only two bookings for live performances. "Let's face it, ballrooms and clubs are a bit of a drag now "said Ronnie "we've done two and a half years of those kind of dates. Hard slog. Anyone that wanted to see us must have done so by now. When I was a kid I never liked who you saw on the TV all the time. I went to see the inner circle groups like Nero and the Gladiators, the Piltdown Men and I used to

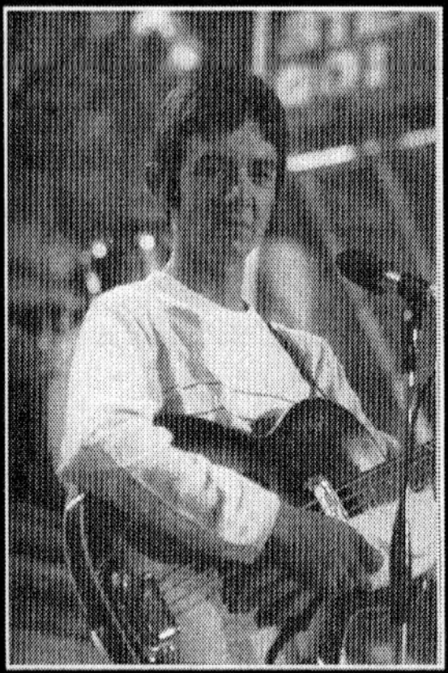

stand with mouth agape while Jimmy Page played guitar with the Crusaders".

"We have to get out and about to find new ideas for our songs. Steve and I took a cabin cruiser, the Maid Maureen, down the Thames recently. and a few ideas for songs came out of that. We got as far as Reading, hit every mud bank between there and Thames Ditton".

"We've got a tour of Australia being negotiated for a couple of month's time and a loon in the Philippines before that. You've got to get out and do things or you find a brick wall when you're looking for new songs. Itchycoo Park was written on our last European tour".

Talking ceased for a while and listening began as Ronnie's vegetarian lunch was brought in by Susie. He set about his cauliflower and cheese sauce while the new Beach Boys album Smiley Smile was playing. This album is going to stand some Beach Boys fans right on their heads because much of the new material and interpretation is straight from Mothers Of Invention land. It might as well have been titled "Music To Get Stoned By" or "How High Brian Wilson?". Let me add, hastily, that it is brilliantly played and has a deliberate ambiguity so that you can enjoy it even if you miss the point. It is a masterful piece of production. A great deal is satirical and Vegetables (in which listeners are invited to write letters naming their favourite vegetables after which eating they will feel better) is one of the most outstanding tracks. Other titles include the dreamy She's Going Bald (Frank Zappa for Pope!), Getting' Hungry, the Mike Love/Brian Wilson opus which was issued as a single here, Wind Chimes, which sounds like what it says, With Me Tonight and an extraordinary instrumental. Ronnie summed it up quite succinctly between mouthfuls of cauliflower "A lot of people won't be able to see the wood for the trees. It sounds as though Wilson recorded the whole thing at home" "I understand he has a recording studio built into his house, that's the way to do it, man. The Beach Boys were getting too intricate and intellectual. There's some nice simple things here, it's nice!"

Following a brainful of Beach Boys I got a mindful of Ken Cordine and his Colours album, available here on Philips. A spoken narrative of the verbal associations of colours ie: "Olive is over-used, Lavender is an old, old, old woman, Burgundy moves slowly. Against musical settings it is a great deal more clever than I can make it sound in cold print. "It's Steve's LP" said Ronnie" great isn't!"

It was about this time that it all began to happen. As Ronnie was lighting a cigarette (he likes to roll his own) his Dad arrived. Mr. "Plonk" Lane proved to be a stocky, bespectacled, grey-haired man with a Volkswagen. He is a very pleasant, down to earth person who has obviously worked very hard as a lorry driver but in no way resents his son's success and

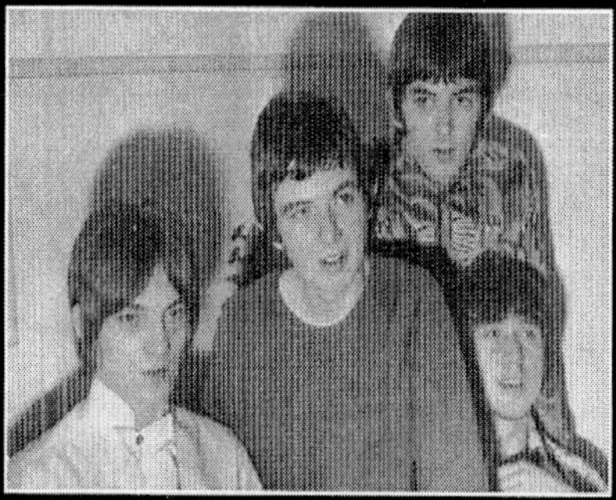

there is a good warm relationship between them.

The discussion began in reference to the Beatles recent TV appearances and their attitudes toward Yoga and meditation. Dad took the part of a very typical parent and Ronnie was careful not to express himself too forcefully and offend his father, but very clearly it illustrated the old and the new attitudes. This discussion, if not verbatim, is a fair reflection of the conversation.

"I don't think Lennon and Harrison should have done those programmes (referring to the Frost Programme), said Mr. Lane. " The average man in the street doesn't have time for all the deep thinking. A lorry driver comes home, watches a bit of TV and then goes to the local for a drink and a game of cards with the lads. He doesn't want to sit there meditating on the state of the world. His Immediate concerns are his family, his wage packet and his car". "And you know as well as I do that all these material things won't bring him happiness" said Plonk "not the car, not the TV or the money. This idea isn't deep at all. All the Maharishi and the Beatles suggest is that people would live better, more effective lives, if they sat down for a few minutes each day and thought about things. Young people are desperately unhappy doing jobs they don't like and now they are asking, why should I? I was unhappy in the factory where I worked. During your life-time you went through two world wars and there wasn't much time to think about things but now there is and the chance to do something about it. "But you're an exception" countered Mr. Lane "you've worked hard and you have talent. Most kids don't even want to entertain themselves let alone anyone else". "You only think that because I'm your son" said Ronnie "the milkman could have done what I've done if he had wanted to know and made the effort. Ultimately what will happen is that the teachings of people like Maharishi will be adopted into the normal education". "But you can't impress abstract and collective ideas upon individuals" said Mr. Lane "it's very difficult to convince a docker that he should be learning Yoga when he's fighting for a wage increase to keep his wife and children". "All this is relative to the individual" said Ronnie "it would help them put things in perspective. It is happening. It will happen. The acorn is there in the ground and from acorns you get Oak trees."

And that ended the debate of Lane versus Lane as I regretfully had to leave. I returned five minutes later to get my raincoat (Ronnie gets more raincoats that way). "Don't put that in the story" grinned Ronnie. Incidentally Ronnie, that red biro you write all your songs with and which you lent me…I still have (I get more biros that way).

Previously published in NME (14th October 1967)

Legendary 60s Mod

About Small Faces at the Goldhawk and his Irish MS Benefit Concert.

It was sometime in Winter 1965, there was a special buzz in the air because they were a top twenty band but I can also recall a definite tension down on the dance floor because let's face it, the Small Faces were not a local band, not like the Who. We felt they invaded our sacred turf coming to the Goldhawk and bringing with them their unmistakeable Cockney swagger all the way from the East End. It was alright to see the Small Faces playing up west in Soho where West London Mods mingled freely with East London Mods but playing at the Goldhawk! Come off it. Id never seen them before and they sounded to me like they were more evenly presented than the Who. I couldn't put my finger on it at first and then it occurred to me that it was their organist playing the Hammond which filled out their surge of sound. It was very danceable, not at all the guttural guitar chords produced by the Who. What hit me was the sheer power of Marriott's voice. It was almost like if you closed your eyes for a second you'd think he was black. I pushed nearer the stage and I couldn't keep my eyes off of him. The veins on his neck stood out like they were ready to pop. I remember going into the toilets before the band went on stage. The usual clique were gathered selling there pills and there was that tell-tale ring of spittle around everyone's mouths. I wanted to score some blues and noticed there in the middle was the bleeding Artful Dodger himself, Steve Marriott. He was small, jumpy, bony, his hair like a creation parted in the middle. I thought "Is this really him? Is the bloke everyone's talking about? He moved over to the urinal and while I waited to use it, I stared at the back of his head at the wonderful hair. I noticed how thin his shoulders were, he was like some geezer who had mitched off school. I realised in a rush of excitement that this bloke was the genuine article, a true little Face.

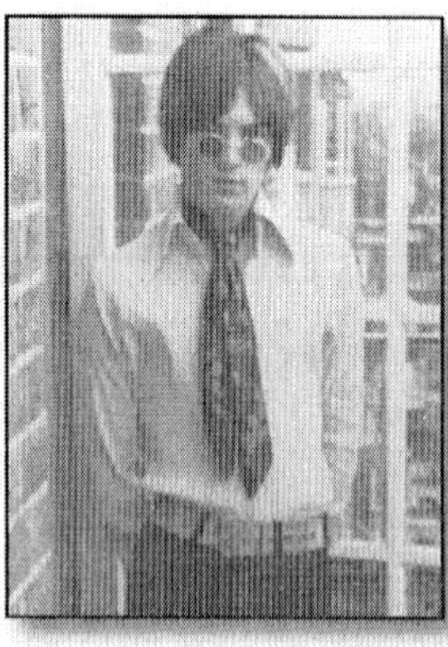

It was after coming back to Cork in Ireland in the very late sixties that I got thinking about my old friend, Ronnie Lane. Pete Townshend did an album with him but Pete told me that Ronnie was difficult to work with. Ronnie was my old Mod mate from Plaistow, how could he be difficult? He was a charmer and I fell under his spell. Pete told me that when Ronnie came down to Eel Pie studios they did a few songs for Rough Mix, which was supposed to be a kind of raiser for Ronnie's complaint, and after a few tracks he insulted Eric Clapton…it was like "I know you're supposed to be a world class guitarist but can you cut the mustard on this very important album?" Poor Eric, he was an obliging man and didn't know where to show his face: he was doing Pete a big favour. Ronnie could upset anyone. I always liked him 'cos

Irish Jack talks.......

he was a cheeky chappie, he even invented a kind of Townshend/Lane scowl on stage at the Marquee. And when he came off stage I challenged him on it and his reply was "You're from fucking Goldhawk, ain't cha?" I said "Yeah, I am, my name's Irish Jack and I'm a mate of Pete Townshend's." He shut up after that.

When I discovered he had Multiple Sclerosis and what it implied, I was devastated. People like Ronnie live forever, so I thought more and more about the boy from Plaistow who had delivered false teeth from a hole in the wall operation in the East End on a scooter…long, long before Whatcha Gonna Do About It. And I thought "I know I'll put on a gig in aid of MS for our local group and for Ronnie. I phoned Ronnie Lane in Austin, Texas and we spoke for over an hour…..wonder why the phone bill was so high! Just hearing his voice made me feel I was a Mod again and back in my beloved Goldhawk Social Club on Goldhawk Road where I saw them. How can I convey to anybody reading this what it was like? And you can see from reading this, when Ronnie Lane says "You old Mod you! " You are a fucking Mod! You are from Shepherds Bush. You ARE from the Goldhawk Road. You ARE from Kelscott Gardens in Askew Road just across the street from Little Percy where your old mate Roger Daltrey is from!! So how much more can I say about my old friend Ronnie Lane? You tell me.

(Letter dated 11th April 1986)

Dear Ronnie
Hi, Irish Jack here. I enclosed this letter in another letter that I've written to Mac and Kim. Well, Ron, I expect that by now you have heard about the benefit concert I'm putting on here in Cork in aid of our local MS Society. If it hasn't been explained to you already by Kim I should point out to you that naturally most of the money raised through the concert will be going to our local organisation and then depending on the amount realised you will receive a token distribution. If it's OK with you I have suggested to Kim in my letter to her that I send the cheque to her and she can then send it on to you. I was very sorry to hear from Kim about what happened at ARMS. I hope it hasn't had any effect on your hard-won morale. Yes, Ron, I've heard from Pete that you're a brave 'un. Good on yer son!

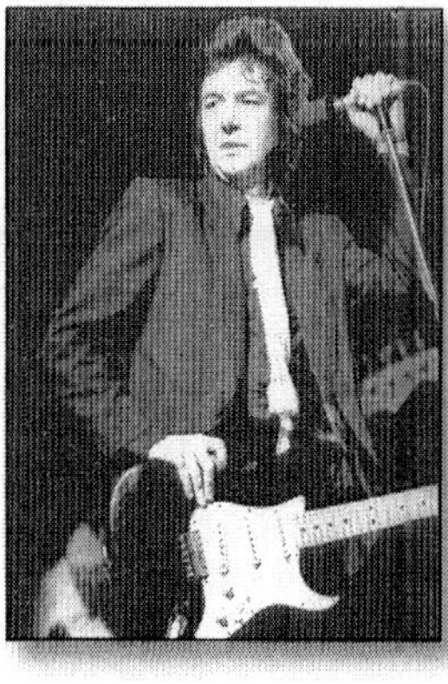

The reason I haven't contacted you earlier was because I thought it best to wait until I actually had the concert organised before writing to you. Now that everything is finally put into place I feel confident enough to be able to put finger to key and let you know exactly what this Irish nutter is up to. Originally what happened was that I wrote three stories about my reminiscences with the 'orrible 'Ooo! The idea was that our national Rock paper Hot Press would run the stories and I would donate my writing fee to your organisation ARMS. Well unfortunately, the editor of this August edition reckoned that my stories were too long. Since they were all about The Who, one on Townshend and two on Moonie and you have a long standing friendship with Pete I thought I would channel all of my efforts into the Benefit concert. I'm working completely alone without any phone in the house. Pete thinks I'm fucking insane to be involved in the music business here in Cork and operating out of half-vandalised telephone boxes. But I'm a man with dirt on the palm of my hands, Ron, and even now at 43 I've got more honest-to-God energy and dreams then I ever had when I spent half me time pilled up to the eye-balls and doing the Dog in the old Hammersmith Palais. My sole transport is a Honda 50!

What I've been doing in the past three years, apart from my normal job as a Postman, is working as a sort of promoter for a local hotel here. Our venue is called Sir Henry's and our concert hall can hold up to 500 people. We've had the likes of John Martyn and The Pogues here plus, of course, the usual top Irish bands like Moving Hearts and Stockton's Wing. In the past twelve months I haven't been involved in any concerts because the hotel got renovated and they decided to just have occasional concerts with an outside promoter. So really this is my first concert for over a year and as I explained to Pete, in my letter, I was really very nervous about approaching bands and the like. But gradually as the weeks went by I began to feel my old confidence coming back and now I'm really looking forward to the night.

To promote the concert some of our DJs on the national radio will be playing Small Faces singles in your honour. They will also mention the fact that you've got Multiple Sclerosis and that our concert will be donating a token distribution to your fund. The local radio station will also be giving away some free tickets to winners in a Small Faces phone-in quiz. A friend of mine, Dave Livingstone actually has a mint copy of Ogden's Nut Gone Flake; some people have all the luck! I'm about to persuade him to lend it to our radio station who'll play tracks from it. I've also written to Pete asking him if he would sponsor our newspaper ad for the concert. It'll be a two and a half inch double-column for our evening paper so I'm just waiting to hear back from him. God, I really do hope he agrees, we've been mates since '62. I've suggested to him, in my letter, that he could sponsor either under his name or else through Eel Pie Sound. Anyway, he only got my letter last week, maybe I'll get lucky.

A friend of mine who lives in New York (yes, another Corkman!), Paddy McCarthy has been in touch with Kim and she told Paddy about your Texas anniversary appearance and also the possibility of you appearing during the Faces re-union. I'm thrilled to hear about that, Ron, and I'm sure that you and Ian McLagan must be looking forward to it very much. Paddy did ring Chesley Millikins office and a girl there spoke to him and said she would give you a ring. Anyway, I've been in contact all the while with Kim, who I first wrote to about a year ago, and Kim told me she is in contact with you all the time.

Ronnie, this is important to me, I don't know whether your complaint allows you to be able to put pen to paper but is there any possibility that as soon as you receive this letter you write me a few brief lines, or send me a telegram, simply endorsing my Benefit Concert and you know, the usual message. A few words from you would go a long, long way to boost everyone's confidence involved in the event and I could then read it out on stage during the proceedings. It would mean a lot to the musicians taking part who will be playing for nothing. Though they are quite young and the music involved will be New Wave they all have a great deal of respect for you and a sharp awareness of the disabilities of MS. You're a legend here, boy! And as well as that, I've had to turn down some bands that were only too willing to give their services to MS and out of sheer respect for you.

Sorry that this letter has gone on and on but consider yourself lucky...Pete usually gets sixteen pages! Anyway, Ron thank you for taking the time to read this rather lengthy epistle. I've enclosed a kind of home-made press release on me which I sometimes use (if I hadn't sent you that this letter would never end). At the risk of a swelled head I've more or less listed some of the "things" that have happened to me. Did you know I spoke in your place at the First Annual Mod Convention in London in 1984? It was my proudest moment filling in for you. I wish you the very best, old son, and would consider it an unforgettable honour to meet you some sunny day. My personal dream is not to own a smashed Rickenbacker on my wall but to see New York. Maybe I'll make it one day.
In Friendship
Irish Jack
PS: Paddy McCarthy, two weeks ago, donated one hundred dollars to my Concert Benefit.

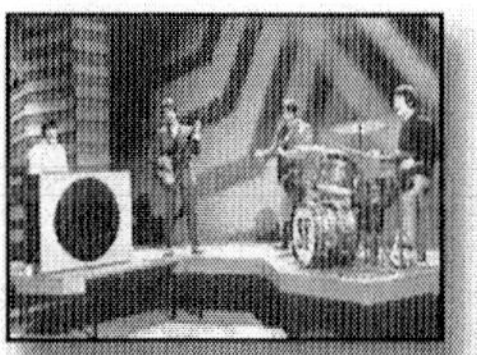

AND Ronnie's reply some six weeks later......
Dear Jack

Didn't receive your letter in time due to our nomadic change of locations but now I'm settled in one place. I would have loved to have supported your efforts with your May concert. I hope it went well and rest assured you will always have my support for any future events. Also, something which I have found which I think is quite interesting is if you suffer from MS it should be known that you are subject to many allergies, even if they are unconscious. That is one of my contributions as I am the best guinea pig that I have access to. I will be sending you more information on Dr. Robert Soll and his allergy strategy. You will also be able to read of the demise of USA ARMS in the future edition of Rolling Stone magazine. My new foundation is: The Ronnie Lane Foundation, PO Box 49190, Austin, Texas 78765. This address is for anyone interested in advice regarding Dr. Soll's approach or for donations to the Foundation. I want to further spread the Doctor's theory.
Please know that I truly respect your efforts over this problem in Cork in Ireland and I wish you my very best.
YOU OLD MOD YOU!
Ronnie

NICE GEAR MATE

A 19 year old fan spends the day with the original Mod"grand"father... A Steve Marriott interview.........(September 1986)

I first met Steve in 1985 after his Packet Of Three gig at the Camden Palace. After following his band around for the next year and having had the privilege of DJing a few times at some of his gigs (twice at the Fox, Palmers Green and once at my local, the Royal Standard in Walthamstow), Steve agreed to do an interview with me for the fanzine I was running at the time called All Or Nothing. He gave me his home phone number and told me to call him the following week to arrange a date and time. This I duly done and this dear readers is what you are about to read. It has not seen the light of day for over 24 years. I hope you enjoy reading it as much as I did conducting it. Now are you all sitting cumftybold two square on your botties? Then I'll begin.....

As I sat on the train speeding my way to Steve's Stanstead Abbotts home, I couldn't help feel nervous. Even though I had already met and known the great man for a few months I just could not shake off the nerves, just couldn't help it. I was about to spend the day with and interview the man whose music, words and style had influenced my life and still does to this day. I still idolise the great fella and will always do so.

As soon as we met those nerves disappeared. It was just like two mates going for a beer. He made me feel so instantly comfortable in his company and he was in a blinding mood, up for a drink and a laugh. There was also a huge mutual respect from the moment he looked me up and down and said "Nice gear, mate" referring to my Mod threads, yes I'd gone dressed to impress well I was going to meet the original Modfather, the guvnor!

We went to his local boozer, The Crown. It was a beautiful sunny September lunchtime and I couldn't help thinking about The Universal. We walked into the bar and it was obvious by the greeting that Steve got, from the owner and the two locals sat at the old Oak bar, that he wasn't a stranger to the place. We had a drink at the bar and this is where the flaw in my drinking plan appeared. Steve asked what I wanted and I, in my infinite wisdom, had a pint of locally brewed wallop about 6 % in volume and Steve ordered a white wine spritzer. Immediately I could see where this might lead. We had a drink at the bar and I got the next one in and we headed out into the warmth of the garden where we settled at a wooden bench table. I started the tape machine and as we sipped our drinks and rolled our fags under the mid day sun the interview commenced.

Firstly, we spoke of his involvement in the Mod scene prior to the Small Faces formation in 1965. Steve recalled "Well, I was just one, mate. It's like you now. There weren't a lot of Mods to begin with, there was only a few. I just loved the clothes. I used to save up all me dough and go down Carnaby Street" I asked what Carnaby Street was like back in the day, as I took another gulp of the pint of diesel I had in my glass. He continued "The funny thing about Carnaby Street was that it was only a couple of dingy little shops and they used to import clothes from Italy and France and a mate of mine,

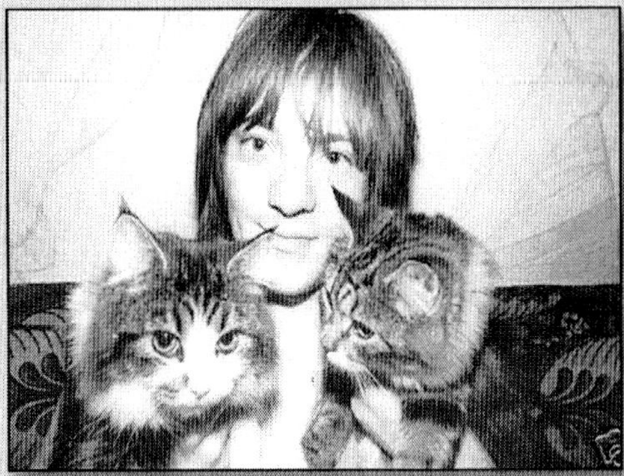

who I used to hang about with at the Square Ring coffee bar in Manor Park, turned up wearing all this gear and he told me where to get it. It was fucking expensive, so I had to save up for it"." In the beginning Mods were new, a never seen before creature. People who were not hip to it gave us a very funny reaction. Me and Ronnie used to get laughed at. We got wolf whistles from geezers on building sites and me ol' man didn't like it at all. I mean it took a lot of courage in those days but, to be honest, I think there's more Mods now than there were back then, in the beginning anyway. Now every gig I play I see Mods but in those days it was a more select crowd. If you went up north there were no Mods to start with but in the end they really took it up. I mean Manchester and Sheffield were totally Mod, 100%. Another snifter of his white wine and Perrier water and he continued to explain with a passion on the subject (remember the old maxim…once a Mod always a Mod). It was nice to be different. That's the way I feel about it anyway. It's all to do with mates as well, I mean you look around and there's gotta be one geezer around who looks a bit different. You have a look, ask him where he got the clobber from, he tells ya and you become a Mod without even realising it. That's the way it went". Briefly dipping into my tobacco tin he carried on "The media called us Mods" he explained "We didn't know what the fuck it was, y'know, we just liked button-downs, same barnet as yours (referring to my circa 1966 Marriott backcomb) and when I look back it was fuckin' great"." But I couldn't do it now. I'd be like a cartoon of me self (laughs), a fuckin' parody. No, I leave it to people like you to carry that flag, mate, 'cos you do it better than I could, if I did it I'd look like an old man in young mans clothes. It would be stupid".

Having a deep rooted love of music myself I was interested to know who Steve's own musical influences were and still are. "Booker T and the MGs, then people like Otis Redding" "So it was the R&B thing then?" I asked "Oh yeah, absolutely. I mean if it wasn't black then I didn't listen to it. That's why I was so surprised when I got done by that black guy the other night (Steve's referring to the other night when a black guy lobbed a glass at him whilst on stage, cutting his hand leaving him requiring stitches), I thought what the fuck, I've been pioneering this music all my life".

During the 1960s there were a lot of bands that jumped on the Mod bandwagon like The Who. They were just lads who were groomed into the Mod thing by one time manager Pete Meadon. I asked Steve what he thought of this at the time. "I thought they were great, mate. At the time we didn't know that did we? It's only in retrospect and hindsight that you can see the way that he and later Kit Lambert kitted them out"." But then you had the legitimate bands like The Action, they were the same as the Faces, just off the streets, not groomed at all. But you've got it dead right, mate. There were a lot of bands like Grapefruit, Johns Children and The Gods; they were groups that were made that way. They were sent out to go and get clothes and stuff from this or that particular shop. There were a lot of rotten, horrible bands who had a lot of money spent on them and they amounted to fuck all really" he pauses to light his roll up "Out of all that quagmire of bands The Small Faces rose to the top because we were legitimate and I think it showed" he finished proudly and I for one couldn't help but agree with him.

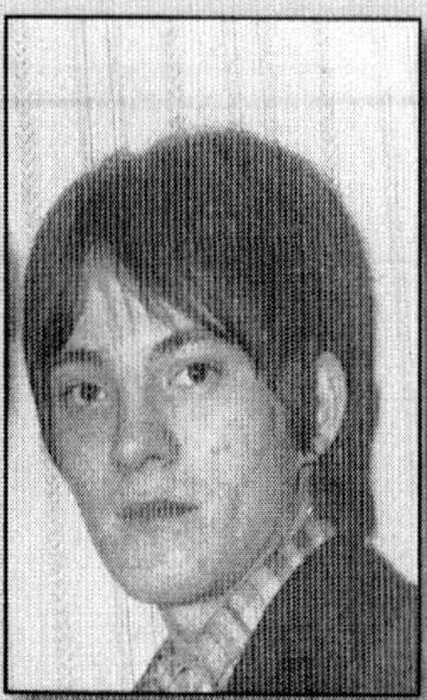

So clothes played a major part in the Mod culture of this time, I asked Steve if the Small Faces ever tried to impress their Mod image onto the scene. "No mate, it's just the way we were. I think we were just a little Moddy band who were that way before we got discovered. Unlike The Who who had everything bought for them. That's how Townshend could afford to smash his guitar every fuckin' night 'cos he had rich management who'd go out and buy him another fuckin' ten or so, whereas we didn't". I then asked him what that period of time during the mid sixties meant to him. This was met by a huge grin and his trademark dirty East End laugh "A fuckin' great time, mate, fuckin' great. Tarts for days, drugs up the arse, marvellous time, mate". He carries on laughing away as if re-running some of the funnier highlights of the time. So what did he feel was his greatest achievement of that time? "Fucking Chrissie Shrimpton!" came his immediate answer as we both fell into fits of uncontrollable ribald laughter. I must say he also looked pretty smug with himself too. Who wouldn't I suppose?

We turned our attention to America and I asked Steve why the Small Faces never toured there. "Dunno mate" he replied shrugging his shoulders "We were scheduled to go there, we were booked to do Fillmore East with The Move. I don't know why we didn't go. I don't even know if The Move went"." I think it's a case of English managers didn't like you going to America in those days because they didn't have control over you. It would have meant English management farming you out to Yank management and vice versa. You see management like control and when they can't get it they get the horrors, like they're gonna get shafted the way they're shafting you".

We paused the interview here while Steve sauntered off to replenish our glasses with yet more alcohol. When he arrived back we spoke about his and Ronnie Lane's song writing. I asked him whether he felt that the two of them had written everything they could together by the time Steve left the band. After reflective thought he replied "Yes!" he paused again deep in thought and then continued "Yeah, we had another stab at it in 1981, when me and Ronnie did another album but it wasn't released. It was alright and we recorded some good stuff but I don't think Ronnie wanted it released. I think he wants to sit on it until he snuffs it or something or maybe that's just my thinking, I dunno. I've got copy tapes but not the masters, they're with Ronnie. We were pleased with it but not a lot of people know we done it. I'll do you a copy of it before you go" And true to his word he did me a copy of them and it is now and always has been one of my most treasured possessions, (the album Majic Mijits was eventually released in the year 2000). As we reflected on his and Ronnie's work we got back to their writing partnership during the Small Faces heyday of the 60s and I asked Steve what he felt Ronnie and himself had tried to convey in their songs. He laughed "Taking the piss. I used to take the piss as much as I could. Itchycoo Park was a piss-take, 'cos we were never too hippy trippy and all that. We used to take the piss out of ourselves and everything. We had a good sense of humour." "You still have" I retorted. "Well God bless ya, mate" he replied as he smiled that beaming Marriotty smile at me. So what did he feel was the best Marriott/Lane song?." Err, fuck knows. To be honest me and Ronnie didn't write an awful lot together. We wrote apart like Lennon and McCartney and Jagger and Richards. They wrote separately and heaped it together". He paused for a few seconds thoughtfully as he took another mouthful of his white wine and Perrier spritzer before looking up and saying "Rene, the Dockers delight was probably the one me and Ronnie laughed at the most and a thing called Happy Days Toy Town off the Ogden's LP, we wrote that together, oh and Itchycoo Park. Maybe those three sum me and Ronnie up. All the rest, well nigh on a hundred per cent of them were written apart. I wrote Tin Soldier, Lazy Sunday, All Or Nothing…stuff like that. Ronnie wrote the more obscure stuff, I tended to write the hits as it were". Again that unmistakeable dirty laugh emitted from the man.

A change of record company in early 1967 saw the band sign with Andrew Loog Oldham's newly formed Immediate Records and to the record buying public it seemed that the Small Faces were becoming more of a studio band. Steve went on to explain. "Well no, it wasn't that as such. We didn't really want to be known as anything really. We were just given the chance to experiment that's all that was. When we were with Decca we were told to make an album in three days. So you did that but with Immediate they were also our managers so it suited their purpose to have us in the studio as much as they could. Basically all we done was to set out to experiment in the studio a little more 'cos in those days you didn't have all the electrical gadgetry that they've got nowadays and it was a big time for experimentation" Again a little chuckle and he continued "We used to have tape loops running round the back of chairs and back onto the machine to get that desired effect. I suppose it could have looked like we were an album band but all we done was live in the studio for a fuckin' year or two".

I asked Steve whether he regretted leaving the Small Faces. "No mate, course not. When something's over it's over, innit mate? It's like people say to me "You form a band, get it to the top of its form and then you leave. Why?" And the thing is I don't like things that are formulated. If something works to a formula then it becomes boring, ya know what I mean? So I like leaving and starting all over again just like I'm doing now with Packet Of Three. We're having a great time. I'm enjoying myself twice as much as I was ten years ago with Humble Pie. I enjoy the band on its way, when it's got that bit of respect going for itself before it gets to the point of boredom. As soon as it's accepted I'm bored with it". The Small Faces finally bailed out in 1969. I asked him if he felt the band had maintained that respect that he had spoken of earlier. "I think so, mate, yeah. I think that I left at the right time. I think that if I'd hung about then we'd still be the Small Faces and not the legends that they are in your mind. We could have stuck it out and got all shitty but we split at a fuckin' good point, mate. On a high, so to speak". "I mean" Steve continued as he dipped into my bacci tin and rolled another cigarette "at the time Ronnie, Mac and Kenney couldn't understand it, it was like "What the fuck! Why the fuck are you leaving?" and I said if I leave now it gives us all a new lease of life. Individually you can go and do such and such and I can do this with all this under our belts and with a bit of respect. I did the same with Humble Pie; I left just as they were peaking out. But that's what you gotta do. As soon as it becomes money and not music you gotta go".

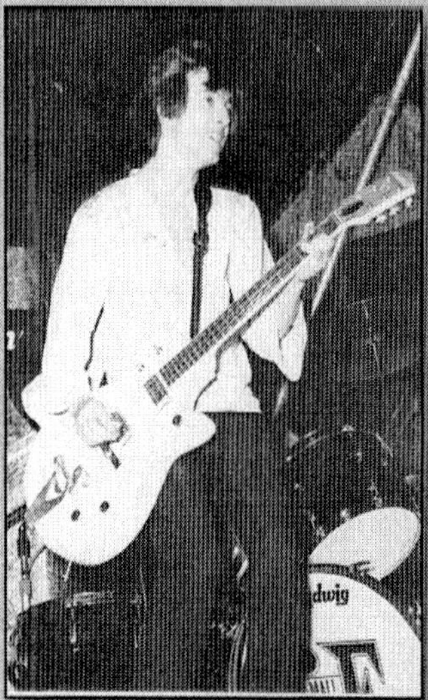

At this point our conversation shifted to the present and the Packet Of Three. I asked him why and when they were formed and how the somewhat delicate name came about." Well, why not?" I was living in America and I came back in '83 'cos me Dad was ill. I came back to see him and he turned out to be alright. I sort of got side-tracked into staying here really by Jim Leverton, who plays bass with me, and a couple of others said "Stick around and play over here for a bit" 'cos up to that point I'd just concentrated on America for years. I thought about it, found meself a new ol' lady, well I say new, she was me bird when I was 16 and it all felt good. So I said "Fuck it" and stayed". Steve once again had a chuckle to himself and looked as if he was re-running some old cine footage in his head. He continued "Why the name Packet Of Three? 'Cos there were three of us and we'd often laughed at what you'd call a three piece and Packet Of Three made us laugh the most. Once again it's the sense of humour thing and not taking things too seriously!" With one single, a new version of the song that started it all off back in 1965, Whatcha Gonna Do About It and an album under the Packets belt, I asked if there was anything else in the pipeline. "Yeah, oh yeah without a doubt. I've got a little studio set up in my bedroom. I've always had my own studio set up be it professional or amateur" Steve got visibly more enthused on this subject and carried on with great animation. "You see with Humble Pie I used to do everything, the whole lot. I'd engineer it, produce it, edit it, the lot and what I'm doing now is stock piling a whole lot of new songs for when we've got the time and the money to go into the studio and do it. But at the moment we don't have either" he said laughing. I asked him what kind of stuff he'd been working on and what we, the fans, can expect. Would it be an R&B type excursion? "Well no not really. It'll be like a continuation of what I've always done…silly old love songs or whatever. I suppose it will be R&B influenced 'cos that's the way I sing and that's the way I am. It's all good stuff, mate" So is there a hankering to break into the charts again? "NO, well it goes without saying really doesn't it? I've got fuck all to prove except when I'm playing live. That's when you've got to prove whether you're good or bad. Frankly records never made me any money anyway, they were just a giggle and lets face it you've gotta live. So that's why I'm playing live so much. Records have never been my living so I don't worry about it. Someone got the fuckin' money but it wasn't me, so who fuckin' cares". We now dipped our toes in the waters of his current live shows and I asked how long he planned to continue playing the smaller clubs and pubs. "Until I can, mate! Until there's no demand or I just physically can't do it any longer (little did we both know how poignant that statement was going to be). I mean it's where I belong, in pubs and clubs. I've done Shea Stadium and Madison Square Garden and frankly I got no satisfaction out of it. It was an experience but a totally unsatisfactory one. It was like playing to a fuckin' great pond. You might as well watch paint dry but when I play a pub you can actually see the people and they can see you sweating and working. You know there's no posing in it and that's what I believe in. I mean I've fallen into that trap of money, where you go and play some fuckin' great big Ice Hockey stadium in America and it's all for the money and not the music. Whereas you play the Walthamstow Standard, you pack it out and the atmosphere is fuckin' electric. That to me is what it's all about. I get a great buzz out of that".

As the afternoon drifted on and the alcohol flowed in abundance, I was beginning to regret my choice of drink as we were by now into our fifth round and this local brewed wallop was making this 19 year old decidedly half cut. We moved on to the subject of Mod revival bands of the day. Bands like The Prisoners, Fast Eddie and The Moment. I asked Steve what he thought of the current crop. "Yeah, they're good. It's very difficult to see, how shall I put it? They're doing everything that I've done. Even the tones on the guitars they use. To me it's a compliment but to be honest I think they've got their influences mixed up. They're more influenced by the Small Faces or whoever whereas we were more influenced by the black R&B and Soul artists. They're not really taking it back to the roots. They're just being influenced by something that was influenced by, if you know what I mean". During this period in time there were a few bands on the scene that were taking their influence from the R&B and Soul that was being spun in the Mod clubs of the time and the acts that Steve had pointed out earlier. I pointed out that there was an underground resurgence of this type of sound. "Well that's fuckin' great" came his reply." What worries me is that the music we had when we were nippers is no longer available. Alright you've got compilation albums but they're not the same. You know we had the more obscure stuff by The Contours and other groups like that. It's hard to get hold of that stuff now, you know, and it's a shame. You don't hear it on the radio, as such, anymore. They are influenced by the more accessible stuff, The Small Faces and The Who, but our influences went way back to early James Brown albums. I asked Steve if he was a big record collector back in the day. "Cor not half, mate! That's how I met Ronnie by playing him all these songs and records. I cabbaged him with sounds as it were".

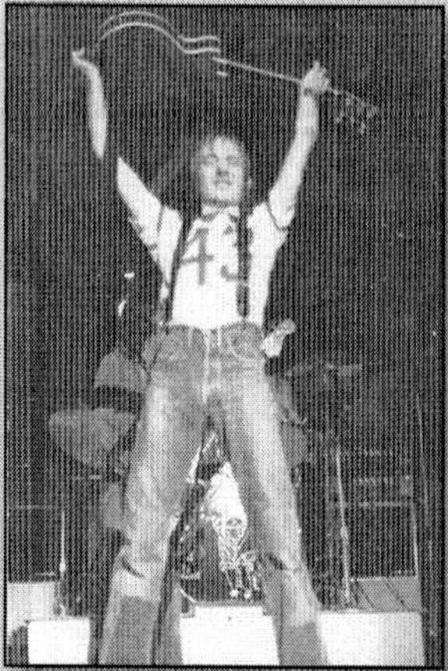

At this stage we started talking again about Ronnie Lane and Multiple Sclerosis the illness that we all know Ronnie had been a long term sufferer of. Steve continued "There's a place in Fort Lauderdale that Keith Richards bought for his auntie, funnily enough, he bought this whole centre for MS and he paid for Ronnie to go there and my job was to take Ron there and look after him. Well I say my job, it was my fuckin' pleasure but it was also something that was pre-arranged. We got a lot of songs together while we were out there as it happens. You see Ronnie's mind is over active but physically he's knackered but he can still write. The way he writes is to tell you something.....do this, do that, play this chord with these words etc etc. He can still do it. Well I'll prove it, as I said I'll give you this stuff, it was recorded in 1981 at the Corbett Theatre in Loughton. We hired the theatre and took Ronnie's mobile down there. But bless his heart, he's knackered really. He's like a car with no wheels, he has to be carried everywhere". I asked when Ronnie had first been aware that he was suffering from MS. "Well his Mum had it, did you know that?" Steve replied "Turns out it's a hereditary illness but he didn't know that. He was told it wasn't. You see when we were together his Dad, Stanley, who was an absolute masterpiece of a man, used to carry Ron's Mum about, wherever, even if she came to a gig, which I think she only ever did once. Anyway, they lived in those big tower blocks in Plaistow, wossname point and Stanley carried her everywhere. MS was all new back then". Bit like Aids now I replied. "That's right, that's dead right I mean it used to worry me. I remember being round Ronnie's flat in Chelsea and she had an attack. Because it comes in waves it retards them and Ronnie would try to make excuses like "Err, sorry mate" and all that but it used to scare me 'cos she couldn't speak. And Ronnie, as I said, was told it wasn't hereditary. So he said to me a few years ago" If I knew then what I know now then I wouldn't have abused my body so much". He wouldn't have done so much Coke, Hash, Speed or drink. He would have left it all alone. Then it was discovered that MS is hereditary but only from Mother to Son. So he didn't know that, he was told not to worry, poor little sod. So, of course, he done everything we all do, which in the long run has paid him back in fuckin' spades".

As the afternoon continued and we were both worse for wear (well I was anyway) I thought I'd ask Steve about the song which I considered to be his best work with the Small Faces "The Universal". I asked about it being written and recorded in his back garden. "It was yeah, on one of those (pointing to my cassette recorder). The dog was barking because my roadie had just turned up to go to a gig. What I done was, I got up and had a boiled egg in the garden. I had my 12 string and I was writing this song and I thought this sounds good I'll slap it down. You can even hear me missus saying "Hello Dave" (Dave the roadie) in the background. We tried to do it in the studio but it didn't work 'cos obviously the way I sung it was totally off the cuff and when you try to do something in the studio you've got red lights, microphones.....and it's just not the same. So we kept the cassette version and dubbed on the trombone. All we kept was my voice, the 12 string and the noises that went with it, the dogs and the car. I love it, it's a great song". So what inspired you to write it? I asked "Dunno mate, really. It was a beautiful day, just like today, the wind was blowing and I thought what a fuckin' lovely day and I wrote it about how I felt at that moment. I just thought (standing up with arms outstretched to the sky and shouting) WE ARE THE UNIVERSAL!!".

With that poignant statement we decided to have another drink which started with a banter-ish argument as to who was going to get the next round in. It was here that we called the interview to a halt and had a few more drinks in the garden soaking up the now mid-afternoon sun and basically just chatting and in an almost role reversed mode Steve started quizzing me on being a Mod, clothes and music etc. until we left The Crown happy, (boy happy!). We went to his nearby house where I was to meet his parents Bill and Kay, two very lovely people, Manon, his partner and their recently born daughter Molly Mae.

As we meandered down the road, laughing and joking, it suddenly struck me in some alcohol blurred daze that we truly are THE UNIVERSAL.

In dedication and memory of one Stephen Peter Marriott. You are truly and sorely missed.

LEE ALSFORD.

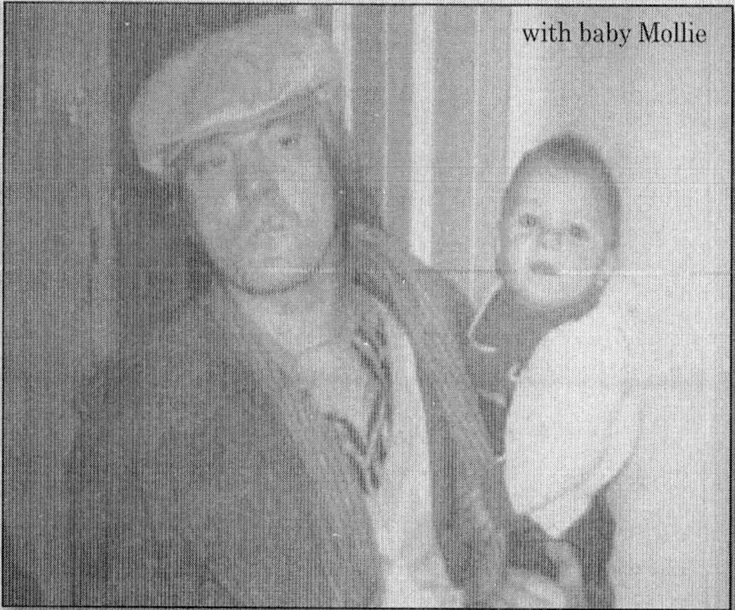
with baby Mollie

HOW I MET RONNIE LANE

His Texan bosom buddie and Butler BUCKS BURNETT tells the tale....

People tend to ask me" How in the hell did you manage to meet Jimmy Page?" I answer with "First I have to tell you how in the hell I met Ronnie Lane" Several at that point will ask" Who the hell is Ronnie Lane?" "Here we go again", I think to myself. You must consider the context, a lifelong Texan, born in 1958 in Dallas, so I was in my teens when the Faces were having their day. I loved Stay With Me on the radio but didn't buy the album and never saw them live. But one day I picked up a used Ronnie Lane LP in a shop and thought "Why not?" I loved it. Then a year later Mahoney's Last Stand came out." Him again!" To this day I consider Mahoney's an under-rated gem. But stick with the original LP or CD; the later CD with all the bonus tracks is rubbish, the flow is destroyed. I started tracking down solo Lane LPs, not an easy task in Texas in the '70s. One For The Road was and remains my favourite. I was working at a record store in 1977 and one day spied the new Rough Mix LP in the racks. Surely I was the only person in America who shouted "It's a new Ronnie Lane album!" I was a pretty big Who fan, too. It was a lonely trek being a Lane fan in Texas. I liked Nick Drake and Fairport, too, so I was used to people asking "Who?"

Cut to 1983; Rolling Stone magazine had a feature story on Ronnie having MS. I was amazed to see a story about him, but very bummed to hear the news. I spent the next week making call after call to the magazine, trying to get a contact address for Ronnie. Most people I talked to were disinterested, but I kept at it and finally a nice young lady gave me the address for ARMS UK. So I gathered notes, money and small gifts from friends and co-workers (I worked at a large music store, Peaches Records), threw some poems into the box and shipped it off. I just wanted him to know we were thinking of him in Texas. About six weeks later I got a letter from Ronnie. The first half was a form letter thanking everyone for their donations and support, but after that was a scrolled message to me which in part read "You are nothing more or less than a sweetheart. I like your poems, have you shown them to God?" I'd shown them to Ronnie Lane- close enough! I wrote him back right away and he sent me another note and then called me one night at 4am to make sure I was sleeping okay. This was my introduction to the Lane humour.

As fate would have it the ARMS benefit tour with Clapton, Beck and Page opened in late November with two nights in Dallas. Again, I was the only one shouting "Ronnie Lane is coming to Dallas!" I was happy to see the other lads as well. The day after the first gig I met Ronnie at a rather posh hotel for lunch. I brought him a dozen roses. While waiting for him in the lobby, I walked around and there at a table was

Kenney Jones and Eric Clapton, so I said hello. Eric asked if the roses were for him and I scolded him with "Certainly not!" They are for Ronnie Lane" He gave me a sad pout so I handed him a rose and we all had a good laugh. Then the elevator door opened and there stood Ronnie Lane, supported by a cane and Boo Oldfield, his girlfriend of the time. We walked a short way to the hotel café and found a table and I gave him the roses. Then Bill Wyman walked up and asked "May I join you, Ron?" "Sure! Meet my friend Bucks!" Bill eyed me with suspicion and sat across from me. A minute later Jeff Beck joined us. We all ordered and I spent the next two hours basically listening instead of talking, a rarity for me. It was easy, their stories were better than mine. Wyman kept telling Beck he was at a jam in 1971 at Steve Winwood's house. "You were there; I've got it recorded on my computer!" "I don't care what you've got on your bloody computer, I wasn't there!" Somehow Elton John came up and everybody tore in. Ronnie got the last laugh with "He's a nice bloke, when he's asleep!" Ronnie invited me up to his room where I recorded a brief interview with him and presented him with a large American flag and thanked him for invading America again. This was important to me, he was royalty, and I felt that he should have a flag upon his arrival. No "official" would ever think of it so I did it. He decided to take a nap so I asked how in blazes I could meet Charlie Watts. "He's in the room next door, tell him I sent you" I said goodbye to Ronnie, kissed him on the forehead. Knocked on Charlie's door.

After a few minutes it cracked open and a very sleepy Charlie peeked through. "Ello?" I quickly realised that he was two things, asleep and nude (at 5pm) holding a hotel wash cloth over his bits. He invited me in if I would wait a few minutes but I felt terrible about waking him, so I excused myself. That night I saw the second show and figured that was the last time I would see Ronnie. Fate had other plans.

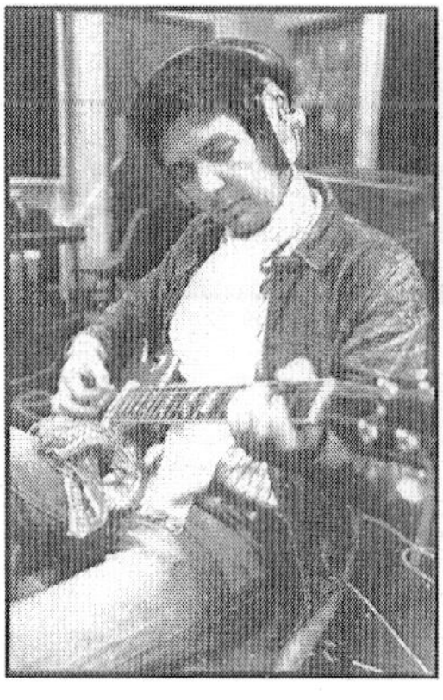

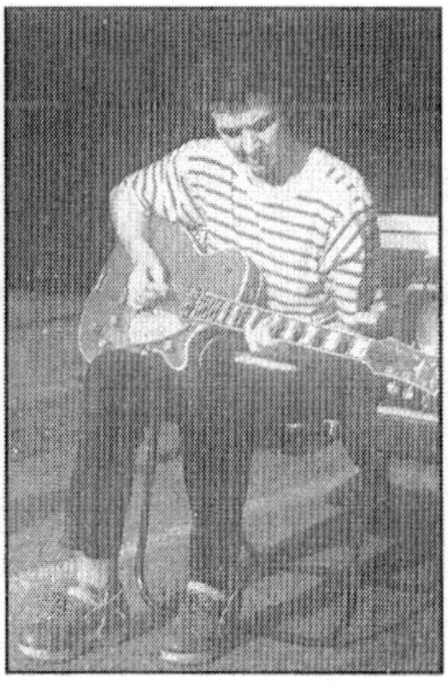

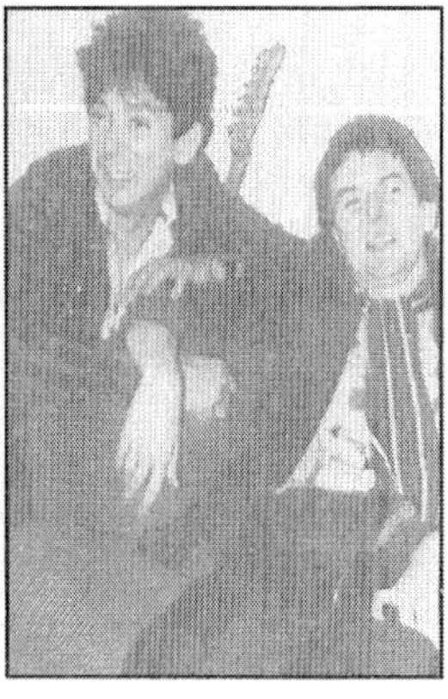

After the tour I wrote to then President Reagan, who was very anti Rock and Roll, and told him about Ronnie's tour raising a million dollars for MS research and told him he shouldn't be so quick to denounce Rockers (or Mods neither). To my utter shock, about two weeks later, both Ronnie and I got letters from Ronald Reagan congratulating Ronnie on the success of the tour. Ronnie called me when he got his and I asked what he thought about the letter. "Oh, it's great…I just snorted some coke off it!" On rare days, everything seemed right with the world. In late '84, against all the odds, Ronnie moved to Houston, Texas and opened ARMS America and hired Mae Nicol, a Houston attorney who claimed to have MS, to manage the outfit. I phoned him in January 1985 and he invited me down, so I went for the weekend and stayed six months. About a week into our visit he hired me to be his Butler. In February Ian McLagan came to town to play at the first ARMS America benefit, so I found myself butlering to two Faces. My God, those two, a dream comedy team. They took great pleasure each day in creating new ways to say the word "cunt". One would look at the other and say "You cuh-yunnt!!" The other might reply "Why thank you you c-c-c-cyant….." One night the Houston vice squad showed up looking for cocaine. I just said "Sorry gentlemen, can I offer you a beer instead?" Ronnie had a good buzz on and told them all to "piss awf". Why they showed up and why we weren't arrested, I'll never know.

In late March The Firm came to town. Jimmy Page gave Ronnie four seats onstage behind a bank of speakers, so we watched the show from ten feet to Jimmy's left. The whole thing had been set up by a Houston photographer Mark Bowman, who proved to be a great friend to Ronnie and myself. The next night Jimmy came to our apartment for a visit. I opened the door when he arrived and said "Welcome to the Lane household, my name is James" he snorted "Yeah, mine too" and walked right past me to Ronnie. He pulled a crumpled box of PG Tips from his jacket and said "I brought ya something" I spent the next few hours keeping tea cups full, always speaking with a posh British accent. Finally Jimmy laughed at something I said and looked at Ronnie and said" Where'd ya get him?" He offered to buy us hotel rooms at the next nights Austin gig and came for a visit in Ronnie's room after the show. We've been friends ever since.

Ronnie asked if I'd help him write his autobiography (I Can Take It, was his working title) and I said yes. So I called Pete Townshend, who offered to get it published. I spoke briefly with Pete and he said " If Ronnie says you're the one then that's fine, but you must understand this is gonna be a hell of a lot of work and I want to know if you're really up for it" I told him I could handle it. We announced the plan to Mae a few days later and she said "No way, Ronnie. You need a big name author for this. Let me handle it. Bucks you're Ronnie's butler, not a writer". By this stage in the game Ronnie was out of money and Mae was paying his rent and had signed on as his manager. A month later she cut my pay in half, so I told her to fuck off and as soon as she replaced me (the next day) I returned to Dallas, very down trodden. She later settled out of court for mismanaging the ARMS funds. Hardly any of the funds raised by the tour went anywhere but her purse, it seems.

It was an amazing and very taxing six months. Though it ended poorly, I was glad to be free of the 15 hour work days. Ronnie soon moved to Austin and we remained best friends until (and after) his death on June 4th, 1997. One night in Austin, my band The Ne'er Do Wells warmed up for him and Alejandro Escovedo, his guitarist at the time. We all sang "Ooh La La" together at the end of the set.

How do I sum it all up? Ronnie was gifted with more than talent. He also had charisma, a very deep spirit, a keen mind and enough British wit to have joined Monty Python. He was absolutely the funniest person I have ever known. In 1993 I videotaped an interview with him. It's the only footage of us carrying on the way we did, each undermining the other for the sake of a laugh. That's what's missing from the fabulous Passing Show DVD. Ronnie's amazing sense of humour.

A few days after he died, I was awoken in the middle of the night. Lyrics were flowing into my head and Ronnie was standing about two feet from my bed. Couldn't see him but knew without a doubt my friend was in the room. I went to the living room and found some paper and pen and he spent the next half hour dictating lyrics to me. Some of you might find that a bit daft, but it was very real and a year later my band The Volares released our first album and the opening track was the song Ronnie had given me that night, "Down To The Lane". Ronnie would visit many more times, often appearing visually right before me, usually when I was stuck for a lyric. We wrote another song together "Old Circus Wagon" and I got Ian McLagan to play organ on it. Ronnie visits now and again as well.

Do I miss him? Hell yes I miss him. He was my brother and we loved and hated each other. Do I want him back? At times. But you must remember that breed of fish that jumps and jumps to finally reach the top of the waterfall and swim upstream. You don't ask one of them fish to come back down do you? Ronnie ain't dead, brown bread...he's gone upstream. He's found his freedom. Screw all the clichés about the afterlife and about him being gone but the music living on. He's alive and having a blast. So let's all be a bit more like him; be alive and have a blast! Because the raver raves on. Never forget his masterpiece "Evolution". It's true story about Ronnie Lane and Dan the Blacksmith. He told me once about writing and recording "The Poacher" Great story

You were saying something about Jimmy Page?.........

TWO BLUE FLAMES IN THE SMALL FACES - OR

"WHAT THE PLUG DOES GEORGIE FAME DO IN A SMALL FACES MAGAZINE?"

By Uli Twelker, with quotes by the late, great IanMcLagan

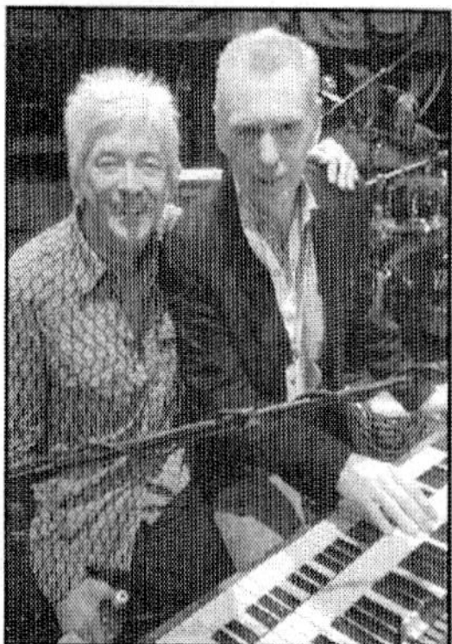

Ask a decent cover band like The Small Fakers to play a crazy medley of "Lazy Sunday", and "The Ballad of Bonnie & Clyde". They wouldn't even have to change their swing groove or tempo, let alone the vibe. Both Marriott/Lane and Georgie Fame love(d) the occasional East End tongue-in-cheek Music Hall connection in their repertoires – while that did not prevent either of these artists to positively hate these famous 1968 tracks "Bonnie & Clyde" and "Lazy Sunday" coming out as singles!

Apart from the Vaudeville/Music Hall connection, there was the Hammond link. Ian "Mac" McLagan had adored the organ with the tone-wheels right from the start – as Stevie did later. For his role model, Ian didn't have to look further than the Flamingo Club in London's Soho, just a (Rollin') Stone's throw from the Marquee Club where the Small Faces reigned supreme. As Mac recalled in your host's Georgie Fame book There's Nothing Else To Do: "I went there a couple of times before the days when I was in the Small Faces, never went there with Steve, Ronnie or Kenney. I was in a different band, The Muleskinners. Georgie was someone I really idolized. I thought he was fantastic! He was very Mod, and he played a great Hammond. In fact, the Hammond that I bought – the first one, which is now in Kenney's house – I got that because I realized that the B3 which I wanted, was too much and too heavy. The L100 was good enough, and it was small enough. It was still expensive, but that's what he played, so I got that. I've got a photograph of me and Clive, of me and Georgie Fame at the Royal Albert Hall when the Faces played there a couple of years ago. He was sitting at his Hammond, and I said 'Would you mind if we had a picture taken with a selfie?' We sat there at the Hammond, and he said it had been 40 years, and I said yeah, it's ridiculous. I never had a photo taken with him before."

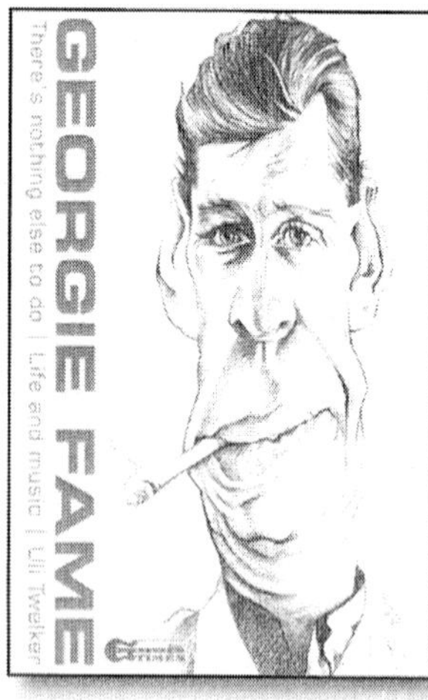

So there was always a certain musical mediating possible between Georgie's Flames and the (Small) Faces: in terms of style, with regard to one crucial instrument, and – spot the headline - in personell too. Fame's long term trumpeter Eddie „Tan Tan" Thornton has never been able to pride himself of being carved in song inside the ranks of the Blue Flames. But once Eddie stepped into Olympic Studios in the leafy London suburb of Barnes to help the Small Faces with the recording of their first Immediate album, during 1967, things got rolling for a song in his honour. Mac in 2009: „Ronnie Lane wrote the short and sweet number 'Eddie's Dreaming' as a tribute to trumpeter

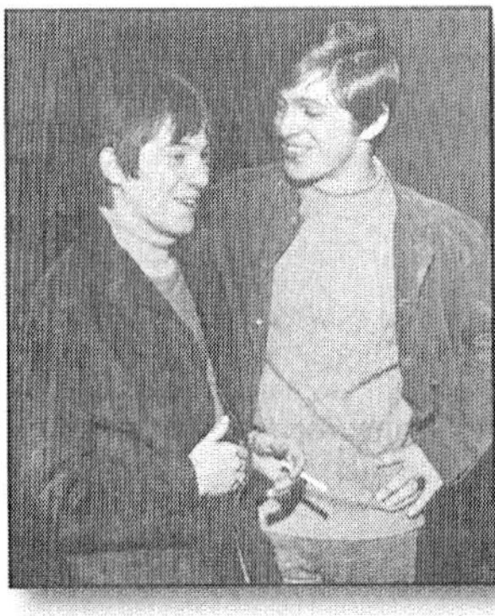

'Tan Tan' Thornton. Eddie played for Georgie Fame – and he had developed this stutter. When he was in the studio with us, he was a little bit high, and when the horns got recorded, he got chatting. But he couldn't get anything out: 'I g-g-got to t-t-tell ya...' We left that in the recording, but over the years, the technicians cut it out, and that killed the joke. Now of course, with the new Small Faces masters, Eddie's stutter is on one of the two versions. A short time ago, I met Eddie again when I played with Billy Bragg in Japan. He always wanted the Small Faces to eat spinach because it was healthy. These days I actually do eat spinach!"

Dreaming Eddie was not the only Blue Flames member to join the Faces Family: their long-time conga man Speedy Acquaye was keeping busy elsewhere, too - on the road and in all sorts of studios, for instance helping the Faces add some colour to their long-suffering album Oh La La, which Rod Stewart seemed to be avoiding at all costs. So Fame's Flames man Speedy proceeded to help with the instrumental "Fly In The Ointment". In Happy Boys Happy!, Roland Schmitt had already described it as a "dynamic instrumental piece, which spotlights Woody's slide guitar, and features an appearance by guest percissionist Niimoi Speedy Acquaye from Georgie Fame's Blue Flames." What's more, the complete Blue Flames brass section had toured with the Small Faces, proof of which can be heard on the live side of THE AUTUMN STONE double album. The Soho-based Ghana man died in 1993, and Georgie Fame helped pay for Speedy's funeral down in his African home of Ghana.

There was yet another link to Lane's Faces: Georgie Fame's fellow Mod and occasional Flamingo visitor Ronnie Lane, after leaving the Faces, signed a deal with Chris Blackwell's Island Records in 1974, just like Georgie did for his Tulsa, Oklahoma-produced Georgie Fame. His eponymous Island album was simply called Ronnie Lane's Slim Chance – why should Ronnie deserve a proper LP title if Georgie didn't get one? Ronnie's album featured the old Fats Domino chestnut from Georgie Fame's Fats For Fame EP, "Blue Monday", which proves that Lane obviously had the same taste in good vibes and heroes, and most probably heard Georgie's version down in Wardour Street.

I N F L U E N C E S

John Hellier talking to Mssrs. Marriott, Jones and McLagan.

WHO ARE YOUR MUSICAL INFLUENCES AND DID YOU EVER GET TO MEET ANY OF THEM?

Steve: Buddy Holly has gotta be the biggest influence on my youth. I used to run about the room wearing a pair of thick glasses, no glass in them just the rims and I had a tennis racket that I used to mime with. I made a record once called Give Her My Regards, I was copying him. It was dire! A rotten record! One reviewer said I was copying Adam Faith.......WHAT! The vocals were very hic-cuppy but that was what Buddy did. Adam Faith did that as well but like me he was just copying the guy from Lubbock, Texas. I dug all of the other American Rock n Rollers as well particularly Eddie Cochran, Gene Vincent, Everly Brothers, Jerry Lee and the black ones, of course, Chuck Berry, Little Richard..... the list goes on and on. Around 1964 my musical taste changed somewhat and I was now digging all the black Soul and R&B artists from America. If it wasn't black and American I wasn't really interested. Now it was all about Booker T, Junior Walker, Marvin Gaye, James Brown and Otis, of course. Later I met and enjoyed playing with some of my heroes, none more so than Jimmy Reed.

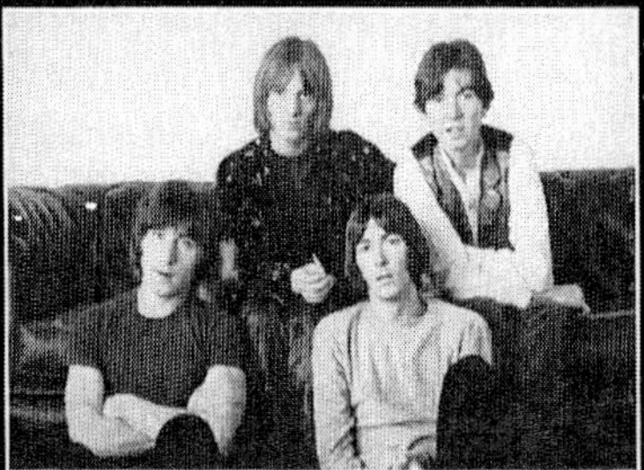

Mac: Stax, Motown, Muddy Waters, Howlin' Wolf and the Rolling Stones. In the early days of the Small Faces we would do stuff on stage like E to D and Come On Children and those types of numbers were just glorified jams. They were never the same twice and they'd be based on old James Brown and Muddy Waters licks. I remember all of us going to the Hammersmith Odeon to see the Stax revue. There was Otis, Booker T, Arthur Conley, Sam and Dave and Eddie Floyd all on the same bill. The curtains opened with Green Onions, it could have ended right there and I'd have gone home happy! The best gig I've ever been to. Otis was great but Sam and Dave stole the show. I got to know Booker T and the boys a bit later on. The last time he played Austin his organ was fucking up. I went to see him after the show and shared a few beers with him and Duck Dunn and Steve Cropper in the dressing room. I told him "Next time you play this town, call me and I'll supply Hammond and Leslie, it's a sweet B3, you'll love it". On the subject of good gigs did I ever tell you about the time I got thrown out of an Elvis Las Vegas show? Yeah, me and Woody for drunken behaviour.

CAN YOUR HEAR YOUR OWN INFLUENCE IN CURRENT BANDS?

Steve: Well yeah, it's very difficult, how shall I put it because they're doing something that I've done. Even the tones on the guitars they use. To me it's a compliment but to be honest with you I think they've got their influences very mixed up. They are influenced by the Small Faces or whoever, whereas we were influenced by the black R&B and Soul artists. They're really not taking it to the roots. What worries me is that the sort of music that we had when we were nippers is no longer available. Alright you can get compilation albums but they're not the same thing. We had the more obscure stuff like the Contours and groups like that. It's hard to get hold of that stuff and that's a shame.

Kenney: I can see a lot of the drummers playing like me which is really strange. I'm incredibly flattered and I can see similarities in Ronnie, Steve and Mac in the look of the bands now, even in Oasis. They're the first ones to admit to it. Of all the sixties bands the biggest hyped bands were obviously the Beatles and the Stones but we were right there in amongst them. Our record company kept releasing these Poppy records but in a way it was our fault we should have put our foot down. Nobody listened to our album tracks which was a shame as they were bloody great. We were a lot heavier than people gave us credit for but we could never shift that Pop image. Funnily enough I'm quite proud of that now because there is strength in the Pop side of music. People realise now it's not just Pop because it's commercial. Pop is just a term and you can actually still be heavy under that label, Tin Soldier being a good example.

Mac: I've worked with a lot of younger bands when I lived in LA. I got more work with younger bands that were familiar with our records. It's like a wave or a cycle. Now people are familiar with our band again but in five years time I'll have to be telling people who we were again. When the Faces split in 1975 we couldn't walk down the street without being stopped. When I moved to Malibu in 1978 I remember going to the market and a boy was laughing at my hair, he didn't think I could hear him but he was talking to his Mum and saying "Look at his funny hair". I'm thinking...wait a minute my hair has always been the same. Two years later kids had hair like mine again and I'm thinking...wait a minute you're probably the same kid that was laughing. Now it's all starting again, I had somebody come up to me yesterday and ask "Are you Rod Stewart?" Gimme a break!

STEVE MARRIOTT interviewed by JOHN HELLIER, MARCH 1985
MAC/KENNEY interviewed by JOHN HELLIER, FEB.2001

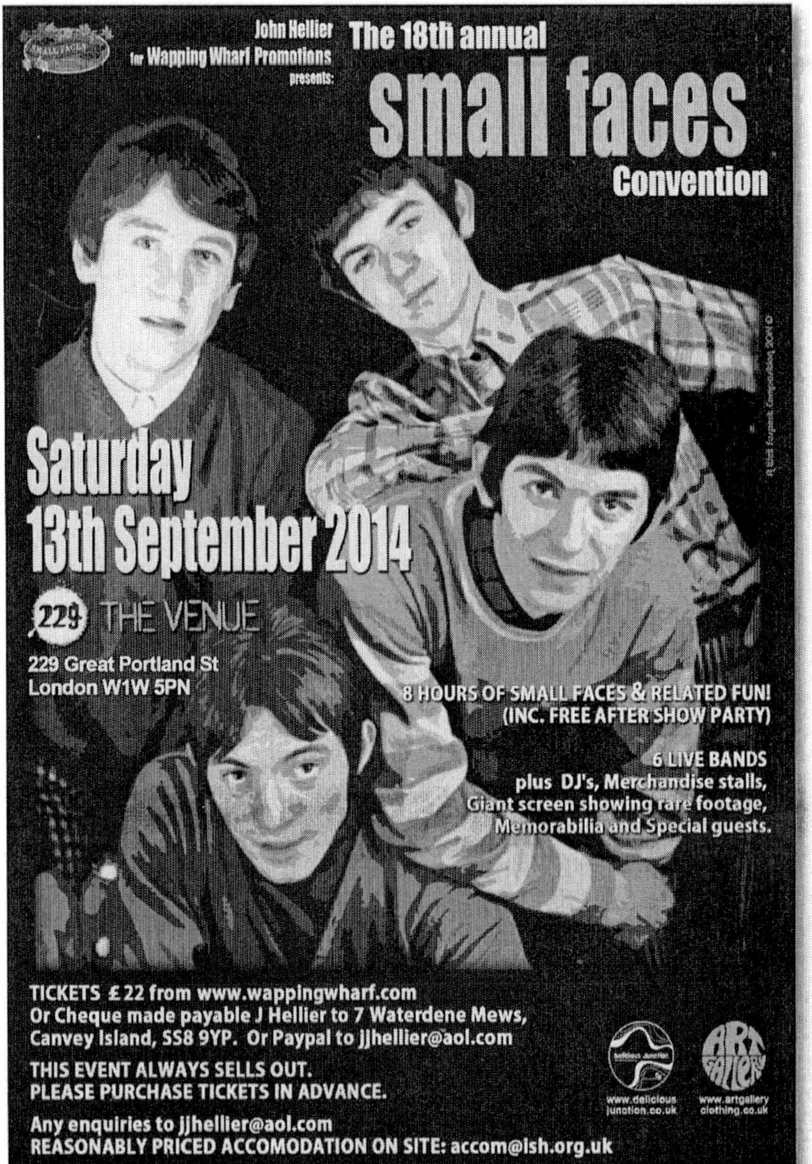
John Hellier
for Wapping Wharf Promotions
presents:
The 18th annual
small faces
Convention
Saturday
13th September 2014
229 THE VENUE
229 Great Portland St
London W1W 5PN
8 HOURS OF SMALL FACES & RELATED FUN!
(INC. FREE AFTER SHOW PARTY)
6 LIVE BANDS
plus DJ's, Merchandise stalls,
Giant screen showing rare footage,
Memorabilia and Special guests.
TICKETS £22 from www.wappingwharf.com
Or Cheque made payable J Hellier to 7 Waterdene Mews,
Canvey Island, SS8 9YP. Or Paypal to jjhellier@aol.com
THIS EVENT ALWAYS SELLS OUT.
PLEASE PURCHASE TICKETS IN ADVANCE.
Any enquiries to jjhellier@aol.com
REASONABLY PRICED ACCOMODATION ON SITE: accom@ish.org.uk
www.delicious junction.co.uk
www.artgallery clothing.co.uk

KENNEY JONES INTERVIEW

PART ONE.....

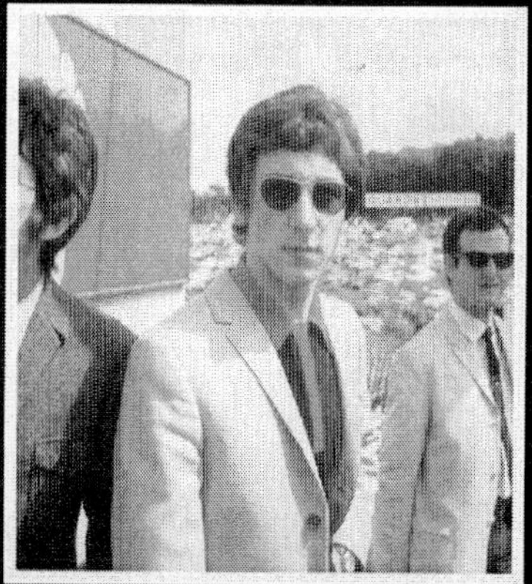

(from Skiffle bands to the Small Faces)

by Mike Dolbear

Ringo, Charlie, Keith, Mitch, Ginger… and Kenney. When the Small Faces charted in March 1965 with 'What 'cha Gonna Do About It', little did we know the little giant soulsters from East London would deliver some of the most exciting hits and inspired performances in rock history. With Dansette turntables and radio stations around the nation spinning their hits 'All Or Nothing', 'Here Come the Nice', Itchycoo Park', 'Tin Soldier', and #1 album Ogden's Nutgone Flake, the Small Faces were stars. Beatles and Stones fans now wailed for these young Mods in Carnaby Street clobber, while musos like Hendrix dug their sound and soul.

<u>Let's roll the clock back to the Sixties. What was your attraction to drums?</u>

A banjo! [laughs] I was twelve and a friend and I were washing a car for pocket money. We were fooling around throwing wet sponges and he popped his head up and said, 'Let's form a skiffle group.' I went, 'Yeah, great!" I then asked him, 'What's a skiffle group?' He said there'd be one on TV – back in the days of black-and-white – so off we went, and sure enough this skiffle group came on at 6:30. It was one of the biggest stars of the day, Lonnie Donegan, and he was playing 'Rock Island Line' and 'My Old Man's A Dustman' [laughs]. He was playing banjo and I went, 'WOW! What a great sound.' And it made a sort of drumming sound: I fell in love with it instantly. Next day we went to a pawn shop next to Bethnal Green station. I'd seen a banjo there a few days earlier, so I dragged my mates over to buy it with no money in our pockets [laughs]. We didn't think about that… it never crossed our minds. When we got there, there was no banjo. The bloke had come and paid for it and taken it back so we left. My friend could see that I was really upset and said that a friend of his has a drum kit which sounded great to me.

And was it what you expected?

It turned out to be a floor tom and an old bass drum with no pedal. There were two sticks and one was broken in half [laughs]. My dad was a bit of a carpenter so we went up to his shed and found some glue – now this was before Superglue – and glued it together. I was impatient waiting for the glue to harden, so I picked it up and the end fell off. That happened a few times. So we ended up banging this floor tom with one and a half sticks. My mother, who was walking home from work, heard the noise and wondered where the sound was coming from. The closer she got, the more she realised it was coming from her house. She threw us out! [laughs]

It sounds like drumming found you.

I must have been subliminally influenced by my Uncle Dave, a mace thrower. He led a marching band and they did processions that went around the streets. I'd run alongside the marching band and pretend I was a side drummer because I loved that sound. After that I rushed back to my dad's shed, which was like an Aladdin's cave. There was a square biscuit tin there. I put it upside down, got two bits of firewood and started banging away. After the banjo and one-and-a- half drumsticks episode, I found a shop called J 60's in Manor Park. (Small Faces and Faces band mate) Ronnie Lane would later buy his bass there. I was thirteen when I went into the shop and asked if they had drums. There were a couple of kits; one was a white Premier Olympic with calfskin heads. It was three drums and looked great. The cymbals weren't terribly terrific and the bass drum pedal had a rubber ball for a beater. It was 64pounds, 9 shillings and tuppence [laughs]. I said, 'Right, I'll have that!' He said I would need some HP to pay for it. The only HP I knew was brown sauce. So I asked, 'What do you mean HP?' He responded with, 'Hire purchase.' I had to get ten pounds deposit and my mum and dad to sign the agreement. I rushed home, but mum and dad were at work. Then I noticed her purse with a couple of tenners. I borrowed those and rushed back to the shop with the deposit. I then asked whether they could deliver. Yes, but they needed my mum and dad to sign the HP agreement. Now you've got to remember that nobody banged our door after 5:00 pm. But at 6:30 pm the door goes and everyone panics. My dad opened it and this bloke walked in and said, 'Where do you want the drums? I'll put them in the front room.' He just took over! Both Dad and Mum were looking at me with their mouths wide open, staring, giving me daggers. They were completely taken aback by it all and didn't say a word. So this fellow set these drums up in the front room and played something. 'Have you played before?' I had no other option than to tell the truth: 'No, not really.' So he said, he would show me something, but I had to get Mum and Dad to sign the HP agreement. I got more dagger stares from my parents. He got some brushes out, did that typical jazz swipe on the snare. Well, I'd never heard that one before! He held out the brushes, waving them and saying, 'Now you have a go.' I looked at my Mum, my Dad, the guy and the drums. Then I closed my eyes and had a go... and was actually doing it! I really surprised myself. According to my Mum and Dad, the look on my face was priceless. They had never seen me light up like that, so they signed the HP agreement and that was that.

How did things go once you had the kit?

That's when the real trouble started: I was hooked. I would get up at 6:00 in the morning and play before I went to school. All I could think about in class was drums, tapping on desks and stuff. Then at lunchtime I would come home, get straight on the kit. At four o'clock I was right out of school and back on the drums again and didn't stop playing until I was dragged off around seven pm. This went on for about three months. I'd watch drummers on the telly and I remember going up to Shoreditch where there was a music shop… not one that sold musical instruments, but they sold sheet music. I bought some and got pictures of Buddy Rich and Joe Morello. Having had dyslexia, looking at the music was all I could do, so I studied the pictures to see how they were holding the sticks. And I would study bits of film and watch bands at the 59 Club in Bethnal Green. I saw The Tornadoes and I was totally in love with The Shadows. From there I started to get into Booker T & the MGs and other soul artists. So it was mainly observing other players and listening to different styles, then miming what I heard. Putting that all together, I found my own style while teaching myself to play.

Do you recall any lighter moments during this learning period?

At one point I realized I was doing too much on the hi-hat and snare and thought, Hey, I've got these other two drums. So I started hitting them and found a whole new dimension. I kept everything fairly simple and remember learning a 'mummy daddy' (double stroke) roll from the sheet music. I went up there on a Friday and consequently every Friday. There was this drummer, Roy, and he was playing swing jazz. He was also a singer; I'd never seen a singing drummer before that. He had that old square Rezlo that came up in between his legs and he had his arms around it. I sat that there for three Fridays in a row, then this drummer, Roy, came up to me and said, 'Are you taking the piss out of me?' I asked what I'd done. 'Why do you keep blinking at me? he asked. I was surprised: 'I'm not blinking at you.' He didn't believe me: 'Yes you are.' Then I realised he had this affliction; when he played a beat he would blink at the same time, and when he did a drum fill, his eyes would flicker faster in time with that fill. So I said, 'Because you're blinking.' [laughs] I then got to know him and said I was just picking up a few tips. When I went back the next week, halfway through the gig he announces, 'We've got a young drummer who's going to get up and play with us,' so I thought; Great! Another drummer, I wonder who. Then he announced me! So I got up, sat there petrified… and I mean really petrified. So I'm behind his kit, a really nice kit, and I remember looking at these three other guys who look like giants. Everything then started to happen in slow motion. Wow! That's when I broke ties with the earth. Years later I learnt to fly helicopter and that's the only other time I've had that same feeling. I thought I was in heaven and really didn't want to get off. And that was it, really; I was blooded… done! After all that the barman came up to me, I was still shaking, and said, 'That was great. Are you in a band?' I said 'No, I'm forming my own,' to which he added, 'My brother is just learning to play guitar. Shall I bring him round next Friday?' Next Friday comes, and in walks Ronnie Lane. That's how we met. He was a couple years older than me and was a plumber's mate, while I was still at school. The rest is history.

Aside from the energy of the band, what attracted record companies to The Small Faces?

Don Arden [notorious manager and father of Sharon Osbourne]! We'd formed a band – me, Steve Marriott and Ronnie Lane – but didn't have a name. We got this guy, Jimmy Winston (Langwith), in the band because his brother had a van, a police 'meat wagon' as we used to call it. Not only that, Jimmy's parents had a pub, the Ruskin Arms in Manor Park, so we rehearsed there. The only problem was that Jimmy couldn't play anything, so Steve had to teach him how to play notes on the organ and guitar – he wasn't with us for long.

What was it like, trying to make the big time in the mid Sixties?

We decided we were going to be professional and played up in Manchester, at places like the Twisted Wheel. We would knock on the door and offer to play for nothing. Our van broke down in Knutsford and we were stuck there for a week whilst it got fixed. I remember that Ronnie Lane was half pissed and fell into the engineer's pit in the middle of the night. We ended up in Warrington and hadn't had a bath in a week! My hair had become a brown colour, which turned out to be rust from the inside ceiling of the van. Great times! [laughs] We ended up in Sheffield and played at The Mojo. We knocked on the door and out comes Peter Stringfellow; it was his club. We were starving, so we said we'd play for nothing. He invited us in, fed us and watered us. We played that evening and brought the house down. A few months later we had a residency for six weeks at the London Cavern, just off Leicester Square. Don Arden's sidekick saw us there and invited us to Don's office the next day. We said thanks, but no thanks. But after talking about it, the next day we did go up and that's when we first met Arden. He looked at us – we're all the same size, all small and cute… we looked the equivalent of four Justin Beibers, and Arden exploited that. We soon had a hit record with 'What 'cha Gonna Do About It' and did "Ready Steady Go". Our first TV was "Thank Your Lucky Stars". That was the first time we'd seen each other on the television. I hid under the table and said to myself, 'I don't look like that!' TV appearances quickly became a way of life, and by that time we had bumped into Peter Stringfellow again. He was a hip mod who would warm up the audience before the bands played; you never saw him on the telly, but that's what he did. We have a lifelong friendship with him even now, and I'll never forget his kindness and generosity. [Stringfellow would go to become a celebrity in his own right, owning a number of major clubs] When we met up with [former Rolling Stones Manager] Andrew Loog Oldham, we broke ties with Don Arden and moved from the Decca to Oldham's new Immediate label. With Immediate we never had to go out of the studio, which was really fantastic, because that meant we had lots of time to experiment. That's how we got phasing (introduced on hit single, 'Itchycoo Park'). I remember Glynn Johns, the engineer, taking tape from the recording machine and looping it around a chair to get this effect on the drums, 'cause we wanted something different. We were the first to do that and other interesting things. After coming through our five year experience… the hit singles, the touring, all the excitement, we had a #1 hit with our album, Ogden's Nut Gone Flake. But we all said, 'How the bloody hell are we ever going to top this?' You have to think in terms of the times, though even now I think how amazing that record was. We'd put all our recording experience and musicianship to the test. One of the things we suffered from – not that we didn't appreciate it – was we were constantly plagued with the screaming girls. It was amazing, we were as big as The Beatles - four albums and approximately twelve hit singles between 1965 – 1968. We didn't have monitors in those days and the screams were so loud you couldn't hear yourself. We became competent players but could never shift that teeny-bop image. Eventually it got to all of us, though more to Steve. All we wanted was to prove we were not that teeny-bop image that had been created for us and exploited by Don Arden. We wanted an image like Jeff Beck or The Yardbirds, 'cause we were always going to see them."

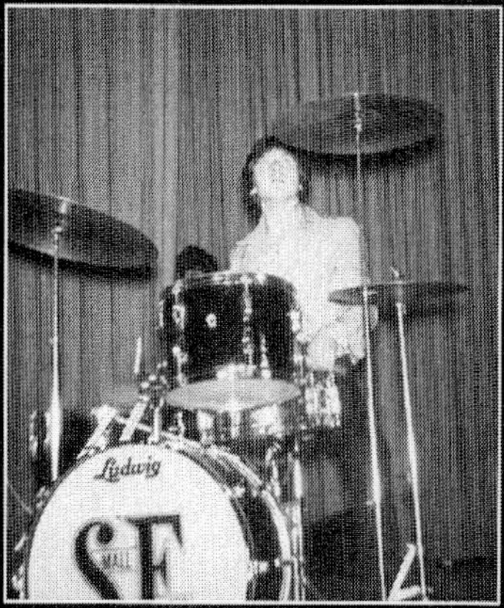

How did the Small Faces end?

The last gig we did was at Alexandra Palace in North London. Steve wasn't happy with the situation and threw down his guitar and walked off stage… we were left dangling. When you're in a band, you're mates and you become part of each other. You get some sort of telepathy going and share your emotions… the music becomes an emotional experience. It's called 'feel'. You feel it together and that's how you bond as a group. When that's lost or one member goes, it leaves a big hole. Steve was like a brother… it was like a marriage break up. He left and joined a band being put together by Peter Frampton called Humble Pie, which went on to do really well.

TO BE CONTINUED.........

KENNEY JONES INTERVIEW

PART TWO.....

(part one published in issue 38)

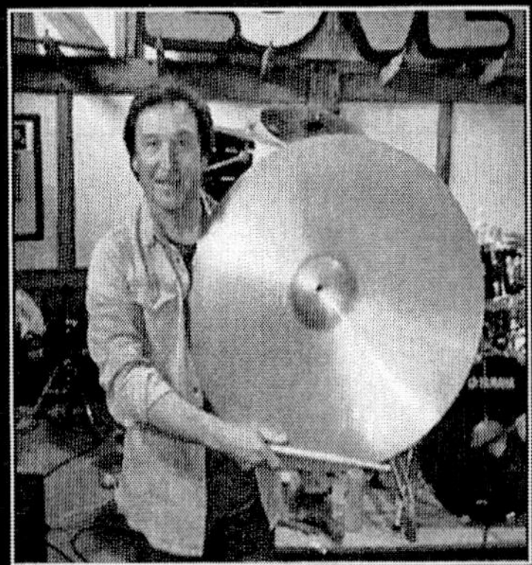

(life after the Small Faces) by Mike Dolbear

With Dansette turntables and radio stations around the nation spinning their hits 'All Or Nothing', 'Here Come the Nice', Itchycoo Park', 'Tin Soldier', and #1 album Ogden's Nut Gone Flake, the Small Faces were stars. Beatles and Stones fans now wailed for these young Mods in Carnaby Street clobber, while musos like Hendrix dug their sound and soul. When the Small Faces dropped the 'Small' and added Ronnie Wood and Rod Stewart, they got big. Globally big! The Faces, boozy and loose, epitomized good time rock 'n' roll, with Kenney's thundering drums on '(I Know) I'm Losing You' a real showstopper. The Who would later choose him, a mate from early days, to be the final quarter of their reformed foursome and first farewell tour. There were other sessions and bands including Joan Armatrading, Chuck Berry, Jerry Lee Lewis, David Essex, John Lodge (Moody Blues), Wings and the Law with Paul Rodgers... But whom he's played with isn't as important as what he's played. The fact is that Kenney Jones is Kenney Jones in the same way Ringo is Ringo: he's the one! And when that casually stumbling fill at the end of 'Tin Soldier' thunders out of the speakers, one is reminded that Kenney Jones epitomizes the creativity of the Sixties, the power of the Seventies, and the spectacle of the Eighties that made rock music so exciting and drumming so great.

But you, Ian McLagan and Ronnie Lane soon resurfaced as The Faces?

Yeah. In those days the Rolling Stones had a warehouse in Bermondsey Street just over Tower Bridge. The basement had a soundproofed room where they stored their equipment. Mick [Jagger] said we could use it, so every Friday we would jam. One day, Ronnie Lane brought along his new neighbour from Richmond, Ronnie Wood. Ronnie and Rod Stewart were playing with the Jeff Beck Band, both on wages, and we thought that was a great band. Woody was playing bass, and I've got to tell you, he's a phenomenal bass player. Well, he wanted to play guitar and step away from bass. I'll digress slightly, but I have to tell you that this was what happened with Ronnie Lane. He had an old Gretsch guitar but wanted to play bass. That experience of playing lead guitar is what made his bass playing so unique and melodic. He was certainly one of the finest bass players I've ever worked with. Okay, back to the story...Well Ronnie Wood joining the band filled that guitar gap. The following week he brought down his best mate, who was Rod Stewart. Rod sat on the amps watching us. This went on for a week. What would happen was we would have a break and go to the Bermondsey Arms and have a few lagers… a bunch of great guys hanging out together. Then we would go back and play a bit more. One day we thought we should put something together instead of just jamming about. We needed a singer, so everyone started singing… all of us would have a go. Ronnie Lane sang, but after Steve Marriott, who had such a big voice, Ronnie's wasn't strong enough. I went up to Rod, bought him a drink and asked him whether he wanted to join the band. He said 'Wow! Do you think everyone would let me?' I didn't tell anyone at the time, but announced the news to the band when we went to [Ten Years After guitarist] Alvin Lee's house for drinks and it didn't go down well. The lads didn't want to experience what had happened before, what with the singer quitting and leaving us. But me, I saw it as the difference between success and failure and experience was telling me that adding Rod would make that difference. In the end I got my own way.

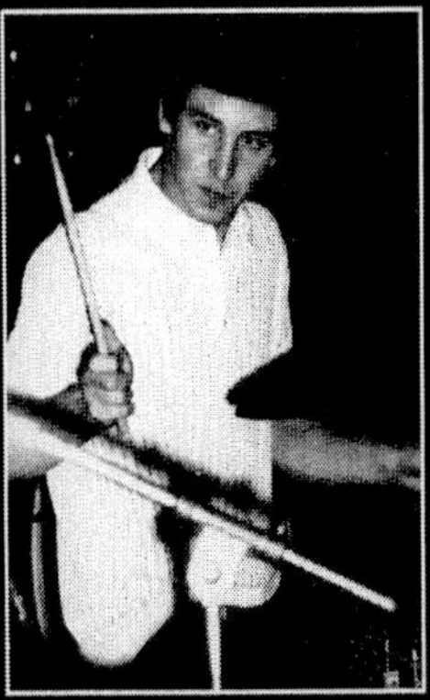

Though Ogden's Nut Gone Flake was never performed 'live', you have been working on an animation based on the album, correct?

Yes, we've just been working on the script again. We had one but threw it out. One of the guys at Metro Goldwyn-Meyer once said that when you're working on a film you have to get three things right and they're the story, the story and the story. You've got to know it's right and if there are any doubts you have to go back and make the appropriate scripting adjustments. New characters have to be created and that's quite challenging. I said years back that this would make a great cartoon and having lived with it for so many years I now have to finish the blinking thing!" [laughs]

What was it about Al Jackson, drummer with Booker T & the MGs, that was so relevant for you?

The one thing I loved about Al Jackson's playing was that he was very simple in his approach; he knew his place and because of that, his playing complemented the rest of the band so much that you wanted to know more about guitarist Steve Cropper and the rest of the guys. Al made everyone shine through. Now some people think that if you play simply then you won't shine through, but you do shine. Al also played just that little bit behind the beat, which was perfect. What listening to Al taught me was that the drummer should know his place in the confines of a band… know how to serve the band and the song.

How did you discover yourself as a player?

Over the years I've learnt is that you can discover yourself, your own style, through your instrument rather than through other people. Influences are good, but don't stray away from your focus. You need to find your strengths and style from yourself; that should be the first and foremost thing. Then you let new techniques complement your style.

Now back to The Faces: How did the collaboration with Simply Red's Mick Hucknall transpire?

The PRS (Performing Right Society) wanted to present an award to The Faces – to the band, but it also awarded to each member individually – at the Royal Albert Hall. In its seventy-five year history there had been only two other recipients of this iconic award: Paul McCartney and Andrew Lloyd-Webber. I called Rod and told him everything and he said, 'I love an award, I'll be there, you can count on me'. Anyway, Rod's management then got hold of me to say that Rod couldn't make it 'cause he's cutting a record or something. Basically he got his dates mixed up. So we called PRS and explained the situation, but they insisted they wanted us there for the award and to do three songs. Andy Fairweather-Low, Paul Carrack and Mick Hucknall were also on the bill, so it ended up that Andy did 'Ooh La La', Mick did 'Stay With Me' and Paul did 'Cindy". Mick was really up for it 'cause he had always been a passionate fan of The Faces. He did 'Stay With Me' because it's one of his favourites. That's how we got together with him. Actually, having Mick onboard is great, but we're still looking forward to doing something with Rod at some point. In fact, we all got together recently... Mick, Ronnie, Rod and myself, funnily enough, all met up and went to watch Bobby Womack performing at Jazz Cafe, who has also been a lifelong friend – we all get along as pals. No one is shunning Rod. Mick is just standing in and we're enjoying it 'cause we want to play... we don't want to wait. Rod understands this.

In 1985 you and the Who played to what must have been your biggest audience which was 'Live Aid'. Any thoughts on that?

I joined The Who back in 1978, three months after Keith Moon died, bless him. We were no strangers to massive gigs. It was an amazing experience for more reasons than just playing there. The excitement and the prestige of being able to take part in such a glorious event was really amazing for me. We had twenty minutes, and in the middle of 'My Generation', when Roger got to that part of the song that goes, 'Why don't we all f-f-f-fade away', the satellite blew up and we did fade away as we were off air for a few minutes[laughs]. The viewing audience saw us disappear in the middle of 'My Generation', missed the whole of 'Pinball Wizard', and it all came back on the next track, 'Love Reign Over Me'. It was great and you have to remember that they were stretching technology to its limits at that time.

Any really memorable highlights that we don't know about?

The indulgence for me at the time was that I learnt to fly a helicopter and co-owned one with David Essex. So that day I took off from my back garden and flew to Battersea, to meet up with two helicopters, Live Aid 1 and 2, and was asked to co-pilot one of them to the playing fields just outside Wembley Stadium. From there we went on to meet Prince Charles and Lady Diana. For me, that really was an unforgettable experience.

You pioneered the big drum and big cymbal sound favoured by the likes of John Bonham and Jerry Shirley. Where did that come from?

One day I walked into Drum City in Shaftesbury Avenue and this guy said Paiste had sent something for me. The lads in the shop had never seen a cymbal like it. It was 26 inches... a 26" ride! It had such a big sound and such a great bell that it became one of my treasured possessions. When I first got it I did a track called 'Rollin' Over' [On "Ogden's Nut Gone Flake"]. Since then I really look for that big sound in other rides. But it was mainly the Small Faces that led me to experiment with cymbals and drums. I had a great band, we had a lot of studio time, and I had a mixed bag of cymbals, some Paiste, some Zildjian. I always had a smaller crash to my left and even used a Chinese cymbal there – Charlie Watts does a similar thing – but it became overpowering and I realised I needed sweeter sounding cymbals. You experience different things in studio sessions and those moments make you want to experiment.

The sticks you use are shorter than the standard drum stick, why's that?

I use Vic Firth sticks but I've always sawn almost an inch off the ends of mine. Over the years drummer friends have said my stick should be longer. I never forget buying longer sticks and it would get stuck in my sleeve. If you find the centre of gravity if gets caught up your sleeve. I obviously found that I like a short stick and I find that I could be snappier with them. For me, a longer stick has a bigger arc which also slows the speed of my playing. I didn't know until sometime later, that it's not only me that does it but Phil Collins also uses a shorter stick. We use exactly the same length stick, I didn't know that and neither did he. Weight wise, he uses a thinner stick and mine's a bit more beefy, a cut down version of a 2B; Vic Firth kindly gets them made for me and they are well balanced.

What about technique and other changes?

Techniques change over the years, and whilst I had my sound with the Small Faces, when it came to playing with The Who, well to start with Keith Moon I did play bigger drums, though not any more, mainly because drums nowadays are louder and are better made. I still have all my kits and when I look at them I wonder how I played them. The kit I use now is a Yamaha. In fact, I just found out that I am the longest serving Yamaha drum endorsee, going back to about 1972, which is incredible. Before that I had the Premier and the Ludwig.

With your polo club keeping you busy, are there future plans, especially the Jones Gang?

With The Jones Gang, there is talk of cutting another album. Besides owning the polo club there's the animation of Ogden's Nut Gone Flake and a Kenny Jones app I'm working on. There's also a book that I'm working on which will be out next year. I've got a lot going on to keep me busy and it's all quite testing, but life's treating me pretty good.

What advice would you give an upcoming drummer?

Ask yourself, can I live without money and fame? You're likely playing 'cause it's something you like and it makes you feel good. In turn, if it makes others feel good, that's a bonus. Get that right and you'll be playing drums honestly, which is the difference between successful musicians and those who fall by the wayside. On the business side there are people you can go to for advice. The Musician's Union are a responsible body of people and a mine of information. In my day, bands were being ripped off left, right and centre, but today you have many avenues to seek information. I know I had to learn how to negotiate and what to charge for a session. Then later, when I made a name for myself, I stopped the hourly rates and started to charge a fee. The thing is to always be fair. There have been times when I would do a session for nothing, purely because I was earning money in other bands and could afford to. The main thing was I wanted to do those sessions and play different music and work with different musicians. It was fun and part of my learning curve. And finally, don't sign any contract without first having it looked at by a suitable lawyer. The Musicians Union and even the PRS can be very helpful.

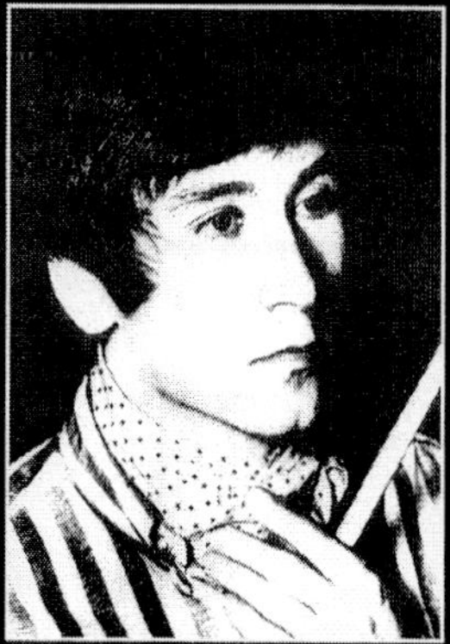

MIDNIGHT OF MY LIFE
A STEVE MARRIOTT SHORT MOVIE

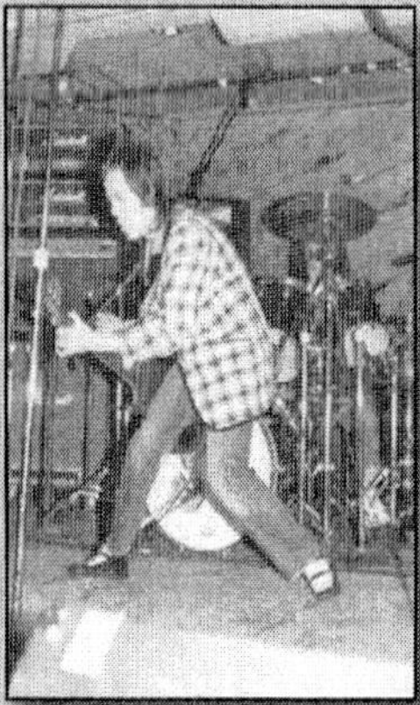

SYNOPSIS: Steve Marriott is one of the British music scenes most revered but widely overlooked vocalists. His life and premature death were marked by the incredible pace at which he lived out his passion for music, performing and partying. Midnight Of My Life is a poignant study of talent, ageing and what success means. This short film describes an imagined encounter, one night in Steve Marriott's final years. It's July 1985 and Rock and Roll's great and good are strutting their stuff at Wembley, all for a noble cause. Meanwhile Steve is propping up the bar of a dingy pub in Putney waiting to play to a small crowd of boozers. While he awaits the arrival of his Packet Of Three, bitter and drunk, an encounter with a young revival Mod restores Steve's faith and reminds him of the true joy of performing.

With Brit actor and director Phil Davis (Quadrophenia, ID) taking the directing reigns, Film superstar Martin Freeman lined up for the lead role, a soundtrack composed by Andy Bell (Oasis, Beady Eye) and John Hellier as consultant how can it fail? Here the film's writer, Nina Gerstenberger, tells us why Steve's story inspired them to make this film...

"Not always what I wanted to be, but it has become a part of me"...... Steve Marriott sings in his 1976 song Midnight Of My Life (from the Wapping Wharf album Lend Us A Quid). There are so many aspects of this great man's life one can identify with, despair over or simply marvel about - his unprecedented talent as a singer, guitarist, and songwriter; the fame he found at a young age and the relative anonymity he experienced during the later stages of his career when he was playing small clubs and pubs; his complex friendship with Ronnie Lane, his cheeky humour and ultimately his tragic and untimely death. So how can all this be expressed in a short film? It can't! Ten feature films might not be enough to tell Steve's amazing story. He was with us for only 44 years, but he lived such an exciting and adventurous life. What we aim to do is to focus on one small, yet poignant moment from Steve's life that says a hell of a lot about his career, his talent, and the man he was. But more about this later.

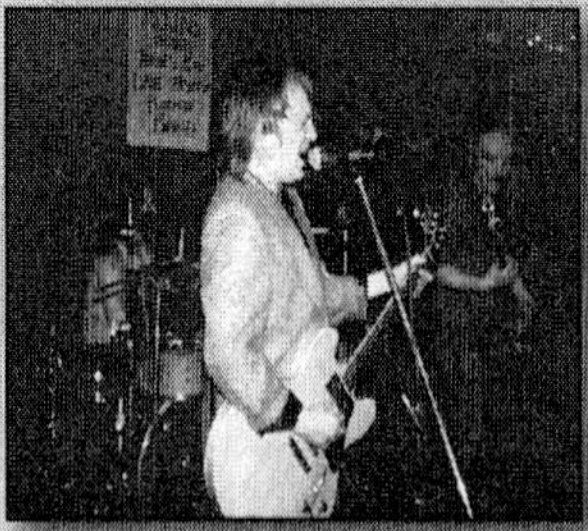

I made a documentary in 2009 about the current Mod

scene in London and bumped into John while filming on Carnaby Street. Before I started the film I had expected a handful of real Mods to still be about, keeping the memory of this great culture alive. I couldn't have been more wrong! I realised two things quickly - the Mod scene is alive today and the music of Steve Marriott is playing a crucial role in making sure that it will never fade away.

John invited me to do an interview at his house and I happily accepted, intrigued about the stories he would have to tell. If he had told them all, I'd still be sitting on his sofa now! Someone should make a film about Steve, John remarked after our chat. Yes, I replied, someone really should. It is a rainy afternoon in 2009 and I find myself in probably the coolest music room ever, cluttered with Steve and Small Faces memorabilia. Oh and that scarf on the wall over there - Keith Richards gave it to Steve as a good luck charm before his audition with the Stones. John Hellier, Mod historian, Steve Marriott biographer, mega-fan and genuinely nice bloke tells me casually. I nod and just stare at the scarf and wonder if I might be able to touch it, maybe when John leaves the room to get me a cup of tea. If scarves could talk, I bet this one would have a few stories to tell!

On the evening of Live Aid in July 1985 whilst Rock Stars, once way below Steve in the pecking order, played to billions worldwide our man played to a small audience in a South West London pub. The irony of this situation touches me deeply and I can imagine that it must have evoked mixed feelings within Steve as well. On the one hand bitterness and disappointment, anger even, because he wasn't up there, but on the other hand gratefulness he was able to do his own thing, on his own terms, and just play his music. So Midnight Of My Life is a film about integrity, about passion, about regrets and ultimately realising why you are doing what you are doing.

The reactions we are getting from Steve's fans could not be more touching and encouraging, proving again how many dedicated admirers of his music there are who want this film to be made. It's an honour to have penned this short story about Steve. I hope you'll enjoy watching our film as much as we will enjoy making it.

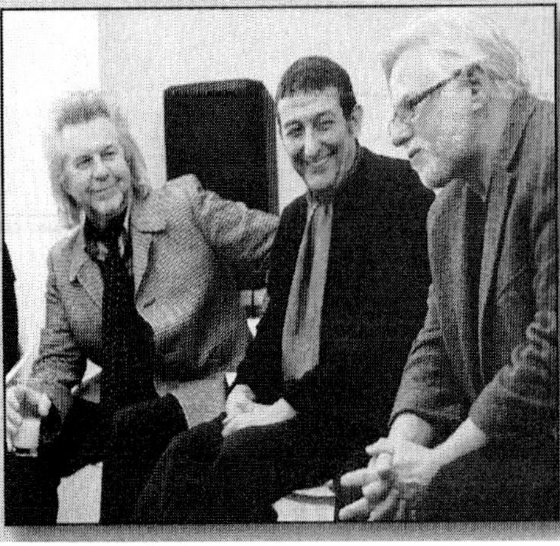

Filming is scheduled for late April with a view to releasing the movie in the summer.

MICK TAYLOR presents......... LAZY SUNDAY, the story

Although history states that "Lazy Sunday" was only meant as an album track and the band didn't want it released as a single, I absolutely loved this song from day one and for a 15-year-old lad I thought it was absolutely superb! It was completely different from what any other band was doing at the time and that's probably why it became such a big hit. It's been said that even The Who were envious of this tune and the use of an exaggerated Cockney voice that they tried copying it and released the song "Dogs" in answer to the Small Faces..... quite a compliment!

Lazy Sunday was inspired because of Steve Marriott's feud with almost every neighbour he chose to live next door too. Steve's love for parties, rave-up's, dogs and cats running about the place and VERY loud music had his neighbours at the end of their tethers and close to lynching him. The whole of the main song though was based on Steve's feud with the Hasselwaithes family in Chiswick.

Ian McLagan, Ronnie Lane, Steve Marriott & Jenny Marriott recall:
STEVE: "I wrote Lazy Sunday whilst having 'difficulties' with my neighbours in Chiswick, West London. I suppose it was my way of getting all the hassle off my chest."

JENNY: "I moved in with Steve and his dog in a small terraced house in Eyot Green in Chiswick, West London, right near the river. He was having a lot of hassle with his neighbours, the Hasselwaithes and that's how Steve ended up writing "Lazy Sunday" about his time there. Mind you I didn't blame the neighbours it must have been hard living next door to Steve. They complained continuously about the noise and rightly so. Steve had installed Wharfdale speakers from Olympic Studios in a living room which measured approximately 14ft by 12ft!"

IAN & RONNIE [Reminiscing together about Lazy Sunday and another reason why Steve didn't get on with the neighbours]: IAN to RONNIE: "Lazy Sunday", was it all Steve? or mostly Steve. He had the idea because he was living in this house in Chiswick and he had dogs, they use to shit all over the balcony. RONNIE: "Cats, dogs, stunk to high hell! IAN: The place stunk. He had this beautiful little house, beautiful carpets, paintings, furniture, and it was all wrecked. He had someone paint "THOR" all over the wall, Thor from Marvel comics. The whole wall was Thor. You could smell the place before you got in there. It was really a pleasure to go round and see him! RONNIE: And then he went round to the bog, in the toilet, he's sat there singing "Wouldn't it be nice to get on with me neighbours, 'cause they make it very clear they got no room for ravers" Ha-ha!!"

Lazy Sunday starts with Ian McLagan lighting the touch paper for a romp of immense proportions with a nifty little Hammond riff followed by Steve Marriott's over the top exaggerated Music Hall, cockney style singing, a good old knees up springs to mind and as Steve is singing Kenney Jones is playing along with

Other versions of interest are:
The "BBC Sessions" version and the Small Faces Mk2 "Live At The Hammersmith '77":
I first heard the BBC Sessions version on a bootleg CD called "All Or Nothing" (also released as J60) which also included studio outtakes and acetate mixes."Lazy Sunday" on the J60 CD is an edited down version and is only 2:23 minutes long. The same version got an official release some years later on the Strange Fruit label [SFRSCD087] titled "Small Faces: BBC Sessions" and was the full version, 3:14 minutes long, cleaned up with crystal clear sound. The take was actually from the BBC show Top Gear played on the 14/04/68. The version was quite funny with sound effects which added hens clucking, geese cackling, bicycle horns, whistles, you name it.... it was probably there! The "Live At the Hammersmith" version is the Small Faces reunion and recorded in 1977. Although Steve has a bit of a sore throat on this track it is still an interesting version for purist collectors.

And nahh, for your delight-tah, the darling's of Wapping Wharf sing ...

LAZY SUNDAY [ORIGINAL ALBUM VERSION]

A-wouldn't it be nice to get on with me neighbours,
But they make it very clear they've got no room for ravers,

They stop me from groovin', they bang on me wall,
[What's going on in there]
They're doing me crust in, it's no good at all...Aahhhhh

Lazy Sunday afternoon-nah,
I've gotten no mind to worry,
A-close my eyes and drift away...

Here we all are, sitting in a rainbow,
[Hmm, hmm hmm hmm hmm hmm hmm]
Gawd blimey, hello Mrs Jones, how's your Bert's lumbago?
[You mustn't grumble]...

[Diddley bay]
I'll sing you a song with no words or no tune-nah,
[Diddly bay]
To sing in your khazi while you suss out the moon, oh yes,
[Diddly bay x 2]
Lazy Sunday afternoon-a,
[Diddly bay]
Yes, I've gotten no mind to worry-a,
Close my eyes and drift away-aa...

[whistling]
A-roo-de-do-de-do, A roo-de-do-de-di-day

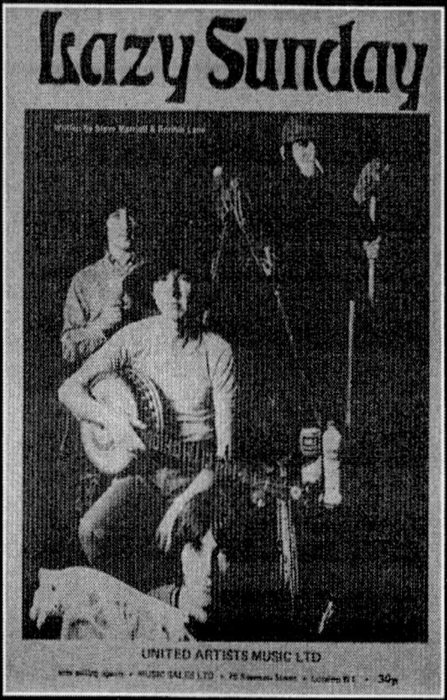

The lyrics for Lazy Sunday were written in Marriott's Auntie Sheila's bathroom. Whilst travelling to his Aunt's house, Steve had been hit by inspiration and on arriving at his Aunt's, Steve grabbed pen and paper, rushed upstairs, locked himself in the loo and scribbled away.

A promotional video was shot for Lazy Sunday and was shot at Kenney Jones parents house in Hainault Road, Stepney, East London. Kenney's mum still lives there. On the video the Small Faces used a real neighbour of Kenney's called Peggy Dawson. It shows her smashing a vinyl album over Steve's head. The Green [where you first see Steve Marriott sitting crossed legged saying "What the f**k] was in fact Steve's (communal) back garden and the beach/water shot was taken on the Thames embankment near his home in Chiswick.

Another video clip of 'Lazy Sunday" was released a couple of years ago on a "Special edition DVD EP". It's from the German TV show "Beat Club" and lasts 2:51 minutes.

Did you know? ... Steve Marriott originally wanted to release 'Song Of A Baker' as the A-side and 'Lazy Sunday' as the B-side but Steve's dad Bill preferred Lazy Sunday for the top side. Andrew Oldham thought so as well.

Did you know? ... the very first time the Small Faces played Lazy Sunday on stage it was at Greenford Starlight Ballroom. Steve says: "We used acoustic guitar on the original record but used electric on stage and unless you're careful you get a lot of feedback problems. Very technical but also very annoying".

For collecting enthusiasts:

I've heard 3 versions of the original "Lazy Sunday" release [Immediate IMO64]:
[1] Stereo version, [2] The Mono version & [3] Early mix version...
Lyric wise there is no difference between the mono and stereo but the stereo version is slightly longer at 3:06 minutes rather than the slightly shorter mono version at 3:04 minutes. Obviously the stereo mix is mixed for a far superior stereo separation sound. For superior quality I recommend the recently released "Ogden's Deluxe Edition" which incidentally includes the 'mono' mix of Ogden's on CD for the first time.
One version I've heard recently is an earlier mix which basically has the Ronnie Lane backing vocals "Diddley bay" missing. It's on a CD called "Lazy Sunday" and is on the 'Success' label [Cat No 2198CD]. This version is 3:01 minutes long.

A-roo-de-do-de-dum, A-re-de-de-de-do-dee...
[Hmm hmm, hmm hmm hmm hmm hmm hmm]

There's no one to hear me, there's nothing to say,
And no one can stop me from feeling this way, yeah,

Lazy Sunday afternoon,
I've got no mind to worry,
Close my eyes and drift away...

Lazy Sunday afternoon,
I've got no mind to worry,
Close my eyes and drift a...
Close my mind and drift away,
Close my eyes and drift away........

MARRIOTT/LANE

~~~~~~

VERY SPECIAL THANKS TO:
The Hasselwaithes family for inspiring Steve to write such a fantastic song! Peggy Dawson, John Reed at Sanctuary for the Mac & Ronnie reminiscing on the BBC "Classic Albums Documentary 1989".

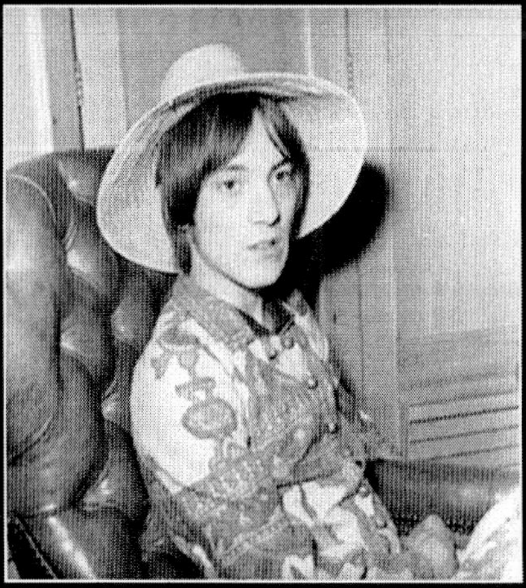
~~~~~~

RONNIE LANE....
the Eric Clapton era

As told by legendary ex McGuinness Flint, John Mayall and Blues Band drummer Hughie Flint

The few months I spent in Ronnie's band, and company, in the Spring/Summer of 1977 were among the happiest, musically, of my career. As Eric Clapton had asked Ronnie to get a band together to support his for a forthcoming U.K. and European tour I was asked to join, along with Charlie Hart, Brian Belshaw, John Porter and Ian `Stu' Stewart, and what a lovely band it was ! We rehearsed at Stu's house in Surrey, then eventually toured major cities in the U.K.

It was good to meet up with Eric again, we had worked together with John Mayall, eleven years earlier, and he had changed quite a lot in that time. He was much more confidant and outgoing, although some of that was down to his fondness for the Gargle – as was Ronnie, his comrade – in – booze !

Ronnie's repertoire was a mix of Faces songs. I got him to include Debris, Slim Chance songs, Ooh La La, etc., and we also did the Stones' Dead Flowers . Every tune was a pleasure to play, Ronnie mostly played rhythm guitar and his voice melted my heart – it still does .

We then embarked on the European tour, starting in Copenhagen and travelling through Sweden, Belgium, France and The Netherlands on the sleepers and dining car of the Orient Express, ending up in Munich. After the gigs some band and crew members slept on the train, while others – myself included chose the option of the various InterContinental's etc., luxury hotels!

It was a pleasure listening to Eric's band every night – the American one with Carl Radle, Jamie Oldaker, George Terry, etc., and at the end of Eric's set Ronnie and the rest of us ambled onstage to sing a rousing Goodnight Irene! And of course Ronnie's wife Katy and Eric's girlfriend Patty Boyd, as The Harlots, went down a storm dancing the Can Can to Ooh La La !

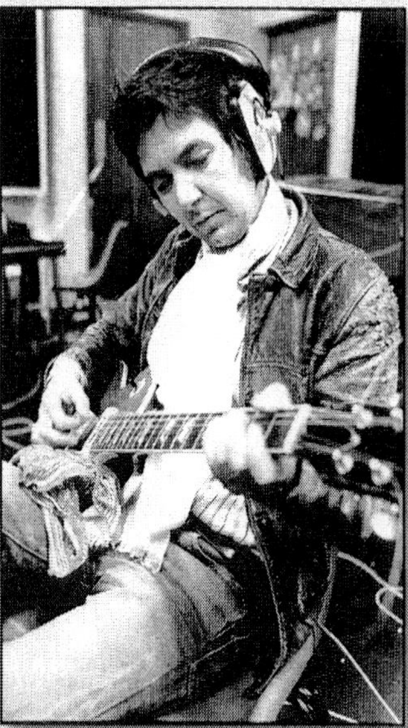

After a short break back home the ever generous Eric hired two luxury yachts, one for the two band's members and the other for the two crews and we sailed from Cannes to Ibiza where we played a gig, then on to Barcelona playing the bull fighting stadium, our final gig of the tour. It was after that gig, back in the hotel that Ronnie gathered the band together and told us that as he wasn't well he was having to let the band go and he was going to take a break for a while. He became *tearful and excused himself.*

Despite all the camaraderie and fun, on and offstage, and the wonderful music, Ronnie had had trouble with his right hand – I had taken him to an Osteopath friend of mine who couldn't do anything for him except advise rest, which of course he couldn't do in the middle of a tour and increasingly, after only a few drinks he would lose control of his legs , often falling down. Eric and the rest of us would drink heavily after a gig, but it became a common thing for a couple of us to have to escort both Ronnie and Eric (usually a little later) to their rooms.

Of course, we didn't know that these were the early signs of Ronnie's MS, but Stu and I were so saddened by Ronnie's news that instead of sailing back to Cannes with the others we flew back from Barcelona to London .

It's no exaggeration, John, for me to say that Ronnie was one of the loveliest men I have ever met, and whose music gave and continues to give me so much pleasure. If, by chance, these days I happen to hear Ronnie's voice singing, I get goose bumps.

SMALL FACES:

THE CASE FOR THE REAL MISSING ALBUM.

It's a great time to be a Small Faces fan right now, there was the release a couple of years ago of the 'Universal De-Luxe' re-issues of all the albums. Topped this year with the magnificent box set 'Immediate Years: Here Come The Nice'. We can also look forward to forthcoming reissues of 'The Autumn Stone' and 'There Are But Four Small Faces.'

With the advent of these box sets we have for the first time information, such as recording dates which shed light on the activities of the band in the studio.

The one thing for me is the fabled lost Small Faces album entitled "1862". The question I ask myself, is it an album that has been lost in the archives or is it just that, a fable? I can find no new evidence to suggest that the boys were deep into producing a follow up to 'Ogden's' unless the forthcoming Autumn Stone re-issue turns up a few more unreleased and unheard gems.

The real case for the missing Small Faces album is the 2nd album they did not release for Decca in late '66 or early 67. When I submitted the idea for this article to JH it centred on a killer album which should have come out middle March 1967 as a contractual filler album to Decca. I then thought of another situation and another lost record which could have come in late '66, if the boys had remained under Don Arden's management. By the way all below is purely speculative and just a bit of fun, but bear in mind most bands do have a couple of LP's that should have been. For example in 1966 The Who had an album pencilled in for release called Jigsaw Puzzle which never came out. This album was totally different to the album which they did eventually release in late 1966 called A Quick One.

Case 1.....In the late Summer of 1966 with the boys riding high in the charts with' All or Nothing' they enter IBC studio to start work on their second LP. It is from these mid-September 1966 sessions that Arden pulls 'My Mind's Eye' as a single to put the final nail in the coffin of their relationship with him. I think the boy's real argument with him was in and around how much time they were given in the studio to perfect their new tunes. Arden, being the old show-biz man that he was, had no interest in this and was just concerned with keeping the boys in the public eye with a hit single and milking cash from live performances. But just say that the boys did not have a problem with the release of 'My Mind's Eye' and stayed under Arden's management? He would have wanted to cash in on the success of the hit singles with an album aimed at the Christmas market of 1966. I reckon they would have released a similar type of album to their debut LP, assembled with the tracks recorded up until early December. I think this could have been as follows:-

Side 1

- Runaway
- My Mind's Eye
- Yesterday, Today & Tomorrow
- That Man
- My Way of Giving
- Green Circles

Side 2

- Tell Me Have You Ever Seen Me
- Understanding
- Patterns
- Plum Nellie
- You've Really Got a Hold On Me
- All or Nothing

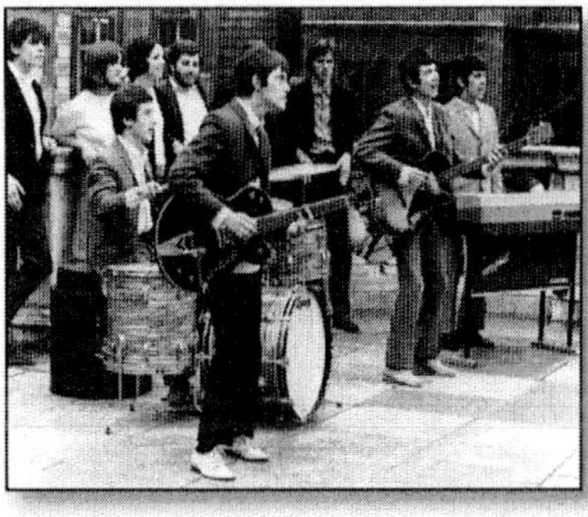

All things considered it is not a bad LP to have released but bear in mind that '66 saw the release of several progressive LPs by The Beatles, The Stones, The Kinks, The Beach Boys and The Byrds to name but a few. This LP would not have been progressive enough and would probably have garnered some good reviews but I am sure the reviewers would have pointed out its short comings.

Case 2.....We all know what really happened in late '66. The boys were sold by Don Arden and were in contractual limbo until Andrew Oldham turned up early '67. They carried on working on a second LP at IBC studio even though Arden wasn't on the scene anymore, the boys would have known that they still owed Decca two more singles and an album from their contract with Contemporary music. With this in mind I think the boys hit Olympic Studios in January '67 to work on an album that would free them from Decca and allow them to look elsewhere for a label quickly. The Here Come the Nice box set reveals that most of the tracks for the first Immediate Album were recorded in early January and February 1967 with a few additional recordings in April. I love the first Immediate LP but when it was released in June the band had moved on yet again as the singles of the Summer of 1967 would suggest and it must have seemed like an album out of step as a lot of music in the wake of Sgt Pepper must have done. For me the big question is, what if the boys had released the following LP in March 67 on Decca, would they have stayed together longer?

Side 1

- Tell Me Have you Ever Seen Me
- Mystery
- Yesterday, Today & Tomorrow
- Things Are Going To Get Better
- My Way of Giving
- Don't Burst My Bubble
- Green Circles

Side 2

- This Feeling of Spring
- I Can't Make it
- Get Yourself Together
- All Our Yesterday's
- Talk to you
- Eddies Dreaming
- Shades Of Green (Green Circles reprise)

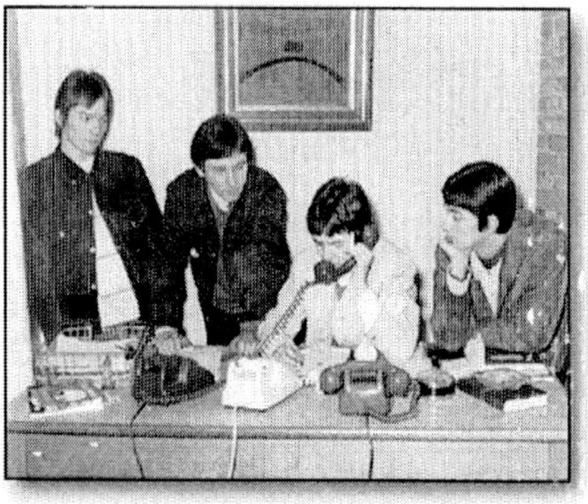

This album would have been a great nod to their Mod Soul days with a hint of what was to follow. In my mind they would have garnered great reviews for this LP and it would have been a major leap forward from their debut album and would of lead nicely into the fun and frolics of the Summer of '67 .We know Oldham was on the scene by this time he could have licensed the recordings to Decca like he did with the I Can't Make It single. This I am sure would have wiped the slate clean and allowed the boys to move on again quickly. As for Oldham he would have probably wanted an LP along the lines of There Are but Four Small Faces for late '67 release and when the boys came up with the 'Ogden's' concept in early '68 they would have bought themselves more time to develop that record into a stage show as did the Who did two years later with 'Tommy'. This would have kept them together to at least late 1969 and who knows into the early 70's.

The upshot is that none of this happened and what we are left with is the most perfect body of work from the greatest London band ever to exist and thankfully now getting the respect and treatment that they always deserved.

Roll on the Decca Box Set

PAUL KENNEDY

FLYING VISIT TO THE HEART OF FRANCE

The SMALL FACES IN PROVINCIAL PROVINS

Those who tend to flick through the excellent Small Faces chronicle Quite Naturally for the summer of 1966 as their reference will already know it. Ever since the May release of the chart bound single Hey Girl, a true sing-along number, our idols had been on the road permanently for live concerts as well as TV appearances.

But there was an undocumented gap between those gigs at the end of June in Sheffield's Mojo Club and the Marquee in London' Soho, namely the 27th June. Obviously on short notice, French television had steered the Small Faces to a live performance at an open air festival near Paris, which manager Don Arden did not want to do without.

Just how this brief sojourn came about logistically is not known anymore. Their permanent minder at the time, incidentally, was road manager and chauffeur Bill Corbett. Presumably, the Small Faces simply caught a plane to Paris and were then carted off to Provins, a mid-size town in the literal sense of its name, which is situated about 50 miles south west of the French metropolis. The picturesque festival site itself could be found in the medieval looking city centre. There, among other acts, the real fab four were supposed to play support to the Yardbirds, who already sported a legion of fans in France and had just been joined by Jimmy Page, as a bass player of all imaginable tasks!

Having arrived in the early afternoon, the available time after the sound check was used for a photo session on the castle premises, within the proximity of its characteristic Caesar Tower, the "Tour de Cesar". The precious contact to the professional lens man Jean-Louis Rancurel, an institution for the French Rock Music scene, had been negotiated by the Belgian music journalist Jean-Noel Coghe. Some of the castle wall shots were used for French EP releases that same summer. Coghe knew the Small Faces via two gigs in Flanders, part of their little tour of the continent in early January of the same year. Ever since then they had been in touch as good friends. Coghe offered his services as a kind of assistant to Corbett and he certainly made himself useful as an interpreter. Eventually Ronnie Lane invited him to their mutual London pad in Pimlico.

Coghe was especially taken with Steve's charisma. "My memory of Steve Marriott has been solidified as such: slight, petite, diffident, but blessed with an unbelievable power and presence. I can picture him in front of me now, approaching the microphone with half closed eyes, moving his left hand to his ear and having that awesome voice splutter out of him with sheer power and exceptional tonality".

The open air festival, held on a Monday, started in the early evening apparently with the Small Faces. It is not documented how long their set lasted and which songs were played but there were certainly those numbers which were already tried and tested live nuggets such as Whatcha Gonna Do About It, I've Got Mine, Sha La La La Lee and Hey Girl. The latter, incidentally, became a national hit over there, complete with French lyrics and sung by Ronnie Bird (aka Ronald Mehu) as the flipside of N'ecoute pas ton coeur.

On stage, the Small Faces were followed by Screaming Lord Sutch with his Savages. Steve Marriott appeared excited with the performance of that wild bunch and, according to eye witnesses; he wanted to take part in the encore but encountered some aggro with the musicians, who were not too keen on his involvement!

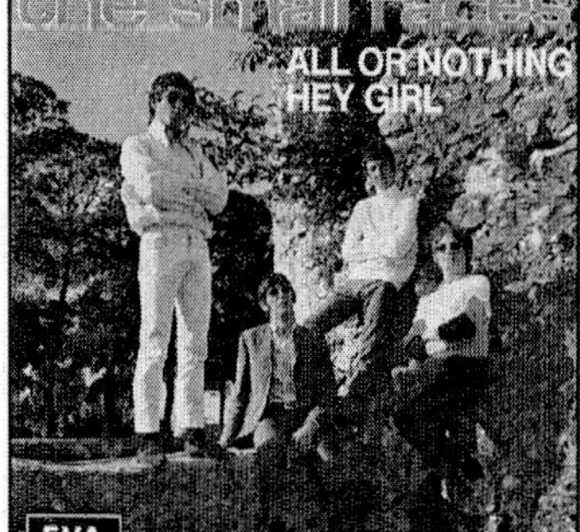

Simon and Garfunkel were also on the bill but when exactly they appeared is not known. It is pretty hard to imagine that those two followed in the footsteps of Lord Sutch! Instead, it can be assumed that now was the time for the Yardbirds to start their set, which was eagerly awaited by the majority of the audience.

Excerpts from their appearance were screened only a few weeks later in the TV series Music Hall de France. Just like Lord Sutch's performance these actually still exist, while the concert by the Small Faces, if it had been filmed at all, is believed to be lost without any trace.

ROLAND SCHMITT

SHA LA LA LA LEE - THE TRUTH!

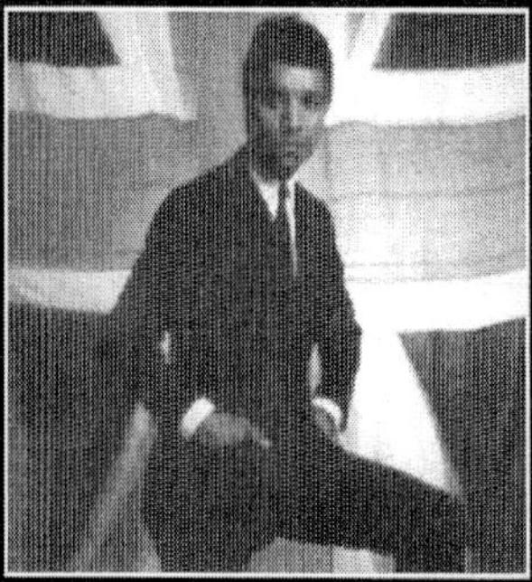

CO-WRITER KENNY LYNCH TELLS THE TALE!

Mort Shuman (who had previously written hit songs for none other than the king of Rock and Roll, Elvis Presley) and I wrote "Sha La La La Lee" in about five minutes! We actually wrote it for Amen Corner. When we delivered the song to their manager he just turned his nose up and said it was too simple and not at all suitable for his band. He then said that he had another group, The Small Faces, and it would be just perfect for them. The Small Faces recorded it with Ian Samwell producing. I was away filming in Rome and Ian sent me a copy. I said " Don't put it out, it's terrible!" When I flew back, the following week, we went back into the studio and re-recorded it.

I said to Steve Marriott "Are you sure you're alright with the key" and he said "Yeah, no problem". When we came to do it, it turned out he couldn't hit the top notes at all, so I did the background falsetto myself.

I flew back out to Rome the next day to continue filming and was still out there when the record came out. It reached number three, I think. The funny thing was that Mort Shuman really hated the song and had said to me "For heavens sake don't put my name on it!" When I told him, later, that it had charted in just four days he said to me "You did put my name on it didn't you?".........

BILL MARRIOTT INTERVIEW

By John Hellier (3rd September, 1995)

To most people who knew him Steve Marriott's dad, Bill, was a man of few words. Here he opens up to talk about his famous son, in what is possibly his only interview ever.

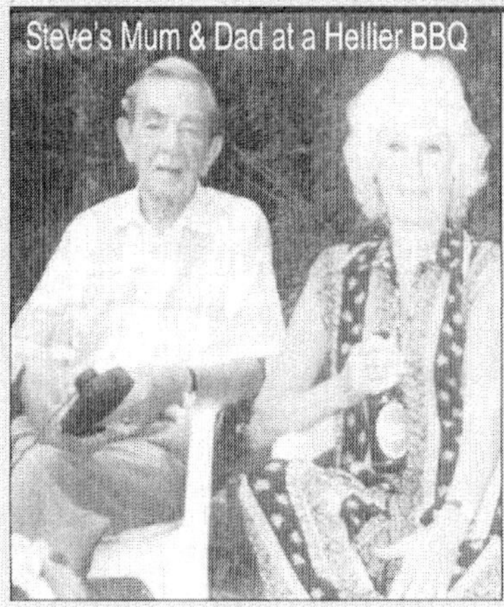

Steve's Mum & Dad at a Hellier BBQ

JH: What was Steve like as a child, when did you first realise he had this unique talent?
BILL: My first realisation was when I bought him a ukulele and to my surprise he more or less played it straight away. So I bought him a guitar and got him a teacher but the teacher said it was useless trying to teach him because he'd developed his own way of teaching himself. Also taught himself to read music. Very good.

JH: What was he like at school and what was your reaction to him burning the school classroom?
BILL: When we went to see his teacher at open day she told us there's only word I can use for Steve "unique". "He's unique, I caught him hanging out the window about four storeys up with just his boots showing" "What's really annoying is that he does absolutely nothing all term and then just a couple of days before exam time he'll swot up and ends up with good results. Most frustrating for all the kids who have been working hard all term and end up with an inferior grade than Steve" "underneath a couldn't care less attitude was a very bright boy". As for the fire we're still not sure whether he did it or not. Somebody put a lit match or a cigarette through a knot in the floorboards and whoosh up it went! (For the true account as told by a schoolmate read "All Too Beautiful").

JH: When did he start singing?
BILL: He started singing seriously when he was about 16. He'd been to Italia Conti previously and done some singing there along with the acting. We were actually very disappointed when he gave the acting up.

JH: Why did he stop acting?
BILL: He was mixing with the likes of Ronnie Lane and other aspiring musicians and his heart was set on music. I remember one acting audition in particular, he never had many auditions but they knew his potential and normally just gave him the parts, but this was for the National theatre and I was so very excited. He came back from it and told us he'd flopped but we found out later that he'd lied. He was actually offered the part but didn't want to be tied up for a year.

JH: Did he enjoy being in Oliver?
BILL: Very much so. All the boys took different parts so it was never boring and Ron Moody (Fagin) was a very, very nice man to work with.

JH: How did he get that part?
BILL: I was working in the print and I saw the Daily Sketch advertising for a boy for the part and I came home and told my wife. We knew he had the cheek and the cockney appeal so my wife took him for an audition. Although they had lots of boys from various acting schools auditioning Steve got the part because he was a natural.

JH: What did the audition involve?
BILL: He took his guitar and played and sung the Buddy Holly song "Oh Boy". When they said, "It's fine" he said "For my next number….." They said "That's enough thank you" and of course, he got the part. He was such a confident child.

JH: Did you always believe he was destined for stardom?
BILL: Oh yes. Even a woman down our street where we lived, who was a fortune teller, told us that he would go right to the top of whatever profession he chose to take. And she was so right.

JH: What did he like about Ronnie?
BILL: They were definitely two of a kind. With the song writing they were there for each other and helped one another out with ideas. Ronnie always encouraged Steve to write. Steve was so prolific in that area, he'd write complete songs in half an hour!

JH: When Steve first went into the pop business did you think it was a bad move?
BILL: No. All the parents thought the same "Well that's what they want to do, let them do it".

JH: Did you try and convince him to continue with his acting career?
BILL: At first we tried to persuade him to carry on with the acting career but soon it was clear to us that it was to no avail. I remember Steve first watching the Beatles on television, must have been around 1964 and told me " The vocals are ok but the playing is crap" I told him "You can't talk like that son, they've made it and you're a nobody" He said "I'll be like them one day, Top Of The Pops and all that" He was right, he made it and I was a proud man.

JH: What was the first sign to you that he was going to make it with the Small Faces?
BILL: "Whatcha Gonna Do About It". I was working at the Evening News at the time and this manager at Decca got a load of big yellow placards advertising the new single. I stuck them all around the Evening News office and got told off about it.

JH: Did you go and watch any of the early gigs?
BILL: Oh yeah, I remember going to see them in local pubs in Canning Town, Dagenham and the Ruskin Arms, of course. After the hit records had begun they moved to bigger venues but we'd always go if we could.

JH: How important was the East End origins of the Small Faces and do you think it brought anything to the sound and the look of the band?
BILL: Quite a lot, I think. They were proud to be East End boys made good. A lot of stars of stage and music have originated from the East End and even way back at Italia Conti Steve was referred to as a second Anthony Newley because he, like Steve, had gone there from a working class East End background and had to pay his own fees with the work that they had got for him. Steve was proud of being an East Ender and never forgot where he came from. In the later years he'd come back and play gigs at the Three Rabbits pub, one of our old locals.

JH: How did feel when the very first single became a hit?
BILL: The wife and me were indoors and it was played on the television, Top Of The Pops I think. It was a very exciting time for us but Steve always made our lives exciting right from the beginning. It was absolutely wonderful when he had a number one hit. We've always followed Steve's career carefully.

JH: What were your thoughts on Don Arden?
BILL: Steve always thought he was a good manager and he introduced him to me. I didn't like him at all right from the beginning. I don't like any managers very much, I'm afraid. I told him so. At least I told him that I've never met a straight manager yet and suddenly I've got a couple of big chaps standing right behind me so I kept my mouth shut. I really didn't trust him. Managers in the pop business are not like the stage agents and managers.

JH: Did you ask Don Arden about the money or lack of it?
BILL: Yeah, I went to see him in his Carnaby Street office and told him I wasn't satisfied with things. Steve was broke but wanted to buy us a house. Arden told me that not only did Steve have no money but he also owed him £3,000. His bank account was minus £3,000! I told him I wanted to see receipts for all this money that he said Steve had spent. He opened a drawer and produced little bits of scrap paper written in pencil "after show party" "champagne for so and so" they were useless; they weren't receipts of any kind. I told Steve "I'm afraid you've been caught, son". He just said, "bless him". That's all he ever said when he was caught by Arden and others "bless him".

JH: Did you approve of Don Arden moving the band into Westmoreland Terrace?
BILL: We didn't object to it as much as the other parents. We had faith in Steve. We knew he was an extrovert but he was not an idiot. They could have done with more looking after; they were still very young you know.

JH: Didn't the management look after them? How did it work?
BILL: Don Arden employed a road manager to look after and organise them, Bill somebody, but I don't think he did a very good job. They were working seven days a week, gigging up and down the country, endless interviews and radio and television work and still they had no money in the bank. Arden would set up clothes accounts for them in all the Carnaby Street shops and tell them to buy as much as they want. Being young, naïve and mod they did. But the bills were paid out of their money not his and he'd already taken something like 40% of their wages beforehand. It was daylight robbery; I don't know how he slept at night.

JH: Presumably you were pleased when they switched management?
BILL: At the time Andrew Loog Oldham seemed like a genuine sort of guy. Steve loved him at first and the boys spent loads of time in the studio and less time on the road which is precisely what they wanted. I don't think Oldham was as crooked as Arden but he was a poor businessman. During the Small Faces time with him they recorded a number one album "Ogden's Nut Gone Flake". It was number one for six weeks and stayed in the top ten for thirteen weeks and still they were broke! They should have made a fortune with that one record alone but nothing. Story of Steve's life, I'm afraid.

JH: What are your favourite Steve Marriott songs?

BILL: "Lazy Sunday" "All Or Nothing" "Itchycoo Park" and there was a great song called "When Will We Be Free" (Alabama 69) which was on one of the early Humble Pie albums.

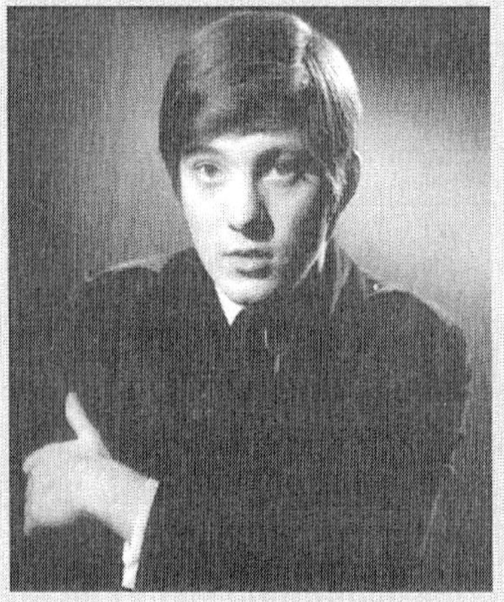

JH: Steve is often underrated as a vocalist. Do you think he was up there with the likes of Jagger and McCartney?

BILL: Oh definitely, I may be biased but he was a great soul singer and don't forget he also played guitar and played it wonderfully well. He had the lot. He auditioned for the Rolling Stones in the 70s but Mick Jagger saw him as a front man and a threat.

JH: Were you, as a parent, worried about the drink and drugs associated with the business?

BILL: Yes, of course. We knew that Steve smoked a bit of pot, well all of them did, but he'd never ever use a needle. Steve for all his good points was a coward. He could never fix a needle in himself so we were never worried about that. Don Arden once tried to tell us that they were all on the needle but we wouldn't buy it. He called a meeting of the parents and the others were all really shocked.

JH: Was Steve disappointed that the Small Faces never made it big in America?

BILL: Yes, I think he was. They had a minor hit with "Itchycoo Park" and they should really have gone over there then but they didn't and I don't know why. Steve's dream of making it in the States did come true but he had to wait.

JH: Why do you think he left the Small Faces when he did?

BILL: He seemed frustrated after "Ogden's" I don't really know why. All these pop singer's use the phrase "I've gone as far as I can go" and I really don't know what they mean. He'd put everything into "Ogden's" and was really proud of that album and rightly so, but to finish then baffled me and I'm still baffled to this day by it.

JH: By forming Humble Pie he presumably wanted to go from pop star to rock star?

BILL: By the end of the Small Faces he was getting into a heavier style but by then the scene was moving in that direction generally. It was what he wanted to do. I didn't like it half as much as the Small Faces but there was no stopping him. Strangely though the early Humble Pie recordings weren't heavy, quite the opposite it had an acoustic feel to it.

JH: Do you think that when he went to America with Humble Pie he changed?

BILL: Well he was a home loving boy and we always told him "don't forget your roots". He did love us and we loved him but America did change his attitude. It made him harder; he seemed to be harder when he came back. He wasn't the softie that he used to be and others such as his wife and Jim Leverton will tell you the same.

JH: Humble Pie were massive in the States but never really made it in a big way in their home

country. Why do you think that was?
BILL: They were indeed massive in America and played all the big stadiums such as Shea Stadium and Madison Square Gardens in New York. We would fly out there for most of those. Magnificent places and magnificent shows. They had American management and were especially groomed for the States. The albums sold in big numbers out there as well.

JH: During Steve's last ten years or so he seemed to be deliberately avoiding becoming famous again. It was almost as if he was happier without it?
BILL: Steve always hated the big star thing, always. Even when he was having number one hit records he would like to mix with ordinary kids. It was difficult when he came back to the East End because all the kids that he knew from way back would treat him like a god and he didn't want that. He was never bigheaded or toffee-nosed. I used to say to him "Steve, you should have all the money in the bank that you want" and he'd just reply, "I've got no interest in money, none at all". Whether he was unlucky or just a bad judge of management I don't know but he bought us this house (in Sawbridgeworth) and one of the last things he done before he died was to put double glazing in for us. We could never grumble he was marvellous to us.

JH: How did you learn of Steve's tragic death and were you surprised by the amount of attention that was given to the funeral?
BILL: I was here at home and got a telephone call from Toni, his wife. She was hysterical and couldn't talk, she put somebody else on the line and we were told. I just couldn't take it in, still can't. We will never get over it. As for the funeral I was too eaten up to see what was happening. I knew there were hundreds of people there and television film crews but was quite oblivious to most of the day. The one guy that really comforted us was Steve's best pal, Joe Brown. Although Steve's later years were low key he still demanded a lot of respect and for that reason alone I wasn't surprised by the big crowd. There were even young kids there on scooters and young girls with just one flower. Touching.

JH: At last, some three years after his death, Steve is getting some deserved recognition, at least for his Small Faces work. Many of today's contemporary artists are citing him as a major influence?
BILL: Well I think that's wonderful. He didn't always get the credit he deserved during his lifetime.

THANKS BILL FOR YOUR TIME AND YOUR MEMORIES.

Sadly Bill passed away a few months after this interview was conducted.

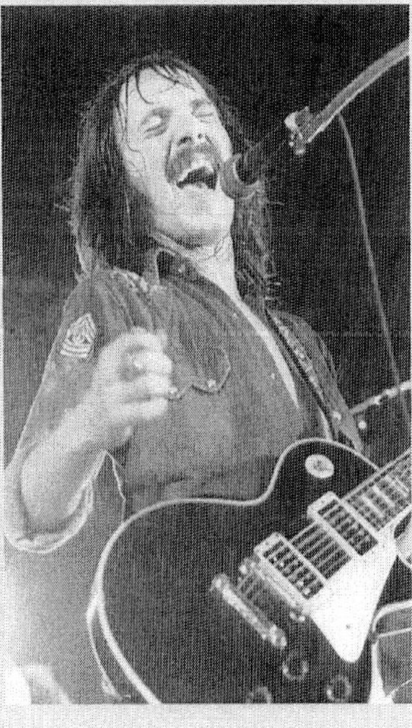

What Better Company?

(A Day In The Studio With Ian McLagan—July 22 2002)

by Nikki Sudden

Every year I like to give myself a birthday present. Sometimes they're good, other times they're fine—the one for 2002 was exceptional… it was a few days late but well worth the wait… My birthday is on July 19—we went in the studio with Ian McLagan three days later.

Mac and I first met in Los Angeles 10 years earlier when I ended up staying at his house in Highland Park for a week or so during April / May 1992—the L.A. riots kicked off a few days into the trip! I'd ended up in L.A. with Radio One DJ, Annie Nightingale, who was visiting California to work on a Mike Oldfield book and needed someone to drive her around. She asked if I'd care to accompany her. "Where are we staying?" "With my friends Kim and Mac!" "Kim and Mac who?" I innocently asked…

Kim McLagan picked us up at LAX and after a few drinks we headed out to 230 San Pascal. Mac has been married to Kim Kerrigan for over 25 years now. Annie and Kim were friends from years back… from when Kim was Mrs. Keith Moon.

Mac and Kim were great hosts. The Faces have always been one of my favourite bands and I've always wanted to play with Mac. He invited me to join him and The Bump Band on stage at the John Bull in Pasadena the night we arrived but I was so drunk and jet-lagged that I didn't realise. The next night we had a few drinks and the conversation ended up getting rather confusing. As Mac so charmingly put it, "The first time I met Nikki I thought he was a fucking idiot… Met him a few more times and realised he was a really nice guy…"

Next time we met was a couple of oceans away in '95—Mac was playing with Rod at the Empire Pool in Wembley. A brief aftershow, "Hi and hello… What are you up to now?" and I didn't even get a signed football! We didn't meet up again till I went to see the Bump Band at the Zodiac in Oxford—November 2000—when Mac was doing his first ever solo UK tour—and the three shows I saw were pretty damn good! Ended up chatting in the dressing room for an hour or so after the show. The next evening in Cambridge I did a brief interview for my still half-finished Ron Wood (If You Gave Him A Chance!) book. The last question I asked Mac was if he'd be up for playing on my next album… "How much are you going to pay me?" "How much do you charge?" "Lots!" "I know that… I don't know if I can afford you…" "Well, I'm so busy I don't have to do cheap sessions anymore… I don't have the time… I haven't been at home for more than four days in a row for months… months and months…" After the gig at first he didn't seem so keen, then after a few drinks he started saying yes. The next time we got together was in Berlin—May 2001 when he was playing with Carl Carlton and the Songdogs. After a lot

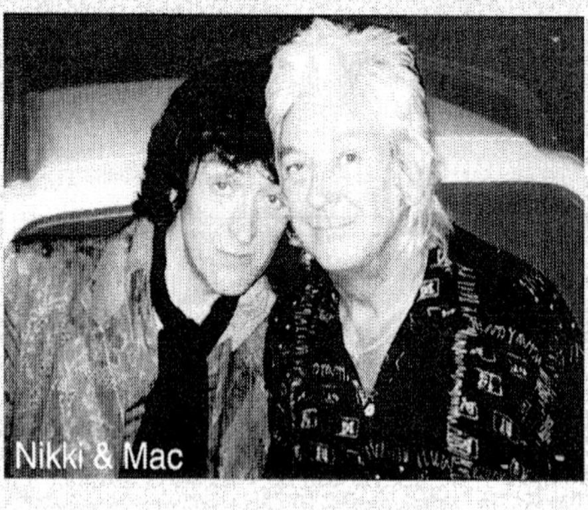
Nikki & Mac

of liasing via email we finally worked out a date when he'd be in England and when I, and my band could get across the Channel from Berlin where we're based. On July 19 we left Germany and drove, drove and drove.

****

Arriving in England our first stop was in Richmond where I showed bassist, John Barry, and drummer, Stephane Doucerain, the ultimate Ronnie Wood collectable, The Wick. A pub lunch and then I drove the final leg home and we slept… The next day we were in WSRS studio for five hours to get the equipment set up, microphones on the drums, guitar amps, bass d/i, vocal mike… Engineer, John Rivers, set about getting the levels on the mixing desk together, that kind of thing. The first number we wanted to record with Mac was a descending 4-chord song that I'd come up with during soundchecks on a European tour a couple of years earlier. Wooden Floor had started off as a number entitled No One Left Alive but quickly evolved with lyrics echoing the Feast of the Passover and the Children of Israel's exile in Egypt mixed with undressing girls on wooden floors. The idea of whatever the song is about seemed quite appealing at the time—and still seems appealing now…

We'd played the number at gigs for a while but I'd decided to drop it from the set until I had a clearer picture of how we should play it. It went through a few changes including the addition of the middle eight… John, Stephane and I had been rejigging the song's arrangement at last minute rehearsals over the past week—trying for a different approach to the way it had been going.

****

Monday morning, July 22—10 minutes to midday—we went to Leamington Spa British Rail to pick up the first of the album's special guests, Ian 'Mac' McLagan. Mac bounced down the stairs as I came up, "Hello, darling! How are you?"

As soon as he got to the studio Mac checked out the organ. He'd mailed me earlier with the comments, "M101 not great, but that's what I used in Small Faces for most Immediate recordings. I can't bring 'my' Hammond and Leslie. We rent in the UK, and they cost big money and just ain't something I can bring. You have to make sure this M100 is in good working order. There's nothing worse than an organ that 'worked when we last turned it on'. I don't want to waste your time and mine." The Hammond worked fine… Then he had a brief chat with engineer John Rivers about miking techniques—we ran through Wooden Floor and the session was off… Even though we'd been playing the song for a few years sometimes it takes until that very last minute when you get the perfect version together. You need the pressure of being in the studio to play your best and being in the studio with my and John Barry's favourite Hammond and piano player certainly helped… I showed Mac the chords on my new five-string guitar. "It's yer basic Keith-chords," I said, "I'm not sure what they're called…"

With the first few run-throughs Mac was working out his part and we were still figuring out the revitalised arrangement. It must have looked as though we didn't really know how the song went. At first Stephane was playing too 'correctly' as though he was trying to impress us—I asked him if he could play a bit looser, a bit rougher round the edges. As soon as he realised that was what was needed he was great… At least the headphone levels were all fine by this time.

Mac made a few suggestions… I asked if he could do an organ 'doodle' after the middle-eight—he did—the track was acquiring soul. In some ways this is what I was paying Mac for—for part of his soul. Everyone threw in a few suggestions and we had another go. Then we played through the middle eight a few times—there was a new part at the end which John Barry had suggested I try the day before. It sounded great when I played it right… sounded even better when the Hammond doubled my part. I can't remember how many takes we did—not many. Three or four tops. But when you get the one it's something you just know. We had the studio for ten hours and I'd noted six songs that I wanted Mac to play on—Wooden Floor hadn't even been one of those!

The next song out of the pot is something I came up with around twenty years ago. It took another twenty before I was totally sure what to do with it… When The Lord is the first 'gospel' number I've recorded… I played guide guitar and sang while the other three carried on. When the song as such had finished I started improvising lyrics, 'The Pharisees and all their tribes / Never tried to run your life…' Searching the sky for lyrics. The usual kind of stuff.

After a while I came up with the line Never Let Me Go, which got repeated a few times. At first I was a bit worried that there was a Dylan song of the same title but then I realised it was a Johnny Ace number that Bob had covered in Renaldo And Clara. Mac was vamping away like a good'un… at one point during the 9_ minute track he drifted into Je T'Aime, the Johan Sebastian Bach / Serge Gainsbourg composition. That's something that'll get cut out of the finished track. The three of them must have wondered how long they were going to have to play this three-chord piece for. I think we did it in one take. Maybe we did a quick run-through first but nothing more. In an email a day or so before Mac had warned that his playing might not be 100% up to scratch for the session. He wrote the following, "I have to warn you that I caught my left hand index finger in a door at home last Friday and though I have been rehearsing here since yesterday, I'm hardly using my left hand so far. It's quite painful as it is, but not broken. I have a day off tomorrow followed by two gigs in a row, Friday and Saturday. I just hope it's back to it's usual use by Monday because playing with Bill [Billy Bragg & The Blokes], I know where I'm going if you see what I mean, and can carefully avoid too much accidental pain, but playing other things can mean random acts of wild imaginings… Anyway, I have a day off on Sunday as well, so I feel it could be OK. This is just to let you know what's happening, I'm not begging off, I just want to give you the best of myself, that's all. So with 4 days till Monday I think we'll be alright." Arriving at the studio he taped up the damaged finger with some special American plaster, "It's quite painful as it is, but not broken." A cry of anguish can be heard at the end of the extended jam! Or maybe it was relief at the thing having finally ground to a halt.

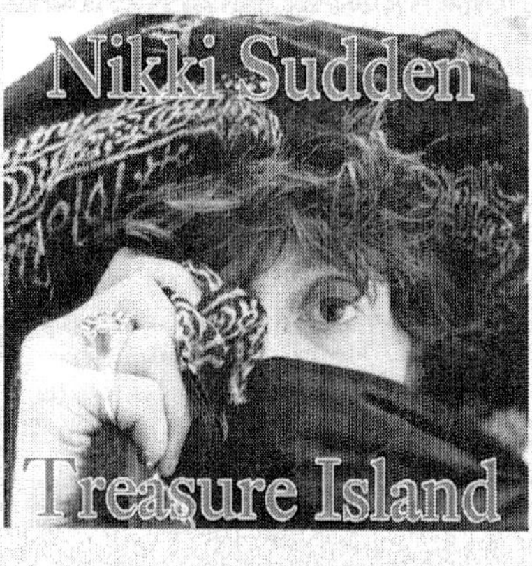

I was thinking what to do with the two songs I now had for the price of one: When The Lord / Never Let Me Go when Mac woke me from my thoughts, "So if that's two songs, Nikki?" he asked. A look of mild (financial) panic must have grazed across my brow… "Oh, it's one piece…" I said in an unconvinced way. "Don't worry, I was joking," Mr. McLagan smiled. That was one relief!

The next song, Fall Any Further, though bearing no similarity at all was partly inspired by the classic last Faces' single, You Can Make Me Dance—spot it if you can! It's more the feel than anything. The title came from a paragraph from All The Rage in which Mac described his father having made a pot of tea for his wife and himself—and carrying two cups, saucers and a newspaper upstairs to the bedroom. He tried an ice-skating sidestep at the turn of the stairs but instead of making the intended move he tripped and tumbled down—tea tray in hand:

"Mum heard the noise, and his muffled groans and jumped out of bed and ran downstairs after him. 'Mac! Mac!' she said. 'Darling let me help you up.' Lying on his back, covered in hot tea and broken crockery, bruised and sore all over, he said: 'No, leave me where I am. I can't fall any further.'"

The line stuck in my head and a few minutes later the basic song was written. The bridge riff dates from the early 1980's. It was called Motown Riff. If you hang onto ideas for long enough they generally fit in somewhere. After a few drinks at the Junction in Cambridge I told Mac the background to the song and generously he said, "Take it! You have my blessing..." I said, "You have to play on it..." And lo and behold he ended up putting down both Hammond and piano on the track!

After the first couple of breeze through numbers Mac must have been getting the impression that the whole session would be a doddle. This track probably made him rethink that thought. Chord and key changes galore litter it's way. I'd been playing This Old Heart Of Mine—the Isley Brothers' song that Rod recorded back when—I had a Rod Stewart songbook with the words and the chords. That's the way songs often come—you're playing one thing when something falls into your head. I asked Mac if he recognised what I'd got the track from—he didn't until I showed him. Basically you double the length of the chords from the verse... then it goes off somewhere else...

There's a little piano motif that Mac plays at the end of the bridge that's just so magic. I thought it was worth the money just for those few seconds—anything else was a bonus. A few minutes earlier I'd asked if they'd used piano on Motown records... Mac seemed struck dumb! "Of course they bloody did..."

****

The fourth track is called Stay Bruised. I played the number through on acoustic to give Mac the rough idea of the feel of the track—I wanted him to start this one on the piano while I played five-string... There's two different ways of doing the song on guitar with a step-down from the C chord to the F—the other way just hints at it—I think this version turned out as a perfect mixture. Once every year you come up with a great love song. This is one of my most recent. Written on a train going from Salzburg to Frankfurt then fine-tuned over the years this was going to be the title track of the album. After we'd done the take I mentioned to Mac that the number was one of my 'LA Rod' ballads—I thought he wouldn't like that and I was right. But hopefully it turned out the kind of way I Was Only Joking might have done had the Faces done it. Mind you the guitar solo, played later by Darrell Bath, is pure Jim Cregan. Whatever it is, it's perfect. Pure, that's what it is.

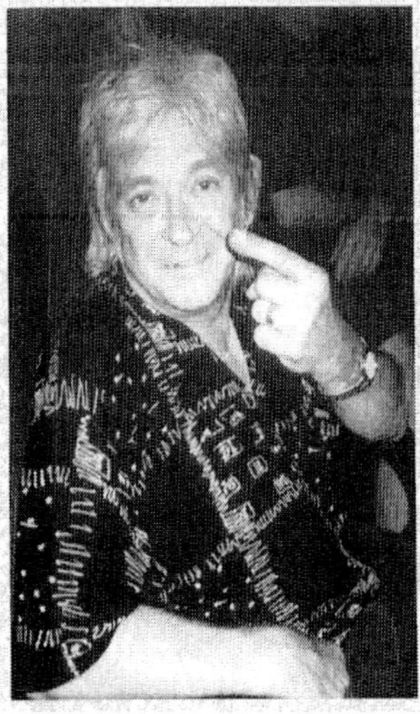

While Mac was doing another piano part I rustled up some food. Over mashed potatoes and whatever I did a second interview with the one-time Face—more questions about a half-remembered past. Then it was off down the studio local, The Talbot, for a couple of well-deserved pints of Guinness. John Barry took the opportunity to further quiz Mac about the Faces. We got to hear the story of Plonk's leaving first hand. I should have recorded the conversation in the pub as well. The relevant tales got remembered…

If there'd been more time—and if I'd had more money I'd have loved Mac to play on the whole album. But he only had one day free—and I didn't have any more spare cash! After a few drinks he agreed to do the last track half-price… As long as I paid his train and taxi fare which I was going to offer anyway. Looking For A Friend took a run through and a take. A pretty basic twelve bar a bit reminiscent of one of Rod's best ever covers—it's pretty difficult to go wrong with a Chuck Berry number. I said to Mac, "Just play Sweet Little Rock'N'Roller!" When Rod had played Aston Villa football ground in 1995 I'd been hanging off the barrier—Mac took solo after solo in that night's version—he knew what I meant.

Looking For A Friend is in some ways the oldest song on the album. In some ways because the 'song' as such was just a half-remembered chorus which I dragged out of my memory at a rehearsal a year or so back. Every time we played it the melody line of the verses was totally different—and sung whatever words fell into my mind. The lyrics of the finished version are one of many… The title has never changed. It originally came together in Wimbledon in 1975. The tracks Mac plays on have his magic piano and Hammond sprinkled all over them. As I wrote to a few friends, "He's played with the Faces, played with the Stones, played with Bob Dylan and now he's played with me…" True enough… And I gave John Barry a day he'll never forget.

****

I took Mac to the station, paid him his money, we shook hands and he trotted off to get the train back to London. With typical British Rail efficiency the 1 hour 40 minute journey back took a good three hours. At least he had time to count his cash! The next day he sent me the following mail:

Hardehar Nikki,

I couldn't believe it. The train was half hour late and only took me to Banbury, then went to Bicester, some other place and then Princes Risborough on a bus, then the last train back to Marylebone

Luckily, I found a taxi eventually and the streets were so empty I've decided to only travel at night in future.

Very much enjoyed y'all, and the music.

Good luck with the project.

Cheers for now,

Mac

****

I'd told my father that Ian McLagan was coming along to play organ and piano. My Dad, who also plays piano and organ, hadn't got a clue who Ian McLagan was. He asked, "Have you got sheet music for him?" "No!" I replied. "Well, how will he be able to play the songs then?" My father was a bit puzzled. A few days later I asked, "Dad, would you like to play on one of the songs from my new album. His immediate response was, "I can't play it without the music." I said, "Dad, it's only four chords!" and showed him the basic timing… So it's ended up with my dad and Lee McLagan's dad playing on the same session. Which I think is pretty cool!

Nikki Sudden And The Last Bandits Rookwood 001
www.nikkisudden.com

IAN McLAGAN INTERVIEW

by Binky Phillips.....December 2013

It was a week before Christmas break in 1967. My friend, Steven T, was 'going home' to England for two weeks. Although born in the USA, Steve's parents were both utterly British. His Dad seemed like a retired Colonel from Her Majesty's Army. Bristled moustache and bristling manner. His Mum was so classically a middle-'classy' lady, with such a proper accent, she seemed like some distant royal. "So, what do you want me to bring back for ya, Binky" asked lovely Steven. "Oh man, Small Faces albums, any you can find. That's it. Small Faces, Steve." Two weeks later, back home in Brooklyn, Steve came over to my house with the first Small Faces album on Decca and the second Small Faces album on Immediate. I paid him the $10 I owed him. By the time I'd finished listening to side one of the Decca album, the Small Faces were immediately the sixth in my Rock Pantheon next to The Who, The Rolling Stones, The Yardbirds, The Kinks, The Beatles. Yes, they were/are that good. The more you have heard, the more you realize that was always where they belonged. When Punk broke out in all its angry ugly anti-glory, only The Who and Small Faces were immune from their sulphuric disdain. It's obvious why. Small Faces were punks. Punks with world-class chops.

Here's we go... One ringy-dingy, two ringy-dingy, three ringy-dingy...
"'Ello, is that you, Binky?"
Binky: "Hey, Mac... Look, this is very odd for me. I'm a musician, not an interviewer, Mac. I want you to know, I had a friend bring me back the two Small Faces albums from London, Christmas, 1967, based on photos of the band alone. Your music blew me away. I am a stone fan of you and your band, so bear with my awkwardness."
Mac: "It's nice to hear your background, very much appreciated."
Binky: "I think the thing civilians find eternally fascinating is Pop Stardom. What's it like being a Rock Star? For better or worse, Mac, that's what you are. I mean, it says so on Wikipedia."
Mac: [laughs] Yes, they've got William as my middle name. I don't know where the fuck they got that from. I've tried to change it, but, it's impossible for me to do it. Who decided I'd be Ian William Patrick? Okay, so, I've decided that's who I am. You can call me Willy."
Binky: "Okay, Willy. Getting back to Pop Stardom, when was that precise moment you felt, 'Oh my God, I've done it!'?"
Mac: "That was the MINUTE I joined the Small Faces, Binky. They were in an office, and as I came 'round the door, Steve Marriott laughed and picked me up. Then, all three picked me up on their shoulders. I'd found my brothers, that's the truth of it."
Binky: "I'd heard that the other three Small Faces didn't even know what you looked like when you joined the band... really?"
Mac: "What happened was, they'd seen a review in a magazine of the band I was in

and it raved about my playing and the fact that I played a Hammond [the best organ ever made]. And there was a photograph of the handsome Boz Burrell, who wound up in Bad Company, who was our singer, with my name under it. So, they thought, 'Well, he's got a Hammond, he plays great, and he's good looking'... [Mac starts heartily laughing]... Hooray!" When they met me, they knew I wasn't the guy they saw in the magazine. Steve said, "Oh well, he ain't good lookin' but, he is short!" [more laughter from both of us].

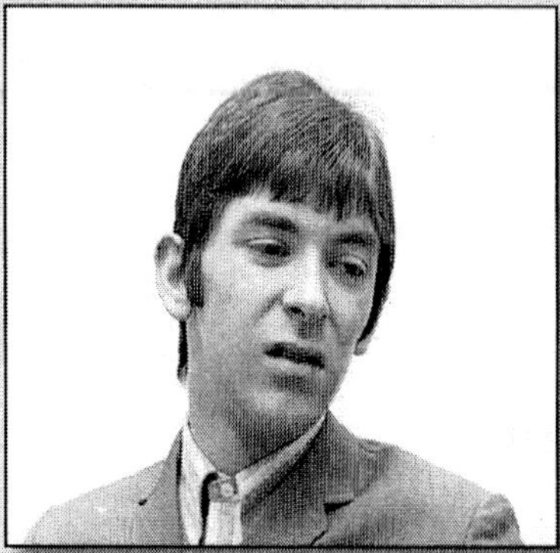

Binky: "Well, if I had to share a prison cell, I think you're better looking than Boz, but, maybe that's just me."

Mac: [more laughs]

Binky: "Leads me into the fashion aspect of the Small Faces, Mac. Even though we only saw you in photos and never onstage, me 'n' all my friends in the States thought you guys were the absolute coolest looking band, the best fuckin' haircuts, the best suits... You guys were just dead impeccable. Was this just the fact that you guys had that much savvy and taste or was some stylist coaching you?"

Mac: "Hell yeah, we had taste. No one picked out our clothes for us." [giggles at the thought]

Binky: "Let me ask you about the songs, Mac. All those Marriott/Lane songs. Can you give me a sense of how those two were writing together?"

Mac: "It varied. For example, 'All Or Nothing' was pretty much all Steve. 'Itchycoo Park' was almost all Ronnie. I mean, we were always together. I heard all those songs going through their growing pains. Lots of songs evolved, rather than, Hey, I've written a song, fellas. One summer, we all had boats and mine was the biggest, so we were always on my boat. Ideas were flowing. And that's how I broke the Marriott/Lane logjam in the song writing department and got writing credits on Ogden's Nut Gone Flake. But, you really need to read the lyrics to 'Itchycoo Park'. It's NOT just about getting high, which is the way Steve turned it. Steve wrote the part about feeding the duck in the pond and all that bollocks, Ronnie is actually singing about Oxford and Cambridge! And what Ronnie was saying was, he didn't have money, he didn't have education, but, he could find beauty in a nettle patch. And not in the 'England's green and fair land' way and all that bollocks. Ronnie found beauty in a nettle patch in the East End of London. Rônnie sang, [Mac over enunciates] It's... All... Too... Beautiful. The only trouble was, the song was so fast, and Steve turned it into [sings like a corny vaudevillian] It's Ah All Tooo Beeeoootifula! Frankly, I hated that. So, I've recorded a version on my tribute to Ronnie, A Spiritual Boy, An Appreciation of Ronnie Lane and I did it the way it should've been done. It's still a 'great hit' and all that, but, it's a better song than you'd normally think."

Binky: "You could be describing John Lennon's 'All Across The Universe'..."

Mac: "Yeah! You know I just heard that the other day. Love that song."

Binky: "So, you were a very young man, a kid really, inter-acting with two of the most spectacularly colourful eccentric influential guys in the history of Pop music, absolute monoliths in England, and almost diametrical opposites. Tell us what it was like to deal with Don Arden, someone who notoriously would keep a pistol on his desk during negotiations, as hard a nut as ever produced in show biz, and then suddenly, be dealing with one of the most creative visionary oddballs that pop culture has ever spawned, Andrew Loog Oldham. Can you tell me about these two guys and how you related to them?"

Mac: "Well, they were both professional thieves."

Binky: "Oh dear." [laughter]

Mac: "Andrew had ideas, y'know. Andrew and I have made friends in recent years and by 'friends' I mean to make peace. I was gonna do it with Don, too. But, then he went and died, so fuck him. I mean, the money is gone. We only started getting royalties in 1997. So, it's just not about the money, it's about the music. That's all I can say. I had great times, too. But, the fact that Ronnie and Steve never got a penny for publishing, song writing, or Kenney and I 'til 1997... it's a tragedy. But, I can't live in the past."

Binky: "It's astounding. It seems like almost every British band got totally ripped off, at least their first few years..."

Mac: "Well, the Small Faces are the only band I've ever heard of who NEVER got paid. Think of it. Our royalties from 1966 til 1997. Can you imagine the millions? Nowadays, it's a trickle. A hundred dollars here, a hundred dollars there, it's piss. The Who and The Kinks wound up doing, okay, y'know."

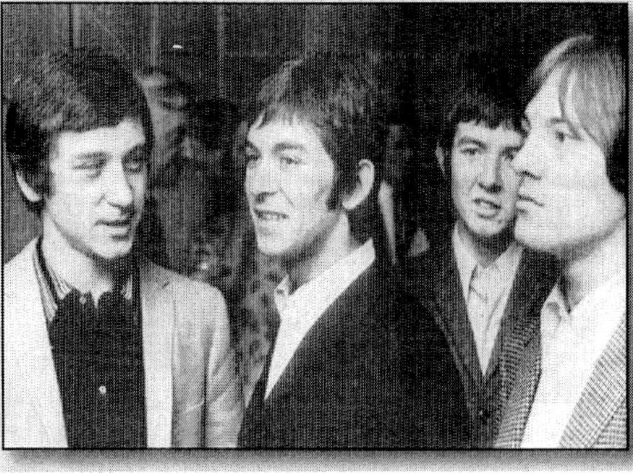

Binky: "Speaking of The Who, when I first heard the Small Faces, Steve's guitar, especially that

you were in the Faces with Rod the Mod and Ronnie "Rolling Stone" Wood, there must've been some wild times on the road in the 1960s, too. Anything strike you as worth divulging for Blinky, Mac?"

Mac: "I suppose that tour of Australia and New Zealand we did with the The Who..."

Binky: "OH GOODIE!"

Mac: "It all started when an Australian band on the same flight as the Small Faces and The Who opened a bottle of beer. Can you believe all the bollocks over that tour started with one open bottle of beer on a plane? Australian airlines had a strict no alcohol policy during flights. All the Faces and Who's knew this and were behaving ourselves. We landed and were promptly arrested! We marched down the stairs out of the plane with our hands high in the air, just mocking them. Then, while we're waiting in the first class airport lounge while the police figured out what to do with us. A waiter came up to us and asked if we wanted a drink! We said, 'Fucking right, we will." Then, after that delay, we got on the plane to New Zealand and when we arrived in Wellington, there were 8 policemen waiting for us. Four for the Small Faces, four for The Who, one for each of us. They escorted us to the hotel. They were with us at all times, so, that nothing 'terrible' would happen. The show that night went fine. It was Steve Marriott's 21st birthday. The police came back with us and by this time we were all on a first name terms. I asked them, 'Would you like to come in for a drink?' They said, 'Oh well, that'd be nice'. They came to Steve's suite, all very nice. Keith Moon came to the door. He immediately picked up the portable record player we were using for entertainment, threw it through the plate glass window... and the policemen RAN! That's all there was."

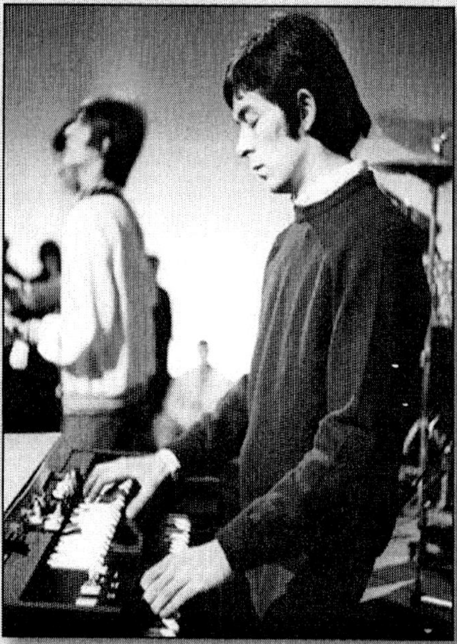

Binky: "They RAN?!"

Mac: "Look, it was a great tour. We played to packed houses, we played great. The Who were fantastic, and all anyone remembers is we got arrested because another band opened a bottle of beer on a plane."

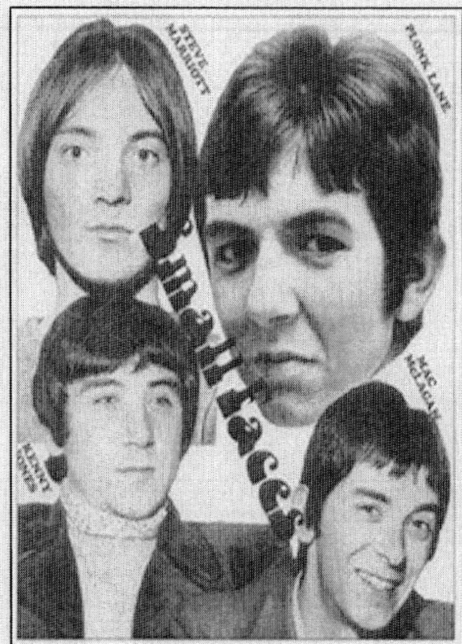

Binky: "Wow. Yeah, I've always heard insane stories surrounding that tour. Glad to hear the facts, sir. Hey, I just want to make sure about something dumb. The name Small Faces came from you all being under 5' 5" and 'faces', the Mod term for a truly cool dude. Is that right?"

Mac: "Yes, that's how I always understood it. There's a story in the box set that tells it differently, but, I think it's wrong."

Binky: " It must've been an odd thing to hear all these unreleased and 'lost' tracks while you were putting together this box set for Charly Records. Any moments come back to you?"

Mac: "Truth is, I haven't heard all of them yet. It's in my phone and I'll be listening on my flight to the UK later today. "Anything" surprised and amazed me. Kenney and I listened to that together and while we remembered it, but couldn't place it. Then, I realized it was the intro to "Tin Soldier" that we never used."

Binky: "Wow, my band, The Planets, has been doing "Tin Solder" for years and years. We just landed a new singer. He's only 26. Yet, when we showed him the list of songs we wanted him to learn, the first thing he said was, 'Wow, Small Faces' 'Tin Soldier'. Cool!'... How 'bout that!"

Mac: "Really! I love that!"

Binky: "Last query, dearie... Someone told me that, as a kid, you somehow convinced a store to sell you your mammoth Hammond organ on instalments and that when your Dad got home that night, he literally couldn't open the front door as the Hammond was totally blocking the way."

Mac: "That's the story that I started my book, "All The Rage" with, Binky. You must get my book!"

Binky: "We ALL must get your book, Mac... and will! Thank you so much, man."

Mac: "Oh, Thank you very much. And, good luck with YOUR band, Binky."

Flat 2 "Reynella"
10 Third Avenuo
Frinton-on-Sea
Essex CO13 9EG

Tel. 01255 674516

31.10.04

Dear Mr Hellier,

First of all, I would like to say how much I enjoyed reading "All Too Beautiful" As an ex-journalist who interviewed Steve and the other "Small Faces" many times during the '60's and early '70's, I thought it a superbly written book and one which captured Steve's complex character to perfection.

I am lucky enough to have only very good memories of Steve, Kenney, Mac and Plonk. Whenever I met them, they were always very helpful and I remember, particularly, Steve's kindness in contacting me, to ask how I was, after I had been in hospital.

However, there was a time when, on visiting him at "Beehive Cottage" I got more than I'd bargained for - namely a "Big Black Dog" (although he was only a pup at the time). I called him Shamus 11 and for the next 14 years he was an integral part of my family.

I remember, too, an evening when Steve turned up unexpectedly on my doorstep with Peter Frampton. I was living at Theydon Bois at the time and they had called in just to have a chat.

Occasionally, I would meet Steve by chance, in Epping High Street and we'd have a coffee together. On one such occasion, he told me he had gone to the market to buy a pair of jeans for Toby. Nothing strange in that, you might think, but his son was only a few weeks old at the time, so I doubt he found a pair small enough to fit him!

From all that I have read about her, Kay Marriott would seem to be a very strong and compassionate woman and I would have liked to have expressed my condolences to her at Steve's funeral but I did not do so as she was surrounded by people and I did'nt want to intrude. Also, I thought she might resent being approached by a journalist.

Once again, I would like you to know how much pleasure "All Too Beautiful" has given me and no doubt to countless others. I would also be most grateful if you could send me a sample copy of "Darlings of Wapping Wharf Laundrette"

Yours sincerely,

Pat Saville

PS. How on earth did you manage to track down my quote re: Steve on Jimi Hendrix (P141)? I thought it had been lost for ever in the mists of time!

SMALL FACES – A CRASHING END!
New Years Eve 1968

London - The festive season was in full swing. Bright lights and colourful decorations adorned the hip clothing shops on London's trendy Wardour Street, many of which featured the latest in fine imported fashions along with kaleidoscopic hippie-ware. With the post-Christmas hangover still ringing, the city's young music fans eagerly awaited the sold-out New Year's Eve show at the Alexandra Palace.

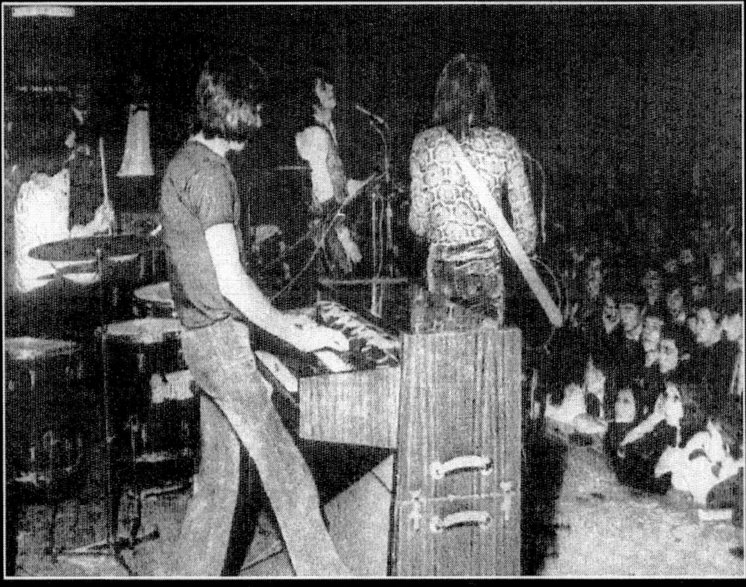

Advertised on light standards throughout the city's West End and heralded as "The place to be", the arrival of the final year of the swinging sixties would be celebrated with a dynamic musical mix of Mod and R&B that featured the father-figure of British Rhythm and Blues Alexis Korner in support of the stylish and cheeky Small Faces. As the tie-dyed, acid-induced haze of the feel-good sixties drew to a close, this memorable evening and potent double bill would bring an explosive end to one of England's most distinguished and popular bands. As the remaining weeks of 1968 dawned, The Small Faces continued working hard while most of their peers were comfortably ensconced in their respective country estates for some much needed rest and relaxation as the fruits of their previous months' labours were released. The Stones, who just a few weeks prior had filmed and recorded their "Rock and Roll Circus", took a break after the December 4th release of their "Beggars Banquet" album while still glowing from their most recent worldwide hit, "Jumpin' Jack Flash". For their part, The Beatles' golden touch remained as they continued to dominate and expand. Their ever-increasing power and influence afforded them the luxury of their own record label as they celebrated yet another number one single, "Hey Jude" b/w "Revolution" (August 30th), the very first release on Apple Records. Meanwhile, the late-summer release of their full-length animated film, "Yellow Submarine", continued its box office looting while being praised endlessly by critics in Europe and North America. Fellow Modsters- turned-high-volume rockers, The Who, enjoyed a brief respite as they prepared to enter IBC studios in January to record a little something called "Tommy". Oddly, a few weeks earlier, on November 20th, Small Faces drummer Kenney Jones joined Keith Moon for the encore performance of "Magic Bus" when the feisty Shepherd's Bush foursome played the Liverpool Empire Theatre. As for The Small Faces, 1968 was a tumultuous year laden with maddening paradoxes. Troubles with Decca, their former label, and financial mismanagement saw them working harder, earning more, yet keeping less, even though the band charted two Top 20 singles during the course of the year ("Lazy Sunday" #2 and "Universal" #16). The band refined its sound as they continued their evolution from Pop/R&B to Psychedelia, finally arriving at a more complete, mature sound with the release of the

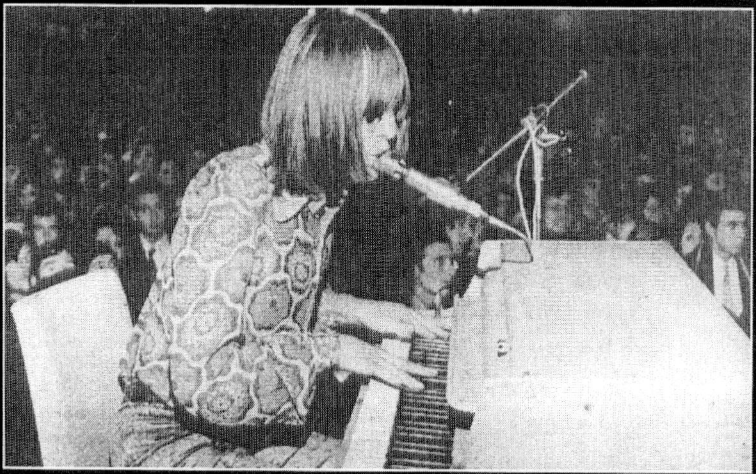

superlative "Ogden's Nut Gone Flake" album, its classic circular fold-out sleeve a replica of the familiar U.K. tobacco brand. Critics lauded the album and the solid song writing partnership that had been cemented between Steve Marriott and Ronnie Lane, this in spite of the fact that strife between the two left them barely speaking to one another. Adding to this volatile powder keg was the incendiary strain of mounting pressure for the band to produce more chart toppers to match the international success of 1967's trippy-hippie anthem "Itchycoo Park". Marriott remained frustrated with both the band's overall playing ability and their collective failure to produce on-stage what they did in the studio. His recommendation to add another guitarist to augment their live shows (he suggested adding one Peter Frampton to the band) was shot down immediately by the others who were satisfied with the band's competence. Marriott's disappointment with the non-musical aspects of the record business also came to a head during this time, his disdain for the press more than apparent during an interview, "As far as the kids are concerned, they love us, but in the eyes of the press we're just dirty, boozing bastards. We were stereotyped as difficult, quite unfairly, because a clause in our contract demanded that the management supply soap and clean towels for us. Is that asking too much?" The seeds of discontent had been sown for some time, and as New Year's Eve rolled around, the unhappiness had grown and flowered.

The line-up of spotty faced youths outside the Alexandra Palace snaked its way down the street and around the block as they anticipated the start of year-end festivities. As a thick evening fog enveloped the switched-on crowd of smartly dressed "faces", the Ally Pally's doors swung open just in time to shelter the eager punters from a cool mist that began to fall. The weather did nothing to dampen their spirits, their mood as optimistic and jubilant as the season. Unfortunately, the same could not be said for the atmosphere within the Small Faces camp. The unsettled and gloomy weather conditions outside the theatre on this New Year's Eve seemed to mimic perfectly the dark and ominous state of affairs between the group's members. Alexis Korner took to the cramped stage shortly after 9pm, offering up his high energy, soulful renditions of the R&B classics he had been sharing with young aspiring musicians since his days with Blues Inc, the training ground and launch pad for everyone from Mick Jagger, Brian Jones and Ginger Baker to Andy Fraser, Hughie Flint and Long John Baldry. The packed room danced away the evening's damp chill and worked themselves into a sweaty, near-hypnotic trance. Everyone was having fun. Things were going well. That is, until the headliners appeared. The pint-sized "Darlings of Wapping Wharf" took to the stage for what was supposed to be a forty-five minute performance. They charged through an impressive set list that covered the group's history from its initial chart success in 1965 ("Whatcha Gonna Do About It?" UK # 14) to the mystical, flowery lyrics of "Green Circles"(1967) and "Lazy Sunday" (1968). The evening was fraught with the technical problems that had irked Steve Marriott from the beginning. Due to the limitations of late sixties portable sound equipment, he found himself unable to hear what the band was playing. The inability to recreate the phasing effects on "Itchycoo

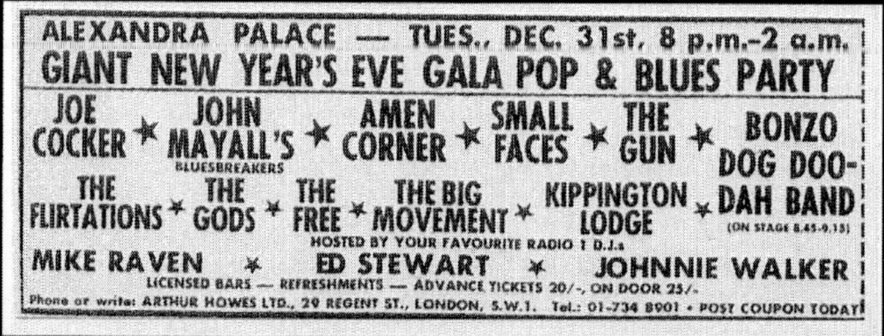

Park" did nothing to soothe the rapidly unravelling nerves of the charismatic, powerhouse vocalist. As the evening wore on, things didn't get any better for Marriott and the frustration began to simmer inside the diminutive Cockney. Ear piercing feedback flowed from the amplifiers as the band tore into "All Or Nothing" and "Rollin' Over", bringing the boys to several unceremonious halts. Things continued to deteriorate, his rage escalating to a furious boil. As the end of their set approached, Marriott was seething. While the band prepared for its final number, and with the new year barely half an hour away, Steve asked Alexis Korner to join them, hoping this would add some much needed levity to the proceedings. This was not to be. A deafening cacophony of distortion soured the closing song. Marriott had had enough. In one wild and vicious swoop, his Fender Telecaster became airborne, landing headfirst and snapping in two, bringing the concert, and his tenure with The Small Faces to a crashing end. A swift kick to the mike stand was Marriott's final act of revulsion as he stormed off the stage, leaving band mates and concertgoers alike shocked and confused. Stunned and bewildered, both Lane and Korner were forced to share vocal duties on that final number, capping off this fateful evening and ushering in an uncertain new year, which by this time, was just a few minutes away.

As his colleagues soldiered on, Steve Marriott quickly found his way to the nearest pub, running into none other than Spooky Tooth bassist Greg Ridley. The two talked about a possible collaboration and by the end of their conversation, Marriott was on the phone to a seventeen year old drummer named Jerry Shirley, who later recalled their conversation: "Steve Marriott called me on New Year's Eve night 1968-1969. He had just come back from a disastrous gig with The Small Faces at Alexandra Palace and asked if he could join our band (Shirley and Peter Frampton were planning to start a new band). My first reaction was, 'Oh dear, what about The Small Faces?' because I was a huge fan, but Marriott was adamant. Then he said, 'By the way, I've got a bass player, Greg Ridley, who wants to come with me'. The pair had been crying on each other's shoulders before Marriott finally decided to call me. Needless to say, I was thrilled." And so, hours after indignantly tendering his resignation from The Small Faces, Marriott had already brought together most of the elements for his next band, Humble Pie. Aside from contractually binding gigs in Germany and the Channel Islands, all future live commitments for The Small Faces were cancelled, including an appearance at The Fillmore East. Shortly after the incident, Marriott spoke of the gig at the Alexandra Palace: "The whole set was diabolical. It was New Year's Eve, Alexis came on stage, and it got worse. It was my fault, but nobody was taking any notice of each other. They were all in their own little universe, it was a terrible mess, a nightmare and as a front man, I noticed the nightmare more than anybody else."

The Small Faces helped to create, portray and perpetuate the designer dressed, scooter driving, pill-popping culture that became The Modernists. They were quintessential Mod figureheads and as author and Who biographer Richard Barnes noted, "The Who became Mods as a career move, but The Small Faces became Mods almost before they became a band. They were real, genuine Mods."

STORY COURTESY OF MARTIN McCARTAN.

WINDOWS,ROCKETS.. AND RONNIE LANE!

John Crocker recalls working in the Selmer Factory at Theobald's Road in the mid-1960's.

Just after Easter 1964 I joined Selmer at their factory situated on the first floor in a building behind the Holborn public library in Theobald's Road, London. I stayed with Selmer until the factory officially closed on 7th February 1969 but this story is focused on a very short period; circa. 1964/65 and because there is plenty of good technical information about the amplifiers etc. produced before, during and after this period I would like to concentrate on some of the people I met and had the pleasure to work with. I started in the test room where the newly wired amplifiers were tested and, if necessary, repaired. The room was of rectangular shape with a large multi-paned metal-framed window, which looked onto John's Mews. As the window was East facing on a sunny day the sun poured into the room in the morning which made it a pleasant place to start work. One of these panes was destroyed by a rocket, but more about that later! There were two doors; one leading to the adjoining inspection room where two or three ladies worked and the other door was on the opposite wall to the window. This door gave access to the rest of the factory and was directly opposite the soundproof test room where the then eighteen-year-old Ronnie Lane worked. The test room had workbenches on all four walls and as would be expected there were various types of test metres, oscilloscopes and all the equipment that was needed to test and repair 1960's amplifiers. I actually happened to start at Selmer on the same day as John Weir, both as test engineers. John had a working background with hi-fi and was technically competent. At a later date he transferred to the Development Dept working with John Hosay and Brian Davis and when the Holborn factory closed he went with the company to Braintree and became Production Manager. I remember when he bought a new red Mini and gave me a lift to work when my car was crook. All the pop stars and royals had a Mini in those days and John was no exception! A year or two ago we made contact for the first time for many years and have been in touch since then. He was and still is always ready for a chat especially if Selmer is the

Ronnie (top right) with his 1964 band The Outcasts

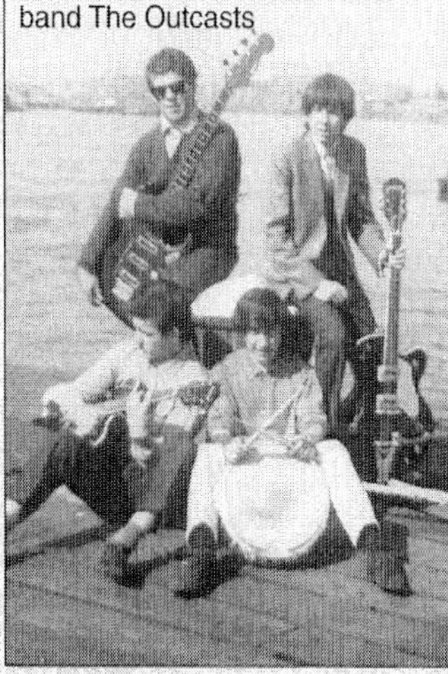

subject. Come to think about it, he is just ready for a chat! An approachable, friendly sort of bloke, he was always willing to give advice and something of an encyclopaedia on all matters Selmer.

The man in charge of the Test Room was Ron Fowler. Ron was born in Brazil, used to live in Jamaica, and looked just like the stereotype Mexican bandit complete with black moustache! It was easy to imagine him with cross gun belts, a large Mexican hat, draped manga, and saying through white clenched teeth "today you live, tomorrow you die, Gringo!!" I don't know if he drank tequila but if he didn't, he should have. He could have easily played a part in one of those spaghetti westerns. Ron fancied himself as a musician. He would borrow a keyboard from the organ department, install it on his workbench and start making a very distinct sound! As his hands roamed over the keys he would suddenly stop and with one hand touching the top of his head, slowly turn round to look at the rest of the guys in the room and say, "Gentlemen, do you agree that I'm improving?" "Yeah Ron, you're a maestro" was the ensembled reply. Ron gave an agreeing nod and continued with the recital. Was Ron any good? Well, that's best answered in the words of Eric Morecambe. He knew all the notes; it's just that he played them in the wrong order! One day Ron was bored and decided to have some fun! Adjoining the test room was another room where a talented man repaired Claviolines. Without any kind of warning Ron announced to the staff in the test room "Gentlemen, I've decided to kill him". The two rooms were connected by a false wall so one lunch time Ron made a small hole in the wall, threaded a mains lead with the wires bared through the hole and connected the other end to a 240v mains outlet. He threw the switch and waited to see what happened when the Clavioline repairer returned from lunch. The more sensible members of the test room saw the danger and persuaded Ron not to go ahead with his little 'joke'. Ron reluctantly disconnected the lead from the mains and pulled it back through the hole. I would like to believe that Ron was not serious!! During this period the US space programme was well under way and the staff of the test room must have been caught up in the excitement. One day we decided to make a rocket. In fact I think we made three. The first exploded before take off, one took a lump out of the ceiling, and another went straight through one of the small windowpanes, which remained un-repaired for years. Dick Twydell, the Works Director, came rushing down from the office and peering through the smoke shouted "what have you f***ers been up to??" Looking like butter wouldn't melt in our mouths, Ron made up some cock and bull story. He was good at that! Fortunately we didn't have any TNT lying around, so we used red top matches (RTM) as the explosive but this didn't have the desired impact so we progressed to RTM-FP (finely powered). This did the job quite well by giving a slower ignition rate. The last rocket was made from bent aluminium. Ignition by putting a match to it proved to be rather dangerous so the problem was solved by remote electronic ignition. (Eat your heart out NASA). Ron was a good leader. Not that he overworked himself but he was on the side of his men if the going got tough. An unforgettable Mexican bandit!

I started at Selmer just about the time of Ronnie Lane's 18th birthday on 1st April 1964. He worked in a supposedly soundproof room made out of some kind of board, which was meant to cut down the sound. This was situated on the opposite side of the corridor to the test room. He used a Fender Strat and Precision bass to test the newly made amps and speaker cabinets. Ronnie would regularly stroll around outside the soundproof room playing 'Green Onions' on the bass, trailing a long lead, which was connected to the amp. He often came into the test room just to wind up Ron Fowler, which I must say, wasn't too hard to do. Ronnie and Ron Fowler had a love/hate relationship. Ron being a fiery character and Ronnie, young and fun loving, was just the bloke to take advantage. One morning when we arrived at work, we found a gift from Ronnie. It was a rope tied in a hangman's noose dangling from above the test room door with Ron Fowler's name pinned on it! Ron Fowler was last seen chasing Ronnie, waving his hands in the air shouting, "I'll kill him" in best Mexican bandit accent. There was the day when Ronnie declared that he was skint and asked if I would lend him a tanner (6d) (2.5p in today's money) for bus fare. I must have had a bit of spare cash that day so I gave it to him. How things were to change for Ronnie! As we all know, Ronnie was to soon to jump from rags to riches when he became a founder member of the Small Faces. Another founder member was drummer Kenny Jones.

At this time Kenny worked at Selmer's with a Polish chap called Felix putting the amplifiers and speakers into cabinets. Although I didn't have much to do with Kenny except for the occasional visit to his area to discuss something related to work, he always came across as a quiet, pleasant and amenable young man. His quietness being in stark contrast to Ronnie! Another man in the test room with a dry sense of humour was George. He worked next to Ron Fowler and back to back with me. Mac was there for a short time. He was a well-mannered, very well spoken West Indian guy. Chris Wright also worked in the test room. Lenny Caton was a very nice guitar player. He was just as much at ease with acoustic or electric guitar styles even at his young age. Sometimes he tested the amps in the soundproof room with Ronnie. I think he played in a band with another chap that we called 'Ginger', who also worked in the soundproof room. I'd be surprised if Lenny didn't make a career out of music. Tom Sayers was production foreman. An episode which I remember well relating to Tom and Ronnie Lane is well told by John Weir elsewhere. Tom always seemed to be harassed in some way and rushing around chasing people, usually young guitar players in the soundproof room! But Tom could also be a nice bloke. After this period several other characters came and went. Notably was Allan Baldwin. He was a young guitar player who worked in the test department. We became good friends but lost contact after Selmer at Holborn closed. After many years we made contact in 2002 with the help of Tim Fletcher. Allan is now a great, versatile musician and technician.

My five years working for Selmer was certainly not the best paid job I've had, but if lots of fun, working with lively, memorable characters and an overall good feeling is part of the equation that make a job desirable then this must surely be the best job I've had. One last word about Ronnie Lane. When I knew Ronnie nobody had any idea what the future held for him. Within a short period he and Kenny Jones were to be founder members of one of the best and most famous bands of the '60's. The Small Faces. Ronnie's exuberant character was always good for a laugh a minute and certainly made life 'interesting'. When I learned of his death in Trinidad, Colorado on 4th June 1997 aged 51 years after a twenty-year battle against multiple sclerosis, I, and no doubt many others who knew Ronnie, were greatly saddened.

But the memories live on....

P.S. I never did get that tanner back from Ronnie. Never mind.

John Crocker

Trivia! Trivia!

DID YOU KNOW THAT..............Eastenders actor Billy Murray, who plays the part of hard man Johnny Allen, once worked as the Small Faces' road manager. Quote from ex-mod Billy "I was their roadie back in 1966. I did it as a mate, they never paid me a tanner. I got my rewards in other ways........

DID YOU KNOW THAT.............Whilst on tour with Roy Orbison in the 1960's the Small Faces took advantage of the Big O's bad eyesight to sneak onstage every night and tune his guitar higher. They then rolled about laughing as Roy's already high voice was pushed up a few gears.

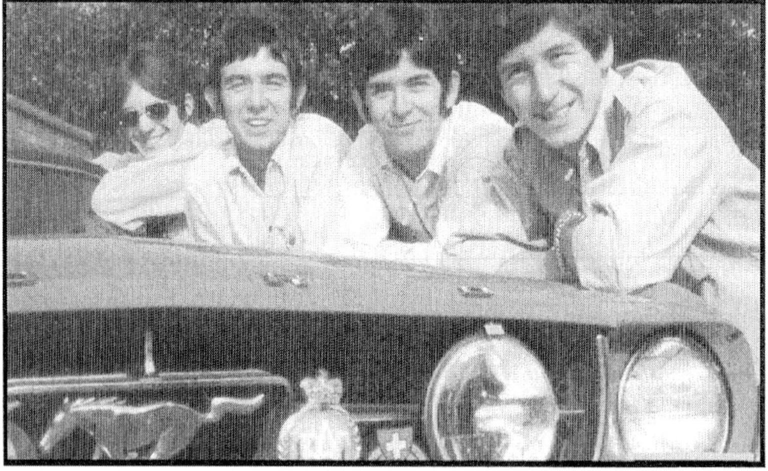

MOD AID 20

THE CD, THE CONCERT and other things!

At long last the cd single is available at all good record stores or through Biff Bang Pow Records website www.biffbangpow.org.uk

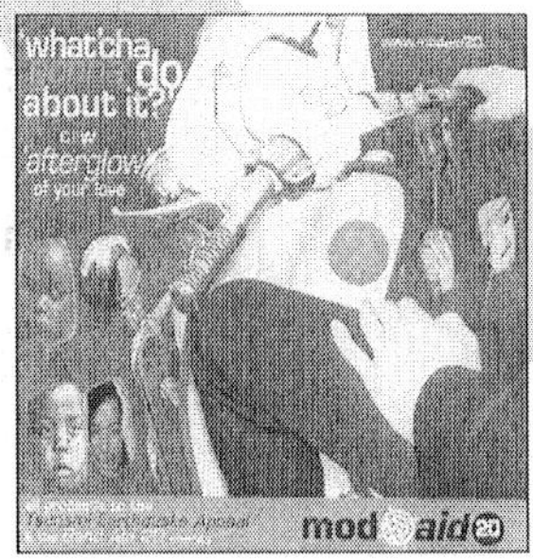

Continuing on from the last issue of Wapping Wharf I'd just like remind readers of the objective of Mod Aid 20. Created by Paul and Karen Hooper-Keeley the aim of the project is to raise much-needed funds for both the Band Aid charity and the Tsunami Earthquake Appeal. Two Small Faces numbers "Whatcha Gonna Do About It" and "Afterglow" have been re-recorded by a whole array of mod superstars both past and present. These include PP Arnold, Chris Farlowe, Ronnie Wood, Steve Cradock, Mark Joseph, Jimmy Winston and many, many more. Small Face daughters Mollie Marriott and Emma Langwith (Winston) were also in on the act. Ian Page expertly produced the sessions and the finished product gives us the following:

1 Whatcha Gonna Do About It – lead vocals PP Arnold, Chris Farlowe, Mark Joseph

2 Afterglow – lead vocals Mollie Marriott

3 Whatcha Gonna Do About It – Mark Joseph (acoustic version)

4 Whatcha Gonna Do About It – the video

Three events have preceded the release of the Mod Aid 20 single. Firstly on 4th March there was a pre-launch fund raising gig at the White Horse in High Wycombe featuring the likes of Rinaldi Sings, Small World and 17Black amongst others. The press launch of the cd was at Filthy McNastys in London on 26th May and featured an acoustic set from Secret Affair's Ian Page, Dave Cairns and Dave Winthrop and finally the "Come Together" all day fundraiser on the 26th June at the South Parade pier in Southsea, Portsmouth. This event featured no less than 14 excellent bands and was headlined by Mark Joseph, surely a superstar of the not too distant future.

For more details about Mod Aid 20 or any of the other superb cd releases on Biff Bang Pow Records please contact Paul Hooper-Keeley info@biffbangpow.org.uk

WHATCHA GONNA DO ABOUT IT

During early Small Faces rehearsals at the Ruskin Arms in East London, Steve had taught Jimmy Winston a little riff that he had "borrowed" from the Solomon Burke record "Everybody Needs Somebody To Love". Marriott later used the riff as a springboard to create a vibrant instrumental.

Having signed for Decca, in the summer of 1965, the band's thoughts turned to the first single. All agreed this was ideal, it was certainly commercial enough. Just one snag! It needed words and it needed them fast. Manager Don Arden turned to the song writing team of Samwell and Potter to assist in the matter. Ian Samwell was a very respected name in the business and had previously penned "Move It" for late 1950s rocker Cliff Richard. A classic British Rock And Roll record by anybody's standards, in fact one of Steve Marriott's previous bands The Frantiks had recorded a version themselves.

The team returned with a set of lyrics entitled "Whatcha Gonna Do About It" (not to be confused with an earlier hit of the same title by American soul diva Doris Troy).

JOHN HELLIER (FEBRUARY 2005)

AFTERGLOW (OF YOUR LOVE)

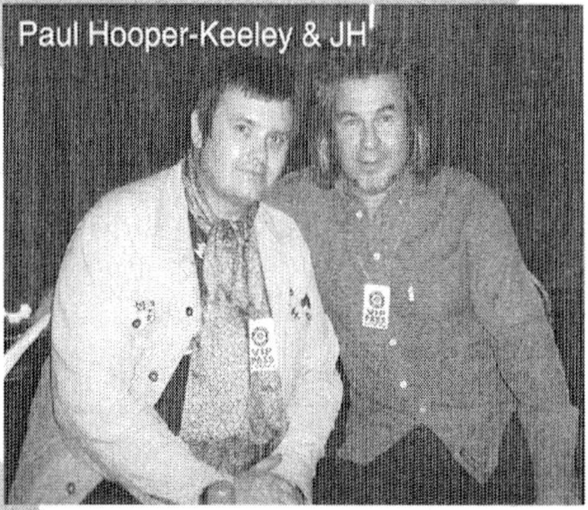

I once asked Steve Marriott of all the songs you've written over the years what is your favourite. He gave me a top five without even thinking about it and right at the top was "Afterglow". He had even put the song back into his set just before he died. Having said that when asked about the song in a 1988 interview Steve, being the Jekyll and Hyde character that he was, dismissed it as "Just another soppy love song for some soppy tart!"

The origins of the song go back to 1967 and PP Arnold claims it was written for her. At the time of Steve writing this song the two of them were an item so who am I to dispute that fact. Although credited to Marriott/Lane this was a solo Steve Marriott song. It starts gently with very soft vocal backing only to erupt into something akin to a volcano! Incredibly strong chorus line and the song is commercial enough to be a massive hit for somebody.

By the time this was released as a double A side single with "Wham Bam Thank you M'am" the Small Faces were a spent force and it bombed. Nearly forty years later the song is revered by most Small Faces fans as one of their finest moments.

JOHN HELLIER (FEBRUARY 2005)

TOBY MARRIOTT INTERVIEW

STEVE MARRIOTT'S SON, TOBY, SHARES HIS MEMORIES WITH JOHN HELLIER, FROM HIS HOME IN THE USA.

(10TH JUNE 2003)

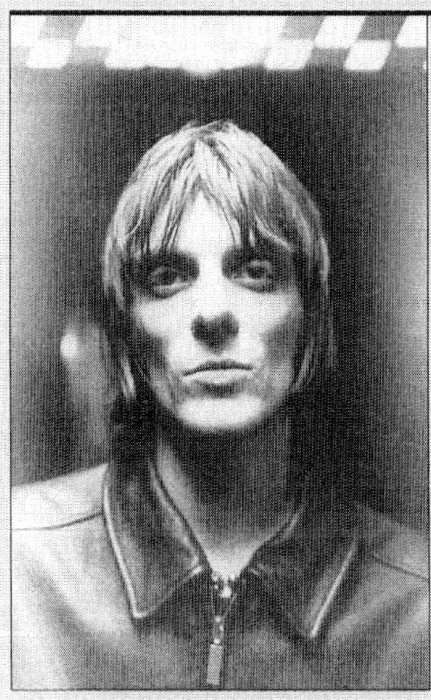

JH What are your earliest recollections?

TOBY I have no recollections at all of Beehive Cottage, too young. Dad went to America in 1978 because the tax man was after him and I was sent to live at my nan and grandads house in Sawbridgeworth in Hertfordshire and from there on it was backwards and forwards between there and wherever mum and dad were living in the States. It was like that right up until 1990 although most of my schooling was in England. The first place that we lived in America was Santa Cruz in California. That was great; we had a real funky house there with a massive garden. As well as me and mum and dad we had Jim Leverton, Dave Hynes and Leslie West (ex of Mountain) living with us. They were dads band and it was called the Firm. They were trying to reincarnate Humble Pie really although it never worked out. Leslie West was enormous, about 30 stone! They made this special room for him and he'd have buckets and buckets of cookies in there. When he weren't about I'd nip in there and help myself but if he found out he'd go apeshit. He just lay in bed all day eating.

The band didn't last long, Jim and Dave went back to England and we moved to Pikes Creek. Not long after that I came back to nans house and mum and dad moved to New York.

JH Where were you living when you next went back to America?

TOBY Atlanta, it was there that mum and dad split up which was sad but a good thing really as they were fighting badly. Dad was going through a bad period with drugs and drink and both contributed to him becoming a violent person. He'd lost all his money and was struggling to get anything together commercially. The man was who he was, all Rock n'Rollers have tantrums, at least all the ones I've ever met, and dad was no different. Anyway mum got herself a job as a flight assistant and things were ok for a while but after about six months things took another turn for the worse and I was packed off back to England again. Up until I was 15 that's all I knew, back and forwards. Another recollection I have of dad is visiting him in Atlanta after he had split with mum. He was recovering from a broken leg and I stayed the weekend. He was pissed the whole time but in a fun sort of way. We were in a bathtub together and dad kept playing this old Rock And Roll record all the time, Tutti Frutti by Little Richard. Over and over again he played it. He was plying me with beer and I got drunk as well. I was only about 7 or 8 but he didn't mind that. Shortly afterwards he moved out into the country, a place called Kite County about two hours drive south of Atlanta. He was living with a 16-year-old stripper called Bunny in a beautiful house, swimming pool the lot!

JH What was Steve like as a dad?

TOBY He was as he was and I didn't know any different. He just didn't understand kids; he was always waiting for me to become 18 so we could get pissed, legally, together. At times he was great, most people thought that he was just a rude little buggar but he was a very smart man, very well read. He loved reading, I remember him reading King Arthur stories to me, and he turned me on to Excalibur and all that stuff. Sounds like I'm making excuses for him but he never really got the chance to be a real father. For a lot of my childhood I was living with my nan and whenever he turned up he couldn't seem to get past my nan! She was very overpowering you know. He was better with Mollie than with me, he was older and a bit more settled by then. My relationship with him was at its strongest a bit later on when he was with Toni. They made more time to see the kids; she had a daughter herself from a previous relationship. I spent a lot of time with them at their home in North Essex. Previously when he was living with Manon (Mollie's mum) it was different again. Manon and nan had quite a barney while I was living at Nans house. I remember dad coming round to get me. He just took me outside and told me that I was coming to live with them now. I lived with dad and Manon at their Stanstead Abbots home for about six months. Dad wasn't around very much, he'd be away on tour with Packet Of Three, and Manon was very strict. After a fairly miserable six months I ended up back at nans house again.

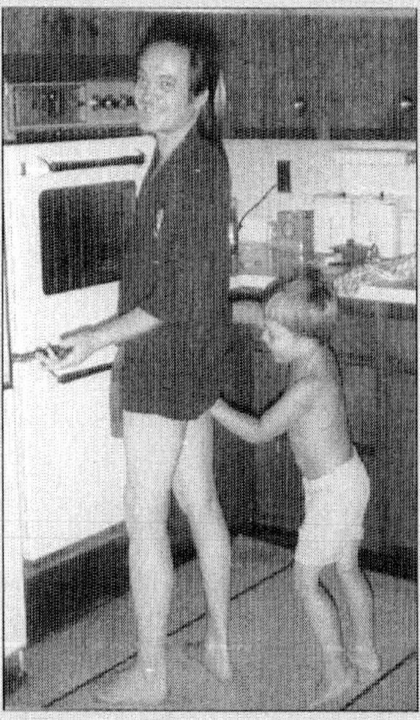

JH Did you see your dad play live and did he encourage you at all musically?

TOBY I remember him bringing me on stage in front of 9,000 people in Macon, Georgia. In later years me and Toni (Steve's wife) used to go and see him play lots. Mostly though I'd just take a sleeping bag and kip in the dressing room. I just wasn't into the music thing at all back then. In answer to the second part of your question, something told me deep down that he didn't want any of his kids involved in the business. Having said that he did give me a Gretsch guitar one time when it was my birthday. He just said, "Here you are" and expected me to play it. Then he'd come back three months later, drunk, and say, "I need that guitar back". I suppose I can relate as to why he didn't want us involved.

JH What music do you remember him listening to?

TOBY If you walked into any of his houses you'd never have known it was a musician that lived there. He never had many albums. I can only remember a Randy Newman LP, the one with the dollar sign and some blues albums such as Muddy Waters and Little Walter and, oh yeah, his favourite album of all time Dire Straits "Brothers In Arms".

JH What was his relationship like with his mum and dad?

TOBY Before I was around I think they were very close. Grandad was very quiet and didn't have the same parental qualities as nan. Dad's relationship with grandad was domineering. Dad would shout at him a lot especially when he had been drinking. I only ever heard him shout at his mum once; he knew with nan he'd met his match. I think he owed them a lot really, I mean they raised me. He did buy them a house though. At the end they had a massive row and they hadn't spoken in months. Toni told me that he would never speak to them again, if dad was pissed off with somebody he wouldn't talk to them for years. It was an inability to be able to talk a problem through. His relationship with them was like that for as long as I remember.

JH Was your dad happy doing the low-key gigs in the 1980's?

TOBY The people that were around him at that time will tell you that they were the happiest days of his life. I'm not so sure, he was fairly content but he had little money. By going to Los Angeles just before he died to do a deal with Peter Frampton tells me that he wasn't as content with life as he made out. Playing music was all he'd ever done and when you've gone from Shea Stadium to East End pubs it's only natural to want to go back to bigger things. At the end of the day the Frampton plans never worked out. Dad was always in awe of Peter as a guitarist but by the end he was every bit as good himself. Apparently while he was over there he got back on the booze and "Melvin" reappeared. After giving it a try for a couple of months he just wanted to get back home and build a relationship with his kids. He hadn't seen Mollie since she was two years old and not seeing her gave him big problems in his closet. Probably what brought this feeling on was the fact that while he was in LA Eric Claptons young child died in tragic circumstances and dad just felt it was time to mend bridges with his own child.

JH Do you think the drink/drugs stories regarding your dad are exaggerated?

TOBY I hear a lot of drug stories concerning my dad second-hand. He never sat me down and told me about the demons. By the 1980's he nailed the Charlie on the head, well cut down on it anyway. Previous to the 80's he'd had a bad problem with it. He was always a massive drinker but he'd even slowed down on that. Ironically his last days were the healthiest ones of his adult life. When I said he'd cut down on his drinking he could still down 7 or 8 pints a day, which was good for somebody, that had previously been doing something like 30 pints a day. Beer that is, not Brandy!

JH What is your favourite Steve Marriott era?

TOBY Definitely Small Faces. Humble Pie were probably better but as far as image and song writing go there's

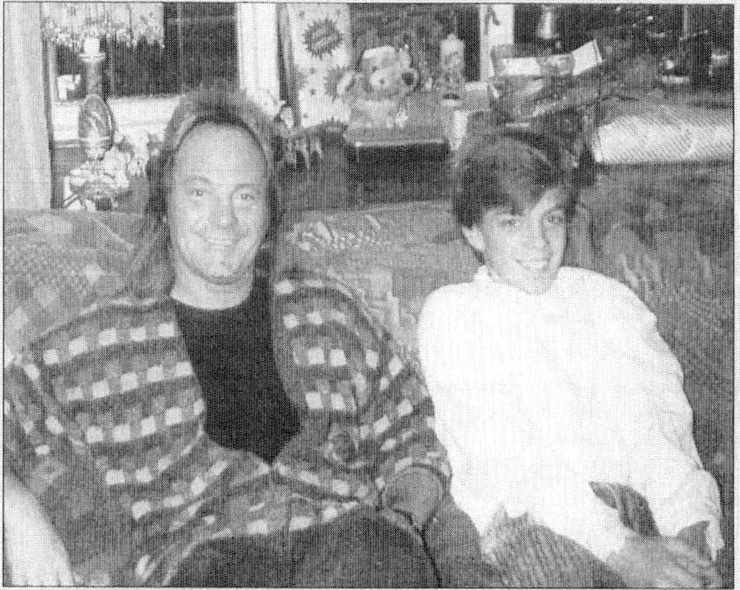

nothing better than Small Faces, well perhaps, with the exception of the Beatles and the Stones. "Ogden's" was a masterpiece and I spoke to Mac about the proposed follow up album "1862", which was going to be recorded in a church hall, next door to Beehive Cottage, that dad wanted to buy. I would have loved to have seen how they would have followed "Ogden's". I think they were afraid of not being able to follow that classic album. I listened to some of the out-takes on the Wapping Wharf album and I absolutely love "Pigs Trotters". Small Faces songs are very hard to play, you'll find that even Grade A musicians can never play Small Faces songs that well. Dunno why! It was great to see the "Ultimate Collection" cd in the charts recently and it got 5 star ratings in the music press. I find it amazing that a band that only made 3 albums can attract the kind of cult following that they have. The mod image is very strong in England much more so than in the States. It is a very English thing isn't it?

JH What are your own plans for the future?

TOBY Well for the last five years I've been pretty fucked up with drink and drug problems. Like father like son eh! During this time I didn't even want to play music at all. But after rehab I'm back and have been playing with a local mod band, here in Atlanta, called "Tender Idols". When I was in England, a short while ago, I was expected to live up to dads reputation and go to the pub and drink 20 pints or so of beer and take drugs and live the whole Rock N Roll lifestyle. Anyway, I've got the passion back now. I got to hang out with Keith (Richards) and Woody last November, that was great. An old manager of mine called them up and they invited me to a gig. Keith's personal manager came and got me and I thought it would be a little handshake and that's it but they invited me back to their room and I spent a few hours with them. They both idolised dad and we spoke about dads audition for the Stones. Anyway I knew a lot of old London pub songs that I'd heard dad sing and the three of us ended up singing those together. They were great guys and spending time with them spurred me on to keep going. If those guys don't make you wanna do it again nobody can.

THANKS TOBY, FOR YOUR TIME AND YOUR MEMORIES.

TRACK BY TRACK

A NOD'S AS GOOD AS A WINK...TO A BLIND HORSE

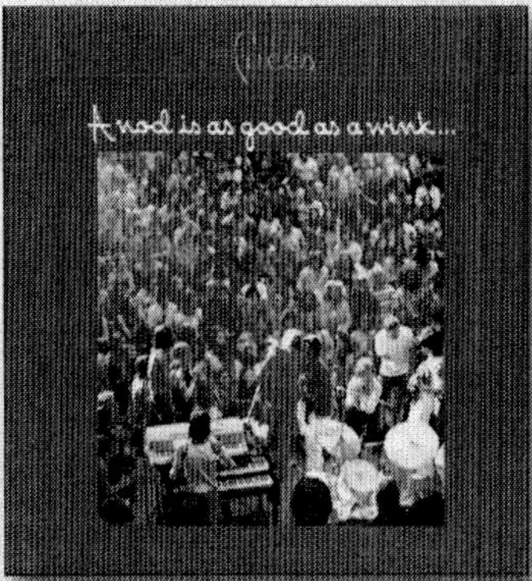

BY THE FACES

UK ALBUM WB K56006
UK CD WB 7599-25929-2

November 17th, 1971 saw the British release of this album which is generally regarded as the Faces finest work. As their co-producer, the band had finally been able to hire Glyn Johns. The ways in which he assisted them in the studio are documented in a little credit on the included giant poster: "We thank you, Glyn, you made all the difference"

MISS JUDY'S FARM: Not only the opener of this album but also the driving force during many concerts. A simple riff based one just one chord, perfectly suited for improvisation.

YOU'RE SO RUDE: A McLagan/Lane composition. Heavy duty boogie type Rock with tongue in cheek lyrics. The parents have left the home visiting Auntie Renee and the teenage couple take advantage of the "love nest" but not for long 'cos Mum and Dad return too soon.....

LOVE LIVED HERE: A deeply sad ballad. Not about lost love in this case, but memories of popular hang-outs such as snooker clubs and pubs which have been demolished since. The text, with its unusual comments on a political matter, was written by Ronnie Lane while Woody and Rod supplied the music.

LAST ORDERS PLEASE: Another song to celebrate the

institution of the British pub, composed and sung, with dobro accompaniment, by Laney. Woody does not only contribute lead guitar but makes an appearance on double bass!

STAY WITH ME: The hit single off of the album. It's a crisp riff rocker by Rod and Woody. The words are rude depicting Rod's adventures with more "horizontal" trades. The start is decidedly mid-tempo but revs up considerably in the wild finale with Kenney using all his powers of drumming.

DEBRIS: Ronnie Lane's homage to his Dad. A tender, somehow fragile song with Rod helping him out on second vocals and harmonies during the higher passages. Ronnie plays dobro again and now it's his turn to use the double bass. This was also the b-side of the Stay With Me 45.

MEMPHIS: Another tribute, this time taking the form of a cover version. Chuck Berry's Memphis Tennessee gets the Faces treatment with Woody trying out a few effects on his electric guitar, otherwise this is filler material which went down a storm in live shows, of course.

TOO BAD: Another highlight from the Faces live repertoire, it comes as straight Rock without compromise. Written by Wood and Stewart.

THAT'S ALL YOU NEED: The intro is reminiscent of Plynth but cannot hide the fact that this is average riff Rock which is just about rescued by Woody's slide guitar showcases in the middle section. For the final onslaught, steel drums courtesy of Harry Fowler are added to the full blown band.

With "A Nod's As Good As A Wink...To A Blind Horse" the Faces achieved their biggest success to date, number 2 in the British hit lists and number 6 in the American album charts. A new US tour became another huge smash resulting in a "Guinness Book Record". Their 26th November 1971 gig at New York's Madison Square Garden sold out quicker than any other gig before.

Album review by Uli Twelker and Roland Schmitt.
Check out their excellent book HAPPY BOYS HAPPY.

ALL TOO BEAUTIFUL....

THE OFFICIAL STEVE MARRIOTT BIOGRAPHY.

An introduction by co-author Paolo Hewitt.

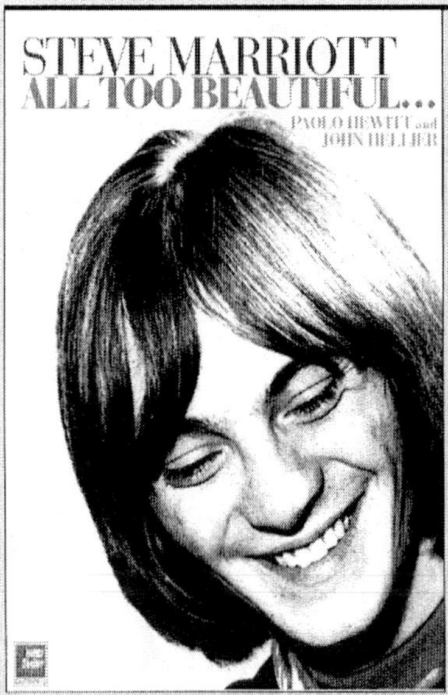

The intention was to begin this book describing Steve Marriott's last day on earth. My idea for the opening scene was the flight taking him and his third wife, Toni, home from America on Friday 19th April 1991, an extremely turbulent journey; the couple argued continually until landing in the UK at around mid-day.

At that point we would meet their friend, Phil Anthony. He collects the couple from Heathrow airport and drives them back to their 16th century rented house in Arkesden, Essex. Phil would leave and we would then watch the arrival of Ray Newcomb, another friend who invites the couple out for a meal at the Straw Hat pub in Sawbridgeworth. We would sit at their table and discover what Marriott ate for his last meal (roast lamb and mint sauce) see his clothes that day (suitably, given his place in mod history, a silver grey mohair suit) and then view the actions that led up to him returning home alone at about 1.30am.

There I would have stopped, hopefully with the reader now eager to know more about this unique man.

I had to jettison these plans. In all honesty, you wouldn't have wanted to be around Steve Marriott on his last day on earth. He was vicious, argumentative and tiresome. He had spent the last two weeks of his stay in Los Angeles terrorising Toni. No blushing violet she but even her feisty nature and her combative stance could not cope with Marriott's onslaught. The man was simply uncontrollable.

Worse, it wasn't the man she married who was carrying on in this manner – it was Melvin, a bald headed wrestler. Melvin was Steve Marriott's alter ego, the other side of his dual personality. Melvin first surfaced around the mid 1970s when Marriott was into his second marriage with Pam Stephens. As all his women soon discovered, when Melvin appeared, big trouble followed. It was Melvin who began the fights, kicked off the arguments. It was scary stuff to be around. When Pam would plead with Steve to stop, he would shout "I'm not Steve, I'm Melvin the bald headed wrestler" and then tear into her some more. In the morning, Marriott genuinely seemed to have no recollection of his actions. His day would be spent wracked by guilt and remorse.

This is challenging and uncomfortable material and to open the book in such a manner would run the very real risk of putting the reader off Marriott completely. We couldn't allow this to happen. Melvin was one facet of Steve, a dark facet but not the whole man by a long chalk. There was so much more to Steve Marriott. Over the last few years, as I have discovered more and more about the man, I could not help but admire his unique spirit, warm to the way Marriott refused to go down, how he allowed nothing in life – the Mafia, the Inland Revenue, the law, the music business – to beat him. Faced with my own day-to-day problems, his life lessons proved to be extremely valuable.

Steve Marriott was a warm, funny man, blessed with incredible talent, energy and charisma. He sang tremendously, he wrote beautifully and he devoted himself to his craft for the whole of his life. He was a true artist. All his life he only did that which his muse demanded, not that which might enrich him.

Music consumed him. He worshipped that beautiful, inspirational force to his dying day. Two, maybe three weeks before his untimely death, he was in a Los Angeles club when he met two fans. He invited them back to his house to play them Inez and Charles Fox records, explaining how great and vital and important this music was. At age fourty four, he was still spreading the word; still acting as standard-bearer for the R&B music he adored so much. He was not alone in his love for this music.

In the 1960s, most British artists that mattered – Georgie Fame, Van Morrison, Brian Auger, Rod Stewart, Eric Burdon, Chris Farlowe, Peter Green, The Beatles, The Stones and many others - felt the same way. They displayed an urgency to promote Black American music to reveal to their audiences its wondrous nature. Rhythm and Blues was the source, the springboard these acts used to forge their own unique music. Today, much to our detriment, that tradition is becoming lost. Back in the day, every young white hipster wanted to sing like Otis Redding or Ray Charles. Fourty years later, the majority of young hopefuls want to sing like "Rock" singers, a breed who always lean more to the histrionic than the historic and for whom the expression "stay in tune" might as well have been written in Russian.

Not Stevie Marriott. He may well have been the best white soul singer this country ever produced. He's certainly in the top three. Ask Oasis's Liam Gallagher, one of the very few singers today worth listening to. When Mojo magazine placed Liam above Steve in one of those Best Singers lists that all publications love, the young buck, who read the piece while sitting in a Primrose Hill pub, screwed up the mag and threw it on the summer pavement outside, in anger. He knew the truth, knew what an instinctive vocalist Marriott was, how he knew when to go soft, when to race ahead, when to unleash the power, when to hold back: knew in fact how best to use all his musical talents, especially in his Small Faces days.

In that period, 1965-1969, Steve Marriott wrote songs that still transport me to this day. "Afterglow" "Tin Soldier" "Autumn Stone" "That Man" "I Can't Dance With You" "Understanding" "All Or Nothing" " If You Think You're Groovy" " The Universal " Donkey Rides A Penny A Glass" – my fingers will tire before the list is complete. His songs were filled with melody, passion, energy, beauty and drive. He was a great arranger as well, imbuing many of his records with a unique musical character. Such was his talent; he could incorporate elements as disparate as East End music hall and screaming rock guitar solos into one satisfying whole.

His writing changed when he formed Humble Pie, did so again in his later years and there is a case that his muse thoroughly deserted him during this latter period. I tend to disagree. There is still enough great music from this period to fill a lengthy CD. Steve Marriott wrote until the day he died, couldn't stop himself. He loved the job. But he loved performing even more.

That's why in his latter years he was able to play the pubs and the clubs for a mere grand a night and not feel too bitter about his fate. Onstage, wherever he was, he became whole, became one. He did feel resentment at other lesser talents who had left him behind to become much bigger stars - the Rod Stewarts of this world – but he did so not out of jealousy but a sense of injustice. Marriott had been raised to believe that talent was the only benchmark. The more the talent, the better the rewards. When he discovered that success in the music business owes as much to other factors – a willingness to schmooze, to play the game, to stay meek, keep quiet, not upset people – he reared up in anger. Pound for pound, he was as good as any of his contemporaries, yet in the end they got the mansions and stadium shows while he got the pub circuit. That wasn't right, it ran contrary to his sense of fairness.

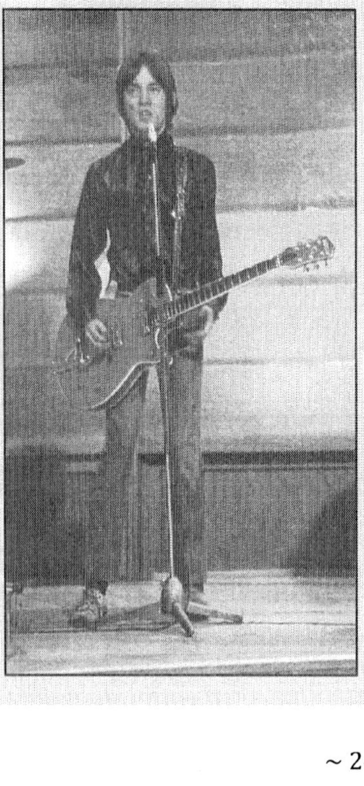

His complex personality didn't help him. On the one hand a sensitive artist who could write subtle and evocative lines such as "All I need are your whispered hellos", on the other hand a man of dirty, ribald humour who displayed no tact whatsoever. His unstoppable penchant for winding up or annoying people in high places inevitably interfered with his career. His first hit combo, the Small Faces were the first to be banned from the prime music show, Top Of The Pops. The reason? Marriott believed the show's producer was retiring and confronted him with the words "I'm glad you're leaving, I always thought you were a major cunt". The producer thanked Steve for the gesture but told the singer he wasn't actually leaving, it was somebody else that was. The next day, a short-lived ban was enforced.

Not that Marriott cared too much. "Fuck 'em" was a phrase he often used throughout his life just as in the same manner he used humour to deflate the pompous and the boring. Many of his actions were hilarious, sometimes surreal. Pouring mint sauce over a neighbours plastic lambs or taking to the stage in a bathrobe are acts worthy of Spike Milligan himself. No surprise then that Marriott, as a child, loved the Goons. In fact in the downstairs toilet at his last home in Essex there was a bookshelf full of Spike Milligan books. The base for his humour was earthy and forged from his East End sensibility. The same went for his appeal to the opposite sex. From an early age, Marriott was a rogue and a charmer.........ask the women.

They loved his cheek, his openness, his shoes and his girl-like features. In the '60s, especially when clothes were his passion, Marriott displayed both male and female qualities, a duality that fascinates and attracts women. On stage or in the studio, he looked like a doll but he sang like a man. He was "all too beautiful".

Marriott's four main relationships were loving and turbulent but none of his long-term partners will have a word said against him. Those who do criticise him, found his energy too overpowering, his actions too wild. His non-stop chatter, his outlandish behaviour, his filthy mouth, it was all too much. Most others, though, warmed to him. For them he had a heart that was big and warm and exceptional.

In reading this book, I hope you can see through his faults and be drawn to Steve Marriott in the way I was. I hope the words inside lead you to his music, that his work gives you the thrill it gives me every time I hear it. I know my co-author, John Hellier, feels the same way and on that particular subject I have to say this. I could not have been gifted a better man to write this book with. Not only was his research absolutely exemplary but John's ability to calmly fulfil everything asked of him, whether it be at seven in the morning or twelve at night, was just amazing. He has been like that all the way through this journey and that means one thing, any success that this book attracts is as much to do with John as it is anybody else.

PH

"ALL TOO BEAUTIFUL"
(Helter Skelter books)........Hardback.

BY PAOLO HEWITT AND JOHN HELLIER

AVAILABLE FROM
www.wappingwharf.com
www.stevemarriott.co.uk
OR BY POST FROM
JOHN HELLIER
at Wapping Wharf address (see page 1)

PIMLICO PILGRIMAGE

It was around Autumn last year that I received an email from a guy called Rupert Trollope. Rupert explained that he was the owner of 22 Westmoreland Terrace in Pimlico, London. This address needs no explanation to Small Faces fans, nicknamed "Party Central", it was their home from Boxing day 1965 to Boxing day 1966, courtesy of manager Don Arden. Rupert bought the house in 1993 for £200,000 (now worth £800, 000) and has been campaigning for a blue placque to be put on the outside of the house commemorating the year our idols (minus Kenney, of course) lived there. Anyway, he invited me over for the full tour and I in turn asked Paolo Hewitt to come with me as it's always been his dream to view this house from the inside. PH also states in his excellent "Young Mods Forgotten Story" book that it is his lifelong ambition to buy the house, but I guess he'll need a lot of help from the lottery to fulfill that one. I met up with Paolo, on Sunday 8th October, and we spent several hours in the famous place trying to relive those heady days of 66. The property is a Victorian terraced townhouse on 4 floors. The rooms are very small and it has lots of very narrow staircases, must have been bedlum with a few dozen people in there at one of the now legendary all nighters. It was strange really because I've been looking at pictures taken inside that house for nearly 40 years and it was kind of eerie in a way just being there. Obviously its been decorated differently but it hasn't been modernised at all and the house and layout is still as it was then. The strangest thing was, before we arrived at the house we had been talking about the Small Faces scalectrix room (it's been well documented that they loved playing with this, for the uneducated it was a toy racetrack with toy battery operated racing cars).......lo and behold the first room we were shown into had a scalectrix track set up in one corner...... The owner wasn't aware that the band had Scalectrix and neither myself or PH had seen one in 25 years and yet there was one set up on the floor!.........spooky or what!
All in all a super afternoon, comparable to the first time I visited Beehive Cottage.

Thanks a million to Rupert and his lovely wife for their hospitality.

JOHN HELLIER

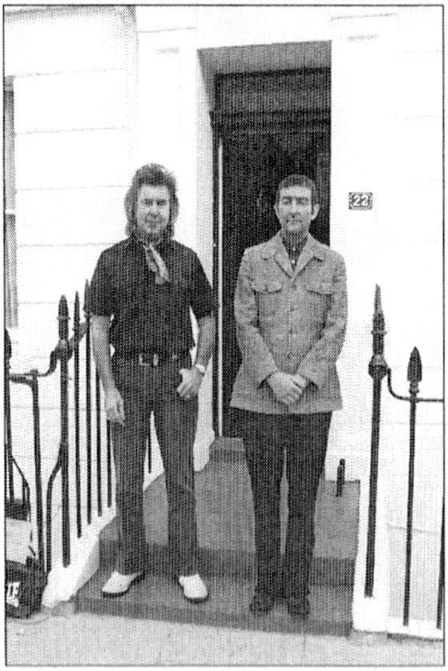

MAC BACK IN PIMLICO

For those that aren't already aware, Ronnie Lane aficionado Rupert Williams is shooting a Plonk documentary. He needed to interview Mac while he was in the country, during April and May of this year. I made a quick call to another Rupert, this one's Rupert Trollope, current owner of that rock and roll residence 22, Westmoreland Terrace........and hey presto and we've set up the Mac interview at this famous house. Mac was ecstatic at the thought of "going home". He hadn't set foot inside the house since Boxing day 1966! Anyway, myself, Rupert and a film crew were all there at noon on Friday 23rd April to greet one of the streets most famous ex-residents back home.

His face was a pleasure to see as he slowly went from room to room taking it all in, according to Mac not very much had changed at all since those days when it was known in the business as "Party Central". He was genuinely thrilled to be there. Eventually he settled down in the sitting room for the interview and what a great interview he gave to Rupert.

Approximately 1.30 pm, the doorbell rings........would you believe it's Paolo Hewitt and Paul Weller. They had no idea we were filming there today, they were just out in Pauls Mini Cooper and stopped off at random! Paolo had been to the house once before with me, several months ago, but Paul had never been. After exchanging pleasantries with all, Paolo gave Paul a tour of the premises pointing out such details as to who slept where etc.etc.. Paul was chuffed, we were all chuffed..........what a great day!

Can't wait for Ruperts documentary, that man is indeed thorough and will leave no stone unturned in telling Ronnie's story.

John Hellier

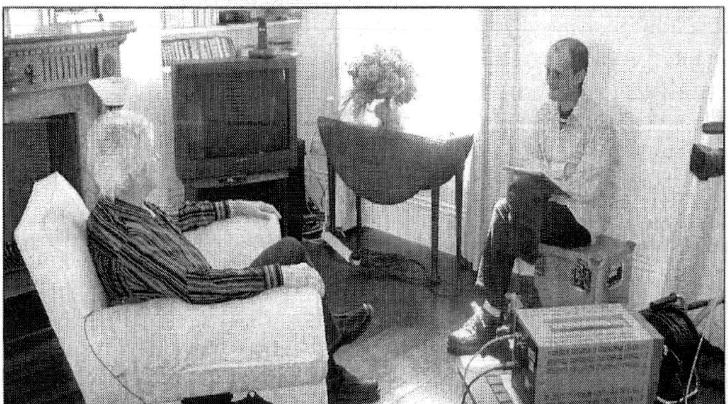

Mac being interviewed by Rupert Williams inside No 22

FEELING LONELY
Steve Marriott's Emotional Lyrics

Whilst recently transcribing the lyrics of Steve Marriott's songs I realised it was as if he was writing his autobiography of what life threw at him and also about growing up in the Small Faces. It's almost as if you could understand what Steve was thinking about on that particular day whilst he was writing down the words. Steve had at times a very dry and witty humour which was very mischievous, but most of all Steve had a heart of gold and could write very beautiful love songs which certainly showed his emotional and romantic side.

At the time of transcribing the lyrics of Steve's songs [not forgetting Ronnie] I had just parted from my wife of 22 years. I was going through stages of anger, depression and emotional breakdowns and while transcribing Steve's lyrics they brought me to tears. A lot of Steve's lyrics were related to love and the partings of relationships and with songs like "Feeling Lonely" "Afterglow" "Autumn Stone" "Get Yourself Together" "Things Are Going To Get Better" they really did pull at the heartstrings. Steve just had a way with words that meant something and it showed what a sensitive and emotional guy he could be.

Indeed, Steve's first wife Jenny would later remark "Steve was devastated when I left and used to call me a lot afterwards. Even when I was married to James, my second husband. James would answer the phone and Steve would say, "Is MY ol' lady there?"

I can really relate to Jenny's quotes above and understand how Steve was feeling. Steve in fact wrote "Tin Soldier" for Jenny and reading between the lines I can imagine he wrote "Afterglow" and "Autumn Stone" for her as well.

In some respects Steve's lyrics helped me to come to terms with life and point me in the right direction of how to get on. For almost a year I had these words drummed into my head which came from the song "Things

Are Going To Get Better" : "Things are going to get better, times change, better later than never, being true to myself makes me see, all the more, things are going to get better. And believe me it did help and especially with the words "Being true to myself makes me see all the more". These days I'm "Happy Boy Happy". I've changed in a lot of respects and I think have become a better, stronger person and have become a lot closer to my children than before, which goes to show "good things can come out of bad things".

I still love transcribing the lyrics of Steve and Ronnie. "My Mind's Eye" was Steve one night sat in a field just gazing at the sky and writing his feelings down. "Become Like You" was allegedly written about the Small Faces manager Don Arden and the way he treated people. The taking of drugs showed in lyrics such as "Here Come The Nice" "Itchycoo Park" and "Green Circles". Steve battling with his neighbours in "Lazy Sunday". "Donkey Rides, A Penny A Glass" based around Steve's Uncle Joe [As told to me by Kay Marriott]. But for me Steve was at his best writing about his emotional experiences with romance and broken relationships. "All Or Nothing", "My Way Of Giving", "I'm Only Dreaming", "Afterglow", "Feeling Lonely", "Autumn Stone" and many more.

I owe a lot to Steve Marriott through his lyrics and would also like to share those lyrics with anyone who may go through a bad time [and even a good time]. I've created a Marriott/Lane web site/e-group non mailing list at: http://groups.yahoo.com/group/MarriottLane/ I believe this to be the ultimate Small Faces lyrics site. The site also includes trivia on alternate takes/demos of the tracks with special thanks to Ian McLagan for the help on "Long Agos And Worlds Apart" plus "Up The Wooden Hills To Bedfordshire" and many thanks to Mike Griffiths for transcribing Stanley Unwin's 'gobbledegook' narration from the 'Ogdens' album - Nice!

FOR STEVE AND RONNIE: FOREVER IN MY HEART.

MICK TAYLOR

One For The Road
Ronnie Lane Memorial Concert

8th April 2004

Following the immense success of the Steve Marriott Memorial in 2001, April 2004 saw the staging of One for the Road, the Ronnie Lane Memorial Concert at London's Royal Albert Hall. This intended as a charity concert in aid of Ronnie's children here in the UK who lost their home in a fire a while ago.

The event took enormous planning, not least in dealing with the Lane family politics, and everyone's gratitude is owed to John Hellier of Darlings of Wapping Wharf, who with big help from Brent Yeomans of 17 Black, organised the concert.

The Royal Albert Hall was an excellent choice of venue. The Marriott event at London's Astoria had sold out quickly and actually broke the venue record for bar takings! Steve would have been proud of that! Even with the greater capacity of the Royal Albert Hall, the evening was a sell-out and the bars were doing brisk business.

Ronnie Lane fans converged on South Kensington from all over the world, while the list of performers included those who had made their name in the sixties, seventies, eighties and nineties, so highly is Ronnie regarded amongst musicians and fans. There were a few notable absentees from the original planned line-up for various reasons. Fellow Small Face and Face Ian McLagan was unable to attend as was PP Arnold. Tributes to Lane were read out from Sir Paul McCartney, with whom Lane had played with Kenney Jones in the Rockestra concerts from the early 1980's. Eric Clapton also sent his apologies. A long-term friend and collaborator of Lane, Clapton was playing Frankfurt the same evening. However, these absentees did not detract from the very high quality of the event. Both Clapton and McCartney sent written tributes to Ronnie which compere John Hellier read out at the start of the evening.

There were three principal phases to Ronnie Lane's musical career (the Small Faces, the Faces and the "solo" years with Slim Chance). These phases were all well-represented,

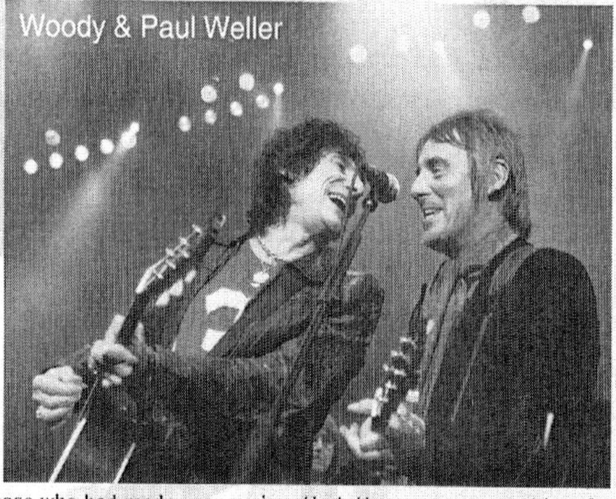
Woody & Paul Weller

ensuring that there was something for everybody.

The first half of the evening focused on the Small Faces, probably the best-known and most-popular stage of his career. Kicking off proceedings were Small World from Essex. The band have played at recent Small Faces Conventions and have proved to be very popular. A short set of Small Faces classics was much appreciated. The Deborah Bonham Band was eagerly anticipated. Deborah was one of the stars of the Steve Marriott concert. Her band included former Humble Pie drummer Jerry Shirley. She has a powerful voice and deserves to be heard further to show she is more than just Bonzo's sister. Her two songs were both cover versions, well covers when Ronnie originally did them. Every Little Bit Hurts is the Brenda Holloway song that became a feature of the Small Faces set, appearing in live form on In Memorium and as a BBC version on the fairly recent BBC

Pete Townshend

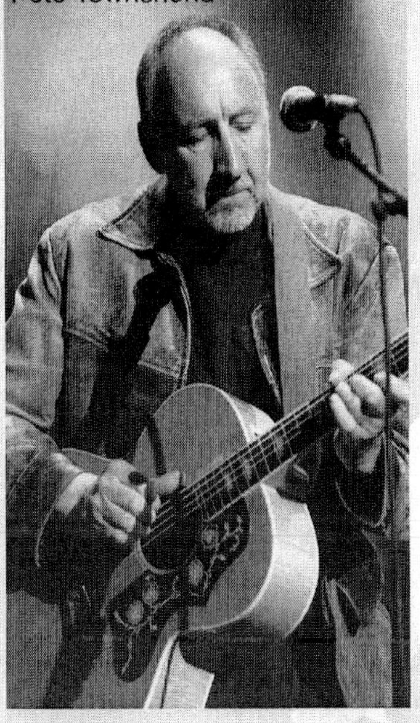

Sessions. The Faces covered Maybe I'm Amazed with Plonk taking lead vocal on the first verse. If Sir Paul could not be be there in person, at least one of his best post-Beatles songs was. 17 Black continue to go from strength to strength. Another regular at the annual Small Faces Convention, Mollie Marriott appears to be almost a member of the band now. Mollie's appearance highlights the support that the Marriott family has for these events. As well as Steve's daughter, his sister and mother, the two Kays, were there along with nephew Little Stevie and niece Lucy. After a pair of tracks from Ogden's Nut Gone Flake, 17 Black were joined by Buzzcocks guitarist Steve Diggle who repeated his performance of Here Come The Nice from 1996's Long Agos and World Apart. Nine Below Zero's Dennis Greaves joined for Hey Girl and What'cha Gonna Do About It. Midge Ure was fortunately allowed two tracks having played just My Mind's Eye at the Steve Marriott concert. Mad John was excellent and was a good choice. Both of his contributions came across very well with just acoustic guitar and distinctive vocals.

Ocean Colour Scene were also on the Long Agos and Worlds Apart CD and reprised their Song of a Baker. A slightly different line-up for this concert featured Andy in place of Damon Minchella on bass and Simon Fowler's cousin on guitar. The opening chords of Wham Bam Thank You Ma'am threatened to lift the dome off of the Albert Hall. A surprise in their set and a real joy was Done This One Before. Guitarist Steve Craddock took lead vocals for the b-side of How Come and did such as a good job that the band is said to be considering adding the track to their live set. The band had been considering playing Traveller's Tune from their third album. This was written as a tribute to Ronnie

The reformation of Slim Chance after 25 years was eagerly anticipated by many. Unfortunately, this part of Ronnie's career is less well-known than the Faces or Small Faces material and unfamiliar to some of the audience. However, interest was maintained by an array of guest artists that joined the nucleus of Slim Chance that had been reassembled by Charlie Hart. To his credit he was able to bring in members from different Slim Chance incarnations including Chrissie Stewart on bass and ex Wings man Henry McCulloch on guitar. The line up also included Geraint Watkins on keyboards, Alun Davies on acoustic guitar and Geoff Dugmore on drums. Cat's Melody and Kuschty Rye were familiar to many and showed that Charlie Hart had done a superb job in getting Slim Chance up-and-running. Another Convention regular Keith Smart joined for Anniversary before Chris Jagger, fresh from his article for The Independent, led the audience through the hit How Come and Anymore for Anymore. Sam Brown made several appearances throughout the evening and her opener Flags & Banners showed the promise of what was to come. She was certainly one of the stars of the evening, both on backing and lead vocals.

Steve Diggle had already made his appearance but more stalwarts of the punk revolution showed that Ronnie's appeal transcended the generations and maybe he was not viewed in the same way as many others of the previous generation. Fresh from an appearance at the 2003 Small Faces Convention and appearances with Ian McLagan, Glen Matlock of the Sex Pistols joined Slim Chance along with Mick Jones of the Clash. They played two Ronnie Lane songs from the Faces days, Debris and You're So Rude.

A huge cheer and a standing ovation met the first appearance of Pete Townshend of the evening. He recorded an album with Ronnie called Rough Mix, but his first choice was a Faces track called Stone. He was followed by another of the class of '77, Paul Weller was joined by Sam Brown for one of the most popular songs from Ronnie's solo days The Poacher and Spiritual Babe, a little known Ronnie Lane number that had appeared on Live in Austin. With an ironic twist, Sam Brown took the lead vocals for The Lad's Got Money with Henry McCulloch leading through One for the Road. Paul Weller and Sam Brown returned along with former Face and a surprise appearance from Ronnie Wood. This ensemble played one of Ronnie's most popular Faces songs and Ooh La La also brought an appearance from two can-can dancers, one of which was John Hellier's daughter, Melanie.

During a short break the audience was introduced to John Unwin, son of the late Stanley Unwin. "Professor" Unwin had illuminated the Small Faces' superb Ogden's Nut Gone Flake with his Unwinese links. His son told us of the view from the Unwin household of the whole episode. He was a Small Faces fan himself and his father had never heard of them. However, Ogden's Nut Gone Flake has gone down in music history and Unwin junior switched into Unwinese to introduce the final band of the evening. A relatively new band but heaps of experience, the Jones Gang features Small Faces, Faces and Who drummer Kenney Jones with Rick Wills and Gary Grainger. They launched into the title track of Ogden's Nut Gone Flake, an instrumental version of the second single I've Got Mine. The band's vocalist Robert Hart and Dave "Bucket" Colwell joined for the Faces' Maggie May. A new song from the band called Gypsy Lane was written by Robert and Kenney and was another Ronnie tribute. This was followed by Itchycoo Park before the band was joined by Love Affair vocalist Steve Ellis for Afterglow. Then it was the turn of a rousing version of Tin Soldier, . Sam Brown returned to sing the Marriott/Lane song If You Think You're Groovy. This was recorded by PP Arnold with the Small Faces providing the backing. A couple more Faces tracks were Had Me a Real Good Time and Stay With Me, featuring the return of Ronnie Wood. Pete Townshend made a second appearance of the evening to sing Heart to Hang Onto, a track from the Rough Mix album. This also featured Sam Brown's vocals. The evening ended with the Small Faces' number one single All or Nothing. Chris Farlowe made a surprise appearance as did former Humble Pie guitarist Clem Clempson.

Overall this was a superb evening of entertainment and an excellent tribute to Plonk. The Small Faces are probably more popular now than ever and with interest in the Faces sure to be revived with the forthcoming boxed set, Ronnie's music is reaching out to people again. Following this event, there is also talk of Slim Chance recording again, but that will be another story.

MARTIN PAYNE

Full Artist & Song Listing

Small World	• I Can't Make It • I've Got Mine • I'm Only Dreaming • Don't Burst My Bubble
Deborah Bonham Band	• Every Little Bit Hurts • Maybe I'm Amazed
17 Black with Mollie Marriott	• Rene • Lazy Sunday
17 Black with Mollie Marriott and Steve Diggle	• Here Come the Nice
17 Black with Mollie Marriott and Dennis Greaves	• Hey Girl • What'cha Gonna Do About It
Midge Ure	• Mad John • My Mind's Eye
Ocean Colour Scene	• Wham Bam Thank You Ma'am • Done This One Before • Song of a Baker
Slim Chance	• Cat's Melody (Rat's Tails) • Kuschty Rye
Slim Chance with Keith Smart	• Anniversary
Slim Chance with Chris Jagger	• Anymore for Anymore • How Come
Slim Chance with Sam Brown	• Flags & Banners
Slim Chance with Glen Matlock & Mick Jones	• Debris • You're So Rude
Slim Chance with Pete Townshend	• Stone
Slim Chance	• Harvest Home
Slim Chance with Paul Weller	• The Poacher • Spiritual Babe
Slim Chance with Sam Brown	• Lad's Got Money
Slim Chance	• One for the Road
Slim Chance with Paul Weller, Sam Brown and Ronnie Wood	• Ooh La La
John Unwin	
The Jones Gang	• Ogden's Nut Gone Flake • Maggie May • Gypsy Lane • Itchycoo Park
The Jones Gang with Steve Ellis	• Afterglow
The Jones Gang with Sam Brown	• If You Think You're Groovy
The Jones Gang with Ronnie Wood	• Had Me a Real Good Time
The Jones Gang with Pete Townshend and Sam Brown	• Heart to Hang Onto
The Jones Gang with Ronnie Wood	• Stay With Me
The Jones Gang with Chris Farlowe on vocals and Clem Clempson on guitar	• All or Nothing

A TRIP DOWN MEMORY LANE

Fan Liz McLean, from the North East Of England, reminisces...

Memory lane eh! Here are my recollections of being a Small Faces fan in the swinging sixties.

I was twelve years old, I had 12 shillings and 6 pence in my pocket, and I was going to buy a record, my very first LP in fact. I walked into the record store and was drawn like a magnet to the cover of the Small Faces first Decca album. There was no question that was the one I was going to have. I don't think I had ever actually heard them before and why I chose that one I have no idea. I took it home, listened to it and that was it, I was hooked. I absolutely loved the music, I loved the way they looked, and I loved everything about them. Pretty soon afterwards the bedroom walls were wallpapered with Small Faces pictures and my poor pre-Dansette record player was glowing from over use. I lived and breathed the Small Faces, I knew every word, riff and drum roll. I could hear every single note of every single song in my head and used to go to sleep each night going through them. If the Small Faces liked egg and chips, I liked egg and chips. If they recommended sticking your head in a gas oven, in mine would go. I loved them all but especially I loved Steve. It was that voice. To a young girl with hormones all over the place it was like Heineken (you know, reaches the parts others don't!). I used to write stories featuring the Small Faces – they always ended the same way - with Steve putting a protective arm around me and walking off into the distance. OK so I was a very young and naïve child! Most of all though it was the music. I just loved listening to it, preferably 24 hours a day. I went to every gig at the Newcastle City Hall, to me that was the ultimate experience, seeing and hearing them live not that you could actually hear very much. I, personally, was not a screamer. I just stood there besotted with my mouth wide open – no doubt waiting for Steve to spot me and put a protective arm around me! This was the era of the package tour where you got to see about ten bands. The sets were pretty short, nevertheless I was never disappointed and you did get to see a lot of bands that you would have otherwise missed. I have the Small Faces to thank for the fact that I saw Jimi Hendrix live, mind you I also got to see Engelbert Humperdinck live, which I wasn't quite so thrilled about. Another thing I remember and I don't know if this was universal or just peculiar to Newcastle (or indeed just to me) was throwing sweets on stage. Obviously I didn't do this when the Small Faces were playing as I was too busy standing looking like a berk, but I do remember hurling sherbet lemons, of all things at the Hollies – not a wise choice to actually hit anyone with, but luckily I was not a very good shot.

It was at Newcastle City Hall that I first saw PP Arnold. She opened the show with her backing band, The Nice. She was wearing a gold tent dress, very fashionable at the time. When she started to sing, I was astounded. I just loved her voice immediately. I wrote to her to see if she wanted anybody to run a fan club but she already one, so I joined. Enid Buckland-Evers ran it and she did a really good job. They had fan club days out that Pat (PP) would go along too, but I never went as I lived too far away (heartbreaking, I know). When I couldn't get a copy of her album "The First Lady Of Immediate" locally, Enid, very kindly, sent me one with a little message written by Pat on the cover. It was my pride and joy. Unfortunately, after I had left home my mum assumed, just because they had been lying around for seven years, that I didn't want my record collection and kindly disposed of the lot, so I'm afraid it is lost forever. It was also around this time that I painted half my face brown with Mary Quant eye make up to see if I looked better black or white! (Well, who hasn't done that)?

I must say I did look on both the Small Faces and PP Arnold as almost personal friends and was deeply concerned about their welfare. I loved the music with a passion and it gave me endless hours of pleasure (still does). Surprisingly, when the Small Faces split up I was upset but not devasted. Steve was happily settled into Beehive Cottage with wife Jenny, so obviously going to live happily ever after. He was going to do Humble Pie and the others would do the Faces. If they were happy,

I was happy and that was that. I didn't even buy "Autumn Stone". I listened to Humble Pie and the Faces but not with the same emotional attachment that I had for the Small Faces. The magic was over; I got on with the rest of my life.

When Steve died I was surprised at how much it affected me, after all I had only rarely thought about him for twenty years. Obviously it was upsetting and such a tragic way to go but it wasn't grief, in my belief system death is just the start of something different, it is as if your life is held up by a solid foundation and a bit that has always been there holding you up drops out and you become destabilised…couldn't put it into words then and still can't. I think I was surprised at what a fundamental and important part of my life he was, even after all those years. When Ronnie died the feeling was not so intense, his death was not so unexpected and if anyone deserved a new start it was Ronnie.

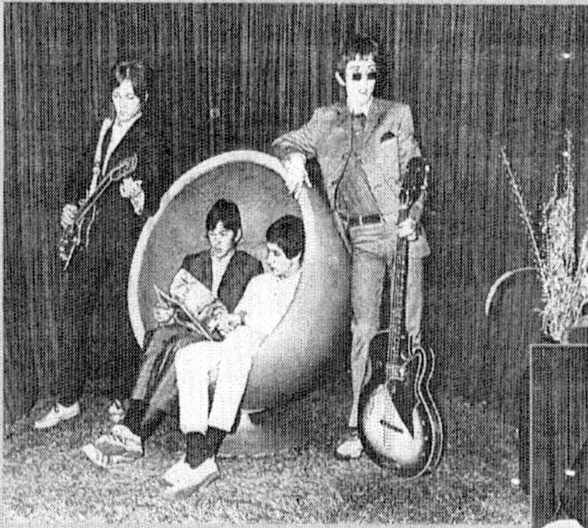

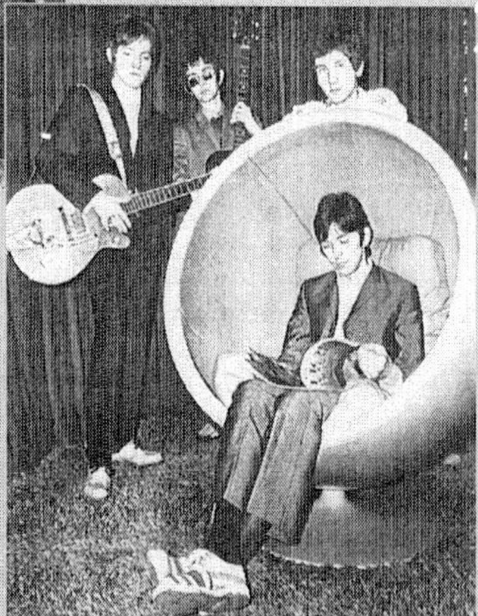

In 1993 I was overjoyed to find the cd re-issue of "First Lady Of Immediate/Kafunta" and find Pat's voice was every bit as good as I remembered. What's more I still knew all the words, much to everyone's dismay, and could sing right through the lot…albeit very badly! Later the same year I bought Steve's last studio album "Thirty Seconds To Midnite". It was a real pleasure to hear Steve sing again and it was still like Heineken! And there was the added bonus of Pat being on the album as well. Later I bought "Clear Thru' The Night" and was very to have re-discovered Steve. A few Christmases ago my mother spotted "Small Faces" "Ogden's" and " Autumn Stone" cd's in a box set and bought them for me as a surprise. I hadn't heard them for over thirty years.... indeed, I'd never heard "Autumn Stone" at all. The effect was amazing, the music! The words! Some I had forgotten about and yet I knew them all intimately. I was transported back in time, emotional attachment and all, I was right back back to the egg and chips and gas oven state. I knew it was ridiculous and I loved every minute of it. What I could see now quite clearly, which I couldn't at the time, was that the Small Faces were not just Steve Marriott with backing musicians, but a unique combination of personalities and ideas that would never be repeated. I was also quite amazed to see quite clearly in the lyrics many of my basic attitudes and ideals, which was a bit of a blow because I had always assumed I had thought of them myself! Still in this state of idolization I listened to "Autumn Stone". The live tracks were from Newcastle City Hall – I was there! (the one with the mouth open). I can actually remember them being recorded with the great big double mikes they used to use. Then I heard "Call It Something Nice", the words, so true, so clever. So there I was in the kitchen, next to the washer, singing away perfecting the words. I had just finished "Don't lean on me or I might let you down" when the washer did something it had never done before or since. It physically switched itself off at the on/off switch in mid cycle. I can only assume one of two things – either Steve and Ronnie were saying "For Gods sake, woman, listen to the bloody words and leave us alone can't you! Or the washer just hates my singing! Either way it did make me think and I have now settled down to sheer appreciation of the Small Faces and their music and the good times they gave me ....And still do.

Liz McLean.

Liz is the editor of the excellent PP Arnold newsletter "Angel Wings" and also runs the PP Arnold fan club. For more details liz@lmclean.fsnet.co.uk

Small Faces Night,

National Film Theatre, London, 14 August 2003

As part of its Mod cinema season, the National Film Theatre on London's South Bank held a Small Faces night, courtesy of Paolo Hewitt. This featured a series of clips and films featuring the band or Steve Marriott. The cinema was packed and many waited ticketless outside. Amongst the guests were Steve's mother and sister as well as his nephew Stephen.

The first part of the programme consisted of clips of the young Steve Marriott as a child actor. These were poor quality clips of films such as Night Cargoes. The interesting point here is that cheeky grin and mannerisms were there even then. The gig clip from Dateline Diamonds was next. Until recently, most of us would not have seen this but the release of the film on DVD and video means that the only footage of the Small Faces with Jimmy Winston (correct me if I am wrong) has a wider audience. The Small Faces are playing "live" in a club where they take the stage fresh from their US tour (??) and play I've Got Mine, Winston playing Rickenbacker guitar. Check out the early Small Faces haircuts here!

The two extracts from the Morecambe & Wise show from 1967 were both played live. All or Nothing was very good but I Can't Make It almost blew the roof of the cinema off. Between the two Morecambe & Wise clips was part of a documentary showing the Small Faces in the studio jamming with segments of an interview with Don Arden ("If I've ever exploited anybody it's because they want to be exploited.") Naturally, this was met with derisions of laughter.

After the promotional films for Get Yourself Together (the police assaulting Marriott) and Itchycoo Park (on the beach) came the real highlight of the evening. Following the release of Ogden's Nut Gone Flake the Small Faces performed in a Colour Me Pop special for the BBC. This included the promotional film for Lazy Sunday and a superb live (in the studio) Song of a Baker. The latter has been shown from time to to time by the BBC as part of its Sounds of the Sixties series. The following live rendition of side two of Ogden's was a real treat. The songs were interspersed with narration from Stanley Unwin that was more extensive than on record and slightly different, especially with his gestures. Basically, played live side 2 sounded so much better than on record! Just try to imagine this!! This live footage showed just how good the Small Faces actually were. There is little live material available from the band today. Somehow this should re-released in its entirety on DVD. It takes Ogden's to a totally new level. The band is so together, not just musically but also in terms of their humour.

The final treat, apart from some brief home movie footage with Marriott in his garden with wife Jenny and dog Shamus who made his recording debut on The Universal, is the My Generation Without Walls special from 1995 on the Small Faces.

Overall, the evening was a huge success with many rare or unseen clips alongside some more accessible ones. There was plenty of cheering and clapping. Ronnie Lane looked even cooler than we thought all the way through (except THOSE sandals). Ian McLagan admitted a shoe fetish but some of the things he was wearing suggest there could be more fundamental problems here (dress, that hat, that collar in Morecambe & Wise slots). This man is dangerous.

Let's hope that these clips do not disappear and they are given a wider audience again.

• MARTIN PAYNE

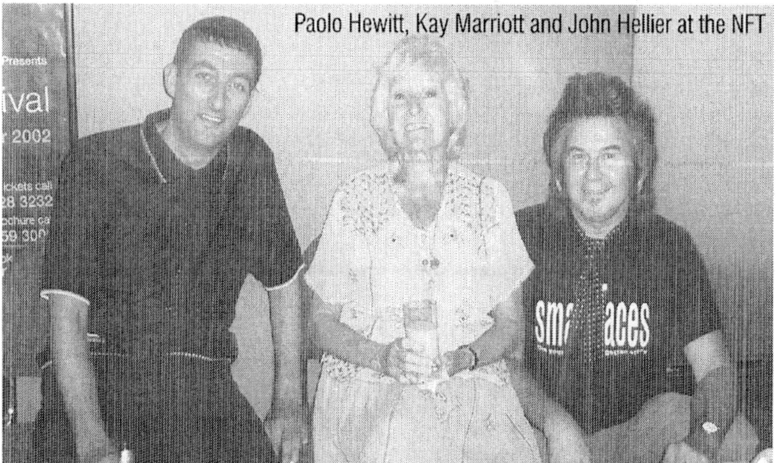

Paolo Hewitt, Kay Marriott and John Hellier at the NFT

HAPPY TO BE PART OF THE INDUSTRY OF HUMAN HAPPINESS

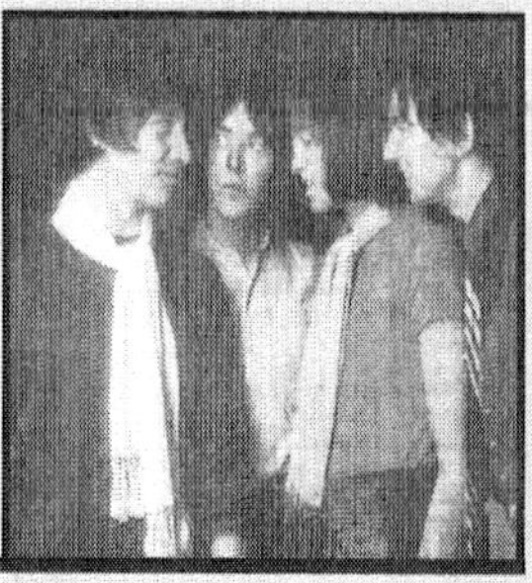

BY PAUL BANES

It's a small world if you'll excuse the pun, but apart from still being Murray Heads publisher (he was also on Immediate) I was Tony Calders assistant DJ at the Ilford Palais from 1962-1967 and went on to work with him at Immediate Records. We effectively had this young, up and coming actor/blues singer called Steve Marriott, managed by Tony, and one Monday night after our evening show at the Palais, in the good ol' Wimpy Bar, we came up with a name for his group, Steve Marriotts Moments. They later did a free concert for me at the Ilford Palais, as did the Who, thanks to my workmate Ray Tolliday who was their press man and later Immediates.

I recently served as a witness for Andrew Oldham in this sordid affair to the ownership of the Immediate tapes. We now seem to be hip and trendy or is that what they call recognition. Whilst I am delighted that the band are now being paid 33 years later, I might point out that the villains of the piece are really EMI, who acquired some of the Immediate tapes when the company went bust, and a couple of other dubious people who should not be mentioned.

What most outsiders ignore when they talk about Andrew and Tony is that not only did the artists get artistic freedom but the artists royalty deals were twice as much as some of the major acts of the day. We did see Status Quo, Donovan and Cat Stevens in our throws, although they were all keen to be part of Immediate, none of them eventually signed. Contrary to our neighbour in New Oxford Street, Dick James, we set up publishing companies for most of our acts i.e. Nanker Phelge and Mirage for the Stones and the Small Faces with their typical east end humour called their company AVAKAK. I registered most of their songs at PRS when I was running Immediate Music under this company.

I tried to help Kenney sort this out a few years ago but I don't think he really grasped the situation for the songs were seized by United Artists, now EMI, at the time of liquidation but they effectively belonged to the band. That said, the re-edition of the back catalogue is water under the bridge as Charly Records have massacred the whole back catalogue since they got their grubby hands on it.

There will never be another album sleeve to match Ogdens Nut Gone Flake, it was and still is unique. Did you know they dreamed up the idea of the sleeve after their New Years Eve television appearance in Bremen in Germany and despite all the adverse comments regarding costs. It was manufactured with a custom built machine in the UK and with a plastic jacket in America where the wonderful Bob Cato convinced CBS to manufacture despite the fact that it was likely to fall out of the racks.

I went to America in 1969 to open Immediates New York office and road managed Humble Pies first US tour later that year, with help from Small Faces roadie, Dave Clark (no, not the drummer!). Billy Nicholls came over to look after Andrews home in Connecticut whenever Andrew wasn't around. I was married while I was over there and Billy was one of the witnesses.

I don't know whether Mac or Kenney managed to lay there hands on any of the Olympic sessions tapes but I know for a fact that they recorded something with Donovan and we did a Christmas single for Immediate with everybody singing including The Small Faces, Chris Farlowe and PP Arnold.

In view of the fact that I came from Forest Gate in East London I was probably more related to Ronnie, who lived in the same area, than Steve who was almost middle class as he had been through the whole child actor scene and was considered a bit "west end".

That said, I am proud to have been part of the "industry of human happiness" and one of those "bastards called Immediate", because we have left behind a legacy whether it be the Small Faces or the Nice or Rod Stewart or whoever. I just hope that all the artistic and creative genius that the artists and Andrew had remains intact and that we don't see anymore of these tacky re-editions on Charly or wherever.

NICE! PB (September 2003)

IT'S ALL TOO BEAUTIFUL

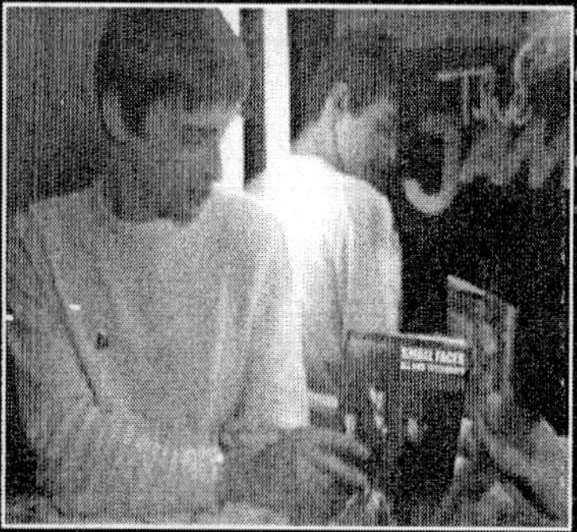

Paul Weller pays homage to "the ultimate group"

I see the Small Faces as the ultimate group, the sort of group you could only dream of being in. They all dug the new music and came out of the mod scene with its brilliant taste and influence, whether that be clothes or Booker T & The MGs. They didn't give a fuck but weren't above taking the piss out of themselves as well as everyone else and the whole music biz charade. They were even the same height! They were destined to be in a band together, which gives them a very uncanny, magical quality. They were also very sussed. Steve Marriott was one of the greatest vocalists to come out of this tight-arsed country.

As their playing got tighter and their songs got better, they developed their own feel, which no one else could or ever can reproduce. Their arrangements were great, complex in a concise way and always dramatic. They also had great lyrics, a lot of humour, plenty of attitude and on most of the records a feeling that everyone involved were totally committed to the group. It's so rare to meet other players who think along the same lines. Most are just into bucks and jerking off onstage. There's very little commitment to the music but you never felt that from the Small Faces.

Charles Shaar Murray once wrote that I had "based my entire career on George Orwell and the Small Faces". I much prefer being me, but I'd have loved to have been in that kind of band when I was younger, to have four people all knowing instinctively what it should be.

I'm still a fan. I like everything about them as much now as when I first saw them on TV in 1967/68 doing 'Tin Soldier' with PP Arnold.

FINEST MOMENTS

Music: Their first Immediate album "Small Faces" and for me their best. In fact, all their stuff in 1967 was great. I'm Only Dreaming, the B-side to Itchycoo Park. I Feel Much Better, Talk to You and Here Comes The Nice, the ultimate mod/pill song. Then there's Itchycoo itself and its humour among and against all the flowerpot men and trendies. And Tin Soldier, my favourite Small Faces tune.

Hair: Steve's haircut around Itchycoo Park (summer 1967) was for me his best look. You have to have a small tugboat to pull this one off, petit but tough. Check that black and white film of them when they are on podiums – that haircut.

Clothes: Itchycoo Park, on Beat Club, for the Paisley jackets and checked pants. All Or Nothing, on Swedish TV, for the coats. Ian McLagan in Quant style PVC, Ronnie Lane in black fur-collared car coat. I Can't Make It, from Beat Club appearance, pre-psychedelic gear. Just hip. Stills from French TV (I think) outdoor show, Steve's wearing a red, white and blue hooped sweater, Kenney is in white Levis and blue suede shoes, Mac is suited with brown and banana yellow weaved shoes and Plonk is in some serious desert boots. Two of these shots are on French Eps with fantastic colour pic covers. Check also the pic on the French Ep of My Minds Eye, where Steve and Plonk are wearing satin shirts with round collars. Also, don't forget the round toed brown and white shoes, circa '68.

Attitude: Mac pouring a pot of piss over debt collectors heads, Steve telling Johnny Stewart (TOTP producer) and Tony Blackburn to fuck off, the lyrics to Itchycoo Park, Here Comes The Nice, Become Like You and the Who/Faces tour of Australia and New Zealand in 1968.

Interview by Paolo Hewitt 1994

Trivia! Trivia!

DID YOU KNOW THAT................during Steve Marriott's low-key later years he'd turn up at gigs and not be known by the management. Once he had to pretend to be a window cleaner to get into his own dressing room. Also he'd chat to members of the audience, unrecognised, about what a twat Steve Marriott was!

DID YOU KNOW THAT.................According to a story in the February 2001 edition of Mojo, immediately following Steve Marriott's departure from the Small Faces Kenney Jones was thinking of forming a new trio with Status Quo's Parfitt and Rossi. Apparently they rehearsed a few times in a school hall in Lambeth. Rick Parfitt says, "Kenney was a right pain in the arse, we couldn't get him to work and when he did he kept playing all the wrong things, as far as we were concerned".

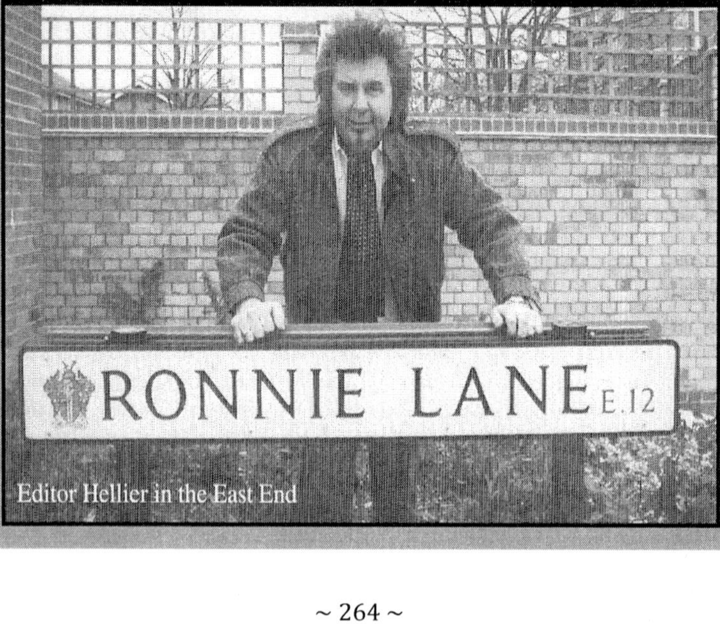

Editor Hellier in the East End

STEVE MARRIOTT – A SMALL FACE

Moody mod, Paolo Hewitt, meets a nice ol' geezer, Steve Marriott. (October 1984)

Yesterday is dead but that doesn't kill the memories. As he sits in the Giaconda Café in London's Denmark Street, some of them start to flit through Steve Marriott's mind.

"This street", he recalls "Tin Pan Alley, was full of studios where bands could do demos. We all used to sit in here and someone would walk in and say, any drummers around? Or any guitarist? A few people would put up their hands. Right you, come on them...You'd go and do the session, get a few bob for it, nip along to the drinker next door, have a few swifties and then back in here for some brown sauce rolls. Lovely days, they were".

When Steve Marriott first started frequenting the Giaconda he was but a mere fresh-faced 16 years old about to embark on a spectacular pop adventure. Within three months of starting The Small Faces with friends Ronnie Lane and Kenney Jones, he would be a nationally known figure, a genuine 60's pop star. With them he would produce a steady stream of songs that could arguably be described best as the epitome of classic British pop, vibrant, raw and melodic, three-minute rushes of youthful energy and vigour. These records have stood the test of time.

Twenty years on and much has changed. Denmark Street now boasts a kind of faded glory, the Giaconda has painted its walls and changed its layout. Steve Marriott is now heavier, scruffier and much, much wiser. From the skinny arrogant 16 year old with a flair for clothes and music, perhaps the only thing that hasn't changed is Marriott's outlook. Even as he approaches 40 he remains the archetypal wide boy, a quick joke always on his lips and a stubbon refusal to take anything, least of all himself, seriously.

After he dragged me into the Tin Pan Alley Club to ply him with scotches – "its all right you'll get them on the expenses" we returned to the Giaconda to start the interview. It's closed, but Marriott isn't put off. "Never mind me old mate" chortles Marriott "we'll sit here". Which is how Steve Marriott and I ended up outside a music shop, sitting on its steps, on a freezing Tuesday afternoon. "Do you mind talking about the Small Faces?" I enquired. "Not at all" he replies "I'm proud of my past" and so he should be.

Steve Marriott's career started not as a pop performer but as a child actor. It was what his parents wanted for him and when, at the age of 13, he landed a part in the production of Oliver, it looked as though their ambitions were going to be realised. "Any kid off the street could

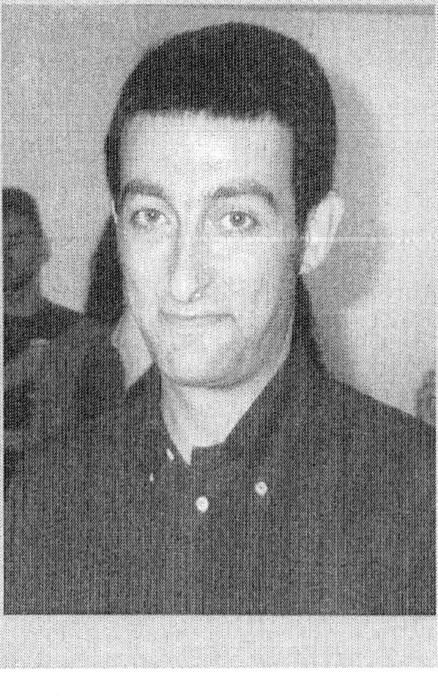

have got a part in Oliver" says Marriott. "It weren't hard. I used to go round the bus stops busking with a ukulele in the East End so they thought I was a born entertainer. They sent me up for this audition and I shit myself as it happens. Played some Buddy Holly songs and got the part. Now the reason my acting thing continued is me school burnt down and I was instrumental in it, in fact I got the blame for it. It's a kids dream really. So there was no school to go to. I ended up going to Drama School, working my way through it and beating up all the rich kids for their sweets."

By the time he was 15 Marriott was an avid admirer of blues music, adored Buddy Holly, worshipped people like Little Milton and Bobby Bland, had become a mod and landed a job in a music shop to finance his interest in clothes, clubs, pills and records. Clothes to us were essential says Marriott. "I don't know why, it's hard to put into words. I've lost that verve, the whole sort of look. I just dress to be comfortable now so it's hard for me to rationalise it. It was a case of all me mates were mods and I was a mod. It's very easy to say that the Small Faces were the leaders of it but we weren't. We were just mods. We come to the top of the pile, but at the same time we were just part of the movement. We weren't no spearhead. Like we'd take pills, stay up at night. It was The Scene club until midnight, the Flamingo for the all nighter and being sick in alleyways, ruining the jacket you'd just paid an arm and a leg for. I just thought everything was just marvellous. I thought we were marvellous. I thought being sick was marvellous, taking pills was marvellous and all the other groups were marvellous, I didn't analyse it, I just went for it.

Steve Marriott was 18 when he formed the Small Faces "You've got to realise", Marriott stresses, "first we formed out of error, it wasn't a planned thing at all. I got Kenney and Ronnie slung out of their group by smashing a piano up in a pub one night. They had invited me along and I went berserk. Me and Ronnie got pissed and Ronnie and Kenney got the bullet. So we said fuck it lets form a group ourselves. But we couldn't get anyone to join the group. The name put them off, I remember sitting in the café next-door, he says nodding to the Giaconda and trying to tout for guitarists. They'd say what's the name of the group, because in those days it was a very, very heavy thing. I'd say (he whispers) The Small Faces and they'd say, what? I'd say The Small Faces and they'd go, fuck off, you've got to be joking. It embarrassed them, so in the end I thought, fuck it I'll play guitar, I knew my way around it but I wasn't proficient at all".

Marriott had met Lane and consequently Jones, through his job at the music shop. All three were young and without a care in the world. All had tried groups before but because they had been the youngest members they had been severely patronised. When they finally did get together, with Jimmy Winston, originally on organ, they had given up on the idea of being successful.

For us to get together it was like sod it, let's not be serious anymore. We'd play the odd wedding and fuck trying to make it. Within three months we had a hit record. The Small Faces secured a residency at the Cavern Club in Leicester Square. At the time they only knew four songs between them but somehow managed to string them out for a good hour and a half. Because we used to do numbers like "Pass The Spliff", Marriott recalls, "we thought we were being ever so cool and we'd wonder why the audience would start cracking up. It was here that they attracted a large mod following – because of their clothes and love of soul music which was reflected in their set – and eventually caused Don Arden to come down and see them. The night before Arden came, Marriott and Lane were involved in a vicious punch-up. It was a bunch of Tottenham boys. Apparently Woodford and Loughton (where Marriott and Lane were then dossing) had done up a bit of Tottenham. "They all bundled out of this van as me and Ronnie were walking home and gave us one of the severest kickings I've ever had. Me, like a tosser, said what's it all about and they came back and gave me another kicking. The next day we auditioned down the Cavern Club and every time Ronnie hit a note his head would bleed, and my lip was out here, my eyes were out here, we must have looked fearsome. But they obviously liked what they saw." Arden took on the Small Faces, signed them to Decca and within three months their debut single. "Whatcha Gonna Do About It" was a massive hit.

What set them apart from their contemporaries was Marriott's voice, a kind of mini version, of people like Sam Cooke and his R & B heroes. It didn't possess much finesse but like all great singers communicated instantly its raw power and passion. In fact one of The Small Faces legacies was to bring to the attention of a large audience their love of black orientated music. "We used to cover songs" says Marriott "and then say fuck that, listen to the original it's much better."

The Small Faces borrowed from this black source, mixed it with their own finite pop sensibility and produced a tremendous surge of sound and blue eyed pop music. Obviously it couldn't last forever. The Small Faces quickly became popular and then idols to millions of girls. "It was fucking terrible." Marriott states. "When I got married I got sacks full of broken records and hate letters from little girls. What you've got to realise is that it's got nothing to do with music and that's the heartbreaking thing.

"If you're at all serious about it – and I think my track record must mean I am – it breaks your heart. Its like no matter what I play, they're not listening." Other things were happening as well. Despite their successful record sales, the Small Faces were still on £20 per week. This didn't bother the band. They had money in their pockets, a gig every night and accounts at clothes shops. But their parents thought different. They approached Don Arden to see where all the money was going. Arden told them that the band were all junkies and were spending the cash on supporting their habits. It was, of course, a complete fabrication. It put our parents off the track and flung them up in arms against us, "Marriott remembers. "I'll tell you something though, without Don Arden there wouldn't have been the Small Faces. We have to say that I think he managed us very well, money regardless. And screw money, money only gets in the way. What he actually did was put us over very well, opened a lot of doors. Without those people you wouldn't get anywhere so thank them for making my name."

The second phase of the Small Faces career saw them leaving Decca and Arden and signing for Immediate records. The mod days were over, the Small Faces were sick of playing to screaming crowds and wanted to expand on their recording ideas. Marriott's reaction to the new emerging hippy movement was to write piss-takes of the longhaired breed. Pop music had entered its serious phase with the Beatles, The Rolling Stones and The Who all writing and releasing concept LPs. Pop was out and suddenly rock was in.

The Small Faces spent a year in the studio recording their masterwork. "Ogdens Nut Gone Flake". When they finally finished it, it called for so many musicians that it was impossible for them to promote it by touring. Also it contravened directly Steve Marriotts ethos, above all it must be a laugh. That's where 'Lazy Sunday' and 'Itchycoo Park' come in, says Marriott. "It was kinda taking the piss out of the intellectuals. It had got like that. Music got intellectual and it was fuck all this, where's the fun gone?" Within the group the tension had finally become unbearable. "We all lost interest," Marriott admits, "It was getting to the point where I was writing songs and I was trying to give them away to people. Ronnie and Mac would say no, we need them. But you don't need crap. Someone else wants to do it, fine but it wasn't up to our standards. Unfortunately it got on our albums." "Also you grow apart for Christ's sake. You're talking about people living together from the age of 16 to about 22 and that's a very important part of your life. We grew to hate each other."

By the time of The Small Faces demise, Marriott's writing reflected his pre-occupation with straight rock music. It was on this basis that he formed Humble Pie. Basically a heavy rock group, they proved most successful in the States. "It was different for me." Says Marriott, "I tell you that at the time it was new. There weren't many people playing that way when we first started to do that. There's millions now, but at the time I thought it was something different. Another challenge and when that got a bit tired, I introduced the horns and black chicks. The rest of the group didn't want the horns and black chicks so they left.

After Humble Pie, Marriott – with 'Itchycoo Park' enjoying a brief resurgence of chart popularity – joined up with The Small Faces again for a reunion tour which he describes as 'shocking," and a couple of LPs which he still thinks are "quite good, quite different." After that he returned to the States and travelled around a lot. Seven years later he returned to England to be

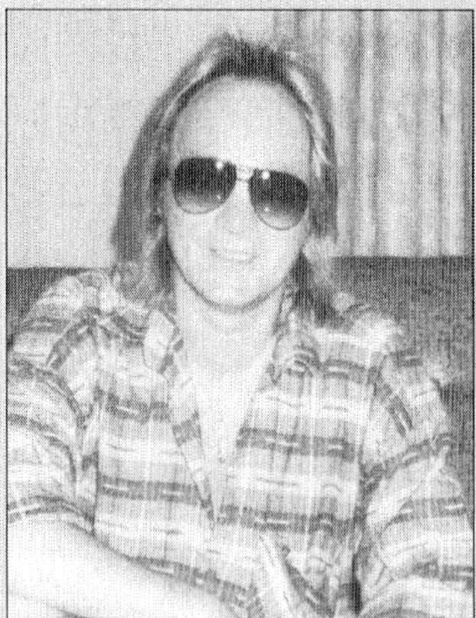

with his family and formed the awfully titled Packet of Three.

After all the turmoil he's been through, he's happy to play the round of pubs and clubs, earn a few bob and stand amazed as a cluster of mods, rock fans and punks attend his shows. Looking back on it all he regrets nothing, even a lack of finance, "What I've had I've thrown up in the air and what's come down I've spent, I've had a great life. If I weren't me I'd be envious. Mind you I wouldn't let me in my dressing room either. I've had everything I've ever wanted out of life. All I'm doing now by gigging all the time is pleasing myself, which is how it started. You see, you realise, by going all round the houses, you're original ideas were dead right. Just have a laugh, you know what I mean? You don't need all this money, it's bullshit. But until you have it how do you know that? We've got a drummer in the band who wants to be a star so bad that I hope he is a star. Then he can look at it and go, "Cor! I don't want all this". As for music today, Steve Marriott believe that a stake through the heart of most bands would cure the problems.

Big Country sound like Bonanza to him, Aztec Camera are "interesting", Paul Young's voice not his material, "is brilliant", and Ali and Robin Campbell from UB40 are "Frighteningly good singers".

Marriott now has his eye on producing. I'll give it my best shot for a couple of years then I have to get into producing. I should pass on any knowledge that I've learnt. You shouldn't keep it a secret." For a man who started his career-playing ukulele for old age pensioners, Steve Marriott has come an awful long way.

"Yeah", he said standing on Denmark Street's busy pavement, "but that's really the story of my life, playing to old aged pensioners. He breaks into his deep throaty laugh and walks off......................Happy boy happy!

OBSESSED

A light hearted look

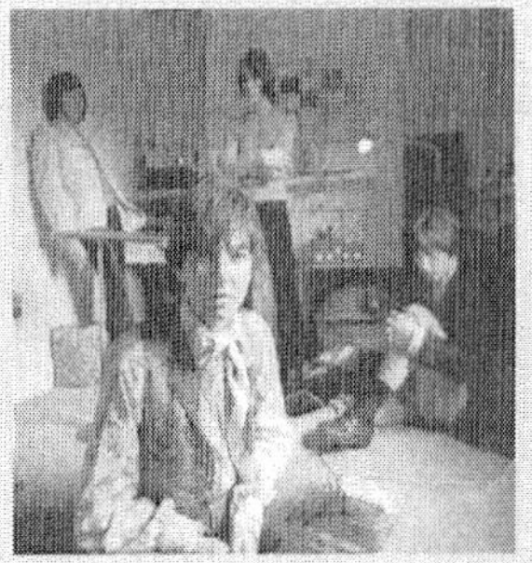

I think I'm obsessed with the Small Faces, so I wrote a list of symptoms that could point to Major Smofey Obsession. If you suffer from more than three of these, you too may be as nutty as me!

Here goes:

1. You often think how nice it would be to get on with your neighbours.
2. You seriously think that Ronald and Frederick are nice names.
3. Your favourite adjective is the word "nice".
4. You find that a nice person is always around when you need some speed.
5. You dream of being as short as Kenney.
6. Your neighbours, despite your valiant attempts to befriend them, have made it very clear that they've got no room for ravers.
7. Whenever you get ridiculously hungry, you go home and make yourself a loaf of bread.
8. You have a tendency to close your breath and hold your eyes.
9. You don't find it strange that Steve Marriott's voice doesn't match his height.
10. You rest your eyes in shades of green.
11. You get high in the most beautiful parks.
12. Your local pub is The Crown & Anchor
13. You're often found groping with stokers from the coast of Kuala Lumpaur
14. You know that pain never hurt anyone.
15. When you visit the local park you will only feed the ducks with a bun.
16. You decide to call your daughter P.P. and your son Arnold.
17. You share your shepherd's pie with any fly willing to talk to you.
18. Whenever you see boxes of All-Bran at the supermarket, you can't help but start singing…
19. You know that there's everything you need to know just resting in the afterglow of your love
20. Your favourite phrase is "Come on children!"
21. Sometimes you feel like a frustrated child.
22. It's all or nothing for you.
23. You beg and plead with people just to leave your bubble alone.
24. You sell all your worldly belongings and shack up in a Victorian Charaband.
25. You get an awful sinking feeling whenever you don't see a full moon in the sky.
26. You understood every word Stan Unwin said on the Ogden's album the first time you heard it.
27. Whenever you're depressed, you find it most relieving to clap twice, lean back and twist for a while.
28. Telling someone to get themselves together never seems quite right without the obligatory "OOH AHH!" bits (Ronnie Lane making nice nice nice noises… woohoo! *thud*).

29. You suffer with déjà vu and often ask people if they've ever seen you.
30. You become a carpenter just because of the vague Small Faces reference.
31. You become a groupie for a Small Faces Tribute band
32. You always sing the rocked-up Marriott Version of You Are My Sunshine.
33. You know exactly what to do if you have an unexpected attack on your nose.
34. You liked your Uncle Joe, what a lovely man!
35. You mind your own and your own minds you.
36. You haven't paid your rent yet.
37. Just for today you thought you'd leave love alone and hold hands with day.
38. You move to Blackpool and sell donkey rides for a penny a glass.
39. Your dream holiday is a weekend in Bognor Regis or Southend-on-Sea after hearing the Steve interview on the BBC Sessions.
40. You eat, sleep and laugh and cry just like the rest.
41. What becomes of you is what's meant to be, so you'll just groove along quite naturally.
42. It's all part of your way of giving.
43. You love arguing with people just so you can shout "What'Cha Gonna Do About It?"
44. Unfortunately, you've been a fan of The Small Faces for so long that it comes out as "What'Cha Gonna Doooooooooo About It?"
45. You call it something nice.
46. Everybody you know says you'll change.
47. Nobody will ever see all that you can see in your mind's eye.
48. You are that wide eyed girl on the wall.
49. You're good to those who take off all their clothes or play guitar
50. You boogie till the rooster crows.
51. You're paranoid about your behaviour and tell people that if you're so bad then please won't they take you away.
52. Your favourite coloured balloons are red ones.
53. You'll only contemplate the idea of a green coloured circle.
54. You know what an Itchycoo is, and why it is so named.
55. You know that it's more than love, it's a way of living.
56. You firmly believe that the only access to Bedfordshire is via some wooden hills.
57. You're a little Tin Soldier.
58. Every little bit hurts.
59. You thought that someone would listen to your reasoning, but now you see they don't hear a thing.

That's all I can think of for now, however if you have been suffering from any other symptoms then please feel free to add to my list.

Anyway, must dash, things to do and all that. Well, actually, I'm lying. I don't have anything to do at all. I just say that so you all think I have a hectic and fulsome life when the truth of the matter is that I don't. At all. I only say I have things to do when I can't think of anything else to write. Unless of course I do actually have something else to do, like for example clean the kitchen, but you'd know about it then because I'd tell you.

And I'm guessing none of you were interested in the above paragraph...

Ah well, can't win `em all! Take care

Spev xxxxxxxxxxxxxxxxxxxxxxxxxxxxx *(aka Heather Wainwright)*

STEVE AND LONNIE

Lonnie Donegan, who died recently, was an influence on nearly all British musicians over the age of 50. His skiffle music in 1956 brought home to a lot of working class kids (inc Marriott, Lennon and McCartney) that you could make music and form a band with very little money.

Steve was a big fan and when he was 12 he learnt that Lonnie didn't live far from him. Lonnie was living in Wanstead (considered then a posh part of the east end). Steve did some detective work and found out the address. Off he went to meet his idol. After he had found the house he pondered outside for a while trying to pluck up the courage to knock. He eventually did so, met Lonnie and got his autograph. When he got home his mum (also a fan), asked how he had got on. Steve didn't look as excited as she had expected him to be. He said yeah he had met the man… he answered the door himself, wearing a white t-shirt with dried egg down the front!!! Steve was gutted to find that his idol actually had egg on his t shirt. It brought home to Steve at an early age that so called 'STARS' are only human too!

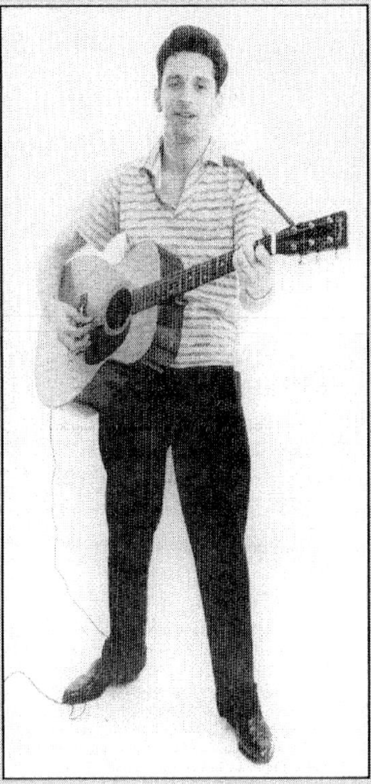

Nice story.

John Hellier

JERRY SHIRLEY INTERVIEW

By
JOHN HELLIER
(14th September 2000)

Humble Pie drummer Jerry Shirley's recollections of working alongside Steve Marriott.

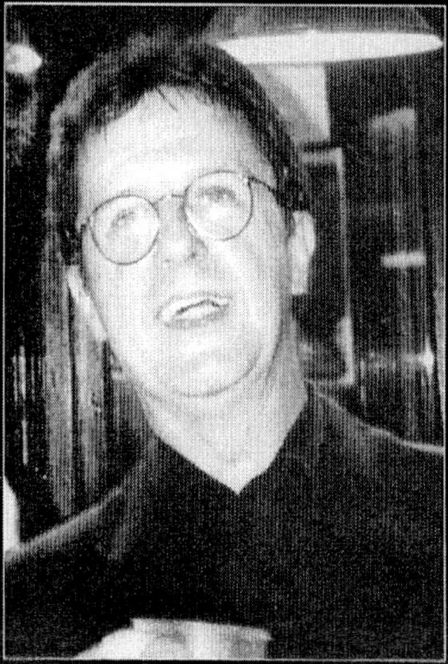

When did you first become aware of the Small Faces?

That would be on Ready Steady Go playing "Whatcha Gonna Do About It". I was completely blown away by everything about the band. Kenney's drumming in particular struck me. It was exactly how I wanted to play, I became a pseudo Kenney I did just about everything I could to be like him. The mod image was absolutely spot on and, of course, Steve's' voice really floored me like it did everybody else. Shortly after that Ready Steady Go appearance I went to see them at the Hertford Corn Exchange. By this time my own little group had become a full-blown Small Faces copy band and we ended up supporting them at the Wolsey Hall in Cheshunt. That's when I first met them and I remember whilst we were playing our set I looked sidewards into the wings and saw Steve and Kenney watching me play and giving me the thumbs up. After the gig Steve actually asked me if I would be there stand in drummer in the event of Kenney being sick or unavailable. It was probably just friendly chat on Steve's behalf and Kenney never did become sick but, of course, it made me feel ten feet tall. Steve and I did become good friends and I would often go to Steve's flat in William Mews, Knightsbridge. This was in 1967 and it was during that period that he gave my group a song to record. We went into the studio and recorded "Tell Me Have You Ever Seen Me" and it was released on Immediate under the name of Apolistic Intervention, we were previously called Little People. Steve wanted to call us The Nice but Andrew Oldham said no. Only a few days later I found out that he'd given the name to PP Arnold for her band.

With the Small Faces were you always closer to Steve than the others?

Not really. I was very good pals with Kenney, we would swap ideas and talk drums. Mac was always very nice although I would only see him and Ronnie at gigs. Ronnie was always a bit distant. I think he had some resentment about us coming in and recording one of their songs. Ronnie was at the recording session but he left halfway through. With Steve it was very much a social thing.

How did Humble Pie come about?

Fast-forward a year or two. Steve had become good pals with Peter Frampton. Peter had told Steve that he was unhappy with his current band The Herd and Steve had offered to help him form a new one. Steve recommended me and I went to Beehive Cottage to meet him. I, in turn, invited Peter to a gig that I was doing in Cambridge with my band The Wages of Sin. He liked what he saw and the Humble Pie seed was planted that night. At this stage there was no intention of Steve being in the group. Nothing really happened for several months until I got a phone call from Steve in the early hours of New Years Day 1969. He told me that he'd walked out on The Small Faces and asked if he could join the new band with Peter and myself. My first reaction was one of total shock. The Small Faces were my favourite band and the thought of them being no more left me dumb. However when he told me that he had a bass player lined up and that bass player was Greg Ridley from Spooky Tooth well that clinched it for me. Greg was the most respected bass player in England and the idea of playing with him was every drummers dream.

How did the name "Humble Pie" come to be?

It was suggested that all band members submit names, we'd write them all down and come up with a shortlist. Humble Pie was one of Steve's suggestions. One of mine was Evil Cardboard, which was the end of a joint. Anyway Evil Cardboard did not get the vote. We all thought Humble Pie was just perfect. It was a reaction against the whole super group thing. The idea of being called a super group without even playing a note was quite disturbing. We were just saying, "Now wait a minute we're only a bunch of lads just starting and want time to develop".

Were there any differences between playing with Peter Frampton and his successor Clem Clempson?

Both are brilliant guitar players. Peter was and still is a very jazzy guitarist whereas Clem was more of a Blues man. Clem joining the band gave us a fiercer edge, more of a dirty blues feel. Clem also became a good mate and he probably fitted in personality wise a bit better. He was one of the lads. Peter is a nice guy, please don't get me wrong, but Clem slotted in better.

What were your favourite Humble Pie songs to play live?

Well there weren't too many that I didn't like. I loved "Hot 'N' Nasty" because of the Hammond organ. "Doctor" was always fun, so was "Hallelujah". There's a couple of songs that we played in the later years that I didn't like doing, one was "Up Our Sleeve". But generally speaking if we didn't like it we didn't play it.

What are your favourite Humble Pie albums?

Probably both "Smokin" and "Rock On". The live album was great but that was a different animal. Also the two Immediate albums have some wonderful moments on them. We were having so much fun in those days.

Was the installation of The Blackberries the beginning of the end for the band?

Yeah it was. It wasn't their fault though. Things that were going wrong behind the scenes just happened to coincide with them joining the band. Steve's life was falling apart at the seams so therefore so was the band. In today's world having black female singers with a white rock n' roll band is an everyday thing but back then it just wasn't accepted by lots of people. You could really feel the prejudice in a lot of the American audiences. I hate any sort of racism. A great shame.

Why the Split?

The disintegration of our personal lives I suppose. We were all doing too many drugs, we'd lost sight of our business arrangements and no one within the band had any control over money matters. But the main reason was that we were making bad records, it all came to a head in early 1975. The rot had set in so deep it was inevitable.

Are there any unreleased A & M recordings?

I don't think so. I suppose there might be the odd one here and there. Oh yeah, there is a version of the old Chris Montez hit "Lets Dance" knocking around somewhere.

How did the early 80's Humble Pie reincarnation come about?

In 1979 while I was living in New York I got a phone call from Steve, who was living in Santa Cruz, to ask if I was interested in putting a band together. I mentioned the idea to David Krebs, a New York manager, and he made us an offer to put Humble Pie back together. Steve came over to my house in upstate New York to see what we could come up with song writing wise. Over the first weekend we wrote "Fool For A Pretty Face" and made a demo of it. We used session bass player Sooty Jones and on the strength of that song and our version of "My Lovers Prayer" we got a deal with Atco Records. I approached Clem to see

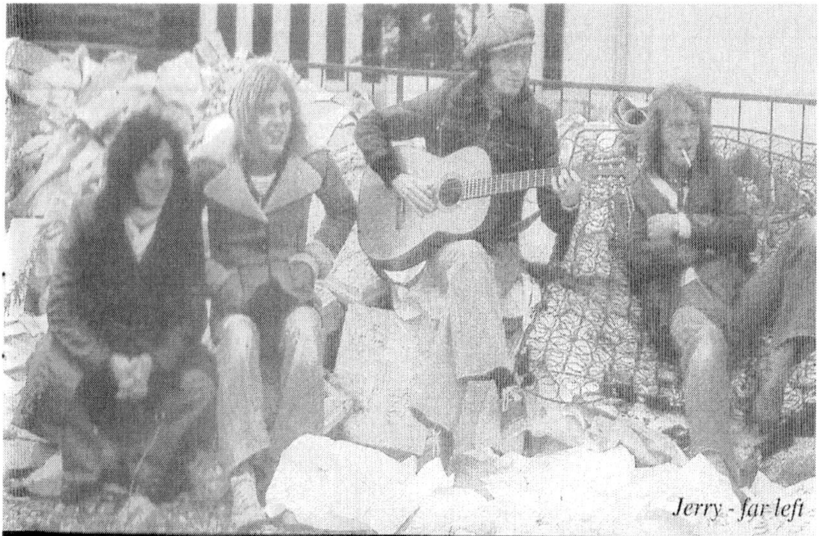

Jerry - far left

if he was interested. He came over to check us out and brought Bobby Tench with him. Clem chose to pass on the idea, I don't think he wanted the hassle of working with Steve again but Bobby stuck it out and that was the line up, me, Steve, Bobby and Sooty.

How did the Packet of Three thing come about a few years later?

Steve called me in 1985 and asked me if I'd like to join the band. The idea of playing again with Steve in small clubs and pubs appealed very much to me. I was out of work at the time and had just moved back to England. It was a fun two years but it ended on a sour note. We came back from a very ugly American tour and Steve decided to change the band and it didn't include me. Shame but these things happen.

How would you sum up Steve Marriott?

He was certainly the most talented person I ever worked with. He was like a brother to me and I was devastated when he died. He always lived on the edge and I was always waiting for a phone call to say that he had died but I never dreamed it would be under those circumstances. He's never got the credit that he deserves. He should be in the Rock and Roll hall of fame because he was the greatest white soul singer that England ever produced. I'm sure if you caught the likes of Rod Stewart and Paul Rodgers in a private moment and asked them who was the main man? They would say Steve Marriott.

Thanks Jerry for your time, that was super.

Jerry went on to form a new version of Humble Pie in 2000 with Greg Ridley, Bobby Tench and Dave Colwell. For full story see issue 20.

Memories Of Ronnie

About three months ago I was in HMV with an old friend of mine, Mike Conry, when we went through the usual ritual of looking for CDs that Ronnie Lane had recorded. Finding the Majik Mijits CD was a bit of an event for us as a) we had been talking about it the night before b) we were together when we found it and c) we had recorded the music in the first place! You can see my name in the top corner of the photo of one of the tape boxes in the sleeve notes. The handwriting is Mike's as he was better at labelling things than I was.

I met Ronnie at the beginning of the 80's. I was working as a structural engineer and had met a friend of Boo's at work. She knew I was passionate about music and introduced me to Boo. At the time they were looking to find someone to help with Ronnie's mobile recording studio LMS and I offered to help out.

I find it difficult to put all of the events in order but...The first thing I helped record was at a pub in Colliers Wood. There was a room upstairs where we set everything up. I was working at the time so most of the recordings were done in the evenings. The band was Chrissie Stewart on bass, Bruce Rowlands (Fairport Convention) on drums, Ian Stewart (Rolling Stones) on piano, Mick Weaver on the Hammond, Neil Hubbard (Roxy Music) on guitar and Ronnie playing acoustic guitar (as best he could). These were the first recordings of Bombers Moon and Ruby (better than the one on the Mijits CD). Ronnie at this stage could still sing pretty well, unlike at Debden. I have no idea what happened to the tapes of this session.

At the end of this recording, I think, Ronnie left his wife Kate who lived in Richmond and moved in with Boo in Kentish Town. This was convenient for me as I lived only five minutes from their house. I became a regular visitor. Ronnie had one of the very first portastudios, a Teac 144? and I used to help him with some of the recordings. I remember the first recording of Son of Stanley Lane. A guy called George Carlis played the sax on the

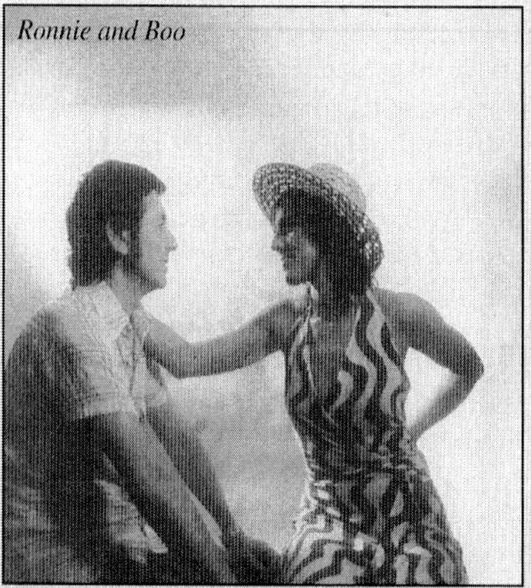
Ronnie and Boo

recording and I remember thinking it had echo's of Night Boat To Cairo. Maybe it was in the air as the church opposite Boo's house was where Suggs married Betty Bright.

I would like to think that Ronnie and I became friends. He was pretty immobile and I used to help him get around. He was still doing gigs and I remember he used to get different musicians to help him. James Honeyman Scott played guitar at the Half Moon in Putney just before he died. (We were all very saddened by his death). I got involved doing the sound for the band and we played some great venues, 100 Club, the Venue, the Rainbow and Glastonbury. We had a gig set up at the Bridge House in Canning Town. Just before the band were due on, Ronnie went missing. I found him in the mens loo leaning against the urinal..he had had another MS attack and was taken to hospital. Jim Leverton took control and led the band through a night of soul covers which was fantastic. Jim has a great voice.

I ended up doing all of the engineering for the mobile and was asked to help out with Ian Dury's band who were doing their own stuff after a bit of a fall out with Ian and Chas. The music was excellent and Ian Horne taught me loads about production, useful for later. I think it was just after this that Kate sold the house in Richmond and moved to Wales taking the children. These were bad times for Ronnie and she said some very hurtful things to him, one of which resulted in another MS attack after a particularly nasty phone call. Actually Kate was a lovely person but break-ups do tend to be bitter.

I got wind of the fact that Ronnie and Steve had met again shortly before their gig at the Bridge House. A while later, I was asked to go to Debden as Steve and Ronnie wanted to listen to some of the tracks from the Colliers Wood sessions. I met Steve and within two minutes he told me that I was going to be their engineer for the next two weeks. This nearly cost me my job as I didn't turn up to work throughout that time and I got a very serious bollocking for it. We set up in the drama school hall with the mobile parked outside. I knew I would need help so I called Mike Conry who was living in Birmingham and he came down the next day. The details of this band you already know but Boo was also there and from time to time Steve's wife Pam used to turn up. I can't remember the name of the people who ran the drama school but the son had a girlfriend who was one of the students there. Steve really had the hots for her and was desperately trying to muscle in. I don't know if he made it but he was persistent as I recall. We set Dave up surrounded by screens in the middle of the room. Dave made a sign saying pump room which was very appropriate. Other screens were made using chairs where necessary and it was a bit Heath Robinson at times

Steve had an incredibly loud voice and I had problems with the mikes distorting. I'm a bit disappointed that one of the outtakes on the second CD doesn't have Steve saying 'I bet that cracked your fucking mike up' after a very lively version of You Spent It. I used to have it on a cassette but can't find it now.

One of the great thrills was to meet Mick Green. I believe it was me who told them all that he had been described as 'semi legendary' in the NME book of Rock. This caused much teasing and questions about why he wasn't fully legendary. Unbelievable guitarist who I still try and emulate to this day. Steve and Ronnie used to joke about him having a Jewish background. I have no idea if he was Jewish or not but the joke took root. On the window of the LMS they used to stick up pictures from the papers and called it (Ray) Clemence corner, there was one excellent picture of Lew Grade with his hands in the air in a gesture of surprise and Steve had written something like 'No Micheal, no another guitar my boy'. The best thing about NATO was Mick's guitar solo. the version on the CD is about half the length of the full take which is a shame. Toe Rag wasn't actually recorded in the bar, it had been done earlier in the day. However, the backing vocals were completed in the bar full of students and we all got very drunk.

I used to drive Ronnie home afterwards, he had this enormous Toyota Land Cruiser to pull the mobile and called it the Tonka. We used to run all the red lights on the way back and never got caught.

Ronnie's voice was very weak by now and not all the final vocals were captured in Debden. I'm not sure how they finally got on tape but someone did a good job.

After that, it all went quiet. Ronnie was looking for help with his MS and ended up in the States. The mobile was sold and that was that. I have met two men in my life that I have admired more than any others. One was the great Catalan Architect Enric Miralles and the other Ronnie Lane. Both had an unbowed spirit, both loved life and both now are sadly dead.

And Boo and Ronnie

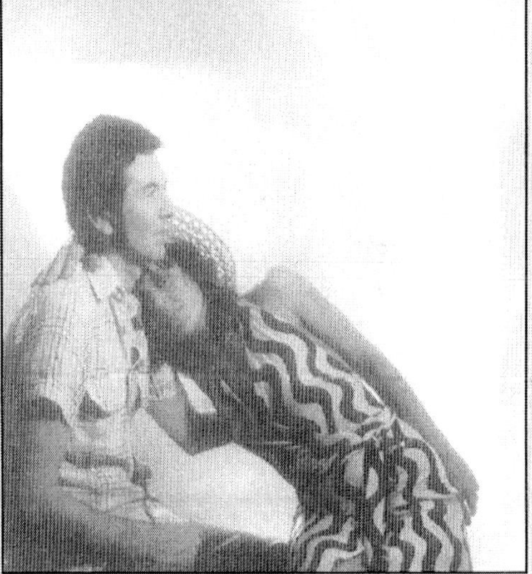

Steve Fisher

JOHN HELLIER INTERVIEW

BY John Kearney (14th September 1999)

WAPPING WHARF EDITOR GIVES HIS VIEWS ON THE EAST ENDS OWN FAB FOUR

When did you first discover the music of the Small Faces and what was the first song that really made an impact on you?

I've been a mega fan right from the beginning. It was 1965 and the first single "Whatcha gonna do about it" had an enormous impact on me. I became quite obsessed with them not only the superb sounds but also the overall image. I used to buy all the pop mags of the day like Fab208, Rave and Jackie just to see what they were wearing and then I'd be off to Carnaby Street to copy them. I was very much into the mod scene back then and I even had my hair straightened (a perm in reverse) to get the Marriott look. Between 65 and 67 Steve was the biggest fashion icon in the country if not in the world.

If you had to choose three songs that were your favourite what would they be?

I really do like everything that they have ever done so to narrow the choice down to three is difficult. However I think I would go with "Whats a matter baby" the b-side of the very first Decca single. A great song and a great performance from Steve. I would add to this two songs from the Immediate period 'I'm only dreaming' and 'Get yourself together'. No particular reason I've just always loved these tracks.

What is your least favourite song by the band?

A very difficult question. There's nothing at all that I dislike but if I'm pushed to name a track I suppose it would be one of the psychedelic ones possibly 'Yesterday, Today and Tomorrow.

Did you ever see the band live and if so where, when, and what did they play?

I saw the band live dozens of times. From the early pop packages, with people like Roy Orbison and The Hollies which were at my local cinemas like the ABC or Odeon in Romford, Essex, to club gigs such as The Marquee, Uppercut and Lotus Rooms all of which were in London. The pop packages only featured a 20 minute set and it was impossible to decipher what they were playing as screaming girl fans drowned the music. The club gigs were very different, they nearly always opened with 'Shake' and I recollect numbers like 'Jump Back' and 'Oo Poo Pa Doo' being in the early set, neither of which were ever recorded by the band. Later on, by '68 numbers like 'Rollin'Over', 'Wham Bam' and 'Song Of A Baker' had been added to the set. One memorable gig that I witnessed was at the Bubbles Club in Brentwood, Essex, in October 1968 when Pete Frampton joined them on stage ....Great times!!

The Small Faces seem more popular now than ever. To what do you attribute the increase in fame?

For some reason the music and image of the Small Faces appears to be timeless. They have been an enormous influence on a lot of today's contemporary artists such as Weller, Oasis and Ocean Colour Scene and these people have become great ambassadors of the band, Paul Weller in particular. Lots of younger fans have got into the Small Faces through Mr Weller.

Are you aware of any tracks that have yet to be released and if so what are they?

Kenney Jones has access to some Ogdens out-takes including versions of 'Be My Baby', 'Love is Here and Now You're Gone' and 'If You Think Your Groovy'. He claims that he's saving them for an ultimate Small Faces box set to be released some time in the future by Castle Records. I would personally rather just see an ultimate Ogdens cd with the bonus tracks attached.

What age group is the music of the band appealing to now?

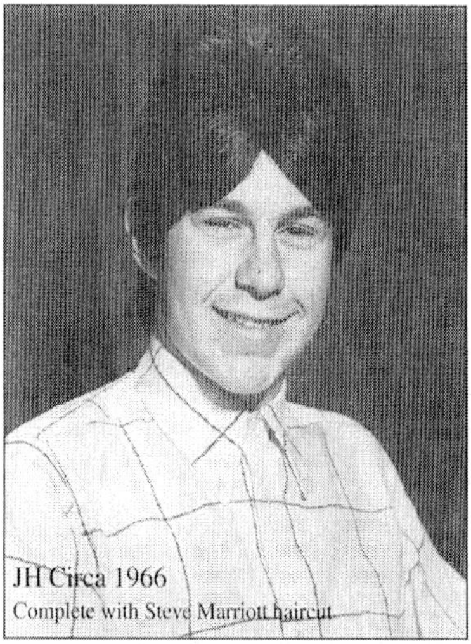

Every year Dean Powell and myself put on a convention at, the spiritual home of the Small Faces, the Ruskin Arms in East London. We fill the place with fans from all our Europe and even the USA would you believe. The ages of these fans vary from 16 to 60! Totally amazing.

In retrospect, looking back at the sixties, how would you rate the Small Faces to the "big boys" like the Beatles and the Rolling Stones?

As writers I would rate Marriott/Lane second only to Lennon/McCartney. As a live band The Small Faces were right up there in the big league. In fact after The Beatles stopped touring in 66 The Small Faces were probably the biggest live draw in the country for a while. Record wise, I think the Immediate albums, Ogdens in particular, rate alongside the very best efforts from the Beatles and Stones.

Since the deaths of Steve Marriott and Ronnie Lane a Small Faces reunion is impossible. However, if Ian McLagan and Kenney Jones decided to pay tribute to their former band mates who would you pick to replace them for say a one off gig?

This is pure fantasy! I would keep it SMALL and keep the IMMEDIATE connection by bringing in PP Arnold and Billy Nicholls.......It would be interesting to say the least.

There is talk of an animated version of Happiness Stan with the addition of new music. Who, in your opinion, would you envisage writing the music and who would you see singing the parts?

I'm not really sure about this one, but there would have to be a place in there somewhere for *Stanley Unwin he's alive and well* and would love to do it. As for writing the music why not Mac, Kenney and Billy Nicholls.

How many subscribers do you have to your magazine?

Wapping Wharf has a print run of 5000. Not bad eh! For a band that broke up 30 years ago. Mind you I cover the whole family tree, which gives me a lot of scope.

The Small Faces musical career consisted of two genres: the 'Decca' band was r & b orientated while the 'Immediate' band was pop and psychedelic. Which appealed to you more?

I love both the Decca and Immediate periods, but if I was to be honest with myself I suppose there's a slight preference for the Immediate stuff.

What can we expect in future from your magazine/website?

"Darlings Of Wapping Wharf Launderette" can go on forever. People regularly say to me "surely you'll soon run out of things to say". This is not so, as the readership increases I get more and more feedback from readers and lots of this goes to future stories for the mag. Recently I've had interesting stories sent to me from members of Steve and Ronnie's pre Small Faces bands and these along with many others provide exclusive material for future issues. I've interviewed such illuminaries as Eric Clapton, PP Arnold, Jimmy Winston, Stanley Unwin, Steve Ellis and many more. **In the next issue I have an exclusive interview with Paul Weller** and I have many, many more interviews lined up for future issues. I also have dozens of unpublished interviews with Steve, Ronnie, Mac and Kenney all of which will eventually see the light of day. According to a reliable source in London "Wapping Wharf" is the best selling 'zine in the UK at present and I intend to keep it that way.

**please note this interview was conducted before the sad passing of Stanley Unwin*

***Paul Weller interview appeared in Issue 15 (still available)*

BIG BLACK DOG
A true tale

Steve was famous for his collection of pets. Visitors to his homes in Essex would sometimes be forgiven for thinking they had landed in a farmyard! And at least one of his London flats, according to a fellow Small Face, smelt like one due to Steve's liberal attitude to giving the animals plenty of freedom!

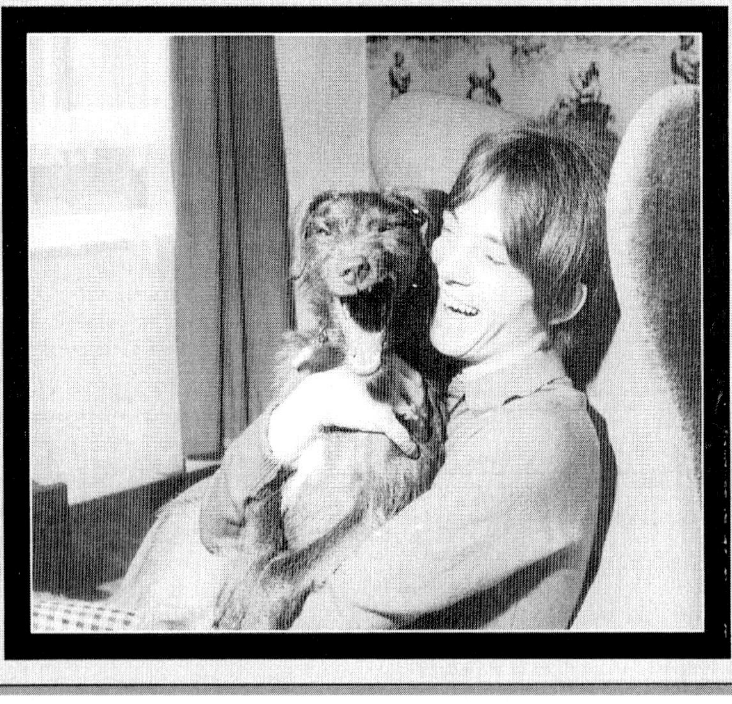

In his career and in his life, dogs loomed large. Yes – honest! Apart from the above titled Humble Pie single, Steve's dog can be heard plainly barking on "The Universal" as wife Jenny returns from shopping. Mind you, how many people record Top Thirty singles in the garden? His most famous dog Seamus became notorious for its ability (taught by Steve) to bark along to the blues records. Pink Floyd were so taken by this that they named a track on their "Meddle" album after Seamus barking on it. (No it wasn't Hound Dog). Also as you'll remember one of Humble Pie's best tracks "Beckton Dumps" has these memorable lyrics.

> I give my lucky dog a stroke
> He just tipped me a wink
> And I know just what that means man
> It means that I need
> to put on his lead
> if I don't want a mess on my jeans man (or G Plan I'm told)
> that's cool – 'cos I know I can trust him
> to grab the fuzz if they bust in
> Git him boy

Classic!!

Marriott was also ejected from a Los Angeles hotel in the mid 70's for befriending a dog, which had escaped from the LA dog pound. If my memory serves the dog was eventually given a home by one of the Blackberries. Anyway – here's the point. Here's the Seamus story On Pink Floyd's album "Meddle" there appears a rather short song much maligned by the Floyd faithful, called simply "Seamus", this acoustic blues number seems to be about nothing more than lying on the porch with Seamus, a dog. Said dog can be heard yowling

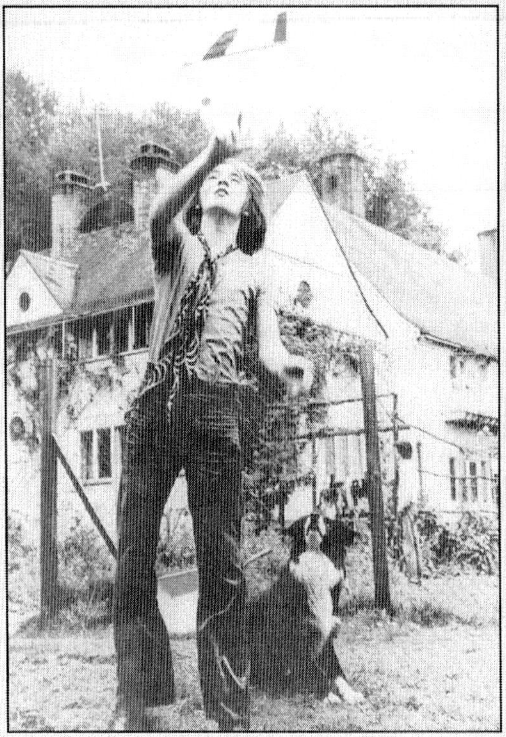

with the music throughout the song.

What then does this have to do with our hero?

Well it turns out that Mr Marriott indirectly had a hand in the creation of this non-epic Floyd filler piece. You see, Seamus was Steve's dog, and it was Steve who had trained Seamus to yowl in a blues-like manner whenever confronted by the appropriate twelve bar chords. When Meddle was being recorded Steve was touring the States with Humble Pie and had left Seamus in the hands of some trusted friends. Here's where fate stepped in.

Dave Gilmour, fully-fledged Floyd guitarist and Leonardo DiCaprio look-alike was a neighbour of those friends of Steve's. Dave had always fancied recording a slow bluesy number and in a fit of pot-induced inspiration Dave decided it would be, the be all of hilarity to take Seamus down to the studio and record with the dogs accompanying vocals.

Now Seamus may have been a blues howler – but nothing on par with Steve himself – so Dave's joke was perhaps good for a stoned chuckle at the time, but thirty years on it appears to have worn a bit thin and one thinks Dave would have been better off smoking straight Camel Lights and recording a few more dozen minutes to "Echoes" instead.

On a related note – when Pink Floyd filmed their "Live at Pompeii" the Seamus number was revived. However Seamus was unavailable apparently and so the song is retitled "Mademoiselle Knobs" after the dog used in Seamus' place. It remains unknown if Mademoiselle Knobs was also a graduate of the Steve Marriott School of Canine singing, or if in fact there is an entire gander of British dog-blues enthusiasts running around playing Howlin Wolf albums for their four legged friends. In which case the Floyd must surely have held auditions for suitable Seamus soundalikes.

"Picture that if you will"

I have heard a rumour that Seamus is headlining this years Convention!

Iain McGonigal

GLEN MATLOCK INTERVIEW

BY JOHN HELLIER (13TH MARCH 2002)

Ex Sex Pistol Glen Matlock talks about his love and respect for all things Small Faces related.

When did you first become aware of the Small Faces?

I suppose it was on Ready Steady Go, when I was a mere boy. It was 1966, I was ten years old and used to listen to pop music on the pirate radio stations. It was Ronnie Lane that made the biggest impression on me. He had this impish thing about him and he was the reason I picked up a guitar in the first place. The bands whole image was a knockout and they didn't look much older than me. They were such a bunch of likely lads, weren't they?

Were you inspired by the Small Faces musically?

Well yeah, more so later on when I became a massive Faces fan but before that I remember working in Malcolm McLaren's shop in Chelsea called "Let It Rock". It was a Teddy Boy shop and he had a jukebox with a lot of rock n roll things on it. I got a bit fed up with some of that stuff so I bought a pile of records from Ted Caroll's Rock On market stall. It was always a bit of a lucky dip as to what you got. I remember picking up 'Wham Bam Thank You Mam' from him and playing that incessantly instead of the Gene Vincent stuff. It was around this time that I first met Paul Cook and Steve Jones and we were all massive Faces fans together. They were both a couple of right tealeaf's, pinch anything. I said "why don't you nick some amps and guitars and we'll start a band". It was alleged that Steve once nicked Keith Richards telly! Anyway, we started the Pistols and were looking for numbers to play. We all had short hair in an age when everyone else had long hair and we were attracted to the mod bands of the 1960's, I suppose we were just looking for a records with a slice of three minutes of magic instead of all the progressive rock of the day, such bands as Yes and King Crimson didn't do it for us. One of the first numbers we ever played together was the Faces 'Three Button Hand Me Down' now that really was three minutes of magic.

What did you think of the Small Faces off shoot bands?

Well, the best gig I ever saw was Humble Pie at Hyde Park in 1971 when they supported Grand Funk Railroad. Blew them off the stage they did! And my favourite all time live album would have to be Pie's 'Rockin The Fillmore', a truly great performance, loved 'I Don't Need No Doctor' and all the between track chat. Steve used to say "It's been a gas." He loved the word gas, all done in an East End accent. The thing with Humble Pie is that it makes me wonder who wrote the songs in the Marriott/Lane partnership because the Small Faces stuff was much more poppy than anything Pie ever did. I loved the Pie but I loved The Faces even more. I also used to go and watch Slim Chance whenever I could I remember them at Victoria Palace during the 'Ooh La La' and dancing girls period. One of my all time favourite songs is Ronnie Lane's "Debris" and one of the reasons I dig it is because at the tail end of the 60's I remember my dad, who had always done manual work, coming home from work telling me his colleagues had voted him in as their Shop Steward. I said "That's great," he said "No that's trouble". I asked him why and he just said I was too young to understand. A few months later there were a lot of redundancies and the first ones to be laid off were the Shop Stewards. So that line in the song "There's more trouble at the depot with the General Workers Union" that really comes home to me.

Is it true that Johnny Rotten was the only Sex Pistol to dislike the Small Faces?

Yeah, that's just about spot on. Johnny did hate the Small Faces he used to call them the Small Faeces. Well that was all right the Sex Pistols would never have worked out the way it did if we had all been the same. Paul and Steve were into the Skinhead thing in their younger days and I was more mod orientated and dug tamla and the whole soul thing.

Which Small Faces songs did you play with the Sex Pistols?

'Whatcha Gonna Do About It' and 'Understanding'. When bands first get together you play numbers because you know how to play them, if you know what I mean. With "Whatcha Gonna Do About It' we'd change the lyrics to "I want you to

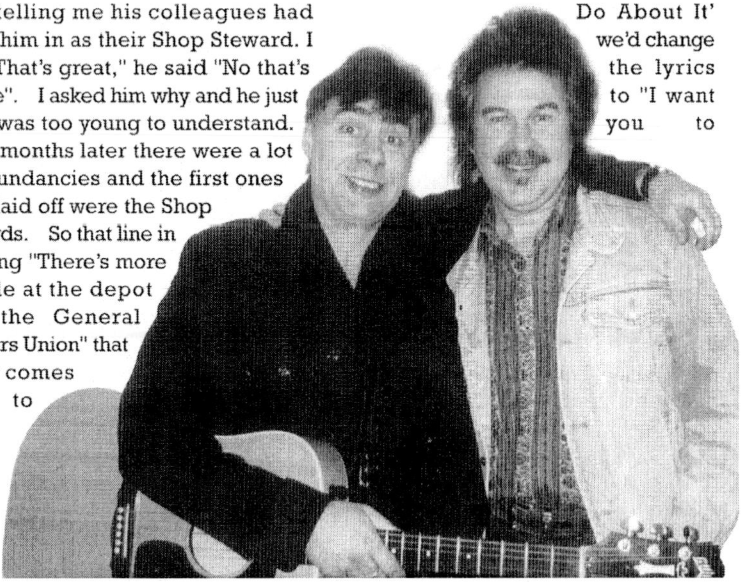

know that I hate you baby". Yeah we played those two songs in our early set, 'Substitute' as well. A track that I particularly liked was 'Talk To You' we never done it but I think that song was a bit of a fore runner for what Steve was writing later on with Humble Pie. His vocals on it are very heartfelt, but my favourite all time Small Faces track has to be 'Wham Bam Thank You Mam'. Later on I remember playing 'Here Comes The Nice' and 'Sha La La La Lee' with Midge. Also I don't know if anyone noticed but the bass line on 'Anarchy In The UK' was lifted from the Faces 'Had Me A Real Good Time'. Another nick was 'Holidays In The Sun' its not Small Faces related and it happened after I had left the Pistols but amusing just the same. That song was a complete re-write of the Jam's 'In The City'. Apparently Sid Vicious approached Paul Weller at the Speakeasy Club one night, shortly after its release, and was taking the piss about having nicked one of his songs. Paul wasn't too happy about it and ended up landing one on Sid who finished the evening in the casualty department of the local hospital. As I said, not Small Faces related but funny.

Did you ever meet any of the Small Faces?

I was lucky enough to play with Mac in The Rich Kids. That came about through an album we were doing down at Barnes. Mick Ronson was producing and we needed a piano player. Mick himself was playing piano and I said to him "Well that's good but its not really what we're looking for" he said "Well what do you want" and I told him that we were looking for a real rock n roll sound. He said "Do ya mean like Jerry Lee Lewis" I said "No something like McLagan plays" he said "Well I can't play like that". Our engineer who was in the room said that Mac was down here last week and that he had his number. We got Ronson to ring him, we were listening to the call. Mick said "Hi Mac it's Mick here" Mac replied "Mick who" "Mick Ronson" Mac still didn't know him so he said "Mick Ronson I used to play with David Bowie". Anyway he came down next day and we got on like a house on fire. He's one of those blokes you can really warm to. He played on 'Here Comes The Nice' and also played with us at the Lyceum Ballroom. It was a Capital Radio promotion gig and Nicky Horne was the DJ and compere. I remember Iggy Pop turned up to check me out as he was looking for a bass player. Anyway, Marriott turned up at the gig as well and he had the right hump because Mac was playing with us. He thought we were trying to nick his keyboard player because he was looking to reform the Small Faces at that time. Steve came back stage and I remember him having a run-in with Iggy Pop about something. Steve from the Pistols turned up as well and I hadn't seen him in years, but the thing I remember most was Marriott in a real stroppy mood. Somebody must have nicked the coke!! I met Steve Marriott later on at a few Packet of Three gigs and we always had a chat afterwards.

The last time I saw him was at the Half Moon in Lower Richmond Road. I always remember that story in the Melody Maker about Steve being broke and was going to have to eat his horse. There was a picture of him with a knife and fork. I saw Ronnie at the Lyceum when Slim Chance were doing a gig there for the 10th anniversary of Time Out. I was right down the front and after a few numbers Ronnie looked down at a set list on the monitor and before he could say anything I shouted out "Pint of milk, packet of Daz and half a dozen eggs". He looked at me as if I was a complete idiot and went into his next song but after that one he looked down at me and said "oh I get it, on the list" or words to that effect. I never got to meet him as such but that didn't matter, with some people you just want to keep what you've got in your mind, if you know what I mean. I met Kenney very briefly last year at a Roxy Music concert. I introduced myself and we spoke a few words, that's all.

What did you think about the way Steve's career went with him ending up playing in pubs?

I've heard it was something to do with the Mob! An East End underground thing. He seemed to enjoy playing those small venues with small monitors. He didn't look like he was doing it under duress, he was born to perform. He probably gave the guys £50 each and all the booze they could drink and pocketed the rest. What a trooper eh! Loved them dungarees didn't he!

What are your own current and future plans?

Well in recent times it was the Pistols reunion thing. A lot of people thought it was just Finsbury Park and Shepherds Bush but it was a big tour, the best part of 100 gigs. In Japan it was Beatle mania all over again, we couldn't leave the hotel. Yeah I enjoyed that. With most bands after they've tasted success they go on to play their hit songs for twenty years until they knock the stuffing out of it. We never did that. It was all new again but this time instead of travelling to a gig in the back of a van arguing with each other we travelled first class, had good gear and big audiences. It was terrible!!! We're doing it again for the Golden Jubilee in July at Crystal Palace. Steve Jones would like to reform the band properly and do a new album, but I don't think so. My current band are The Philistines and we're working on a new album due for release in September. We recently supported Ronnie Wood at the Shepherds Bush Empire that was really something else. It was a full house and we went down really well. Working with Ronnie reminded me of how Steve Jones used to go to his house at the Wick in Richmond and scrawl "Steve Woz Here" messages on the wall.

Thanks Glen for your time, it's been most entertaining.

HUMBLE PIE - THE IMMEDIATE YEARS

BY
JOHN HELLIER

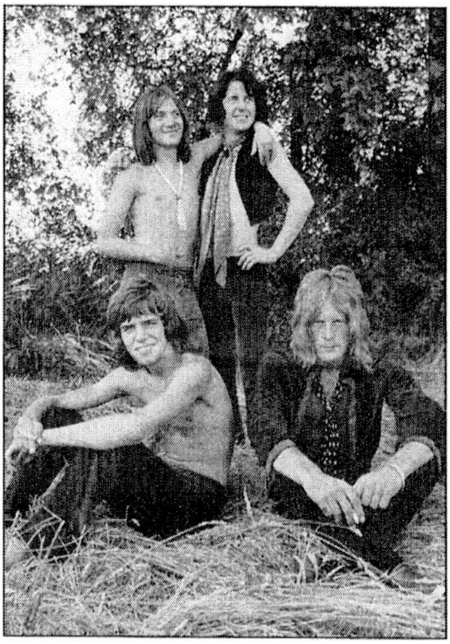

Like so many so called "Supergroups" Humble Pie never quite lived up to the media's high expectations, well certainly not here at home in the UK anyway, They did eventually rival the likes of Led Zeppelin as the premier English hard rock export to the USA where they went to achieve "stadium filling" status. But this story really dwells on the birth of the band and those first two magical Immediate Albums.

The story starts in summer 1968, Steve Marriott and Peter Frampton had become pals after touring together. There were patent differences in their personalities, Marriott being the typical rock and roll party animal while Frampton was more middle class and in comparison very quiet but that didn't matter there was mutual admiration for each other. Although both were experiencing chart success with their respective bands, The Small Faces and The Herd, they both felt trapped within the pop star image. Peter, tagged the face of '68 by Rave magazine, was particularly unhappy with the material he was being forced to record with The Herd and Steve tried incessantly to hussle him into The Small Faces, having decided that an injection of this type was what the band needed if they were to continue. However, Messrs Jones, McLagan and Lane didn't share Steve's enthusiasm and were having none of it. Eventually it was decided that Steve would help Peter form a new band and introduced him to young drummer Jerry Shirley, with whom Steve's friendship went back to 1966 when Jerry's band Little People (the name bearing an obvious Small Faces pun) supported The Small Faces at a gig at the Wolsey Hall in Cheshunt, Hertfordshire. Jerry recalls "Little People were a full blown Small Faces copy band and at that Cheshunt gig I remember

Steve and Kenney watching us from the wings and giving us the thumbs up! I became very friendly with Steve and we would socialise together at his flat in Knightsbridge. It was during 1967 that Steve had recommended my band to Immediate Records and suggested that we record one of his songs "Have You Ever Seen Me". Andrew "Loog" Oldham liked us but suggested a change of name. Steve said call them The Nice but Andrew said no its gonna be Apolostic Intervention which we didn't particularly like but we were in no position to argue. Incidentally five minutes later he gave the name The Nice to PP Arnolds backing band! We recorded the song at IBC with Steve not only producing the record but also adding bass guitar and backing vocals. Anyway, the single bombed and The Small Faces went on to use the song on their own album. Some time after that while I was playing with a band called Wages of Sin I got a call from Steve asking if I would be interested in forming a new band with Peter Frampton. Peter was a name in the business and yeah, of course, I was interested. After meeting Peter at Steve's Essex cottage he came to see me play at a gig in Cambridge and it all started from there really. At this stage there was no suggestion at all of Steve joining the band himself, that came in the early hours of new years day 1969. I received a phone call at 2am from him telling me that he'd just quit The Small Faces and he would like to join the new band with Peter and myself. I remember having mixed feelings, The Small Faces had always been my favourite band and I guess I was pretty gutted at the thought of them being no more but at the same time the idea of being in the same band as Steve was obviously appealing. It was even more appealing when he told me that Greg Ridley, from Spooky Tooth, was keen to join as well. Greg was probably the most respected bass player in the country at that time. It would have been every drummers dream to play with a bass player like Greg. Yeah, that really did it for me. That was the birth of the band that night.

Jerry goes on to talk about how the name Humble Pie came about. "It was a joint effort really between Steve and myself. Each one of us would put suggestions on a piece of paper, the intention was to draw up a short list and select from there. Amongst Steve's suggestions was Humble Pie and as soon as I saw it I thought that's absolutely great. I guess I was so enthusiastic about it that the others followed suit. Humble Pie was perfect. We were being called a supergroup before we'd even played a note and we all found that quite disturbing to say the least. The name itself just says now wait a minute we're just a bunch of guys just starting and we want time to learn and develop".

The band signed for Immediate Records and that in itself was a superb move. Immediate was the first independent record company in England and it was the type of label that gave new bands such as Humble Pie complete freedom in the studio. The whole set up at Immediate could be likened to Tamla Motown in the USA in the 1960's. Everyone was treated equally from the big wigs down to the little guys (like Apolostic Intervention!) and, again similarly to Motown, artists would willingly give up their own time to guest on each others recordings. While it lasted Immediate was the place to be in the late

1960's. Jerry recalls time spent in the studio "Most of the recording was done at Olympic in South West London, working there in those days was a wonderful learning experience, we used established engineers such as Glyn Johns, Alan O'Duffy and Eddie Kramer, all wonderful producers. While we were working in studio two you'd have guys like the Stones or Jimi Hendrix in studio one. It was quite something for a young drummer like myself to meet all those sort of people. Yeah! Immediate was a wonderful learning experience".

By the spring of 1969 Humble Pie had locked themselves away in the Magdalene Laver village hall, deep in the Essex countryside, rehearing new material for their first album. It was during this time that Steve received a phone call, right out of the blue, from ex Rolling Stone Brian Jones. Brian expressed an interest in joining Humble Pie and was invited down to Magdalene Laver to see the new band. But within the few days between the phone call and when he was gonna come down, he turned up dead!

The single "Natural Born Bugie/Wrist Job" and the debut album "As Safe As Yesterday Is" were both released during the first week of July, each charted immediately ('scuse the pun'). The single peaking at no.4 and the album at number 16 in their respective charts. "As Safe As Yesterday Is" was a fine debut album with many stand out tracks including "Alabama 69", "Buttermilk Boy" and "A Nifty Little Number Like You".

The band made it's live debut in August 1969 on the Radio One in concert show "Symonds On Sunday" and followed that with a tour of Belgium, Holland and West Germany in which they headlined over Deep Purple. Afterwards came a UK tour, incidentally the support act on this tour was a little known newcomer by the name of David Bowie! (I wonder whatever became of him!!). Even at this early stage Marriott and Frampton were becoming unhappy with the "Supergroup" tag that the music press had burdened them with. Because of this they looked towards the USA where they felt that they would be more readily accepted for who they were rather than what they used to be (neither The Small Faces or The Herd had ever made any major impact on America). Later in the year Humble Pie toured the States for six weeks as the opening act for Santana. A learning experience indeed!!

While the group were in America the second Immediate Album "Town And Country" was released. This LP reflected Peter Framptons influence more than its predecessor. It was altogether lighter and had a more acoustic feel to it. Unfortunately, the reviews weren't particularly kind and with the band out of the country and unable to promote it, it sold poorly in comparison to the first album. There were no singles issued from it although I've always felt that their wonderful revival of, Steve's boyhood hero, Buddy Holly's "Heartbeat" could have been a hit record. By late 1969 Immediate Records were in a dire financial position and by the time Marriott and Co. returned home from America both their record and management companies had gone into liquidation.

1970 saw Humble Pie moving to the States and a whole new era opening up for them over there. Although they continued to make wonderful albums the two Immediate ones always had that little bit of extra magic to them, probably due to the fact that at the time of recording they weren't a touring band and had spent much time experimenting "in the country" with new ideas.

As recent as 1999 a whole batch of previously unreleased Humble Pie recordings from their Immediate period were discovered in the tape library at the legendary Abbey Road Studios. The recordings not only include unfinished backtracks and alternate versions of familiar material from the first two albums but also new (!) songs including one absolute treasure. Jerry takes up the story "The real find of this collection and probably the biggest star of any Humble Pie session is a version of Ray Charles "Drown In My Own Tears". This was Steve's favourite song of all time. If Steve had to spend time on a desert island with only one record it would have been Ray Charles live version of this wonderful song. We did a version as identical as possible to the original which Ray recorded for his live album in Atlanta, Georgia in 1959. We brought in a big brass section and the arrangement was absolutely beautiful. I didn't realise the track had survived and in multi track format as well, I honestly thought it had got lost in magnetic heaven! Finding that track after 30 years was indeed a dream come true for me".

Yeah, that track is worth the price of this anthology alone. Listen and I'm sure you'll agree. Enough said Eh!

HUMBLE PIE 2000

Saw Humble Pie at the London Astoria on Wednesday 11th October. They were superb, all the old favourites and more! As well as the expected 30 Days in the Hole, I Don't Need No Doctor etc. etc. we were treated to Pie classics never performed live before, such as Red Neck Jump, Strange Days and 79th And Sunset. Obviously they're never gonna replace those unique vocal talents of Mr. Marriott, they know that themselves but Zoot Money and Bobby Tench are established vocalists in their own right and they exercise their own style. It was especially nice to see Greg Ridley back where he belongs after a quarter of a century in retirement. Greg loved every minute of it and he told me after the gig that he was ready to do another gig that same night, he enjoyed it that much. Greg is recovering from a throat cancer operation but he still managed a few vocals here and there. A diamond geezer, as they say.

As time moves on the band will be featuring new original material written by all five members and will develop along those lines but for the night it was just super to wallow in all the nostalgia of those 70s classics.

SET LIST: Four Day Creep * C'mon Everybody * Fool For A Pretty Face * Stone Cold Fever * Natural Born Bugie * 79th And Sunset * Don't Think Twice It's Alright * Hot n Nasty * Strange Days * Redneck Jump * Don't Fight It * Hallelujah I Love Her So * 30 Days In The Hole * I Don't Need No Doctor.

Get to see them when you can ....Deep Joy, John H.

STEVE MARRIOTT INTERVIEW

BY
JOSS HUTTON (1989)

It has been said that you should never meet your heroes. Well, I've gotta say that, in my experience, it can go either way. The one person who simply blew me away with their integrity, lust for life and overall friendliness was Steve Marriott. Back in 1988 and '89 I must've seen Steve playing around pubs in Leicester about three or four times. He was always approachable and giving of his time to his fans, even to a spotty teenage git like myself, and would spend hours just talking and drinking in the bar before hitting the stage. Ensconced in a booth with a brandy in a hoarse voice, that was frequently punctuated with expletives, he'd regale me and my friends with tales of love & lust, record business shenanigans and many libellous stories, all of which are too risqué to print here. Steve would then grab his guitar, kiss his wife Toni and join the rest of his band on stage.

Despite the fact that his surroundings weren't always the most salubrious and that the PA might be a little on the duff side, he always gave the most to his audience. The following interview was conducted by post shortly before his untimely death in a house fire in 1991. I'm sure it will bring a smile to the face of anyone who, as I did, stood in front of Steve as he belted out 'Afterglow' or his version of 'Five Long Years', during which he frequently challenged the world to try and 'put this bald little motherfucker down'.

What's the current situation regarding The Small Faces' back catalogue? Will there ever be a 'definitive' retrospective compilation released?
The Small Faces' catalogue is scattered amongst various fat cats. I didn't really make any money as it wasn't my prime consideration at the time. As to the compilation, your guess is as good as mine!

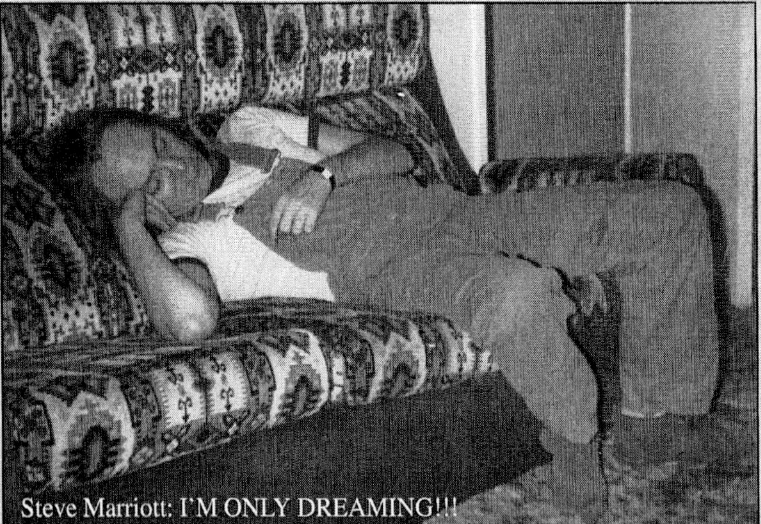

Steve Marriott: I'M ONLY DREAMING!!!

What's your favourite Small Faces recording?
'The Universal'.

Are you still in contact with any other members of the band?
I don't really see any of them anymore but we send our love through mutual acquaintances. I don't really know what they're doing, although I can tell you that Ronnie lives in Austin, Texas, Mac does session work and Kenney plays with The Who, when and if they work.

Back in the 60's, who were the bands you really enjoyed seeing play live?
Touring blues artists from America, Jimi Hendrix, The Spencer Davis Group, The Action and The Who.

What sort of stuff are you listening to at the moment?
I listen to Blues and R&B. I always have.

What's your all-time top ten?
Watch Your Step - Bobby Parker
Drown In My Own Tears - Ray Charles
Blues With A Feeling - Little Walter
Plum Nellie - Booker T & The MGs
I'll Never Get Out Of This World Alive - Hank Williams
Please, Please, Please - James Brown
First Time I Met The Blues - Buddy Guy
Mannish Boy - Muddy Waters
Land Of A Thousand Dances - Chris Kenner
That'll Be The Day - Buddy Holly
Hurt By Love - Charlie & Inez Foxx

You've recently been playing with Leicester based R&B band The DT's, how did you hook up with them?
They were the support band for the Packet Of Three at The Five Bells, Northampton in 1986 and later they came to see and have a drink with us at JB's in Dudley. In September 1987, Simon, the DT's harp player rang me to ask if I'd jam with them in Leicester. I did and was so impressed that I asked them to tour with me, internationally, as from February 1988.

Why did you split with the Packet of Three, was it amicable?
I decided to leave and pursue a more R&B flavoured direction, as regards to touring. As far as I'm concerned, the split was amicable.

Do you feel more comfortable playing in pubs and clubs, rather than the large halls you used to play in, is it a return to your roots?
YES!

Your sets are mostly made up of covers these days, except for a few Small Faces numbers, was this a conscious decision? Will we be hearing any new Marriott songs?
I'm just doing the numbers that I enjoy. There will be more originals added as we go along.

You get a large cross-section of people at your gigs, do you think it's down to curiosity, the music or your past reputation?
I think that it's a mixture of all three.

Why do you think that so many people are still big fans of your music after close on 25 years?
Because it's good music, at least I'd like to think so.

How do you feel when a fifteen year old kid comes up to you and says that you're his hero?
Old!

What are your plans for the future?
I've got no actual plans, apart from to take each day and any offers as they come.

He was one in a million and I never did get to buy that brandy I owed him.

Dear Joss,

Hope this does you OK. Send me anymore questionnaires and I'll throttle ya! You CUNT!!!

Good Luck

Steve

LAMBRETTA CLOTHING

SPONSORS THE SMALL FACES CONVENTION 2000

If the 1999 convention was largely remembered by fans for the superb PP Arnold performance this one will surely be remembered in years to come as THE STANLEY UNWIN SHOW. Stanley, at 89 years of age, made a superb guest appearance and had the 400 strong audience in hysterics with his performance using his very own Unwinese language to the full. A super show! Also the fans were treated to a very moving Steve Marriott tribute speech from Humble Pie sticksman Jerry Shirley who finished by playing a long lost recording of Steve with Humble Pie performing the Ray Charles classic "Drown In My Own Tears". A quite breathtaking performance from Steve which demanded total silence from the usually noisy audience, you could have heard a pin drop!

The music for the evening was supplied by The Threads, Keith Smart, The Phrogs, Small World, 17 Black and Afterglow also mixed in with this were sounds from our mod heroes themselves supplied by DJs Doug McLauchlan and Mark Baxter.

This event gets bigger each year and it was just superb to see fans of all ages there from not only all over Europe but Canada and the USA as well. The Small Faces themselves were well represented with members of Steve's and Ronnie's family in attendance. From Steve's side there was his mum and sister, Kay and Kay, also niece and nephew, Lucy and Stephen. By the way, it was great to see mum Kay bopping away at the front to the live bands. It was also lovely to see the Lane clan again down from Wales, wife Katie, sons Luke and Reuben and of course the lovely Lana.

Yeah, another success and we will do it all over again in 2001!

Dean Powell and myself would like to thank the following for their invaluable assistance and help, our other halves Julie and Gill, Doug McLauchlan, Mark Baxter, Dave Clark, Sarah Robinson, Top Guard Security and Jack and his staff at the Ruskin Arms.

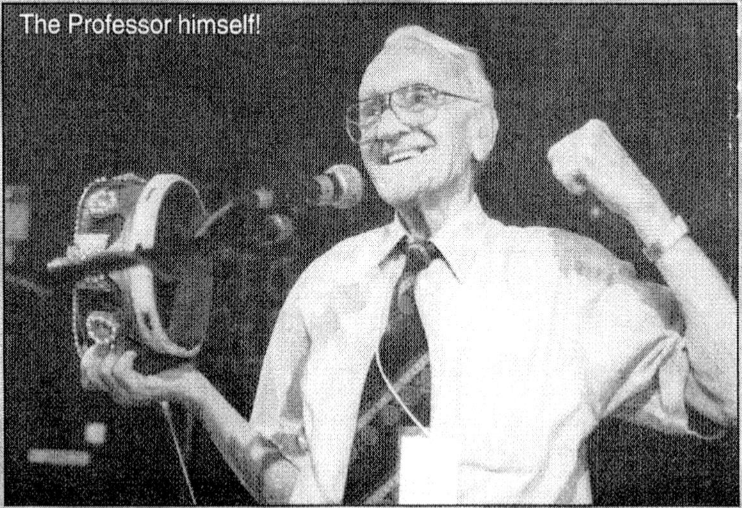

STANLEY UNWIN EXPLAINED

by John Hellier

Are you sitting comfort-boldly, two-square on your botty? Then I'll begin............ If Shakespeare is Britain's greatest writer, then Stanley Unwin must be considered to be Britain's greatest speaker. No other man has ever succeeded in talking a complete gibberish which paints such a fantastically clear and beautiful picture. Stanley evolved his strange language, Unwinese, whilst reading bedtime stories to his children. In the days of radio wireless, Stanley had a perfect medium by which to deliver his strange tales to a public that lapped up every word, revelling in its beauty and accrediting him the appellation of Professor. Now in his 90th year Stanley is still active and is best remembered for his appearances in Carry On Regardless and Chitty Chitty Bang Bang also his contribution to the Small Faces concept album Ogdens Nut Gone Flake where he narrates the tale of Happiness Stan.

Britain is a country bored of it's own language. While Johnny Foreigner marvels at the prose of Shakespeare, Shelly, Wordsworth, Dickens and Hardy, your average provincial town joy-rider type of minger would rather reject the mother tongue in favour of Supermarket Sweep (a nation of shopkeepers, natch) and You've Been Framed (Are peoples lives really that boring that these video clips are supposed to be funny?). Before the Buggles released "Video killed the Radio Star" there were some phonetically challenged terrorists that believed that the way to keep our language alive and vibrant is to subvert it. Spike Milligan, Viv Stanstall, Jake Thackery - the last believers in the power of nonsense, a sad kind of humour that is only made and understood by the British themselves. And standing like a colossus above them all (Albeit a reluctant one) is the linguistic lobotomist himself, the self-styled Professor of Unwinese, Stanley Unwin esq.

Stanley, like many of his disciples and mimics, is a shameless and enthusiastic supporter of the most influential medium of the spoken word - Radio. Indeed, the young lad Stanley was to be found tinkering with the crystals while a radio reporter for the Beeb in the 1940's and 50's. Stanley is a true veteran of Radios Golden Age, when the nation tuned into the wireless to listen to The Goons, Round the Horne and Steptoe & Son. It was in this environment that Stanley began to infiltrate the public consciousness with his inimitable brand of spoken nonsense, the non- language that is Unwinese.

Developed from the bedtime stories he'd made up for his kids and a love of Edward Lear, Unwinese is, for all its linguistic pretensions, a load of bollocks. Stanley is the first to admit it. Yet like all the best maulings of the English language, there is a coherent stream of thought running through Stanley's distorted syllables. When Stanley says "And they dancey round, all loony loony rotator", you miss it literally, but you get it descriptively. Stan will tell you that he has more in common with a jazz musician than any great intellectual - yet, at the age of 89 he has started to use a word processor as a minor concession to the demands of the modern media industry in which he still works. Once exposed to an audience used to listening, Stanley became a star of radio shows and commercials, influencing comedians and comic writers such as Spike Milligan, Peter Cook, Freddie Starr and Monty Python. It was almost inevitable that the hippies would try and get in on it.

In that hazy, love ridden time that was the late 1960's Stanley was approached by the Small Faces, a band beloved of mods throughout the ages. The Faces felt they had a credibility problem, every band was making concept albums because they'd smoked pot and got it a bit wrong on bottom lips. Anyway the result was "Ogdens Nut Gone Flake", an album considered to be their finest hour. A psychedelic masterpiece, "Ogdens" is the story of Happiness Stan as told in impeccably delivered Unwinese by the master himself. Lets face it, the heads and the freaks loved it because it did their heads in. Stanley achieved instant cult status for life which still amuses him today.

So what happened next? Well, Stanley appeared on numerous TV commercials he's a natural performer and looks great on the telly. Happily, Stanley is unbothered by his fame and is extremely modest about his achievements. He has worked with mutual admirer Spike Milligan on the Great Bong, has been played out by Sasha to a packed club and has done jingles for Kiss FM. Not bad for a man in his 90th year.

Professor Unlow recitely kindly. Delivering joyful roundness on all-gathering (sitting quietly-softly), hanging-roundlow. Deep Joy. Goodly Byelode.

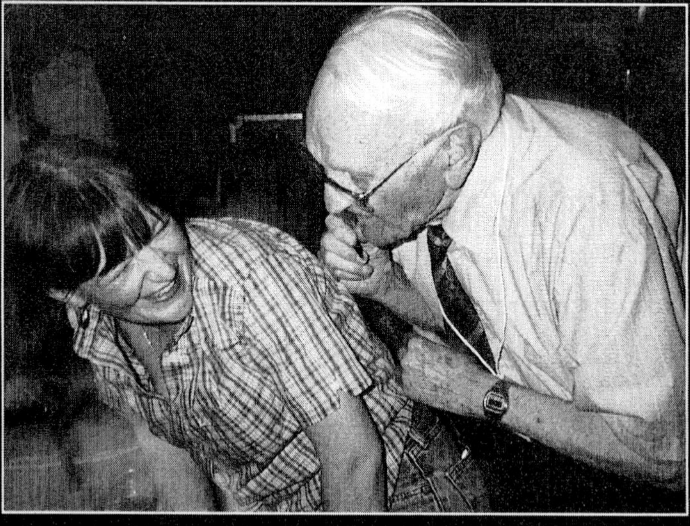

Stanley putting his signature on a fans back at last years Small Faces convention

STEVE MARRIOTT MEMORIAL EVENT
London Rocks !!!

To merely say that the memorial concert was a success is to make the understatement of the year. It was magnificent, beyond belief! There together were the sharp suits of todays mods, the greying bouffants of yesterdays mods and the balding, beer bellied Ben Sherman brigade all united in their love of a man whose talent should really have been celebrated years ago. The concert itself was sold out some six weeks before the event and on the day touts were having a field day selling tickets for three figure sums.

Toni Marriott, Chris France and myself first met in September 2000 to discuss the possibilities of the gig. When the Astoria was booked there was still a question mark as to whether we could fill it. How wrong could we be. In hindsight we could have booked the Royal Albert Hall and still sold out.

On to the concert itself. It was intended to be a tribute to Steve's whole works from the heady days of the 60's pop star to the pub rock hero of his later days and this is what was achieved admirably with stars such as Paul Weller and Noel Gallagher paying tribute to their hero. The evening got off to a great start with Small Faces Convention favourites 17 Black. They performed four Small Faces numbers including the blinding "Don't Burst My Bubble", they were followed by 60's mod legends John's Children with lead singer Andy Ellison climbing onto amplifiers and spraying the front row with water. High jinks indeed but just the sort of thing Steve would have loved. Next up The Mods a London band with excellent credentials, as well as a few numbers themselves they provided excellent backing for ex Love Affair man Steve Ellis. Steve reappeared several times during the evening and proved to be a class act.

After a short break the house band took to the stage and what a line-up they presented. On drums Who star and Ringo's son Zak Starkey, guitarists Bobby Tench and Dave 'Bucket' Colwell both members of Humble Pie 2000, keyboards were supplied by Who man John 'Rabbit' Bundrick and last, but certainly not least, Rick Wills on bass, the tallest Small Face ever! This excellent band provided backing for such acts as the soulful Debbie Bonham, Steve Ellis (again), Simon Hickling, Dennis Greaves and an appearance from Steve's son Toby (playing Steve's very own Gibson) with vocalist Max Ireland. As if this wasn't enough backing vocals were provided by none other than Immediate stars Tony Rivers, Billy Nicholls and Ant Thompson who were joined on stage by Steve Marriotts daughter Mollie and her band D2M.

Could things possibly get any better! Well after another short break it was the turn of Steve's legendary 70's band Humble Pie, but with a difference. For the first time ever on stage together the line-up included both Peter Frampton and his predecessor Dave 'Clem' Clempson along with original bass player and drummer Greg Ridley and Jerry Shirley. This was history in the making and the set was very well received by the 'elder' statesmen in the audience.

Next up a complete contrast, Band Aid star Midge Ure entertained the audience with an acoustic version of "My Minds Eye". A brave step by Midge but a successful one. Half way though the song he had the whole audience singing along with him.

The atmosphere was near electric at this stage and when our all-star band appeared the whole place erupted and what a line-up it was with original Small Faces Ian McLagan and Kenney Jones, Oasis stars Noel Gallagher and Gem and the mod father himself Paul Weller. These were joined on stage for the encore of "Tin Soldier" and "All Or Nothing" by Steve Ellis, Jerry Shirley and various members of the cast on backing vocals. WHAT A SHOW, ABSOLUTELY FANTASTIC only one person was missing.............

I didn't actually see anyone crying at the sheer poetry of it all but it was emotional stuff believe me.

John Hellier

P.S. An amusing bit of trivia is the fact that the bar takings at the Astoria broke all records at this event. Steve would have loved this........... CHEERS MATE!

FULL SONG AND ARTIST LISTING

17 Black:	Don't Burst My Bubble Wham Bam Thankyou Mam Hey Girl Rene
Johns Children:	Lazy Sunday It's Too Late
The Mods:	Sha La La La Lee
The Mods plus Steve Ellis:	Understanding Song Of A Baker Afterglow

Houseband featuring: Bobby Tench guitar, Rick Wills Bass, David Colwell guitar, Zak Starkey Drums, Rabbit Bundrick keyboards, Billy Nicholls, Tony Rivers, Anthony Rivers backing vocals.

Houseband (Bobby Tench lead vocals)	Fool For A Pretty Face
Houseband plus Simon Hickling:	Big Train
Houseband plus Dennis Greaves	Whatcha Gonna Do About It Five Long Years Phone Call Away
Houseband plus Debbie Bonham	I Can't Stand The Rain If You Think You're Groovy Black Coffee
Houseband (Tony Rivers lead vocals)	Itchycoo Park
Houseband plus Steve Ellis	My Way Of Giving
Houseband plus Toby Marriott, Max Ireland, Mollie Marriott	30 Days In The Hole
Humble Pie (Peter Frampton, Greg Ridley, Clem Clempson, Jerry Shirley)	4 Day Creep Natural Born Bugie Hallelujah I Love Her So Shine On I Don't Need No Doctor
Midge Ure (acoustic)	My Minds Eye

The All Star Band featuring: Paul Weller guitar/keyboards, Noel Gallagher guitar/keyboards, Ian McLagan organ, Kenney Jones drums and Gem Archer bass.

The All Star Band	Become Like You (lead vocal Weller) I'm Only Dreaming (lead vocal Weller) Get Yourself Together (lead vocal Mac) Here Come The Nice (lead vocal Gallagher)
The All Star Band plus Steve Ellis Vocals & Jerry Shirley drums	Tin Soldier (lead vocal Steve Ellis) All Or Nothing (lead vocal Mac/Weller)

DID YOU **KNOW?**

WHILST BROWSING THROUGH THE LOCAL LIBRARY, I came across a fascinating book called *British Music Hall*, which is basically a history of the genre.

But, even more fascinating was a piece of sheet music featured in the book called **Hitchy Koo!** Did they have mods in 1912? **Hitchy Koo** was apparently a new American dance craze and the song was performed by *The American Ragtime Octette*.

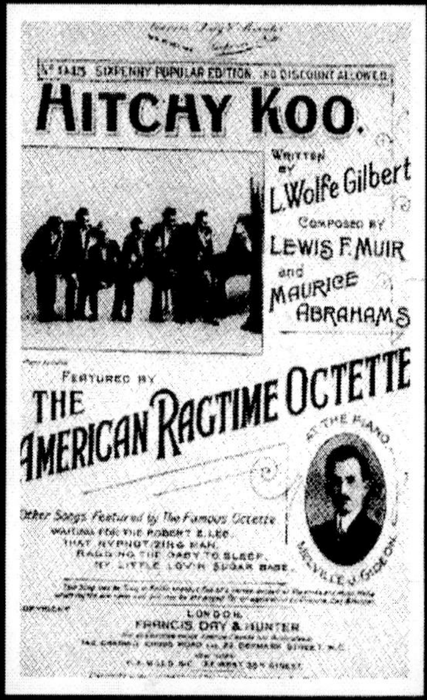

But that's not all. On the opposite page was a list of all the performers who appeared on the Royal Command Performance at the Palace Theatre in the same year (1912). Of the many music hall performers appearing, one was called **Marriott Elgar** and another was **Lupino Lane!** Doubly fascinating!

DID YOU KNOW...

BACK IN 1964 STEVE'S BAND *THE MOMENTS*, played a gig in front of a packed audience of mods at the village hall in Dagenham. When Steve appeared on stage the crowd laughed at his elfin-size and long hair and began throwing things at him, generally taking the piss. Steve, unperturbed, opened with **House of the Rising Sun.** He started to sing it in a very soft style until he reached the second verse then let loose those great lung-busting vocals, to the shock of everyone in the hall. At the end of the gig everyone who had jeered came over to apologize to him! Rightly so!

TRIVIA • TRIVIA • TRIVIA • TRIVIA

IN RECENT MONTHS 'COLLIBOSHER' has been the theme to *Sportsnight's Magic Memories* series. And if you were watching BBC's *The Underworld* episode concerning the Kray's you would have heard a blast from **Tin Soldier** playing in the background. Also **Watcha Gonna Do About It** was the number playing in a pub juke-box in another BBC programme *The Riff-Raff Element.*

IN THE SHUTTER - BUT SOME OF US ARE LOOKING AT STARS

A STORY BY DAVID WEDGBURY

If fame is having your picture in the papers then David Wedgbury must rank as one of the most famous people of the sixties. David who? That's probably because he was on the other side of the camera, taking the pictures.

Anybody who ever flipped through record racks or owned any Decca albums in the sixties and early seventies would be instantly familiar with his work. David Bowie, Marc Bolan, The Rolling Stones, Eric Clapton and The Who have all flashed past his Halledblad shutter. Remember the chalked smiley faces cover of the Small Faces first album and the picture of the lads walking the crocodiles in the rain outside Westmoreland Terrace? Well that was him.

David wrote this story back in September 1994 and tells of when for £9 a week and all the black and white film he could use, he rubbed shoulders with the famous but not yet rich.

I joined Decca in 1961 when I was employed as their staff photographer. This was just before the Beatles happened in 1963 and up until then I was essentially photographing American artists that were coming over here on tour, The Everly Brothers and people like that. Then when the Beatles had their first hit in January 1963, (Decca having previously turned them down - the famous Dick Rowe) - They went really mad and regretted very heavily not having signed them so they went after everything that walked about on two legs and played a guitar, they were desperate to try and replace them.

They succeeded to some extent in that they got the Rolling Stones and the Who and subsequently the Small Faces.

Decca House was by Lambeth Bridge on the Albert Embankment. It was a great marble nine story building and across the road in an old Doulton pottery factory we had our art studio. The studio was just beginning to do fledgling LP covers and so forth and I was literally photographing groups morning, noon and night. I might do two or three different artists per day and I always had to have in the back of my mind a whole range of locations worked out because with photographing three bunches of people in the studio every day we'd soon run out of ideas.

So this is really one of the first sessions I did with the Small Faces (shows picture of them huddled together under a variety of lampposts wearing loud check jackets). I was always very impressed with the Small Faces because they came along and were impeccably dressed in this mod gear with a very definite image and nearly all the same size, same look. When taking photographs of groups you'd often have a 'sore thumb' in the band that stood out and was unphotogenic, or had a squinty eye or was much taller than the others I mean Jimmy Winston was, if anything, slightly heavier than the others so that's why he ended up at the back.

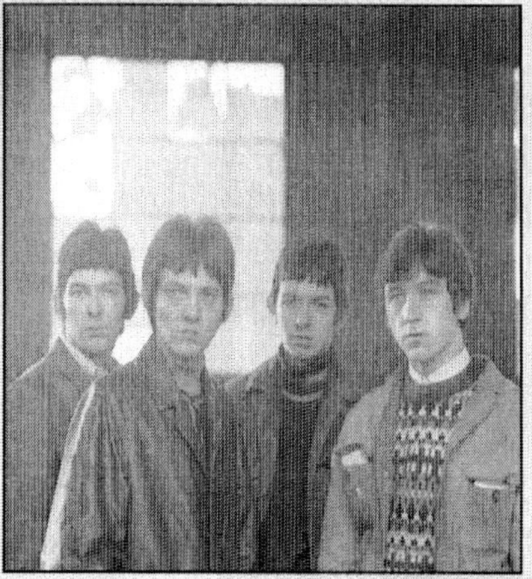

But I can remember this session fairly clearly, we used to have a guy called John Cockell who wrote the standard Decca biographies, these were the things that went out on initial promotion with ten by eight black and white glossy photographs, so the magazines could have something immediate to print. It was always linked to a single release with the groups favourite likes and dislikes, favourite car, favourite food, favourite film star, all that crap. Anyway they arrived at Decca in June/July and the routine was that they came into the office and John Cockell interviewed them to come up with the material for the biographies then we'd pop out to the location. We drove down to the South Bank site, I'm not sure who was driving their car, I think it was Ronnie Lane, and he was driving one of these Ford popular, sit up and beg, type cars. John and I were in a little blue mini. The four of them came with a little scruffy dog, real sort of mongrel with a wiry furry face.

We drove in convoy to the site and drove into the South Bank car park and John suddenly said, hey they're driving out again, and got out and yelled after them. It turned out they didn't have the money to pay the parking fee. We obviously picked it up on Decca expenses and managed to complete the session successfully.

A sharp band needs an image conscious photographer and I was always pleased to photograph the Small Faces and their consummate group identity gave me ideas. Perhaps one too many as it happens.

John Cockell and I were very excited by the Small Faces and their imagery and we were going around clubs in Manchester, Liverpool, all over the place looking at groups and we decided to chance our arm in pop management. We were looking for a Small Faces type group to base our efforts on and we advertised in Melody Maker and New Musical Express saying that we had contacts in the record industry and were looking for a group along the lines of the Small Faces. We had a multitude of responses and one came from a group in North London who were managed by the father of one of the band, a Jewish gentleman called Bertie Bacon.
We went along to this factory in Tottenham full of beds and blankets and cheap furniture he

manufactured. At the back of the factory was a group of five lads with guitars and drums and a guy on the organ and they did a kind of audition for us, ran through a few numbers, and we were really impressed with them, they sounded quite strong and looked very good with one exception, the drummer we thought he was a bit big and overweight - because we were so keen on the right image. So Bertie Bacon said, what do you think? And we replied there was only one thing we were unhappy with and that was the size of the drummer. He said, well I regret to have to say this but he's my son and I'm financing this.

They went on to become the Love Affair and we managed the group for a while on Decca and later CBS where they had three hits.

(The Love Affair, you may remember were fronted by a half-pint hardcase with similar physical and vocal characteristics to Steve Marriott, his name was Steve Ellis).

Let me tell you a bit about the session which was to become the cover of the Small Faces first LP.

We again went just round the corner from the Albert Embankment and went under a half lit railway arch where the light just comes in from one side. We gave them sticks of chalk which we brought at the local shop and they drew all the faces themselves, so they are Small Faces faces. I think maybe there was one on the wall and they said, look at that wouldn't it be great if we could have a wall full of them. I got the chalk and away we went. Their first Decca album sleeve was born.

As a quietly spoken gentleman it's hard to imagine David marshalling all those inflated pop egos to pose for his studied, stylish portraits but then you can't always judge an album by looking at its cover.

Sadly not long after this article was written David passed away, aged 60 years, his work is best chronicled in his book "As Years Go By" published by Pavilion and features amongst others, pictures of Small Faces, Marianne Faithfull, The Rolling Stones and The Who.

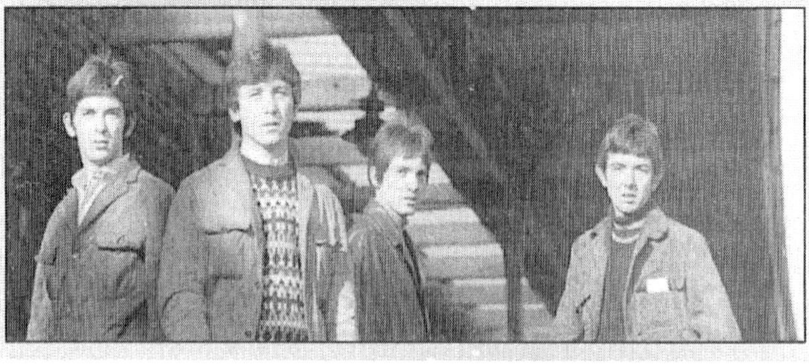

'Lazy Sunday'

MANY THANKS TO STEVE'S AUNTIE **SHEILA** FOR ALLOWING US TO PRINT THE LETTER BELOW!

Dear John,

Many thanks for sending me your fanzine No. 5 and sorry to have taken so long to reply. I think it is really excellent and congratulate you on such a good piece of work.

I'll try and give you this anecdote, but will probably have to abandon it because of interruptions (I hope you haven't heard it already).

When we lived in East Ham, Steve was at a flat in Chiswick and came over for lunch one Sunday. It was a nice sunny day and I had pulled out all the stops to provide his favourite food - roast beef and Yorkshire pudding, etc., Anyway, he turned up, getting out of a taxi with his then wife, Jenny, and one of his Alsatians (whose name I've now forgotten, but I think it was one of his first, and was called Lilly - something like that). Anyway, as soon as he arrived, he said he had to go to the bathroom because he was "in the middle of a song, and just had to get it finished." Of course, I didn't take too kindly to this, thinking of my special lunch and hoping it wouldn't spoil, and also thinking to myself that it was something like a scene from a Cole Porter film, where the composer is finishing off a masterpiece.... So, upstairs he went and we dutifully sat down and waited, stroking the dog, etc., Finally, and after not much time, down he came with bits of a cigarette packet over which he had scrawled the words to "LAZY SUNDAY" - which he literally had written in his head in the taxi, driving through the East End.

Of course, we were all absolutely thrilled and delighted that one of our favourite Steve numbers should have been written en route to us and finished in our bathroom - spoilt lunch or no spoilt lunch.

All best wishes,

Yours sincerely,

Sheila.

BILLY NICHOLLS INTERVIEW

BY

JOHN HELLIER (22ND MARCH 2001)

Immediate recording artist Billy Nicholls was not only a good friend of all four Small Faces but also played and sang on many of their Immediate sessions. Here he talks about his relationship with the band and also of his own plans for the future.

J.H. When did you first meet the Small Faces?

B.N. I first met the Small Faces at the offices of Immediate Records in New Oxford Street in 1966

J.H. What were your first impressions?

B.N. We were introduced to each other and we instantly teamed up, to me they looked like a bunch of elves giggling and laughing. We had the same sense of humour and musical appreciation.

J.H. What was it like working at Immediate and what did you make of Andrew Oldham?

B.N. I loved working at Immediate Records. I was paid £20 a week to write songs. My office was a meeting place for lots of people, who just wanted to hang out and play. Andrew Oldham was not like a boss, he played harder than most of the visitors to my office, and more dangerously. He took chances as a producer and with most other things in general.

J.H. How did you come to work with the Small Faces?

B.N. It was a natural coming together. There was rarely a moment when we were not socialising or playing.

J.H. Which tracks did you feature on?

B.N. I can't remember all the tracks that I sang on. It would be safe to say I sang on most of the tracks on "Ogden's Nut Gone Flake".

J.H. Which member were you the closest to?

B.N. I was close to all of them at that time, especially Mac and Ronnie, but eventually spent more time with Ronnie Lane. He introduced me to some of his friends who were followers of Meher Baba.

J.H. What are your favourite Small Faces tracks?

B.N. I don't have any favourite Small Faces tracks. I think "Ogden's" would be one of my all time favourite albums. But then I would, wouldn't I?

J.H. Tell me about your album "Would You Believe" why is it so valuable and what roles do the Small Faces play on the album?

B.N. Ronnie and Steve produced the title track, the Small Faces were the band. Steve and Jerry Shirley played on "Girl From New York" and Steve sang backing vocals on "It Brings Me Down". It's a rare vinyl album because it was never released. I never signed a contract and so have never be paid. Typical!

J.H. After Immediate Records demise did you keep in touch with any of the Small Faces?

B.N. I kept in touch with all of them and did a pub tour of Ireland with Ronnie.

J.H. What did you think of the off shoot bands such as Pie, Faces etc. etc. and did you get to work with any of them?

B.N. I really loved Humble Pie and The Faces. I spent a lot of time with The Faces and they came to stay with me whilst on their first tour of the States at a house in Connecticut. It was there that they first rehearsed "Maybe I'm Amazed" and a weird and wonderful time was had by all and sundry.

J.H. Can you hear the Small Faces influence in contemporary bands?

B.N. Yes and also on my son Morgan's album "Organised".

J.H. What have you been doing since 1970?

B.N. I have recorded four solo albums and worked extensively with The Who and Pete Townshend. Recently I have been recording with Morgan. Very exciting!

J.H. What are your current and future plans?

B.N. I want to carry on writing, producing and recording. I hope to release at least three albums in the near future, some retro some not. My latest album "Penumbra Moon" is soon to be released via the web. The Website has been a great success, the feedback had been extremely encouraging. If you want to take a look it's www.nicholls.co.uk

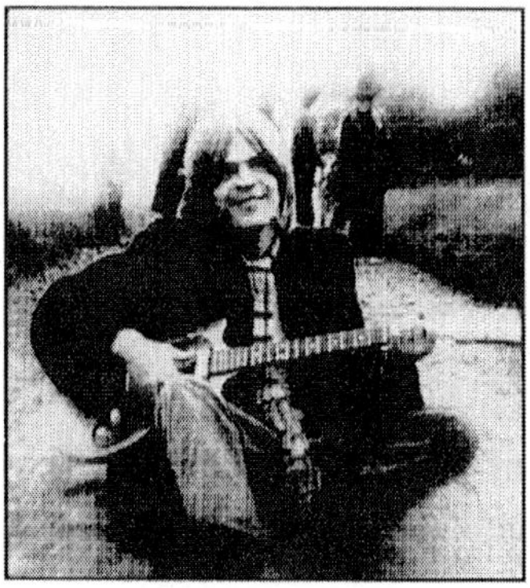

THE FACES STORY

(1969 - 1975)

Steve Marriotts departure from the Small Faces left the other three in a penniless limbo. Lane had been doing some jamming with Ronnie Wood who had left his job as bassist in the Jeff Beck Group. This was allegedly due to Beck's hire and fire attitude to the band members. Still remaining as vocalist in that band, was Wood's good friend Rod Stewart. Woody fancied concentrating on his guitar playing and at Lane's invitation began to rehearse with the remnants of the Small Faces. Gradually Rod Stewart began to appear more frequently at these rehearsals, as his own disenchantment grew as to his future with Jeff Beck.

Ronnie Lane feared losing control of the new band for whom he had written most of the numbers. However he eventually agreed that the band needed a strong vocalist and Stewart did not require much encouragement to join. The new band played a couple of gigs under the name of Quiet Melon, in a loose line-up featuring Art Wood - Woody's elder brother - amongst others. Warner Bros. gave them a contract, but the band were obliged to keep at least part of the original name. Indeed in the States, their first album came out under the old name of Small Faces. Immediate, their original label had backed Steve Marriotts new venture, Humble Pie.

Work started on the Faces debut album, to be called First Step, in December 1969. Of all the tracks on it 'Three Button Hand Me Down' gave the best clue to the direction they were to take. As McLagan said at the time, they neither wanted to be "all showbizzy", not "hippy-trippy". The track reflected the raucous pub sing along style of their alchohol-fueled live performances. Their first shows were in England in the spring of 1970 and were not very successful. This seemed to encourage their enthusiasm for a good drinking session in the pub before going on stage. By necessity, they soon learned how to play whilst lying flat on their backs.

In the US, Stewart and Wood already had a following from the Jeff Beck Band, which unlike the Small Faces, had toured there extensively. Building initially on the Beck Band's popularity in Boston, they toured as a support for both Lee Michaels and Savoy Brown. The Faces became a tough act to follow.

Back in Britain in June '70 they did half a dozen supporting gigs, again without achieving much, so in October returned again to the States. This time it was a largely headlining tour, selling out from East to West.

The second album "Long Player" had now been completed. It contained the track 'Bad 'n' Ruin' which epitomised this stage, as it was about coming back home after a successful US tour and not being recognised. Dogged by this in the UK, they returned for a third US tour in only ten months. Now it was headline stadium gigs.

The next tour of the States was already planned, this time to be even bigger, in support of Rod Stewart's third solo album, "Every Picture Tells A Story". His solo contract was signed with Mercury's Lou Reizner in late 1968 and was to create much future tension between Stewart and the Faces. On these albums he only regularly used Wood and McLagan from the Faces. By October '71, this solo album and the hit single 'Maggie May', were at No.1 on both sides of the Atlantic. Most new Rod Stewart fans drawn by this solo success were unaware of his dual role, even though it was generally the Faces who mimed with him on TV appearances for the single. Resentment began to grow within the band. Ron Wood reflected, "If people didn't know Rod was in the group, hard luck, but if it had to be forced on them, then it got a bit out of hand".

These two successful tours of the US in late '71 launched Stewart and the Faces to true stardom. They even had their long overdue breakthrough in the UK with several big festival appearances. The end of the year saw the release of the third album "A Nod's As Good As A Wink", generally accepted as their finest. It was co-produced by Glyn Johns, whom Lane had wanted involved from the very beginning. With it they at last achieved UK chart success with a No 2 slot in the New Year of '72. The single 'Stay With Me' reached No.6.

Despite or perhaps because of this success, the band became much less publicly active during the rest of 1972. They did a few small US tours, playing the big stadiums. A full UK tour wasn't planned until December and there was to be no album to back it up. Instead they toured on the back of Stewart's fourth album "Never A Dull Moment". This is undoubtedly the solo album most influenced by the Faces. Indeed the first track 'True Blue', was recorded at the same sessions as were to produce the fourth Faces album "Ooh La La". The second side also contained three tracks that were to become regular live Faces numbers - Etta James' 'I'd Rather Go Blind', Sam Cooke's 'Twistin' The Night Away' and Jimi Hendrix's 'Angel'. This last number became the great sing along anthem for British Faces fans. From Stewart's previous album, only 'I'm Losing You' was really a Faces track. As ever, the live versions tended to put the recordings to shame.

The next release, 'Cindy Incidentally', did not appear until February 1973. A year had passed since the previous single 'Stay With Me' and it was not supported by an album. It topped some charts but only managed No.2 in the UK. 'Ooh La La' was not released until April and although few would have suspected it at the time, it proved to be the last studio album. The reviews were poor and Stewart distanced himself from it.

The first side was dominated by rowdy Stewart/Wood compositions which were clearly in the Faces party traditions, but had begun to lapse into cliché. Side two was largely Ronnie Lane territory, with his more introspective, folky style. Older Faces fans enjoyed the album, with the newer Rod Stewart fanbase finding it less accessible. The lack of cohesion seems to have been down to the divisions within the band. Rod Stewart did not attend the first two weeks of sessions. Songs were written only whilst in the studio, most originating from a riff. Some also felt that Stewart was holding back his best material for his solo efforts. Ronnie Wood stated he hadn't ever been aware of that, but couldn't vouch for what might go on in Stewart's head. In Wood's opinion they wrote songs with Rod in mind, or specifically for the group. When Stewart did finally turn up to the sessions, he often didn't like the key they were in, or the melody, or the lyrics. Many songs were thrown out or reworked. The title track was symptomatic of the problems. Neither Stewart nor Lane could settle on a key for it, so it was eventually sung by Woody.

It finally became too much for Ronnie Lane. Aside from personal considerations, he felt the emphasis was now all on Stewart and not on the band. On 'Ooh La La' it was his songwriting that had received the bulk of the criticism and he had been replaced by Stewart in the writing partnership with Wood. Lane left to form Slim Chance, a band much closer to his more folk roots. He was replaced by Tetsu Yamauchi, who had previously been best known for a short spell in Free. Tetsu was first and foremost a bass player and many felt the band had a tighter, more rock-based rhythm due to him. He was also happy to party - an important consideration for the Faces.

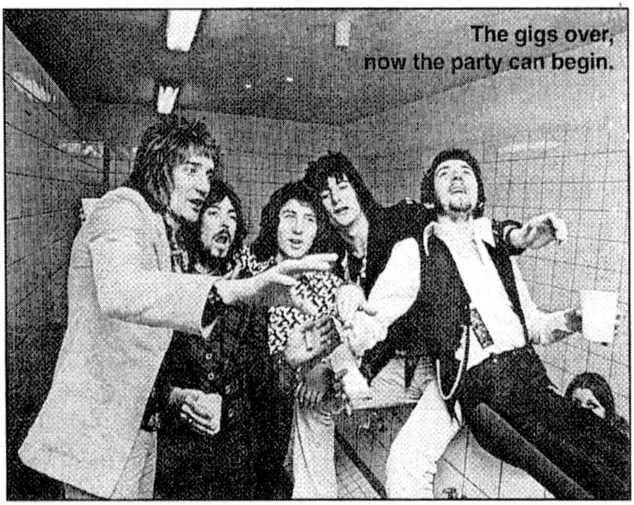
The gigs over, now the party can begin.

In October of 1973, 'Poolhall Richard' was released. The single was a hit and although certainly energetic, it was a bit brash. The B-side was a live version of the Temptations' 'I Wish It Would Rain' and had much greater subtlety. A live album had always seemed to be an obvious choice for a band that excelled on the road. When it finally arrived in January 1974, "Coast to Coast/Overture And Beginners" was a disappointment. Ominously enough it bore the label Rod Stewart/Faces and proved to be the last Faces album. It had been recorded during the last three dates of the October '73 US tour and was pretty much a standard Faces set of the time. The release probably only occurred as part of a deal between Mercury and Warner Bros., over the ownership of Stewart. It certainly didn't catch the band at their best. Most critics found it unbearably sloppy and musically embarrassing. Fans tended to find it an enjoyable but not significant record.

The New Year of 1974 also saw the group conduct their first tour of the Far East. It came straight after a successful UK tour the previous December but between March and September '74, the band played only two more gigs. This inactivity was partly due to the Warner/Mercury dispute which delayed Stewart's new album "Smiler". However by this time, Woody also had solo plans. April marked the beginning of sessions as he assembled a host of Stones and ex- Beatles plus some well known session musicians. The recording became 'I've Got My Own Album To Do'. The title saying much about the motivation. Despite the variety of musicians, and indeed egos present, every track contained Woody's distinctive stamp. Musically the album was a success, but it didn't see much chart activity. It did however define Woody's transition to the next stage of his career. On the 13/14th July '74 Wood gave the material its first live airing, before the album release, with two shows at the Kilburn Theatre in London. Again musically the shows were a success, but with none of the old material to bind them to the audience, the crowd were a little restless. This was particularly true on the second night, when Woody's band were very late on, in old Faces style, but without the familiar numbers to win the crowd back.

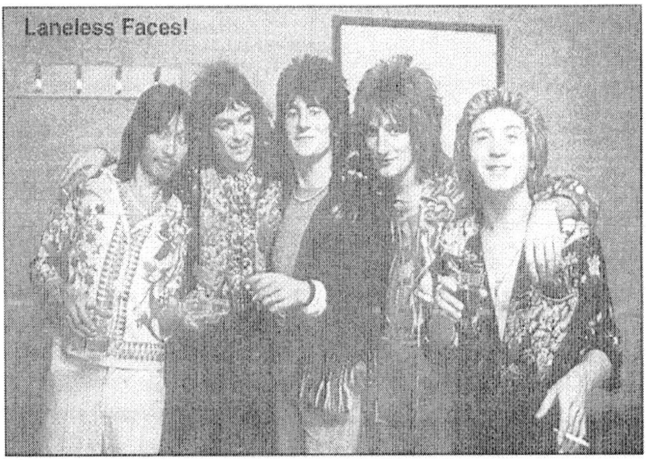

Rod Stewart's "Smiler" came out shortly after Woody's album, in early October '74 and comprehensively eclipsed it in the charts. "Smiler" was Stewart's last offering on Mercury and followed much the same song choices and songwriting formulae as his previous solo albums.

At the of the year, the Faces recombined for their longest and possibly best UK tour. They had warmed up with several weeks in Europe, where they had faded in the memory, struggling in small venues. This had

returned the group to the most lean and tight that any of them could remember. It was at this time that they recorded their last single 'You Can Make Me Dance, Sing, Or Anything', with 'As Long As You Tell Him' on the flipside. These were recorded in just two days and were of superior quality to any of their output for a long time.
This new energy drove a tremendous tour and by January 1975 the Faces were back in the studio laying down tracks. Hopes were high for a quality album. Instead of finishing any numbers, the group went to the States to tour. Studio time was booked in L.A., but nothing constructive was achieved as recording time inevitably slipped into party time. The tour ended and Rod Stewart stayed in the US, initially for tax reasons. This meant that the rest of the group would have had to join him if the album was to be finished. This all became academic as Stewart began to record "Atlantic Crossing". Also Wood took his own sessions left over from '74 and worked with Bobby Womack to create his second album "Now Look".

The fate of the Faces had been pretty much sealed back at the end of 1974, when Mick Taylor left the Rolling Stones. This left a gap in the Stones which Ronnie Wood felt destined to fill. In the end, the Faces just about survived to the end of 1975. During April, it was announced that Woody was to tour with the Stones in the US, but that it was only to be a stop-gap for them and that he remained in the Faces who would tour later in the year.

Stewart had released his first US recorded album "Atlantic Crossing", in the summer. It largely dispensed with his old formula and was much more smoothly produced. In August the Faces began rehearsals in Miami for a US tour, advertised with Stewart's name above that of the Faces. Stewart wanted to be able to recreate "Atlantic Crossing" live, the group wanted a Faces tour. Stewart wanted a string section and rhythm guitarist, the group suggested a string synthesiser for McLagan. Stewart got his strings and an extra guitarist, but not Steve Cropper whom he had wanted. Instead Wood brought in Jesse Ed Davis.

The tour during September and October was a great success financially and musically. It ended on November 1st and the band headed their separate ways. During December, press speculation was rife with group members commenting and denying. Rod Stewart seemed to create the final crisis by publicly quitting, saying that he couldn't continue with his lead guitarist "on loan" to the Stones. Wood insisted he was keen to record at least one more album whatever. The band booked time in January '76 to record without Stewart. Warner Bros. were still happy to promote the band, but would only put up studio money if a tour was guaranteed to promote the product. Wood did not feel he could make that promise. IT WAS ALL OVER NOW!.

Alwyn Davies (1997)

COUNTRY BOY (MEMORIES OF RONNIE LANE)

I was 18 years old when I met Ronnie Lane. It was the year after the great summer of '76 that England still talks about today. They'd remember the summer of '77 for more than just the weather. I'd met a girl and out of whatever reason moved in with her across the other side of the country. It was virtually in a different country. Right on the borders of Shropshire, Herefordshire and what was then, Montgomeryshire, Wales. I'd been playing guitar since about 11yrs old, seeing Jimi Hendrix on T.V. when they re-released "Voodoo Child" the week he died saw to that. So I was hot shit by this time, even other people said so. What the hell was I doing moving to butt**** nowhere? It didn't take long, however, when I got there to find the old and young hippies still trying to work out the Steely Dan & Little Feat riffs. So singer, guitar, bass and drums, me trying to teach them how to play R&B, blues and rock 'n roll, the singer thinking he was Peter Gabriel or some other hippy.

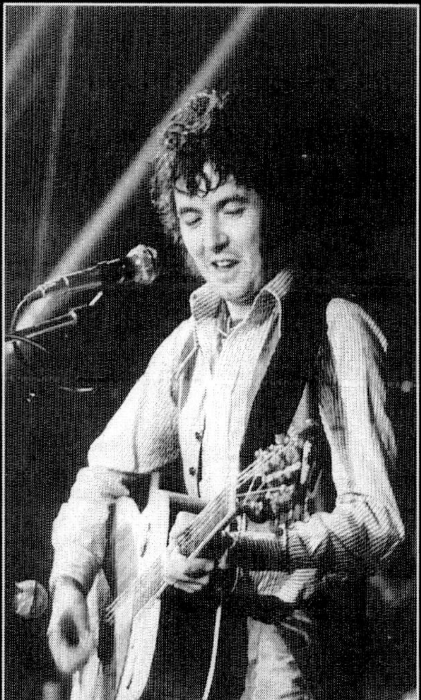

Then one day Ronnie walked into the pub. I'd got a job from my next door neighbour, labouring for him as he had the contract to refurb the brewery outback and build a beer garden. We'd nearly finished and they'd kept me on to help out behind the jump. I sussed him straight off. The Faces, man! Our drummer was so old he could remember before the Small Faces. After a while we got to talking, met him at couple of parties and finally blagged a support spot for him at a local boozer up in the hills - the Drum & Monkey (or as Laney would have it, The Horse & Trouser). We were called some half-arsed name like The Rhythm So and So's so after the 1st gig Ronnie sold me for a fiver the name he'd been calling his mob - Harry Earthquake & the Tremors. So we copped his gig and the name - nice one, mate. At one lunchtime session in the pub as I was closing up (in those days 2.30pm last orders) he asked me up to the farm he'd got on the hill by Rowton. "Let's get a few beers and have a strum". O.K. mate, you're the boss. After that I think he took a shine to me. Lent me a Twin Reverb when the bass player took back the amp he'd lent me, another guitar to use live 'cause I used to hit it too hard & kept breaking strings. But mostly, "why do you keep playing with those guys? Go play with other people". By this time the romance was pretty much over and definitely taking second place so I'd taken

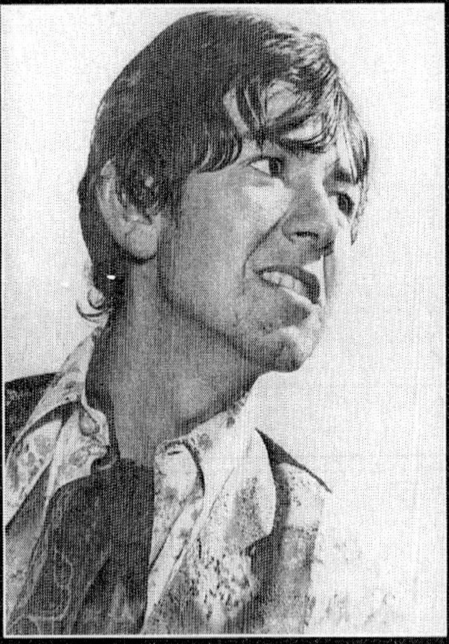

at weekends to hitching to London with the guitar and crashing on peoples' couches. One week back in the west Ronnie introduced me to Nico Korner, eldest son of Alexis Korner who lived most of the week in a converted chapel in Knighton, just across the border. Nico, like his dad, was a guitar player so we started hanging out and playing and through him and his dad I ended up moving permanently to London spending a month on Alexis's couch in Queensway. All due to Ronnie... Typical. A good, honest bloke. If you were straight with him, no problem (God knows, enough people had tried to have him over, over the years...). The other guys I'd played with up in Wales couldn't understand it. They'd brownnosed him, told him all the bullshit, got nowhere. He'd just help someone out if there was no big deal about it. Me? I was too grateful to say much. I just got me 'round in. That was enough. He did this for loads of guys, nothing special about me. I thought he was sick of the attention from people just looking for what a name could do for them, regardless of who it was.

What I'll always remember about him was him insisting that the thing he was most proud about his whole career was his songwriting. Never mind the strong, swooping basslines, that great earthy voice: Ronnie Lane - Songwriter. I only saw him once after I left Wales for good. It was a pub gig in town. He just walked up, shook me hand, said "hello, mate what're having?" Nice one, Ron.

Phil Dobbin 2001

TRACK BY TRACK

HUMBLE PIE

By....

HUMBLE PIE

Original UK vinyl release A&M AMLS 986

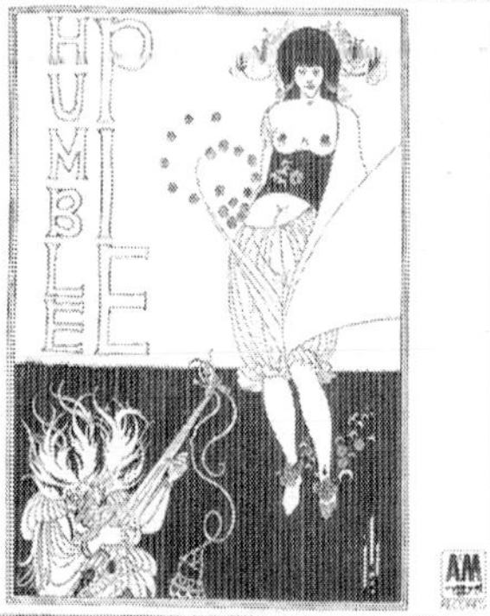

The third Humble Pie album and first on A&M Records was released at the end of July, 1970. The first two albums, both released on Immediate Records didn't sell very well at all and the musicians in the band knew they were capable of something better. The new collection of songs simply titled "Humble Pie" proved to be much more satisfying. The album sleeve, instead of using a band photo, depicted English artist Aubrey Beardsley's famous 1894 motif which Jerry went on to adopt for his bass drum logo.

By this time the band had been together around a year and in that time they had become a closely-knit unit, both musically and on the friendship plane. The press had called them "Supergroup" and their first concert tour was a mistake. It was too near to the old package shows that went round the cinema circuit to give the band a new identity so they turned to the States for respect.

Lead guitarist Peter Frampton takes us through the album one step at a time and by the way, there's no side one and side two, it's this side and that side!

LIVE WITH ME: The line up on this one is Greg on bass, Jerry drums, Steve guitar and me on organ. We each sing a verse. We all wrote the words to our own verse so it's just a Blues about how we felt at the time. Steve plays electric piano on it as well. I like the way this one builds. It was just a blow but we turned it into an organised number. We do this on stage. It's a good sound technically. Glyn Johns, who engineered our sessions really helped with the sound and it's much better than on previous albums. He was very much part of the team.

ONLY A ROACH: This is Jerry's one, it's the first time he's sung as well. There are two friends of his playing on this from a band called Cochise. A guy called Willie plays drums and BJ Cole plays steel guitar. Jerry's on guitar, Greg bass, Steve tambourine and me on piano. We all sing in the chorus. It's nice to have a drummer who can write and sing a number like this.

ONE EYED TROUSER SNAKE RUMBA: Steve and I play guitar, Jerry drums and Greg bass. We all sing on this and it's a group composition. We do this on stage, it's just a dirty song really. Dirty fun, all I can say really.

EARTH AND WATER SONG: This is my song. It's a personal song about me and Mary (soon to be his wife) or me and everybody if you like. I play rhythm and lead guitar, Steve's on piano with Jerry and Greg on drums and bass. Parts of this were written when we were in America last year. I completed it when we got home. It's nice because all our individual songs on this album have their own styles but when we club together we have a different style again.

THAT SIDE....
I'M READY: This is two guitars, bass and drums with three of us singing. The words are by Willie Dixon and we've written our own music to them. You know, it's just an old standard we've re-arranged and put a new riff to. It's a good opener for this side and we'll be doing it on stage.

THEME FROM SKINT and SEE YOU LATER LIQUIDATOR: These two are linked together . This is Steve's bit. It's auto-biographical, the story of Steve's life. BJ Cole s playing steel guitar on this. I suppose the feel is very country but Steve has always been into that. It's just going back to his roots really.

RED LIGHT MAMA, RED HOT: This is a group effort with words by Steve. We played together and he put the words over the top. It's got a nice natural fade that we kept. We'll be doing this on stage as well when the album is released.

SUCKING ON THE SWEET VINE: This is Greg's song. Steve is playing bass this time. Jerry is on drums and Greg and I played acoustic guitars. BJ Cole plays steel guitar but somehow he makes it sound more like a 40 piece orchestra. He just plays overtones that fill the sound. I put some twiddly guitar on this track. It could be a nice close to the album the way it drifts out but it doesn't matter which side you play first.

For me the most attractive thing about this album is the variety of style in the songs which Peter thought was missing from the first two albums. The album was a slow but increasingly steady seller and was met by the music press with critical acclaim.

ALBUM REVIEW BY PETER FRAMPTON,

speaking with Tony Norman (July 1970)

STAN LANE INTERVIEW

JOHN HELLIER speaks to Stan Lane at his Essex home (11th February 1996).

STAN LANE, elder brother of Ronnie by seven years, is now something of a legendary figure amongst Small Faces aficionados. It was he who was responsible for introducing Ronnie to Kenny in the first place and he was always there or thereabouts throughout the turbulent 4 years that the band were together.

Stan, these days, has his own farm in the Essex countryside and a while back I had the pleasure of looking through the contents of one of his barns. I was totally gobsmacked to discover not only Ronnie's guitars, stage cloths and original Small Faces amplifiers but a treasure chest full up with unreleased demo tapes from Ronnie's mobile studio, the L.M.S., complete with note books containing hand written lyrics to songs. It appeared that the majority of these recordings were from about 1979/80. Perhaps one day Stan and I can get this wealth of material filed into some sort of order, listened to and, who knows, possibly released for the whole world to enjoy!!

Anyway on with the business and by the way this is something of a Wapping Wharf exclusive as its Stans first ever interview. (Its taken 30 years!!)

J.H. STAN, STARTING RIGHT AT THE BEGINNING, I UNDERSTAND YOU WERE RESPONSIBLE FOR INTRODUCING KENNY TO RONNIE. HOW DID THIS COME ABOUT?

S.L. I worked in a pub in Bromley Street, Stepney called the British Prince. Kenny used to stand outside the door. When the drummer used to go for a beer I used to call Kenny in and he'd fill in on the drums. He wasn't old enough really to be in the pub. I though he was a good drummer and told Ronnie about him. Ronnie came up and met him and thats how they got together.

RONNIES EARLY BANDS WERE THE PIONEERS AND THE OUTCASTS, RIGHT?

Yeah and they used to play in the church hall at Forest Gate by the Princess Alice.

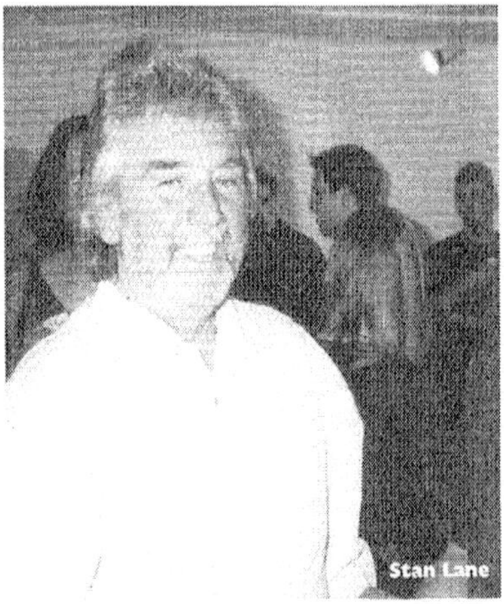

Stan Lane

DID THOSE BANDS WRITE ANY OF THEIR OWN MATERIAL AND DO ANY DEMOS EXIST?

No. None that I know of. Before all that I got Ronnie a job in Selmers. He used to test all the guitars in there, that got him to learn the guitar better and then he went on to the fairground at Battersea.

WHAT WERE THE EARLY SMALL FACES GIGS LIKE AND DID YOU GO TO ANY OF THEM?

I used to go to all of them. I used to drive them around in an old Bedford van. They used to sit on beer boxes in the back. But once they'd done Sha la la la lee the management took them over.

DID YOU GO TO ANY OF THE GIGS ONCE THE HYSTERIA STARTED. SCREAMING GIRLS AND ALL THAT?

Yeah. I used to go to them.

DID YOU EVER GET CHASED DOWN THE STREET, BEING RONNIE'S BROTHER?

No, they used to run past me! (laugh) I went to the Goldhawk rooms, where I had an argument with Don Arden. When I said that he was ripping them off he just said oh! I'll buy them all an E Type Jag each and all that. He had his heavies there like Pat Meehan. They all stood round me while I was saying it to him, so I thought to myself I had better shut up.

DO YOU PLAY ANY INSTRUMENTS YOURSELF , STAN?

No. I tried to learn the guitar, but couldn't.

HAVE YOU EVER TRIED TO WRITE A SONG?

No cause then I started up my own business and I opened up a snack bar in Stratford and they used to come in on their way to a gig. They used to have the chauffeured limo pull up outside and they all used to come into the café.

WERE ANY OTHER MEMBERS OF THE FAMILY MUSICAL?

Dad used to play the piano. Uncle Charlie, I think, used to play the piano. Renee, Dads sister, she was a good singer.

WAS SHE ANYTHING TO DO WITH "RENEE, THE DOCKERS DELIGHT"?

No, No that was Auntie Renee. I think it sort of all come from that though, you know. Yeah, I think it all come from that.

STAN, DID YOU GET INTO THE MOD SCENE YOURSELF?

Oh Yeah Yeah, You see I was 7 years older than Ronnie. When he was 17 I was 25. I was a Teddy boy, as well.

ARE THERE ANY PARTICULAR MEMORIES YOU HAVE ABOUT THEIR DAYS LIVING IN WESTMORELAND TERRACE?

They were always hungry. Me and my first wife used to go over there and do them a bit of grub. Georgie Fame used to come round and have beans on toast! And Speedy the bongo drummer. I made them a bit Scalectrix. I made all the cars for them. I've still got all the cars. I ain't got the scalectrix but yeah, Ive still got the cars. I put in my own motors and all that.

J.H. WHAT ABOUT THE STORIES OF ALL NIGHT PARTIES AT WESTMORELAND TERRACE. WERE THEY EXAGGERATED?

Well no, I think they used to have them. There used to be all the girls sitting out on the steps, waiting to be dragged in and slung out again! (laugh) But yeah! Then they all went to live in Marlow, in a rented house over there. A lovely house! I went there, they were all smoking joints. An awful smell, you know.

WHO WAS HAPPINESS STAN BASED ON?

I suppose it was Stanley Unwin.

WE THOUGHT IT WAS YOUR DAD?

Well it could have been my dad. "Debris" was written about dad. We used to go down Brick Lane and sort though the odds and ends. That song was written about Brick Lane

HOW DID THE SMALL FACES SPLIT, IN 1969, AFFECT RONNIE AT THE TIME?

Well I think that him and Stevie couldn't get on anymore. Stevie took off to do his Humble Pie bit and Ronnie went and got Stewart and Woody. They jumped at it and that was the start of the Faces. I went to a lot of their gigs and they were absolutely fantastic.

WERE THE FACES DAYS DIFFERENT TO THE SMALL FACES DAYS?

Well I went to the Rainbow rooms everytime they played there. That was in Tottenham, no, Finsbury Park. But the best gig I ever saw was the one at the Odean, Edmonton. I was on the balcony there. They done it one Christmas and eh, it was absolutely fantastic. All the hair creeped on the back of my head. I was in the balcony and the balcony was moving. A bit frightening! All the confetti was coming down and the lights were swirling. It was just like an act. It was so amazing! I'd like to go through it again.

STAN, TELL US A BIT ABOUT RONNIES PASSING SHOW?

I went with him up to Carlisle. He hired the equipment from a firm called Luckings. It was all Pre-war lorries and half of them were falling apart on the way. They just used to be like showmen. They'd put the tent up and that started off in Marlow ten went to Bath, Shrewsbury, Carlisle and Newcastle. I didn't go to Newcastle but went as far as Carlisle. They were all good gigs. But Luckings, the circus people, were supposed to go up a month ahead billing up. But they weren't going up 'til 3 days before so consequently nobody knew they were there.

WHAT WAS YOUR ROLE, WERE YOU THE ROAD MANAGER?

No, I just wanted to be with him and be in the fun of it all. See, I was married and had a daughter so I couldn't keep going away, you know what I mean. Plus I had my own business I was running. They lived in a caravan and it was a part of the gypsy thing before he moved to the farm.

WHAT DO YOU FEEL ABOUT RONNIE BEING SO FAR AWAY, ESPECIALLY AS HE IS IN ILL HEALTH?

What do I feel. Well I wish he was nearer so I could help him. But even when he lived here, he had to go and live in Wales, which was a long way. I couldn't be with him then the multiple schlerosis was coming on and he used to keep going out and kept getting drunk, you know and I really couldn't help him.

THANKS STAN FOR YOUR TIME, YOUR'E A GOOD MAN!!!

WAPPING WHARF EXCLUSIVE!

Mac

A 'shortarse' speaks!

Wapping Wharf **EXCLUSIVE!**

THE FOLLOWING IS AN EXCERPT FROM **IAN MCLAGAN'S** BOOK. WE WOULD LIKE TO THANK MAC FOR OFFERING **WAPPING WHARF LAUNDERETTE** THIS EXCLUSIVE.

We were booked for three nights in Scotland but the van broke down on the Friday morning and couldn't be fixed till the next day so that blew Friday night's gig out. Our manager, Jack Barry, reckoned if we could get up there by Saturday night we could still walk away with a few quid and maybe even pay for the van repairs. Now, Boz didn't take things too much to heart, like he wasn't one to lose sleep worrying over minor details like a career or money, simply because he didn't have either one and couldn't get himself moving even is he did. He liked a laugh more than anything else and was an amusing bloke but he could be very exasperating because although I like a laugh as much as anyone, I really wanted to play. I was a professional after all!

Well finally the van was fixed and Scotland here we come, but after several hold-ups in traffic we broke down again, this time on the North-Circular overpass. Boz found it hilarious, giggling like a schoolgirl. I was not amused and he wasn't bothered one bit. I learned the first rule of show business that afternoon and it's simple, just show up. I mean if you're not there you can't expect to play and get paid. In a blinding flash I saw everything clearly.

I've had enough of this shit! I said and reached for my bag, "See you later." I got out of the van, walked down the off-ramp and thumbed a lift home. I never thought about it, I just knew I couldn't carry on like that. Later, I felt depressed, but I knew I'd done the right thing. The next night, the Sunday, I went to see Irene, my girlfriend of the

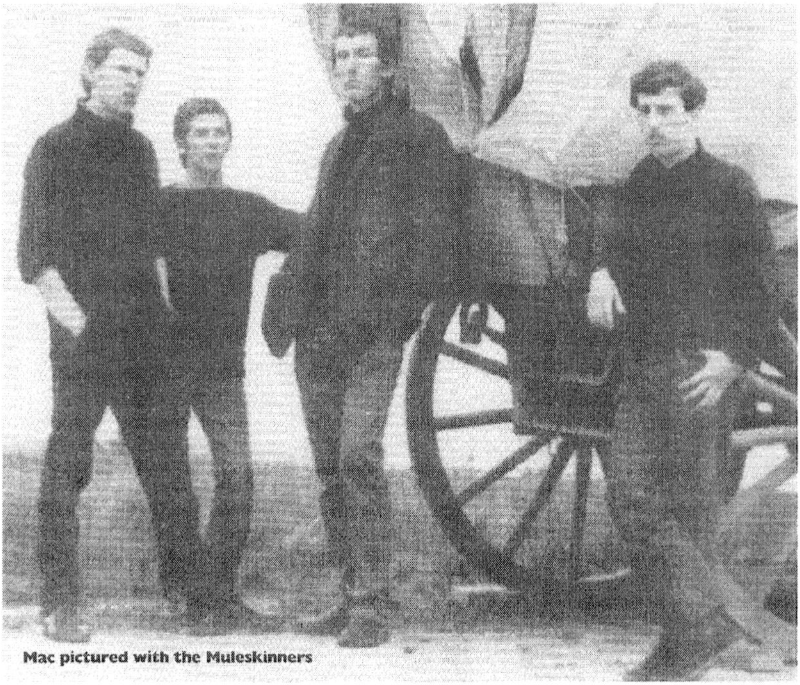
Mac pictured with the Muleskinners

moment, who lived in Manor House at the other end of the Piccadilly Line. I was in a very subdues mood. After pouring my heart out to her, travelling back across town to Hounslow, I bumped into Phil Weatherburn, our neighbour Gillian's cousin.

"Hello Mac, how's the band?"

"Rotten, I just quit."

"Your should join the Small Faces."

"Bloody funny Phil." Ha, Bloody Ha.

"Have your seen them, they're really great?"

Actually my Dad had turned me on to them a few months before. They were on "Ready Steady Go" one Friday night as I was getting ready to go out.

"Here Ian, look at this lot, will you?" he shouted from downstairs. "You look just like him" he said, pointing to Ronnie Lane. They looked and sounded incredible! It was their first single on Decca, "Watcha Gonna Do About It." It was Summer, 1965 and they were rockin'.

They were Mods, not like me, the art student type in brown corduroy jacket and blue jeans without a pot to piss in.

"Yes Phil I've seen them, they're brilliant but they've got an organ player".

"What's his problem?", I'm thinking. Well, I said goodnight to Phil and now I was really depressed. I was adrift. I had no idea what to do next. Home. To bed. To dream.

I woke the next day, Monday, November 1st, unemployed and deflated. What a fuckin' idiot. I'd left the band without thinking it out. If they'd thrown me out I might've felt better, but I'd done this to myself.

The phone call came about 10am.

"Hounslow 7353" I said, quick as a flash.

"Is Ian McLagan at home?" He said in a thick Manchester accent.

"Er, yes".

"This is Don Arden, I'd like to talk to him about a job."

I'd only been out of work since Saturday, what luck!

"Yes, I'm Ian" I said.

"I've got a band that needs a keyboard player, can you come in to the office today?"

"Y'yes" I mumbled, My brain was becoming jelly. This was Don Arden. I had heard of him, he was an "Impresario", whatever that meant. He was somebody in the business.

But this was November 1st 1965, the day that changed my life, and I was impressed.

I agreed to meet him at his office at noon. Who the hell did I think I was?

Actually, I thought of myself as a professional musician at this time. Let's face it I wasn't doing anything else, and I could dream couldn't I? Mum and Dad must've thought otherwise but they never said a word, they backed me up. I realise now they put me through art school when most kids had to go straight out to work, and this after my brother Mike had gone to University. That's two kids not earning anything. So we weren't the best bets for success and at the same time they weren't giving either of us hell. God bless 'em.

I zoomed up to Carnaby Street on the 'tube', climbed the stairs above John Micheal's shop and walked into the outer office of Don Arden's little empire. The receptionist asked for my name and as I didn't know which band I was going to work with and if it was a session or a full-time job I told her I didn't know anything other than Don Arden had called. On the wall were 8 x 10's of all his artists: The Animals, the Nashville Teens, Small Faces and the Clayton Squares. Now I knew Alan Price had been replaced by Dave Rowberry in the Animals only recently and the "Teens had Chris Hawken, who was a fantastic piano player. I thought it had to be the Clayton Squares because it couldn't possibly be the Small Faces, could it? I found out subsequently that the @Faces organ player, Jimmy Winston, hadn't been playing long, his brother owned the group van and he used to try and hog the stage when Steve had a far better voice. His days were numbered. I found out later they'd seen an issue of "Beat Instrumental" that had reviewed a Boz People gig, raved about my organ playing and mistakenly included a photo of Boz with my name under it. They never seemed to notice I didn't look much like my photograph.

Meanwhile I waited and waited. Nothing. All afternoon it went on. Every now and then someone would pop their head round the door, look at me, pretend they hadn't and disappear. I know now it was Steve, Ronnie and Kenny. All the time I'm thinking, "Which Band?" Hours went by. Later I found out one of the reasons for the dipping and diving was that the receptionist was going out with Jimmy and they knew she'd tell him if she found out what was going on. Plus, I think they wanted to get the van back before he did a runner with all the equipment. Quite a Shakespearian plot!

Around 5 o'clock Don called me into his office. He was a short, fat, smily boy. A greasy, bearded Manchester Jew, he sat me down in front of his sidekicks, the outwardly friendly Ron King who ran the agency, the mean, poker-faced Pat Meehan, who was the booker and the camel hair coated vastness of 'Old' Bill Corbett, ex-boxer and heavy turned driver. Don asked me how much money I was getting. I was getting about a fiver a week, but with a straight face I said, '£20'. because that's what my Dad was earning at the time, a very fair wage. '£20 a week? You start at £30, but you'll be on probation for a month and after that, if everything goes well, you'll be on an even split with the lads.'

'Which lads?' I said

'Small Faces, of corse.' I was in Heaven.

'You're to tell no one, O.K? Right, be back here at 6 o'clock sharp'.

'Fine, yeah, can I tell my parents?'

'Tell 'em you'll call them in a couple of weeks and explain everything then.

I couldn't think straight. I left and wandered up the street not knowing where I was going, then I found myself on Wardour Street and I went into The Ship just down from the Marquee and ordered a pint of bitter and a packet of crisps while I tried to get to grips with my new life. I was buzzing. I wasn't supposed to tell anyone but I wanted to shout it out. I was dying to let my Dad in on it but he wouldn't be home for half an hour so I savoured the pint until I could call him. I was too excited to think, but I knew I was finally in a great band and I was going to be very rich, or at least famously poor! When he answered the phone I was too worried about ruining my chances so I only said quickly that he and Mum shouldn't worry, that I'd got a job, it was good money, I wasn't allowed to tell them anything but I'd call them in a couple of weeks, He was great.

'Are you happy'

'Oh yes!' I almost spilled the beans, but caught myself in time.

'I'll call you when I can and tell you all about it'.

'O.K, take care of yourself.'

I walked back to Carnaby Street on a cloud, my head was spinning from the beer.

The receptionist had become unfriendly, I suppose she'd figured it out. I was asked to go straight in to Don's office. Hew shook my hand with an insincere smile, then these three geezers came round the door, laughing and grinning at each other and they picked me up! What a funny bunch, Steve, Ronnie and Kenny were all short like me, between 5'5" and 5'6". I hadn't realised from the name that they were short-arses too. We got on well immediately. While we were driven to he hotel we talked about music and influences we shared which was basically Muddy Waters, Booker T. and the M.G's, Ray Charles, etc, and I knew we were going to get on well. We stayed at the Russell Square Hotel in the West End, which was a big deal to me, but they were past being excited about hotels and were more excited about, and interested in, talking to me, We quickly got to know each other better that night. They were all over me, asking questions, calling room service and pouring drinks and I was a bit intimidated at first. No one had scrutinised me like this before and I wasn't yet used to it.

Steve was a fantastic, larger than life, cartoon of a person. He'd studied drama as a kid and was the original Artful Dodger in Lionel Bart's cast of 'Oliver' that played in the West End. You can hear him on the live recording of that show which proves he was a natural for the par, it was type-casting. He was a very intense person, like he'd say something funny then scream with laughter before you could properly grasp what he'd said, and I'd be exhausted trying to keep up. Ronnie was a funny guy too, and he was excitable, but he was a little more relaxed then Steve and much easier to get to know. Kenny on the other hand was quieter but no less funny, and when he got a word in edgewise he was hilarious. Never mind the Monkees, these were the Marx Brothers of rock'n'roll. Of course I realised soon enough that they were all on leapers, that they were high as kites, bouncing off wall. I'd taken them for innocents and they though I was too. They didn't have to worry, they hadn't done anything I hadn't done already. ■

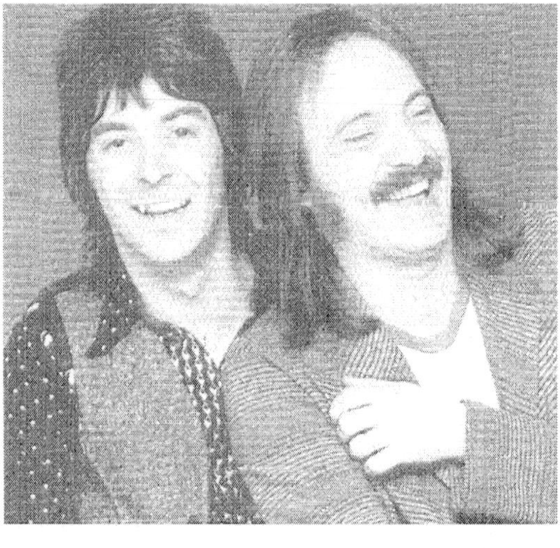

Ian McLagan 1995

Of course, this is just a taste of that one day thirty years ago, there's lots more but I thought you might enjoy the significance of it.

All the best Mac. By the way at the beginning of this story I was in Boz and the Boz People.

AN INTERVIEW with JIMMY WINSTON (PART ONE)

John Hellier speaks to Jimmy Winston at Jimmy's Essex Home 8th. September 1996

Yet another Wapping Wharf exclusive! Original Small Faces keyboard player Jimmy Winston gives his first interview for over 30 years. Jimmy was a founder member of the band and previous to that had spent a couple of years at the East 15 drama school training for a career as an actor, After his departure from the band he formed his own group Jimmy Winston and the Reflections (they released a fine version of Sorry she's mine in 1966) which later developed into Winstons Fumbs (Real crazy apartment 1967). In 1968 Jimmy returned to his acting roots and appeared in Hair, at the Shaftsbury Theatre in London, for a year. During the 1970's he went on to do lots of TV and Film parts including the part of Shura in the television series Doctor Who. There was another single from Jimmy in 1976 'Princes ball' on Decca records, after which Jimmy set up his own business in 1980 supplying recording studios with sound equipment.

Jimmy still writes and plays and we here at Wapping Wharf were privileged when he accepted our invitation to appear as a special guest artist at the Wapping Wharf Small Faces convention in London in January 1997, Thanks Jimmy!

J.H. JIM, STARTING RIGHT AT THE BEGINNING, WHAT DID YOU DO PRIOR TO FORMING THE SMALL FACES?

J.W. Well I think the truth really was prior to that period I really wanted to be an actor. It was music at school and bands when you left school . I played in a couple of bands and then about 17 or 18 I started to do some small parts in films as an extra. I did that for about a year or so and I really did get the taste to do some acting, but you can only go so far in extra work, a line here and a line there and you end up doing loads and loads of nothing really. But I did get the buzz to go to drama school and I suppose when I was about 20 I started to set it up and get more serious. I realised you couldn't go any further doing the extras stuff and I did end up going to the Theatre workshop drama school for a couple of years. I went to do a proper course and got a grant and I stopped everything else and actually did that for a couple of years. In fact it was the week I left drama school while I was doing some work in my dads pub the Ruskin Arms as a compare and singing with the resident band, that was when Steve came into the pub and we met.

TELL ME ABOUT YOUR OWN MUSICAL BACKGROUND AND HOW YOU CAME TO JOIN THE SMALL FACES.

As I said I'd done my training at the theatre workshop and was getting ready to get an agent and do the things you have to do after drama school. Then one night while I was singing in the pub in walked Steve and Ronnie. They were having a few beers and Steve wanted to get up on stage and play harmonica. He played a bit and then we got chatting about some ideas over a beer and really that was the night the band was launched. I hadn't met Kenny then because he wasn't there. Myself, Steve and Ronnie sat around and got fairly plastered on ideas and all the possibilities. But its really weird because of that whole period of drama school and I was all geared up to go on from there and at that moment I was about to throw it all away to play in a band. At that time I had a little house in Stratford and we went back there afterwards and carried on the good night. Yes, it was that night that the band was born. At that point there was only enthusiasm and goodwill.

IN THE EARLY DAYS YOU PLAYED A RICKENBACKER, WAS THERE ANY REASON FOR THAT, THAT WAS BEFORE TOWNSEND PLAYED ONE, WASN'T IT?

No, he already had a Rickenbacker. It was then quite an unknown guitar, but a few people were using it. It had a very interesting sound especially the 12 string electric version which was nice. I don't think anybody tries anything that they haven't seen somebody else using. We all used to go into the Music shops around the east end and dribble basically, because we were all using our hire purchase cheapos and all of a sudden in front of us would be all the Rickenbackers and Gibsons. You could use a dozen different electric guitars and they'd all sound pretty much the same, but the Rickenbacker had a slightly distinctive sound, like a Gretsch it had a different tone about it, it was quite nice and as I said the 12 string was great. That's how that came about really.

WHY THE MOVE TO KEYBOARDS?

Well to be honest I was an out and out guitarist, but Stevie wanted to play guitar, he had already kind of geared himself for that and Ronnie Lane only played bass and, of course, Kenny on drums. In a way what they needed was a keyboard player. I'd never played keyboards, so when people want to unjustly say he wasn't a very good keyboard player I can nearly agree. It was a case of finding what you needed for these initial songs, a lot of what was happening was quite simple to play on keyboards actually, it wasn't very elaborate. On certain tracks I used to play guitar anyway, especially some of the ones I used to sing.

HOW MUCH REHEARSAL TIME WAS ALLOCATED BEFORE THE BAND BEGAN PLAYING LIVE?

About 24 hours (laugh) I mean it wasn't a lot of time. I suppose within a couple of days from that first night we'd set up a rehearsal. The great thing about that moment was that we merged instantly. There was no conflict at all at that early stage. What I liked about that time was that we would get together and just sit around and play acoustically. We didn't have to set up with 2000 watts of power. It was like an instant idea that was quite good then we just took it into the hall to try and tidy it up and make some sense of it all. But within just a couple of weeks we were doing a raw set.

CAN YOU TELL ME ABOUT THE VERY FIRST GIG?

The first gig was our local youth centre up the road in East Ham. They didn't know what to expect. We kind of bluffed our way through. There was only about 5 songs in the set, but with different variations we got away with it. Oh yeah, it was the Kensington youth centre, that's it. It went down kinda well, I think in retrospect the raw stuff in the early days was very good. I've been listening to some of these new compilations and I think those early things are the theme for everything else. E to D was probably the first thing we ever played. It was just like a raunchy instrumental. I think E to D features in half their songs.

WHAT NUMBERS WERE IN THE SET AT THAT TIME?

Apart from E to D, there was you need lovin, Baby don't do it all the raw stuff really. They all had a certain kind of feel about them, like a jam that became a song.

HOW SOON AFTER THE FIRST GIGS DID THE BAND START ATTRACTING THE PRESS?

Well it did happen very very quickly. After the youth club gigs it was only a short period before we done the first gig at the Cavern Club in Leicester Square and I think we got a 4 or 6 week residency on a Saturday. It wasn't really until the Don Arden incident that the press got involved. After about 4 weeks we got quite a following. There was no real press, as such, just a poster outside on a board with your name on it.

AFTER THE FIRST HIT YOU BECAME TAGGED WITH THE TEENYBOP IMAGE. WHAT DID YOU THINK OF THAT, AFTER ALL YOU STARTED OUT AS A RAUCOUS R & B BAND?

It certainly didn't bother me. The thing that this makes me think of is Stevies comments, much later, about screaming kids being mistreated, You couldn't hear what you were doing and it all became a kind of mess in the end, There was people getting hurt and kids getting pushed about and all that is terribly sad. The early teen thing was quite nice as the fans were always younger than us, The kids go wild as older more intellectual people are more sober about how they respond to you, so they don't come around so quickly. As the band gets bigger they then say yeah, I quite like them. But they don't make the fuss, that the kids do.

HOW DID YOU COME TO MEET DON ARDEN?

During our Cavern Club residency Pat Meehan, his assistant came down and had a nose at the band. He was obviously very interested. He didn't say a lot but he did invite us to go and meet Don Arden in Carnaby Street.

WHAT ARE YOUR FEELINGS ABOUT DON ARDEN. WHAT POSITIVE THINGS DID HE DO FOR THE BAND?

Well really its probably all been said and nothings been said! He was a friendly sort of rogue in his own way. We were very young and gullible and he kinda looked like what we were looking for. I suppose then if you met someone who was normal and nice having a cup of tea with you, you wouldn't have any faith in him. There we were sitting by his big desk, he was in a serge suit with one thing and another he certainly had the look. With respect to the man he just had that ability to market something. The problem was that he wasn't sensitive enough and aware enough to think long term. Everyone should have got what was due to them for the efforts they put in. I'm sure he could have still earned a good living by doing this. He was a business impresario he could take something which he had no feeling for and still go and sell it. I've always found that quite sad. Did you know he made a record once, I've heard it, 'My Yiddisha Momma' or something like that.

WHO WAS YOUR CLOSEST FRIEND IN THE BAND?

I don't know if that can be answered. What you've got to remember is from that first interesting night at the Ruskin Arms when we first met we had no pre-history. Steve and Ronnie hadn't known each other long. It's not as if you've known someone from school, it was all absolutely fresh. My energy was with Stevie really because he was very similar to me in a way. He had a lot of drive, a lot of attitude and there was a lot of things he wanted to do. With great respect to Ronnie and Kenny they were slower and just coming out of their shell, they hadn't been out there doing so much. Me and Stevie had both been at it for a few years to find something that would carve into a career. Our energies were definitely higher, so in a way we fascinated each other. It was kinda good in respect that we could bounce off one another and get a lot going quickly. Yes, I would say I was closer to Stevie because I'm drawn to things that have a lot of interest about them and he did have that.

CAN YOU DESCRIBE THE MUSICAL TALENT OF EACH INDIVIDUAL MEMBER?

At this particular time Stevie was also learning the guitar. He wasn't a good guitarist. Everyone was slightly raw to be honest. Ronnie and Kenny had played together in a band. What united us was that we all had a love of the same sort of music. Because the focus on the music was good, you started learning good ranges. Stevie was determined to get his guitar style and I think that's where his vocal thing came from as

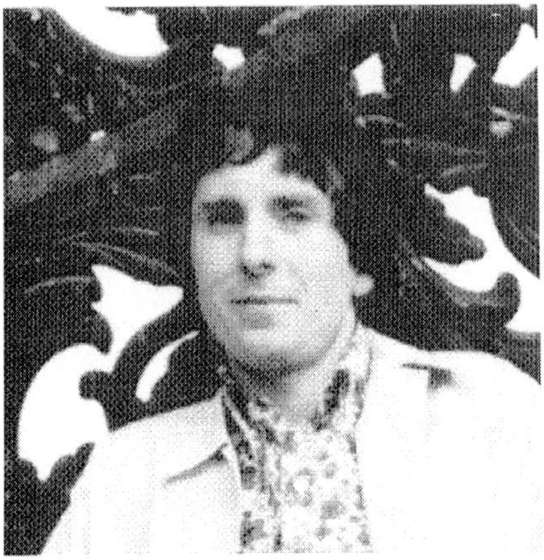

well. He liked so many good singers. He listened to their interpretation and style and how they performed and when you do that it grows on you all the time, you know.

WHERE YOU A MOD BEFORE JOINING THE BAND AND WHAT DID YOU THINK OF THE IMPORTANCE OF THE MOD MOVEMENT AT THAT TIME?

I suppose I was really, I actually had a lambreta just for the record. What you had was two kinds of mods in a way, you did have the movement and the jacket and all of that. But if you were in the music business you had the other style of mod, you had the performance side of the mod. It didn't mean to say it was derogatory it was just that you'd tidy it up a bit. The band never ever consciously turned round and said here we're a bunch of mods lets dress like this. Never, ever occurred to you we were actually wearing what we were wearing. It wasn't really until the Don Arden time, when we had our own accounts in the Carnaby Street shops, that we started picking our clothes and generally tidying up. We then became better quality mods with a little bit more flare. Once the first record was released we became involved in lots of P.R. things and we became more conscious of the whole mod image. There was Don Arden saying 'Look tidy up boys and make me a lot of money'. Up until Don Arden it was all a lot more raw, like The Who if you like. The Who were representative of the kids on the street.

WHAT ARE YOUR RECOLLECTIONS OF 'DATELINE DIAMONDS'.

Not a lot. Half the time we'd go in and do a few days work but we didn't know what was going on. It was kind of a P.R. thing really from Don Arden and it was a thing obviously aimed to help launch the band certainly not aimed as a career move. We would do odds and ends of shots but we had no idea how they were going to mix together and what the logical steps of the sequence were. In a strange way it was exciting because running around and doing something in a film is exciting. But at the end of the day you think to yourself 'what was all that about'.

WHAT TV SHOWS DO YOU REMEMBER DOING WITH THE SMALL FACES?

Ready Steady Go was the first one and was also the main one. I think we did two or three of those, but there were quite a few others afterwards, a few one off shows but I can't remember them by name. There were certainly people that we took up a kind of friendship with like Sonny and Cher. They were sort of climbing at the same time as us. I remember that Ready Steady Go went out live so whatever blunder was made was on there, it was living proof. It's not being blasé to say that when you've done something 4 or 5 times everyone gets used to it, but those first few shows everyone was running on overtime. Before we formed the band I used to watch the show and think 'Cor wouldn't it be great to play on there'. All the different shows that we did were exciting in their own way but the Ready Steady Go ones stand out in my mind the most. They had Gary Glitter moving the crowd around. He was a crowd arranger! Various artists used to introduce the other acts, I remember Eric Burdon introducing us as the New Faces! I never liked him after that, I don't know whether he done it on purpose or not. Silly really.

WHAT MOMENTS WITH THE SMALL FACES BRING THE BIGGEST SMILE TO YOUR FACE, ANYTHING IN PARTICULAR?

It's interesting that they are still talking about it now. My period with the band was relatively short compared to the whole of their time, but it was the initial time. One day something is completely impossible and the next day it occurred. For everybody in the band these early days were good times. We were all young and naive yet we all just got on with it, we were given a free licence if you like. I loved those times because they were less complicated and they were, to me, what The Small Faces were all about. It was great to be on stage performing something we've only been doing for 2 weeks and getting away with it. It was a bit later on when things started getting a bit more sophisticated and clever when it began to go downhill.

HOW MUCH MUSICAL INPUT DID THE BAND HAVE IN TERMS OF PRODUCTION AND ARRANGEMENT ETC.?

Well in the early days everything. The songs were kind of self arranging really they'd be written and put together in the middle of the night somewhere. We'd be sitting around playing acoustically with Kenny playing drums on his knees. We'd get the rough outline that way and then take it into the studio to tidy it up.

DID YOU PLAY ON THE WHOLE OF THE FIRST ALBUM?

No, I recorded a certain amount of tracks that ended up on those early Decca releases, but not everything.

WERE THERE ANY PARTICULAR FAVOURITE SONGS?

Not really, I suppose if I had to pick anything it would be the ones I did myself. I suppose that sounds a bit selfish. Things like E to D I loved, the good thing about that was that it could go on for about ten minutes or so it you had to fill the space. Don Arden got Ian Samwell in to write the first single 'Watcha gonna do about it'. In fairness we did need a pop song that had a lot of bounce, energy and cheek in it and I suppose we weren't writing that sort of song at the time. Our songs were more raunchy and that frightened Don Arden. He couldn't see any commerciality in them and he was probably right. They were just right for the stage act but not for the first single.

HOW DID YOU FEEL ABOUT BEING LEFT OFF THE COVER OF THE FIRST ALBUM?

Well unfortunately it was to be expected. When the split came Don Arden wanted to change it as rapidly as possible and carry on undisturbed, so I think it was fairly predictable. Oh yeah, it did peeve me a bit at the time.

BECAUSE YOU WERE THE ONLY TALL MEMBER OF THE BAND DID THE OTHER GUYS EXPRESS ANY DISPLEASURE WITH THE WAY YOU LOOKED?

When things were fine, No. I was a couple of inches taller and also a couple of years older that's just the way it was. In some ways I suppose I was a little bit more streetwise and maybe done a few more things than the rest of them. But lets be honest here, if you look at bands and say I'm sorry that person can't come in the band he's an inch and a half taller than the other one, well, I mean, lets all give up now. That's pathetic really. You've got to have your major fall out first and then all these silly negative things come to a head. I mean we were out one night when a friend of mine came up with the name 'Small Faces' it was conceived for the band as it was then and it was fine. All these funny little bits were written in after the event really. It's always freaked me out really, the very thought of manufacturing a group of people all five foot five tall weighing two stone! Its really not what Rock and Roll is all about is it. as I say these things were created later on by less enlightened folk. But Don Arden yes he would look at four T-shirts all size 32! In real terms the band in the early days never thought anything about it. It's only later on in moments of bitterness and anger that you can come out with this crud!

To be Continued...

AN INTERVIEW with JIMMY WINSTON (PART TWO)

By JOHN HELLIER (Sept. 1996)

(Part one appeared in Wapping Wharf issue 10).

Jimmy Winston, sometimes referred to as the Pete Best of the Small Faces, gives his first interview for 30 years.

J.H. DID YOU QUIT THE SMALL FACES OR WERE YOU FIRED? WAS IT OVER PERSONAL OR MUSICAL DIFFERENCES OR A COMBINATION OF BOTH?

J.W, It was the combination of a few things. There's the notorious old story concerning my brother and his van. He loved the band and he was keen. Like the rest of us he didn't have a lot of money but with the few hundred pounds that he did have he offered to buy a van and do the roadying for us. We just wanted to play; we had no transport and certainly didn't want to have to drag the equipment on the underground. We were earning virtually nothing at the time and agreed to give him 10%. He was going to buy the van, insure it, tax it and do all the driving and things like that. Everybody agreed that was fine. I thought so as well. Seeing as I was a couple of years older than the others and the tallest!, it was me that always went and got the money after a gig. I'd automatically take my brothers 10% out first and pay him. The rest of the band got a bit grumpy about this, I don't know why. It was one of those incidents where I got stuck in the middle. I did get into conflict with Ronnie and Steve over this. I'd always been close to my brother and they weren't being fair to him. I think they used this later as a bit of a lever. Against all good advice we ended up signing for Don Arden. He certainly wasn't happy with the 10% contract. Don Arden saw it as 10% of a lot of his earnings and I think right from the beginning he was trying to do something about it. So right from day one Don Arden had a problem with me because I sided with my brother. Somewhere in the scheme of things that's what occurred. Don Arden called me to his office and told me that this is not going to work and suggested that I put another band together and he would record us, He kind of gave me an

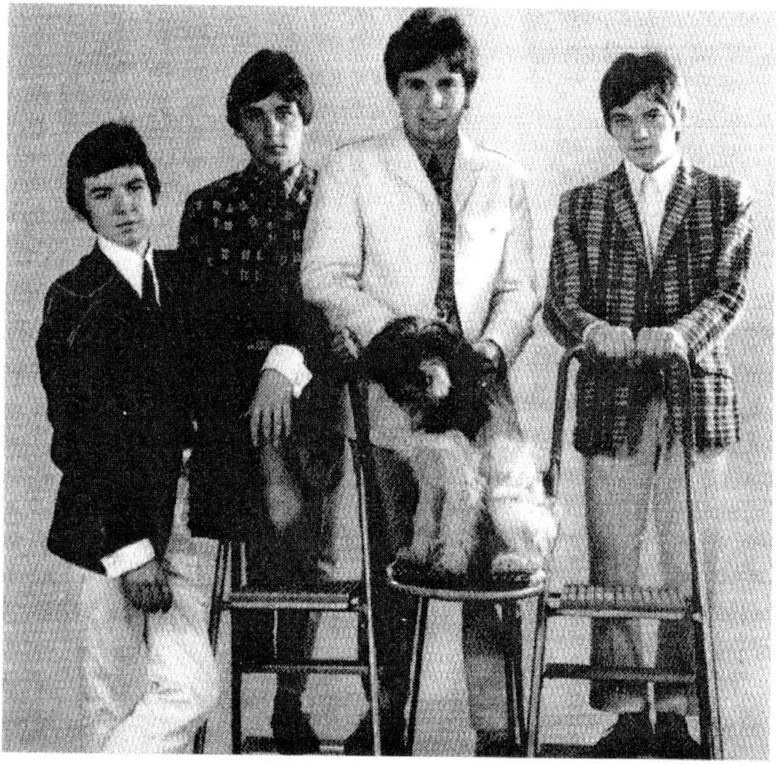

alternative. He said we would be able to go straight into the studio and promised a lot. I wasn't particularly happy about the situation The Small Faces were doing well and looking like they had quite a good future but at the same time we were not getting on well, there were lots of rows and it was becoming a drag. In retrospect I'd have been better off leaving Don Arden and going somewhere new.

WHAT WAS YOUR OPINION OF THE SMALL FACES AFTER YOU HAD LEFT?

In a way I was disappointed and angry because things had gone on behind my back. I felt very let down I'd done as much as anybody else to get the band going and it was already successful. I look back now and I realise that I've done a lot of things over the years that I probably wouldn't have done. It hasn't been all doom and gloom. I liked Stevies work, he was young, pig headed and selfish but very talented. At the end of the day that's what it's all about. I suppose deep down I wish things could have been sorted out better, perhaps it could have been with a different type of manager.

DID YOU EVER SEE THEM LIVE AFTER YOU LEFT?

No, I was a bit uptight with them and of course I had the opportunity to go straight ahead with putting another band together. It was the only thing to do really. Incidentally my first "Reflections" were a bloody good band.

HAVE YOU EVER MET MAC AND WHAT DO YOU THINK OF HIM?

Never met Mac. To be honest with you it's not his fault. I suppose I could have nothing against him and in the same respect he can have nothing against me. He just ended up in a good gig but with respect to the guy he ended up in something that was already going. So a certain amount of birthing and whatever sets something in gear had already happened.

OF ALL THE SMALL FACES NUMBERS, AFTER YOU HAD LEFT THE BAND, ARE THERE ANY THAT YOU WISHED YOU COULD HAVE BEEN INVOLVED WITH?

I liked Ogdens. I also liked the physedelic side of the band. With 'Winstons Fumbs' we actually got to physedilia before them. Although Ogdens was good it could have been even better. I mean the idea of the cover, the idea of a smoke that's probably how the band started. To end up with this being their mini masterpiece based on that, was great. Even back when I was with the band we mucked about with our own kind of language, Stanley Unwin was our history and the fact he ended up on there was quite funny really. There are some things on that album that Steve didn't like, 'cause by then he was getting into raunchy rock. Some of the commercially funny stuff although it was done tongue in cheek was starting to embarrass him. I think he wanted more cred in a true music sense that's why it all folded shortly after Ogdens. I like good pop with ideas and fun so from that angle I really liked the album.

WHEN YOU WERE WITH THE SMALL FACES DO YOU REMEMBER PLAYING ON THE SAME BILL WITH ANY OTHER MAJOR ARTISTS OF THE TIME?

We never played with The Beatles. They tried to play with us many times, but we turned them down (LAUGH). In the early days we used to meet other artists on TV shows, that's where we met Sonny and Cher. I ended up dating Cher's sister! After a lot of gigs we would end up in a club somewhere and it was in those that bands would meet up. I remember going to the Bag O'Nails Club in Soho and you'd have people like Otis Redding and Jimi Hendrix sitting on the next table. All the band members congregate in places like that and you met a lot of interesting people in the privacy of the night (LAUGH).

HAVE YOU SEEN PAOLO HEWITTS BOOK?

I've got certain sensitivity to that time and I really don't take to the bull too much. I made myself sit down and read it, front to back. I knew that you would get certain clips about the break up and all the same old bullshit coming out. Even though it angered and pissed me off a bit I read it 'cause I thought I'd get up to date with what they're doing. What does come out is that as everyone gets a bit older people get a bit blasé and things that were once just little conflicts have now been blown out of all proportion. Just before Paolo's book came out I got a call from John Pidgeon to ask it I would contribute to a radio documentary that they were doing. I decided to participate otherwise people will always be talking about the same old things.

(P.S. in 1997 Jimmy also contributed to Wapping Wharfs own book 'Quite Naturally').

WHAT HAVE YOU BEEN DOING FOR THE LAST 30 YEARS?

After the Small Faces I fronted the Reflections and Winstons Fumbs. We toured around Europe, interestingly enough we played a big venue in Paris with Johnny Hallyday, who the Small Faces went on to work with. We ended up living in Paris for a while. By late '67 I had the yearning to go back to acting. I went to the Theatre Royal at Stratford one night and had one of those quantum leaps! I was watching a show and actually fell in love with it; I just wanted to act again. I met Joan Littlewood that evening and she offered me an audition for a new show that she was putting on. The following week I attended the audition, I passed and by the next week I was acting again. After that I did "Hair" in the West End of London for a year which was followed by a thing called "Rablai" at the Roundhouse. From that came lots of TV bits including "Dr Who" and "Hazell". In the mid 70's I got another band together and did a couple of recordings for Decca including "The Princes Ball" single. I kept writing throughout the 70's and had various publishing deals. In the early part of the 70's the first type of home recording equipment came about. I got one of the first 4-track reel to reel machines and after that it all developed rather quickly. I started to get bits for other people and other people wanted help with home recording equipment and by 1980 it had kinda took off. I set up my business properly. I still wanted to play but by understanding the technology and maybe have some of the technology it could only help. It was a healthy time for music and home recording and anyone who could do their own thing, it was the right time.

DO YOU STILL PLAY NOW, JIMMY. DO YOU STILL DO GIGS?

Yeah, I play mainly acoustically. For people that I know, situations that are OK. For people who like what I do. I like situations like that. I like writing acoustically. Everything begins on a guitar you can elaborate on it later.

WHAT ARE YOUR THOUGHTS ON THE AMAZING RESURGENCE OF INTEREST IN THE SMALL FACES AND CAN YOU HEAR THEIR INFLUENCE IN TODAY'S BANDS?

Yeah, I think it's good. I'd say it's desperate to put it mildly. I think the industry in the UK needs an enema badly. There's always been the good bits, we know that, but when the recession hit this country the music business clamped up and went very tight and mean and wouldn't get behind anything, so they kept picking things that were cheap to record and put out. Just a bunch of people with a drum machine and odds and ends. We had a long period of no creativity. The last few years or so it's just starting to break again and I feel there's more to come. I'm glad to see guitar bands with bit of attitude again. Shades of 1965 Small Faces and The Who.

WHAT SORT OF MUSIC DO YOU LISTEN TO NOWADAYS?

To be honest with you my taste hasn't changed very much. Its grown there's a little more courage about what I like now. I love the earliest roots of rock and roll, soul and blues. I like good pop writers as well. I like people who can strut with ideas. I like writers who have something to say about life and survival, people like Jackson Browne. Don't mind a bit of opera, not all of it. Anything that touches me basically (LAUGH). The only music I've never gotten into is Traditional Jazz. I like Modern Jazz and Fusion Jazz also real Folk music. I like country, as well, a lot more than I used to. If you write you tend to listen to stuff with an angle, you go out with a basket to collect ideas. You would be a liar if you said you didn't. Everybody learns from previous examples and ideas. I love the Eagles, at their best they go into a whole new chapter of writing. My influences are certainly wide and varied. It's the only way!

THANKS, JIM FOR YOUR TIME; IT'S BEEN VERY INTERESTING.

A **LEGEND** IN HIS **OWN** TIME

by Pam Jenner

(June 1991)

I FIRST MET POP STAR STEVE MARRIOTT in a coffee bar near Epping in the mid 1960's.He was an 18 year-old fresh from stage school who was just making a name with his band The Small Faces.

A diminutive young man with a pixie face, Steve was full of boundless energy and a single minded determination to make it to the top in the music business.

I last saw him only a few years ago at a gig at the Sawbridgeworth Memorial Hall, near Bishops Stortford, with his band Packet of Three. He hadn't grown much - except outwards - and his face had a heavily lived in look but he still had that amazing voice and larger than life stage personality that could enslave any audience.

Although he became known nationally and internationally Steve was always regarded by the people around Saffron Walden and Bishop's Stortford as their local rock star.He played at the Rhodes Centre, Bishop's Stortford, in the 1960s for Stansted entrepreneur Alan Goldsmith.

'They were on their way up at the time and were always very popular,' said Alan owner of Mountfitchet Castle.

He played for Alan more recently at a 'Legends of the 60s' event at North Weald airfield when he appeared with the Packet of Three.

As he sat with other old stagers in the dressing room I remember him laughing and saying modestly: "Legends? We're all legends in our own minds".

Steve was always very reticent about himself.

"I'm a bit of a bore to most people," he said in the early days. I don't mix socially and don't think I'm the awkward sort of person some people try to make out that I am."

BORN IN EAST LONDON IN 1947 Steve had a flourishing career as a child actor and appeared in Lionel Bart's musical 'Oliver' in the West End.

Although a Londoner, Steve loved the country and once said: "I think anyone who has ever lived in a town has a hankering to get out of it."

He maintained that if necessary he would live in a tent to make sure he had a home in the countryside.Although he had only lived in Arkesden a comparatively short period of time, Steve had maintained an association with this area over many years. He loved animals and when he lived with his first wife Jenny in Moreton near Ongar in a 16th century thatched cottage he had three dogs, a number of ducks, six cats and even a pet cow.

Steve's career certainly had its ups and downs. He had just returned to Arkesden from a two month trip to America for recording sessions and had great hopes for the future.

It seems ironic that he should die now, just when he was on the point of finding new popularity as a result of the 1960s revival.

Steve will certainly be missed by local musicians and ageing rock stars alike and the publicity that his death has received has shown that he was far more than just a "legend in his own mind". ■

Trivia! Trivia! Trivia!

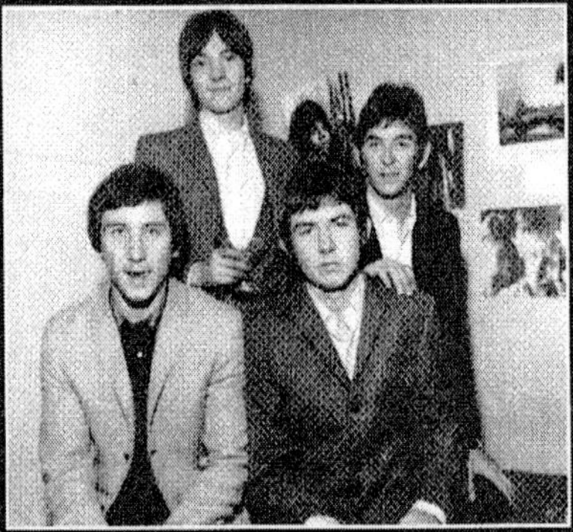

● **DID YOU KNOW THAT ...**
Respected archivist Keith Badman has recently discovered a piece of film featuring Tom Jones live on stage. So what, you may well ask! Well behind Tom is a giant screen and for some unknown reason there's rare 'Top of the Pops' footage of the Small Faces miming to what we think is "Tin Soldier". Seeing as all of 'Top of the Pops' 60's material was wiped many years ago this makes this a particularly special find for Small Faces aficionado's. Well done, Keith !!

● **DID YOU KNOW THAT ...**
Pink Floyd wrote and recorded a song about Steve Marriott's dog, Seamus. It appears on their album "Meddle" and the track is called simply "Seamus". Apparently, Steve taught the dog to howl when the blues was being played. You can hear Seamus himself on the disc!

● **DID YOU KNOW THAT ...**
Ronnie Lanes "Anymore for Anymore", which was the title of his first solo album, was written originally for the Faces. A very early version, recorded in Ibiza in 1972, has recently been discovered amongst the many tapes that Ronnie's brother, Stan, possesses. It has recently been made available by New Millenium, as a bonus track, on their "Anymore for Anymore" CD re-issue.

● **DID YOU KNOW THAT ...**
During 1967 Steve Marriott moved home no fewer than six times! He was constantly besieged by over zealous fans and eventually resorted to renting accommodation under the alias of Fred Smith!

● **DID YOU KNOW THAT ...**
In 1990 Itchycoo Park was used in a TV advertisement for toilet paper! The same year Steve surprisingly put the song back in his live set with his last Packet of Three line up, which featured Steve along with bassist Jim Leverton and drummer Sticky Wickett.

P.P. ARNOLD INTERVIEW

by John Hellier (26th July 1998)

P.P. Arnold is one of the pioneers of black music in this country. She has done it all. A soul singer from the age of four when she sang in the Baptist church, she's sang Rock and Roll, Rhythm and Blues, appeared in West End musicals and toured with dozens of illuminaries such as Eric Clapton, The Small Faces and Billy Ocean. She's made classic soul singles such as 'Angel Of The Morning' and 'The First Cut Is The Deepest' and was known as Immediate Records 'First Lady'. Her story also has more than a fair share of tragedy and despair. P.P. lost a daughter in the 1970's and suffered a terrible accident in 1986 when she was crushed between two cars. In recent times she's worked with Ocean Colour Scene and appeared on their hit single 'Its A Beautiful Thing'. In the summer of 1998 she released an excellent single 'Different Drum'. A great song written by ex-Monkee Mike Nesmith.

These days P.P. (real name Patricia Ann) continues to write beautiful songs and has recently taken up the piano. 'It's as if I've been playing it for years'. Aside from her music Pat is very involved in nutritional food herbs. A very health conscious person.

J.H. Starting right at the beginning , how did you first arrive in England?

P.P.A I came over with the Ike and Tina Turner Review. 'River Deep Mountain High' had become a big hit and they came over in 1966 to tour with The Rolling Stones. I was an Ikette

J.H. What was it like working with Ike and Tina Turner?

P.P.A. It was great, quite an experience. I started in 1964, it was the first big opportunity for me. When I met Ike and Tina I was seventeen with two kids. I was pregnant at 15 and my daddy pulled out a shotgun! It wasn't a happy marriage, neither of us wanted to be married. Our parents forced us into it. It was quite an abusive marriage. Basically, I woke up one morning and prayed to god to help me. I had had to leave school which I loved, if I had become a legal secretary my dad would have been the happiest man in the world. My husband, David Arnold, wouldn't work so I had to take two jobs to feed the kids. During the day I worked at a clothing firm, in California, as a clerk/typist. In the evening I would pick up the kids from my mum, cook their dinner, put them to bed and then it would be out on the night shift. I worked in an egg factory where I separated the egg white from the yoke for the bakery. It was awful! That was my life. On Sundays I would do all the scrubbing and housework, I was a real life Cinderella! My dad said I had made my bed and would have to lie in it. So I was doing just that. Out of the blue, I got a phone call from my brother's ex-girlfriend and she knew Gloria Scott, one of the Ikettes. Ike and Tina had two sets of Ikettes, one that went on the road with them and another set that they would send out on tours with Dick Clark. Gloria was one of the Ikettes on the Dick Clark tours. She knew that Vennetta was leaving and she and Maxine were trying to get the gig. They asked me to go along with them, I had only done one session previously and that was with Bobby Day, the Rockin' Robin guy. In order to go to the audition with Gloria and Maxine I had to tell my husband a lie, he would never have allowed it. Anyway, the next thing I knew I was at Ike and Tina's house for the audition. Tina loved us because we were all like little motowny looking girls, so she said yeah you got the job. I thought well not me there's no way I can go on the road I'm married with two kids, I only came up here to get out of the house. Tina insisted that she wanted all of us and invited us to see the show before we made up our minds. I went to see the show, it was absolutely incredible, totally mind-blowing, but when I got home my husband, David, was waiting for me. As soon as I got through the door he hit me hard. But it seems like when he hit me that time he knocked some sense into me, because from that minute I was gonna do it. I saw it as an opportunity to get out of the situation that I was in. I asked mum and dad for their help with the kids, I hadn't told them previously about all the abuse but now I just blurted it all out. Four days later I was in Columbus, Ohio at my first gig with The Review. I toured with Ike and Tina for a couple of years and one night in 1966 while playing at the Galaxy on Sunset Strip in walked these two English guys. It was Bill Wyman and Charlie Watts, we were told that these guys were in the Rolling Stones. They dug the show so much that we were invited over to England to tour with them. So there it was. Out of the Chitlin Circus and into the Albert Hall!

J.H. How did you come to stay in England?

P.P.A. Well we toured the country and were having big fun. I was now eighteen and free and in London in 1966. I just planned on having loads of fun and that's what I did, had loads of fun. The Stones were great, when I first saw Mick Jagger on stage it just cracked me up. I was in stitches, you know, he was such a character and this guy was singing the Blues! We used to take the piss out of them and they would take the piss out of us. We just had loads of fun. Mick and I became very good friends, we were friends throughout the tour. It was a great tour and a very good experience for me working with Ike Turner. Ike was a great bandleader and a great musician. Tina was there but Ike had made Tina, Ike directed everything. It was his show, he ruled with an iron hand. Anyway, I had mentioned to Mick that I was going to leave when we got back to the States and Mick mentioned it to Andrew (Oldham) and it was Andrew who asked me if I would stay in England and sign up to his label, Immediate Records. So I spoke to my mum on the phone and told her about this because she was looking after my kids. She was okay about it so I decided to stay. Once again opportunity had knocked so I thought I'd try it. I got hooked up with Immediate.

J.H. How did you first come into contact with the Small Faces?

P.P.A. Well that was at Immediate, in the office at 69, New Oxford Street that's where we all used to hang out. Immediate were really happening, it was one of the first independent labels. The first time I met the Small Faces, I loved them. We were all the same age, same size and into the same music. Even though I was close to them all, my relationship was with Steve. We had a strong bond, we had a lot of love. We were like mates, I was the new black girl in town so everybody was trying to get it on but there are only certain people that you connect with. Mick was one and Steve was another. I was also very close to Jimi Hendrix, who was also a black American in London. We had a lot in common, he was like my brother. The enthusiasm at Immediate was marvellous. One big happy family. Yeah, it was great we'd all meet up at places like the Speakeasy, Bag

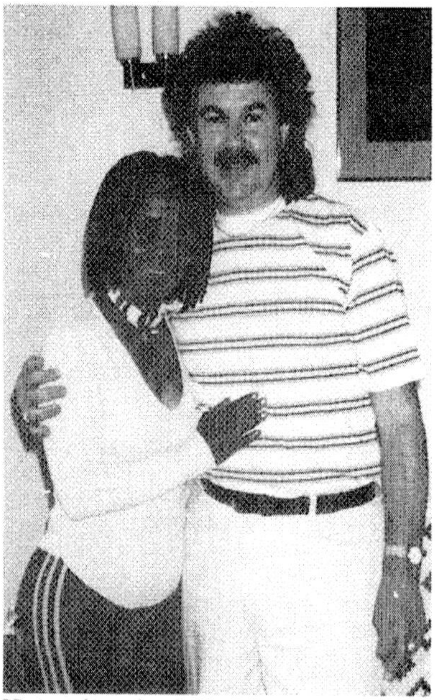

PP pictured recently with John Hellier at her London home.

O' Nails or Cromwellian.

J.H. How did you get to record 'If you think your'e Groovy' and do the Small Faces play on the record?

P.P.A. That song was written for me and yeah, the band were on it. I also done 'Tin Soldier' and 'Itchycoo Park' with them. I was going to do 'Afterglow' but then Steve took it back, he liked that one. He liked 'Groovy' too but I wouldn't let him take that back. I remember doing a video on a beach somewhere near Brighton with the Small Faces and my own band The Nice. We had planned on doing a lot more stuff together but Immediate went bust and everybody went their own way. It was a shame because we were trying to make Immediate a bit like Motown in England where all the artists work together and collorabate together but everybody had their own separate scene as well. It worked. At around this time I also worked with Rod (Stewart). I was kinda hanging out a bit with Rod for a while, but we didn't get along too good. We were arguing all the time. I remember we did a song called 'Come Home Baby' and we had a big row in the studio. It was really funny it was over a key thing! One key was too low for him and too high for me or something. Once he had chosen the key he wanted I learnt to sing it in that key. Soon as I had learnt it he decided to change it again. Then I never saw him again until just a few weeks ago at TFI Friday and he didn't even recognise me! I also did lots of stuff with Chris Farlowe like 'Handbags And Gladrags' and 'Reach Out I'll Be There'. Mick was producing him. Chris is a great singer, A soul man!

J.H. Did you like the offshoot bands, Faces, Humble Pie etc?

P.P.A. Yeah! They were all great. I did some work with Humble Pie. The thing is I've done so many sessions in my life it's difficult to remember everything.

J.H. Can you hear the Small Faces influence in today's contemporary bands?

P.P.A. I've worked on different projects and with different bands such as Ocean Colour Scene, Paul Weller and Primal Scream. I've been on tour with Ocean Colour Scene and I done a 25 minute set of my own with MickTalbot. When I was on stage I'd look out into that audience and I thought 'My Babies'. They were so into those songs. They made songs like 'First Cut', 'Angel Of The Morning' and 'Groovy' new for me. Those songs have held me in peoples hearts. There were times when I just wanted to do new material, but those songs are my legacy. The kids in the audience really made me love that stuff again. Some of my old material like the 'Kafunta' album has never been performed live. When, years later, I listened to that album I realised just how good some of those songs are. I was listening to 'Welcome Home' just yesterday with Chip Taylor, what a beautiful song. As for influence, Yeah, its great. I can hear the influence of The Small Faces, Beatles, Stones, Hendrix, Kinks and The Who in it. I can hear the influence of the era. Yeah, the influence is there. They can't get rid of it can they. There's no generation gap anymore.

J.H. In the late 70's the Small Faces reformed without Ronnie, What did you think of that?

P.P.A. Yeah, I went on tour with them. I had gotten the feel for touring again after touring with Eric Clapton. Yeah, I remember that tour, it was crazy. I had left England and gone back to the States in 1974. I had returned to England to sell my house and I run into Steve somewhere. He said he was going back on tour and he asked me to go out with them. I remember riding in a Land Rover. Steve was very lively on that tour, It was a different chemistry than the first time around, but it was good. I wouldn't want to compare it. I remember one gig at the Rainbow in London when somebody broke into the dressing room and stole all our belongings including my passport. Eventually I got home after the tour and two weeks later my daughter was killed so my memories of the time are of tragedy and grief.

J.H. You were involved with Steve Marriott's 'Thirty Seconds to Midnite' album in the late 80's. How did that come about?

P.P.A. Steve contacted me to do it along with Vicky and Sam Brown and Margo Buchanan, I did the 'Clapping Song' with Steve. Its a great track. Steve experimented with technology and used drum machines but his soul was very much in it. It was a good album. I really admired Steve he had never stopped playing and never stopped gigging.

J.H. Do you still keep in touch with Tina Turner?

P.P.A. I'd like to. I did write her a letter, I took it to the stage door. I just wanted her to know that I'm still here and I think about her. I still respect her and maybe one day we'll have a one to one. I wanted to also let her know how much that one day in her life changed my life. Whether I played any significant part in her life is another thing, but she played a major part in my life and my history as an artist and I wanted to let her know that. She acknowledged my letter but I haven't got to speak to her.

J.H. What other things have you done since Immediate folded?

P.P.A For a while Robert Stigwood was my manager and I worked with Barry Gibb. Following on from that I toured with Eric Clapton and Delaney and Bonnie. Also on that tour was George Harrison and Billy Preston. I opened the tour with Ashton, Gardner and Dyke. In 1974 Fuzzy Samuels, myself and our baby son decided to go back to America as the whole scene in England had changed. We had a band called Axis, a Jimi tribute. The line up was similar to Chaka Khan and Rufus. Before that EMI had offered me a deal to record as Starfucker! I was insulted. As I said before, while I was in L.A. I lost my daughter, that tragedy separated me from a lot of things for many years. I came back to England in the eighties and it was after meeting Andrew Lloyd Webber that it was suggested that I audition for the West End Show 'Starlight Express'. I had previously been in Jack Goods 'Catch my Soul' in the 1970's. That was ok but I get bored doing shows. I've never had any acting lessons and I find after a few months I'm ready to move on. Anyway the audition for Starlight Express involved Roller Skating. I lied and told them I could Roller Skate. Well I could Roller Skate but I couldn't 'Roller Skate' if you know what I mean. I had three weeks tuition with Sammy Samwell who was about 75 but he was a British Skating Champion. Anyway, I got the gig. More recently I done another show 'What's On This Island' which won an Olivier Award in 1994. But its not really for me, I'd much rather just sing a song.

J.H. What were your thoughts when you heard that Steve and Ronnie had died?

P.P.A. The thing with Steve and Ronnie is I just love them and as far as I am concerned they are very much alive and well and living in my heart. Its as if Steve's right here with me. I think about them all the time also Jimi Hendrix and Brian Jones. Brian was really kind to me when I first came to England. Brian was really cool he really understood that I was 6,000 miles from home and I didn't have many friends, I was homesick. Nobody talks much about Brian these days, a shame he was such a great musician.

J.H. Well thanks for your story, Pat. It's certainly a fascinating tale!

P.P.Arnold has got lots of new material in the can for a new album and hopefully a deal can be sorted shortly. There are also plans afoot for New Millenium records to possibly do a live P.P.Arnold album. More about this in a future issue.

P.P.Arnold still possesses THE best female soul voice around and I know there's still lots more to come from The First Lady.

P.P.ARNOLD-A GLITTERING STAR AND A ROCK AND ROLL SURVIVOR!

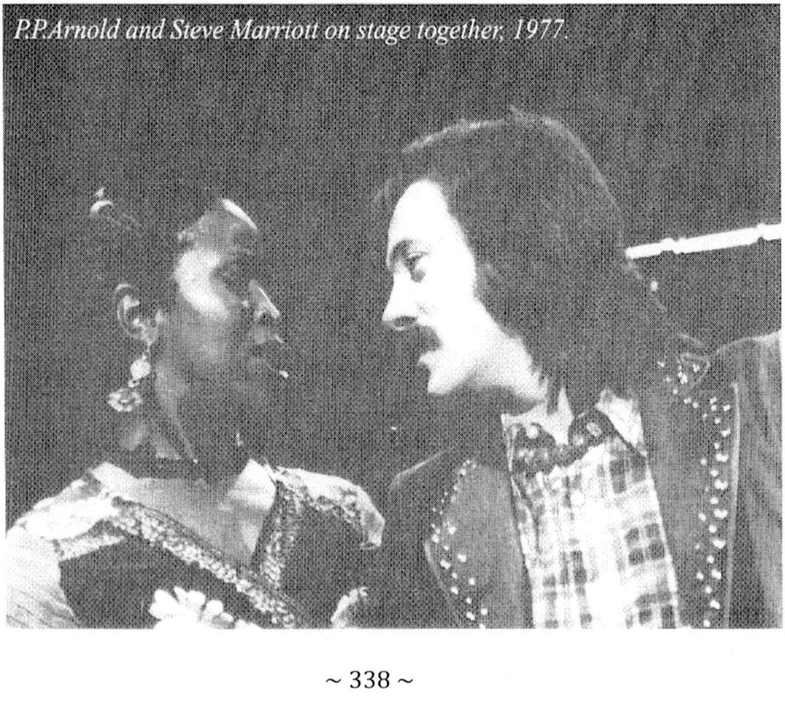
P.P.Arnold and Steve Marriott on stage together, 1977.

Small Faces

by John Hellier

Live '68

IT was during a cold November evening in 1968, that I took the short journey by train from my home in Romford to see The Small Faces at The Bubbles Club in Brentwood, Essex. The Bubbles Club was situated in a large, dingy, dimly lit, disused warehouse with incredibly basic facilities. There was a permanent, musty smell to the place and a general feeling of dampness. But, amidst all the gloom, I must say the acoustics were absolutely brilliant! I suppose some comparisons of this unlikely venue could be made with Liverpool's famous *Cavern*.

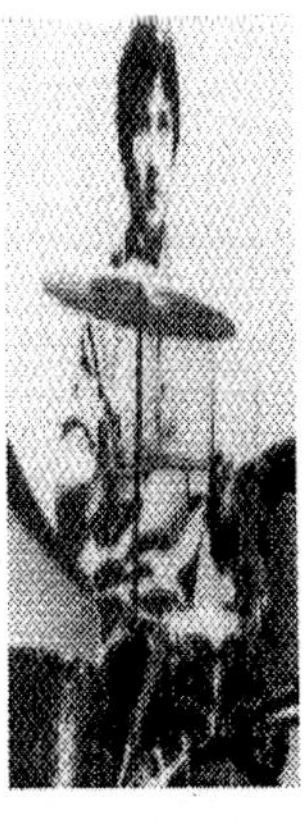

Anyway, I paid my 5/- (25p to younger readers) and entered the darkness. There was no stage lighting as such, in fact there was almost no stage! The bands were set up in a corner, on a platform no higher than 6" off the ground, with just a wooden barrier separating the fans from the group. But what incredible value for money (5 shillings!) Only a couple of weeks previous, I had been here to see The Who for the same price and, in the short time this venue was open, both Jimi Hendrix and The Move performed there.

As I went in and pushed my way down to the front, the support band were already playing and surprise! surprise! it turned out to be The Kult, a band I had previously played with myself. It was a heavy, progressive type of thing that the majority of the audience appeared bored with, and many of them soon began shouting and chanting for Steve and the lads. After what seemed eternity Kult finished and The Small Faces roadies immediately began setting up. We were kept waiting for 20 minutes or so before our favourites casually strolled out onto the boards, amidst a barrage of cheers.

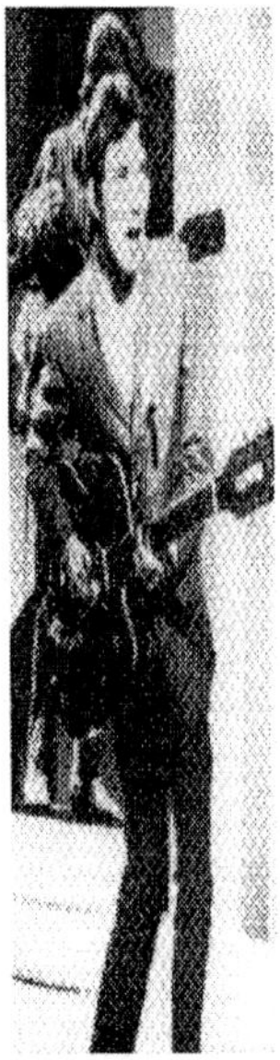

Steve, with cigarette in mouth, greeted us with the words, "fucking cold out there ennitt!" He must have meant it, as he was dressed in an ankle length overcoat which he kept on for the whole gig. Ronnie (or Plonk as he was known then) was attired in a floral waistcoat, green velvet trousers and a silk neck scarf. Kenny was looking very sober in a dark jacket and open neck shirt. They spent a few moments tuning up before crashing into some heavy rock 'n' roll. Unlike previous concert tours that I had seen, they didn't feature any of the hit singles and the only numbers I recognised at the time were *Rollin' Over* and *Wham Bam Thank You Man.*

It was real 100mph stuff; the fans were lapping it up, mesmerised by it all. Gone was the hysterical girlie audience of '66. This was late '68, *Ogdens* had been top of the album charts for some time and the fans were now a fairly even mix of male/female. Anyway, back at the gig, the biggest surprise of the evening was about to happen.

After having been on stage for 20 minutes or so, Steve told the audience that he wanted to bring on a friend and, to the surprise of most of the fans, on came 'The face of '68, himself', The Herd's Peter Frampton, dressed in a short black leather jacket and jeans. I wasn't totally surprised, as there had been much speculation in the music press about the possibility of Steve and Peter Frampton forming a 'Supergroup'. This only added fuel to the fire. Frampton took a back seat, but played some nice lead guitar and spent most of the evening on stage with The Small Faces.

I was particularly amused to see that he was wearing the same two tone shoes as myself, newly purchased from Ravel that day. Anyway, enough of that! The band spent 90 minutes or so on stage and encored twice. By the end of the set, the fans were at fever pitch, reluctant to let them go. But finally the band left the stage, as the lights went up.

As I left the building and made my way outside into the cold winter's night, my ears were still ringing (they were still ringing for a couple of days afterwards). It had been quite a night! I sat shivering on the platform waiting for the last train back to Romford, and pondered over what had certainly been the heaviest performance that I had witnessed from the lads. It was really quite similar to what Humble Pie would be doing 2 or 3 years later.

Although I didn't realise it at the time, this was to be the last time I would see The Small Faces together. Only a couple of months afterwards, following Steve's now famous New Year's Eve walkout, the band split. All the rumours in the music press regarding Steve and Peter Frampton proved to be true, with the formation of Humble Pie! ■

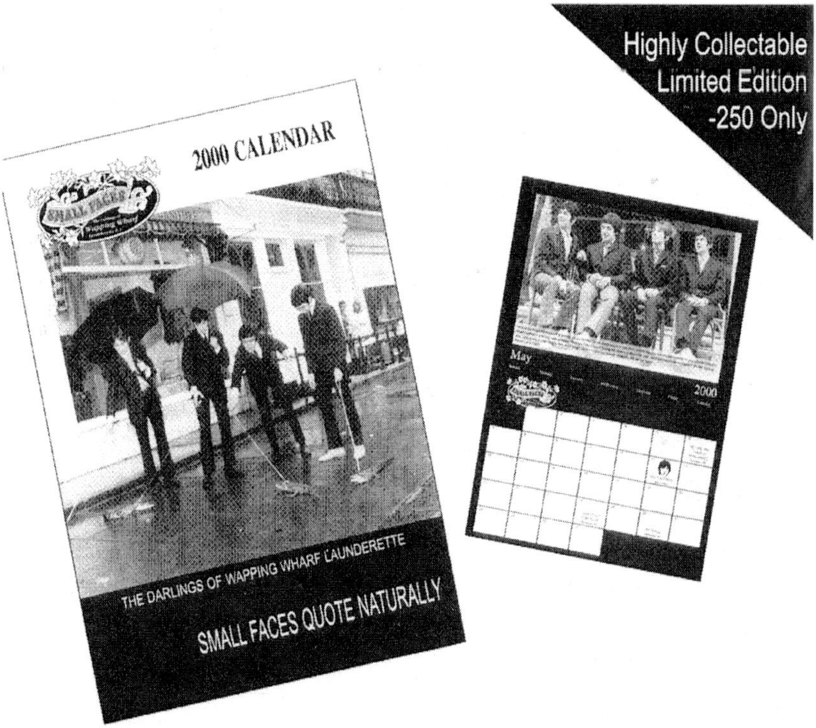

The Darlings Of Wapping Wharf Launderette

SMALL FACES QUOTE NATURALLY

2000 Calendar

Features 13 fab photos, essential dates and amusing quotes from the East Ends own fab four.

Reduced £6.00 including p&p

Available from: John Hellier, 7 Waterdene Mews, Canvey Island, Essex SS8 9YP

TRACK BY TRACK

Small Faces - The BBC Sessions

Strange Fruit CD SFRSCD087 Vinyl SFRSLP087

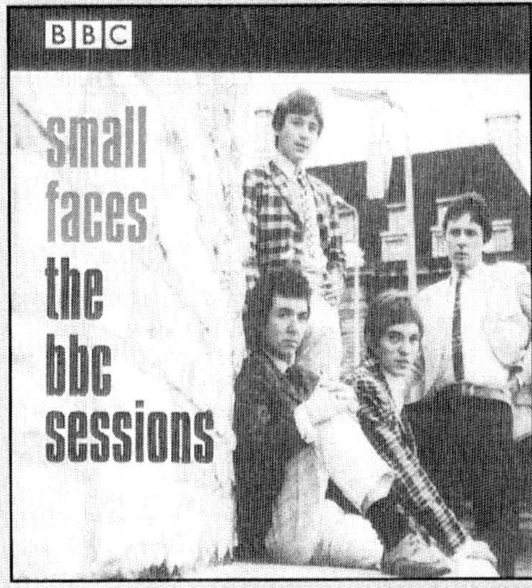

It was with great delight and some trepidation that I agreed to do this review. I mean the Small Faces at the BEEB! Something I'm sure many lifelong fans have wanted to have in their collection yet I must admit I was only 10 when the last of these tracks was recorded.

Wow, what an album; yes I know several of the tracks have been knocking around on various bootlegs but it is great to bring them all together with decent sleevenotes (courtesy of one John Hellier) and some excellent photos but more importantly: infinitely superior sound quality.

So what have we got? Well possibly the best "live" Small Faces album you could have. Pulled from five studio sessions done for the BBC from August 1965 to April 1968 with three tracks from each session, from the very early days through the whole range of mod-dom, flower power and on to the end, although there is a heavy leaning to the very first Decca album. What is missing here, thankfully, is the perhaps understandable over enthusiasm of their screaming female fans, which so marred the In Memoriam live side.

Whatcha Gonna Do About It

It's appropriate that this should be the opening track as this is where it all began. Their first release and their first hit, it made the Top Twenty in September 1965. The first of three tracks with Jimmy Winston on keyboards - pretty faithful rendition of the original although more guitar driven than organ. Incidentally, co written by Ian Samwell who was responsible for writing Cliff Richard's very first hit Move It, back in 1958.

Jump Back

First time I've heard this rare but albeit brief track, which features some excellent guitar playing from Steve. Harmonies are somewhat ragged but overall this number works well and is obviously an absolute must for completists. Not sure, but wasn't this written by Rufus Thomas?

Baby Don't You Do It

The last of the three tracks from the

April 1965 sessions, nice rhythm work from Messrs. Lane and Jones. Quite a dramatic little piece. Written by Brian Holland, Lamont Dozier and Eddie Holland who were responsible for some of Motown's greatest hits, this particular song made the US Top 30 for Marvin Gaye in 1964.

Shake

The first of three tracks from March 1966. Written by Sam Cooke, it was a hit for Otis Redding in 1967 the year in which he tragically died in a plane crash. Drums appear to be mixed somewhat low while the lead vocals are very upfront. Steve's vocal on this is much more raw than the studio version. Nice organ sound from Mac who features for the first time on this album.

Sha La La La Lee

Written by Kenny Lynch and Mort Shuman, this was the follow up to the overlooked second single (the Marriott/Lane penned I've Got Mine). Great intro, much heavier than the poppier single release, with its high pitched backing vocals (supposedly that of co-writer Lynch). Reputedly not one of the bands favourites although a great pop song, went on to make No.3 in February 1966.

You Need Loving

Closely resembles the Willie Dixon song You Need Love and precursor of the Led Zeppelin sound? Is considerably shorter than the studio cut although very similar. Great closing vocal from Steve: follow that, Mr. Plant.

Hey Girl

First of the tracks from the May 1966 sessions, an even livelier version of the high-energy pop song that became their fourth single release and the first Marriott/Lane song to chart, got to No 10 the same month.

E - D

(Occasionally known as Running Wild). I prefer this darker version to the studio cut. With its eerie backing vocals, great workout from the whole band. One of the albums highlights for me. (The B side of the doomed Decca release Patterns, that failed to chart).

One Night Stand

This is very similar, almost identical, to the original. Change in tempo from the previous numbers. Short and sweet and works well. I always did like this number.

You Better Believe It

From the August 1966 session. Another Kenny Lynch number, co-written with Jerry Ragovoy. Not the greatest mix on this track, which seems to have been cranked up to give a more live feel.

Understanding

The B side of All Or Nothing. This is a brilliant and more energetic version of a less well-known song that demonstrates the strength of each of the band members. Hard to believe it was only a B side and never made it on to an album at the time.

All Or Nothing

The Small Faces only No1! Possibly my all time favourite track, its hard to match up to the original, but this does come close with Marriott's vocals taking on a more melodic tone.

If I Were A Carpenter

From April 1968, the last of these sessions. Love this, had never previously heard a "clean" version of this before i.e. minus all the screaming of the In Memoriam/Autumn Stone release. Two great organs: Steve's lungs and Mac's Hammond driven by the pulsating rhythm of Ronnie and Kenney. Just when you think it's over it swirls back but all too briefly. Could listen to this over and over again. Written by the American singer/songwriter Tim Hardin who wrote a number of songs for Bobby Darin but is probably best remembered in this country for writing Reason To Believe, the first of Rod Stewart's hits back in 1971.

Lazy Sunday

Perfect "live" rendition of this classic track. Would be very difficult to ever top the original, but oddly the backing tracks and various accompaniments on this make it a fascinating addition. It almost begs the question; was this really live?

Every Little Bit Hurts

Passionate vocal performance from Steve and superb keyboard work from Mac topped up with great backing vocals from PP Arnold. Written by Ed Cobb, was a minor hit for the Spencer Davis Group in 1965. A great way to close the album, well musically at least!

Which brings me to my only gripe about this album, which is that the interview introductions should have been exactly that - possibly inserted as individual tracks before each of the relevant songs, but hey who's complaining.

Jump Back is the only track, that to my knowledge, was not previously available in any format. But this is more than just about unavailable tracks, it is an excellent "live" collection which will not only be an invaluable addition to any Small Faces fans collection but also as an excellent insight/overview to any new fans or anyone interested in British bands of the 60's.

Checking various sources it is apparent that this is by no means a complete BEEB collection. I am aware of at least two tracks You Really Got A Hold On Me and an instrumental version of Get Ready, which I believe originate from these sessions. I am sure others are aware of possibly even more from the many various BBC recording sessions. Anyone for Volume Two?

Brian Finlay.

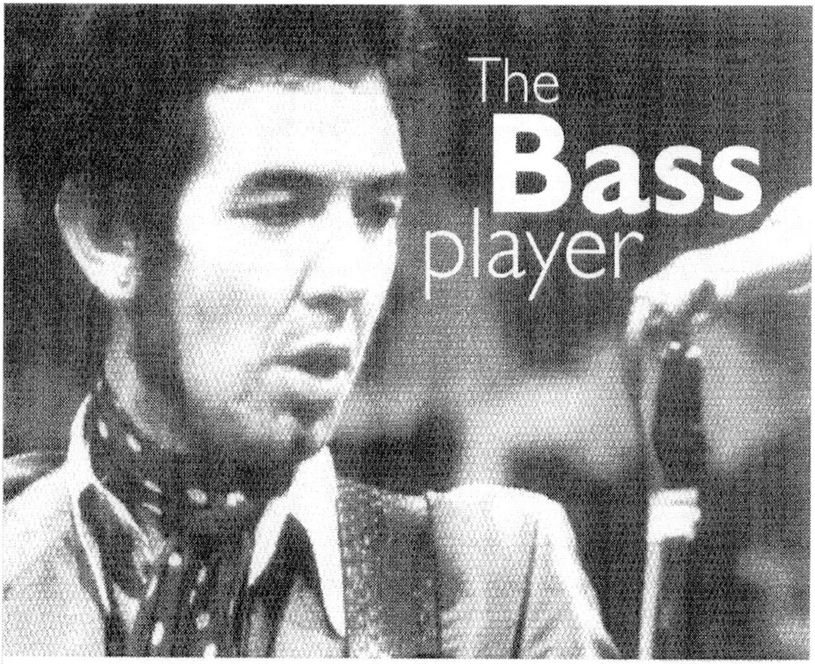

The Bass player

Ronnie Lane

Plonk's bouncing style of bass-playing was a driving force behind **The Small Faces'** sound. Taken from an article in the magazine 'The History of Rock' here is a tribute to his immense talent.

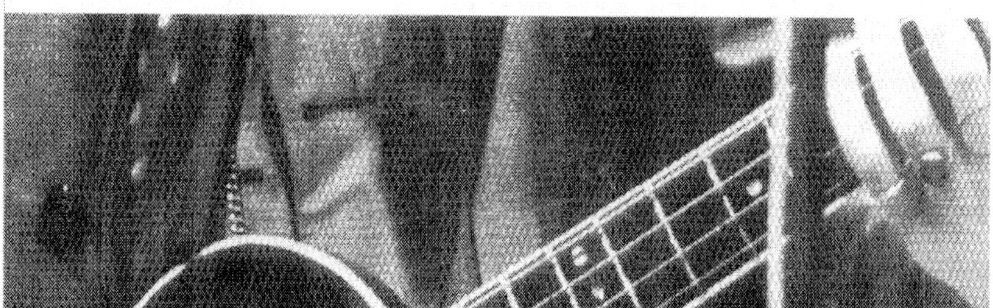

Ronnie Lane was a unique bass player; lacking the tall, lanky build of the Stanley Clarke/Jaco Pastorius stereotypes of today, Lane managed to cope with the bass-guitar by means of a melodic flair and a pulsating right-arm technique. A diminutive figure, Lane started out as a guitarist but soon moved over to the four-stringed instrument, reducing the extra span necessary by favouring medium or short-scale instruments, the best known of which is probably a single-cutaway Zemaitis model used in the latter days of the Faces.

He is one of the few players never to have been a regular user of any of the classic basses such as Rickenbackers or Fenders, although in the early days of the Small Faces he favoured a then-fashionable semi-acoustic instrument.

The Small Faces' first single, **Whatcha Gonna Do About It,** was an unspectacular, if competent, debut for Lane's playing; the song was a re-write of Solomon Burke's **Everybody Needs Somebody To Love** and the imaginative, bouncing style of bass-playing developing in the States seemed to have influenced Lane; his refusal to play the obvious bass line became more apparent with every Small Faces release.

A potentially tame song such as **Sha La La La Lee** was electrified by Steve Marriott's wailing, bluesy vocal with Lane's bass pumping away underneath. Some players plucked their strings, others twanged, but Ronnie Lane used to pump; he slung his bass low, necessitating a straighter right arm and therefore a more rhythmically attacking approach.

Lane's bass lines were surprisingly agile and he was quick to explore the higher frets. On **Itchycoo Park** the bass was almost a lead instrument on the verses, and on **Tin Soldier** and **Afterglow** the melodic and upfront bass virtually competed for attention with the lead vocal. The impact of the bass on these records was due not only to Lane's playing but also to his production; most of The Small Faces records were produced by Marriott and Lane and sound fuller and more solid than most other records of the time. Lane's role in the band was far more than just that of a bassist; he co-wrote most of their songs with Marriott and featured strongly as a harmony singer, taking the lead vocal on the 1968 hit **The Supernatural.**

One of the reasons that Ronnie Lane's playing was able to develop into a more melodic style with a less orthodox rhythmic approach was due to his partnership with Small Faces drummer Kenney Jones. Jones' playing was tight and fairly straight forward, allowing Lane room to elaborate; the drummer, nevertheless, had his own sound which, coupled with his distinctive use of cymbals, made him as much of an individual as Lane.

The combination of the two resulted in a tight, driving and instantly recognisable rhythm section. When Steve Marriott left to form Humble Pie in 1969, Lane, Jones and keyboardist Ian McLagan stayed together as the Faces, recruiting guitarist Ron Wood and singer Rod Stewart.

The Faces were the ultimate good-time bar-room band. Arguably, they were in their element in their early days, playing small venues, the pint-sized Lane grinning through his beard as he staggered between the gangly, hedgehog-haired figures of Stewart and Wood, his playing as solid as ever – despite the fact that the group claimed never to have walked onstage sober.

Lane and Jones made up for what they lacked in consistency of tempo with drive and momentum. Songs such as **Had Me A Real Good Time** remained loose from start to finish, without actually managing to miss a beat, while on Paul McCartney's **Maybe I'm Amazed,** Lane's playing was at its most expressive.

There are too many classic Faces tracks to highlight the best of Ronnie Lane's playing, although his fill on the opening passage of **Stay With Me** is probably one of the most copied tricks of all time. His approach to extreme tempos was as daring as his style on

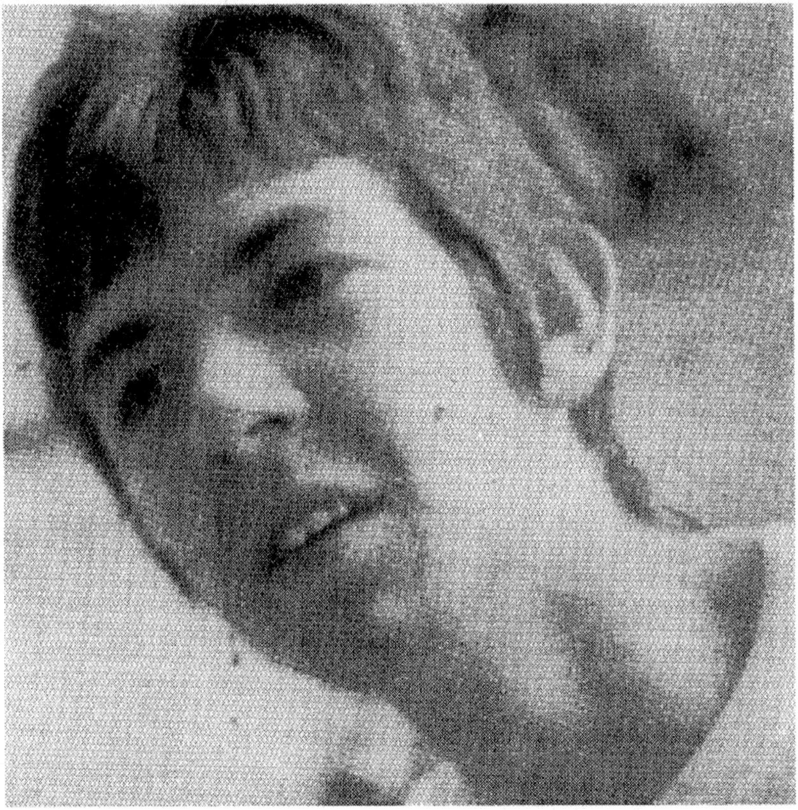

the customary swaggering rhythms that the Faces favoured: on slow numbers he had a tendency to leave huge gaps or to finish a melody line when Stewart ran out of words; on fast tempos, where Jones was at his best, Lane was more than able to cope. On **Bad'n'Ruin, Too Bad** and especially the fade out of **True Blue,** he contributed stuttering, off-beat lines that locked in with Jones to provide a smooth pulse-beat that carried the other instruments and vocals with it.

Boosted by hard work and Stewart's success as a solo artist, the Faces became a big-name act worldwide, enjoying increasing record sales and touring the states with a spectacular portable stage. After the release of their fourth album, 'Ooh La La' (1973), Lane decided he'd had enough and left the Faces to start up his own band, Slim Chance, which reflected a more pastoral, down-to-earth style. In his new role as lead singer/front man, he reverted to playing rhythm guitar.

Tragically, Lane's guitar-playing days are numbered by the onset of multiple sclerosis but hopefully, he will still be able to write and sing. He has already made a valuable contribution to the vocabulary of the bass guitar; there are few bassists around who can simultaneously inject a song with melodic twists and pumping momentum as ingeniously as Ronnie Lane. ■

Night Cargoes

LOST IN THE ARCHIVES, NIGHT CARGOES WAS AN ADVENTURE FILM STEVE APPEARED IN CIRCA 1962. **HUGH JAMES** ACTOR AND PLAYWRIGHT RELATES TO DAVE CLARK HIS EXPERIENCES ON THE SET WITH STEVE.

HUGH, TELL US ABOUT NIGHT CARGOES?
It was for Saturday morning pictures, you'd join the Granada Picture Club as a grenadier and there was two hours of cartoons, nature, personalities and finally the adventure story. Night Cargoes was a Serial of eight 1/4 hour episodes about piracy on the South Coast.

SO WHEN DID YOU DO THIS?
We filmed between April and June 1962 at Franchan Ponds, it was great cos there were several horses on the set and Steve and I would go riding in between shooting. It was pure guess work for me and Steve – one day we were tanking across the downs, I was on a Hunter and Steve was on this Pony going like the clappers. He had this riding style that I can only describe as a 'Sack of Potatoes' all his legs and arms going in different directions, the girth snapped, the saddle slowly slid round on the horses sweat and Steve was still riding until he fell off, laid down and burst out laughing.

IT REMINDED ME OF THE PRINCE AND PAUPER
Yeah, I was the little rich kid staying at the aunts while he was the cockney poor kid, there was some girl called Waveney Leigh who played along side us who was a pain in the arse. They put us up in some hotel and we were chaperoned by this woman who was built like Hattie Jacques, a formidable character.

PRESUMABLY YOU KNEW HIM AT ACTING SCHOOL?
Yes there were three or four of us around the same age, Colin Spaull the actor was one of them, who were at the Italia Conti School in Lendore Road, Clapham. Steve was never without his guitar, always working out riffs and trying out different styles. We'd knock about with a football at dinner time and hang around this Greek Cafe at Clapham North cos it was the only one with a Pin Table.

THIS MUST HAVE BEEN AROUND THE TIME OF THE FRANTICS?
Yes and the Moments, they didn't have proper Roadies in those days, Colin and I would help set up the gear and Colin would do the MC-ing. Steve played drums well and he'd show me a few things before the gig started. I've still got a pair of Drumsticks he gave me somewhere which I depped with in a band called Contagious Disease, we were awful.

WERE YOU A MOD?
By default I suppose really, when they were in the Small Faces Steve would take off his gig cloths which he'd wear just the once and leave them in a pile and he'd say have what you want, so Colin and I would go around in these mod clothes and Colin had a Yellow Triumph Herald Convertible with Vitesse double headlights which was pretty cool, it was great for the girls! It was also nice to knock around with another fellow shortie.

DO YOU REMEMBER THE GIGS?
The fights more like, we were from South London, Steve from the East End and the lads around Shepherds Bush would resent them for doing so well, many's the time we used to come out of a gig and there would be a punch up because you were on someone else's manor.

DID YOU KNOW THE FAMOUS PIMLICO HOUSE?
Yes I remember it was spartan, very much a boy's house, we used to leave at around 7 or 8 in the morning after playing Scalextric all night. It had four tracks and covered the whole floor with cushions around it and a biscuit tin in the middle with the drugs in, loads of Baked Beans, Heinz Spaghetti and beer for the pit-stops.

WAS IT A MAD HOUSE?
No it was a bolt hole from the madness of the riotous gigs, you could calm down even though the Scalextric was taken seriously.

HOW DO YOU REMEMBER HIM?
As easy, straightforward and a lot of fun. He found humour in all sorts of things and although he was never destined to be a good actor he was always a great guitarist.

THANKS FOR YOUR TIME, HUGH.

PAUL **WELLER**

Afterglow

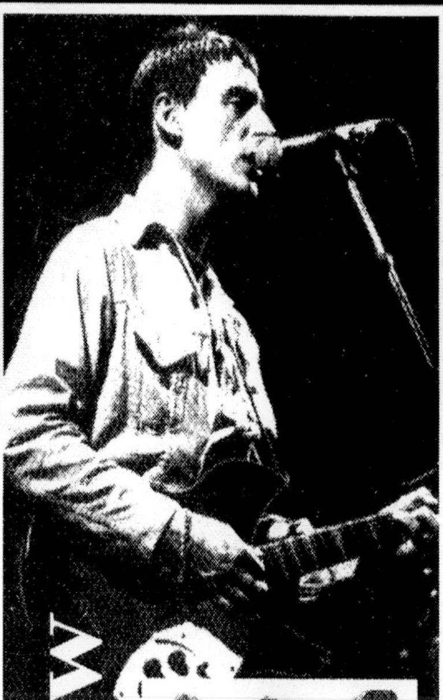

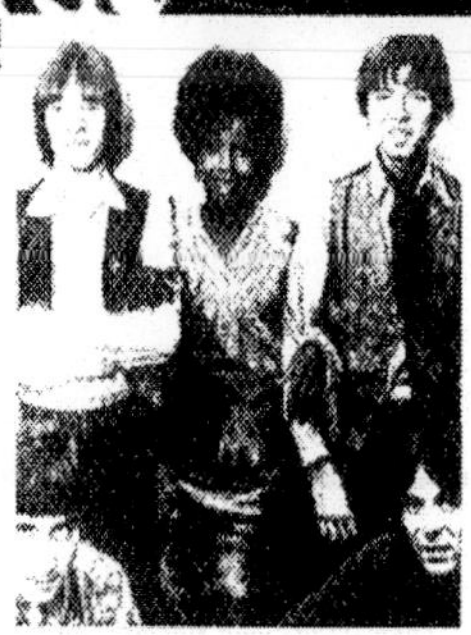

The Small Faces with P. P. Arnold.

Many thanks to 'Cool' fanzine for allowing us to reproduce the articles on pages 14/15.

One of my first musical memories was seeing The Small Faces on TV, probably on Top Of The Pops. It was them performing § with P. P. Arnold and possibly even live (or live vocals?). Although time (and nostalgia) can blur the truth and reality, as I remember it, P. P. was at the opposite end of the studio and facing Steve Marriott. Any way, even as a seven year old, I was pretty impressed, so much that even after about 25 years, the image is still with me.

I never met Steve. Though I had the chance to a couple of times, I was too overawed; too nervous. I'll always regret the fact that I didn't at least shake the man's hand or tell him how much his music meant to me.

And now he ain't around, at least physically, I regret it even more. But one of the great things about music is the legacy an artist leaves us, a musical legacy that can last forever.

I still get a rush from hearing Tin Soldier, Autumn Stone, Grow Your Own, I'm Only Dreaming or Afterglow. I could go on and I'm sure you all could too.

Stevie was an amazing vocalist, real grit, real blues and an extremely unsung hero on the guitar as well. I really do rate him right up there with Keith Richards and Pete T, as far as rhythm guitarists go, very under-rated.

Just before his death he'd cut six or so tracks with old Humble Pie man Peter Frampton, and whether good or bad, whether we love them or not, let's hope they see the light of day and add to the legacy... ■

HE'S THE KEEPER

Paul Weller recently wrote this song about Ronnie Lane. It's his own tribute to the great man himself. Paul has given Wapping Wharf very kind permission to reproduce the lyrics here below:-

He's the keeper
Of the lantern
Stone believer
It's a passion
And he knows it
He's the keeper
Hanging wishes
Up upon the stars
As he waits for love
As he waits for love

Flying without a hand
Trying to brave the hand
Something about the man
Is about to make a stand!
With nothing but liars and thieves
Trying to purchase thee
Where are you meant to go
But fly away
high away

He's the one knight
On a knackered stallion
His rusty armour
So undervalued
Does he know that,
He's a reason
He's asleep now
But never gone
He just waits for love
Yes he waits for love
He's the keeper

Hanging without a cloud
Hoping to draw a crowd
If he's willing to take a chance
Come on people make a stance!
From tiny acorn grow
All kinds of seekers
And where are they meant to go?
But fly away
High away

In the maelstrom of indecision
Shine! Believer!
Find the season
He helped to grow it
He's the keeper
Hanging wishes
Up upon our stars
As he waits for love
Yes he waits for love

He's the keeper
Of the lantern
He's the message
In the midnight
Of your madness
In the backlog
Of conversations
We never had
As we wait for love
Yes we wait for love

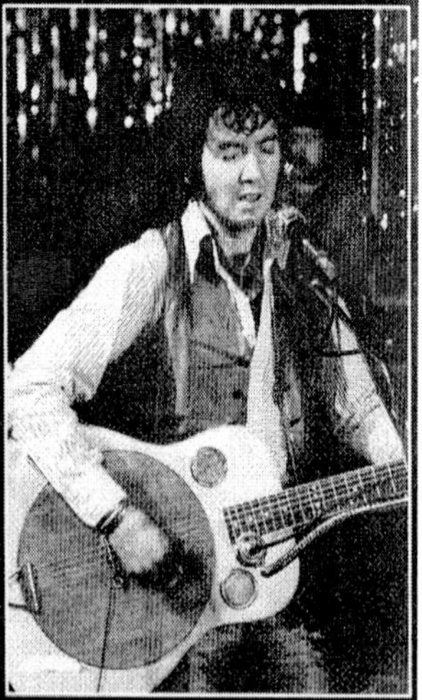

ERIC CLAPTON

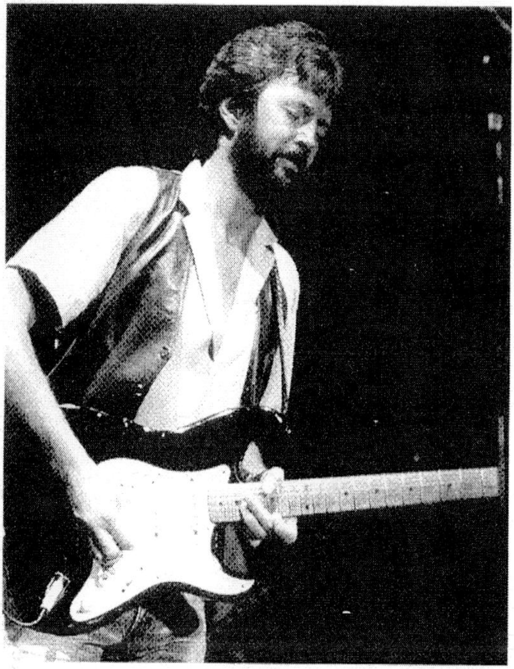

INTERVIEW

Eric Clapton speaks exclusively to John Hellier about his relationship with Ronnie Lane.

25th July 1997

J.H HOW DID YOU COME TO MEET RONNIE IN THE FIRST PLACE?

E.C. I first met Ronnie back in the 60's in Denmark Street I was up there looking for a guitar and the Small Faces were rehearsing downstairs in a little studio. We all went for a cup of tea, I think I was with Cream at the time. I used to see them around a few times, I went to see them play, we did a lot of gigs together. Was I with Cream, I can't really remember who I was actually with at the time, but it was in those late 60's days. Then I got to know him later through Woody, Ronnie Wood. I bumped into Laney at Woodys house then we just started to hang out a bit more. He came over to my place in the country in his gypsy caravan that he was towing around behind a bus. Then I went off with him to Wales, it was then that we really began associating a lot together. We used to play at The Miners and The Drum and Monkey. We also used to play down at my neck of the woods, we played The Cranleigh Village Hall quite a lot with a band that I had called "Eddie and the Earthquakes". It was just a little pub band. We even became blood brothers down at Fishpool with a kitchen knife!

WHAT DO YOU RECALL MOST ABOUT RONNIE'S PASSING SHOW? DID YOU ACTUALLY GO ON THE ROAD WITH THEM?

I didn't really get a chance. In order to do that I would have had to turn away from my own thing. We always understood that we would get together and then split up when serious business called. So I don't think I ever saw the Passing Show actually at work while he was touring with it.

DID YOU EVER RECORD ON RONNIE'S MOBILE STUDIO?

We did a lot of stuff, we did "Wonderful Tonight" on that and another song called "Next Time You See Her". I recorded the original demos on the mobile. Also "Annie" and all the things off of "Rough Mix". Yeah, all the demos were done there and then I took them to Olympic.

WHAT PART OF RONNIE'S OVERALL CAREER APPEALED TO YOU THE MOST?

The Passing Show. It was either that or what I saw with the original Small Faces when Steve was with them. To be honest I was never a fan of the Faces with Rod Stewart and all that. I thought Laney was the one who kept it all together, he was the heart of the band. In this day and age there seems to be so many nostalgic reunions and kind of retro stuff going on, but they've missed the point, a lot, with Laney. He deserves a lot more.

DID YOU KNOW OR PLAY WITH ANY OTHER MEMBERS OF THE SMALL FACES?

Yeah, with Kenny Jones and Ian. Kenny came out and done that tour when we were trying to raise money for ARMS. Kenny was the drummer on that tour and Ian I've played with on several occasions when I've been in the studio and there's been a jam going on. Nothing too serious. Really Ronnie was the one I was attracted to as a man. He was, the funniest, the most creative, he was the strongest personality of the lot. He used to drive the band from behind in a way.

DID YOU EVER GET TO KNOW STEVE MARRIOTT, AT ALL?

I never actually got to hang out with Steve. Never got to know him.

WHEN WAS THE LAST TIME YOU SAW RONNIE?

It was in America, a few years ago, while I was on tour. He came to see me in Dallas I think or it might have been Houston. He was pretty angry, I mean he was funny but he was fed up. He really wanted to see the show, but it was a very frustrating experience for him. I think it was the predicament of being backstage with all the normal things that he would have been very much a part of. He was in a lot of conflict, you know. He was very angry about his own condition and it was sad and very hard to be around him 'cause you could feel his pain. After that I didn't see or hear from him until I heard of his demise.

HOW WOULD YOU SUM UP RONNIE IN A FEW SENTENCES?

A burning star of the 60's. English Rock and Roll owes a lot to Ronnie because he really was one of the core people who took it very seriously. He wasn't in it for anything else other than the music.

WHAT ARE YOUR OWN PLANS FOR THE IMMEDIATE FUTURE?

I've been in the studio for almost a year trying to make a good record. I've never worked this hard in making a studio album before. I don't know why it suddenly became so important but I really want to make a good one, so I'm taking my time. We are going over to Japan just to try out a few of these new songs.

RONNIES BROTHER, STAN IS HOPING TO STAGE A TRIBUTE CONCERT FOR RONNIE IN LONDON NEXT YEAR. WOULD YOU BE INTERESTED IN PARTICIPATING?

I had my relationship with Ronnie and that I will treasure. It's a very sacred thing. Other than doing this I haven't felt obliged to do anything else. But, Yeah, I saw Stan in the park last Easter Sunday. Yeah, pass my number on to him and we'll talk about it.

WELL THANKS VERY MUCH FOR YOUR TIME, ERIC. I'LL SEND SOME COPIES OF THE MAGAZINE ON TO YOU.

OK Thank you John, Keep up the excellent work.

Part two of the Jimmy Winston interview has been held over and will appear in Wapping Wharf issue 12

Dear John,

Thanks for your letter, I really enjoyed reading Wapping Wharf #6 and hope you'll send me the newest issue when it comes out and the previous ones if you've got them. I'll enclose $20 to cover postage. Let me know if it's not enough.

By the way, you might let Stuart Wright know that the reason we never toured the States had nothing to do with either my hash bust or Steve's guitar playing. Don Arden, our manager, put forward a tour so implausible and gruelling that he knew we'd turn it down. You see, in the States he wouldn't have the tight grip over our money which he had in the UK. It was as simple as that. He came to us with that tour in 1966 and I wasn't busted until November 1967, when we were with Andrew Oldham who never even planned a tour of the USA for us, unfortunately. And Steve was a silly bastard to say anything against his own playing, he was fucking great!

Anyway I thought I'd clear up that little misconception and I'm looking forward to reading more from Stuart, give him my best when you speak to him.

If you want to know the truth, the whole truth and nothing but the absolute truth from the horse's mouth then you'll have to wait till I've finished my book. I've been at it since May and I'm maybe half way through it as I write. This is going to open a few wounds, make you grin and give an insight into the goings-on in front of the curtains, behind the scenes and in the bedrooms of the short and stylish!

All the best,

Ian McLagan

Ian McLagan is looking for a few good original photographs of the band for his soon to be finished book 'Autobiography of a Short-Arse'. Please write to: Ian McLagan, PO Box 739, Manor TX 78653-0739, USA.

County Borough of East Ham Education Committee

MONEGA JUNIOR MIXED SCHOOL

REPORT on Stephen Marriott. for School Year 1956/57

3rd Year — No. in Class 39

A B C D B Stream — Position 9th.

SUBJECT	Grade in Stream	REMARKS
ENGLISH Composition	C	During this school year,
Comprehension	B	Stephen's main aims ~~have~~
Reading	B	been to do as little work,
Spelling	B−	and be as great a nuisance,
Usage	B	as possible. He does not
ARITHMETIC	D+	seem happy unless he
HISTORY	B−	is the centre of attraction.
GEOGRAPHY	C−	He has achieved 9th
LOCAL STUDY	C−	position in class by not
NATURE	B−	even trying. If he applied
RELIGIOUS INSTRUCTION	C	himself to his work, he
WRITING	C−	could be at the top, or
PHYSICAL EDUCATION	C	perhaps in the A stream.
MUSIC	·	I hope that next year
ART	C−	he will reverse his
CRAFTS	C−	outlook, and make a big
	·	effort to improve his
		standard of work and also

SCHOOL CLUBS & OTHER INTERESTS	GENERAL REMARKS
Member of Boxing Club.	his behaviour.
	W. A Beech.

Trivia! Trivia!

DID YOU KNOW THAT..........Ozzy Osbourne has written a song called "See You On The Other Side" about two dead people, one of whom is Steve Marriott.

DID YOU KNOW THAT...........Glen Matlock claimed, when being interviewed on TV's Classic Albums series about the Sex Pistols "Never Mind The Bollocks", that he based the chords of their hit "Pretty Vacant" on the Small Faces song "Wham Bam Thank You Ma'am"

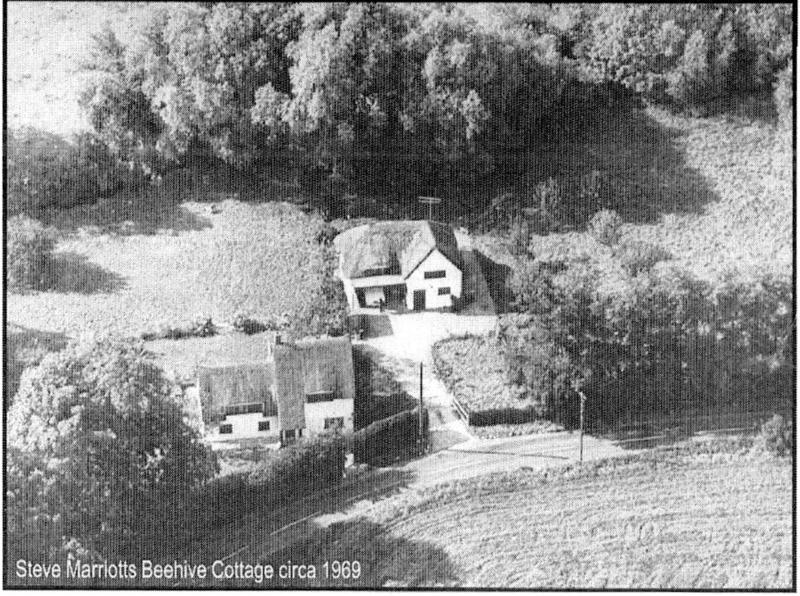

Steve Marriotts Beehive Cottage circa 1969

STANLEY UNWIN INTERVIEW

BY
JOHN HELLIER
(14th September 1998)

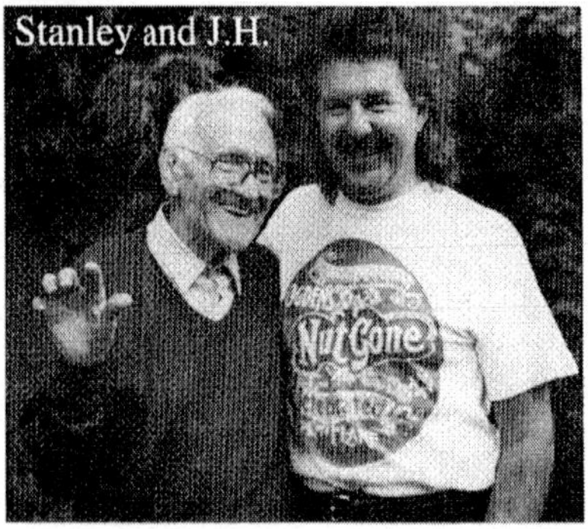

Stanley and J.H.

To his fans Stanley Unwin needs no introduction but for those unfortunates who have remained unaware of his unique humour and only know him for his work on Ogdens Nut Gone Flake here is a quick run down on the man himself.
He's 88 years old and his show business career spans six decades. He's a comic, film star, author and practically everything else you can think of. Very much an artists artist revered publicly by stars as diverse as John Lennon and Tommy Cooper.

STANLEY UNWIN, MASTER OF THE SPROKEN WORD!

J.H. How did the famous 'Unwinese' language come about?

S.U. You call it Unwinese, I'm glad you do, John. A BBC producer was at my house and he heard me telling the children some fairy stories in a different way. They weren't listening anyway,except the youngest one who said that's not quite right Dad, it's not Goldiloppers and it doesn't begin with once a polytyto. As I said the girls weren't really listening. This producer said to me after the girls had gone to bed, "I want to use that, its different, I like it". I said "No, I don't think we should use it as we are mucking about with the language and we'll get things thrown at us". "Oh no, you don't understand" he said and he was the first one to use it. He was a nice man, fresh out of a German prison camp, his name was Peter Caerns. There was another chap called Gerald Nethercott he was a BBC public relations official and it was he who said lets call it Unwinese, which I rather favoured better than Gobbledegook or Double Talk. By the way Freddie Starr and Jim Davidson do Unwinese as good as I, they're excellent. So that was the origin, John. Deep Joy!

J.H. How and by whom were you approached to do Ogdens?

S.U. I'd had a call via my agent and I considered it a compliment to be asked. My agent said that this group called The Small Faces are recording somewhere in London and if they gave you a straight script would you transfer it to Unwinese. I thought I'd give it a go and I drove down to Barnes in South West London. When I arrived I first met Ronnie Lane with their producer, a chap called Glyn Johns, and they gave me the script. I read it through once and I said what about giving me some phrases, they gave me 'where you at man' and 'stay cool' and things like that, so I popped those into the dialogue. It was about this rather mad character who lived in a cave and thought the moon was made of half a cheese or something. It was such fun to do but it was all over pretty quickly, you know, and then the album came out. I remember getting a lovely card from Ronnie Lane saying something like 'thanks for being such a groove, we're knocked out with it, hope you like it'. Yeah, that was the first pop group thing that I got involved with. Ronnie said that he had heard me saying the Sunnyglow and Purimost on a TV Advert for Gales Honey. He said that they had cottoned on to that. It was fairytale stuff and that's what they liked. Happy Days! and then out came the album with the tobacco tin motif.

J.H. What can you remember about doing the Colour Me Pop TV special with The Small Faces?

S.U. Yes, we went down to the BBC Studios in Lime Grove. You know what John, I was amazed at that video you gave me I was so pleased to get it 'cos here I have a visual record of the time I spent with The Small Faces. I can hardly recall doing the show really, I can't remember how I done the dialogue, I can't remember having an autocue, but when I saw the video I was tickled. My only positive memories are of doing the recording not the TV part. Whether they borrowed the cloak from the pantomime I had just done I don't know, but the crown I was wearing definitely came from that. That was made especially for me because the original crown was made of brass. It was heavy and hurt my head so the director of the panto said we'll make you another. It was very comfortable and it looked nice too, in fact this crown is still in my possession.

J.H. What was your relationship like with The Small Faces and which member were you the closest to?

S.U. It was a very warm relationship. Everyone was in tune with what was going on. There were lots of chuckling, laughter and replacing of words. There was a lot of ad-libbing going on, I couldn't understand all of what they were saying as they had their own sort of language themselves. You see I'm very interested in communication of all sorts, any languages. I can speak quite a bit of Russian but I can't do any Chinese. Chinese is a language of sound. If you rise up at the end of a sentence that means something positive and if you go down at the end of a sentence something not very happy is going on. Deep Folly!. Anyway, I suppose Steve was the one I was closest to. We didn't correspond or anything like that but I met up with him a couple of times. I remember we worked on a TV thing called "The Tube" together at Tyne Tees. It was there that I met Jools Holland he asked me to comment on all the equipment in my customary Unwinese. What a wonderful feed he was. I've always been interested in Jazz and the way they improvise. In fact, some Jazz musicians think that the way I talk is improvisation on language almost the same way as Jazz. Because they are conveying musical ideas in sounds it gives this little hep feeling. With language its quite a different feel but its still communication.

J.H. What did you think of the finished album?

S.U. Well, it was done in one quick take. The producer was quite superb John Glyns, I mean Glyn Johns. Deep Folly! Well, of course, I was chuckled. It was a new thing for a start, it flowed and was continual. It was a good story, a little weird story which one has to listen to again and again to get the best out of it. I still don't know whether it was worked out by any individual or whether it was all of them cooking up the story. Ronnie was the one who seemed to jump about a bit more than anyone else. It was an awful shock to hear of him going the way he did, Steve as well.

J.H. Have you kept in touch with any of the band members over the years?

S.U. Well, Kenney Jones sporadically. He's now running a Polo Club south of the Thames somewhere. We appeared together recently at Tyne Tees studios on The Doctor Rock Show. It was great to see him again and have a chin wag and he suddenly gave the interviewer a short burst of Unwinese. He's on the wave length! Yes, just Kenney. Steve and Ronnie are gone. It would be nice to meet up with Mac one day.

J.H. Ogdens is a legendary album in Rock circles. Are you aware of its importance?

S.U. Well as you know I'm getting old, 88 next year and there's a diminishing awareness of what's going on around you. But every now and then you get a feeling that something rather special has happened and I have that feeling with this album. Its 30 years old and still around. I only done a little bit on the record and was paid a set fee. I don't get royalties, only needle time on the air. That doesn't worry me unduly I am just happy to be associated with it. May the Small Faces be long remembered. Deep Joy!

J.H. Some of the band regret not having put the story of Happiness Stan on the stage. Apparently Pete Townshends 'Tommy' was influenced by it. What do you think of that?

S.U. It would have been fun, on stage with the cloak and crown eh! We could have added a few things to it and dramatised it a bit.

J.H. What have you been doing since Ogdens?

S.U. Lots and lots of things John, chat shows, radio and TV work, films, local charitable work and I used to do quite a bit of after dinner speaking, not so much these days as I find it very tiring. After doing 'Chitty Chitty Bang Bang' my agent introduced me to Gerry Anderson who said that he wanted to use me as a live parson, wearing a dogcollar, in with his puppets. I got very involved with that. There were 13 episodes and it was great fun to do. I met all the people who made the puppets and I remember driving a lovely old Model T Ford around London. The Model T only had brakes on the rear wheels and two gears. I was chased at one point and nearly turned the darn thing over! The Gerry Anderson people hold regular conventions and exhibitions, there's one on at the moment down in Eastbourne. They've got a puppet of me on the door. I did some dialogue to put into the puppets mouth welcoming people to the exhibition.
When I went into show business one of the first people I worked with and became close pals with was Ted Ray and I'll always remember one of Ted's lines about me, he used to tell people 'Don't give Stanley too much to drink or he'll start to talk straight".

OH DEEP JOY!

J.H. Well thanks Stanley, you're a true gentleman.

Last Chance To Dance

(The Small Faces on tour in Germany and Austria, January 1969)

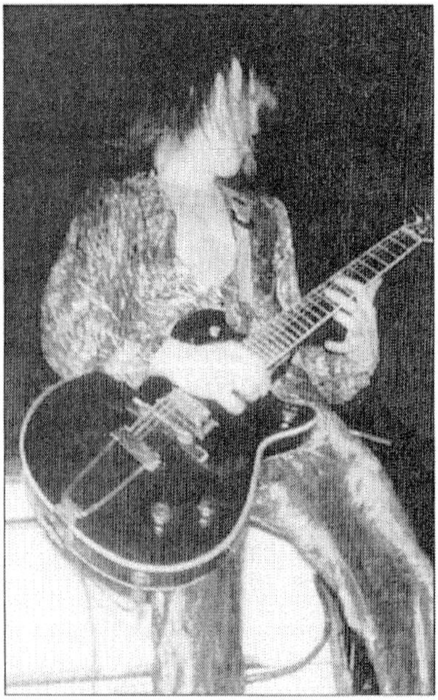

When Steve Marriott left his mates during the gig at the Alexandra Palace on the 31st December the Small Faces couldn't break up simply. Above all they were obliged to do a tour with concerts in Germany and Austria. 1968 had been the most successful year in Germany for the Small Faces. "Ogdens Nut Gone Flake" had reached number 6, staying 16 weeks in the album charts. So the German fans were eager so see and hear them playing their hits and songs from "Ogdens".

The contract was signed around October '68. The tour was presented by the legendary German magazine "Underground" who published a special (and now very rare) tour programme. The tour itself was realised by Konvera, a Munich-based agency in co-operation with the Arthur Howes Agency Ltd., London, and Eckart Rahn Productions, the German branch of Immediate Music. It was announced as "First German tour"! of the Small Faces.

The tour programme mentioned the provided songs: Here Come The Nice, Itchycoo Park, Tin Soldier, Lazy Sunday, The Universal, Wham Bam Thank You Mam, Talk To You, All Or Nothing, I Can't Make It, Song Of A Baker and Afterglow. It is proved that during the concerts they also played You Need Loving, Every Little Bit Hurts and Long Black Veil (from The Band). The Small Faces were supported by Status Quo and The World Of Oz. Status Quo made a good job but played very loud whereas World Of Oz didn't appear! So they had a substitute, the young Austro-Canadian folk & blues singer Jack Grunitzky (aka Jack Grunsky), in the mould of Dylan and Donovan.

The band flew out from London Airport to Munich where the tour started. Ian McLagan remembers: "That was the only time we made any money playing live and that was because I took over the finances. Everybody was ripping us off but once I took care of the cash we made some money. As for the tour, I don't remember it being strained or anything."

On Saturday 11th January the Small Faces played at the Munich "Kongress-Saal Museum", a dreaded hall because of its bad acoustics. In a concert review these problems are mentioned. The Small Faces played obviously as loud as Status Quo and harder and more variable than on their album 'Ogdens Nut Gone Flake'. They performed their clear

compositions with erotic and aggressive spontaneity. Especially Steve Marriott, totally direct and wild like a dervish, they were excellent musicians with a lot of feeling for spontaneous creation.
Next day (Sunday 12th January) they flew onto Vienna where the Small Faces performed at the old venue "Konzerthaus". Austria's biggest Small Faces fan Peter Grundei met the Small Faces there and he was very impressed. "And then, they came on stage. Young girls were screaming and they started to play, from 'Rollin' Over' till the encore it was a thrill. For the encore the audience streamed to the front of the stage and the light went down. I remember Steve playing "Every Little Bit Hurts" on the piano, "All Or Nothing", and an unbelievable "Tin Soldier". What more would you like!" (There's still a tape in circulation!)
Then the Small Faces flew to the north of Germany, to Hamburg, where they had time to get acquainted a bit with the legendary night life. On Tuesday, 14th January, they gigged at the "Musikhalle". Ian McLagan remembers: "The tour was fine, and as we knew it was our last go around we put everything in to the shows. We had eight (?) gigs in as many nights to play and after four (?) shows in a row we had a day off, after the first gig in Hamburg. I paid everyone their week's money in cash, put my little orange schoolbook away and with wads of German marks bulging in our pockets, we headed for the red-light district for a night of nis, nuf and reeb, or beer, fun and sin." If you want to know what really happened this night read Mac's autobiography (All The Rage, page 140-141).

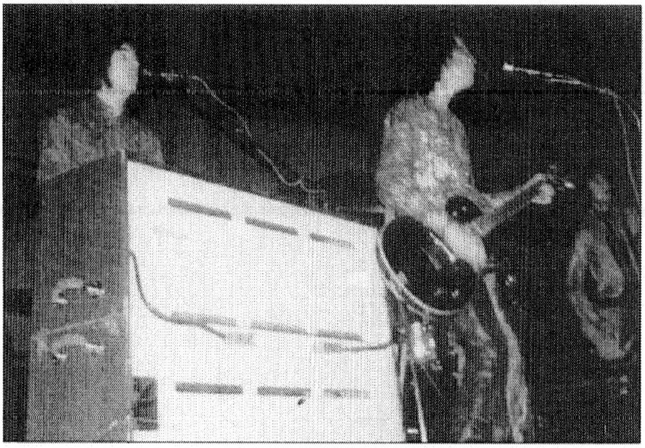

Next day they went to Hanover. Ulrich Poluschinsky, a fan who saw this show (on 16th January at the „Niedersachsenhalle"), wrote a short commentary for the mag Bravo (title: "Roughnecks with good manners") and told that the Small Faces offered him a glass of whisky! He was allowed to take some pictures of them. Ulrich mentioned about rumours that Steve wanted to leave the band. The picture shows Mac (with moustache!) and Steve playing on his harp on their way to the stage.
The tour ended the 17th January in Berlin at the "Deutschlandhalle". All in all it must have been a pleasant trip. On the 18th January the four returned to London.
Six weeks later the German press published, what the UK already knew, that the Small Faces would disband.

Roland Schmitt

IN WITH THE TIN CROWD

The story behind that famous round sleeve

The circular gatefold tobacco tin inspired artwork for the Small Faces 1968 swansong album is one of the finest and most elaborate sleeve designs in rock history. The idea stemmed from one Mr W.W. Townsley.

Tony Calder, Andrew Loog-Oldham's right hand man at Immediate, takes up the story.

"I was working with Townsley at Decca. He wanted to try out a round sleeve. We were against it, it'll roll off the shelves we said. When I mentioned it to Ronnie Lane years later, he jumped at the chance. Ronnie was also the main spur behind the tobacco tin concept. Ronnie suggested the notion to Andrew, Andrew phoned up Liverpool based manufacturers Ogdens' and they were most obliging. They sent over a big old-fashioned book of labels for their smokes. The band pored over them and Steve picked out the design for the brand Ogdens' Nut Brown Flake, immediately changing the word brown' to gone."

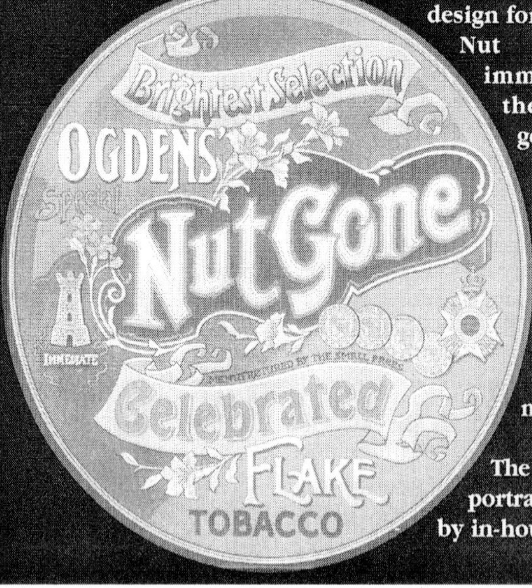

"It was a little joke," laughs Kenney Jones, "We called it Nut Gone because your nut's gone if you smoke the stuff - you know marijuana."

The inner sleeve featured portraits of the band taken by in-house photographer at

Immediate, Gered Mankowitz. Theatre designer Sean Kenney created the actual mechanics of the sleeve, he explains "I took the photos, deciding to reflect the guys characters, Mac was shot in my studio in Mason's Yard, Piccadilly. In the background you can see Steve in his cap, smoking a cigarette and holding a scrubbing brush. Ronnie is playing Ian's banjo and Kenney's holding a glass. The Steve and Ronnie portraits were taken in Steve's Chiswick flat, I'm not sure where we took Kenney."

For Andrew Loog-Oldham, however, the eye-catching packaging wasn't enough. He launched a controversial ad campaign based around the Lords Prayer. "Britain was still a religious nation," remembers Kenney. "John Lennon had angered everybody by saying The Beatles were bigger than God and now the Small Faces were being sacrilegious too. The ad really did cause a hoo-ha."

This time the blame fell with Beach Boy Brian Wilson. "Andrew was on the phone to Brian," explains Calder. "Brian told him he wanted people to pray to his music. This got Andrew thinking. He was already wearing a Jesus robe and wanted to turn the office into the shape of a cross with two fountains of red water either side of his desk. We had complaints from various churches but nothing too devastating".

CIRCULAR DESIGN AND COINS

Because of their shape, the records would literally roll off the shelves. There was one advantage to this. "Fans would buy multiple copies," laughs Kenney. "They had to replace their broken ones." In the end the circular cover was housed in a plastic sleeve to secure its place on the shelf. The four coins reveal each band member's name. Steve Marriott is The Phantom Street Whistler, Kenney Jones - George The Cleaner XV111, Ian McLagan - Maximillion III, and Ronnie Lane is Leafy Lane.

ILLUSTRATION AND CIGARETTE PAPERS

According to Tony Calder, Ian McLagan commissioned his former art school chums, Pete Brown and Nick Tweddell to illustrate the inner sleeve with the simple brief, "to represent the psychedelic times we live in". They chose to draw this elf smoking a pipe. Gered Mankowitz took the shot of the open tobacco tin revealing the cigarette papers inside. Kenney Jones explains, "It was Steve's idea. That's because the whole box is 'sussed' - suspect. The suggestion, if you read between the lines, is to get yourself a little bit of Ogdens' Nut Gone Flake, roll a joint, put the LP on, listen and get involved with it".

KENNEY JONES INTERVIEW

By
John Hellier (11th December 2001)

How much rehearsal time was allocated to the band before they started playing live?

Can't remember that far back. I remember us kinda rehearsing at the Ruskin Arms. Rather than call it rehearsing we were actually just discovering ourselves. We just loved each other and were excited about playing together. It was quite electric really we didn't need a lot of rehearsing we had this telepathic thing. We just knew what each other were going to do. Strange eh! Even when we started recording I don't ever remember actually learning the songs. Steve and Ronnie would come up with a chord sequence and away we'd go. It was never a jam session though, all the songs were arranged it was so incredibly easy.

Do you remember if there were any songs in the set that were never recorded by the band?

I remember Jump Back and Oo Poo Pah Do. But we were only doing 20 minute sets back then not like later on. We played a lot of our own favourite songs in the studio when we were just jamming.

Do you remember the very first paid gig?

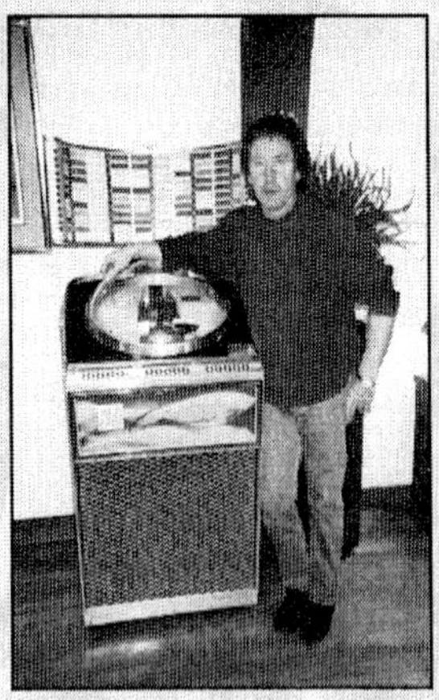

Before the Cavern in Leicester Square I remember a little youth club in Forest Gate, I think it was Saint Katherines. It was right near where Ronnie was living at the time on the Romford Road.

After the first hit you became tagged with a teeny bop image. What did you make of that after all you started out as a raucous R & B band?

Well we had no control over it, because we were all the same size and dressed as Mods it just took off. The mod thing wasn't a gimmick it was us. At first we thought it was a bit of all right but after a while all the screaming girls got us down, we couldn't hear ourselves play on stage. A lot of that got in the way, it was very annoying. We were plagued right from the beginning with managerial problems. We had our own ideas of what we wanted to do but we were pointed in the direction of commerciality. Because we were always doing TV shows we just dug ourselves in deeper and deeper. When we joined Immediate we took on a different direction, we had matured by then. The sound got tighter and for me personally I was really enjoying it and my drumming became very distinctive. The early Decca stuff was just wild but by the Immediate days I had been doing sessions and stuff and I discovered the real me. I just adored the Tin Soldier, Green Circles era. I am just re-discovering it now I'm back to playing a four drum kit just as I did then. It was my eldest son who remarked that the double bass drum set-up that I played later on with the Who was now old hat. Even when I played Zak's kit at the Steve Marriott Memorial gig I disposed with one of his tom toms and lowered the cymbal. I do play a lot, lot better with less.

What are your feelings in retrospect of Don Arden and Andrew Oldham. What positive things did they do for the band?

Well Don Arden I always thought was a necessary evil. His side kick Pat Meehan came to see us at the Cavern Club in the West End and told us he thought we had something special and invited us to Don Arden's office in Carnaby Street the next day. When we met Don Arden we were impressed, he managed the Animals and the Nashville Teens and he was like a big teddy bear really, a father figure I suppose. He told us he'd put us on a percentage and a wage. He was very enthusiastic and made us feel real good about ourselves. It was Don who was responsible for Jimmy Winston's departure. Jimmy was always trying to overshadow Steve on live gigs. While Steve was doing his bit Jimmy would be in the background waving his hands and whatever and because he was that much taller and that much older he stuck out like a sore thumb. After Jimmy had departed it left a big gap, we desperately needed a good keyboard player and that was where Mac comes in. The first rehearsal with Mac was like heaven. From a drumming point of view it was magic we were sounding just like Booker T & The M G's! The fact that he was the same size as us was just a coincidence. In some ways it would have been better if we had all been different sizes. Mac was superb, we used to call him posh because he was from Hounslow not the East End. With Andrew Oldham we got lots of studio time. I remember Immediate would pay 50% and we would pay 50%. With freedom in the studio we were allowed to relax and experiment. The Small Faces were never afraid to experiment.

Which moments with The Small Faces bring the biggest smile to your face. Anything in particular?

Dunno really! Just being with them, Westmoreland Terrace and all that. Very brotherly relationship. We were just a bunch of piss takers really but we all helped one another.

Why didn't the Small Faces tour the USA on the strength of the hit single Itchycoo Park?

Ask Mac! Mac had a previous drug offence and therefore we couldn't get a permit. It did slow us down in a sense. The Small Faces did actually go to America, we didn't perform but we landed on US soil on the way back from Australia. We got fogged in and had to land in Honolulu and then got diverted to San Francisco. It was still foggy and we ended up staying the night in a hotel. No immigration, no passport control, no customs……nothing. They put us on a bus and we went to a Holiday Inn between the airport and city centre. My first impressions of America were when I turned on a TV in my room and they were showing that now famous clip of a Vietnamese Soldier being shot in the head, blood everywhere. Got back on the plane and came home. I arrived home from that Australian trip with Australian crabs they were upside down ones anyway!

In retrospect do you think the band could have gone on a bit longer and if so what direction do you think it would have taken?

I wish we had been a little bit more grown up at the time. If we had have played Ogdens' live it would have boosted our confidence so much. We were labelled as a pop band, which definitely got up Steve's nose more than we realised. I wish we had been more like The Who in the fact that when they have problems they stick together until they've overcome them. Steve just thought well how do we top Ogdens' and he was off. Ogdens' was a masterpiece if we had played it live we would have gone to even greater things. I reckon we were on the verge of crossing the great divide and becoming a heavier band.

What are your favourite Small Faces singles and albums?

I really like the second single "I Got Mine", very Who like although that was not intended. We wrote this single ourselves and it bombed. I remember Don Arden telling us he was getting in Kenny Lynch and Mort Schuman to write the next single as he couldn't afford another flop. I remember we recorded the follow up "Sha La La La Lee" at Decca in West Hampstead. I also remember Kenny Lynch saying to me "Never play anything you can't mime to!" I felt sick when he said that. After that single we started writing our own stuff again and thank God it was successful. Another single I loved was "If You Think Your Groovy" that was us, with PP. Favourite album well, that's got to be Ogdens'.

Next The Faces. The ultimate kicking band. Mac was once quoted as saying that the Small Faces were simply the apprenticeship and that the Faces were the real thing. Do you also think along those lines?

Not at all. Mac would do because he wasn't a founder member. The best band and most creative one was the Small Faces. I still listen to the Small Faces to this day and it always brings a smile to my face and now I've become a Small Faces fan. I look at it from the outside looking in. The Faces were fun, a party band. We all loved it but it wasn't creative. There were no really great songs. We could have done a lot more if had pulled together more as songwriters.

Towards the end the band were being billed as Rod Stewart and The Faces did this anger yourself and the other guys?

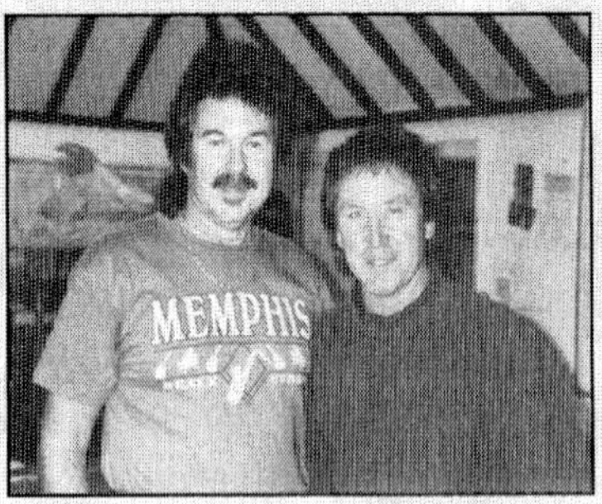

To be honest it did get up everyone's nose. It was Billy Gaffs (our manager) idea with Rod's support. It was within Rod's power to curb it a lot more, but he didn't. What we were doing effectively was going around plugging Rod's solo records so we became almost a backing band. All the best songs were saved for Rod's solo albums so the Faces suffered in that respect. If the band including Rod had pulled together we could have come up with some fantastic stuff.

What is your favourite Faces album and why?

I like "First Step". The album features a definite link between The Small Faces and the Faces. I wouldn't say it was necessarily my favourite--- in fact I haven't really got a favourite Faces album. They're all very much in the same mould.

What are your thoughts on the Small Faces reformation in the late 70's?

It was great when Ronnie was there. I regret it to this day, if Ronnie had stayed it would have been okay to a degree. If only Ronnie and Steve hadn't argued so much. Marriott had become super cocky, he'd always been cocky but he was piss taking all the time and going through a spitting stage. I think he was a bit insecure at the time, don't know why maybe it was because his hair was falling out, yeah let's put it down to that.

How did you come to join the Who and how did you feel about replacing possibly the most flamboyant drummer in Rock & Roll, Keith Moon?

Keith Moon was irreplaceable. I went into the Who with that in mind. I had been doing a lot of session work and then I got a call from Bill Curbishly, the Who manager, he told me that following Keith's death the band was going to pack it in but they had had a change of heart and wanted to continue and wanted me to join the band and nobody else would be considered. At the time I had put a new band together which was very much in the Eagles mould and I was very happy with it. But anyway I decided to go the office to meet Pete Townshend. We had a drink and a good old laugh and Pete told me that the band wanted to try new things and he also told me that he felt Moonie had been holding them back. Although everyone was devastated at Keith's demise they now had the chance to do something different. My ears pricked up. They said that The Who and Small Faces had been through a lot together and I'd done a lot of work with Pete anyway. They put it in such a way that I really couldn't say no. I then learnt their repertoire which was much more complex than I had first thought. This gave me even more admiration for Keith Moon. I wasn't gonna change my style for anyone and when I did join the band the whole sound got tightened up. Perhaps a little bit too tight! As I got to know the numbers I feel that I did loosen up a bit.

How many world tours did you do with The Who and how many albums?

Loads. Working with the Who was the hardest I had ever worked drummer wise. Some of the concerts would go on for three hours. I became super fit and I loved it. I certainly loved working with John and Pete. I don't think the band fully understood how I was dropped in at the deep end. They should have come to my aid a bit more. No one could replace Moony there is no better drummer, not even Zak whom I taught how to play. With Zak, Moony was his mentor and he plays pretty much exactly the same, which is not particularly what Pete wanted. I have no regrets what so ever about playing with the Who, they were great years.

Was your departure from the Who down to personal or musical differences or a combination of both?

I don't think Daltrey ever got used to the new Who. I always had a problem with Daltrey. I think Daltrey missed Keith a lot more than John and Pete. Daltry became intolerable and eventually the band split in 1982 although we got back together for Live Aid a few years afterwards.

What have you been doing since then? And can you tell me about your current activities?

After Live Aid I got together with Paul Rodgers, which was just the two of us. The idea was to bring in different musicians at different times. We were called The Law and we made two very good albums but then we decided to knock it on the head because Paul didn't want to tour. That ended in 1992.

Then my Polo Club got bigger and because it is in my back garden I tended to play more and more. My sons were also playing, one of them has been playing since he was three. Any little bit of spare time I had I would jump on a horse and play polo. The club developed itself really, its now THE premier polo club in the country. We hold various charity games here and one thing and another. It's a polo and country club with a licensed restaurant that is open to the public.

With regards to the Ogdens' animation project. I have been working with a couple of guys from Liverpool. They are about the same age as me and massive fans of the Small Faces. At first I was totally against computer animation but I realise now I've got to tow the line and that's how it has to be. We are still working on a story line and how it develops all depends on who we use to be in the film. Pete Townshends' on standby to write a couple of songs for it. We're currently looking at the Small Faces back catalogue and may well use some of those songs in the story if we feel that they fit. Completion of the project is still eighteen months to two years away but it will definitely happen.

Nice records was originally set up as a charitable fund for Ronnie in 1995 and The Small Faces tribute album achieved success in that direction. I thought, back then, I can't stop at that and now is the time to re-establish the label and it will be styled along the lines of Immediate. Immediate was a very good label apart from the fact that they didn't pay you. I'm doing a charity record at the moment called "It's All About The Children" I'm doing this with my new band and it will feature on Nice Records.

I am very passionate about my own Small Faces charity. It's Small Faces for Small Faces, a children's charity. I am not interested in particular charities for particular illnesses. All a child knows is I'm not well can you help me? It's for mental, physical, underprivileged...just about anybody who needs help whatever. It's an all children's charity we'll give to any needy child. The new charity record features not only my new band but also Paul Young and Ronnie Wood.

The new band consists of Gary Grainger, Boz and Robert Hart. Robert was the vocalist who took over from Paul Rodgers in Bad Company. This guy can really sing, why the world has never heard of him I really don't know. We used the charity single as a means to start working a lot more together so it's effectively my new band. We'll being doing gigs, albums, the lot. The only thing we haven't got is a name. Maybe Wapping Wharf readers can come up with something.

THANKS KENNEY FOR YOUR TIME AND GOOD LUCK WITH BOTH THE CHARITY AND THE NEW BAND.

THE **JOHNNY HALLYDAY** SESSIONS

IF YOU WERE READING the December '94 edition of *Record Collector*, you probably caught the article on rock band Foreigner titled *The Secret History Of......* This mentioned an album which Foreigner's Mick Jones produced called 'Johnny Hallyday' by the French rock star Johnny Hallyday in 1969 which featured several Steve Marriott/Ronnie Lane compositions. After a bit of painstaking research we found that The Small Faces had actually backed Hallyday on every track! So read on for 'The Secret History of the Johnny Hallyday Album'.

Steve Marriott had already decided to quit The Small Faces on New Year's Eve 1968, when he threw down his guitar in frustration at a gig at the Alexandra Palace. But the band still had contracts to fulfil and gigs were booked for the first couple of months of 1969.

The band had also promised to play on Hallyday's new album. Hallyday was no stranger to The Small Faces, for he had covered **My Way of Giving** back in 1967 for one of many hits in his native France. After a gig in Jersey The Small Faces, along with Peter Frampton, (who had been playing with the group and who Marriott had wanted in The Faces, but the others vetoed it) set off for Paris to lay down backing tracks. On hearing the album **Quiet Melon**, which has a very late sixties 'progressive' feel, the music stands as a missing link between the later period Small Faces and the very early Humble Pie. Similarly it was the transitional bridge between the Marriott-less Small Faces and The Faces and Rod with Woody.

The opening track **Rivière....Ouvre Ton Lit** was a Mick Jones/Tommy Brown composition which lifted the album off in heavy fashion. However you get the feeling that Marriott and Lane had a say in the writing of the song, as it ends with exactly the same riff which repeats itself towards the fade of The Small Faces instrumental **Collibosher.**

Track two **Voyage Au Pays Des Vivants** is another Jones-Brown number which leads us to Marriott & Lane's **Amen**. This is basically a French language re-write of **That Man**, (courtesy of G.Thibault) although the record sleeve gives the English title as **Bang Bang** which was either a mistake of Steve's or Ronnie may have provided new lyrics.

Track four, **Viens** (Jones-Brown) is followed by probably the most interesting track, for Small Faces fans at least, called **Reclamation**, or **News Report**, to give it its full English Title. The song is a Steve Marriott number written especially for the Hallyday sessions and sounds very much like an early Humble Pie out-take! **Reclamation** is followed by **Regarde Pour Mou,** which roughly translated is **What You Will** which turned up on Humble Pie's first album a few months later.

It would be interesting to know if The Small Faces had actually recorded **What You Will** in demo form for Hallyday. It's pretty fair to say that Humble Pie's first album is not far off how The Small Faces might have sounded had they not broken up. The remaining tracks are **Je Te Veux, Je n'ai Besoin de Personne, Je Suis Né Dans La Rue,** (all by Jones-Brown) and **Les Anges De La Nuit** (by Hallyday-Revaux).

Probably all the parties involved were under contract and the best way to avoid legal complications was to keep it quiet! And in the mists of time, amongst all the upheavals that were to follow, the whole affair simply became a lost memory.

The album, released in April 1969, stands as the last thing The Small Faces recorded together as a band. If you think that it'll cost a fortune to obtain such a rarity, then you're sadly, or 'gladly', mistaken.

The original album (Phillips 844 971) would set you back a mere £10, if you can track it down. Failing that, try tracking down a C.D. called 'Inedits' which came out in 1993 (Phillips 512 501) which I've been told contains all the tracks mentioned above. It's also priced at £10. Happy Hunting!

Wapping Wharf would like to thank good ol' John Jordan over the pond in Sunny Florida (lucky bleeder) for his invaluable information. *Cheers Mate!* ■

P.S. The Album is available again on an import CD.

DENNIS GREAVES INTERVIEW

BY

John Hellier

(11th September 1999)

Dennis Greaves, lead vocalist/lead guitarist with R & B favourites Nine Below Zero (once described as The Jam play Muddy Waters!!), speaks here for the first time about his love and admiration of the Small Faces,

J.H. When did you first become aware of the Small Faces?

D.G. Well it was my dad really. My dad loved Steves voice. Apart from The Beatles he only liked two singers from the 1960's and they were Andy Fairweather-Lowe and Steve. I remember buying My Generation and he didn't like that but when, at the age of 10, I bought Itchycoo Park he remarked that he dug the voice. Normally when I bought singles I thought I won't share that with him because he won't understand it but with the Small Faces it was different. Yeah, Itchycoo Park was my first Small Faces record, I've still got the original Immediate single. After that I bought Lazy Sunday. Another amazing single, I never thought anybody could sing with a cockney accent and still manage to sound extremely COOL!

J.H. Did they have any influence on your own career?

D.G. Oh yeah, definitely. When I was young I always liked things that were blues orientated. I loved the Stones, the Who and the Small Faces. I now love all the same people that Steve Marriott was himself listening to as he was growing up. When Steve put his later bands together in the 1980's all he ever did was the Blues. He may have stuck a couple of Small Faces numbers in the set but he himself had gone right back to his roots. His roots were the major thing that connected me with him. The image, of course, was absolutely perfect. After that I started to dig out some of my Dads 60's clothes, that's how I got into the mod scene. When the punk thing started I didn't like that. I suppose Nine Below Zero got in on back of the mod revival thing. When I look back now at some of the New Romantic fashions of the early 80's they look so fucking dated. If you look at a picture of Nine Below Zero taken at that same time it'll look as though it was only taken last week. I used to go to Max Cohen the tailor in the East End. He would have all these books with original 60's cuts in them. I had a two tone tonic suit made there for my wedding in 1979. Yeah, I loved the whole mod thing also the suedehead image from the late 1960's. I loved the 60's clobber and of course The Small Faces were perfect for that. I didn't study it as much as Paul Weller would probably study it but yeah I loved it.

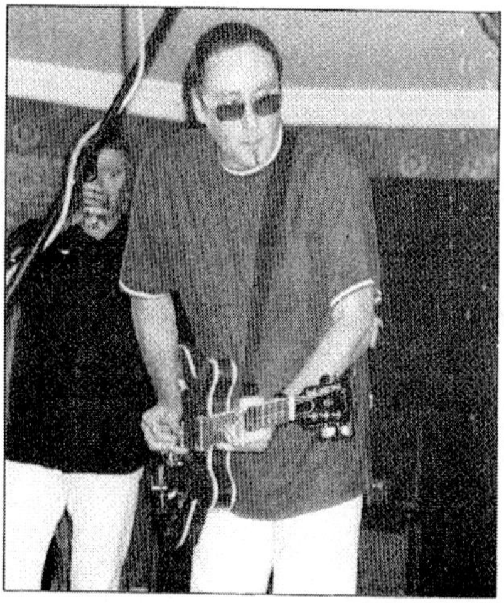

J.H. Did you ever meet any of the band?

D.G. One of my big regrets is not meeting Steve. Steve loved our drummer Brendan O'Neill. He wanted him in his band. He loved his drumming. Brendans got that Chicago feel, he played over there with Rory Gallagher. I've met Kenney, he came to the Olympic Studios while we were doing our second album with Glyn Johns. Kenney was terrific I remember him not liking our snare sound and he tuned it for us just right, very tight. He was also part of the reason Nine Below Zero toured with The Who in 1981 so yeah, I owe him quite a lot. Then a bit later on me and Gerry (McAvoy) went down to his studio and had a jam with him. Quite a thrill! I've never come across Mac and Plonk but as I said before my biggest regret is not having met Steve.

J.H. How did you rate Steve as a vocalist?

D.G. Well he's number one isn't he. Recently I had the opportunity to meet and write some stuff with Peter Frampton and he was telling me that although they argued like anyone else as soon as Steve opened his mouth on stage everything was forgotten. His voice was just fucking brilliant! There isn't another white man who can sing like that and his size! Such a big sound from a little body. I'm just so envious of that voice, definitely the number one. As for Peter we got on great I met him at a song writing seminar and a couple of our co-written songs will appear on a forthcoming album of his.

J.H. How did you rate Steve as a musician?

D.G. He was great but very underrated. With most bands the rhythm section revolves around the bass and drums, but with The Small Faces and Stones it revolved around the guitar and drums. Steves rhythm guitar and Kenneys drums were well locked together and Plonk was happy plonking around it. Similarly Keith and Charlie were doing the same things with the Stones. Although Steve wasn't doing a lot of lead guitar back then what he did do was terrific. He was mainly a rhythm player with Mac adding the frills on top. In later years he was stepping forward and giving it some. I suppose it was because the voice was so good that the guitar playing was a bit overlooked and also, don't forget, he wasn't a half bad song-writer as well. I've always regarded Peter Green as being the perfect package by that I mean voice, musician and songwriter but Steve is right up there with him.

J.H. What did you think of the off shoot bands, Humble Pie, Faces, Ronnies Slim Chance etc. etc?

D.G. Well I loved Ronnies work with Pete Townshend also loved his How Come single. Humble Pie I liked and The Faces with Rod were just terrific.

J.H. What are your own plans for the future?

D.G. Well we as a band have just formed our own record company ZED Records and we've started by reissuing the first three Nine Below Zero albums on CD. We're in the process of negotiation to get my other band The Truths album back from EMI. All in all we've got about 9 or 10 albums lined up. We started the company on 9/9/99 and it gives us total control over our career. It has been frustrating but I'm pleased now we've got it sorted. At last I've got my house in order and I now know where everything is. Everything I've done throughout my career is now in my hands. We've got a very strong fan base and like the Small Faces situation we've got the cult thing about us, which is nice. Nine Below Zero have always been approachable with less of the pop starish stuff. I love being in the band but I don't like a lot of the shit that goes with it. But having control is fantastic first we'll sell through the fan club and then on the shelves. We're getting a website designed at the moment and the next five years are secure and in this business that's a good feeling. There's good solid business people around us and a new album Refridgerater available in early 2000 featuring 12 new numbers. Gigwise we're busy, we're very big in Europe, Scandinavia in particular. Italy and Germany also have a strong base of fans. We had Simon Hickling in the band for a while. As you know Simon had played previously with Steve Marriott and that apprenticeship is good enough for anybody. He used to amuse us for hours on end with his Marriott tales. I used to love 'em!, they were very funny. Yeah, I'm still gutted about not having met the man. Many people who knew both Steve and myself seem to think we'd have got on famously, knitted together with our love of the same music, The Blues.

Thanks Dennis for your time and good luck with Zed Records.

RONNIE LANE INTERVIEW

BY

ALLAN VORDA

(5TH APRIL 1987. HOUSTON, TEXAS)

A.V. What did you do musically prior to the Small Faces?

R.L. I knocked about with a couple of bands that played in public houses or drinking taverns. We could never get a bass player. Down on the East End of London it seemed nobody wanted to play the bass unless he was a real loser who couldn't play a lead instrument. They thought they could play the bass cause it only had four strings. That was the attitude toward the bass. I was a mod at the time and I was listening to Booker T & the MG's and I was into the bass. I started listening to the bass. So I thought, fuck it, I'll play the bass! I had already learned to play guitar - not very well - but I could get my hands around a song. So I talked my old man into buying me a bass guitar in 1963 or 1964. Strangely enough, that was the turning point. I went to this shop to buy the bass guitar that I had seen in the window and this little guy came up to me who was serving. I said "I'd like to have a look at that bass over there". And he said "Oh that's the best bass in the shop. That's a great bass!" He was very enthusiastic and keen about Tamla Motown. I liked him. Anyway, that's how I got to meet Steve Marriott.

A.V. Was Marriott with another band at that time?

R.L. He was with Marriott's Moments, but it was kind of an on off situation. We started talking about music and what we got out of it. He had a great record collection at home including stuff on the Sue label. It was an independent label in England that did some pretty cool records. I think they did some stuff by Ike & Tina Turner. He also had Bobby Bland, James Brown and lots of Motown. This was an education for me because until then I had been hand-strung to the English music scene which didn't have the depth the Americans had. This opened my ears considerably. I had just bought the bass and I suggested we start a group. That was it.

A.V. How did you get the name Small Faces?

R.L. We used to go out with this chick from Kensington. We used to go over there and smoke some dope. You know what I mean? Anyway, we had a gig up the Cavern Club in Leicester Square, but we didn't have a name. So we smoked a bit of dope and wondered what we should call ourselves. She said "Why don't you call yourselves the Small Faces?" You see we didn't have the money, but we considered ourselves mod-oriented. A mod in those days was a face. We weren't very big and she said we should call ourselves the Small Faces. Actually, I was a bit pissed off with it. I was pissed off at being small anyway and then to have the band named that also.

A.V. What was the name of the girl who named your group?

R.L. I can't remember, I think she was a girlfriend of Steve Marriott or maybe Jimmy Langwith, the first organist of the Small Faces.

A.V. You mean Jimmy Winston?

R.L. Ah, his name was Jimmy Langwith, Jimmy Winston was a load of bollocks!

A.V. How did the other members join the group?

R.L. I had been playing with Kenny Jones in those loser-type bands that played the public houses. My brother, who had a job in a public house, spotted Kenny Jones. Kenny would sneak in on Saturday and sit in the drummers place. He was fourteen and not supposed to be there at all. Stanley Lane said I should come and see this guy because he was good. So I did. And he was good. So Kenny Jones was the drummer and I was the bass player. I told Steve Marriott I had a Grech Tennessean guitar that my old man had signed an H.P. agreement on.

A.V. Is there any connection of the Small Faces name to the High Numbers/Who song "I'm the Face"?

R.L. That was part of the whole mod thing. I'm a Face.

A.V. Any connection to the Byrd's song "Eight Miles High" which states: "In strange places/small faces are known"?

R.L. No. It came left wing and had nothing to do with me. You'll have to ask the bleedin Byrds.

A.V. There is also a reference by Robin Trower in the title track of his Bridge of Sighs LP to "Itchycoo Park" that states: "Over Bridge of Sighs." Any knowledge about this.?

R.L. No. The term "Bridge of Sighs" came out of an old British magazine that was in the hotel room when we were on tour. I was reading it because I was bored. The Bridge of Sighs is a place in Oxford where people used to be led across before they were executed. Actually, it has nothing to do with the song, but I thought it was a great term to use in the song. I was just digging for some lyrics. They also had in the same article the Dreaming Spires of Oxford, but Itchycoo Park wasn't in Oxford but down on the East End of London. It's known as artistic license.

A.V. Rumour has it that the Small Faces did not play instruments on the early releases, true or false?

R.L. Absolutely false. We never did a Monkees. If we hadn't played, they would have been much better records. What you got was what was happening.

A.V. In retrospect it is so strange the Small Faces were so popular in England yet virtually unknown in the United States. America never really got to know the Small Faces?

R.L. They never did because the manager obviously did not have the good of the band in his heart. He was just taking it for what he could while he could. We lived pretty good, but we could have gotten better as a band if we had come over. Speaking personally, playing in America made me a better musician. The intelligence of the audience was higher. The American audiences know what you're doing more than English audiences.

A.V. By 1967 your songs began to have psychedelic or drug overtones. How did this evolve?

R.L. We went to a party and got spiked with LSD. We didn't even take it voluntarily. Blew my bloody mind! The lyrics for "Itchycoo Park" came from that experience where I wrote, "It's all too beautiful" I couldn't believe it! Where had I been all my life? The whole thing is all laid out there. And it is all too beautiful! I went out into the street and people were coming past me with these long faces, and

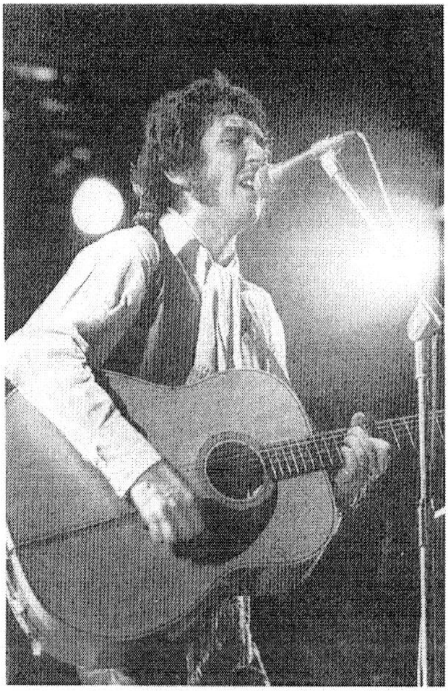

I cried! I couldn't believe all these people didn't realise what a fantastic gift they had. I burst into tears. That's when Glyn Johns came to my rescue. He took me out in his E-type Jaguar and drove me around to help straighten me out. It was a bit of a long drive. I had been scarred deeply by what I had seen where all these people were ignorant of their gift.

A.V. Ogdens Nut Gone Flake - tell us about that?

R.L. "Wouldn't it be nice to get on with my neighbours." All that came about because Steve Marriott had this flat down by the river Thames. He did aggravate his neighbours. He played his records loud all night long. He had lots of cats who would shit everywhere in his neighbour's gardens. Marriott was a terrible neighbour. "Lazy Sunday" came about when Marriott got stoned and wrote the song in the toilet. One of the lines are, "Sitting in the carsey, while

I suss out the moon". Another true story. Ogden's Nut Gone Flake is from a well established tobacco company in England called Ogden's. We were thinking if they ever legalise this stuff we smoke then Ogden's would definitely want to market it. Ogden's used to market this tobacco call Nut Brown Flake, but we sort of fantasised they would call it Nut Gone Flake! It would be good dope and your nut would go! The round cover, which I think was the first ever used, was a disaster because it would fall out of the record bins. You said the album is a sort of cult classic. So it should be.

A.V. After Marriott left the name become shortened to the Faces, why was this?

R.L. Because I wanted to drop the Small! I was tired of always being small in person and on stage.

A.V. What about making the Faces LP A Nods As Good As A Wink To A Blind Horse ?

R.L. Nods As Good As A Wink was an album when we were hot! We had been playing a lot in America and it had really tightened us up. The Faces got to be so good that I myself would stand on one side playing the bass and I was in awe of the band I was playing with! We had a good time on the road. There was a lot of good living and a lot of bad living!

A.V. How did the Faces break up?

R.L. I don't know how the Faces broke up because I wasn't with them then. I had fallen in love with this woman, madly in love, by the name of Kate. I had the audacity to break the band's rules and take her on the road with me to America. So the band sent me to Coventry.

A.V. You mean the city outside London that was bombed badly during World War II? The band actually sent you there by yourself?

R.L. No, not actually. It's an expression in England. If you're "sent to Coventry", it means nobody talks to you. I don't know why the band did this, but no one would talk to me. So I said, "Fuck this! I'm leaving this group." They didn't take me seriously because we were earning quite a lot of money, but I did.

A.V. So the band pretty much kicked you out even though you were a founding member of the Small Faces and the heart and soul of the Faces.

R.L. I suppose I was. Yes, I was. You can say that but I can't.

A.V. You then started a new group called Ronnie Lane's Slim Chance which included a troupe of jugglers and fire eaters call the Passing Show.

R.L. I was trying to make Kate's dream come true. She was part of that group, but I lost all the money I had made with the Faces. Mick Jagger once called me an incurable romantic and I think he was right. Kate and I aren't together anymore. She's in Wales with my two sons.

A.V. How did you become afflicted with multiple sclerosis?

R.L. I left home when I was sixteen to get away from my mother who had M.S. all my life. She took it very negatively. My dad had encouraged me to play the guitar before I had even thought about it. He said, "If you know how to play the guitar, you'll always have a friend." I did learn to play a little on an acoustic guitar and he was so tickled with it that he went out and bought me a cheap little Broadway electric guitar. He brought it home and was bursting to give it to me. My mum said "Why did you buy him that? He's never going to do anything with it!" She was so negative. It made me determined to do something with it and I bought her a house five years later with the money I earned from playing the guitar. I was always told all my life that I wouldn't get M.S. like mum because the doctor said it wasn't hereditary. Then my father died. I was still under the illusion that men don't cry, so I didn't cry. Nine months later I got M.S. My mum also got M.S. when her mum died. I decided I was going to go to America to get to understand this bloody disease. My mother said, "You'll never walk again." So I thought, "Yeah, it's going to be just like the guitar." I can't walk yet, but I think I'll get there. I've found out a lot about M.S. It's aided and abetted by the mercury in the amalgam filling in your teeth! The fuckin' doctors in this world! It's unbelievable! When I had all my fillings changed to plastic the effects were remarkable. I'm left now with the weakness of someone who has had M.S., but I don't have it anymore. I'm not slurring my speech and I'm not as easily fatigued. It's all pretty much gone because my fillings were changed and I stopped eating food that I was allergic to.

A.V. What was the Faces reunion like at Wembley Stadium?

R.L. That was Rod Stewart's idea. He paid for my ticket and also paid me well even though I didn't really do anything. We had Rod Stewart, Ian McLagan, Ronnie Wood and myself

A.V. How did you come to live in Austin?

R.L. I came over to Houston to give this lady the million dollars to start up ARMS Foundation. I used to talk on the phone in the office and get on the line to the poor people and try to rally their spirits and to hang in there. Which was all hard because I was finding it very hard to hang on in there myself. I had such an unfortunate experience in Houston because of this ARMS problem. I remember a black guy on the ARMS board yelled at me during one of the hearings: "Who are you? King Lane! King Lane is it! King Lane are you!" What an asshole! I thought I just want to get out of here. I ended up in Austin because of Chesley Milligan. I knew him when I was in the Small Faces and he was real bad and we were real bad together. He was the manager of Stevie Ray Vaughan in Austin, but he used to come see me and say, "Keep the faith, Ronnie!" It was great and I needed that.

A.V. What are the former Small Faces and the Faces doing?

R.L. Ian McLagan has a band in L.A. Kenny Jones is out of the Who and flying his helicopter. Obviously he's got a lot of money servicing and gassing his helicopter. Steve Marriott had a band called Packet of Three with Jimmy Leverton and Jerry Shirley which is very subtle. A packet of three is how they sell condoms in England.

A.V. Steve Marriott and Humble Pie came to Houston about five years ago and had to cancel because of Marriott's "health" problems. He just recently appeared in Houston at Cardi's about six months ago as Humble Pie with Jimmy Leverton and Jerry Shirley. He looked pretty good and really sang his guts out.

R.L. Steve was his own worst enemy. I've always told him that. I hope he has got it together this time around. He always could sing.

A.V. What about Ronnie Lane and the Tremors and any future recording plans?

R.L. I will probably play with the Tremors as well as with other bands. There are a lot of musicians in the Austin area that are really good. Something called a kettle of fish. This whole trip is a learning experience. It's all too beautiful!

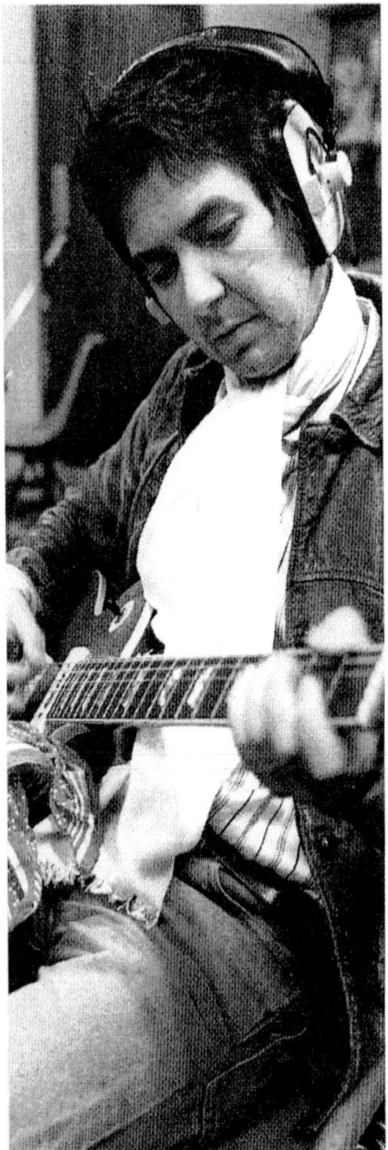

If I'm So Bad, Why Don't They Take Me Away ?

A fans eye view of why Steve Marriott quit The Small Faces to form Humble Pie.

After 32 years this is probably still the most vexing question to Small Faces fans, and interestingly enough, never covered in detail in any books or other publications beyond just a few paragraphs. Maybe it's as simple as how his mother Kay has described it on at least a couple of occasions, that Steve had "given his very best". And it's this sense of not being able to outdo what they had already achieved that I think is central to why he left. In all likelihood, however, it was a mixture of a whole number of things. People may well have their own views and disagree with mine. Please do, in fact ! But I've laid out my own perceptions and my own thoughts on it.....

Certainly, Ogdens was pivotal. The Small Faces didn't take it on the road - and probably should have done, Stanley Unwin and all, although the technology didn't exist at the time to readily reproduce it on the road. As the album became a mini-phenomenon, the group were all struck with the above "how will we top this ?" feeling. Ian McLagan admits to being a bit daunted and scared at this point. So here is probably one of the main strands of Steve Marriott leaving and going on to pastures new. He said "It made perfect sense to knock it on the head. It had taken us a year to make. We'd done all our growing up in that time (Marriott was 21 when Ogdens was released). And that's the main reason people still sit and talk about Ogdens now." I happen to agree with this last comment

From one or two other Marriott interviews, you also get the sense that there was naturally a lot of pressure in being the frontman. Given that he asked to join "Frampton's" new band (Humble Pie) and was content to push Peter into the spotlight is quite illuminating. Jenny Marriott said recently that Steve would come to dread the start of new Humble Pie tours. "I can't be that person they want me to be (onstage)" but what a job he made of it, nonetheless ! It's strange to even consider Steve with this very human frailty - common to many other famous artists who experience stagefright - and the absolute opposite of the confident cockney persona he appears. Steve also said that the Small Faces were "thrust" by Arden into the spotlight before they were ready. Not that they were complaining at the time - but were constanly bombarded on the public through every form of media, especially television and teenage magazines. I think, part of what was going on was a reaction to four years in the constant spotlight ! Also, by his admission, Steve became very introverted for a couple of years, again the opposite of the public perception - and it took a couple of years in Humble Pie for the "real" Steve Marriott to burst out again fully, and even that was after a lot of coaxing and gentle pressure from Manager Dee Anthony . Live was certainly another big part of the problem - after several years when the screaming finally got less, the Small Faces could hear the problem. In an extensive Goldmine interview, Ronnie Lane said "In actual fact, when the Small Faces calmed down a bit, we heard ourselves............and that's why Steve Marriott left the band." More importantly, Steve felt stifled by their chart success. He didn't appreciate the expectation that no matter where the

Small Faces would play a concert they would be expected to play their hit singles. Anyway, he had started this because he wanted to be a musician - not to be a teen scream. And, unknown to many people, there was a re-signing cash dispute with Immediate - and it suited Oldham to keep them in the studio. He had a record company, and didn't need the hassles of tours, nor was he experienced in them - so live they suffered.

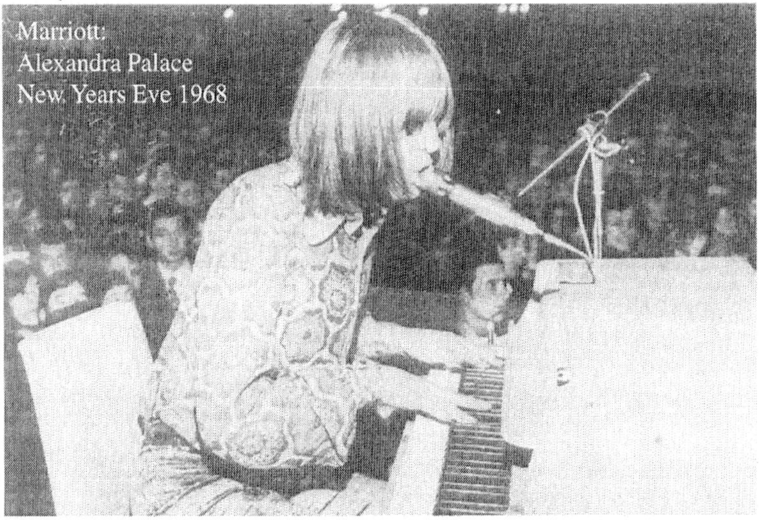

Marriott:
Alexandra Palace
New Years Eve 1968

In the meantime, picture the scene....music was going underground. Very soon Led Zeppelin would be the biggest act in the world (with a fair bit pinched from the Small Faces, but that's another story!!). Live concerts were changing from package tours that owed a lot to British Variety shows, to virtuoso performances. Musical tastes were also becoming much heavier. Hendrix, Cream and the Who at this point are perfect illustrations of what I'm trying to say. In fact, Led Zeppelin, Cream and other groups like Free were taking rock fused with American blues to the forefront of the new music. America beckoned. The biggest market in the world. and home of Steve's musical roots. Even as a teenager in Manor Park he was renowned for his record collection, largely based on American blues and soul. All of this would have had an effect. I really think this was also the start of Steve's insecurity about his guitar playing (especially handling the guitar and singing chores live). Certainly proficient, from a standing start of picking up the instrument only a few years earlier, Steve was not yet the very good guitar player he would become later in his career, and it must have a source of some doubt as to how to make the next big leap with the Small Faces to make them the live powerhouse which would take America by storm. Remember, having been compared to the Who throughout their career, the Small Faces had just seen firsthand in Australia the raw powerhouse the Who had become on stage. The world would see this at Woodstock, and the Live at Leeds testimony on record. "They slaughtered us" said Marriott. Steve's girldfriend shared a flat with Jimi Hendrix' girlfriend, and the two musicians had bumped into one another there a few times. Steve was very well aware of that whole scene.

His solution, as everyone knows, was to bring Peter Frampton into the Faces. The refusal of the others to agree to this proved another main catalyst for Steve's departure. Certainly the live work, and little bits of studio work done with Frampton had Steve moving the Small Faces in a much heavier musical direction. Steve said "Ronnie Lane almost collapsed when he heard Wham Bam Thankyou Mam". Marriott would later claim that he and Humble Pie pretty much invented Heavy Metal - whereas Ronnie remained very melodic. Did he think that the Small Faces, with their English Music Hall undertones were just too English for the U.S. ? To make matters worse, the coolest band on the planet had become cornered by the relative flippancy and commercial success of Itchycoo Park and Lazy Sunday, a cockney "joke" song which they had seen as an ace album track, but not a single release depicting where the group where at. A sorrowful Marriott said that at this point it had got to "where I couldn't sing a 12 bar blues any more, which was very distressing" In the meantime, the Small Faces were aghast at the Frampton suggestion. They had confidence in Steve as a frontman, which was warranted, but also considered him a better guitarist than Frampton, which was not true, despite the "fire" that Steve had always undoubtedly possessed in his guitar playing.

Either way, Steve was not going to get the help outside the studio he felt both he and the band needed. It's worth remembering that five years later, in a similar position regarding how to move Humble Pie forward, Steve's typically original action was to create an absolutely unique blend of hard rock and black soul with the Blackberries. (Note the extremely high position of Eat It in a recent poll of Humble Pie albums !). When the other Humble Pie members wouldn't agree to these ladies joining permanently, that really hastened the end of Humble Pie. Now, much has also been made of the relative failure of "the Universal" single (No 16 in 1969) in the story of Steve leaving. I'm in a quandry on this point. Yes, there's no doubt that Steve was very pleased with this song, and particularly the lyrical content, which was never his strongest suit. There's no doubt that his confidence was dented by its relative lack of commercial success, and he stopped writing.

In fact, although he would write some beautiful songs over the years, he would never again be a prolific writer, nor scale the heights of his Small Faces repertoire. Uli and Roland quote Steve in "Happy Boys Happy". "It killed me at the time. I didn't think that anyone believed in what the song was, which was just a very clever play on words type of song and, I thought, a very clever song. And the reviews said it was either a stroke of genius or a terrible mistake. And because the song wasn't a hit in a big way it was considered a terrible mistake." However, and despite "The Universal" being a top song, a quirky sound, and being put together in thirty minutes one morning in Steve's garden it was never going to make it the polished single to take the Small Faces onwards and upwards. I prefer to believe it was put out as a kind of cool anti-song. As a complete counter-balance to the unhip of Lazy Sunday.

Another often quoted rumour is of Steve's alleged comment of wanting to play with "better musicians" or "real musicians" I don't know. Let me only make this comment............ Humble Pie offered plenty of opportunity for ad lib and hanging loose, but always within an overall structure - and at their core they were the tightest kick-ass band I ever saw (and I saw them all!). On the other hand, whenever I saw the Faces, they were characterised by their very looseness. A great band in their own way, loveably shambolic, a party guaranteed, highs and lows depending on the night you caught them. But at a different point on the spectrum from the tight as a drum unit led by Marriott. In fact, so loose were they, in Glasgow the crowd used to do more singing than Rod - and he let them !

Let me sign off with these thoughts

❑ Playing live was one of the cores of the issue. Kenney Jones reflects that at rehearsals they played only album-oriented material. At gigs the Small Faces would find that the singles were expected. Yet they considered themselves like the Yardbirds or Zoot Money rather than a pop group. All the Small Faces got pissed off when they went to see other groups they considered as rock or blues. They should probably have continued the experiment of taking Georgie Fame's brass section on tour. This could have pointed a way into a post-Ogdens tour. But it was expensive, and given that there was still screaming (witness Newcastle City Hall) they stopped it.

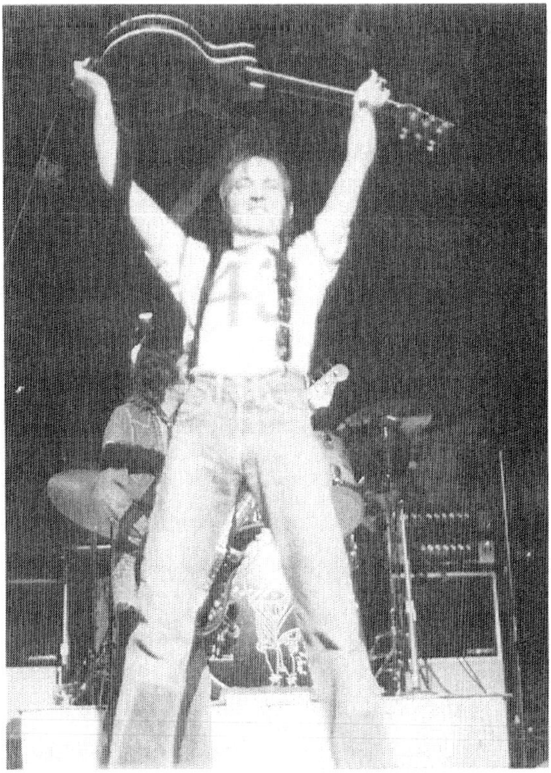

❑ The Small Faces had always been sharp, cool and innovative. Starting with the RnB mod culture, to pop music tinged with traditional music hall roots, through psychedelia and concept album, all the way to the early Humble Pie feel of the fledgling Small Faces 1862 album tracks. But they were cornered as a singles band. Whatever they did next had to be geared for the US, and at the time the group weren't even guaranteed entry given Ian McLagan's previous minor drugs conviction.

But, ultimately, Marriott's clear cut comments are revealing. "It was definitely the right thing to do (leave). No question" In reality, they had all grown up. Everybody older and wiser (roughly having gone from 18 to 22 years old). They had lived too long, for four years, in each others' pockets. Even living together..... It was time to move on.

Stay Cool !

Iain McGonigal

Guitar-o-graphy!

STEVE MARRIOTT AND HIS GUITARS

Whoever spotted the tiny Rhythm'n'Blueser in his recent years – sunk in a comfortable motor-suit and holding his treasured, huge Gibson 335 – couldn't help smile : upright, the instrument looks about as high up as the chord thrashing Marriott musician. Having got used to an axe, Steve could be faithful to a model all through his career (we're still talking about guitars): "I'm terrible. On stage I always use one guitar until it's completely worn out. I don't like putting one down to strap on the next one – it's difficult enough staying in tune with the keyboard (back in 1987, he was referring to Mick Weaver, OFFICIAL RECEIVERS). With two spare guitars and possibly a few acoustics as well I'd be tuning up all the time!"

In spite of stage comfort, Steve had been an avid collector of guitars all through his career. Up to his sudden departure from Atlanta, Georgia in late 1983, and afterwards back in Britain, he would gather a treasured range of guitar gems. Some of these will be presented here (not only) for specialists:

ELECTRIC GUITARS

(in alphabetical order):

DWIGHT:
In the summer of 1971, Steve got this unusual, licensed reproduction in the USA. The Dwight is similar to the Epiphone Crestwood, "a strange mixture", as he told us in December '71, "with an Epiphone body and a Gibson pick-up. The way the pick-up is wired gives it extra volume and tone. It is an older pick-up which they have discontinued owing to the hum level, but for Rock'n' Roll it's one of the best pick-ups you can get."

EPIPHONE "CRESTWOOD":
This small, flat model Steve used in the early days of HUMBLE PIE. According to him, it was Epiphone's answer to the Gibson Les Paul Junior. Steve got one of the makes with the white, flat pick-up: "It didn't have as much 'poke' as the Dwight. Now I use it as a spare", he'd claim in the Fillmore.

FENDER "ESQUIRE" 1955 :
Steve bought this model, which was never really popular in general, around 1972 as another spare for HUMBLE PIE gigs, paying 80 dollars for it in Chicago. But because of it's extremely clean sound, he only started using it on stage with the SMALL FACES in 1977. He liked the sound of its simple pick-up, especially when compared to the treble pick-up, of his Telecaster. He used numerous mid-range sounds but didn't like its bass range. Steve played the Esquire with Ernie Ball strings and connected the guitar to a Fender Twin Reverb – what a contrast to the "larger than Steve" Marshall stacks of the early SMALL FACES and HUMBLE PIE days!

FENDER "STRATOCASTER" NO. 62, 1953 :
A rare find that the Fender company was taken with so much that they actually tried to buy it back from Steve. But for him that was exactly the right noise to hold on to it. He loved its neck, which at the time used to be more rounded at the back. Steve still didn't use it on stage, because the sounds were "too syrupy" for him. In the end he screwed its neck off and had it assembled to his "Telecaster"!

FENDER "TELECASTER" :
This one had been bought in 1965 for Ian McLagan to get him to mime to the TV-playback of "I Got Mine", which had been recorded with his predecessor Jimmy Winston. Once "Top of The Pops" was done, Marriott used it himself, applying "Humbucker" pick-ups.

GIBSON "LES PAUL JUNIOR" 1956 :
This flat guitar Steve was given as a present stopping in San Francsico on a PIE tour by a generous fan – Steve called the phenomenon "love, peace and guitars" – but on stage he played it very rarely.

GIBSON "LES PAUL" ORIGINAL :
This wasn't a flat model, but a fat, cello-type guitar with a "cutaway" for reaching high notes – and a beautifully ornate scratch plate. Steve rather regretted that he'd given this guitar to Alexis Korner in the mid 70's.

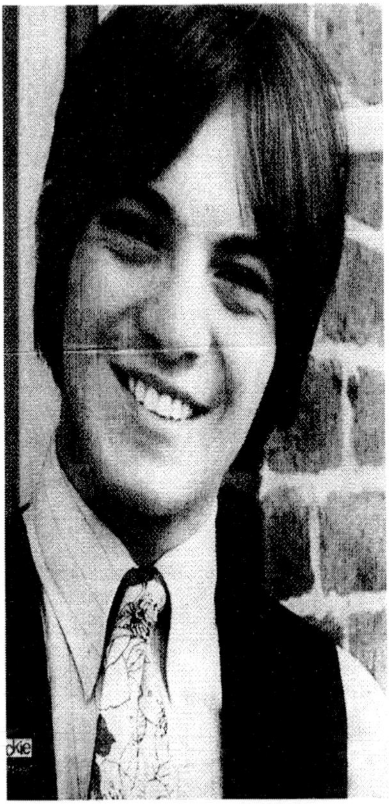

GIBSON "LES PAUL" CUSTOM 1957 :
Steve's famous black one from the HUMBLE PIE days, bought in Cleveland, Ohio. Steve took out the central pick-up of the three it came with, because it was in his way when picking. Later, this beauty with mother-of-pearl inlays in its neck was offered with just two pick-ups, exactly the way Steve had altered it.

GIBSON "MELODY MAKER" :
A completely symmetrical, flat E-guitar which Steve had used as a spare for his Epiphone Crestwood before he got his Dwight.

GIBSON "ES 335" :
Another big, chello-type guitar which Steve used to play on all his numerous tours from 1983 with PACKET OF THREE – a present by his childhood sweetheart and then girlfriend Manon Pearcey. In the Eighties, Steve would only take this and his Ibanez "Artist" on the road with him. Contrary to the Gretsch "Eddie Cochran", the ES 335 has two "cutaways", in that respect it resembles the Ibanez "Artist" again.

GRETSCH "EDDIE COCHRAN" :
This collector's item Steve was able to purchase in St.Louis, Missouri, for only 300 dollars. The dealer called Steve after he had seen a picture of him with THE SMALL FACES and kept it for a year before Steve was able to pick it up, stopping over on tour. It's an orange hollow body with a "G" brand mark – burnt in! The only other known copy is owned by Jimmy Page. Orange Eddie Cochrans aren't so rare, it's the brand mark that counts. The real Eddie Cochran had flat, black Gibson pick-ups built in his "G", but Steve kept the original Gretsch ones. He was very proud of the guitar, but never used it live because of its feedback.

IBANEZ "ARIST" :
A kind of Ibanez answer to the Gibson ES 335, even if the neck top and the bridge have their own design. Steve used to rate Ibanez guitars because you hardly had to break them in. On the other hand he missed its top/treble presence, but raved about its "out of phase" position. In any case, he was sufficiently over the moon with the company that he posed for a commercial Ibanez poster in 1982/83.

IBANEZ "HOWARD ROBERTS" :
Towards the end of the 70's, Marriott preferred Ibanez guitars to Gibson makes, because he realised that its constructors had the necessary know-how and on top of that had bought huge supplies of Gibson wood. Steve had used the "Howard Roberts" as early as 1967 for "Itchycoo Park", with very light strings.

IBANEZ "LES PAUL BLONDE" :
What Steve liked most about this copy was that a solid body guitar had a maple neck. But the pick-ups he found too dirty for SMALL FACES MkII purposes, so he meant to replace them with double-pole Fender pick-ups. Who knows if he ever did?

OVATION "BREADWINNER";
For this designer's wet dream – in subtle "Starship Enterprise" style – Steve also posed in Musicians' trade magazines, during his ALL STARS phase in 1976. For Marriott, the "Breadwinner" was the perfect studio guitar, because he was able to get every (im)possible sound of it, "messing with tones and boosts". The neck is flat and wide, but feels surprisingly comfortable according to Steve, similar to a "Dan Armstrong". ■

IN THE NEXT ISSUE: **ACOUSTIC GUTIARS.**

TRACK BY TRACK

SMALL FACES
OGDENS NUT GONE FLAKE

Immediate IMLP 012 (Original UK Pressing 1968)

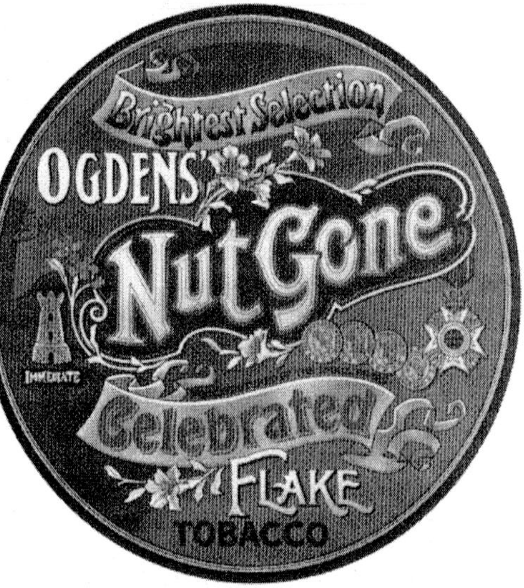

This album review was first published in the New Musical Express dated 25th May 1968. Side one is reviewed by none other than RONNIE LANE himself and Side two is reviewed by the NME's Keith Altham.

Side One

A few words from Mr Ronnie "Plonk" Lane about the first fantastic side of this album which includes no less than four tracks which were considered to be singles at one time and three others which deserve to be. Straight from his long run in Dusseldorf, Herr Lane!

OGDENS NUT GONE FLAKE is an instrumental on which we use strings sparingly. We've always wanted to release an instrumental single - this is heavy. A nice one.

AFTERGLOW a new idea for lyric - it's about "Love" but we've jazzed it up a bit to make it a hit. Features Maurice Ponk on the introductory vocal and Mac on the electrical harpsichord with a rhythm refrain by the Queens. Recorded at the same session as "Lazy Sunday."

LONG AGOS AND WORLDS APART. This is Mac's song - he wrote and he sings it and it's a mid-tempo-shuffler - very straight and very nice. We recorded it only a couple of weeks ago.

SONG OF A BAKER. This is my song. I wrote it and I sing it - it's all about a geezer who wants some bread. Acoustic guitars - a straight forward load of XX??XXX!

RENEE. This is a filthy song which we wrote and will never get any plugs on the BBC. I used to have one called "Daisy" who lived downstairs from me. It's a happy, happy raver which is absolutely revolting and we all love it. Steve does a very fine vocal.

LAZY SUNDAY. Is the original all time Small Faces hit single which we hope you will still like - we do.

Side Two

One listen to the mind-blasting adventures of Happiness Stan, which is one continuous band including six new Marriott and Lane compositions, is likely to reduce the average reviewer who attempts to convey the clever effects and electrical inspiration to a gibbering heap. Writes Keith Altham.

Professor Unwin's voice is first heard enquiring if we are all sitting "comfortybol two square on your botties" before "HAPPINESS STAN" crashes about our ears. Stan lives in the land of greens and coloured dreams, deep inside a rainbow. His big problem is that he cannot understand the mysteries on the other side of the moon and this Steve sings to the thrashing accompaniment of piano, organ, drums and harpsichord.

Unwin comes back to take up the story of how "once upon a polytito, dangly in the heavenly bode Stan was all smashed and flaked," and that takes us into ROLLIN' OVER. A solid, raving sound that could only be the Faces with shades of Jerry Lee Lewis on piano and that hard, rasping vocal of Steve's emerging from the barrage of beat with some brass mixed in for good measure.

Our next track concerns the story of THE HUNGRY INTRUDER a fly who comes to share Stan's shepherd's pie! Strings and cellos in this one with those beautiful "soppy" nursery rhyme lyrics which only the Faces can make meaningful. Lots of nice sounds and an acoustic guitar that sounds like something else.

With a rolling of the magical sleeve, Stan turns the fly into an insect big enough to transport him to the other side of the moon and so to THE JOURNEY. This really is a kind of "Organ into Space" bit with the kind of inspired electronics that defy the printed word.

Once upon the moon they discover a character known as MAD JOHN, who sings with the birds in the morning and listens to the wind at night - he's considered not quite right! But John as this joyous little opus points out has "sussed" it out and "loves all haters until their hate turns to fear."

These last two tracks are my favourites because of the sentiments expressed and clever simplicity of the music. And it is quite alright if you do not have a clue what I'm talking about because you have to hear it - you have to hear it.

The final song is HAPPY DAYS TOY TOWN and is John's song. A beautiful song in big boots and a red nose which quite plainly says what it is all about as "Little Boy Blue" "Knees up Mother Brodie" and "Jackie Jill" all join in at Stanley Unwins invitation and Marriott, Lane and Co give a stirring rendition of the immortal line - "Life is just a bowl of All Bran!"

A magnificent side to an album full of western promise - the first real attempt at a musical space-age, fairy-tale. A portent of even greater things to come.

Also included in this review was a mention that either "Be My Baby" or "If You Think Your'e Groovy" may be included on Ogdens. Neither were and both remain unreleased to this day.

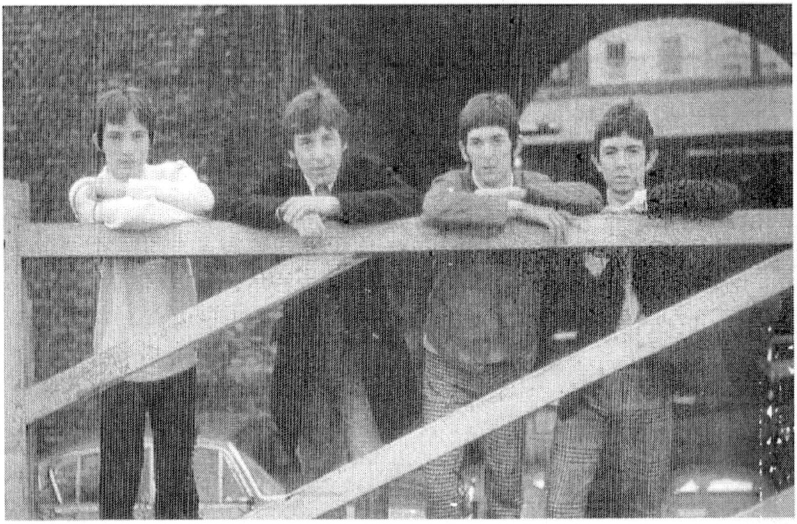

TOTALLY SMITTEN!

An original 60s fan reminisces about her lifelong respect and admiration for the East Ends own fab four.

I regard myself as a lifelong fan, back as far as "Whatcha Gonna Do About It" in 1965, when I was only 13 years old.

I saw them live only three times, in 1966,67 and 68. The first time being at the Grimsby Mecca whilst "All Or Nothing" was at number one, in those days you could get really close to the bands on stage. With my friends we sat for about three hours guarding our places right at the side of the stage. We felt our reward had come when the manager (my friends brother) came from backstage with some change and sent two of us to the shop for some cigarettes for Steve Marriott. Imagine that! When we came back we were allowed to give them to him. Steve touched my hand and I never wanted to wash it again. After getting his autograph we went back to defend our front spot places in seventh heaven.

When the Small Faces did come on stage, around 10 o clock, the ballroom was heaving and being right at the front we were pushed and literally squashed right into Macs stool......that's how close we were. I was actually sitting next to him for the whole of the exciting performance. Mind you he swore at me a few times for almost knocking him sideways on to the floor!

I was totally smitten, I bought everything on vinyl, every newspaper and magazine if only for a few words about them. My bedroom wall was covered in pics and right through Grammar school I wore a gold locket with pics of Steve and Mac inside and I do actually still have this to this day. Every time a new Small Faces record came out I'd be late for school after having queued outside Gough and Davys record shop in Grimsby to be the first to get it.

Due to parents wanting to redecorate, all my pics had to come off the bedroom wall. At one point I had over 600 of them and they all went into the pages of many scrapbooks. I filled about six of them over the years. Due to many house moves, the first scrapbook has vanished, which was and still is a great disappointment as that one had all the very early stuff in it. About six years ago I gave some of them to a fellow fan in Hull but I still have a few of those original scrapbooks tucked away under the bed. I've bought the music several times over and over again on cd but I still have all the original vinyl.

The last time I saw them live was at a ballroom in Luton, in Bedfordshire, in August 1968. By then there was no screaming and you could hear the silence when Steve sung "If I Were A Carpenter". I was still besotted, but 1968 was in some ways a parting of the ways, Steve got married and I discovered real boyfriends!

Their influence has stayed with me, every boy I went out with could have come out of the same mould. My husband-to-be was typical......a scooter riding mod, devotee of the Twisted Wheel club but unlike Steve Marriott he was tall, well 5' 8". I always used to tell him that he smiled like Steve.

We are still married after 30 years and our two sons seem ok about being brought up on a musical diet of Small Faces, Northern Soul and a sprinkling of R'n'B. There's hardly been a week go by in all these years when the Small Faces aren't given a good blast. I never forget their birthdays or anniversaries, but keep them to myself.

I really enjoyed Ians book. The first section on his life in the band was amazing. I remembered all the incidents and I kept thinking I've got the clippings on that somewhere. I wrote to him via the publisher but got no reply.

I've always loved their music and on rare occasions have shown off my scrapbooks, they really have been an enormous influence on my life. I remember in the 1980s going to a wedding where my son was a page boy. I left, mid evening, to find a tv set to watch Steve on Mike Reeds "Pop Quiz" and went back to the reception afterwards.

I remember being in Asda

car park when I heard the news of Steves death. I was totally numb and saddened, to this day I have never read about it. I know what happened and that is enough.

Ronnies death came to me via the Radio Two news. I remember working for Barclays bank in the early 1980s and one of their London branches were organising a collection or sponsorship for Plonk and MS.........all very sad.

I was obviously a fan club member when it was in Carnaby Street, that was cool and also through my many letters to magazines such as Rave, Fab 208, Record Mirror and Jackie I made many good pen friends such as Sheila and Sandra in Barrow In Furness, Janet in Southampton and Hilary in London. All mad Small Faces fans.......if any of you read this, please get in touch.

Well, there you go, I think I have trawled through my life and loves, all part of growing up I guess. Through those formative years it was me, the Small Faces and the pirate radio stations, London and Caroline. It was those things that made me the person I am today. Thanks guys...........love you all !

As a footnote, around 1967 in Jackie magazine Steve was asked his favourite meal. He said, macaroni cheese complete with his recipe. Of course I learnt how to cook it and still cook it regularly to this day. It's become a bit of an in joke over the years but yeah, I still cook Macaroni cheese the Steve Marriott way.......it's true!

SUSAN PRIESTLEY
(June 2003)

DRESSED TO KILL.......

A 13 PAGE PHOTOGRAPHIC TRIBUTE TO THE BEST LOOKING BAND EVER!

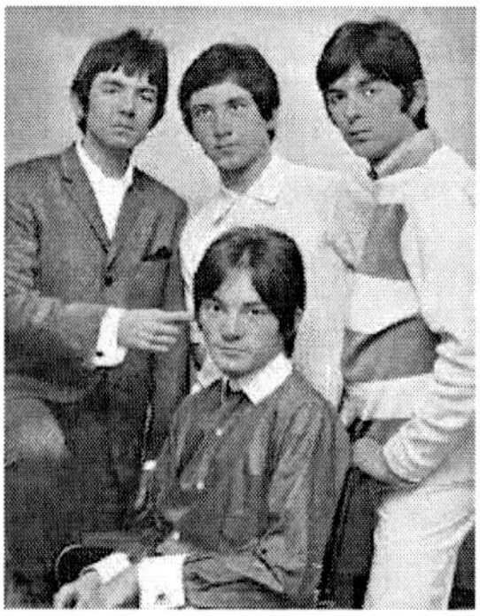

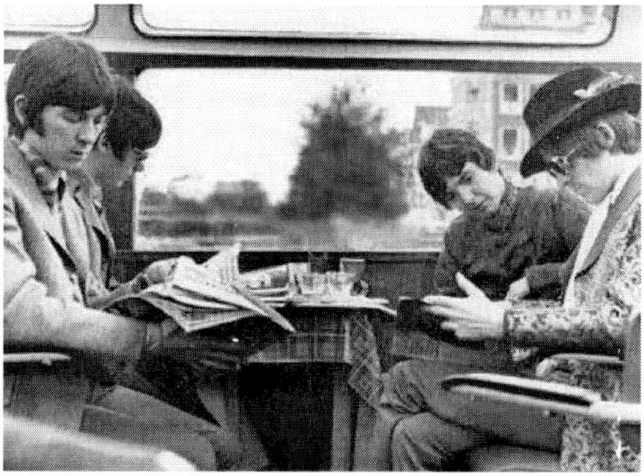

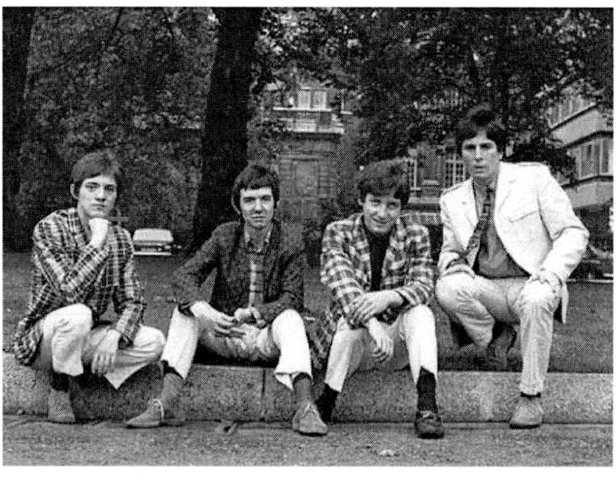

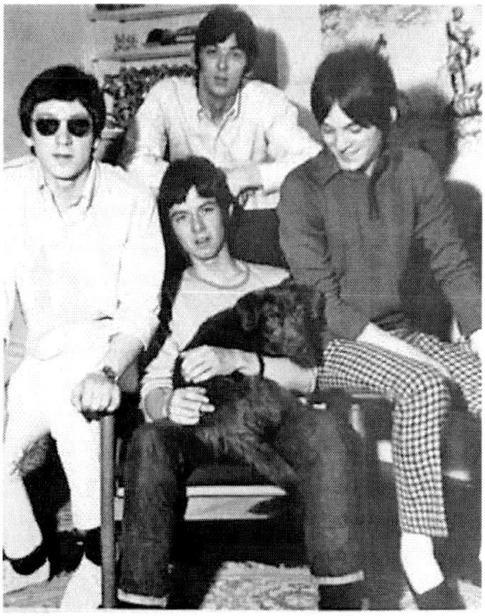

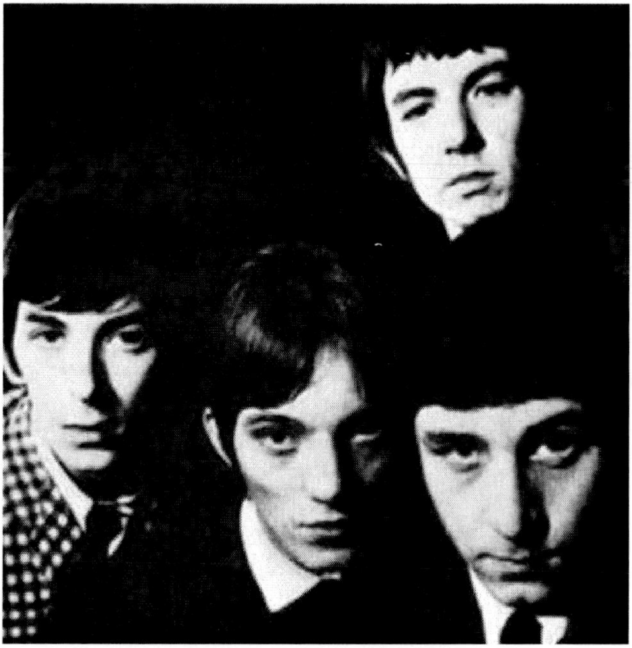

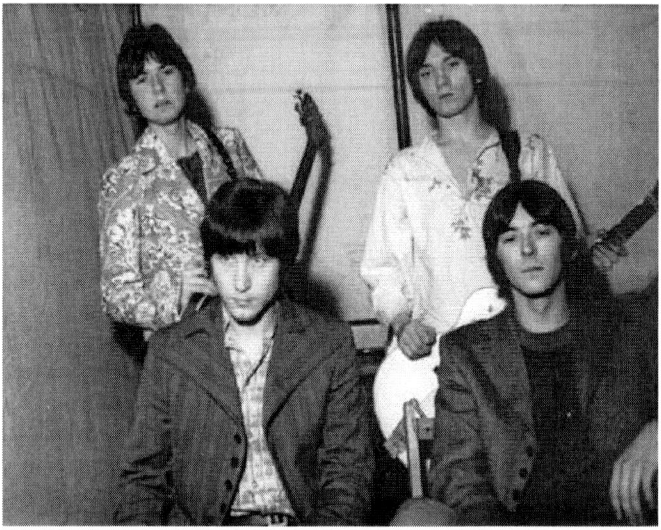

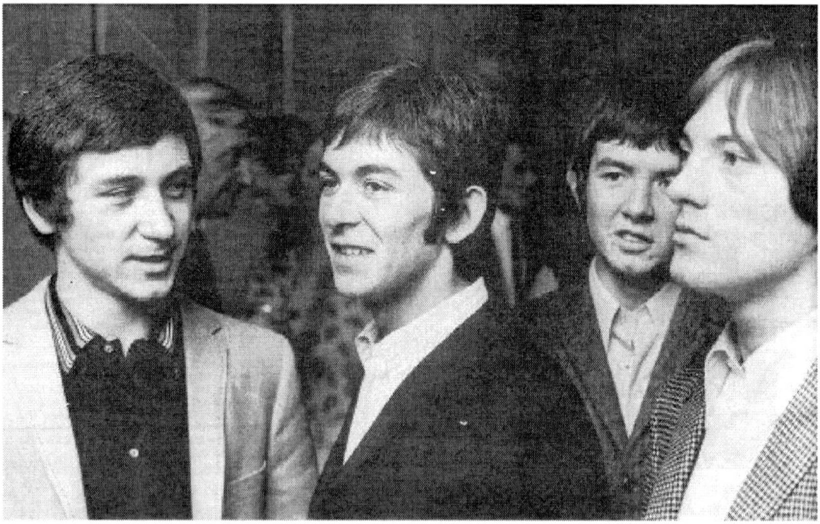

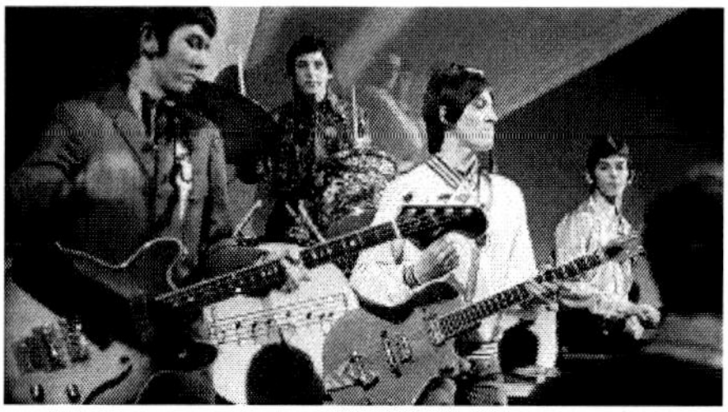

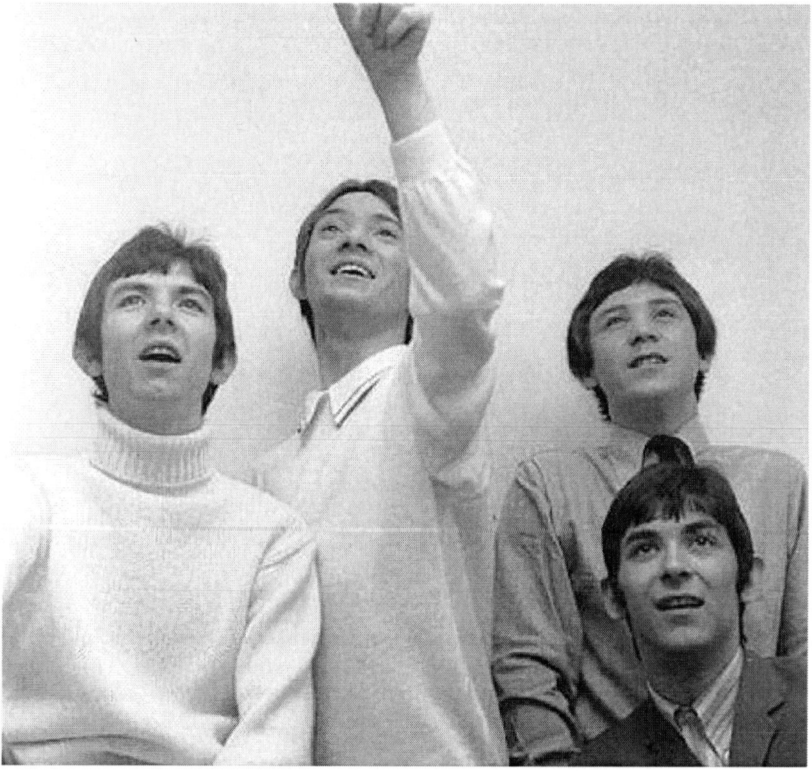

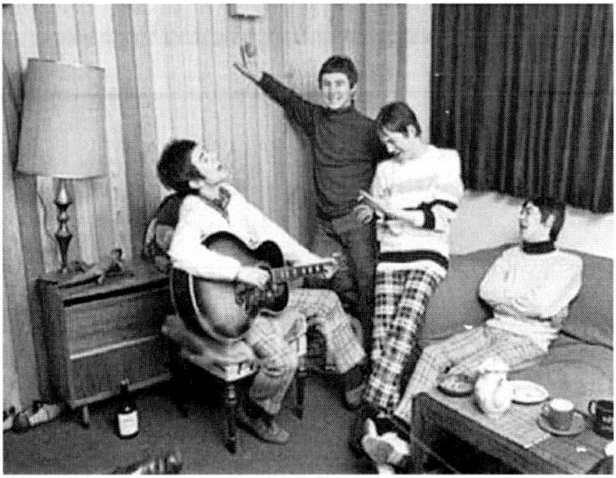

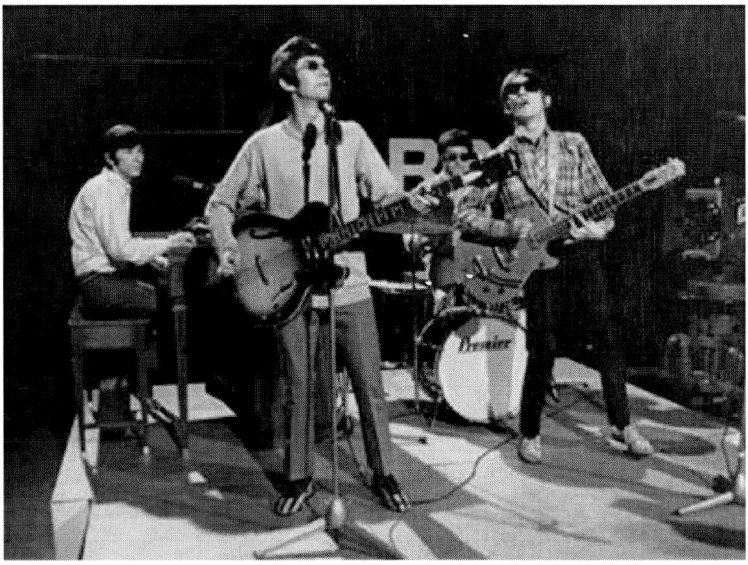
Premier

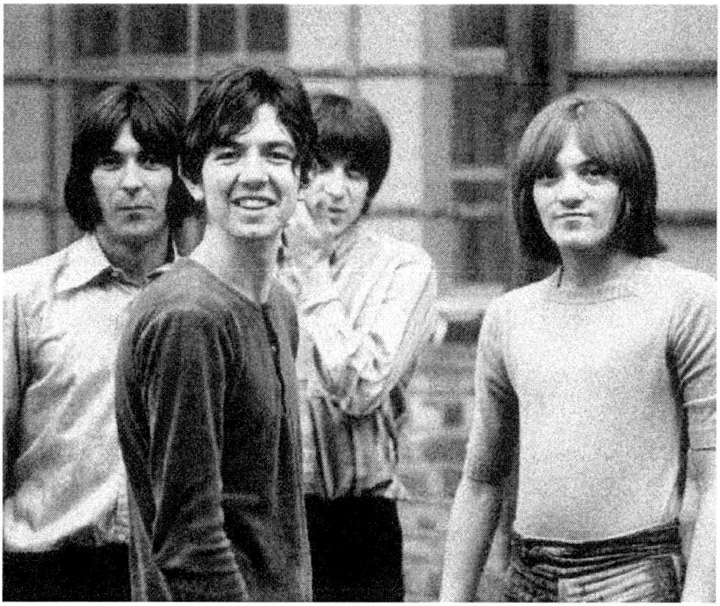

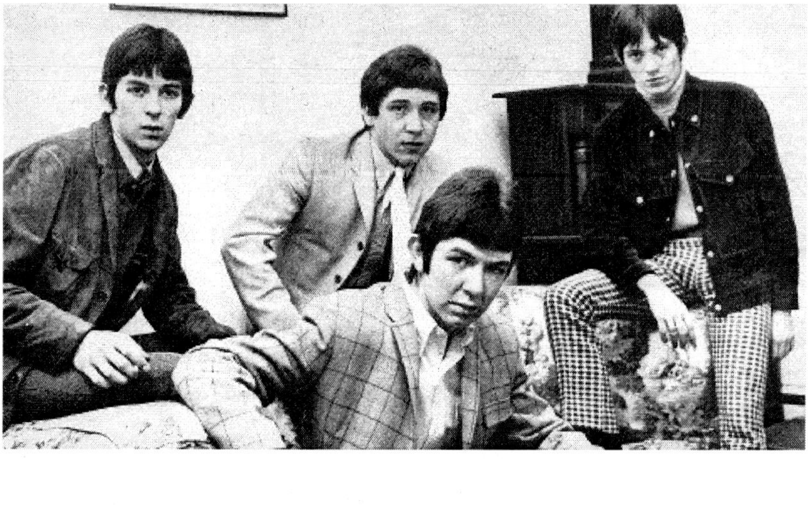

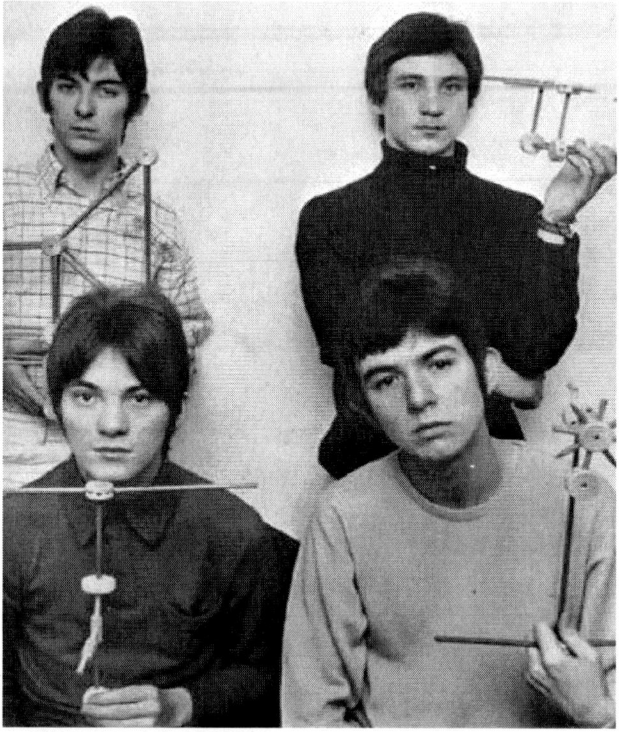

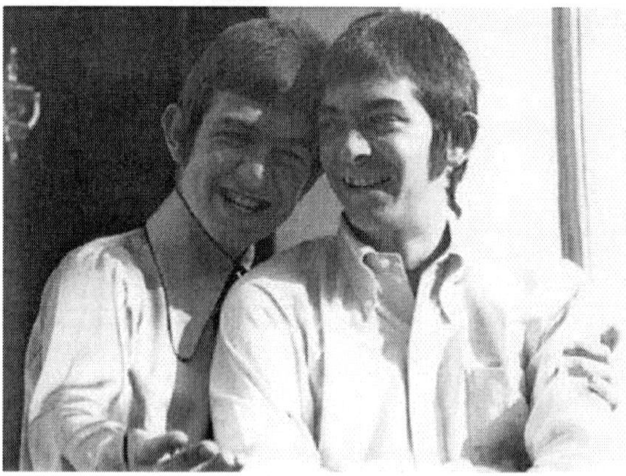

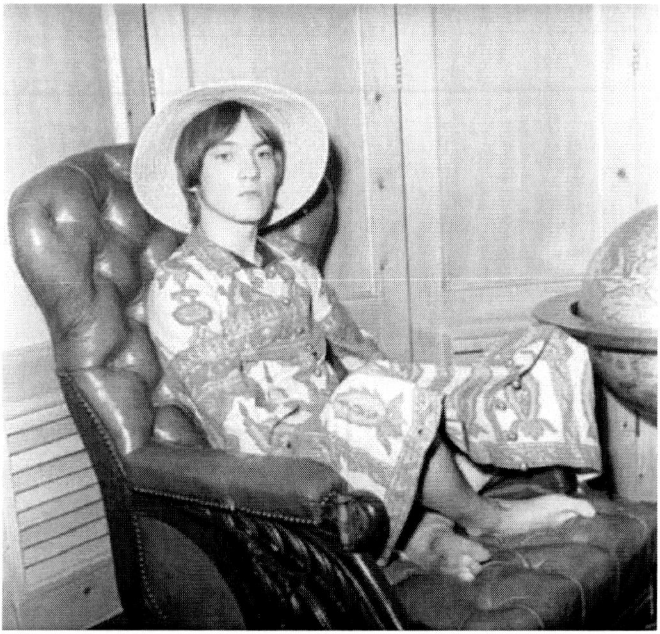

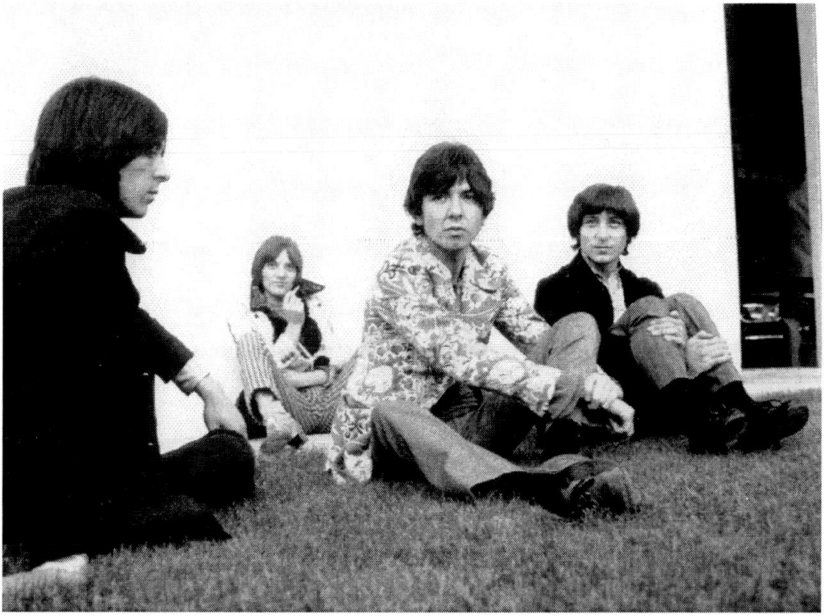

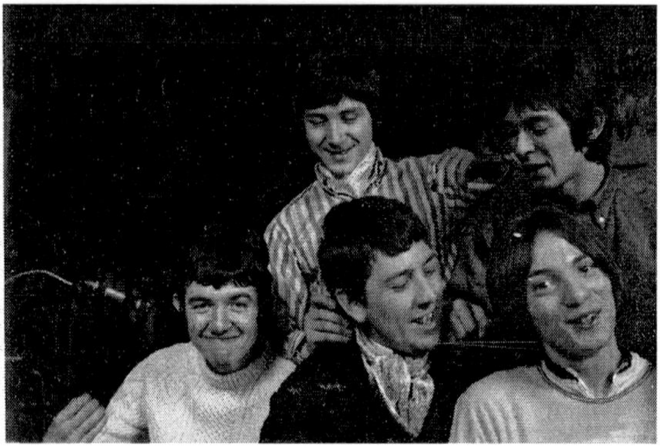

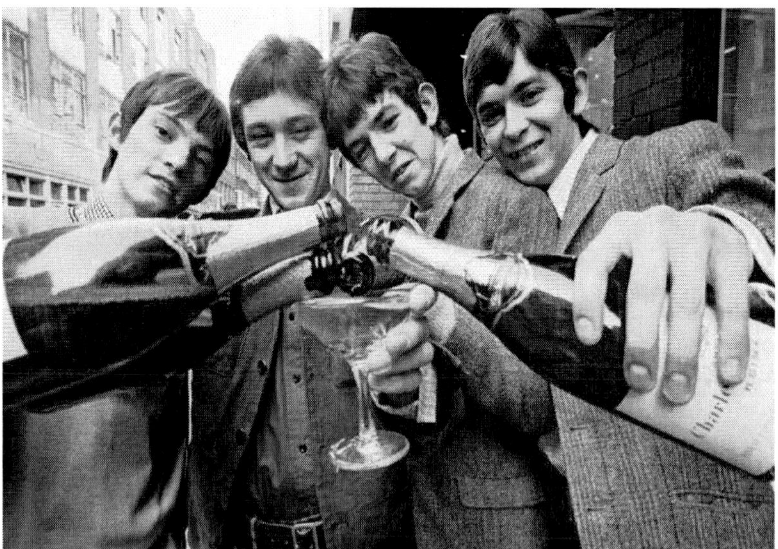

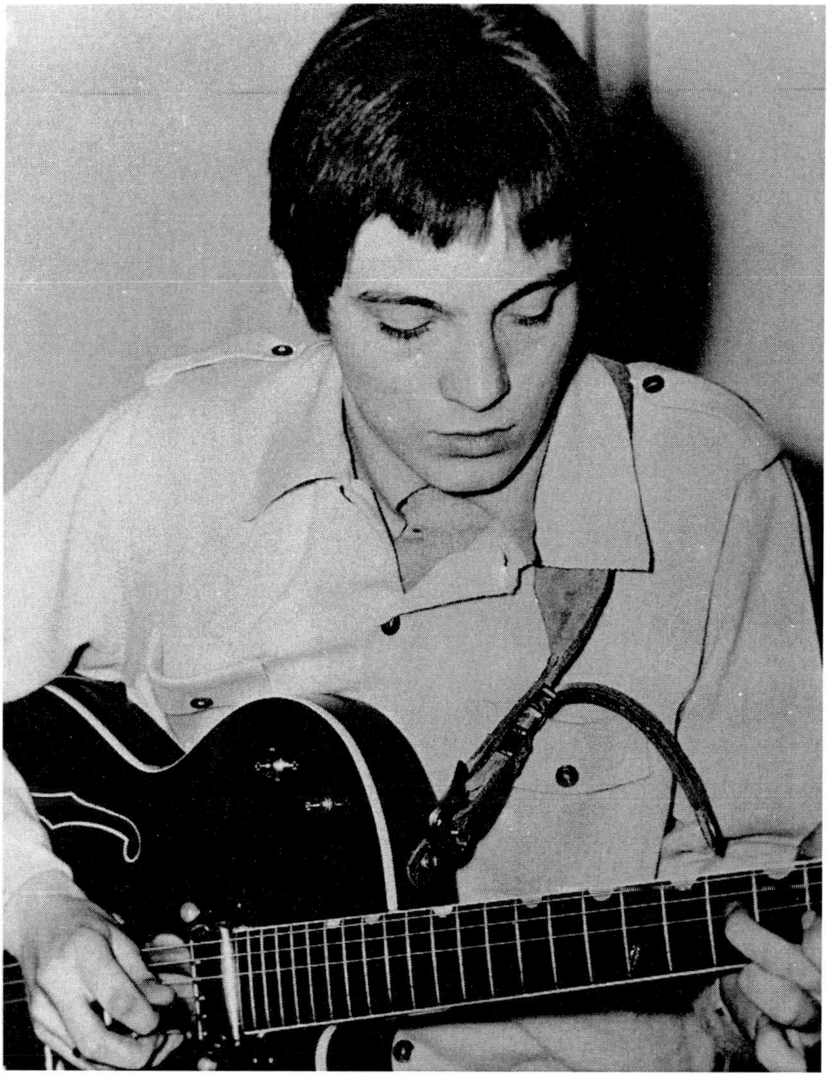

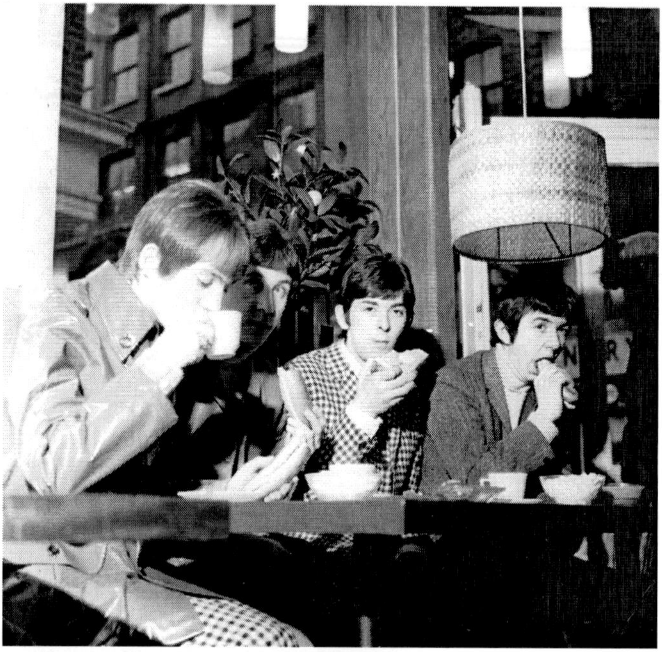

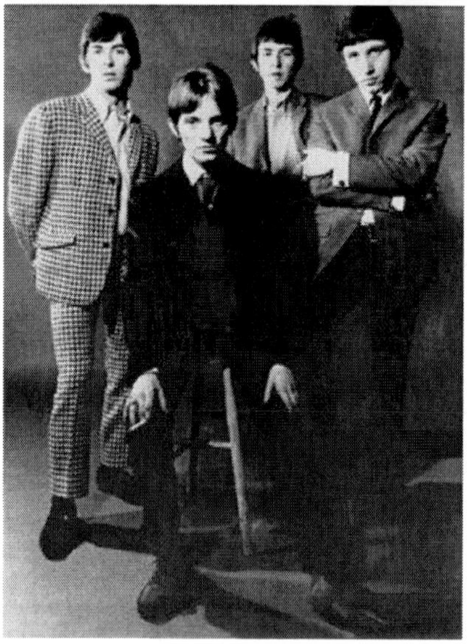

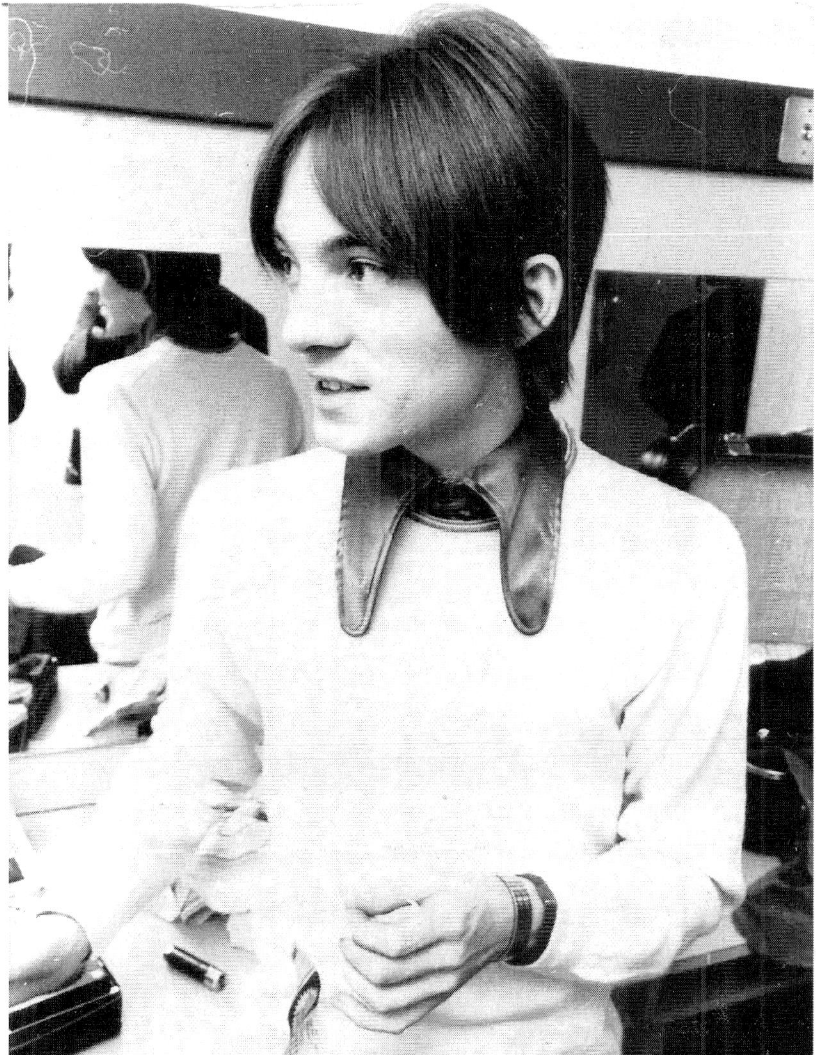

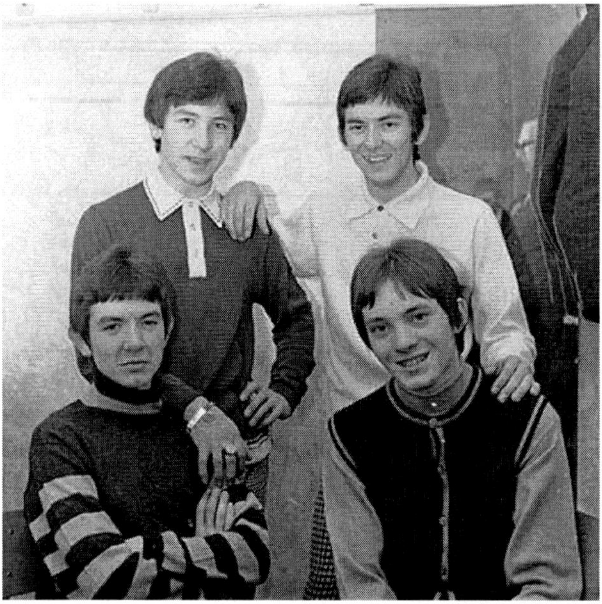

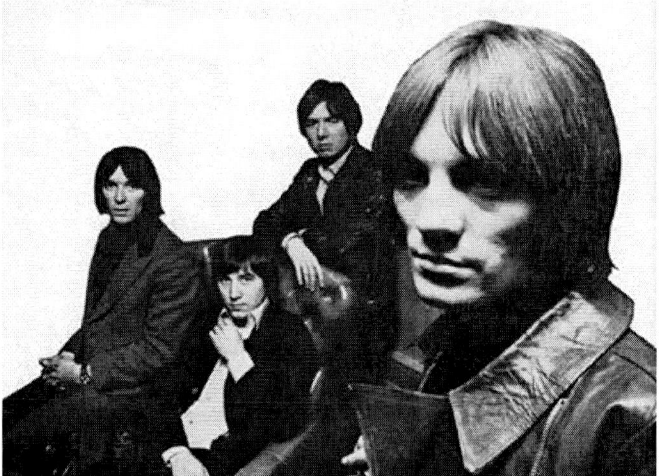

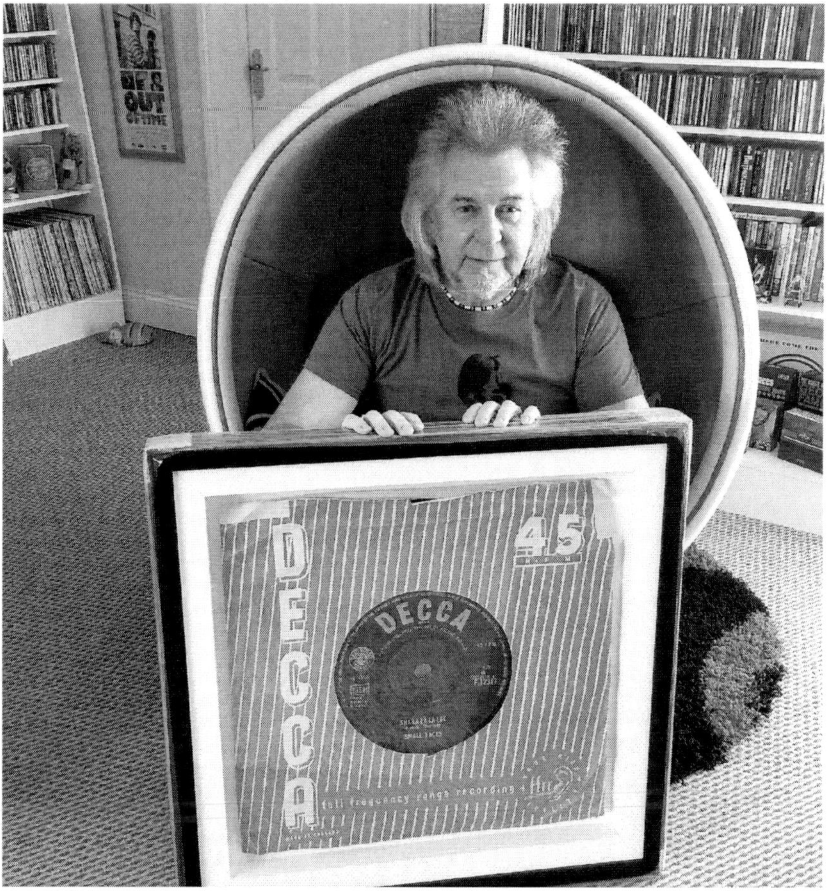

JOHN HELLIER www.wappingwharf.com

Check out the website for all things Small Faces/Mod related. Books, CDs, DVDs, original 1960s/1970s rare memorabilia ....and more!

........and now for your delight,
the darling of Wapping Wharf launderette, Ronald 'Leafy' Lane.